ECONOMIC HISTORY
OF EUROPE

HARPER'S HISTORICAL SERIES

UNDER THE EDITORSHIP OF

GUY STANTON FORD

EUROPE
WESTERN ASIA
AND NORTHERN AFRICA

	Lowlands below 600 feet
	Highlands above 600 feet
	Highest Regions and Arctic Regions
	Mountains
	Forests
	Marshes
	Deserts

Scale of Miles
0 100 200 300 400 500 600

ARCTIC

ICELAND

Arctic Circle

SCANDINAVIAN HIGHLAND

G. of Bothnia

BRITISH ISLES

NORTH SEA

BALTIC SEA

LOW

English Channel

GREAT

FRANCE

Loire R.

PLATEAU OF FRANCE

Danube

CARPATHIAN

Mt. Blanc

ALPS MTS.

HUNGARIAN PLAIN

ATLANTIC

PYRENEES

Po R.

Danube

OCEAN

Duero R.

Ebro R.

BALKAN M.

Tagus R.

CORSICA

ADRIATIC SEA

Str. of Gibraltar

BALEARIC IS.

SARDINIA

MEDITERRANEAN

CRETE

ATLAS MOUNTAINS

SICILY

S

Tropic of Cancer

LIBY

SAHARA

DESE

Niger

L

R.

L. Chad

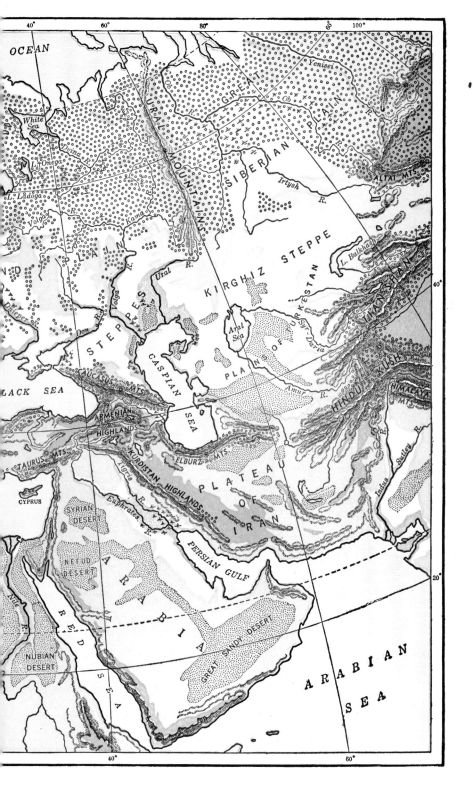

ECONOMIC HISTORY

of

EUROPE

By Herbert Heaton

PROFESSOR OF ECONOMIC HISTORY
UNIVERSITY OF MINNESOTA

REVISED EDITION

HARPER & BROTHERS
Publishers · New York

To My Wife

CONTENTS

Maps and Charts

EDITOR'S FOREWORD

A new edition and a foreign translation of Professor Heaton's account of European economic history are sources of satisfaction to an editor no less than to the author and publisher. Such evidences of approval reflect not only the popularity of the text but the growing importance of economic history as a subject of study. As a result Professor Heaton has seized this opportunity to embody the most recent research, to rewrite and rearrange certain chapters, and to expand the treatment of early modern conditions and of Russia. For the American student with this text in hand, and with a competent teacher to develop its potentialities, European economic history has a special value. Here in his own country he can see the slow centuries from tribal economy to a world bank telescoped into the brief history of his own land. He is living where he passes swiftly from the full daylight to the dawn of industrial development when his airplane glides down to let him trade on an Indian reservation. Through the history of this slow evolution in Europe he can see the development from simple to complex societies, from home to region, to state, to interdependent world-wide economy. And it is the economic history of Europe which will best enable the student to understand the most significant feature of the last three centuries, the dominance of the smallest continent over the vast areas of all the others. Its commercial and industrial expansion has carried with it language, literature, law, and political institutions as spiritual cargoes, even more important than the products of Europe's mines and factories. The disciplined constructive historical imagination of the student of this volume, supplemented by all his studies in the social sciences and the humanities, can build his own understanding of western civilization. When he comes to the end of the story, to his own day, where Professor Heaton leaves him, he should be better able to write the next chapter, which is his to write as a citizen of the nation that is heir to all the values, spiritual and material, made plainer to him by this text and by his whole college education.

GUY STANTON FORD

PREFACE

The first edition of this book, published in 1936, was an attempt to survey the economic development of Europe from the emergence of the ancient civilizations in the eastern Mediterranean to the depressed early 1930's. Working under the shadow of those gloomy years I could not escape excessive preoccupation with the problems raised by World War I and its aftermath. Yet I tried to avoid writing a mere preface to the morning's news, and gave the ancient, medieval, and early modern periods the space which they merited because their story was interesting and their contribution important.

The book was intended for students, especially American students, who had done little previous work in the subject, apart from a brief excursion to a medieval manor or through the Industrial Revolution in a general course on European history. I therefore omitted discus- sion of those controversial or detailed topics which belong to the higher altitudes of economic historiography. At the same time I tried to present the findings of the energetic researchers who were amplifying our knowledge and revising our interpretations at an appallingly rapid rate. And I urged teachers to watch the periodicals referred to in the bibliographies, to read the articles and book reviews, and thereby see how new questions were being asked or how old ones were being given new answers.

Though the present edition resembles its predecessor in scope and character, it is in large measure a new book, completely rewritten. Two things are responsible for the changes. In the first place, much economic history has been made since 1936. Some of this has been described, and while it is still too early to get all the economic aspects and consequences of World War II into focus, some of them have been examined.

In the second place, much economic history has been written since 1936. The war stopped much research and printing. It claimed the lives of some scholars; the leading French economic historian, Marc Bloch, was shot by the Germans because of his part in the French underground resistance. Yet some work went on—the first volume of the *Cambridge Economic History* was published as the bombs rained down on London, even though part of the first printing was destroyed "by enemy action"; the British *Economic History Review* continued to appear all through the war, and a new periodical, *The Journal of Economic History,* was born in the United States in 1941. Since V-E Day the presses in France have striven to make up for lost time. The result is a further widening of our knowledge at some points and a reinterpretation at others. "How quickly History changes," wrote a French scholar in 1947, "and what a magnificent testimonial that is to its vitality!" In the following pages I have attempted to bring students as close as possible to the frontier on which this new work is being done; but it is still a frontier that moves.

My thanks are due Dr. Guy Stanton Ford, editor of this series, for his valuable suggestions and criticism of my manuscript; to Professor Rodney Loehr, William Herbert Ford, and my wife for aid in getting the book finished. Acknowledgment for the use of maps which are not original has been made in footnotes. For the map of medieval commerce and trade routes I am indebted to Professors Sellery and Krey, *Medieval Foundations of Western Civilization.* The map of the parish of Weston Subedge is from C. R. Ashbee (ed.), *The Last Records of a Cotswold Community* (1904). For permission to use quotations I wish to thank the publishers of the following works: Carl Stephenson, "The Problem of the Common Man in Early Medieval Europe," in *American Historical Review,* April, 1946 (The Macmillan Company); Sylvia Thrupp, "Social Control in the Medieval Town," in *Journal of Economic History,* supplement, December, 1941 (New York University Press); Eileen Power, *The Wool Trade in English Medieval History* (Oxford University Press).

HERBERT HEATON

University of Minnesota
June, 1948

ECONOMIC HISTORY
OF EUROPE

I

INTRODUCTION

THE CONTENT OF ECONOMIC HISTORY

Economic history describes man's efforts through the centuries to satisfy his material wants. It is concerned with the age-long sequence of wants—efforts—satisfaction, with wealth-getting and wealth-using. The wants start with the fundamental needs for simple food and shelter; but to these, which man shares with other animals, has been added a desire for more elaborate food and dwelling place, for clothing, comforts, and luxuries. Beyond these physical wants there may be the wish to accumulate still more wealth for its own sake, for the income it will bring when invested, for the sense of security it affords, or for the economic, political, or social power and prestige it may confer. There may even be a continuing want of something to do, an inability to be idle and enjoy leisure, or such an intense interest in one's work that the thought of abandoning it is unwelcome.

To satisfy these wants, effort is necessary on the part of most people. The number of idle rich and idle poor has rarely been large in any society or period. In the 1930's census statisticians announced that about 40 per cent of the inhabitants of the United States and about 45 per cent of those of Great Britain and Germany were "gainfully" employed or occupied. The remainder were chiefly children or young persons, whose working years would come in due time when the period reserved by law for their education came to an end; or they were housewives, who would certainly resent being regarded as "ungainful," unemployed, or unoccupied. In less advanced countries the working force was a larger percentage of the total population, since women and children had a greater part in industry and agriculture. In all centuries until the nineteenth, childhood and housekeeping enjoyed no exemption from the obligation to help produce the family income.

The nature of the effort depends on at least three factors: the physical environment, the equipment and knowledge available

1

(which might be called the technological environment), and the social environment. Consequently "the movement of economic history" is the result of interplay between "physical resources, the technologies developed for the use of resources, and social institutions" (Usher).

The Physical Environment. The work men do is determined by the character of the soil and what lies under it, by proximity to river or sea, by the nature of the flora and fauna, and by the climate. Men cannot earn their living by coal mining in areas that have no coal seams, by growing grapefruit inside the Arctic Circle, or by cutting ice in winter out of a tropical river to sell to summer visitors. They cannot alter the temperature or the rainfall. Yet while they have had to adapt themselves to their environment they have been able to change it to some extent. Some parched lands have been irrigated, floods tamed, waterlogged wastes reclaimed. Grasslands have been turned into plowed fields, and regions of primeval forest have been cleared. Grains have been sought that will grow in areas of low rainfall or short frost-free seasons. Some regions unfit for agriculture have proved to be rich in minerals. Waterfalls have been harnessed to provide power. This ability to change the physical surroundings and to discover uses for what seemed worthless becomes most marked as we approach the days of the modern engineer and scientist; but the ancient and medieval worlds were far from helpless.

Technology. The economic activities of any time and place are also limited by the stage of development of equipment, skill, and knowledge of what to do and how to do it. Stone Age men had no tool capable of felling the trees which covered much of Europe. Once iron had been found and a good axe made, many areas could be cleared; yet that might avail little until a plow had been devised that was strong enough to break the heavy clay in which some trees had grown. A few men in the Middle Ages earned their living by mining coal or ores, but mining could not become an important occupation until powerful pumps were at hand to prevent mines from being flooded, until safety lamps allowed men to work far underground, and until better methods of smelting and refining metals had been discovered. It was little use producing great quantities of heavy goods until a way had been found to transport them cheaply, or growing large amounts of perishable foods until refrigerated boxcars or ships were available to deliver them in edible condition at the end of the journey. Alongside the advancing technique of mining, agriculture, industry, and transportation there was need for improved techniques in trading, banking, transferring money from buyer to remote seller, and in keeping accounts in such a way as to tell whether the work was producing profit or loss.

For thousands of years the accumulation of equipment and technical knowledge was very slow when compared with the pace of the last two centuries. Tradition or conservatism often was more evident than change; there was no apparent conviction that a better way of doing things was possible, and no determination to find it; the innovator might be disliked as a threat to the established order; and each generation passed the technique on to its descendant in much the same condition as it had received it. Yet this conservatism must not deceive us into thinking that nothing new was added until modern times. Curiosity or the urge to meet some pressing need did lead men in most centuries to make discoveries and inventions, and these became a permanent heritage. If we have rapidly developed new knowledge, equipment, and power to produce during the last two centuries, this has been possible only because of innovations made by our near or remote ancestors.

Economic and Social Institutions. Man does not live by bread alone; neither does he live alone. He has always been a social animal, a member of some group or groups. The most intimate of these is the family. It meets the need for companionship of the other sex; it provides a working team, with some division of labor; it is capable of creating a sense of solidarity, and is kept together by many other considerations, including the fact that the human infant is helpless and dependent on parental care for a far longer period than is any other kind of animal.

We can imagine an isolated family that has no contact with the rest of the world, is free to do as it wishes, owns all that it uses, produces all the commodities it consumes—and has to do without those it cannot produce. Such a picture would not be entirely unreal. Many family groups, especially in rural areas, did produce most (if not all) of the foods and manufactured articles they consumed or used until relatively recent times. But the family has rarely been isolated, a world to itself. Its members are part of a larger community, ranging from a village or small town up to a large territory with a numerous population, linked together by political ties and means of transportation, and with threads going out to a still wider area.

The existence of such communities influences the workaday life of their members. In the first place, division of labor is possible, with each individual concentrating on a particular task, selling his labor or product, and buying that of other specialists. A region may devote itself to producing some commodity for which it is best qualified and exchange its surplus for the goods it needs. A trading class arises, transportation and marketing facilities become necessary, and a monetary system emerges. Production can thus become commercial in purpose; its aim is not an output of goods to be consumed by the producer, but of commodities for market. The size of that market determines how far the producer will specialize or become commercial. A small community would not give full employment to a maker of doll's eyes or microscopes, or provide an adequate income for a man who did nothing but tan leather or sell one kind of commodity. Yet it has been a rare thing for even villages to be completely devoid of some production of goods for local or distant sale.

In the second place, the problems of organizing and directing production or trade become larger in a community than in our imaginary family group. Organization involves the assembling and application of capital and labor to the work that has to be done; and of course it implies the existence of an organizer who initiates an enterprise (or carries on one already in existence), who decides what to do, directs its doing, and shoulders the risk of profit or loss. The world's work is done in millions of enterprises of different kinds and sizes. The man who runs any one of them has been called an *entrepreneur*. This word could be translated as "enterpriser," or better still as "undertaker," a term which was often used in early modern times by people who "undertook" to provide a water supply, canal, or other service. But "undertaker" has not yet shaken itself quite free from its nineteenth-century use to describe the man who conducted funerals, and meanwhile "entrepreneur" has become deeply rooted in the economist's vocabulary.

If the entrepreneur owns and provides all the resources, capital, and labor that are required, the problem of organization is simple, but the size of the business will be small, as in the case of a peasant proprietor, small craftsman, or little storekeeper. Such self-supplying economic effort is, however, rare; the peasant proprietor, for instance, may have a large supply of family labor and may own some land, but often he has not enough capital or land. Consequently the entrepreneur usually has to draw on others to supply what he lacks. If he has much land he may buy slaves to work it, use serfs, or hire farm laborers. The craftsman may supplement his family labor force by training apprentices or employing journeymen, and augment his scanty capital by borrowing money or getting his raw materials on credit from a merchant. The larger manufacturer may provide only material and hire men to work on it in their homes with their own equipment; or he may obtain buildings, equipment, and material and gather his employees under his own roof. If he does the latter it is probable that he has to supplement his own capital by entering into partnership with someone who has funds to invest, by borrowing from a bank, or by floating a joint-stock company and selling stocks or bonds. It is possible to find instances of entrepreneurs who have worked with borrowed capital in rented premises with hired labor on materials that belonged to other people.

This division of ownership of the factors of production raises the problem of the distribution of wealth created by joint effort. In essence it is a question of (a) the costs to be paid by the entrepreneur, in wages, interest, or rent, (b) the price he gets for his product when he takes it to market, and (c) the profit (or loss) left after meeting his costs. Custom or law sometimes pegged costs and prices, but the more commercial a society became the more likely was the purchaser of labor, capital, or goods to give no more than he must and the seller to get as much as he could.

Behind the shares that go to the different factors in production are the people who receive them. If a large number of enterprises in any area or period are organized in the same way, these people may constitute recognizable classes—landlords, planters, slaves, serfs, tenant farmers, peasant proprietors, farm laborers, merchants, big industrialists, craftsmen, wage earners, investors, and so forth. The members of these classes, or of some smaller special section within a class, may become conscious that they have common interests to protect or advance, common grievances or problems. In good times they join hands to improve their well-being. In hard times they feel that they are not getting a just share of the wealth they are helping to create, or that the way and standard of living to which they are accustomed is in danger. Their discontent, suffering, or envy of the more successful and powerful may find expression in organized protest, in plans for joint action or regulation, in agitation for reform and help from the state, or in an attempt at a revolutionary change in the economic and social order. The history of all periods reveals individuals trying by voluntary group or class action or by joint pressure on the state to secure an improvement (or prevent a deterioration) in their share of the community's income.

Religion and Politics. Every society has its priesthood and its polity as well as its economy. There is political enterprise and religious enterprise, each with its own aims, standards of value, and organization, as well as economic enterprise. As exponent of a certain view of life and code of conduct, the church may influence the wealth-getting and wealth-using methods of the faithful. As an institution with a "plant" and "personnel," it needs income, which may be obtained from its own property and by contributions from the laity. Christianity and Mohammedanism, the two religions which have most influenced Europe, both affected economic life by their large property ownings and their commandments; but neither of them imposed such restraints on enterprise as were placed on India by some aspects of Hinduism—for instance by the caste system.

The influence of the political authority has been felt in at least three important ways. (1) The state has nearly always been engaged in some economic enterprises of its own. Ancient and medieval rulers had large estates, mines, and workshops. In our own day a government may own railroads, ships, light and power plants, factories, banks, the postal service, and a great variety of other activities. In Russia it owns them all. (2) The state has always protected, aided, and regulated the enterprise of its people. It has protected them, more or less successfully, against external attack and internal violence. Its laws have determined their rights and obligations by defining such things as property and contract. It has helped them by providing roads, harbors, lighthouses, water supplies or controls, currency, and many other facilities. It has favored them against the foreigner by imposing tariffs or prohibitions on imports, giving bounties or subsidies, discriminating against foreign ships, and sometimes by seeking favors for them abroad. At the same time it has always imposed regulations on the individual's dealings with his fellows, in the interest of dependents, consumers, rivals, debtors, creditors, or the state. (3) It has claimed a share of the income produced by its people, and sometimes of their capital, through its

power to tax or to confiscate, and of their time by its power to conscript them for military service, road work, or other kinds of labor.
The state's approach to these three functions has varied. In the
eighteenth and nineteenth centuries the Western world asserted
with some success the idea that the individual was the master and
the state the servant. The task of government was to advance the
welfare of its citizens and help them to enjoy their individual rights.
This concept is, however, one of limited time and space. More centuries and countries have been dominated by the opposite view:
that the state was supreme, that its people were "subjects," and that
economic means should serve political ends rather than that political
means should be directed toward economic ends. The claim of
twentieth-century totalitarian governments to exercise absolute
power over economic and all other aspects of life is in close accord
with earlier attitudes concerning the relation between ruler and
ruled.

A fuller definition of economic history is now possible. It is the
story of man's efforts to satisfy his wants, in a natural environment
capable of being adapted to some extent to suit his needs, with
technologies which have gradually increased his power to produce
or transport, and in a framework of institutions, some of them the
result of natural economic or social growth and some the outcome
of deliberate lawmaking by a political unit which has far-reaching
power to aid, control, command, and appropriate.

The economic history of Europe is worthy of attention for at least
three reasons. In the first place it is concerned with the life of
virtually the whole population, which is not always true of political,
military, intellectual, or even religious history. It is a story of movement, sometimes slow but occasionally rapid, at times upward for a
brief or lengthy period and then suddenly or slowly downward for a
long or short spell. It is a tale of varied developments, thanks to the
diverse resources, differing stages of technical development, and
contrasted political or social institutions and outlooks. At its best it
is a story of high achievement, human ingenuity, and far-reaching
innovations as men sought to make their economic efforts more
economical by putting scarce resources to the best possible use. At
its worst it is a record of greed, conflict, and destruction.

In the second place, economic developments have had a powerful
influence on every other aspect of Europe's history. Historians have
long asked, "Why did some event take place, why were conditions

as they were, and what caused them to change?" The answer used to be found in legal, political, or religious ideas, court intrigues, victory or defeat, some act of God or gods, the character of some man or the influence of some woman. Karl Marx (1818–1883) brushed such explanations aside and replaced them with his *economic interpretation of history*. If, said he, you wish to understand any epoch or chain of events, the only key that will unlock the door is the economic. Men earn their living by working in society. The nature of the work, the prevailing mode of production and exchange, and the social relationships which arise therefrom form "the base on which is built up and from which alone can be explained the political and intellectual history of that epoch" (Engels). Economic organization and methods create social classes, color ideas, shape forms of government, dictate policies, and write codes of conduct. The government is the servant of the most powerful economic class, and laws are the expression of the will of that class. All struggles are class struggles, all wars have economic objectives. Further, all change is due to alterations in methods of production and consequently in the relations between social classes.

This thesis had the defect of all attempts to explain complex results by one simple all-sufficing cause; but it did attract attention to factors which historians had ignored. The influence of economic forces on other sides of life is now universally admitted; or rather it is recognized that the different forces interact on each other, with the economic predominant at some times, the political, religious, intellectual, or military at others. A purely non-economic interpretation of the earth-shaking events of the first half of the twentieth century would be as fantastic as one which was solely economic.

In the third place Europe's economic history is important because of the influence that continent has exerted on the rest of the world. Europe was the birthplace of most of the developments in technique, organization, and ideas that have given the economic life of today its chief characteristics. It was the source of the stream of population and capital that flowed out to settle and develop the New World. Its influence was ubiquitous, and few parts of the other continents could resist some degree of Europeanization. Its preeminence has been weakened during the present century by growing strength without and tragic divisions within. But it still houses at least a fifth—the most energetic fifth—of the world's population. Its resources—physical and human—are great. If those of the west and center should prove to have been irreparably damaged by the two great wars, those of the east are large and have not yet reached the peak of their exploitation. In the early 1930's an American geographer wrote, "Europe, more than any other continent, holds in its hands the destiny of mankind" (Bogardus). He may still be right.

The Prelude to Europe. The Contribution of Prehistory and of the Near East

European economic history might be labeled Chapter III in the story of man. Chapter I covers a quarter of a million years or some such incomprehensible period of prehistory. During that time the human race emerged as a distinct species of animal, learned to walk erect, and hence was able to turn its forepaws into hands. It discovered various new ways of working, found new products worth making, fashioned tools, and thereby added greatly to its ability to satisfy wants. In those developments Europeans seem to have played a minor role. Chapter II begins at least five or six thousand years ago when, in the favorable environment of Egypt, Mesopotamia, and perhaps northwest India, men used the accumulating technical heritage to build elaborate economic and political societies. Chapter III starts about four or five thousand years ago when we get evidence that the discoveries and developments of western Asia and northeast Africa were influencing the inhabitants of that peninsula of Asia which is called Europe. A very hurried skimming over the first two chapters is a necessary prelude to a study of the third.

Chapter I is inconceivably long, but its achievements laid the foundations of most of our basic occupations. Primitive man increased his ability to secure food in three ways:

1. He collected wild plants, nuts, fruits, grasses, and slow-moving animals or insects in much the same way as the other animals did, but added to the list of his victims by devising hunting and fishing traps or weapons which helped him to capture strong beasts or those which were fleet of foot, fin, or wing. He thereby expanded greatly the range of his catching and collecting, as well as his power to defend himself from being caught or collected.

2. He domesticated some animals. By 5000 B.C. most of the farm animals of today had been tamed. The dog helped in hunting, in rounding up flocks or herds, and in keeping guard. Cows, goats, sheep, and swine were useful for their flesh and hides; alive, the first three gave milk, while sheep and some goats yielded an annual

fleece of fibers that could be turned into cloth. The ox became a draft animal with the invention of the plow and the wheel. The ass and the camel were useful though rather capricious draft animals, but the horse was of limited value. It gave speed to attack by cavalry and chariots and could carry officials or couriers quickly over long distances; and mare's milk was a staple drink of horse-keeping nomads. But there were no satisfactory types of horse for draft work on field or road until at least the early Middle Ages. Further, until about 800 A.D. the harness was attached to a collar high up on the horse's neck instead of resting on its shoulders, and a heavy strain almost choked the animal. The horse was less sure-footed than the ox in slippery places; it was more liable to sickness, it ate more, and some Europeans did not care to eat its flesh when it was dead. Hence the ox was the more valued and versatile animal; it shared with house, wife, and ass the honor of mention in the Tenth Commandment, and in some religions was regarded as sacred.

3. Man (or more probably woman) began to cultivate some wild grasses, grains, roots, and fruits that had formerly been collected. The latest evidence suggests that barley and emmer (a kind of wheat) were first sowed and reaped some time before 6000 B.C. in what is now called Iraq, on the banks of the Tigris and Euphrates rivers. The practice spread to Syria, Egypt, and the Danube Valley, and by 2000 B.C. had reached France, Britain, and Spain. From the cultivation of grain to that of vegetables, vines, and fruit trees was a natural series of steps once the basic discovery of preparing the soil and planting had been made.

Cultivation added a third source of food supply, but it was not necessarily an abundant source. A pointed stick or crude hoe was a poor tool for breaking ground, and much labor was needed to prepare a small plot. With the invention of the plow the plot could be expanded into a field, yet even in the Middle Ages and later a plow team spent a long morning turning one acre of land. Harvesting, threshing, and grinding remained slow, laborious manual processes in many regions until medieval or modern times. Further, there were not many areas, especially in Europe, which could be plowed without a preliminary expenditure of much labor in wresting control of the soil from the natural vegetation by felling trees. For all this hard work the yield might be small if the soil was poor, if there was too much or too little water, or if a patch of land became exhausted by continuous cropping. Only in a few favored spots—the valleys and deltas of the Nile, Tigris, Euphrates, and Indus—did nature give much help, by providing an annual flood from a swollen river and by leaving a layer of rich silt behind when the waters subsided. Water, silt, and sun made agriculture easy and rewards rich. In Europe there were no such rivers, the work was far harder, and the crop was much smaller.

The Development of Industries. While man was improving his methods of procuring food he was accumulating tools and learning how to use them to convert raw foods and materials into something more edible or serviceable. His earliest equipment was fashioned from wood, flint, bone, horn, fiber, or hide. From these materials he made hammers, knives, scrapers, awls, and needles as well as his weapons and hunting or fishing gear. He learned how to make fire, thus opening up possibilities for baking, grilling, or smelting. Pottery appeared, to provide containers in which food could be stewed or boiled and liquids could be stored. Brewing and wine making soon provided the liquids. Cloth came to supplement or supplant skins as clothing. Tanning added to the variety of labor and commodities.

The age that developed pottery, clothmaking, and leatherwork was also the one that domesticated plants and animals. It now had nearly all the basic occupations and commodities, and since some of the latter could not be made by any ordinary amateur a class of skilled craftsmen emerged. It had also learned to exploit the subsoil, for the best flints were obtained by mining. It had developed some exchange, as the flints, furs, fish, and shells found in certain areas were wanted by people in other regions.

Some important aids and materials were still lacking, of which the wheel, sails, and metals were the chief. These came in course of time. The wheeled vehicle was well known in advanced communities by 3000 B.C., there are pictures of vessels using sails before that date, and some metals had been found a thousand years earlier. But the metals most easily procured—gold, silver, copper, and lead —were scarce and soft. Scarcity made them desirable for ornaments, softness limited their use as tools or weapons. Copper made "a fairly efficient dagger, a rather mediocre ax, and a poor knife" (Kroeber); but when bronze was produced, somewhere before 3000 B.C., by putting a pinch of tin into molten copper, a hard metal became available. Bronze and its two ingredients were, however, too scarce and costly to be generally adopted, and were enjoyed only as weapons or decorations by the rich or as tools by a few craftsmen. The peasant still used stone or wood implements.

Iron came into the military and industrial picture much later. There is little sign of its widespread use until about 1500 B.C., and the early supply seems to have come from the Hittite area of northeastern Asia Minor. From that time and place its use as weapon and tool spread far afield, for the supply of iron ore was larger and more widely scattered than was that of copper. By 1000 B.C. the Iron Age was well begun. Its warriors had better weapons and more of them than the bronze-using aristocracy which they overthrew. Farmers who could not afford bronze managed to acquire iron axes, plowtips, or reaping hooks, and craftsmen were able to build up their kit of tools. Yet the methods of smelting iron, of making it malleable, and of turning it into steel were crude and laborious, yielding little return for much effort. For the mass of mankind metals of all kinds remained scarce commodities until at least the end of the Middle Ages and were far from abundant until the nineteenth century.

Appropriation Without Production. One important method of acquiring an income has been omitted from this survey. Some men lived by appropriating the products, property, or persons of others. In its simplest form this kind of enterprise might be kidnapping and robbery on land or piracy at sea. On a more ambitious scale it included the raids or invasions which organized tribes or larger units made on flocks, herds, farm settlements, and cities, bent on seizing what was transportable or on settling in the captured region. Its most widespread manifestation was the sway which religious or secular rulers established over the land, labor, person, and income of their own people and of those they conquered.

Where the process was simple raid or robbery, the robber gathered up labor or the products of labor just as his ancestor had gathered up the wild products of nature. Where the method was one of rule, the priest or king resembled the domesticator of animals and plants. He protected his subjects, directed their movements, and might improve the conditions under which they lived and worked. He thereby made it possible for them to increase in numbers and to work more effectively; but his claims on their labor and products were large and constant, and it was unlikely that they were left in possession of any great surplus when their simple necessary wants had been met. Throughout the rest of this book the influence of those who used spiritual, political, or physical force to appropriate without directly producing must be kept constantly in mind.

The River Valley Civilizations. Man's growing technical capacity in agriculture and industry reached its first known mature development in Egypt and western Asia. By 3000 B.C.—and probably much earlier—the inhabitants of the deltas and valleys of the Nile and of the Tigris-Euphrates were skilled in tillage and handicrafts, resided in villages, cities, palaces, or temples, traded at home and abroad, were ruled by elaborate governments, possessed highly organized religions, and had evolved a system of writing, a knowledge of numbers, and a calendar.

In each region everything depended on the river. All around lay desert; but the great stream rose high each year because of tropical rains or melting snow in its upper reaches, overflowed its banks, soaked the ground, washed out some of the salts that were in the soil, and then retreated, leaving an annual top-dressing of silt. Under such conditions even simple farming methods might produce fairly good harvests. As the methods were improved and as erratic natural irrigation gave place to a measure of water control, the yield could be made almost incredibly large. Some records from Mesopotamia suggest that the average crop from barley fields was over eighty times the amount of the seed that had been sown.

This high productivity had important consequences. The farmer could produce more than he needed for his own larder. Therefore the labor of part of the population provided sufficient food to maintain the rest of it and to permit the existence of manufacturing, trading, priestly, and ruling classes. If nature is stingy or man's methods are poor, the labor of all (or nearly all) may have to be concentrated on the land in order to provide a bare subsistence, and there is little spare time or man power for other activities. This was the situation in most parts of Europe until modern times. The river valleys were more fortunate; the agricultural rural base was strong enough to support a substantial industrial, commercial, religious, and political urban superstructure.

High productivity had its price. Individual enterprise by farmers cannot construct or maintain the large earthworks or water controls that are needed for efficient irrigation. A large river—whether it be the Nile or the Mississippi—can be tamed as water system or as waterway only by some ruler who has command of the supplies of material and labor required for grand-scale projects, and who has authority over the distribution of the precious fluid. In the ancient world such a ruler was bound to be a despot, master of the whole economy as well as of the polity; and since he usually was the chief servant of some local god or gods, he was also the religious master, a priest-king. The improvement of river-valley farming was therefore closely connected with the growth of governments. In Mesopotamia some priests became kings of city-states along the riverbanks and then occasionally welded these states into larger kingdoms. In Egypt the absorption of twoscore small states into two kingdoms and then into one made it possible to treat the 750 miles of the lower Nile as a vast royal project. When governments were weak or were overthrown by invasion or civil war the waterworks were neglected and fertile lands lapsed into desert or swamp.

The rulers were also substantial entrepreneurs. Kings, temples, and nobles owned large estates, drew produce from their farms, mines, and workshops, and made profits from their trading or financial enterprises. They used slaves or hired laborers and gathered the yield into their own granaries, cellars, wardrobes, or purses. In Egypt the king's properties were so large and fruitful that they tempted every invader and rebel. His workshops supplied pottery, clothing, and luxuries for his household. He sold the surplus from his own fields and shops, along with that which he received as rent or taxes and that which he claimed the right to buy at a price fixed by himself. The domestic sale of some goods and all foreign trade were his monopoly.

In Mesopotamia the temples were the early landowners. They directed irrigation, assigned each person a piece of land, advanced him a loan of rations and seed out of their storehouses, and then claimed much of his produce as rent, interest, principal, or tithe. Some of these goods, along with those made in temple workshops, they sold abroad for commodities needed by the priests or the community. Even when a merchant class arose, the temples still conducted much production and trade. Markets were under their control, banking was one of their functions. Church and state were thus deep in "big business." They would not have been scared by being called socialists or restrained by being labeled monopolists.

The large incomes collected by crown, priesthood, and nobility supported a luxurious life which lifted industrial production high above the level of peasant handicraft. Palaces, temples, pyramid tombs, giant statues, and fortifications took the art of building and sculpture far beyond the mud or brick hovels of the farmers and the city poor. Since the gods demanded that the dead be well dressed and their resting places well furnished, the tombs yield evidence of the high level of arts and crafts in these early civilizations. From those of Egypt have come pieces of elaborately patterned textiles, pottery, and glass. The goldsmith's and jeweler's skill is measured by the gold coffins or statues, and by the combinations of precious metals, precious stones, and enamels. Cabinetmakers decorated furniture with inlays of gold, silver, ebony, and ivory, while painters and dyers mixed colors that are still vivid after five thousand years. The Mesopotamian tombs tell the same tale of skilled luxury production.

Trade and Trade Routes. Few of the materials needed for these articles could be obtained at home. There was virtually no timber or deposit of ores in the river valleys, no ivory, precious stones, spices, or perfumes. To secure them, Egypt must go armed and take them by force, or develop foreign trade. She did both. Almost every year witnessed a campaign which had as one object the collection of supplies for industry. As trader she sent out grain and eventually in Greek and Roman times became the most famous granary of the Mediterranean area. Linen, glass, wool, and vegetable oils were also exported, along with a commodity of which Egypt enjoyed a monopoly—papyrus. The lower river and delta were lined with big rushes. If these were split, flattened, dried, and gummed together, they made a sheet called papyrus. This was Egypt's writing paper and was in demand abroad, eventually as far west as Spain and Belgium. The literature of Greece and Rome and the works of the Christian Fathers were written on it.

Some of Egypt's imports, especially of metals, came across or along the Mediterranean from Europe, and some, such as gold and ivory, from central Africa. Many of them came from Asia, including Syria and Asia Minor, and the routes along which they were carried remained vital arteries of trade long after the Pharaohs were forgotten and the cities of Mesopotamia had been buried in silt or sand. The map on p. 16 shows the main lines of intercontinental trade. The most southerly route went overland from the lower Nile to the top of the Red Sea, then down that hot humid waterway and along the coast to the Persian Gulf and India. Eventually, in the first century B.C., navigators discovered that the monsoon winds would blow them from the Red Sea mouth across the open ocean to India

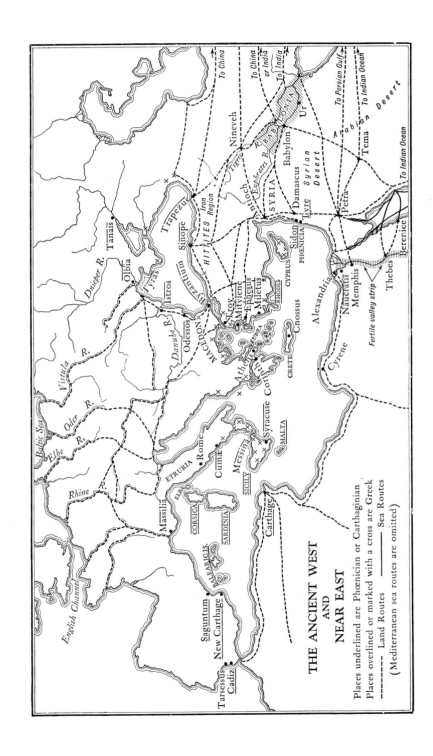

THE ANCIENT WEST
AND
NEAR EAST

Places underlined are Phœnician or Carthaginian
Places overlined or marked with a cross are Greek
———— Land Routes
------- Sea Routes
(Mediterranean sea routes are omitted)

at one season of the year, and blow them back at another. When that fact became known the first important transoceanic route could be drawn on the map.

The other eastward routes were by land and river. The "Great Road" which was most generally used started at the Nile delta, crossed the Suez isthmus, and turned north to Syria. There it forked. One arm went up to Asia Minor, to the land of the Hittites, to Ephesus, or to Troy, which was one springboard to Europe. The other arm swung round the semicircular top end of the Syrian desert to the Euphrates or Tigris. From that point one could descend the rivers, past the irrigated lands and the cities—Babylon, Erech, Ur, and the rest—to the Persian Gulf and India. Or one could cross the rivers, go through spots which later were to have romantic names like Kashgar, Bokhara, or Samarkand, work through the mountain passes to India, or keep going due east to China, the land of silk.

The growth of trade stimulated—and in turn was stimulated by—the development of a trading class and of a medium of exchange. This was especially true in Mesopotamia. Of its traders we know something, thanks to the discovery of baked clay tablets on which they made their business records; and we see them, as well as most other kinds of workers, through the clauses of the Code of Hammurabi compiled about 2100 B.C. From such evidence a picture emerges of a people whose economic organization and practices are highly developed. There is great division of labor. Clear ideas prevail concerning property and contracts and govern the relations between landlords and tenants, employers and workmen, borrowers and lenders, buyers and sellers. There are laws regulating apprenticeship, mortgages, leases, promissory notes, seed loans, interest rates, and partnerships. Punishments are prescribed for doctors who operate unsuccessfully, tenants who neglect to keep their dikes clean, prices that seem exorbitant, interest rates that are excessive, jerry-builders whose work does not stand up, and other sinners against the private or public welfare. The use of credit is well established, and that of precious metals for payments of all kinds, including wages, falls just short of producing a currency.

This complex economy and society existed four thousand years ago. It reveals what could happen when a fairly simple farming technique and an ambitious state water control combined to wring a large product from potentially rich soil. "Society persuaded or compelled the farmers to produce a surplus of food-stuffs over and above their domestic requirements, and by concentrating this surplus used it to support a new *urban* population of specialized craftsmen, merchants, priests, officials, and clerks" (Childe). The persuasion or compulsion came from an elaborate religious and political system. Whether that system took more products from the peasant than its waterworks had added to his crop, we cannot say. It is, however, highly probable that the peasant standard of living on the river banks was higher than that of those Africans and Asiatics who lived away from the fertile valleys and whose life was doomed by their environment to be that of wandering pastoralists or hunters, with intertribal war and infanticide as devices for preventing population from outstripping the scanty supply of resources.

A GENERAL NOTE ON BIBLIOGRAPHY

At the end of most chapters a list of books and articles will be found. Most of them are in English, but a few French and German works have been included. Articles from the *Encyclopaedia of the Social Sciences* have been listed; also many from periodicals. Teachers might with advantage enlist the support of their classes in preparing a card index catalogue of the articles on economic history which are contained in such periodicals as are available in their libraries. This catalogue should have the following journals as its base:

> *Economic History Review*, cited hereafter as *Ec. H. R.*
> *Journal of Economic History*, cited as *J. Ec. H.*
> *Journal of Economic and Business History*, cited as *J.E.B.H.*
> *Economic History*, a supplement to the *Economic Journal*, cited as *Ec. Hist.*

The first two publish lists of new books and articles. Articles on European economic history occasionally appear in the *Economic Journal, Economica, American Historical Review, American Economic Review, Journal of Political Economy, Quarterly Journal of Economics, History,* and in the kindred French and German periodicals. In pre-war days France had two periodicals, *Annales d'histoire économique et sociale* and *Revue d'histoire économique et sociale.* Publication of the former has been resumed under the title *Annales.* The most useful German publications used to be Schmoller's *Jahrbuch* and the *Vierteljahrschrift für Sozial-und Wirtschaftsgeschichte.*

BIBLIOGRAPHY

The Content of Economic History

Clapham, J. H., *The Study of Economic History* (1929).
East, G., *Historical Geography of Europe* (1935).

"Economic History" and "Economics: the Historical School," in *Encycl. of the Soc. Sc.*, vol. v.

Fleure, H. J., *The Geographical Background of Modern Problems* (1932).

Forde, C. D., *Habitat, Economy, and Society* (1934).

Gras, N. S. B., "Stages in Economic History," *J.E.B.H.*, May, 1930.

Heaton, H., "The Economic Impact on History," in Strayer, J. R. (ed.), *The Interpretation of History* (1942).

Johnson, E. A. J., "Tools for the Economic Historian," *J. Ec. H.*, supplement, December, 1941.

Sée, H., *The Economic Interpretation of History* (Eng. trans., 1929).

Sombart, W., "Economic Theory and Economic History," *Ec. H. R.*, 1929.

Tawney, R. H. (ed.), *Studies in Economic History: The Collected Papers of George Unwin* (1927), part i.

Usher, A. P., *History of Mechanical Inventions* (1929), chap. 1.

PREHISTORY AND THE ANCIENT NEAR EAST

Breasted, J. H., *The Conquest of Civilization* (1926).

Bromberg, B., "The Origins of Banking," *J. Ec. H.*, May, 1942.

Cambridge Ancient History (7 vols., 1923–28) contains many chapters on economic conditions and has good bibliographies.

Childe, V. G., *What Happened in History* (1942), chaps. 2–7.

Clay, A. T., *Business Documents of Murashu, Sons of Nippur* (1898–1912).

Gras, N. S. B., *Introduction to Economic History* (1922), chaps. 1, 2.

Harper, R. F., *The Code of Hammurabi* (1904).

Knight, M. M., and others, *Economic History of Europe* (1926), chap. 1.

Kroeber, A. L., *Anthropology* (1923), chaps. 6, 14.

Lutz, H. F., "Babylonian Partnerships," *J.E.B.H.*, May, 1932.

Myres, J. L., *The Dawn of History*, chaps. 1–8.

Neuberger, A., *Technical Arts and Sciences of the Ancients* (Eng. trans., 1930).

Petrie, W. M. Flinders, *Arts and Crafts of Ancient Egypt* (1923).

Rostovtzeff, M., *A History of the Ancient World*, vol. i: *The Orient and Greece* (1925), chaps. 5, 10.

Smith, G. Elliot, *Human History* (1930).

Woolley, C. L., *The Sumerians* (1929).

The Old Testament, especially in the books Genesis to Judges, gives a good picture of a pastoral people.

Encyclopaedia of the Social Sciences: Articles on Anthropology, Archaeology, Famines, Grains, Hunting, Migrations, Nomads, Prehistory, Slavery.

II

THE ECONOMIC EMERGENCE
OF SOUTHERN EUROPE

During the last three thousand years of the pre-Christian era southern Europe gradually emerged as a well-populated region of developed agriculture, of industrial, trading, and political cities, and of rich culture. During the same period the people in central and northern Europe also advanced considerably in their ability to wring a livelihood out of their environment; but they lagged behind the southerners in many respects, their environment was quite different, and their story is therefore deferred till a later chapter.

Southern Europe was influenced and aided by its proximity to the economies of Asia and Egypt. From those regions came migrants and traders. Pastoral people might overflow from the semi-arid steppes of central Asia if their own numbers or those of their livestock grew too large, or if drought cut down the supply of food and water. Farmers in the Nile delta, Syria, or cultivated patches of Asia Minor might feel the urge to move if their homeland became too crowded or disturbed. Miners and craftsmen sought mineral deposits or customers farther west. Kings, nobles, or tribal chiefs went to conquer, for migration was often invasion. Merchants pushed their way to new markets or sources of supply.

The Ways to Europe. Three main thoroughfares led to Europe. In the north was a vast flat expanse, without a single natural obstacle except rivers, from the foot of the Indian mountain rampart in central Asia round the top of the Black Sea to southern Russia. From there one could go on to the Balkans, the Danube Valley, and through the Alpine passes to Italy; or, working northward, one could traverse the plains of central Russia, reach the Baltic, and pass across Germany to the Rhine and points west—provided one did not mind the strangely damp or rainy climate. In the middle, Asia Minor was a land bridge which came within sight of Europe at the narrow waters of the Dardanelles and the Bosporus. Along these two land routes men were moving to trade or settle long before 3000

B.C. But it was the southern route, the seaway along the Mediterranean, which played the most important part in the economic
emergence of Europe.

The Mediterranean is over 2,200 miles in length. Its two great
offshoots, the Adriatic and Aegean seas, and its large annex in the
Black Sea combine with the peninsulas of Greece and Italy to give
it a very long coast line. Chains or clusters of islands supply steppingstones from Cyprus to the Balearics. Landlocked and narrow,
it has little tide, and in summer its surface is fairly smooth except
when a hot strong wind blows from the Sahara desert. On calmer
days the winds may be light and fitful. Thus it was desirable for
ancient ships to have plenty of oarsmen for getting them in or out
of port and for moving the vessel when the wind was lacking or
contrary. In winter cold winds from the north made sailing so unpleasant, and the rain clouds hid the stars so often, that it was wise
for vessels to tie up from November until early spring. Yet, given
improved ship designs and simple sails to supplement oars, the
Mediterranean was increasingly traversed after 3000 B.C., by vessels
which worked along the coast or moved from island to island,
carrying goods and passengers.

The coming of the metal ages made such navigation essential,
since Europe had the minerals and other commodities which the
Near Eastern peoples lacked. Some of the islands and parts of the
mountain mass of the mainland were relatively rich in metal deposits. Cyprus gets its name from the Greek word for copper, or
vice versa. Elba had iron, Spain was a treasure house of silver, gold,
copper, and iron, Greece had silver and lead, and there was copper
or gold at other points in the Balkans. Many Aegean islands were
rich in marble suitable for statues. Farther north there was tin in
Bohemia and Britain, and gold in Ireland. From still farther north
came the amber which was picked up on the beaches of the Baltic,
and the furs of the Russian forests. These two commodities were
brought southward down the rivers which flowed into the Black
Sea. In that sea were shallow areas providing rich fishing grounds,
while on its northern shore the land was capable of being turned
into grainfields or vineyards.

Traffic in these European materials was established long before
2000 B.C. The second fortified city of Troy was built in 2400 B.C. to
collect loot or levies from the people who were crossing the Dardanelles to and from Europe or were passing through the strait to pick

up amber, furs, and fish at the Black Sea ports. By that time Crete was exploiting its position in the center of the eastern Mediterranean to trade with all points of the compass. A regular though small traffic was bringing metals southward from central Europe and the British Isles and sending traders or craftsmen northward to teach the barbarians how better to extract or refine the ores. During the next millenium (2000–1000 B.C.) the trade routes became longer, the Phoenicians strengthened the links between east and west, and important migrations went as far as Italy. In the last millenium B.C. the Greeks roamed far afield in the eastern Mediterranean as colonists and traders, Carthage developed the western half, and the ancient world reached its climax when Rome welded the two halves together in a great political empire and trading area.

The Mediterranean Environment. We cannot measure how far the economic life of Mediterranean Europe was shaped by natives who learned new ways or by immigrants who already knew those ways. But we do know that this life was obliged to differ in many important features from that of the pastoral peoples of the Asiatic steppes and from that of the river-valley dwellers. The differences were determined by the topography and the climate. The topography of southern Europe is one of hill, mountain, and valley. The map at the front of this book shows very little land colored green (i.e., less than 600 feet above sea level) on the north shore of the Mediterranean. Rarely does a valley cover a large area; the Po basin in north Italy is the only one of any size. Equally rarely does a coastal plain possess much width. Spain is mostly mountain and plateau. The Italian peninsula is a ridge of mountains that slope or tumble down to two seas. The Balkans are a maze of mountains, plateaus, and very small plains. In Greece the ranges cut the country into a jumble of isolated valleys and thrust promontories out into the sea, thus making the coast an alternation of forbidding cliffs and deep indentations, and scattering the water with islands where the hills have been broken off from the mainland.

Over these valleys, slopes, and highlands the "Mediterranean climate" prevails. That climate, which is found between 30° and 45° latitude in such other parts of the world as California, southern Australia, and South Africa, has only two real seasons—winter and summer. The winter is rainy and cool in low or sheltered places, but snowy and cold at high altitudes or where there is no protection from the north winds. The summer is a time of drought broken by a rare thunderstorm, of burning winds from the Sahara, blinding sunshine, parched brown grass, and, if you are a wise southerner instead of a stubborn Anglo-Saxon, of afternoon siestas. The winter rains vary considerably from year to year; in addition they are heavier in the highlands than in the lowlands, on the windward side than on the lee side of the hills, and in the north than the south. The summer rains seldom exceed one or two inches in any month. Water is therefore not embarrassingly abundant, but rather likely to be seasonally or unpredictably deficient.

These two factors, topography and climate, shaped Mediterranean life throughout the centuries. There was food for livestock that were sufficiently nimble-footed and strong-legged to roam on the high ground or in the fairly abundant forests; hence the goat, sheep, and hog loomed large in the rural economy, and the man who looked after them figured romantically in classical stories, though in actual life he often was a kidnapper and brigand as well as a herdsman. But for cattle the supply of summer food grew scanty as the grass became brown and parched. The cultivation of hay or alfalfa on irrigated land might ease the scarcity, but this practice would absorb resources of land, water, and labor which were too meager to be earmarked for that purpose. Since the cost of feeding draft animals was heavy in comparison with the service they rendered, man power, including slave power, was in great demand, meat and dairy produce occupied a small place in the diet, and the supply of manure was inadequate.

The area capable of easy cultivation was small, and the period of what one might call simple farming—plowing, sowing, and reaping —was limited to the winter, since the climate was too hot and dry for summer crops. On plains and lowlands the uncertain or scanty seasonal rainfall called for the development of "dry farming" methods. Fields were sown only in alternate years. They must be carefully drained to take away the surplus water in winter and frequently plowed during the year they were lying fallow in order to keep the soil pulverized, thus letting the water penetrate the soil on rainy days and preventing excessive evaporation during the summer. This involved a great demand for labor, especially for the three or four plowings and cross-plowings each year; yet the reward was a crop only every other year.

Even perfect farming on the lowlands could not meet the demands of a large population. The cultivated area must be extended up the hillsides, both for grains and still more for olives and vines. This was a dangerous step, for when forests were cleared and the surface was broken the soil was washed away when the rains came. To make matters worse, this soil settled down in the bed of the lower river-course, impeded the water's outlet to the sea, and created coastal swamps which were infested with malarial mosquitoes. Hillside farming therefore involved great outlay of capital and labor in making terraces that looked like a set of broad stairs, in rendering the drainage adequate, and in checking erosion.

Land which needed so much care was too precious to be sown with grain or any other seed that yielded a small output per acre. It was therefore planted with vines and olive or fig trees. These were able to live through the hot dry summer because their roots went deep to tap the subsoil moisture and spread widely to absorb that which had been stored in the soil by the cultivator's endless working of the surface. They took some years before they came into full bearing, but their life was very long, their yield per acre might be large, and they did not lie idle every other year. Hence the olive and grape were staple Mediterranean crops. Olive oil was the butter and lard, the lamp oil, and the cold cream. Wine held the place now occupied in northern latitudes by water, tea, coffee, and beer. Grapes and figs, eaten fresh or dried, were the chief fruits; even foxes, according to Solomon and Aesop, liked grapes. The fig tree generously gave two or three crops each year.

The central problem of Mediterranean agriculture was therefore that of conserving water and soil. If in spite of laborious efforts there was not enough moisture, more must be made available by artificial irrigation from reservoirs. The farmer's interest in water was supplemented by that of the towns. The growth of Mediterranean cities was impossible unless waterworks were constructed. Hence while Egyptians faced the task of controlling a seasonal superabundance of water, southern Europeans had to conserve a scarce supply by thorough cultivation of the soil and by erecting great public water systems to convey the water from remote places in the hills. The farming, engineering, and construction jobs were far more difficult in Europe than they were in the alluvial river valleys.

At its best the cultivation of many Mediterranean regions could not provide a rich livelihood for a large population. There were, however, two other ways in which the food problem of an area might be solved. The first sought to relieve the lack of land or food by establishing colonies at unoccupied or primitively inhabited points on the Mediterranean or Black Sea coast. The colonists could grow enough to feed themselves and have some to spare for shipment to the mother city-state. The second concentrated agriculture on the intensive production of wine and oil to supply the domestic market and to create a surplus for export. At the same time industries were developed; minerals were vigorously mined and turned into metalware, wool and flax were made into cloth, clay into pottery, marble into statuary. The forests of live oak which flourished on the cool and wet higher hill slopes provided lumber for ships. These carried away the surplus wine and oil, the exports of manu· factured articles or of metal and marble, and returned with the grain and fish of regions which had a surplus of those primary products. By such an export-import economy a small area with a city as its industrial and commercial center could provide a better living for more people.

Crete. The first known European community to practice this com· bination of enterprises was Crete. That fairly large island had most of the necessary economic assets: temperate climate, some fertile well-watered soil, large forests for the shipbuilder and lumber exporter, some copper and clay, some shellfish from which dye was extracted, and a location near to Greece, Asia Minor, and Egypt as well as on the seaway to the west. Immigrants brought the skills and a knowledge of the market demands of their Syrian and Egyptian native lands. For at least a thousand years (2500–1500 B.C.) Cretans exploited these assets. They sailed to the islands and coastal harbors of the Aegean, trading, freebooting, or fighting. They went east to Cyprus, Syria, and the Nile delta. In the west they visited Sicily, Sardinia, Elba, and the other islands, and even passed through the Strait of Gibraltar to Tarsessus (near the present Cadiz), where Spanish metals and British tin were picked up. In addition to their metal cargoes they traded in wine, oil, grain, lumber, and manufactured goods—especially pottery of all qualities—produced at home or picked up in foreign ports.

The discoveries made by modern excavators show that this varied activity was richly rewarded. Some traders rose to be merchant princes or kings of the ports which blossomed into cities. Their palaces contained workshops and warehouses and were equipped with good drains flushed with water. For a long time they dominated the commerce and politics of the coasts and islands of the Aegean; but trading and fighting cities eventually grew up on those coasts, developed the arts of industry, weaponmaking, and war, and overthrew the Cretans (about 1400 B.C.), only to be themselves engulfed soon afterwards by invaders from the north.

Phoenicia. After disaster descended on Crete some centuries elapsed before any other European people took up the work she had been doing. That time gap was filled by the commercial enterprise of the Phoenicians. Their country—a narrow belt of the Syrian coast, with Tyre and Sidon as its two chief ports—rivaled Crete in its happy combination of natural resources and good location. Its hillsides were covered with cedar, cypress, and oak trees, there was some metal underground, the coast had fairly good harbors from which the Nile delta was only about a week's journey, and the country was traversed by the Great Road from Egypt to Asia Minor and Mesopotamia. But there was little land fit for farming. The Phoenicians therefore had every inducement to become manufacturers, middlemen, seamen, shipbuilders, colonizers, and pirates. They carried on much of the overland trade between the two river-valley civilizations, taking the goods of the one to the other and adding their own lumber or metals. They handled the copper of Cyprus and the iron of Asia Minor. Stepping into Crete's shoes (or ships) they gathered the Aegean trade into their arms. Farther west they established colonies in Malta, Sicily, Carthage, and at Gades (the later Cadiz) to collect the products of the faraway mines.

Of their outposts Carthage, established by 800 B.C. on the northeast tip of Tunisia, became the most famous. It took possession of the western end of Sicily as well, thus standing astride the narrow water which divided the two halves of the Mediterranean. It could therefore make trouble for the Greeks when they came west to plant colonies or for the Romans when they developed a desire to expand beyond their own peninsula. It turned the western Mediterranean into a Carthaginian lake by placing trading posts at strategic points, making alliances with native chiefs, and using some of its profits to build warships or hire mercenaries. Those profits came from both sides of the sea. Europe supplied raw materials and minerals. Africa provided gold, ivory, ebony, ostrich feathers, precious stones, and slaves, brought by caravan across the Sahara or fetched by ships which went along the coast to West Africa. The land around Carthage produced plenty of wheat, wine, and oil. Carthage thus had all the ingredients for trade in the west as well as along the routes that led back home to the mother country or the Nile.

The Phoenicians added industry to commerce. They copied Mesopotamian and Egyptian methods and patterns, devised their own, and seem to have produced some goods which were cheap enough to be purchased by the poorer sections of the population. They became especially skilled in finishing and dyeing cloth. Insects collected from oak trees were ground up to produce a scarlet dye, and the famous Tyrian purple was made from tiny shellfish. Few dyers knew how to obtain this color, for the process was kept a top secret. Purple cloth was therefore rare and costly and became the fabric usually associated with the raiment of royalty.

Phoenicia lost some of her commercial opportunities when the Greeks developed their own ships, industries, and traders. Many of her people migrated to Carthage when Asiatic emperors marched westward to threaten the lands where Europe, Asia, and Africa met. There was still work to be done and profit to be made, for these empires needed western materials, the contact between the Mediterranean and the Orient became closer, and Egypt continued to be a rich field for Phoenician shipping and trade. But the business with Europe and that between the various parts of Europe gradually passed into European hands, especially those of the Greeks.

Greece. The Greeks that we know from their literature, ruins, and objects dug up by archaeologists were not the first people to occupy the southern part of the Balkans, the islands of the Aegean, or the west coast of Asia Minor. They were the last of a series of waves of immigrants which had swept over that region from the north or east during the preceding two thousand years. Each wave probably destroyed the rulers and subjugated the people it found in possession; each then settled down to tending livestock, cultivating the soil, mining or quarrying, developing industries, and living in or near towns which were political centers of small city-states, ports, and nests of pirates or warriors. The towns fought each other, and all might be destroyed when the next wave, armed with better weapons —of bronze and later of iron—or possessing better tactics or superior numbers descended upon them. But the old occupations were not quite obliterated; there were enough people left alive to carry them on, the new rulers soon developed luxurious tastes, and the invaders might add something fresh to the stock of productive capacity.

Some such disturbance between 1200 and 1000 B.C. brought the Greeks to the lands and isles of the Aegean. They were probably pastoral, possibly farming, and certainly fighting people equipped with iron weapons. They settled down to herding and grain growing; the picture we get in Homer is one of fields and flocks, with grape or olive growing still an infant occupation, and with little trade. But soon the pressure of population exerted its influence. Scarcity of land or food led to colonization. Between the eighth and sixth centuries B.C., groups of colonists swarmed out from Miletus, Corinth, Megara, and other cities. They went to the shores of the northern Aegean, the Dardanelles, and the Black Sea. Turning west instead of north, some of them descended on Sicily and southern Italy—"The America of the Greeks" (Glover)—while a few went as far as Sardinia, Corsica, Marseilles, and Spain. Others planted themselves on the North African coast, the Nile delta, and Cyprus. Some colonies failed, but hundreds succeeded. Miletus alone made nearly a hundred settlements, and as some colonies in turn founded others, the Greeks finally squatted round the Black Sea and the eastern half of the Mediterranean like frogs round a pond.

The colonists farmed or fished to supply their own wants and to build up exportable surpluses. They exploited mineral deposits or bought the metal from natives who worked mines farther away, and served as distributing points for imports from the parent city. In the fullness of time some colonies became large city-states with their own mature economies. Syracuse in Sicily had grown by the fifth century to be the third largest city in the Mediterranean; only Carthage and Athens had larger populations. But most of them remained economically "colonial," exporting their food and raw materials and depending on the mother city for some of their manufactured goods, of their capital supply, and of their shipping services.

Meanwhile the Greeks who had stayed at home gave increasing attention to the production of oil and wine, the development of manufactures, and the exchange of these staples for imported grain, fish, and other commodities which could not be produced so cheaply or abundantly on the spot. The expansion of industry and commerce caused the cities to grow larger, and thus created a good domestic market for the cultivators who lived around them.

Reliance on imported food was greatest in such large cities as Corinth and Athens. Corinth looked westward to her colonies in Sicily and southern Italy for her grain. Athens depended on Egypt and southern Russia, and it has been calculated that at one time four bushels of wheat were imported for every one that was grown on the soil of Attica, the peninsula of which Athens was the capital. By the fifth century the food supply was therefore a major issue in Athenian diplomacy and domestic politics, since any interruption of imports would have brought starvation to a population estimated at about 300,000 persons. Friendly relations were fostered with the Scythians, who grew grain on the north shore of the Black Sea and caught the fish which ranked second only to bread as a solid article of food in the Greek diet. Control of the Dardanelles was sought by making treaties with those who ruled the land around Troy or by maintaining a large navy up there. The route to Egypt was kept open by constant attacks on the pirates who infested the eastern sea. Since the food ships were laid up during the winter, public officials must provide sufficient storehouses, see that adequate supplies were put into them during the fall, and prevent speculators from cornering the market.

Land Problems. The Homeric economy had been largely self-sufficing, with the land divided into large and small estates. The former were worked as units by slaves or cut up into small farms tilled by tenants; the latter were cultivated by their owners. So long as the land's chief task was to feed those who owned and farmed it, problems of ownership, costs, and prices were not important. But once production was directed toward market and profit many difficulties could arise. The large unit might be more efficient than the small one. If there was a keen demand for land the tenant's rent might be raised. The small farmer has always in all countries been short of capital, and obliged to resort to some lender for the funds he needs to expand his acreage, to buy animals, seed, equipment, or pest killers, to tide over lean years and poor harvests, and to carry him through from the beginning of his year's work to the sale of his product. He usually seems a worse risk than does the large operator and therefore may have to pay a higher rate of interest. Since he buys his supplies on a small scale he pays the retail rather than the wholesale price; and as he sells on a small scale he may get a lower price for his product. If his receipts exceed his costs, all is well, and he probably borrows still more next year; but if his income is less than his outlay he is unable to meet his debts.

In Greece, as in all countries, there were good years, and even longer periods, which yielded a net surplus. But when the years of deficit rolled round, inability to pay the creditor resulted in loss of the land, in enslavement of the debtor and his family, or in both. The Greek small farmer knew well the truth of the assertion that "Greece and poverty were always foster-sisters." The outcome in Greece resembled that in other lands and times. Distressed farmers cried out against the men they regarded as their oppressors. The villain of the play was the landowner who operated large vineyards and olive groves, sold much produce, plowed his profits back into his estate, and lent money to small owners or tenants. With him was coupled the city merchant who made loans and foreclosed the land or seized the farmer's goods and person when the debtor defaulted. The aristocrat and the bourgeois were thus the common enemy in the class struggle. Since they controlled the politics of the city-state, that struggle was largely political. The malcontents threw their rebellious weight behind some existing leader or sought salvation in some lawgiver or tyrant who appeared above the battle, gained control, and took drastic action to redress the grievances. Yet the fruits of victory soon went bad, for the play of economic forces nullified the political reforms. Old debts were canceled, but new ones were quickly incurred. The land was cut up, but eventually the bits came together again. Escape from one misfortune did not insure the farmer freedom from future worry.

The Athenian story of agrarian reform is the best known. Solon the Lawgiver (594 B.C.) softened the law of debtor and creditor, canceled many debts, restored foreclosed land, liberated those who had become slaves through debt, forbade such enslavement in future, and limited the area of land any person might own. Yet Pisistratus had to do the whole thing over again half a century later. He went farther, and therefore pleased the small men more, by exiling many landlords, distributing their estates among the poor, and providing cheap state loans. But within two centuries the land round Athens was back in large estates farmed in highly developed capitalistic fashion.

Greek Industries. In Homer's picture the household makes the things it needs. Even the great men take a hand at manual work in the intervals of hunting, traveling, and fighting; Paris helps to build a house, Odysseus is skilled in shipbuilding and making furniture, a queen spends her days weaving, a princess does her brothers' laundry. In later centuries this production for use continued to play a great part in supplying family needs. The farmer's household made goods because it had some spare time but little surplus produce available to buy them, while on the large estates and in the temples freemen, slaves, and women worked, often in special workshops, to supply the demands of the residents. In the cities, however, production for the domestic and external market gradually expanded. Textiles, pottery, and metal goods were the three chief wares, and each town developed a reputation for the quality and style of its products. During its best centuries Athens sent its distinctive types of high-class pottery to markets as far away as Mesopotamia, Gaul, and Spain. Production was carried on in the homes or workshops of the craftsmen or by groups of free or slave workers gathered under the employer's or owner's roof. Some of these groups were comparatively large; we know of one Athenian shieldmaker who had 120 men at work, and of another firm with 160 slaves working together. But usually only a handful of men were engaged.

Slavery. Greek industry, like every other form of enterprise, relied heavily on slave labor. It has been estimated that slaves comprised a third of the population of Athens. Slavery was "a constant factor in the social and economic life of the Near East and Europe throughout the entire period of ancient history" (Westermann). It was taken for granted as part of the labor structure. The supply of slaves came from many sources—prisoners of war, persons snatched by pirates or slave raiders, defaulting debtors and their families, and children of slave parents. The slave trade was one of the oldest branches of commerce. Some towns, such as Delos, were famous slave markets, public auctions supplemented private dealings, and governments collected a sales tax on every transaction.

Since slaves were drawn from varied quarters, their races and qualities were diverse. The slave might be white or colored, come from any of the "barbarian" lands around the Mediterranean, or be a native-born Greek. He might spring from almost any section of society, possessing only the simple rural training of a south Russian farmer or the great technical or professional skill he had acquired in some city. His duties were as varied as his origins. On the land he tilled a small farm, or toiled in great fields or vineyards under the eye of an overseer. At the oar of a galley, in a mine or quarry, his life was likely to be arduous, disciplined, exhausting, and short. But if his qualifications equipped him to work as policeman, domestic servant, craftsman, salesman, or clerk he might receive wages, work alongside freemen or freedmen, and hold a position of trust or even of authority. He could marry and own some property. Sometimes his master set him up in a business and gave him a fixed fraction of the net receipts, while occasionally he won emancipation either by saving up to buy it or as a reward for faithful service. There is one famous case of a Greek banker, himself an ex-slave, who liberated his chief clerk and later bequeathed to him both his bank and his widow. Yet the fact that slaves sometimes revolted or ran away suggests that the lot of the unfree could be unpleasant.

Commerce and Currency. Greek foreign trade was virtually all sea trade. It needed capital for ships, cargoes, and operating expenses for journeys which might take months to complete. It ran the natural risks of storm and of navigation on seas dotted with islands or along rockbound coasts; but in addition there was the ever present danger of attack by enemies or pirates. The risks were divided in various ways. The ownership of a vessel might be split up into fractions, each the property of a different person. In trading ventures at least two parties were usually involved; one did the traveling, buying, and selling while the other lent or invested the funds. The trader risked the loss of his life, the stay-at-home financier the loss of his capital. If the venture failed because the ship and goods were sunk or captured, the capitalist's funds vanished. If it succeeded he got his "sea loan" back with a high rate of interest; or his investment was returned to him along with a fixed share of the profit. Such loans and partnership contracts were not invented by the Greeks; they were well known in Mesopotamia, where kings, landlords, and temples joined forces with traveling traders; and they financed trade till at least the end of the Middle Ages.

The Greeks did, however, make one invention of vast commercial importance. The river-valley traders had used precious metals as media of exchange, but their unit had been a stated *weight* of copper or silver. The metal was cast in bars, and a pair of scales was needed to weigh it. Even then no one could tell how much of the bar was silver and how much was base metal. The next step had been taken when some temples put out bars or round pieces of standard "fineness," and stamped on them the head or figure of a god as a guarantee that they contained a certain proportion of silver. The quality of the metal was thus known, but scales were still needed. Yet although this was being done by 2000 B.C., it was about 700 before the next step was taken. By that time stamped coins, containing a definite quantity of electron (a natural alloy of silver and gold), were being minted in Lydia in Asia Minor. Tradition makes King Croesus the author of this innovation, which dispensed with weighing in favor of counting.

Soon the leading Greek cities were issuing coins of gold, silver, or copper. For developing its currency Athens was especially well endowed. Mt. Laurium, about twenty miles from the city, was rich in galena, a silver-lead ore. The lead was used for roofs, pipes, and domestic utensils, thus causing lead poisoning to be prevalent. The silver was turned into money. The Laurium deposits were state property, but private enterprise mined them, paying a royalty to the state, employing thousands of slaves, and exhibiting great ingenuity in mining and refining methods. The public revenue and private profit drawn from Mt. Laurium helped to finance the fighting strength, economic energy, and cultural wealth of Athens; but the mines wrote a dark page in the history of slavery.

The coming of money had many effects. In the first place, the circulation of coins of small value helped the small producer, for he could now take money instead of goods for the few wares he had to sell. In the second place, coins helped to change the character of wealth. Real estate, grain, slaves, and livestock were no longer its sole or chief measure. The new form of wealth could be more easily accumulated, stored, and consumed; or it could be allowed to grow by being invested or lent—which meant that it could more easily be borrowed, a dangerous new facility for governments and peasants alike. In the third place, since each city-state issued its own currency, there were scores of coins with different names, weights, and standards of fineness. Consequently a human ready reckoner, the money-changer, was needed to tell the relative values of these coins and to change foreign ones for native currency.

The money-changer sometimes became a money-lender, and by the fifth or fourth century B.C. he was a fledgling banker. He received deposits from those who wished to thwart thieves or to put their money out to work earning interest. He made loans on the security of valuables deposited with him or of farm and workshop products. He transferred money from one depositor's account to that of another, or from his bank to another on receiving an order to do so. He was rarely just a money merchant but handled goods, conducted manufactures, and invested in ships. Often he was an alien, used but hated by the natives, and since foreigners were forbidden to own land his energy and capital went into building a fortune instead of building a country estate.

Politics and Economics. Economically and politically Greek life was that of the city-state. The unit was a city with a small rural area around it. A large plain or river valley can fairly easily become united, with beneficial consequences; but a region of small valleys, mountains, and islands is cut up into compartments, and the sea does not make a solid bond between them. Greece therefore housed scores of separate states. A single island might be subdivided; there were six states on Lesbos, an island about forty miles long and thirty wide. It is in the nature of cities to be rivals, and if they are sovereign states their commercial competition may overflow into armed conflict. So it was with ancient Greece, as with medieval Italy. East of the Aegean the chief rivals were Samos, Miletus, and Rhodes; on the west side Chalcis and Eretria wrestled for control of the copper deposits of Euboea; Corinth resented any attempt to break into the preserve it had pegged out in Sicily and south Italy; and everybody envied the commercial success of Athens. Occasionally rivals came to terms, but the agreement was fleeting. Geography, history, and competition produced "an ineradicable political wrong-headedness" (Michell) which prevented the Greeks from uniting and led them to swear, sometimes "by heroes male and female, by springs and rivers, and by all gods male and female," their enmity toward other Greek communities.

The one force that might be expected to bring unity was the danger of attack from without. Yet when the Persian Empire had absorbed Egypt, Syria, and Asia Minor after 500 B.C. and decided to add the Greek islands and peninsula, joint resistance was not forthcoming. Athens was left to bear the brunt of the attack. She drove the invaders back, built up an anti-Persian confederation, and then turned it into an Athenian Empire of allies and dependent states. This step brought her great gain, as for instance in the tribute which was paid to help maintain her navy for the common defense. But those who paid it grew weary of the imposition, while outsiders were angered. Sparta feared her military strength would be endangered, and Corinth felt the effect of Athenian commercial inroads in the west. The Peloponnesian War (431–404) was therefore an attack upon Athens, and its success wrecked the most ambitious attempt to unite Greece from within.

The Hellenistic Period. When unity did come it was imposed from without by two barbarians. Philip of Macedon marched down from the near north (in about 350 B.C.) and absorbed all the peninsula except Sparta into a realm that stretched to the Danube and the

Bosporus. His son, Alexander the Great, conquered Asia Minor in 334; then in three years of whirlwind campaigning he overthrew the Persian Empire and built in its place an empire that reached to the lower Nile, the Persian Gulf, and the banks of the Indus. Greece thus became part of a vast domain which included virtually all the regions whose history we have been examining.

Alexander's empire was a military creation. It broke into three large pieces—Egypt, Asia, and Macedon—and a number of smaller ones after his death in 323 B.C. But the policies he had begun to pursue were not abandoned. The rulers of these kingdoms were, like Alexander, strongly imbued with Greek ideas and culture. Their armies, like his, were filled with Greek mercenaries or with barbarians who had at least a Greek veneer. Hence, like him, they looked to Greeks for aid in organizing and administering the conquests and in developing their vast resources. Greeks already dominated eastern Mediterranean trade, but their influence became now so strong and wide that historians have christened the period and the region *Hellenistic,* which can be translated as "Greekish."

For the Greeks the opportunity came as a godsend. Their economy had been sickly and stagnant since the end of the Peloponnesian War. Export markets had shrunk, thus causing unemployment and inability to pay for food imports. Slavery had swallowed up more victims of debt or of intercity war, and many small landowners had lost their farms. Greeks therefore swarmed eagerly from their impoverished city-states into the conquered lands as soldiers, settlers, traders, and officials. In each capacity they were welcomed by the new rulers. On the land they were given holdings and stimulated to improve methods of cultivation, or they were placed in charge of royal estates and told to make them more productive. In the old towns, cities, and garrisons as well as in scores of new ones that were established they took charge of production, business, and finance. Alexandria, founded by Alexander in 331, rapidly became the economic and intellectual metropolis of the whole Hellenistic world. Greeks had much to do with handling the goods that flowed into its harbor from places as far away as China in the east, central Africa in the south, Spain in the west, and the Baltic in the north.

The rewards of the Greek rulers, officials, and entrepreneurs were large. Some of them were well earned, for great energy was put into developing the natural resources of the conquered areas. Boats were built larger, postal services established, harbors improved, lighthouses erected, and pirates more vigorously suppressed. In the river valleys the water controls were overhauled, especially in Mesopotamia, where they had been allowed by the Persians to fall into serious disrepair.

Some of the rewards were the result of the discovery of a vast hoard of gold and silver in the vaults of the dethroned Persian emperor. Alexander promptly dishoarded it. He gave large bonuses to his soldiers and spent much of the remainder on public works, the erection of new cities, administrative expenses, and luxuries. The release of this enormous purchasing power stimulated the demand for goods of all kinds, but probably especially for building materials and luxuries. It caused prices to rise; the scanty evidence available suggests that they may have more than doubled in about twenty-five years. It therefore increased traders' turnover and profits, helped to create a new-rich class, and produced some fabulous fortunes.

Some rewards were the result of the system of government which the new rulers took over from the conquered. The Pharaohs had conducted vast enterprises and exercised wide control over the production and distribution of goods, while the Persian emperors ran state industrial or trading monopolies as well as great estates. The conquerors made little change in the systems they found in operation. The Ptolemies, who were the new kings of Egypt, merely installed Greek efficiency experts to make them more productive, claimed labor, produce, and the sole right of sale, and added a state banking monopoly. In this comprehensive system there was plenty of room for well-paid managers, officials, and tax collectors.

Little wonder then that a Greek poet advised a heartbroken lover to "Be off to Ptolemy, and with him you will get high pay and plenty of adventure!" It is doubtful, however, whether this emigration of Greeks added much to the economic welfare of their native cities. The craftsmen who stayed behind may have found good markets for their products in the conquered lands. Greeks who did well abroad may have sent some of their earnings or profits to their relatives at home. Rhodes and other cities of Asia Minor shared in the good times, while Delos did an expanded business in slaves, with a capacity for handling 10,000 sales in a day. But there is little to indicate that cities like Athens or Corinth participated in the prosperity of the Hellenistic areas to the east.

That prosperity did not last forever. The wave of rising prices and profits caused by the dispersion of the Persian treasure subsided when the money was all gone and seems to have led to a decline in prices which must have been as disastrous to enterprise as the upward movement had been stimulating. When the leaner years came, the kings of Egypt and western Asia fought each other or strove to injure each other's economies; they tried to raise taxes and to meet deficits by inflating the currency. Peasants occasionally grew weary of the extortion of their masters, and either resorted to revolts or downed their tools and staged sit-down strikes in the local temple. The weakness of governments was reflected in the revival of piracy. Efforts at reform and recovery were insufficient. There was not enough political or economic strength left in the Hellenistic world to resist the Romans when they came east to see and to conquer.

BIBLIOGRAPHY

Calhoun, G. M., *Business Life of Ancient Athens* (1926).

Calhoun, G. M., "Ancient Athenian Mining," *J.E.B.H.*, May, 1931.

Calhoun, G. M., "Risk in Sea Loans in Ancient Athens," *J.E.B.H.*, August, 1931.

Childe, V. G., *What Happened in History* (1942), chaps. 8–11.

Gardner, P., *History of Ancient Coinage, 700–300* b.c. (1918).

Glotz, G., *Ancient Greece at Work* (Eng. trans., 1926).

Glover, T. R., *The Ancient World* (1935), chaps. 1–3, 6, 7, 10, 11.

Michell, H., *The Economics of Ancient Greece* (1940).

Rostovtzeff, M., *History of the Ancient World* (1925), vol. i, chaps. 12, 13, 16, 20, 23, 25.

Rostovtzeff, M., *Social and Economic History of the Hellenistic World* (1941).

Schoff, W. H., *The Periplus of Hanno* (1913).

Toutain, J., *The Economic Life of the Ancient World* (Eng. trans., 1930), parts i, ii.

Usher, A. P., *History of Mechanical Inventions* (1929), chaps. 2, 3.

Westermann, W. L., "Greek Culture and Thought," in *Encycl. of the Soc. Sc.*, vol. i, pp. 8–41.

Westermann, W. L., "Warehousing and Trapezite Banking in Antiquity," *J.E.B.H.*, November, 1930.

Zimmern, A. E., *The Greek Commonwealth* (4th ed., 1924), parts i, iii.

Encyclopaedia of the Social Sciences: Articles on Agriculture (parts i and ii), Archaeology, Barter, Colonies, Commerce, Commercial Routes, Irrigation, Land Tenure (Introduction, Primitive Societies, Ancient World), Slavery.

III

THE ROMAN WORLD

At first glance the Romans scarcely seem to merit much attention by the economic historian. The city of Rome was never a great commercial or industrial center, but rather a sponge which absorbed tribute, a consumer of goods taken from the conquered. The country around it had no distinctive features or occupations. The Romans made few basic contributions to the technology or organization of agriculture, industry, or trade. They have been called "the prime borrowers of the ages" and do not seem to have invented even those methods of warfare which brought them such success.

Yet they did write an important chapter in the economic development of Europe. Their military achievements and political organization deeply influenced the social environment. Their invasion and occupation of western Europe helped to raise the level and widen the area of that region's productivity. Their conquest of the eastern Mediterranean brought peace to the turbulent run-down Hellenistic world. By merging east and west into a political unit as well as a great trading area, they gave the people of the Mediterranean lands and some who lived far away from its shores a chance to get on with their work in an atmosphere more favorable than had been known before. While those people paid a high price—for the Romans did not come bearing gifts—any other ruler might have been just as expensive without being nearly so encouraging.

The Early Roman Economy. The Romans appear first, about 800 B.C., as farmers living in Latium, a mixture of marsh, plain, and hillside in the middle of the west coast of Italy. They may have been wanderers who had chosen to settle there because it was one of the very few districts which had a river, the Tiber. North of them were the Etruscans, who had probably migrated there from Asia Minor, bringing well-developed methods of agriculture, mining, industry, and trade. In the barren mountains to the east were wild hillsmen, ever ready for a raid on the fertile coastal lands. To the south were various other Italian groups; Greek colonies were dotted on the heel and toe of the peninsula or in Sicily; and beyond them, across the narrow waist of the Mediterranean, was Carthage, rapidly becoming mistress of the western sea.

Society in Latium was less advanced than was that of the Etruscans or Greeks. It was headed by a king and a military class of patricians who ran the government, did the fighting, and in their spare time managed their estates. If those estates were large, the land was tilled by slaves or by tenants who paid rent in kind, cultivated their landlord's home farm, and went with him as camp followers to war. The plebeian class was on a lower level economically and, for a while, politically; it was composed of small landowners or tenants, artisans, and traders. Below it were the slaves. All classes lived chiefly on the product of typical Mediterranean farming: flocks grazed on the hillsides, hogs sought food in the forests, while cultivated fields yielded wheat, oats, grapes, olives, and garlic.

For this rural region Rome became the center. Its site was good for defense or trade. Ravines and the Tiber made the famous group of seven hills easy to protect. The river was navigable by seagoing vessels as far up as Rome; but there an island and shallow water forced ships to unload their cargoes and also provided a spot where the stream could be forded or bridged. All roads by land and sea therefore led to Rome, and during the sixth century, when Latium was under Etruscan control, the town became a thriving community of traders and craftsmen. In about 500 B.C. Rome freed herself from that control and became a republic. During the next 250 years she extended her own overlordship north and south. She became head of a league, alliance, or federation of mid-Italian cities which eventually controlled the whole peninsula and the Po Valley.

From Italy to Empire. While the Romans who thus consolidated 50,000 square miles of Italian soil were chiefly country dwellers, the wars fostered industries to supply weapons or ships and developed a class of army contractors. Trade was facilitated by the union of the various regions and by a provision that the citizen of one place was to enjoy the right to trade in all the others. But the patrician was still the leading figure in Roman society. To him agriculture, politics, and war were the only occupations fit for a gentleman.

There was plenty of gentlemanly unfinished business awaiting his attention, for when Rome absorbed the Greek colonies in the south she became a close neighbor and possible rival of commercial Carthage. Soon the rivals were at war. The first stake was Sicily, rich in grain, oil, and sulphur, with Carthage in control of its western end. In the First Punic War (264–241 B.C.) Rome won all Sicily and destroyed Carthage's sea power. In the Second (218–202 B.C.) she broke Carthage's hold on Spain, cooped her up in North Africa, and thus became mistress of nearly all the lands around the western Mediterranean. In the Third (149–146 B.C.) Carthage itself was destroyed by fire, the population was enslaved, and Romans seized the rich wheat fields, ranches, vineyards, and olive groves that lay beyond the charred city.

By this time the Roman state was well on the way to becoming a huge empire. Its armies were already at work in the eastern Mediterranean, for Corinth was destroyed in the same year as Carthage. The boundaries moved relentlessly outward over the barbarian northwest and the disrupted Hellenistic east. At their widest expanse (see map on p. 41), they stretched from the Atlantic Ocean and the north of Britain—wisely omitting the Scottish Highlands and Ireland—to the fringe of the Sahara, the upper Nile, and the Persian Gulf. The Rhine and Danube marked the continental northern frontier, but for a time the camps were well beyond that line. Almost a third of Europe was inside the imperial fence.

Economic Aspects of War and Conquest. The building of the Empire took up nearly five centuries of intermittent warfare. The period of expansion beyond the Italian mainland was spread over about 235 years (264–30 B.C.), and during that time at least 130 years witnessed campaigns important enough to merit mention in college textbooks on Roman history. Since war was such an important form of public enterprise, some analysis of its costs, returns, and consequences is necessary, but far from easy.

The Costs. War imposed at least three important costs: (1) the peacetime maintenance of the army and navy; (2) the expenses, human and material, of actual campaigns; (3) the defense and administration of conquered territories.

1. The early Roman army consisted of the patricians, who alone could afford horses, chariots, armor, and weapons in an age when metals were scarce and costly. Soon, however, infantry became important. This led to the establishment of a national militia, in which all able-bodied men were liable for service. The actual fighting was to be done by those who owned sufficient property to be able to provide their own shields, lances, and javelins; but poorer men were also drafted and these were eventually supplied with weapons and

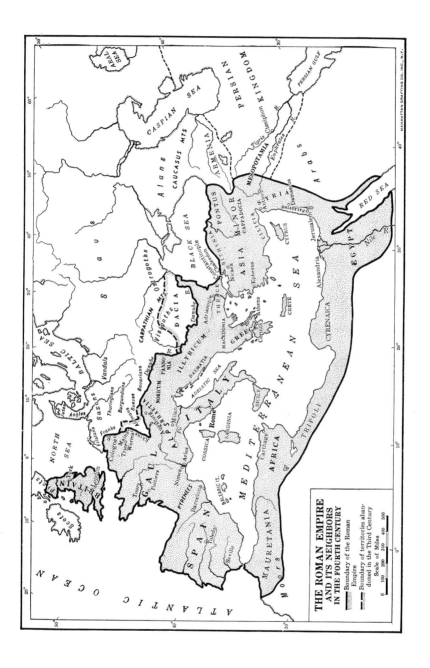

THE ROMAN EMPIRE
AND ITS NEIGHBORS
IN THE FOURTH CENTURY

Boundary of the Roman
Empire

Boundary of territories abandoned in the Third Century

Scale of Miles

0 100 200 300 400 500

paid a wage while they were away from their work. When the wars moved away from Italy less reliance was placed on conscripts and more on volunteers, who enlisted for as much as sixteen years, were equipped and paid, and received a bonus of money and land when they retired. By the first century B.C. the commanders were still members of the patrician class, but the ranks were filled with mercenaries, whose maintenance was a heavy charge on the state.

2. Some campaigns were very costly. The First and Second Punic Wars lasted twenty-three and sixteen years respectively. One Roman historian asserted that during the Second Punic War the Romans mustered over 700,000 men. At the Battle of Actium (31 B.C.) the Roman forces consisted of 80,000 men and 400 warships, and in the following year Augustus was faced with the task of demobilizing about half a million men. Some of the great battles caused heavy losses; at Cannae (216 B.C.) 25,000 Romans or allies were killed and 10,000 captured out of a total of 50,000 men; at Arausio (105 B.C.) 60,000 men are said to have been slain. The destruction of property during the Second Punic War was enormous; fields were laid waste, villages and towns were burned, and the Italian soil deteriorated rapidly from neglect. The total loss of life, of capital goods, and of man power diverted from productive work must have reached vast dimensions during the centuries of conflict.

3. The defense and administration of the captured provinces was an abiding cost. Some conquered provinces were allowed to retain a great degree of self-government, but others might need to be kept in order by a display of force. The chief burden was the defense of the frontiers by maintaining garrisons, building roads, and erecting administrative centers. Any land which had been damaged or depopulated during its conquest or which had become run down before it was taken would need a large influx of population and capital if it was to be restored to productivity. An undeveloped region would yield little revenue to its captors until it had been supplied with capital, settlers, roads and harbors.

The Fruits of Victory. In the early wars on the Italian peninsula the chief reward of victory was safety from further attack by Etruscans, mountaineers, wild Gauls who occupied the Po Valley, or rival cities. Once Italy was safe, the fruits of victory over external enemies fell into three main classes. In the first place there was the booty that might be picked up. Rome never unearthed a hoard of treasure comparable to that which Alexander found in Persia; but the defeated Hellenistic monarchs and their subjects, like the wealthy men of Carthage, had plenty of precious metals or stones, horses, sumptuous furniture, and other articles that could be seized. In addition there might be swarms of prisoners to be enslaved. When victorious armies returned home from the east they brought with them lavish spoils of all kinds; but those who conquered Spain, Gaul, or Britain found much smaller pickings.

In the second place, victory conferred the right to collect tribute. This right had been exercised by all the imperial predecessors of Rome. Egypt, Babylonia, the Hittites, Assyrians, Persians, Athens, Alexander, and his successors, all had imposed on subjugated peoples the obligation to contribute regularly to the conqueror's coffers, and counted tribute as an important item on the revenue side of their budgets. Rome followed this example during the expansion of her control over Italy; but she did it in a very small way, preferring to regard the cities around her as junior allies. The high cost and heavy debt of the First Punic War brought an end to such generosity, and the imposition of tribute became a regular practice. Originally the levy was one-tenth—a tithe—of the crop, but poll taxes and sales taxes were added later.

In the third place, the public lands (and desirable private ones) of a defeated people and the property of a dethroned ruler might be appropriated. On the public lands it would be possible to settle Rome's landless civilians or veterans. From the estates, mines, vessels, workshops, and trading enterprises of the ex-monarch income could be obtained and passed into the Roman treasury or the pocket of its emperor. In the east this kind of transfer brought considerable revenue to the new owner; but in the west much development of resources was required before there could be any large profit.

Finally, the collection of these claims on the income or property of the vanquished called for a little army of administrators of high and low degree, for ships in which the tribute in kind could be carried to Rome, and for capitalists who were willing to finance the collection of the levies, the regeneration of wasted lands, the development of new ones, the contracts for roads, and the ships.

Effects of the Wars on Italy. The Second Punic War damaged the Roman economy so severely that no mere restoration of pre-war conditions was possible. Many farmers did not come back. Those who did return often found ruined or neglected farms, and either shirked or failed at the task of restoring them. Many drifted to the towns or joined the parties that went out to found new colonies. Those who resolutely tried to resume the old life in the old spot might succeed if they were producing chiefly for their own subsistence; but if they were working for market they faced keener competition from the grainfields of Sicily or from the large estates that were being built up elsewhere.

Imported grain and the large estate overshadow much of the subsequent history of Italy. After the First Punic War Sicilian tribute brought about a million bushels of wheat yearly to Rome. As other grain-producing areas were subjugated, cereals from Sardinia, Egypt, Spain, North Africa, and the Black Sea lands reached Rome in tribute or trade. When Carthage was destroyed, Romans who obtained the land made North Africa into a great exporting granary. The conquest of Egypt increased the already large flow of grain from Alexandria. When this influx reached Rome it might glut the market and depress prices; sometimes it was sold at less than the market price; and in any case it made profitable grain growing in Italy well-nigh impossible for the small farmer.

If the small producer turned to products which were less exposed to foreign competition, he might find himself facing severe rivalry from the expanding agricultural enterprise of his own richer compatriots. These men consisted partly of the old patrician senatorial class—already large landowners, and sometimes made wealthy through moneylending or war contracts. When a law of 220 B.C. forbade them to engage in trade, public contracting, or banking, the patricians turned to land as an outlet for their energy and capital. In addition to them there was a growing class of businessmen who had made fortunes by feeding, equipping, and transporting the army, constructing public works, farming taxes, or lending money as well as in ordinary trade. They put some of their wealth into land for profit or prestige, bought the farms of men slain in war, foreclosed mortgages when they had the chance, and kept pieces of the public domain which they held as security for loans to the state.

To these old-rich or new-rich the empty devastated lands, especially those of southern Italy, presented both challenge and opportunity. The government allowed (or persuaded) them to lease large expanses at low rentals after the Second Punic War, and repeated this plan after the capture of the lands around Carthage. Usually each big tract was operated as a unit, a *latifundium*. The character of the soil, the scarcity of labor, or the obvious folly of trying to compete with imported grain might cause it to be turned into a cattle or sheep ranch, and a ranch must be large if it is to provide grazing facilities all the year round. But the wars which killed off many Roman freemen brought in swarms of slaves, who might be sold cheaply if the market was glutted. Given cheap land, cheap labor, and plenty of capital, the *latifundia* could be developed as vineyards, olive groves, and even grainfields in addition to the ranches. Some *latifundia* reached vast dimensions. A thousand-acre unit might count as small; and when one owner died in 8 B.C. he left 4,000 slaves, 3,000 yoke of oxen, and 257,000 other animals.

The slaves worked the ranch or plantation in gangs under the supervision of their owner or of his bailiff and overseers. The treatment varied, but sometimes was so brutal that it led to slave revolts. How efficient the system was one cannot say. Columella, who wrote about agriculture in 50 A.D., reported that on large grain farms the slaves treated the oxen badly and stole whatever they could. He believed, however, that if the land was fertile, the region healthy, and the bailiff capable as well as honest, slave labor might be more remunerative than farming by free tenants. But the use of slaves was profitable only so long as the supply was abundant and the price low. When the wars gave place to the *Pax Romana* of the first two centuries A.D., the supply diminished, the price rose, and slave cultivation became too costly.

War and its aftermath thus deeply affected the Italian countryside. The influx of tribute in kind caused the peninsula to become dependent on imported grain, forced the small farmer to turn to the production of crops or animals which required more capital or labor, and faced him with competition from the plantations. It is likely that he fared better than one might gather from the contemporary documents. These records generally deal with complaints and discontent. When conditions are good there are no complaints, and hence no documents to delight the eye and distort the perspective of later historians. There were probably many small and middle-sized farm owners or tenants who made ends meet without great difficulty. But the larger owner and operator occupied more of the countryside than he had done in simpler centuries, and the opportunities for small-scale enterprise were poor enough to drive many men from the land to the colonies or into the towns.

In the towns, especially in Rome, victory brought little benefit to industry but great opportunity to men of business and money.

Craftsmen had to face the competition of the superior wares that came in from the Hellenistic cities or of those made by skilled workmen who were brought from the eastern industrial centers and set to work as slaves in the town or country houses of the rich. The humble occupations, such as baking, weaving, building, and the like, continued, but the luxury trades were apparently supplied by imported goods or workers.

The chief opportunity for townsmen came in handling the tribute from the provinces. At first the levies were collected by the provincial governor and sent by him to Rome. He was a member of the senatorial class, his power was almost unlimited, and his opportunity for extortion was almost infinite. His aristocratic plunder-preserve was invaded when the two brothers, Tiberius and Caius Gracchus, launched a political campaign (133–121 B.C.) to benefit the urban poor, the peasants, and the commercial class, all at the expense of the senatorial interests. The urban poor were supplied with grain at half price; they and the landless peasants were to be provided with farms on pieces of public domain taken from those who held more than a prescribed maximum; and the middle class was given more political power as well as a chance to handle the provincial revenues.

This chance was given by passing a law (123 B.C.) which put the collection of the taxes in the eastern provinces up for sale by auction to the highest bidder. The successful financiers agreed to pay the central government a fixed sum of money annually for the next five years. They then set out to collect as much as they could. They gathered the tribute in kind, employed ships to carry it to market, and often bought the aid of the provincial governor in order to make the venture more profitable. Since tax collecting was now purely a business venture run for profit, the middle-class bankers, merchants, and capitalists who managed it exploited the provincials to the utmost. When their income was threatened by attacks on the provinces already in Roman hands they persuaded Pompey to go east, overthrow the attackers, and add more provinces in Asia Minor, Syria, and Judaea (67–63 B.C.). By this step the revenue from tribute was almost doubled, and those who collected it benefited accordingly. But their policies were unpopular both in the province which they exploited and among the senatorial families which had been squeezed out of their share of the spoils. When the republic was overthrown the new emperors abolished this farming of taxes and tried to stop the planting of unscrupulous political or military commanders in positions of power.

If Roman capitalists were criticized for waxing fat on the rewards of conquest, they could retort that the proletariat was not being forgotten. The Roman treasury was so full of tribute that after 167 B.C. direct taxes ceased to be levied on Italian citizens, and in 122 Caius Gracchus began the monthly distribution of grain to the Roman poor at half the market price, taking the other half of the cost from the public coffers. After 57 B.C. the grain was given free, and by that time 300,000 people were getting free bread and circuses.

Economic Conditions in the Empire. The establishment of imperial rule in place of republican ended the confusion, corruption, and strife which had bedeviled the last century of the republic at home, restricted provincial plundering, and ushered in two centuries of comparative peace and prosperity. For the first and last time in their history about 1,300,000 square miles of land became a political unit. Apart from occasional trouble on the land frontiers their occupants need not fear attack. The destructive intertribal wars which had been regular features of life in Gaul and Britain came to an end, as did the conflicts between the fragments of the Hellenistic east. Piracy was wiped out, and a strong navy made the Mediterranean much safer for ships, passengers, and cargo. Land travel and transportation were aided and accelerated by the network of roads. A courier could now travel from Rome to the North Sea in about a month. Thanks to the patrols which extirpated highway robbery, he could carry treasure in safety.

Interprovincial trade was made easier by the introduction of uniform coinage, weights, and measures, as well as by the spread of Roman law. In comparison with earlier and later conditions the Mediterranean became a free-trade area such as the world was scarcely to know again until the coming of the United States and similar federal unions. There were many internal and municipal levies on commodities, and some provinces were forbidden to produce goods which might compete ruinously with those of Italy. But in general duties were for revenue rather than for protection, and products which could bear the costs of transportation therefore had a far wider market at their command.

The Western Provinces. Roman occupation stimulated the economic development of the northern and western frontier regions. Garrisons and administrative towns provided markets for farmers and craftsmen, retired soldiers became settlers, officials developed estates, Italian capital was invested in land, and new methods or equipment were introduced to the natives. In Britain Romans tapped more of the lead, iron, and tin deposits, directed some of their roads to the mining regions, introduced flax, fostered grain growing in the southeast, and sent wheat to feed the garrisons on the Rhine. Gaul was a larger and richer field; its southern regions were Mediterranean, its north was in a different climatic zone, and both parts were already fairly well cultivated when the Romans entered. It had fertile grain and pasture lands, vineyards, saltworks on the west coast, iron ore in the north, and good river communications. Under Roman stimulus its blacksmiths made fine arms and armor, its wool and flax served a flourishing cloth industry, its wine became so good that export had to be forbidden in the interest of Italian producers, and its potters evidently broke into the Italian market, for an unopened case of Gallic pottery has been found in the ruins of Pompeii.

Spain was Rome's chief metal mine. It has been estimated that during the centuries of Roman occupation Spain yielded an annual average of over 300,000 ounces of gold. The silver mines at New Carthage (the present Cartagena) employed 40,000 workers, and the iron ore deposits of Bilbao were vigorously exploited. Along the coast grain, wine, oil, and fruits were produced, with improved irrigation methods; sheep grazed on the central plateau; and hogs found food in the forests. Spain took a long time to conquer but was well worth the trouble. Roads, colonies of veterans, and large capital investments all helped to Romanize the country in customs and language.

The Rhine and Danube frontiers were fixed by strategic considerations. Inside them were areas capable of greatly expanded use of soil and subsoil; beyond them was a "barbarian"—but not necessarily barbarous—population which might buy and sell, and the two rivers had long been used for the carriage of goods across the continent. The early camps at Cologne, Mainz, Vienna, Basel, and elsewhere had to produce or import the things they needed, but they soon secured craftsmen and began to make pottery, glass, and metalware. Meanwhile some Germans inside and outside the frontier acquired new tastes as consumers, adopted new farming methods or products, and picked up some handicrafts. When that happened, wine, pottery, glass, arms, and coins crossed the rivers to be exchanged for amber, furs, slaves, hides, cattle, goose down, and red or blonde hair for Roman ladies' wigs.

The Eastern Provinces. In the eastern Mediterranean there was nothing that the Romans could teach the natives, since Hellenistic skill in production and trade, as well as in arts and sciences, was superior to that of the west. But Rome did provide a respite from war, brigandage, and piracy. The cities on the Greek peninsula had been hammered hard in the period of their conquest and never regained their old commercial strength. Athens settled down to be a pleasant little university town, a home for retired businessmen or officials, and a tourist center where visitors gazed on the classical monuments or bought reproductions of the works of the great masters. Asia Minor did much better, thanks to its natural resources, its competent craftsmen, and the widened opportunities for trade in the west. If tribute had to be paid to foreigners, that was nothing new, and peace was worth its price.

When a Greek queen, Cleopatra, was displaced by a Roman emperor, Egypt was in bad shape. In every other addition to the Roman Empire a portion of the land was earmarked for the emperor's use and income, and was known as the *fisc;* but in Egypt the whole country went to him, since it had always been regarded as the personal property of its ruler. Until he died in 14 A.D. Augustus did much to restore its productivity by repairing the water controls; but he also increased his demands for forced labor and for rent or taxes in grain. His successors raised those levies still higher, until eventually they went too high and exhausted the country. When that time came, in the third century, individuals who could not or would not pay fled from their homes. To prevent this, a scheme was devised of making some group—at first the family but later the whole village—responsible for the dues of each individual. The next step was to forbid any peasant to leave his holding or his occupation; he became bound to the soil and the job. That kind of bondage, as we shall see, spread like a plague from Egypt and became part of the imperial policy in Europe.

Trade of the Empire. Trade within and without the Empire was in part the normal exchange of goods and services between individuals; but it was also influenced greatly by the government's needs, receipt of tribute, and consequent spending power. We see the effect of the latter most prominently in the city of Rome. The capital's income consisted of the provincial tax payments, supple-

mented by the profits of Roman capitalists or traders and by the
revenue which landowners drew from their estates but spent in the
metropolis. Rome had few export industries. Her workers milled
flour, baked bread, finished cloth, made luxury goods, erected buildings, unloaded ships, amused the populace, did domestic service, or
served in government offices. Her only export was Roman law and
government. Yet her buying power was enormous. It is estimated
that possibly 6,000 grain ships entered the Tiber each year, bringing
5,000,000 bushels from Egypt and twice as much from other granaries. The imports of other necessaries and luxuries must have been
very large. In the provinces the towns which housed the local troops
and officials had similar but smaller power to pull goods in without
exporting much in return.

Europe could not supply all the luxuries the Empire needed. Asia
provided spices, incense, ointments, drugs, cottons, Indian metalware and precious stones, Chinese silk, dyes, horses, parrots, and
wild beasts for the circus. Access to these wares was made cheaper
by the discovery in the last century B.C. of the behavior of the mon-
soons. A direct transoceanic trip between the mouth of the Red Sea
and India now became possible. A vessel could leave an Egyptian
Red Sea port for the Orient and be back within a year. Trajan cut a
canal between the Red Sea and the Nile in about 100 A.D., thus providing continuous water carriage between the Mediterranean and
the Indian Ocean; but seagoing vessels could not use it, and its value
lay in the provision of a water portage in place of camels. The other
routes to Asia via the Euphrates and the Persian Gulf or overland
through Persia were also used, but they involved heavy freight costs
and might be made unsafe by brigandage or by the rise of any
strong power which did not like Rome and Romans.

How important this interprovincial and external trade was in the
total economy of the Empire we have no way of estimating. The
needs of the towns and cities were admittedly great; there were
enough rich and middle-class buyers to provide a market for oriental
produce; and the grain trade was "big business." Yet certain restraining factors must be kept in mind. The carriage of wine was
limited by the supply of cheap earthenware or skin containers,
though barrels seem to have come into use during the early Christian
era. Transport costs on land were heavy, and although shipping
costs were much lower it was unwise to use the sea in winter. Given
the necessary raw materials and some skilled immigrants, it was

cheaper for a province like Gaul to develop its own glass or pottery industry than to import wares from the older Italian or Greek industrial centers. It might even pay a large landlord to acquire craftsmen and have goods made on his estate rather than purchase and cart them from town.

Oriental trade was restricted not only by high freight charges but also by Europe's inability to offer many goods which the East could not produce for itself. Amber, coral, some metals and metal goods, a few kinds of cloth, glass—the list was short. Gold and silver were welcome in India then as now, and thousands of Roman coins, found in Indian and Chinese ports, indicate one way in which the West paid the East; but there were limits to that method of payment. Long-distance trade was therefore confined to goods of small weight and size but high value which the rich could afford to buy; interprovincial traffic in bulkier commodities might be larger where river or sea transport was available; but the overwhelming majority of transactions were local in scope, while the total volume of goods that entered into commerce was almost certainly far less than that which people grew or made for their own consumption.

Industrial Life. Rome made few important contributions to industrial organization, processes, or products. Her construction industry was her best-developed occupation, but it produced few revolutionary changes. The task of supplying water to cities during the summer drought called for reservoirs, aqueducts, and pipe lines. One of the nine pipes serving Rome brought water sixty miles. The building of temples, forums, triumphal arches, amphitheaters, stadia, markethalls, baths, and villas with central heating required a high degree of skill in architecture and surveying, the use of new materials (especially cement and long iron beams), and the marshaling of much capital and labor. Yet even the construction industry suffered at times from defective methods or fraudulent contractors. When Pliny went to Bithynia as governor he discovered that a costly aqueduct had proved worthless, that the walls of a theater had cracked before the building was finished, and that those of a gymnasium, though twenty-two feet thick, were too weak.

In other industries Rome's contribution was insignificant. This may have been due to the superior technique of the eastern Mediterranean craftsmen, and also to the standards of value which ruled the Roman mind. War, politics, and agriculture continued to be the only tasks to which aristocrats would turn their hands. Industry and trade were untouchables, partly because slaves did much of the making and selling. We may hesitate to attach too much importance to this attitude, and in any case there were plenty of middle-class entrepreneurs available to stimulate industrial or commercial originality. Yet it is true that technical improvements have been most marked in those countries or periods where the fashionable view was friendly to them, e.g., eighteenth-century England, seventeenth-century Holland, or medieval Venice.

Slavery. The list of ungentlemanly occupations spread beyond industry and trade to entertainment and most kinds of services. It included doctors and schoolmasters, whom Juvenal put in the same class as painters, bath attendants, fortunetellers, and tightrope walkers; also charioteers, actors, gladiators, and even architects. Many occupations were thus left to the plebeian, alien, slave, or freedman. Slavery was as widespread in Italy as in Greece. In the shipyard, on the land, in the building, mining, metal, pottery, textile, and other industries slaves did much of the work. For a long time they ran the water and fire departments in Rome. They kept shops, were secretaries, managers, or bank clerks, and some advanced to high administrative posts. Cato bought boys, trained them, and then sold or used them in his own industrial enterprises. When fire swept a residential section of Rome, Crassus bought the ruins, purchased 500 skilled building slaves, and erected blocks of apartments which helped to make him the largest landlord in the city. As a side line he bought youngsters, trained them to be readers, writers, managers, and waiters in his trade school for slaves, and then sold them. Slaves often became freedmen, accumulated great wealth, occupied civic offices, and presented buildings, statues, or public spectacles to their cities. By the third century probably a quarter of the members of the municipal councils were freedmen.

Italian manufactures were usually carried on in the home or small workshop. There were some large units. In Rome baking, fulling cloth, and making bricks gathered many men onto one spot. A publisher employing slave writers could produce 500 or 1,000 copies of a best seller in a very short time at a low price. There was a pottery in Etruria which had nearly sixty artists and perhaps twice as many other workers. The mines and some smelting works operated on a relatively large scale. Yet the advantages of large- over small-scale production were slight, because the equipment was simple and the processes were manual. The little workshop covered most of the industrial landscape.

Guilds. In all ages men, especially townsmen, have banded together to defend or promote their common ideas, faith, economic interest, or pleasure. Men producing the same commodity, using the same wharf or market, living in a street devoted to one kind of industry or trade, traveling to the same fair, or buying the same raw material may be rivals; but they have certain common interests to advance or dangers to avert. They therefore form associations, and one name for such bodies is "guild." There were guilds in most of the ancient cities. They need not be strictly economic in purpose, and many were concerned chiefly with the religious or social welfare of their members—a mixture of friendly society, burial brotherhood, and luncheon club.

In Rome guilds (*collegia*) appear by about 200 B.C. Some became embroiled in the political wrangles of the late republic and were abolished by the early emperors. Later they were allowed to be formed under license, and eventually there were eighty of them in Rome alone. Many of them were groups of poor free or freed workers; these cared for a member when he was sick and gave him a decent burial when he died, but there is no evidence that they dealt with such matters as wages, apprenticeship, or working hours. The guilds of builders, bargemen, barbers, smiths, pork merchants, wine dealers, etc. were more wealthy or powerful, and sought to promote economic gain as well as good fellowship.

The Disintegration of the Empire. During the first two centuries of the Christian era the lands within the Empire enjoyed a large measure of peace and prosperity. There were some extravagant, vicious, or incompetent emperors, but during the second century a series of able, intelligent, and hard-working men were at the helm. The latter kept the frontiers intact, preserved relative peace and order inside them, and thus maintained conditions favorable to enterprise. Middle-class merchants, financiers, contractors, and investors prospered, as did the large landowners. How far peasants and craftsmen shared in the good times we cannot measure. The decline of slavery probably improved their lot, and the demand for both consumers' and capital goods must have kept building, metal, cloth, and pottery workers busy, whether they were bond or free. Some of the great construction jobs were frankly relief work which added little to the productive capacity of the Empire, and in that respect they resembled the provision of free food for the urban poor. But they were not all done to "make work."

After about A.D. 200 the picture changed for the worse. No simple explanation, or even simple description, of what happened during the next two centuries is possible. Political, military, economic, and social factors played their part, interacting on each other. The questions that concern us are: What happened to the polity; what happened to the economy; how did each affect the other; and what did the barbarians do to them both?

The first and fourth questions are the most easily answered. The government and the army, which had put the Empire together, did not expand it any farther; rather it failed increasingly to be able to defend the frontiers or to maintain peace and order inside them. The task of holding 6,000 miles of frontier grew heavier when barbarians pressed harder from the north and a new Persian power emerged in the east. For its discharge the Empire depended on army and emperor. But the army had become less and less Roman, or even Italian; the legions were filled with provincials and barbarians all the way up to the top officers. To these men the stimuli to loyal service were pay and booty, with a piece of land as a bonus on discharge. If such rewards were not forthcoming, an army might melt away or revolt. Emperors depended on this kind of force for their support, were chosen by the rattle of swords, and were dethroned by its violence. Between 217 and 285 there were twenty-nine emperors—occasionally at least two at a time—of whom only one died in bed. Civil war between imperial rivals led to plundering of town and country and encouraged Germans and Persians to attack. In the mid-third century areas beyond the Rhine and Danube had to be abandoned.

Diocletian (284–305) tried to rescue the Empire from this tumult by drastic reforms. Realizing that it was too large to be managed by one man, he took steps which led to its division into two parts, each with its emperor. Constantine, who ruled the eastern half—the region east of the Adriatic—from 306 to 337, built Constantinople as capital of his territory. That city was well placed for defense and trade. Its lands included the richer and more developed part of the Mediterranean economy. For a thousand years it carried on with varying success the imperial laws, ideas, and for a time the bread and circuses transplanted from Rome. (See Chapter IV.)

In the western half there was no power capable of coping with the barbarians when, after filtering in for a long time as individuals or small tribes, they came in force. When legions were withdrawn from Britain and the Rhine just after 400 to deal with trouble in Italy, the way was open for the wanderers to swarm over Gaul, Spain, England, and North Africa. When Alaric caused that trouble in Italy by asking for more land for his Visigoths and was refused, he sacked Rome in 410. When Odoacer in 476 made a similar request and got the same answer, he deposed the emperor, took the title of king for himself, and appropriated land for his followers. Rome's rule of the west had ended. Of the whole story Professor Charlesworth says, "It is hard for us to realize the sheer overwhelming weight of numbers in the barbarian invasions; one may ask what defensive system, lacking modern machinery, could possibly have stemmed the simultaneous pressure of barbarian hordes at so many points. The marvel is not that the Empire was in so poor a state in the fourth century, but that it was in any state at all."

The second and third questions—what happened to the economy, and how did political events influence it—are not so easily answered. The economy was predominantly agricultural; on it a relatively small industrial and commercial superstructure and a large, costly political system had been superimposed. Nature had not been ungenerous in providing natural resources, but the equipment for their exploitation was simple and did not use much power other than that drawn from human muscles. It took many man-hours or days to keep the soil in good condition, make a piece of cloth, fashion a sword, decorate a vase, or transport a load of goods. Productivity was low, and the Romans did little by technical invention or improvement to raise it. At most they let more people work in peace by stopping the destructive intertribal wars in the barbarian west or the conflicts between the rulers of the Hellenistic east. They then put capital or better methods of work into the development of the west and restored such things as the irrigation systems of Egypt and Carthage. The wealth of the middle and landed classes and the revenue of the government were drawn largely from this extended or restored productivity. But if anything happened to lower output and income or to increase the government's demand on it, the whole economy was bound to be damaged.

The damaging developments came in force during the third century. Plague, civil war, and barbarian attacks destroyed capital and labor in nearly every province. Labor became scarce on the land, and the trade of the towns suffered. Yet the imperial demands on the shrunken income could not be abated but must rather be increased. A larger army was needed, a larger civil service was required to cope with problems and administer policies which sought to stop the rot or to bring recovery. When the Empire was divided, two administrations had to be maintained. In short, the state must take more out of less.

The Financial Problem. To meet the cost of government there was the yield from the state mines, public domain, Egypt and other pieces of the *fisc;* there was the profit from imperial monopolies of some trades and industries; there was booty, no longer the plunder from newly conquered foreigners but rather the property of victims of civil war or of persons who had offended the emperor; there was debasement of the currency in years of unbalanced budgets; there was taxation; and there was forced unpaid labor.

The taxes included poll tax, land tax, customs duties, sales and inheritance taxes. The collection of some of them was the duty of the municipalities which comprised one of the four pillars—emperor, army, civil service, and municipality—on which the Empire rested. Like the Greek city, the Roman municipality controlled the surrounding land. When tax time came it was assessed for a certain sum, and the city fathers were responsible for the collection of that amount from townsmen and adjacent country dwellers. If they failed to collect it, they must meet the deficit out of their own pockets. In the good old days this liability caused no disquiet, for the town's trade and the rural output were satisfactory. Town and country got on well together, and the large landowners spent much of their time and money in the city. But the disturbances of the third century impaired the ability of the municipalities to raise what was required of them. Civil war, invasion, pillage, or plague hurt their trade. Depreciation of the currency and the consequent inflation of prices hurt it still more. The expansion of industrial production on some estates reduced the traffic in manufactured goods. Yet from this smaller commerce and income the government demanded more than ever and must have it if the Empire was to meet the costs of keeping itself in existence. Consequently the urban middle class saw its trading enterprise stagnate and its capital or income sucked into the public coffers. When its members tried to escape from their civic magistracies or from the town itself, the positions were made compulsory and hereditary.

From some townsmen unpaid labor was demanded. The *collegia* may have begun as voluntary groups, but now the government saw in them a useful device for discharging such public functions as transporting and preparing the doles of bread, wine, and oil. Guilds were therefore formed for occupations which did not have them. The *collegia* were given a monopoly of their respective businesses, and their members were exempted from military service. In return they were drafted to give unpaid service to the state, and the group was made collectively responsible for the taxes of each member. The shipping guild must carry grain free from Egypt, the bakers must make bread free, the cloth or munitions makers must supply products at cost price, some guilds must maintain the postal service, and others must operate the fire brigade.

As the needs of the state grew heavier, so also did the burden of these *munera*. When the victims tried to escape from guild, trade, or town, a decree forbade them to move, and made membership in the guild—and therefore the occupation—hereditary. The guilds' affairs were supervised by some local official, whose interest was less in the production of wealth than in seeing that his imperial master got what was needed. There is a limit beyond which the state cannot appropriate the income of private enterprise without killing the enterprise. Unfortunately that limit is usually invisible until it has been passed. Consequently the guild policy, like the tax policy, reduced the income on which it was depending. Craftsmen and traders did escape from the towns, urban industries and trade were weakened, and the towns declined still further.

Back to the Land. As the four imperial pillars weakened, the land reasserted itself as the one abiding source of income. We left the countryside at the point where great estates had been built up or had been carved out of the public domain. In the outer provinces, such as Spain, Gaul, Britain, and Rumania, there was much granting of land in large units as well as smaller gifts to veterans. Many a recipient of a substantial estate—or *villa* as it might be called—developed the production of goods for sale to neighboring towns or garrisons, for export to other provinces, or, in the case of Spain and southern Gaul, to supply Rome.

To his enterprise the large landowner might bring a considerable amount of capital and energy. Slave labor might continue to be used, but when peace reduced the supply and raised the price of slaves their use in cultivating *latifundia* became less profitable, and landlords must find some other way of working their estates. In many cases they seem to have reserved part of the land as a domain, and rented the rest of it in full-size holdings to free tenants (*coloni*) or in smaller plots to slaves (*servi*). These men paid their rent by handing over a fixed share or a fixed amount of their produce, and also by doing a certain amount of work on the domain. Thus the landlord got his estate cultivated without having to spend money buying slaves or using its produce to feed them, while the tenant got the use of a piece of land for his own sustenance.

Originally the *colonus* was legally free in all ways, especially in the liberty to leave his landlord and seek a farm elsewhere. But in 332 a law was passed forbidding him to move away and threatening to load him with chains "in the manner of slaves" if he tried to do so. He became bound to the estate as the townsmen were bound to their trades and the city fathers to their offices. This bondage soon became hereditary. It was imposed to insure that estates did not lose their labor supply or the state its revenue. If there was to be any hope of a steady stream of food and taxes the cultivator must stay where he was and keep on working. In return he was secure in the possession of a holding, for while he was bound to the land the land was also bound to him. As a method of satisfying wants in a crisis which was becoming chronic, the colonate might meet the needs of cultivator, landlord, and state.

As the state, including the municipality, slipped out of the picture, the control of local life passed into the hands of the landlord. In troubled times free peasants, runaway slaves, and harassed townsmen flocked to seek protection under his wing. He became the neighborhood's ruler as well as landowner, fortifying his villa, policing the area, collecting taxes, and trying cases in his own court. His estate became in effect a self-sufficing economic and administrative unit, with its market, church, mill, and jail, and with industrial as well as farm workers. The threads which bound it to the outside business and political world became frayed or broken. Rome began as a society of patricians, small farmers, and slaves. The Roman Empire in the west ended with a class of great landowners exercising far-reaching power over *coloni* and slaves, with stagnant or decaying towns, and with a commerce that was shrinking fast and far.

Yet the thousand years of Rome were not all undone as if by a complete turn of the cycle. There was much solid substance left to serve as the foundation or to be built into the fabric of medieval society. As we shall see in the next chapter, the catastrophe was very far from complete.

BIBLIOGRAPHY

Bailey, C. (ed.), *The Legacy of Rome* (1923), chaps. 4, 13.

Barrow, R. H., *Slavery in the Roman Empire* (1928).

Cambridge Economic History of Europe (1941), vol. i, chaps. 2, 3.

Charlesworth, M. P., *Trade Routes and Commerce of the Roman Empire* (1925).

Childe, G., *What Happened in History* (1942), chap. 12.

Clausing, R., *The Roman Colonate* (1925).

Duff, A. M., *Freedmen in the Early Roman Empire* (1928).

Fowler, W. W., *Rome* (Home University Library).

Frank, T., *An Economic History of Rome* (2nd ed., 1927).

Heitland, W. E., *Agricola* (1921).

Loane, H. J., *Industry and Commerce in the City of Rome, 50* B.C.– *200* A.D. (1938).

Lot, F., *The End of the Ancient World* (Eng. trans., 1931), part i.

Rostovtzeff, M. I., *Social and Economic History of the Roman Empire* (1926).

Rostovtzeff, M. I., *A History of the Ancient World*, vol. ii: *Rome* (1927).

Rostovtzeff, M. I., "The Decay of the Ancient World and Its Economic Explanation," *Ec. H. R.*, January, 1930.

Thompson, J. W., *Economic and Social History of the Middle Ages (300–1300)* (1928), chaps. 1, 2, Bibliography.

Toutain, J., *The Economic Life of the Ancient World* (1930), parts iii, iv.

Varro on Farming (Eng. trans., 1912).

Warmington, E. H., *Commerce between the Roman Empire and India* (1928).

Westermann, W. L., "The Economic Basis of the Decline of Ancient Culture," *Am. Hist. Rev.*, July, 1915.

Westermann, W. L., "Industrial Slavery in Roman Italy," *J. Ec. H.*, November, 1942.

Encyclopaedia of the Social Sciences: Articles on the Roman World (vol. i), Agrarian Movements (Rome), Colonate, Guilds (late Roman and Byzantine), Land Tenure (Ancient World), Latifundia, Manor, Slavery (Ancient).

IV

THE MAKING OF MEDIEVAL
ECONOMIC SOCIETY

Of economic society during the thousand years we call the Middle Ages our knowledge is scanty until we approach the halfway mark, and even when A.D. 1000 is passed it is easier to ask questions than to answer them. The broad outlines of the story are, however, fairly clear. In the first place, there was no violent or complete break between the ancient and medieval worlds. "A flourishing Roman civilization was not swept away by wild hordes of barbarians" (Dopsch), if for no other reason than that the civilization was no longer flourishing and the barbarians were not all wild. The Eastern Empire carried on in spite of all attacks. The Christian Church, which was gaining strength as the Roman Empire disintegrated, went on extending its spiritual and material authority. Some Mediterranean cities continued their sea trade, and new ones arose. Even in the Western Empire the collapse of Rome's rule did not destroy the ways of working the soil, the organization of rural society, or the industries based on local supplies of raw material. The picture therefore is one of transition, sometimes turbulent, rather than the violent death of one civilization and the painful birth of a quite different order.

Medieval Economic Trends. In the second place, it is becoming possible to see the broad trends of economic activity during the Middle Ages and to divide the story into four main periods. The first runs from the fifth century through the seventh. During that time the migratory peoples settled down in the lands they had chosen or into which they had been pushed, and turned to the exploitation of the pastoral, agricultural, and industrial resources of their new homes. Kings brought some measure of unity and order, the church converted more heathen and spread its organization wider, while abbots shared with kings and lords in the work of colonizing empty areas.

After about A.D. 700 this process of settlement, development, and colonization was disturbed intermittently for about three centuries by new migrations. Mohammedans rode out of Arabia to conquer or harass the Mediterranean world from Syria to Spain. Vikings left their Scandinavian homes and descended on northern regions, from Iceland and Ireland to Russia. The Slavs who lived east of the Elbe became restless. Magyars swept on horseback across eastern Europe to the Danube Valley and even beyond. Internal political troubles added to the disturbances and destruction caused by the marauders. In such circumstances this second period, and especially the years 850–950, saw the economic and political progress of the first period checked and partly undone in some regions.

The uproar eventually subsided, and during the eleventh to four-teenth centuries Europe made important advances on all economic fronts. There was relative freedom from civil strife and invasion. As population took its chance to grow, farmers filled up the best lands of the west and then swarmed eastward to develop those regions east of the Elbe or north of the Danube basin which until that time had been primitively occupied by Slavonic peoples. Superior agri-cultural methods were introduced by these migrants, and mineral deposits were seriously exploited. Commerce expanded greatly, not merely in its old Mediterranean home but through the mountain passes or river valleys that led to the north, as well as by land and sea between the various parts of the north. Some industries grew large to make the cloth and metalwares needed by local or remote markets. Prices rose. The organization of commerce and banking became more complex, and capital investment increased. Towns which were centers of trade and industry loomed larger over a countryside increasingly occupied in producing food or raw ma-terials for market. This period, and especially that part of it be-tween about 1150 and 1350, was thus one of expanding and matur-ing economic enterprise.

All good times of expansion come to an end, and the Middle Ages were no exception. From about the second quarter of the fourteenth century there was at least a century in which circumstances were far less favorable for agriculture, industry, and commerce. Famine and plague undid much of the earlier growth of population. The east-ward movement came to an end, and Europe soon faced another in-vasion from the east. Wages rose, taxes grew heavier, but prices stood still or declined, and some enterprises became less profitable. Wars between newly forming (or formed) states, between cities, or inside states harassed many parts of Europe. There was progress at some points, but in many varied ways the advance of the earlier period came to a halt and there was some retreat. The Middle Ages ended in stagnation tinged with gloom.

In the present chapter the events of the first two periods will be examined. Since northern Europe plays a larger part in them than it did in the ancient world, it is high time to leave the Mediterranean for a while and survey the north and its inhabitants.

The North European Environment. Behind the Mediterranean coastal lands lies a great divide of hills and mountains stretching from Spain, reaching its highest point in the Alps, encircling the Danubian plain, and filling up the Balkans. This region has had its own characteristic economic life in the forests which cover the lower and middle slopes, on the pastures of the plateaus or of the grassy belt between the trees and the snow line, in the farms, orchards, or vineyards of the valleys, on the grainfields and ranches of the Danubian basin, in the spots where minerals are found, and in the towns that have grown up on the roads or rivers. The highlands have not been impassable to armies, migrants, or traders. The Morava and Vardar (or Maritza) valleys provide an exit from Danubia to the Aegean; passes lead through the Alps from northern Italy into Austria, Switzerland, and France; the high expanse in southern France is easily by-passed along roads leading to the Bay of Biscay or to central and northern France, while in the east the Russian rivers run round the end of the barrier.

The northern slopes of these high lands lead down to a great plain. Starting at the foot of the Pyrenees and the Bay of Biscay, it sweeps northeastward across France, eastern and central England, Belgium, Holland, Denmark, and southern Sweden. Its far rim is either sea or the mountains of Wales, western England, Scotland, and Scandinavia. In the center it embraces the northern half of Germany. Then it broadens out to cover virtually all Russia from the Arctic Ocean to the Black Sea, and after a partial interruption by the Ural mountains it sweeps across Siberia to the Pacific coast of Asia. One can go by train from Bordeaux to the Urals without passing through a tunnel.

Only rarely is the plain broken by hills, and these rise gently but never go high. In places the land is below sea level, as in Holland. In eastern England, Flanders, Holland, along the German coast, and in the Pripet marshes of western Russia it is so flat that rivers flood easily, and seasonal or permanent swamps long impeded settlement. The soil varies greatly in quality, from the deep rich black earth of the Ukraine to the gravel, sand, and other coarse material once deposited by glaciers along the south coast of the Baltic. The regions of swamp, sand, and glacial debris were of little use until they had been drained or their soil properties had been changed. There was some work of this kind during the Middle Ages, but much of it had to wait for modern engineering equipment and knowledge of soil chemistry.

The climate of northern Europe changes as one passes eastward. On the western fringe Atlantic cyclones and the Gulf Stream give a temperate climate to areas which lie in the same altitude as the southern half of Hudson Bay. Snow, frost, and heat are equally unusual; the Englishman can rarely use his skates, outdoor work is possible the year round, and in the more genial parts cattle can be left in the fields all winter. The same oceanic influences bring plenty of rain throughout the year, with fog and clouds, long springs and leisurely falls. But the Atlantic loses its influence once the Rhine is crossed. The climate becomes less temperate and humid and more "continental," with smaller rainfall, harsh winters, and short hot summers. In the far north arctic conditions prevail. In the southeast the rainfall fades away as we cross Russia and approach the arid steppes of western Asia.

Variations in soil and climate gave great diversity to the landscape, to the capacity of each region to carry population, and to the occupations of the inhabitants. Apart from the stern, barren far north, the choice lay between life in swamps, on grassy plains, and in forests. The swamps swarmed with wild fowl and the fishing might be good. The grasslands were easily traversed or settled, their soil was not too heavy to be broken, and in their natural condition they offered food for livestock. But these open and fairly dry lands formed a small part—possibly a fifth—of the total area; the remainder was wet or wooded.

The forests stretched across the whole continent, and someone has said that a squirrel could have traveled from Moscow to the Atlantic coast, passing from tree to tree without ever touching the ground. They provided many kinds of food for man and beast, the trees supplied material for building, and the ferns or bracken which grew under them served as bedding. If they were cleared away, the land was usually fairly, but not exceedingly, good for crops.

Northern religions regarded the forest as the home of bad-tempered gods, and a pagan would have to be completely converted to Christianity before he felt it was quite safe to fell the giant trees. This temperate humid forest zone was the distinctive feature of northern Europe, in contrast with the semi-desert areas of the Near East or the rather different kind of forest that was found in the region of Mediterranean climate. The northern trees grew easily; the work of removing them was heavy; and if a cleared area was neglected for any considerable length of time the trees reinvaded it. The fight to convert forests lands into grain and grass producers has therefore been one of the main tasks of northern agriculture.

Most of northern Europe's many rivers were navigable. Their estuaries provided safe harbors and permitted seagoing ships to go far inland. In many cases the sources of streams which flowed in different directions were so close together that a traveler could enter the continent at one side, go up one river to the head of navigation, make a short portage to another, descend it, and emerge on the opposite side of the country or continent. In France all the rivers except the Garonne radiate from one central area; in England the Trent, Mersey, Severn, Avon, and Thames are not far apart; in Russia rivers which flow into the White, Baltic, Black, and Caspian Seas rise in the Valdai Hills, while southwest Germany is near the upper courses of the Rhone, Rhine, and Danube.

Northern Europe has rich assets in its subsoil and its seas. There was never any great discovery of gold, but most other metals were available, and by the end of the Middle Ages coal was being used in a small way. The seas were shallow, and therefore good fishing areas. They were not very wide; their coasts were dotted with good harbors; and they were rough enough to breed a race of hardy seamen.

If we add up the units of this environment, the total explains much of the workaday history of northern Europe during the last two thousand years. Nature was not hostile, but she was far from lavish. The northern European must work hard all the year round for bed, warm clothing, simple board, and a little pocket money.

The Northern Peoples. When the Romans went north they found three main groups of people, divided into countless tribes with different names. In the west, occupying Gaul and the British Isles, were the Celts. In mid-continent, from the Rhine to the Vistula, were Germanic or Teutonic tribes possessing such names as Franks,

Goths, Angles, Saxons, Burgundians, Alamanni, Vandals, and Lom·
bards. In the east were the Slavs, a mixed people already well ac·
customed to seeing their land overrun by invaders from Asia and
destined to see still more inroads during the centuries that lay
ahead.

How these people lived depended on the nature of the country
they occupied. Archaeologists tell us that they possessed all the
skills, knowledge, and equipment needed for hunting, river or sea
fishing, pastoral and agricultural pursuits, mining and metalwork, or
for the production of pottery, leather, and cloth. Their ancestors
had passed through the Stone, Copper, and Bronze ages, and they
were fairly well supplied with ore deposits for the latest age, that of
iron. During at least two thousand years such northern goods as tin,
copper, gold, amber, and furs had been moving along well-estab·
lished routes to the south. But this trade was certainly far less im·
portant than was the herding of livestock, the cultivation of cereals
and flax, and the production of manufactured articles for home use.

Even in the Later Stone Age (say about 2000 B.C.), some north·
erners had been living in hamlets or small villages, in houses partly
below ground level, with barns, tilled fields, and grazing lands
around the tiny community. They did not need to know how to ir·
rigate, for the rainfall was abundant; but after two or three crops a
piece of lightly tilled land ceased to be productive and must be de·
serted in favor of new plots. As the local land supply was exhausted
or as population grew, it might be necessary for the whole group to
move on. Similarly those who gave most attention to herding might
wish to stay in one area, yet be obliged to go farther afield if over·
stocking or bad weather rendered their pastures inadequate. Hunt·
ing produced the same urge to move if the supply of wild animals
ran out or if rumor reported there was abundant game elsewhere.
Fighting was an attractive and normal occupation, more exciting,
honorable, and potentially remunerative than tilling soil or follow·
ing cattle. If a tribe grew so large that it needed more land it went
out to conquer some. If it heard that a fiercer or stronger enemy was
approaching from the east or north it moved west or south in order
to keep ahead of the impending storm. Finally, the production of
annual crops did not tie men to the soil as did the cultivation of vines
and olive trees in the south.

In the Germanic regions there was consequently "at least as much
perpetual motion . . . as there was permanent settlement" (Koeb-

ner). This statement by a distinguished scholar suggests that there was much settled life. In Gaul the settlement was probably far more important than the motion. The Celts, like Americans in the late nineteenth century, had reached the sea and could go no farther. In Gaul the Romans found well-developed estates, belonging to aristocratic tribal chiefs, and many villages of farmers. They added to the number of both by establishing villas and settling veterans in Gaul as well as in Britain and along the Rhine and Danube frontiers. They allowed Germans to come into the Empire, or brought them in, to supplement the native labor supply, to help the large proprietors and soldier-settlers, or to develop new tribal settlements of their own. Many of the farming veterans were themselves Germans who had fought in the legions as mercenaries. Some of the immigrants were prisoners of war. Others had come voluntarily, as did Scots and Irish into England or Europeans into America in later days, seeking work on the land, jobs as domestic servants, a place in the army, and even a chance to rise to high official or military position.

This piecemeal peaceful immigration was supplemented by various trading, political, and religious contacts across the frontier. It taught many Teutons new ways of earning a living and of living, before the large-scale movements began about 375 A.D. Within two centuries following that date "in every part of Europe peoples had poured into one another's areas of settlement" (Koebner). The great *Völkerwanderung* was a migration of tribes and even of confederations of tribes, led by chiefs and fighting forces, with families, livestock, and such other property as could be moved. Pressure from the east had something to do with starting the wave, while the weakening or actual withdrawal of Roman garrisons from the frontiers removed any serious obstacles from its path.

By the second half of the sixth century the wanderers had settled down and we can see the extent of their migrations. In the Mediterranean area the newcomers were in charge of Spain, southern France, Italy, and for a time the western half of North Africa. They occupied the Alpine regions and the upper valleys of the Rhine and Danube. But their main concentration was on the western part of the great plain, from the Elbe to the Bay of Biscay and the North Sea. The Angles, Saxons, and Jutes had crossed that sea and taken possession of England. The lands east of the Elbe and north of the Danube, deserted by the Germans, had become occupied by Avars in the Danubian valley or by Slavs on the Baltic part of the plain.

Economic Effects of the Migrations. In all lands the newcomers were interested chiefly in securing land, and took what they wished. Their leaders claimed the empty spaces, the imperial public domain, and the estates of large owners who had been killed or had run away. If, as was often the case, they were pagans, they annexed lands which had been given by Christian emperors or subjects to the church; but when they became converted they made ample amends for this sacrilege. They granted land to their chief supporters, who in turn might provide holdings for their followers. Sometimes they seized the villas of surviving Roman or Gallic landlords; but often they were content with two-thirds of the land or of the produce from it, and left the original population to carry on undisturbed. Consequently, in Italy, Spain, and Gaul much of the economy was taken over as a going concern, and the structure of rural society remained as it had become during late imperial days. In the ex-Roman Empire the Teutons did as the Romans had done; they were heirs rather than destroyers.

On the outer fringe—in Scandinavia, England, the Low Countries, and the region between the Elbe and the Rhine—Roman influence was weak or non-existent, the climate and soil were northern, and the Germans therefore continued to develop their own economy and society. The economy became a more balanced type of mixed farming. As settled life became normal, the building of more permanent homes and the development of garden plots or plowlands grew more desirable. The homes were clustered in a village, rather than scattered over the countryside as is often the case today. From this residential core the farmer went out to work his portion of the arable land. He might have a piece of meadow or get a share of the hay crop that was cut from the village meadow. The rest of the locality—and probably by far the largest part of it—was common pasture land, waste, swamp, woodland, or forest. Here he collected wild vegetables and fruits, hunted, obtained wood or turf, and turned his livestock out to seek food.

This village pattern, with its small area of plowed fields or meadow set in a wide expanse of unimproved common pasture, waste, or woodland, became general throughout northern temperate Europe wherever soil or climate permitted such little communities to grow up. In warmer areas vineyards supplemented the grainfields, especially in France and the Rhine Valley. On bleak plateaus (such as those of central Spain) and on slopes where cultivation was difficult isolated farms or hamlets prevailed, occupied by men whose chief occupation was tending flocks and herds. On the coasts and in the swamps fishing took up most of men's time. In the forests a few individuals might make small clearings and eke out a lonely existence as woodcutters or charcoal burners; but real settlement in timbered country called for large-scale operations in felling trees and breaking the ground. Such operations had to wait until the more easily settled open and fairly dry country had been filled up and until some king, lord, bishop, abbot, or group of peasants decided to embark on the enterprise. (See Chapter VI.)

Early Medieval Northern Society. It used to be believed that the Germanic tribes were bands of free and equal warrior-farmers or pastoralists who owned the soil in common and ran their economic and political affairs in a voluntary democratic sort of way under chiefs who were chosen to direct affairs in peace and war. From that happy state of liberty and equality they were supposed to have been degraded later on into subjection to feudal lords and kings. This picture has, however, become discredited as the product of "romantic imagination and a mis-reading of the sources" (Stephenson). The extremely scanty literary evidence concerning the Germans before they moved and the earliest documents—mostly seventh century or later—dealing with their life in their new homes reveal a society headed by a fighting aristocracy which was maintained by lower classes of peasants. Professor Carl Stephenson, one of the most recent examiners of the evidence, reaches the following conclusion:

In early medieval Europe the common man was at most a simple peasant. Though recognized as free, in that his body was not owned, he would normally be the humble follower of a lord—a tribal chieftain, a successful conqueror, a prelate of the church, or some other gentleman. To this lord the peasant, and his children after him, would very likely be bound by a personal tie that involved the performance of customary service. The latter would be agricultural rather than military—and so, according to the standard of the day, servile rather than honorable. The lord, as a member of the warlike aristocracy, would scorn all manual labor; like his ancestors, whether barbarian or Roman, he would gain his regular sustenance from economic dependents. The peasant would be expected to spend his life working the soil, either that of the lord or a plot to which he himself had some sort of hereditary title. In time of need his lord, or perhaps the king, might indeed call upon him for military duty of a sort. As a warrior, however, he would be considered quite inferior to the gentleman who made fighting a profession.

This social pattern resembles in its essentials that which archae-ologists deduce from the evidence they have found in prehistoric settlements and cemeteries in northern, central, and western Europe. Professor Childe, for example, says that Bronze Age graves (not later than 1000 B.C.) in Denmark and southern England reveal "an aristocratic world with richly developed upper-class life based on organized luxury trade and the labor of the lower classes." He speaks of Iron Age war chiefs who rose to affluence and led Celtic war bands, armed with weapons made of the cheap iron that was now available, to sack Rome in 390 B.C. and to invade regions as far apart as Asia Minor, Spain, Brittany, and Cornwall. In the almost chronic warfare of the period leadership by the best and by the best-armed fighters was essential. There was abundant tradition, as well as human nature, to decree that the best be sustained by the labor of the rest of the population.

If, then, the migrating Germans consisted of an upper class of fighting men, each with a small band of armed retainers, and of a herding-farming lower class which might go as far down as slavery, those who went into Gaul and Italy found in the villa, with its owner-ruler, *coloni*, and slaves, a state of affairs not very different from their own. Those who settled elsewhere took their own social system with them, but since it was one of class differentiation the distinctions of rank or status ran through the more settled society in the new home. That society, as ever, had its political, religious, and economic facets. It included a monarch, who was king of the terri-tory and not merely of the people, king of France as well as of the Franks, of East Anglia as well as of the East Angles. The need for a military class did not diminish; frontiers had to be defended or pushed farther out, and fighting prowess depended increasingly on possession of costly armor as well as of a great horse strong enough to bear the load of man and metal. There were problems of internal peace and order that called for some kind of administrative ma-chinery and officials. Finally, there was the church, requiring a con-siderable income to provide the houses of God and sustenance for His servants.

Land was the source, virtually the only important source, from which the income of the ruling, fighting, administrative, and religious classes could be obtained. As few opportunities existed for raising revenue by taxes, the king lacked adequate funds for meeting his own expenses or for paying salaries to a civil or military service. He therefore must have estates of his own, as did every ruler from the Pharaohs onward, from the cultivation of which he could draw much, perhaps most, of the produce he used or consumed. As landlord in chief he granted lands to his military leaders, favorites, or officials in gratitude for past services or in expectation of those to come. The recipient pledged himself to give a certain amount of military aid (knight service) each year with a prescribed number of men, to provide armor and food for himself and them during the campaign, or stoutly to defend the piece of frontier allotted to him. He might also promise to make certain payments in money. To sustain him he received a "benefice" in the form of land. He in turn might make grants of land to his retainers under similar conditions of knight service. Some of them repeated the process until we reach a grant which was too small for further subdivision.

Piety, a troubled conscience, and the desire to win or retain the friendship of the church led the king and his subordinate landholders to make grants to bishop, abbey, or pope; but these also might carry obligations of knight service, which some militant churchmen enjoyed discharging in person, even though they were permitted to use only a heavy-headed mace instead of a sword or lance. Meanwhile attempts to build up a system of paid local officials were not very successful. The Frankish kings put local administration in the hands of counts, and England had its sheriffs. The counts received no land or salary and were expected to live on part of the court fines or other money which they collected for the king. Their position gave them opportunities to be highhanded and acquisitive, while their interference was resented by large landlords. The latter therefore sought, and in troubled times took without asking, immunity from such intervention by the king's representative. They thus became virtually free from central control, lords as well as landlords of the people who lived on their estates.

As a way of providing for civil and military needs this plan looked simple and sound. Its success depended on the ability of the ruler to keep a firm hand on his subordinates. In an age of slow travel and communication, this was not easy. A strong king like Charlemagne made the system work fairly well by limiting the benefice or the count's appointment to the life of the grantee, by issuing detailed instructions, and by sending inspectors round to see that all was in order. But when weak kings were on a throne, when civil war broke out or invasion broke in, the controls failed. Men made their office or benefice hereditary, ungranted land was seized, immunity was claimed, counts grabbed estates, and a private army might cease to owe allegiance to anyone but its immediate master. There were periods before Charlemagne and still more after him in which weakness at the center allowed these things to happen. The principle might continue to be recognized that the vassal held his benefice—or his *feodum* of fief as it began to be called—under a contract which imposed duties and restraints on him; but even then he enjoyed considerable immunity and political as well as economic power over those below him in the social scale. He was lord and landlord. As lord he protected, governed, judged, and taxed his dependents. As landlord he claimed payment for the use of his land. In both capacities he received income.

Of the men who worked that land and provided the income we know very little until we approach A.D. 1000. Some of them were slaves, doing domestic work in or around their master's household, but the use of slave gangs to cultivate *latifundia* had become unusual. Slavery was slowly passing out of the picture. Most cultivators belonged to one of two other classes—serfs and freemen. Their status and workaday life will be examined in the next chapter.

In its political and military aspects this pattern of society is called feudalism. In its social and economic aspects we call it the manorial or seigniorial system, since the manor or *seigneurie* was the unit of organization, ownership, and administration. It has been described as "a form of government, a structure of society, an economic régime based on land proprietorship" (Thompson), and all three facets need to be kept in mind, since "feudal society did not understand purely economic relationships" (Bloch). As a form of government it carried some income-producing perquisites, since the lord could tax the inhabitants of his estate and could levy fines in his local law courts. As a social structure it was a strongly marked class system which divided the population into a landed monarchy, aristocracy, and church on the one hand, and a mass of peasants on the other.

As an economic regime it was an arrangement for meeting the wants of all classes, for producing and distributing goods and services, and for defraying the costs of government and religion in a predominantly agricultural world which had few towns and little commerce. It embodied a division of labor which was well expressed in the declaration that "The House of God is tripartite. Some work, some fight, some pray." It was even better expressed on the signboard of those later English inns which are still called "The Five Alls." On this board are pictures of five men, and beneath them is the inscription: "I rule all. I judge all. I fight for all. I pray for all. I work for all." If the ruler, judge, warrior, and priest were to do their work well, they must be supported by the labor of peasants and craftsmen.

How they did it will be seen in the next chapter. Meanwhile we must examine the economic effects of the new migrations which disturbed much of Europe during the eighth to tenth centuries.

The Northmen. The great age of Viking movement began about 700 and lasted for more than three centuries. The migrants were getting out of a land which offered scanty resources for herding or tillage. Denmark was a low sandy peninsula with a climate that was often bleak. Southern Sweden had some room for pasturage and plowing, but the soil was patchy, thin, and stony. Norway had still less to offer the farmer. Consequently the forest and the sea must supplement the meager returns from the earth. The Swede was a farmer who owned a boat, the Norwegian was a fisherman who had a little farm. Collecting and catching played a large part, hunting and trapping brought food and furs, the forests yielded tar, and there were some rich mineral deposits. On the shores of the Baltic there was amber to be picked up, in the North Sea were herring and cod, while out west were whales, seals, and walrus.

Some northern wares had for centuries been taken southward to be exchanged for the wine, salt, fine textiles, and other products that Scandinavia lacked. The northern traders also gathered up produce from Russia, and either sold it in such markets as Copenhagen or Wisby (on the island of Gothland) or took it up the streams that flowed into the Baltic and North seas. The sea was a place for piracy as well as for fishing, and in lands beyond it were goods that could be obtained as booty or by barter. The boundary line between trading and raiding was as faint on the surface of the North Sea as on that of the Mediterranean. A Viking grave found in an island west of Scotland contained a chieftain's sword, spear, battle-ax, and pair of scales.

For their roving the Norsemen developed good ships and sound seamanship. When speed was essential they used long narrow craft, seaworthy in the rough northern waters, propelled by oars and big woolen sails, and yet so shallow in draft that they could be sailed far upstream into the invaded land. When trading was more important than fighting, broader slower vessels were built to carry many people, sheep, cattle, and cargoes. They had no decks to offer shelter, but woolen sheets were stretched over the boat at night to keep its contents warm or dry. Navigation was limited to the summer, when darkness scarcely descended on the northern latitudes. Stars and sun served as guides, but when these were not visible the direction of the wind or the color of the water gave clues.

With such scant aids to navigation the Norsemen made their way across the North Sea or braved the Atlantic to reach Iceland, Greenland, and some unrecognizable point on the coast of North America. During the eighth and ninth centuries political unrest and possibly overcrowded population led them to do so with increasing force. Their reputation soon became so foul that congregations in French churches added a new clause to the Litany: "From the fury of the Northmen, good Lord deliver us!" For decades the long ships descended on the coasts of the British Isles, the Low Countries, and France with sickening frequency. Towns, villages, and abbeys were attacked, even as far upstream as Paris on the Seine and Mainz on the Rhine. Ireland and Scotland were plundered. Some raiders went on to the Bay of Biscay, through the Strait of Gibraltar, even to Marseilles and Pisa. While Dane and Norwegian scoured the western seas the Swedes went eastward to the Gulfs of Finland and Riga, up the streams into Russia and then down the rivers that flowed into the Caspian or Black Sea. While Pisa was hit from the west in 860, Constantinople was attacked from the north in the same year. The Norsemen seemed ubiquitous.

The economic effects of these onslaughts gradually changed in character. During the ninth century, when the raids were most numerous and fierce, there was much destruction or redistribution of wealth. The western targets were the rich farm and vineyard districts of the Rhine and French river valleys, the fairs and market towns to which food, salt, wine, and manufactured goods went to be sold, or the Low Countries regions which made metalwares and woolen cloth. Some towns were completely destroyed, some rural communities and abbeys were wiped out, booty was seized and tribute levied in wine or money. This sacking and plundering injured the economy of the areas which endured it; but it did not wreck that economy completely or annihilate it, even when the damage done by the Vikings was accentuated by that of civil war and Hungarian invasions. Some towns carried on or rose from their ashes, some merchants survived, production continued or revived, and the old pattern of trade was redrawn.

The invaders contributed something to that restoration. In the first place, raids sometimes led to settlement. Iceland and the islands north or west of Scotland were colonized as fishermen's farms and sheep ranches. The east coast of Ireland attracted some settlers, so that Dublin, Limerick, and other towns became important Scandinavian outposts. In England Alfred the Great was able to prevent the Vikings from seizing more than the northeastern half of the country (about 880 A.D.); but in that region the Danish leaders quickly divided the land among their followers, who promptly turned from ten years of fighting to cultivating the soil. In the second place, some of the invaders settled down to trade. This development of settlement and trade was well illustrated in what became the feudal duchy of Normandy, granted by the king of France to the Norsemen's chief in 912. Natives and newcomers cultivated the land; traders of Rouen, the capital of the duchy, and of other towns trafficked by land, river, and sea in wine, salt, fish, and cloth; and meanwhile those who still had fighting in their blood went from Normandy to capture Sicily and southern Italy (1016–1079) or to conquer England (1066).

With a foothold in so many countries the Norse traders could range far afield. The North Sea nearly became a Scandinavian lake, and the Baltic became one entirely. Swedes and Danes penetrated the Slav lands to get furs, wax, hides, and slaves and to traverse the ancient routes to the Black and Caspian seas. They went in armed bands and built fortified trading posts, of which Novgorod became one of the most famous both as a great fair and as a point from which one could go fairly easily across to the upper waters of the Volga or of the Dnieper.

The Volga flowed in a leisurely way to the Caspian. On the shores of that sea the Varangians—as the Slavs called the Scandinavians in their midst—could meet traders from central or eastern Asia, thus establishing strong ties with that far-flung Moslem world whose activities will be examined in a moment. The Dnieper was an easy waterway to the Black Sea. On its middle course, at a point near the confluence of many tributaries, stood Kiev, the center to which the Slavs brought their produce from plain, marsh, forest, and cradle— for many Slavs became slaves. Each June a great canoe flotilla started downstream from Kiev. When it reached the Black Sea at Kherson (Sevastopol), the goods were sold to Greek merchants or were carried on to Constantinople, where the furs, honey, wax, amber, and slaves were exchanged for silks, spices, wine, fruit, and metalwares. The Norsemen had long been interested in this trade through the heart of Russia, but in the ninth century they swarmed in great numbers into Kiev as merchants or mercenaries, and soon

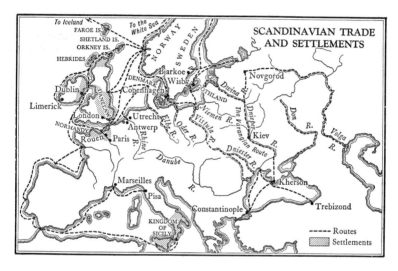

were ruling the Dnieper basin as well as running its commerce along what has become known as the Varangian route.

The Northmen's trade and political power were thus spread like a fan, with one tip in Iceland, the other in the Caspian, and the handle in Wisby. Scandinavians were the middlemen of northern Europe until, in the twelfth and thirteenth centuries, they were elbowed out by traders from German towns. By that time their trade with the Black Sea had been injured by Tatar invasions of Russia and by the competition of Italians from Genoa or Venice.

The Moslems. The Viking disturbances in the north fell on a continent which had for some time been worried by intruders from the south. When Mohammed died in 632 he had founded a religion which inspired its Arab devotees to embark on a far-reaching career of conquest. They quickly gained the mastery over Asia as far east as the borders of China and the mouth of the Indus. They took Egypt and Syria from the Eastern Empire, absorbed the whole of North Africa, and in 711 crossed the Strait of Gibraltar to conquer Spain and Portugal. Their northward sweep was checked at Tours in France in 732, and they were pushed back into Spain. By land or sea they ravaged and for a time held part of the coast of southern France and Italy; they penetrated to the Alpine passes and stayed there till nearly 1000 A.D.; they burned Rome; they captured nearly all the important Mediterranean islands—Cyprus, Rhodes, Sardinia, Corsica, and Sicily.

The Moslems—or Moors, Arabs, and Saracens as they are variously called—thus linked the two ends of the Mediterranean and controlled the island steppingstones. They did much damage during their advance, and there was frequent fighting on the fringe of their empire as well as piracy on the sea. Yet like the Norsemen they turned fairly easily from raiding to trading and settlement. They granted tolerance to the conquered people, and thereby allowed Egyptians, Syrians, Jews, and Spaniards to carry on their normal life without much interference, subject only to the payment of higher taxes by those who refused to become Moslems. Mohammedanism regarded trade as a worthy occupation; ties of rule and religion facilitated long-distance trade and travel; and since the Asiatic end of the Moslem world possessed many industrial or agricultural skills, methods, and products which were superior to those of the European end, the west benefited by the lessons it learned from its new masters.

Spain and Sicily were the chief beneficiaries. The Moslems developed their resources more than even the Romans had done. In Spain the irrigation systems were renovated and extended. New methods of cultivation were introduced. To grapes, olives, and grain were added products brought from the east—rice, sugar cane, cotton, oranges, mulberry trees for the silkworms, peaches, lemons, strawberries, roses, asparagus, and an improved kind of spinach. Industries were stimulated by immigrant eastern craftsmen. Paper, carpets, shawls, and fine leather goods were made at Cordova, fine sword blades and armor at Toledo. The mineral deposits were tapped harder, the silver mines reopened, and the central plateau became a great ranch. Intellectual life drew inspiration from eastern Moslem centers. Cordova in the tenth century was the most civilized city in Europe and probably the cleanest; at any rate it had 70 libraries and 900 public baths. In Sicily the silk industry developed, and Palermo became one of medieval Europe's greatest cities.

The relations between the Moslem world and Christian Europe are still obscure. It used to be contended by Professor Pirenne and some others that the Saracens broke the threads of trade between the two halves of the Mediterranean by their grip on the African coast and on Sicily, and by their pirate ships; that spices, papyrus, and other eastern wares disappeared from western markets; that grass grew in the streets of western ports; that the pope's ban on trade with the infidel kept Christian and Moslem apart; that these interruptions of commerce, followed as they were by the Viking and Hungarian invasions and the civil wars, reduced western Christendom to a self-sufficing economy with little domestic trade and virtually no foreign contacts; and that the revival, or even the rebirth, of commercial life, with a merchant class and trading towns, did not begin until about 1000 A.D.

This picture of commercial annihilation is now regarded as too dark in every respect. Like the Vikings in the north, the Saracens in the south damaged but could not completely destroy town life or commercial contacts with the outside world. Ports built walls to defend themselves from attack. If ships were menaced by pirates, that was nothing new in Mediterranean waters, and it seems safe to assume that they were armed to defend themselves. The papal ban, with its threat of excommunication of those who trafficked with the heathen, would not apply to non-Christians and therefore would not deter those "Syrians" or Jews who since Roman imperial times had conducted most of the trade between western Europe and the Near East. For Christians, smuggling was a normal way of evading prohibitions of this kind then as later. Italian cities, such as Amalfi and Salerno, soon came to terms with the Moslems and traded with North Africa, Egypt, and Syria. Further, if the seaways west of Sicily were blocked, eastern goods could go up the Adriatic, since the Saracens did not control the entrance to that sea; or they could pass along the Varangian route or up the Danube and thence to central or western Europe.

It is therefore hard to believe that the appearance of the Moslems in the west brought complete or prolonged economic paralysis to that part of Christendom. Soon we find many personal and intellectual contacts between Spain and her northern neighbors. Moslems took French wives, bishops of Liége in the tenth century were enthusiastic students of Moorish astronomical works, and young Christian scholars were sent to Spain to be taught mathematics. If the north wanted the best in science, medicine, agriculture, industry, or civilized living, it must go to Spain to learn; and there is no evidence that the school doors were closed against it.

The economic relations between the Moslem and Christian worlds have recently been reviewed from a fresh angle by a French scholar, Maurice Lombard. His thesis has two main themes. In the first place, the conquering Moslems released great hoards of treasure, chiefly gold, from the monasteries, churches, tombs, and royal or private accumulations in Egypt, the Levant, and Persia. At first the gold was taken as booty; then came the yield from taxes levied in gold and then the ornaments taken from the tombs of the Pharaohs. In addition to dishoarding this treasure, the Moslems tapped gold deposits in the Urals, central Asia, Ethiopia, the upper Nile, and in the Sudan (the region which stretched south of the Sahara from the Nile across to the Atlantic). Thus they poured a stream of precious metal into circulation and into commerce in all parts of their world, from India to Spain.

In the second place, their world was not self-sufficing. There were commodities they were obliged (or were disposed) to buy from Europe: white slaves of both sexes, furs, tin, metalwares and arms from the Low Countries, lumber for ships, woolen cloths, and some luxury goods made in Constantinople. Some of these they obtained from the Varangians who brought them down across Russia; some were bought in Constantinople. Some were taken to Egypt or the Levant by Venetians, while Spain obtained what she wanted from France—Verdun was a gathering point for slaves destined for the Spanish market—from England, or from the Baltic. In return the Moslem supplied some luxury cloths and other products, but paid partly in gold. Some of this metal, flowing into Europe via Kiev, Venice, and Spain, was hoarded or made into jewelry, some circulated in trade, and some went to Constantinople to buy the luxury wares western Europeans desired. Thus the Moslem and the Christian world traded with each other, and in that traffic most parts of Europe felt the beneficial effect in one way or another.

In time, during the eleventh and twelfth centuries, the Moslems' power was whittled away by internal weakness and external attack. They were dislodged from the Alpine passes. Italian cities fought the pirates or grew strong enough to negotiate favorable trade treaties with their rulers. The Normans conquered Sicily and southern Italy. In Spain the Moorish frontier was gradually pushed southward by Aragon and Castile, and by 1250 it included only the southern belt, Granada. Long before that date the west had gone east trading and crusading.

The Magyars. The third and last disturbers of early medieval Europe were the Magyars. Moving from Asia into southern Russia during the ninth century, they rode into the Danube basin about 900 and then penetrated as far as northern Italy and southern France. West of the Danube they crashed into areas that the Frankish king Charlemagne had conquered or brought under his control during a series of powerful drives which had carried the bounds of his empire to the Oder River in the north, to the middle Danube in the center, and to the top end of the Balkans in the south. To this eastern belt Charlemagne had introduced Christianity and encouraged settlement on more efficient lines than those known to the Germans or Slavs who inhabited the country. On estates which he took for himself or on wild land given to nobles, bishops, and abbeys, the forests were cleared, peasants were induced to migrate from the northwest by being offered attractive tenures, and the native population was taught better farming methods.

The Magyars destroyed much of this frontier settlement before they were eventually checked in battle in 955 and forced to retreat to the region which became Hungary. Meanwhile the Frankish Empire had broken up after the death of Charlemagne in 814. The western half, which became France, was torn with civil war and hammered by the Norsemen. The eastern half, which we might label western Germany, was more fortunate; yet it had its political and religious troubles, and some time elapsed before its rulers and people were in a mood to resume the drive to the east.

The Eastern Empire. By parting company with the poorer and indefensible west the Eastern Empire shed liabilities without losing many assets. Constantinople was a better imperial commercial metropolis than Rome had been, for it served as the hub of many busy trade routes and was nearer the centers of wealth production in the eastern Mediterranean. For a time the Empire held its rich territories intact, and Justinian (527–565) took back Italy and the coasts of Spain and North Africa. But his successors had to yield Egypt, North Africa, southern Spain, Sicily, and Syria to the Saracens, while Lombards evicted them from most of Italy except the south. Yet even at the worst the Empire continued to hold Asia Minor and much of the Balkans.

As the political and economic heart of the Empire, Constantinople grew to great size. There is talk of its housing a million people; if that is true, the housing and sanitation problems (with dogs for scavengers) must have been acute. The court, church, bureaucracy, army, and navy provided a large market, while some tribute flowed in as it had done to Rome. Slav and Scandinavian products came from the north, metals from central Europe, cloths and metalware from the industrial cities of Asia Minor and the Levant. Grain arrived from Egypt and oriental goods were brought over one of the long trade routes. When silkworm eggs were smuggled from China in 552, despite the efforts of the Chinese to maintain their close monopoly of the silk supply, production of silk fabrics soon became important in the Levant. Like every great emporium, the capital developed a variety of manufacturing and processing industries. Craftsmen and traders were organized in guilds which were subjected to strict regulation and taxation by the state; but the compulsory hereditary membership of Roman days was abolished, and when Justinian discontinued the free distribution of foodstuffs the more burdensome forced labor services vanished.

A fairly efficient bureaucracy carried on the government even in the days of incompetent emperors or in face of hard blows on the frontiers. It maintained a navy to fight pirates, a police system to keep the peace in the towns or on the roads, a corps of inspectors to watch both native and foreign traders, a code of law which fitted commercial needs, and a stable currency. Some emperors were eager and energetic in reforming the government or the economy. Heraclius (610–641) recognized that the Empire could not defend or finance itself so long as it depended on a system of large landed estates worked by *coloni* and spent much of the public revenue to hire mercenary foreign troops. This plan did not provide enough men for the army or enough money to meet the cost of defense. He therefore established military settlements, populated by natives who were given land in return for fighting services. Alongside these he offered land to free peasants, whose obligation was to pay taxes. Thus he provided a peasant militia to fight, and a taxpaying peasantry to produce revenue. This system gave new strength to the Empire but did not last long. By the tenth century the land was passing into the hands of rich merchants who invested their surplus funds in real estate, of successful peasants who bought the holdings of their less able neighbors, of landlords who wished to add to their domains, and of the church. By 1000 A.D. the familiar pattern of great landlords and dependent peasants had reasserted itself.

Early Medieval Trade. The ending of imperial rule in the west caused a decline in the amount of interprovincial trade, such as the movement of grain, wine, oil, and metals. But some long-distance traffic continued, especially in luxury goods and in those special products of one region which were in demand over a wide area. Even local trade may have fallen off less than we used to think, thanks to the Romanized tastes of many barbarians and the survival or revival of some towns which had become regional clusters of consumers and artisans during Roman times.

The long-distance traders of the late Empire had been lumped together as "Syrians." They might be Jews, Greeks, Armenians, Persians, Alexandrians, or any other kind of easterner. These men continued throughout the early medieval period to link the eastern and western parts of the continent; some, more adventurous, roamed over Asia as well, and the bounds of their business were France in the west and India or China in the east. They traveled around the towns as far west as Bordeaux or Paris, displayed their wares in fair, court, or abbey, supplied metalware and fabrics to cathedrals, and sold cottons, spices, perfumes, precious stones, and crucifixes. In exchange they took metals, furs, slaves, and other commodities from the western colonial frontier. As traders, financiers, musicians, and travelers the Syrians were known everywhere and had their own special quarters in the chief cities. They went west by sea from Constantinople or some other eastern port; or they traversed the middle of Europe, passing along a road which came from Asia into Russia and then ran from Kiev on the Dnieper through Cracow, Prague, Regensburg, and Mainz to France. Eventually the Syrians faced the growing competition of the Italian cities; but for three or more centuries they were Europe's leading middlemen.

The Italian Cities. Even in the worst days of migration or invasion some of the Italian cities managed to survive and to continue their industrial or commercial work. Some of them grew as centers of consumption, when a bishop or duke made his home there and goods flowed in from the neighboring countryside to feed the inhabitants of palace or castle. Some were market towns for an agricultural or pastoral region, and some revived or were newborn because they commanded the approach to Alpine passes which led to the increasingly settled lands of the north and west. Most of the leading ports still belonged to the Eastern Empire and had access to its markets, while on occasion Constantinople would seek the naval aid of an Italian city and offer in return freedom from port or customs dues in imperial harbors.

For a long time Amalfi, on the ankle of Italy, was the leading port. It was almost an outpost of Constantinople, but it made terms with the Saracens and thus gained entry to their ports as well. Its coins and the clauses of its maritime code were acceptable everywhere. Other southern ports, such as Bari, Naples, and Salerno, creep back into the records. But rivals were growing up farther north, at Genoa, Pisa, Lucca, Pavia, Milan, and Venice. As markets expanded beyond the Alps in the Rhine and Danube valleys, in the Low Countries and northern France, these towns overshadowed their southern forerunners, for this overland trade between north and south became very important.

Pisa and Genoa belonged to classical times. They suffered severely from invaders, but always came back. By the early eleventh century they were strong enough to drive the Moslems out of Sardinia, Corsica, and the Balearic Islands, just when the Normans were overthrowing them in Sicily. They thus obtained greater freedom in the western Mediterranean but did not go much into eastern waters until the crusades made the Levant the attractive terminus for all westerners.

Venice. Venice had no classical history. She was a medieval product, born of the migrations. When Attila and his Huns swooped down on Italy about 452, fugitives from towns around the top of the Adriatic took refuge on the mud flats and sandbanks off the mouth of the Adige and Brenta rivers. They caught fish and collected the salt left behind when the sea water in the lagoons evaporated during the summer. They found markets for these wares; refugees from later invasions swelled their numbers; and their island home was made impregnable. By the early eighth century their traders were working up the valleys and going through the passes into France or central Europe.

Even before that century they had built ships, sailed down the Adriatic coasts, and established trade relations with Constantinople and the Levant. With the Saracens they reached an agreement by which Egypt became a good customer for the iron, lumber, and slaves that Venice gathered in from the Balkans or beyond. To Constantinople Venice turned quite as eagerly. Her great opportunity came when the emperor sought her help against the Sicilian Normans, and repaid her with the Golden Bull of 1082. This document gave her for a hundred years the right to trade, duty-free, in any part of the Empire. Venetians were thus probably on a better footing than were the native merchants. Soon the crusades were to pour wealth into her lap and make her famous as "Venice the Golden." But already she was a great port, gathering in the raw materials and slaves of Europe's north-central and northwestern frontier, supplying in return oriental or Eastern Empire wares, and in addition selling fish, salt, glass, and various manufactured articles of her own production.

The Church. As the imperial power declined in the west, the spiritual and material power of the church grew. After Christianity was officially tolerated in 313, gifts of land by the emperor and the laity grew rapidly. The erection of buildings, the maintenance of a priesthood, and the discharge of such duties as education and charity called for large transfers of property and income from the hands of royalty, nobility, and commonalty. The Visigoths made the church the largest landowner in Spain, and Frankish kings were so lavish that by 700 probably one-third of France was in church hands. As monastic orders were founded—the Benedictine in the sixth century, the Cluniac in the tenth, and the Cistercian in the early twelfth—still more grants were made. The pope at one time held nearly 2,000 square miles of Italian wheat, forest, olive, or iron lands; some French bishops in the ninth century held over 100,000 acres, while in Saxony a nunnery held 11,000 farms and a monastery had 15,000.

Over these vast properties pope, bishop, and abbot ruled as lord and landlord. From them they drew a large income by cultivating the land or by letting it to free or unfree tenants. Much of the income was received in produce; some of it was consumed on the spot, but surpluses were sent to market. Wool, lumber, minerals, salt, wine, grain, flax, and oil from religious estates entered the stream of commerce. Lordship included control over local markets or fairs, a monopoly of milling, the right to operate a mint, the administration of justice, and other revenue-producing assets. The church also received income from its spiritual services, and a great variety of payments had to be made by the laity or by the lower clergy to the higher. The tithe, a tax levied to maintain the church, took one-tenth of a person's produce. Then there were fees of all kinds: for marriage, for saying masses, and for trials in ecclesiastical courts. Finally, the pope collected taxes and levies from his subordinates. A new bishop had to pay his whole first year's income to Rome, kings and princes might be obliged to pay certain dues, and the number of claims increased as the papacy grew stronger after about 1000 A.D.

By that date the church was well on its way to being "a governor, a landed proprietor, a rent collector, an imposer of taxes, a material producer, an employer of labor on an enormous scale, a merchant, a tradesman, a banker and mortgage broker, a custodian of morals, a maker of sumptuary laws, a schoolmaster, a compeller of conscience—all in one" (Thompson).

BIBLIOGRAPHY

GENERAL

Cambridge Economic History of Europe (1941) vol. i, is the authoritative work on late Roman and medieval agrarian life. For the early period see chaps. 1–6.

Cambridge Medieval History (7 vols.) is a valuable reference work.

Cave, R. C., and Coulson, H. H., *A Source Book for Medieval Economic History* (1936), is a good selection of extracts from medieval documents.

Dopsch, A., *The Economic and Social Foundations of European Civilization* (1937), is a vigorous assertion of the continuity of Roman and later conditions. Beginners should read the Table of Contents and Chapter 13; advanced students should examine the whole book.

Kulischer, J., *Allgemeine Wirtschaftsgeschichte des Mittelalters und der Neuzeit* (1928–1929), vol. i, chaps. 1–7.

Nussbaum, F. L., *A History of the Economic Institutions of Modern Europe* (1933), chap. 1.

Pirenne, H., *Economic and Social History of Medieval Europe* (1937), Introduction and chap. 1.

Sellery, G. C., and Krey, A. C., *Medieval Foundations of Western Civilization* (1929), chaps. 1–7.

Stephenson, Carl, *Medieval History* (1935), chaps. 1, 2, 3, 6, 8, 9, 11.

Thompson, J. W., *Economic and Social History of the Middle Ages, 300–1300* (1928), chaps. 1–15. Very useful bibliographies and maps.

Special Subjects

Arnold, T., and Guillame, A. (eds.), *The Legacy of Islam* (1931), chaps. 1–3.

Bloch, M., *Les caractères originaux de l'histoire rurale française* (1931), chap. 1.

Boissonnade, P., *Life and Work in Medieval Europe* (Eng. trans., 1927).

Heyd, W., *Histoire du commerce du Levant* (French trans., 1895).

Kendrick, T. D., *History of the Vikings* (1930).

Lipson, E., *Introduction to the Economic History of England* (1915), vol. i, chap. 1.

Pirenne, H., *Medieval Cities* (Eng. trans., 1925).

Vinogradoff, P., *The Growth of the Manor* (1911), chaps. 1, 2.

Vinogradoff, P., "Foundations of Society," in *Cambridge Medieval History*, vol. ii, chap. 20; also "Feudalism" in vol. iii, chap. 18.

Articles

Bloch, M., "Comment finit l'esclavage antique," *Annales*, January and April, 1947.

Brutzkus, J., "Trade with Eastern Europe, 800–1200," *Ec. H. R.*, 1943.

Lestocquoy, J., "The Tenth Century" *Ec. H. R.*, 1947.

Lombard, Maurice, "L'or musulman du vii⁰ au xi⁰ siècle," *Annales*, April, 1947.

Moss, H. St. L. B., "Economic Consequences of the Barbarian Invasions," *Ec. H. R.*, May, 1937.

Stephenson, Carl, "Feudalism and Its Antecedents in England," *Am. Hist. R.*, January, 1943.

Stephenson, Carl, "The Problem of the Common Man in Early Medieval Europe," *Am. Hist. R.*, April, 1946.

Vasiliev, A., "Economic Relations between Byzantium and Old Russia," *J.E.B.H.*, February, 1932.

Encyclopaedia of the Social Sciences: Articles on Charlemagne, Commerce, Commercial Routes, Feudalism, Land Tenure, Manorial System, Migrations (Ancient and Medieval), Village Community.

V

THE MEDIEVAL COUNTRYSIDE

If an occupation census of Europe had been taken in the eleventh century it would probably have revealed that quite 90 per cent of the people were country dwellers who drew their livelihood from farming, herding, fishing, or the forest. An air photograph taken at that time would have revealed a sprinkling of villages, linked together by rivers or unsurfaced roads and separated by expanses of forest, moor, or swamp. There were some towns, but few of them housed more than 10,000 persons. A second picture, taken in the mid-fourteenth century, would show that the villages had grown larger, more numerous, and also more widespread, for Europeans had pushed their frontier outward by clearing, draining, and settling new areas. There would be more people on the roads, rivers, and seas, carrying food or raw materials to towns which had increased in number, size, and importance. But a photograph taken about 1450 would reveal that little further expansion had taken place during the preceding hundred years.

Any attempt to describe the countryside during those centuries is beset by two difficulties. In the first place we have to examine the greater part of Europe's 3,750,000 square miles, and not merely the Mediterranean lands. In the second place the inhabitants of that wide expanse refuse to fit into one standard pattern or to stand still. There is variety and there is change. Consequently, as a distinguished student of medieval rural life once remarked, "In the history of land problems there is no sin like the sin of generalization," and "There is no heresy about the Middle Ages quite so pernicious as the theory that they were unchanging" (Levett).

In the early days of teaching economic history it was customary to describe a "typical" manor and give the impression that all rural life was of this kind. But a vast amount of research has been done since then, for the field is an interesting one, the documents are abundant in some countries, the work calls for great patience and skill, and the results may be revolutionary. From such arduous labor

Professor Eileen Power emerged with the conclusion that "manor" was a term about as descriptive as the word "mammal." After equally arduous effort Professor Kosminsky defined the manor as a community in which unfree villagers (villeins, serfs) cultivated their lord's domain as the price of their serfdom and of their use of a holding of land. He then discovered that even in the English Midlands, the stronghold of manors, only about 60 per cent of the territory was "manorial" in 1279. The remaining 40 per cent was nonmanorial; it had no unfree tenants, or it had no domain, or it was all domain and had no villein holdings. In France and other continental regions research is revealing similar diversity. After reading a recent study of the seigniorial system in Lorraine, one reviewer threw up his hands and exclaimed, "The more we look at things the more they appear complicated" (Perroy).

Diversity was due to many factors. While most Europeans probably lived in villages, some regions were so hilly, devoid of good soil, or heavily timbered that villages could not be sustained and settlement was that of solitary herdsmen or shepherds. Some areas had better access to market than others and were therefore more involved in commercial agriculture than in subsistence farming. Large landowners, whether lay or ecclesiastic, were more likely than small landlords to run their estates and especially their domains more rationally and systematically—and also to keep those records from which we learn most of what we know about the subject. Some areas had never been quite feudalized; their farmers were more free from lordship and even from landlordship. Some regions had been recently settled, and their tenants had been offered liberal terms of tenure in order to lure them into the wilderness. Finally there was a time element; the expansion and prosperity that characterized the period from the twelfth to the fourteenth century produced or maintained conditions which were unsuitable to the stormier days preceding or the lean ones following it.

Domain and Villagers' Holdings. The diversities just indicated were largely variations on the same theme. That theme was the sustenance of Europe's population—kings, nobles, churchmen, monks, and peasants—by the produce of the soil. The first four classes owned the land. The first three were too busy with their own full-time military, religious, and political duties or with their pleasures to do any farming, and while monastic movements usually began with such slogans as "To work is to pray," they were prone to let success turn the motto back to front or to concentrate on work which was not earthy. How then were the estates to be operated to provide the owner with his income?

Three methods were conceivable. The first was cultivation as a *latifundium*. But such cultivation with slave labor was now out of the question, and with free or servile labor it was probably impracticable, if for no other reason than that the owner would have to house, feed, and clothe the workers and their families. Experience showed that when villagers did harvest work for their landlord the food and drink supplied to them sometimes cost more than the work was worth. Further, a busy landlord with many manors would be compelled to rely on a bailiff to manage and direct the operation of each estate, and bailiffs who were both honest and competent were not easily found. In general, the balance was tilted against this method of estate management except possibly in times of good prices and buoyant markets.

The second method, at the opposite extreme, was that of dividing the whole estate into peasant holdings. The landlord could then live on the rents and other dues he collected from his tenants in money or produce. In certain circumstances this arrangement was attractive. It relieved the landlord of the troubles and uncertainties inevitable in large-scale farming; it gave him a regular and virtually constant income. The payments in produce might be sufficient to meet the food requirements of his household, while those in money could be spent to satisfy his other needs. Tenants who lived on estates which were far from his normal habitation would sell their produce in some market and remit their rents to him in cash. So long as they did that, they would enjoy considerable freedom of action in their farming operations. But there would need to be markets available in which the tenant could sell and in which the landlord could buy what he desired. If prices declined the tenant would receive less for his produce, while the landlord would get more for his money. If prices rose that situation would be reversed.

The third method, a middle course, seemed preferable (or inevitable) under the conditions which prevailed in the early Middle Ages and proved to be so adaptable that it survived in some regions until nearly the end of the medieval period. Part of the estate—perhaps as much as a half—was retained as the landlord's domain. On it was the manor house, chateau, or castle in which he and his family, house servants, officials, possibly some craftsmen, and probably some fighting retainers lived for part or the whole of the year. In the domain was a substantial expanse of farm land. The rest of the estate was in the hands of the villagers. They paid for the use of it by cultivating the domain, by handing over some of the produce of their own fields and livestock, and possibly by paying some money. Thus the landlord's establishment was sustained by the direct yield of produce from his domain, supplemented by that which he received as rent or other dues. The peasant's household lived on the net proceeds of the labor he was free to devote to his holding and of the work done on it by the other members of his family.

This division of land and arrangement for its cultivation ran through the various layers of rural society. Kings kept certain estates for their direct sustenance and enjoyment. Charlemagne is said to have held more than sixteen hundred of them. When William the Conqueror shared out England he kept about a fifth of the country. In most of these kingly properties a royal farm was worked by the peasants; its produce, along with that collected in rents, was consumed by the local officials, by fighting men, or by the king and his entourage when they visited the area. Charlemagne finally established a capital at Aachen, but was rarely there, while William never had a fixed capital. Both kings traveled round from one important estate to another, eating what had been produced there as well as supplies brought from neighboring domains.

As with the king, so with the subordinate landholders. The larger ones moved round with their retinues, consuming the produce and rents of their domains and enjoying a variety of hunting scenery. A landlord who stayed put all year and depended on the yield from the one estate on which he lived would rank low on the feudal social scale.

The church and monastic estates were also divided between domain and peasant holdings. In their early days the Benedictines did much hard labor on the land in the remote places to which they retreated, but later they became too tired, rich, or feudal. Gifts of settled land and parts of villages came to them. In days of turmoil peasants and craftsmen flocked to their gates in search of sanctuary, while in times of peace settlers were induced to come and clear the abbeys' wild lands. Hence the monks were able to live on the labor or produce of these laymen. The Cistercian order, founded in 1092, resolved to evade this softening of fiber. Its rules forbade the acceptance of gifts of villages or serfs. Its brethren must do all their own clearing, farming, herding, manufacturing, building, and domestic services. But these tasks were quickly delegated to lay brothers (*conversi*), who did the work, supervised that of hired laborers, or served as stewards managing domains tilled by tenants.

This domain economy may have been the most prevalent form of estate management, but it could not be universal or eternal. Some lords held properties which were too far away or too small to be worth visiting, and the produce from them might cost too much to transport to a point at which the landlord could consume it. In such cases there might be no domain; tenants would occupy the whole estate and remit their rents in money to their landlord. Further, even where there was originally a domain the owner might decide that it was less troublesome and more profitable for him to abandon its direct cultivation. He therefore let the tenants have part or the whole of it and lived on the increased rent in money or kind which they paid him. When an estate was pulled into the stream of commercialized agriculture, its owner would then have to decide whether he would expand domain farming for market or leave his tenants to take the risks and do the work. His decision will be examined in the next chapter.

Village Classes. When William the Conqueror's commissioners surveyed England in the Doomsday inquiry of 1085–1086, they squeezed all the villagers into four categories—*freemen,* who comprised 12 per cent of the population, *villeins* (38 per cent), *cottars* or *bordars* (32 per cent), and *slaves* (9 per cent). Each label covered a great variety of grades and shades of status or tenure, but the classification is helpful. The number of slaves engaged in domestic service or on the land was small and was probably declining. Slavery was gone from England by 1200, from France somewhat earlier, but it survived in Mediterranean lands much longer. Hence most villagers belonged to one or the other three Doomsday categories.

Economically the freemen and villeins were usually—but by no means always—farmers who held enough land to keep them and their household fully occupied and to provide a family income. The holding of the cottar or bordar was quite small—a plot of garden or one to five acres of arable land. It could not occupy all his time or yield sufficient to keep him alive. He might, however, be an industrial worker—carpenter, miller, blacksmith, weaver, tanner, or baker; but he was more likely to be an agricultural laborer, who worked for wages on the land of the larger farmers or of the landlord. The size of this pool of virtually landless labor was not very much less than that of the villeins and freemen combined—32 per cent against 50 per cent of the Doomsday population. For other parts of Europe no comparable figures exist, but we know that there were many men who held very little land and who lived chiefly by the sale of their labor or industrial skill.

The villagers differed in the size of their holdings, but the freeman differed from the others in his *personal status* as well. He must bear arms, while the villein did not. He could give his daughter in marriage, put his son into the priesthood, or sell an animal as he wished; a villein could do none of these things without getting his master's permission and paying a fee. More important economically, the freeman might hold his land on payment of an annual quitrent in money or produce, often a quite small one. If he had to pay partly in labor, it was not a regular weekly assignment, as was the villein's, but only a few days' work at such busy times as harvest. He did not do such heavy work as threshing the grain with a flail, or such dirty work as forking manure; the villein was often said to hold his land "by fork and flail." He was not tied to the land, but could terminate his tenure when he wished, or could bequeath his farm to his son. The villein was bound to the soil, as were his children after him; yet his heir had to pay a heavy price for stepping into possession of the holding and another one for inheriting the livestock or equipment.

Some such distinctions were found in most parts of Europe. France had its *vilain franc* or *vilain libre,* who resembled the English freeman, while its *vilain serf* was the counterpart of the villein. Economically the chief difference lay in the greater claim which was made on the labor, produce, and income of the villein than on those of the freeman. When the lawyers began to puzzle about the distinction, they decided that the lord's claims on the freeman were limited, but those on the serf were unlimited. The "will of the lord" (*voluntas domini*) prevailed; it could impose heavier burdens on the villein or reimpose any which had been removed. The freeman could appeal to the king's court (in England at any rate) if the landlord tried to get more out of him; but the villein had no such judicial protection.

The villein had, however, one stubborn line of defense in "the custom of the manor" (*consuetudo manerii*). He was a "customary tenant." Any arrangement, privilege, or obligation that had been accepted "since time whereof the memory of man runs not to the contrary" had thereby gained in his eyes the immutability of the hills and the right to continue unchanged. Its basis was not a document, but human memory and the testimony of the village graybeards that the custom was at least as old as they were. Any attempt of the landlord or his bailiff to curtail a time-honored custom would run head on into "the tenacious memory of the illiterate" (Cam), into protest and perhaps into revolt.

That *consuetudo* and *voluntas* might clash is obvious. That they must do so is not so obvious. What mattered to the landlord was the yield he obtained from his estate. While he might try to squeeze every possible bit of labor, produce, and money from his tenants, discontented peasants would be unproductive or might run away to the towns or frontier. We distort or discolor the picture if we assume that every landlord was a selfish monster and every peasant a sweet-souled innocent. Some landlords were greedy, and in some periods there was strong inducement to extract more from the peasants. But there is plenty of evidence to show that the medieval peasant, like his descendant in all countries, was tenacious of what he held, eager to hold more, and so fond of litigation that he welcomed a fight in court as a popular form of amusement and a lively break in village monotony. In one instance a bailiff was bribed not to collect a certain important levy. When he quit his post the malpractice was uncovered, yet the villeins endeavored to insist that non-payment of the levy was now the custom of the manor. Eventually many customs were written down in the manor court roll or some other document and thus were placed on record.

The Tenant's Dues. *Labor Services.* The tenant paid his rent in one or more of three ways—labor, produce, and money. If the estate had a large domain the labor services (or *corvée* as they might be called in France), would be the most important. The villein who held a *virgate* or *bovate* in England, a *manse* in France, or a *Hufe* in Germany had enough land to meet the needs of his family, probably between twenty-five and thirty-five acres of arable. For this he might have to work three, four, or even five "days" weekly on the domain. If he had no family to do some of this *week work* for him, his own land would suffer; but where the virgate supported grandparents, parents, and grown-up sons along with their wives and children, the family labor supply would be large enough to meet the demands of domain and virgate. Further, the "day" was usually only half a day—a long morning or afternoon.

This week work took care of the normal daily and seasonal routine of the domain, such as plowing, sowing, harrowing, weeding, carting manure from barn to field, repairing the manor house and its buildings, scouring ditches, trimming hedges, building fences, patching the roads, and taking the landlord's produce to market or to the manor where it was to be consumed. But during the very busy seasons—haymaking, shearing, and especially harvesting—the villein had to give more days, possibly four or five instead of three, and might have to bring many or all the adult members of his family. This overtime labor was known in England as *boon work*, and sometimes extended beyond farm duties. If the lord of the manor went hunting the villeins must beat up the game. When one English abbot went fishing, a horn was blown to call the villagers to his aid. When the lord moved on to his next estate his baggage had to be carried part of the way. Thus the villagers were expected to cope with whatever demands for labor arose, subject only to their ability to resist new or strange expressions of the lord's *voluntas* by appeals to the custom of the manor.

The boon works might be unpopular, since they had to be done just when the peasants were anxious to get in their own crops. The landlord salved the sore by providing meat or drink, or both, and by giving a present or bonus when the work was completed. The custom of the manor decreed whether the work should be a "dry boon," for which only such solid food as bread and cheese should be provided, or a "wet boon," in which the meat, fish, or thick pea soup was washed down with ale or cider. At the end of haymaking the peasants might be allowed to take home as much hay as they could carry on a scythe; or the lord's best sheep save one might be turned loose in the meadow and the villagers could have it for a barbecue supper if they caught it before it escaped through the fence. Harvesters might be given half a sheaf of grain for each acre they reaped. When the abbot mentioned above had finished his fishing, he took half the catch and the villagers got the rest; but "if any great pike of four or five feet or more falls to the villagers' share, he can have it for sixpence."

The total amount of labor due from tenants might be quite large.

It came from many hands, and could be grudgingly given or badly done. The task of organizing it from day to day, of directing it, and of keeping account of what services each tenant rendered must therefore have been far from easy. It was usually entrusted by the landlord, or by the bailiff who managed the estate on his behalf, to the reeve. The reeve was a villein, generally a substantial one. He was chosen by the lord, sometimes from a list submitted by the villagers, but in places he eventually was elected by his fellows. Every detail of the manorial economy came under his supervision, but his job as foreman of the labor force was one of his most onerous duties, especially since he had to balance the interest of his land-lord in getting the work done against the wishes, wills, and possible stubbornness or laziness of his fellow villagers. Sometimes he took bribes and bullied or browbeat those who did not buy his favors; at times, like the bailiff, he quietly robbed his master.

Payments in Money and Kind. Payment of rent in cash depended on the tenant's ability to obtain money by trade. We are probably safe in believing that at certain periods or in remote places the amount of trade and of money available was small, but we may doubt deeply whether money was absent from circulation in any developed rural community. Payment in produce was easier. At quarter day or on some holy day the villagers delivered such cash and commodities to the manor house as were called for by the terms of their tenure. Eggs and poultry were part of most rents, especially at Christmas or Easter. Christmas cake, a Yule log, a lamb or ram, wine, cloth, clothes, grain or malt, cheese, salt, and plowshares or horseshoes from the blacksmith are mentioned in the rent rolls. One tenant gives a quarter of seed wheat from his new crop at Mich-aelmas; a peck of wheat, four bushels of oats, and three hens at Martinmas; a cock, two hens, and 3*d.* worth of bread at Christmas. The tenants of one manor pay £4/11/4 in money, and "to the love feast of St. Peter" bring ten rams, 400 loaves, 40 platters, 34 hens, and 260 eggs. In Poland the peasant farmers provide grain, honey, fish, flax, and poultry, while the peasant craftsmen bring wheels, wooden mugs or dishes, earthenware tubs and bottles. A Swiss village sends its landlord 300 cheeses each year.

In most instances the payment in kind was a fixed amount, but sometimes it was a fixed fraction of the tenant's produce. The use of fractions was best known in the payment of the tithe to the church. It was also found in areas where the landlord supplied not merely the land but also the vines or olive trees that were growing on it, and possibly the fertilizer or pest-killer, the seed for grain-fields, and some implements. In such cases the peasant worked on a sharecropping arrangement.

The payments in money or kind frequently covered more than mere rent. They contained elements of taxation and were made to a lord rather than to a landlord. The English serf might have to "give an aid or tallage according to the quantity of his land and beasts." In France the lord had greater taxing power, and levied the *taille* on the produce of all his tenants. Often he collected the tithe as well, for he had gained control of the local church, and the village curé received a scanty portion of the tribute paid by the faithful.

Some servile payments were occasional. *Merchet* was the fee paid by a serf on the marriage of his daughter or by widows when they remarried. It was one of the commonest badges of unfreedom, but it had an economic justification when a person was marrying out-side the manor and thus was reducing the local labor supply in the present generation as well as in those to come. If the villein's son was to be trained for entry into the clergy, the lord might justly claim compensation for the loss of a worker and future father. Though bound to the soil, serfs might run away, and it proved difficult or costly to try to bring them back. Hence they might be al-lowed to remain absent from the manor on payment of an annual fee known as *chevage*.

On the death of a serf his lord claimed *heriot* and *relief*. Like many manorial claims, heriot sprang from an ancient practice; when a man died the fighting equipment which had been supplied him by his chief was returned to its owner. The serf no longer fought, but somewhere in the past his ancestors may have been supplied with farming equipment and livestock by a lord. Heriot was therefore the claim to the chattels and beasts he left behind. In most cases it had become limited to the best beast or chattel, but in some places it ran to far more; on the Welsh border, for example, it included the villein's male horses, his pigs, goats, bees, carts, copper utensils, webs of cloth, salted bacon, etc., "according to the custom of the country." The widow or son might be allowed to buy them back, and in addition must pay relief, which sometimes amounted to one year's rent, in order to take over the deceased serf's holding.

Fees on the sale of livestock, on the business of innkeepers and wine dealers, and on the beer brewed for sale by villeins were part of the landlord's sole right to hold or authorize markets. Those on the transfer of land were the price paid for winning his approval of a transaction which affected the use of his property. The lord's control of local justice had a real economic value; the various fines and fees paid in the manor court went into his purse and proved that *Justitia magnum emolumentum est*—Justice is a great source of income.

The peasants paid in money or produce for the use of the public utilities which were provided by the landlord, such as the village flour mill, wine press, brewery, oven, dye vat, sawmill, or fulling mill. Villagers originally ground their grain on a flat stone or in a hand mill, pressed their grapes by stamping on them in a tub, and fulled their own cloth by rubbing it in soapy water or by walking on it in a trough. But by about 1000 A.D. some French landlords had put a *ban* on such domestic practices, and claimed a monopoly of ownership and operation of mills, ovens, and wine presses. This claim to *banalités* spread widely. Stubborn resistance checked its general acceptance in parts of Germany and France, but in England the lords prevailed. Some monasteries built large mills—one had six pairs of stones—and pressed hard their determination to force the villagers to use them. The mill was one of the earliest instances of a substantial fixed-capital investment. Often the lord leased his monopoly to someone who thus became the official miller, dyer, baker, or fuller for the village. This man may have done the work better than it could be done by hand or foot; but his clients resented the price he charged and usually regarded him as a rogue, whose shirt was "the boldest thing in the world" because "it clasps a thief by the throat daily."

The Tenant's Holding. In return for these varied payments the villager who was not a mere cottager received a house, garden plot, appropriate farm buildings, a holding in the arable fields, a share of the meadow or of the hay that was cut from it, the right to graze livestock on the common pastures, and permission to get peat, wood, and food for himself and his animals from the woodland or waste. In a balanced mixed farming village the amount of arable land he held might range from twenty-five to thirty-five acres. In early times the peasant's holding, like the feudal vassal's fief, was probably not divisible but must either be handed back to the landlord or pass on to the next generation intact. By the thirteenth century this integrity had been weakened. The ambitious and successful villager could then increase his holding by renting more land, while others failed and had to let some of theirs go.

The Arable Fields. On pages 98 and 99 are two maps of villages, one in western England, the other in the middle Rhineland. Both belong to the early nineteenth century, yet they reveal two general features that were found in the Middle Ages over many parts of temperate Europe where the mixed farming village prevailed. The first feature was the division of the arable land into fields, which were then cut up into long narrow strips, often about 220 yards long and 22 yards wide. The second was the scattering of the villager's arable holding in strips located in most or all of these fields. The alternative to this ground plan, found in some parts of France, England, and the Mediterranean area, was the compact square or oblong field or farm, worked in one piece by a person whose home might be on it instead of in a village. But the "nucleated" village, with its inhabitants living in a cluster of homes and going forth to work on their scattered arable strips, was more widespread. It developed as far east as Russia, and was visible on the landscape in many parts of eastern, central, and western Europe in the late nineteenth century. It appeared in the cleared settlements of pioneer New England, and recent photographs show something that looks remarkably like it in the heart of savage New Guinea.

Many explanations of these striped fields have been offered. Here are some of them:

1. When a village was founded and its inhabitants brought a piece of land into cultivation, each family obtained a part of it. In course of time new fields were added to the arable area and each farmer got his portion of each field.

2. Plowing was done cooperatively, since few farmers owned plows and fewer had sufficient oxen to make the team of six or eight beasts required to pull the plow through heavy soil. If one field was plowed and each farmer held a piece of it, he could then get on with his harrowing and seeding while the next one was being prepared.

3. Different parts of the arable land had different degrees of desirability. They were good, fair, or poor, near or distant, swampy or well drained. In dry seasons lowlands might fare better than hillsides; in wet seasons the position was reversed. Distribution of the holding over a wide expanse provided insurance against vagaries of the weather.

4. Periodical redistribution played its part. In some places arable

Map of the
PARISH OF WESTON SUBEDGE
(Gloucestershire) in 1840

The strips are arable land; the other
large areas, with the exception of
Weston Park, are common pasture.

It seems safe to assume that in the
Middle Ages a smaller part of the
parish was in arable strips, and more
of it in pasture.

Long Furlong
Every Years
Field

Long Stretch
Long Field

The Meadow

Poden Hedge
Furlong

Inn Field

Ashbrook
Furlong

Vetchy
Furlong

Witch Leys

Long Furlong Field

Gravel Field

Linch Field

Lays Field

Linches

Park
Farm

Cow Pasture

Weston Park

Park
House

Dover's Hill

Kincomb
Farm

Far Hill

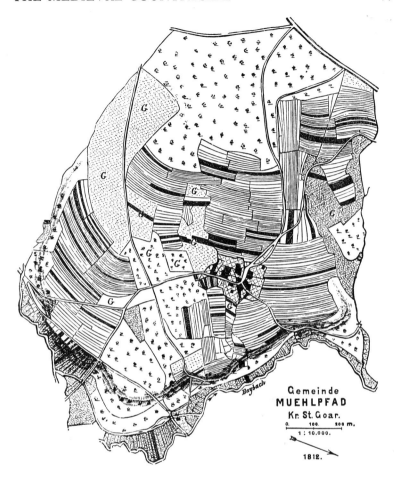

Village of Muehlpfad (St. Goar District, Middle Rhineland in 1812)
G = Gemeindeland (commons). The shaded strips represent one
man's holdings. One man held 21 Morgen (acres) in 105 parcels.

lands were shared out, at first yearly, but later less frequently and
only when the number of claimants had changed substantially. If
the number of farmers rose greatly without a comparable increase
in the village's arable area, then each claimant might get a narrower
slice in each field at each reapportionment.

There may be some measure of truth in all these suggestions,
especially the first two. But there may be a technical explanation of
the long narrow strip in the kind of plow used in some parts of

northern Europe. The Mediterranean plow was little more than a pointed stick which was pulled by one or two oxen, scratched a shallow groove in the light southern soil, but turned no furrow. When the ground had been plowed one way it was then cross-plowed. Hence a small square field, perhaps forty yards each way, was the normal unit for Greek and Roman farmers. Such a plow could not be used in the heavy wet soils which were common in parts of northern Europe, though a slightly sturdier type would be suitable for light soils, of which there were quite a lot in the north.

About the beginning of the Christian era we hear of a heavy plow, mounted on wheels and built to turn a furrow, in use in the upper Danube Valley. Its adoption in northern Europe seems to have been slow—a matter of centuries—and it never displaced the light simpler plow pulled by a couple of animals which was adequate for many types of soil and in addition was much cheaper. But after 1000 A.D. the wheeled plow drawn by about eight oxen was used more and more to turn the heavy clay lands which became available with the clearing of some forest areas—oak trees, for example, usually flourish on clay soil. Consequently a late medieval field might consist of a collection of long furrows, which reflected the dis-tance a team could pull the plow before it had to halt for a rest; and when we finally reach a settled unit of area, the acre, which seems to have been the amount of land that a plow team could treat in a long morning's work, was a furrow long (furlong) and about four rods, poles, or perches wide, i.e., twenty-two yards.

The arable strips may originally have been roughly equal in size or in the time required for the plowing, and a full villein might therefore hold about thirty of them, each about an acre in extent, scattered about the various fields. But by the thirteenth century at latest, division among children or transfer to others was cutting the strips into shorter lengths or narrower ribbons. Half- or quarter-acre strips abounded. In one English manor a quarter-acre piece, 240 yards long and 5 yards wide, had been cut into sections 24, 156, and 60 yards long, each held by a different tenant; six acres were divided among ten tenants in twenty patches, and the whole village had more than 2,000 separate strips or sections of them.

Village Cooperation and Control. The cultivation of this mingle-mangle of arable pieces on an individualistic basis was impossible. If each farmer was free to decide for himself when to plow or harvest and when to leave his land fallow, a formidable array of hedges or fences would be needed—which was absurd. The strips lay side by side, and often there was nothing permanent to serve as a boundary line between them. The plowlands of the lord's domain and of the church glebe were usually scattered among those of the tenants. Some peasants lacked enough oxen or horses to make a plow team, some had no plow, some had not enough arable land to justify the possession of either, and none had sufficient livestock to justify the employment of one member of the family as full-time herdsman. Cooperation in plowing and in tending livestock might therefore be inevitable, and regulation of cultivation was essential.

How cooperation and regulation were effected is not clear. Where the lord had a large domain, including many strips in the arable fields, his influence in making the villagers work together and his voice in control of the plowlands would be strong. Where there was little or no domain the villagers would be their own masters, making their own rules in some kind of peasants' meeting. The rules fixed the dates for the beginning of plowing and the end of harvesting, as well as the order in which the different fields were to be cultivated. They decreed when the grainfields and meadows were to be thrown open—or become *vaine pâture* as the French called it— so that livestock could come in to graze on the stubble or second growth of grass. They governed the starting of hay cutting, and forbade anyone to pick peas before the horn blew in the morning or after it blew at night, for fear his hands might stray over the plants of other tenants. There were punishments for those who let their cattle wander into the crops, stole a furrow of their neighbor's strip, or committed any one of scores of petty or high offenses. The villagers appointed shepherds, cowherds, vine-guards, and swineherds, controlled the use of the pastures, and took some care of roads, drains, and bridges.

The Two- and Three-Field Systems. One regulation—that of rotation of crops—was taken for granted even if there was no specific rule. We saw (Chapter II) that Mediterranean farmers combated soil exhaustion and scanty rainfall by planting a field with crops one year and then letting it lie fallow the next. This was a "two-course" rotation; or if we think of one field under crops while another was fallow, we call it a "two-field" system. In temperate Europe there was no lack of rainfall, but soil exhaustion was possible. In the early days of Teutonic settlement a piece of land might be broken, planted for a few years, and then allowed to revert to grass or weeds. This practice was satisfactory so long as there was plenty of suitable new land waiting to be broken. Like the American pioneer farmer or planter, the early cultivators of northern Europe could "mine" the fertility from one patch and then go on to another mine. In time, however, the supply of virgin soil near a village would be depleted, and some plan must be adopted to conserve what was available. Hence the two-field system found favor, then possibly the three-field.

The two-course rotation was as far as farmers in many parts of France, Germany, and England had advanced by the thirteenth century. Agricultural experts urged the superior merits of the three-course system, but in the three countries just mentioned there was probably no more three- than two-course cultivation. In the three-field rotation, all the strips in each field gave two crops of wheat, rye, oats, barley, or peas; then they lay fallow during the third year, and were plowed two or three times in order to keep down the weeds and enable the field to renew its strength for the next two cropping years. This rotation—crop-crop-fallow—took more out of the soil than did the two-course alternation of crop and fallow. Its use may therefore have been limited to the areas of richer soil.

Ancient and medieval writers or progressive farmers knew that manure would replenish the soil and might even permit the farmer to dispense with the unproductive fallow year. But the use of manure was limited by the available supply. Since the cattle roamed far afield over pastures, waste, and forest in search of food, they scattered manure over a wide area rather than on the fields where it was most needed. The supplies collected in barns, pigeon or poultry houses, and other places did not make up the deficiency. Hence the plowlands yielded small crops, and when man's food requirements had been met there was little arable fodder to spare for helping to carry livestock through the cold northern winter. Considerable numbers of animals must therefore be killed each fall for lack of winter food. Hence we have one of history's most important vicious circles: the scarcity of manure restricted the supply of fodder; this prevented the building up of larger herds; this limited the supply of manure; this restricted the supply of fodder; and so on round and round, with half or a third of the arable land lying idle each year.

The three-course rotation was the best plan that could be devised, yet the pictures of it which were painted by medieval farm-writers have been described by Professor Levett as a "vain imagination," "what they hope rather than what they expect to see." In some areas the fields near the village—the *infields*—were worked on the two- or three-course rotation, but those which were farther away— the *outfields*—were too distant to merit the time and labor involved in carting manure to them. They were therefore plowed up, cropped for a few years, and then allowed to go back to pasture or waste.

The cultivation of the arable fields imposed heavy demands on the time of the villager. Plowing, at the rate of one acre a day, took up much time; a villein who held ten acres in the fallow would spend thirty long mornings giving them the customary three plow- ings. The furrows would then need to be broken by hand or by harrows made of tree branches in a frame. Harvesting was another long job. In 1380 it took 275 people two days to harvest an English manor farm of 250 acres, i.e., 2.2 man-days per acre. Some figures are available from which we get a rough idea of the reward for this labor. The records of English manors show that a yield of four or five bushels for each bushel of seed was the normal harvest. This is vastly below the eightyfold yield of barley in ancient irrigated Mesopotamia. It is also about a third that of English wheat harvests today and suggests that "a threefold increase in productivity of seed seems to measure broadly the difference between medieval and modern farming" (Beveridge).

Meadow and Common Lands. After the arable fields the most important piece of land was the meadow, since the peasants de- pended largely on its hay crop for their chief winter fodder, espe- cially if the climate was such that the cattle must be kept indoors during the coldest months. The hay crop might be shared among the holders of arable fields, the meadow might be divided into sections and distributed annually by lot, or each peasant might have per- manent possession of one piece; but annual reallotment seems to have been most common.

Like the arable fields, the meadow was protected against stray- ing beasts by a fence, hedge, or ditch. Like them after harvest, it was thrown open when the hay had been cut in order to let the cattle graze on the second growth of grass. But around the rest of the village land there were no barriers. All that was left was open common. There the livestock roamed in search of food, and the peasants obtained much that was important for their work or sus- tenance. On the regions of natural swamp or treeless plain the open pastures might be ample, but where settlements had been carved out of forest lands there would be little clear country, and the animals would have to hunt chiefly among the trees. The forests "were the peasant's providence. They fed his horses, unless there was some local rule against it, his cattle, his sheep, his goats, with their leaves—eaten green in summer and gathered dry for winter—and the grass of their open glades. His pigs ate the acorns and beech-nuts" (Parain). For himself the forest yielded wild fruits, berries, nuts, and other foods, wild animals, lumber, and ferns or other kinds of litter for the beds of himself and his animals. Thus the common lands were one of the three angles—arable, meadows, commons—of the rural triangle.

The right of pasture was in theory proportionate to the size of the tenant's arable holding, and must provide food for as many animals as were necessary for plowing and manuring his arable strips. So long as there was abundance of commons for all men and beasts, no regulation was necessary. When the abundance vanished, control became inevitable. In its simplest form it might impose a stint to the effect that "None shall oppress or overcharge the commons or wastes by putting more goods thereon in summer than they can, out of the profits of their farms and tenements, keep in winter." Or there might be closed seasons, when animals were excluded from the forest to prevent them from injuring new growths, young trees, or fruit crops. But two more serious difficulties developed which led to much friction between lords and peasants. In the first place, as population grew there might be need for more cultivated land near the village, and this would have to be cut out of the commons, whether clear or timbered. In the second place, the feudal nobility spent much of its spare time hunting. If the peasants overcrowded the forests with livestock the food for the wild animals, and even the animals themselves, might disappear.

On these points there could be a conflict of interests between peasants and their lords. The lords asserted their claim to do as they wished with the common lands. How they spread settlement on them will be examined in the next chapter. The protection of the forests as hunting grounds and as sources of income for the landlord became an acute problem in many regions along the forest belt. In England large areas were earmarked as royal forests, subjected to special laws and courts, and protected by heavy fines or severe punishment of those who cut down trees, killed deer or certain other beasts, or spoiled the privileged animals' food supply by unauthorized grazing of livestock. Yet in spite of the reduction in the extent of forest available and the restraints on its use, the timberlands continued to be an important source of supplies to the peasant all through the Middle Ages.

Effort and Income. Agriculture in northern Europe possibly gave a lower return to effort than it did on the sunny slopes of the Mediterranean and certainly a smaller one than on the silt-covered banks of the Nile. The cultivator must be satisfied with a meager reward for hard work. His wife was a Jill-of-all-trades, doing her bit in farming and manufacturing as well as her domestic and motherly chores. Child labor was normal, with boys and girls carrying a full share of miscellaneous tasks. The whole household worked, yet from its labors emerged incomes which left little over when necessaries had been supplied. The fact that three adult generations were often crowded into one small house suggests that the reserve of capital and labor for building homes was scanty, while the small supply of personal and domestic effects mentioned in wills (when such documents appeared) shows that even comparatively well-to-do peasants were able to acquire few worldly goods.

The scanty income and the slowly accumulated capital might be wiped out by war, famine, and pestilence. War brought loss to the areas over which armies moved, taking what was movable and destroying what was not. Such conflicts as the investiture struggle in Germany (1075–1122), the civil war during Stephen's reign in England (1135–1154), and later the Hundred Years' War (1337–1453) caused much destruction of life and property, increased taxes and feudal levies, and provoked outbursts of robbery by powerful and poor alike.

Famine was more serious, for it affected larger regions, and defective means of transportation prevented the importation of supplies from distant areas to counteract local scarcity. If the weather of medieval Europe resembled that of today, periods of good harvest never lasted more than two or three years and were then followed by two or three years of poor or bad weather. In addition, there were longer cycles marked by a few decades of relatively good seasons and then by a lengthy term of miserable climate. The eleventh century had black patches of widespread famine. Southern England had great storms, floods, and geological disturbances between 1287 and 1293, floods in 1307, famine in 1314–1316, and a long drought in 1325–1326. The famine of 1314–1318 affected almost the whole continent. Grain prices in Antwerp rose more than 300 per cent between late 1315 and June, 1316. As ever, starvation was followed by pestilence; underfed peasants and townsfolk died like flies, wars were suspended or converted into campaigns of brigandage, plow teams were slaughtered for meat, rats and mice were eagerly sought for food.

Even when the ground had not been prepared by famine, the "plague" still came. Pneumonic plague was directly infectious, but bubonic plague was spread by rats, or rather by the fleas which got it from the rats and then passed it on to human beings. Medieval houses of wood and mud provided fine homes for the flea-infested rat in town and village alike. Of the plagues which did much damage, the worst became known as the Black Death. It reached the Crimea from Asia in 1346, spread over Europe during the next four years, and burst out again at various times between 1360 and 1400. The first attack was probably the worst in its severity and range of devastation—from the Black Sea to Iceland. It struck unevenly, hitting crowded towns, seaports, and monasteries severely, but probably treated the villages more lightly. According to the latest estimate, the first outbreak reduced the population of England—about 3,700,000 in 1345—by 20 per cent, while later ravages brought it down to about 2,000,000 in 1400. The short-run result of such epidemics was economic and social confusion; the long-run effects will be examined in the next chapter.

Village Varieties. The picture painted in this chapter would not be accurate in all its details for any single village at any one time. No brief account can convey an idea of the great variety of conditions or organization prevailing in rural medieval Europe. Even in a small country like England the striped arable lands covered only the midlands and south; in the southeast men worked compact holdings, while in the west and north, where animals fared better than crops and population was thinner, scattered homesteads or hamlets dotted the pastoral areas. In France north of the Loire villages stood in the center of open fields, vineyards, and common pastures; but elsewhere the arable holdings were broad oblongs, homes were scattered, and village control might be almost unknown.

The relations between lord and tenant were as varied as was the landscape. In the English midlands and south, villein holdings and domains predominated, especially on the great abbey and church estates. Yet even there Kosminsky finds that 30 per cent of the territory was held by free tenants against 34 per cent by villeins. Throughout this chapter we have talked of the village and the manor as if they were geographically the same thing, with one lord for the whole village. But the lands of one village were frequently owned by two, three, or more lords. The French *seigneur* had far greater political and judicial power from which to derive income than did the landlord in England, Germany, or most other parts of Europe. In short, medieval country life was infinitely varied. Yet through it all ran the common thread of a peasantry that worked to maintain itself and toiled or paid to sustain its economic, military, political, and religious superiors.

BIBLIOGRAPHY

See end of Chapter VI.

VI

RURAL CHANGE AND EXPANSION

In the preceding chapter medieval rural society was presented as a composite photograph. In this one it is treated as a moving picture. The countryside was affected by four main developments. The first was the growth of population up to about 1340. This led to the more thorough use of land in or on the fringe of old village communities and to an extension of settlement into undeveloped or ill-developed areas. The second was the growth of towns, commerce, and some staple manufacturing industries, the expansion of the trading class, and the improvement in industrial, commercial, and financial methods. This was reflected in an increased local or distant demand for food and raw materials, and a rising price level, with a consequent growth in the attractiveness and importance of commercial agriculture. The third comprised a variety of changes in the military, political, and judicial position of the feudal landed class. These combined with economic factors to affect the landlord's relations with his tenants, the way he obtained and spent his income, and his material welfare. The fourth was the check to population, prices, prosperity, and expansion after the mid-fourteenth century.

The Growth of Commercial Agriculture. Agriculture has always contained a large degree of production for sustenance rather than for sale. The division of the output into subsistence crops and cash crops is well known even today. At the same time the farm family may still convert some of its raw produce into goods to be eaten, worn, or used. Only within the last fifty or hundred years have baking, brewing, or the making of clothes, rugs, candles, soap, butter, cheese, bacon, jam, and pickles declined as domestic industries, especially in rural homes. To this list of usufactures the Middle Ages added the production of cloth, leather, boots, furniture, wooden platters or spoons, and farm utensils. The great household of king, bishop, or lord had its team of specialized craftsmen to make many of the things it needed, and most of the goods which the peasant household consumed had been produced or made by the family.

Yet self-sufficiency was probably never complete either in the homes of great and small or in the village community as a whole. No people in historical times was ignorant of the possibilities of trade or of the use of money. The alternatives were not either trade or no trade, money or no money. They were differences of degree, of more or less trade, of greater or smaller money transactions. There are too many industrial workers and sellers (especially of ale) mentioned in medieval manorial records to allow us to believe that the villager did everything for himself. Similarly no village was so situated that it could produce everything it needed. Iron must be brought in for the blacksmith, salt for curing or pickling meats, tar for treating sheep scab, fish from the coast, and dyes for the homespun fabrics. There might be no stone in the district suitable for the millstones. The nobility or gentry up in the manor house had some tastes which called for the purchase of high-grade cloth, weapons, saddles, armor, spices, and cosmetics, while the commonalty found much to desire when the peddler opened his pack full of strange goods from afar.

If some goods came in, others went out. They might be the transportable part of the domain produce or of the rents paid in kind which had to be sent to the absentee landlord's residence. But when we pass 1000 A.D. the effect of the growth of trade and of towns becomes more and more apparent. All towns were centers of consumption of foodstuffs, but those which developed manufactures needed to import raw materials as well. Their inhabitants might till fields and tend livestock in or around the town, but if the population grew large it must obtain supplementary supplies from surrounding villages or even from remote regions.

The growth of market demands could influence the behavior of landlord and tenant alike. The peasant who was near a town might devote some of his energy to producing goods which he took to the weekly market. If he lived farther away he might produce a food crop or raw material which middlemen would buy and take to market. If he was a free tenant with a light load of labor services, there would be little to prevent him from pursuing this policy. If he was a villein he might desire to convert his labor dues into a payment of money or kind, so that he would have more days to give to work on his own land. He might wish to get his arable strips out of the mingle-mangle, and fuse them in a compact field which he could till as he wished. He might desire to acquire more land for the expansion of his subsistence and commercial enterprise, employ hired labor, and use more capital.

Landlords responded to the commercial possibilities in two ways. Some of them were content to let their tenants take the initiative, and cooperated by converting labor services into payments in money or kind, by cutting up and leasing the domain to new tenants or to expansively minded old ones, and by carving new fields or meadows out of the commons and wastes. Thus their income would come increasingly from rents. But more energetic landlords, especially the large lay and monastic owners, expanded and exploited their domains as large commercial farms. To obtain the necessary labor they insisted that tenants do their full week work and boon days, tried to increase the amount of the labor dues, and hired any labor that was available. To obtain additional land they might strive to get hold of the peasants' fields, annex pieces of common, and reclaim wastes. To obtain capital they borrowed heavily. Their domains became large grain or cattle farms to feed towns, or big sheep farms to feed looms.

A third class—the town merchants—contributed something to the commercialization of the countryside. To these men land had a fourfold attraction. It might yield good returns on the capital invested in its purchase, equipment, and improvement; possession gave social prestige to its owner and permitted his fortune to lose the odor of leather or herrings; a country estate allowed the family to escape from the pestilences which beset towns during the summer; and the merchant's capital might profitably be used in financing production as well as the trade in the product.

These effects of the growth of towns and trade explain much of Europe's medieval rural history. We see them first in Italy and the Low Countries.

Town and Country in Italy. By 1300 Italy was well sprinkled with towns or cities. Some of them, especially in the north, were large by medieval or even by later standards. Milan, it has been estimated, housed 175,000 persons, Florence and Venice had over 100,000 each, while others ranged from more than 50,000 to less than 10,000 inhabitants. The largest communities could not meet their food requirements from the adjacent territory. Venice on its islands had to cross water for most of its supplies, Florence could draw food for only five months in each year from the surrounding country, and both cities had to go as far as Sicily for much of their grain. Most parts of Italy produced farm commodities for market, but the south and Sicily had the greatest surplus to spare.

During the centuries since the end of the Western Empire much of the land had been in the hands of lords, churches, and abbeys, whose tenants tilled the fields, vineyards, and olive groves of the domain, paid fixed dues in money, and handed over a fraction— from a quarter to a third—of the produce from their own holdings. Landlords dominated the countryside from the castles they had built, often on high ground, for protection against attack from land or sea. The villagers' homes were clustered around the castle, the little community might be enclosed by a wall, and the peasants went out of the gates daily to work their fields on the lowlands.

As towns and trade grew, some landlords—and probably some villagers—used these strongholds as bases from which they plundered or imposed heavy tolls on the goods that passed by road or river to the towns. During the eleventh and twelfth centuries these impediments were removed by force or by bargains between town and castle. Florence subdued the five fortresses which commanded nine miles of the River Arno as well as scores of other troublesome spots. The lords were compelled to live in the city for part of the year, and the administration of their estates was put into the hands of civic officials. Serfdom was wiped out. Some landlords were far more intelligently cooperative, and played an active part in the trading, political, military, naval, diplomatic, and social life of what were becoming city-states. They joined hands with the monasteries and the cities—the two great consumers—in spending money to solve the age-long problem of too much or too little water. Embankments and improved river beds prevented streams from overflowing and thus eliminated many swamps. Irrigation reservoirs and channels widened the area capable of summer cultivation. Canals linked up rivers in the Po Valley to make the carriage of produce easy and cheap. Some towns enclosed land and abolished commons as a prelude to intensive farming. Merchants acquired estates and sank capital in their improvement.

All these developments combined with the growing demand for land and its products to make good soil costly. The holdings in north and central Italy were small, but called for much labor. They were tilled by owners, customary tenants, and leaseholders, but increasingly they seem to have been operated on a sharecropping arrangement which Italians called *Mezzadria* and the French called *métayage.* The landlord provided the fields, vineyards, and pasture, and also such capital goods needed for their cultivation as the seed and the ox for the plow. The tenant usually was too poor to supply more than labor, and cattle were too expensive for a small man's purse. Having provided so much, the landlord decided the kind of work that the tenant must do, supervised operations, and at harvest time claimed a fraction of the crop, often a half. The method was in effect a partnership in which one member provided the capital while the other supplied the labor. If the harvest was good both benefited; if it was bad, both shared the disappointment. In the south larger farms and ranches were the rule, carrying on the tradition of the Roman *latifundium* even into modern times.

The Low Countries. On the other side of Europe the relations between town growth, industry, commerce, and rural change were equally strong. The position of present-day Belgium and southern Holland at the mouth of the Rhine, Meuse, and Scheldt made the region the meeting point of great inland routes from east and south and of sea lanes from the British Isles, France, and Scandinavia. In Roman times its wool, hides, dairy produce, hams, and geese were sent as far as Rome. The ore deposits of eastern Belgium gave rise to important iron and copper works. English wool and local wool or flax fed flourishing textile centers, while coast dwellers caught herring or plied their trading vessels on the North Sea. The Germanic invasions may have disturbed production and trade, but both quickly revived. The Vikings came to plunder what they knew to be a rich land, but recovery gradually came, population grew dense, and Pirenne estimates that by the twelfth or thirteenth century half the Belgian people lived in towns. The need for food and raw materials was therefore too great to be met from the local soil.

The Low Countries were actually low. Much of the northern part was below sea level or was sandy heath; it could not be made safe or fit for cultivation without a great effort for its protection and improvement. In Belgium the inland region (Brabant) was higher, drier, and richer, but along the coastal area (Flanders) the water had to be fought. The land was owned by abbeys, bishops, and lay lords in the usual kind of large estate, but the serf's obligations became fixed at an early stage in terms of money rather than in kind or labor services. As the urban demand for farm products grew, prices rose steadily higher. The peasant who produced for market prospered, but the landlord became poorer as the purchasing power of his income from fixed customary payments fell. Two ways of escape were available for him: (1) He could free his serfs, and then let them have their holdings back on short leases at rents which could be raised, if conditions were good, when the lease came up for renewal. (2) He could increase the area of rent-producing land and the number of rent payers by attacking the wastes, swamps, heaths, and woodlands of his estates.

Both methods were used. The first led to the fairly early disappearance of serfdom in favor of a free leaseholding tenantry. The second called for patient, persistent struggle, for great outlay of capital and labor, and for a refusal to be daunted when river or sea, scoffing at human effort, swallowed up land. From 1050 onward the Count of Flanders mobilized peasants to fight the inundations along his coast, and his example was followed by other lords. It was heartbreaking work, for time after time the North Sea broke through the sand dunes built by nature or the embankments piled up by man. In 1135 it flooded part of Flanders again, and farther north took the first bite toward making the Zuyder Zee. In the thirteenth century there were over thirty serious encroachments.

Faced with recurrent disasters, many Low Countrymen emigrated to England or Germany; but those who stayed behind kept up the fight, and accumulated such skill in the work that they were eagerly sought after wherever men wanted to save or reclaim land. If landlords could not afford the cost, city merchants lent them the money or bought their estates. Soon much of the Netherlands was owned by rich townsmen who poured capital into sea walls, dikes, drainage channels, and pumps worked by windmills. The rescued land was used at first for sheep runs or goose farms, but as soon as possible it was converted into meadows or put under cultivation. The damp climate and the rich reclaimed soil produced plenty of grass for large herds of cattle. The farmers therefore had enough manure and were able to replenish the land without letting it lie fallow. On the land thus saved from periodic idleness they planted turnips and other fodder crops, which in turn allowed more beasts to be fed all the year round. In this way they broke the vicious circle described in the preceding chapter. Careful cattle breeding, improved meadows, and better gardening methods were all part of that expenditure of much labor and capital on little land which made Belgian and Dutch intensive agriculture a model for the rest of northern Europe.

Rural Change in France and England. France and England moved more slowly toward better use of the soil and to new relations between landlord and cultivator. They were less dominated by town growth, their land supply was relatively larger, they did not feel so much the pressure of population on limited rural resources, and they were not so worried by lack or excess of water. Yet the influences noted in the early part of this chapter were at work. For example, the population of England rose from a little over 1,000,000 in 1086 to about 3,700,000 in 1340. Domestic trade was stimulated by the food demands of Paris and London, while there was a great expansion in the export of French wine and English wool. By the thirteenth century prices were buoyant, production was mounting to its peak of the early fourteenth century, and agriculture was increasingly profitable to those who practiced it for market.

Political factors influenced economic trends in both countries. There was less war than in earlier centuries, and military exuberance was drained off to the crusades. The English landlord gradually lost his fighting importance as his king became less concerned with the defense of England but more with keeping the feudal vassals in order and with fighting abroad. The crown therefore welcomed a change in the way landlords fulfilled their obligations. Instead of paying for their land by appearing, fully armed and accompanied by a specified number of knights, ready for service for a certain number of days each year, the great barons were allowed to pay *scutage* (shield money), which the king could use to hire mercenaries. The top men therefore did not need the military aid of their own vassals but were ready to take money instead. So it might go on all down the line; *scutage* displaced knight service, and the landed class became partly demobilized.

At the same time the English lord was losing some of his power as local judge and ruler because of the growing strength of the central government. Hence he had more time to devote to the management of his estate, to hunting, drinking, national politics, and other diversions. In France the royal grip on the feudal lords was much weaker; consequently the landlord's powers and income were greater than in England. The seignior showed less interest in actually running his estate or in cultivating a domain, and more in what he could collect as rent and as income from *banalités,* court fees, and taxes. Thus the French seignioral system was better organized on the political side and less exploited for economic ends than was that in England.

The French Rentier. This difference in power and attitudes helps to explain a marked contrast in the response to the opportunities for commercial farming. In England small cultivators and great land-lords alike poured produce into the stream of trade, but in France it was the tenant rather than the landlord who heeded the call of the market. The French farmer was therefore able and willing to seek more land and more freedom, and to pay for both. The land became available as the lord cut up his domain, thus providing additional acres for old tenants, offering holdings to new ones, dispensing with any need for labor services, and allowing his people to pay what they owed in money or kind. As Bloch puts it, a villager's tenure, which had once been a source of man power, was now a source of rent. Money might also buy freedom from any irksome claims or marks of bondage. If the cash did not talk sufficiently loudly, other factors forced the landlord to listen. His villeins might run away to the towns or to some new village that was being developed in the wilderness; or they might band together in a village revolt. But no matter what kind of persuasion was used, the result was usually the same. The peasant eventually gained a hereditary tenancy on terms that were fixed. He paid an annual quitrent called *cens,* and so be-came a *censier.* He was still liable for certain other dues—*taille,* transfer fees, and the like. But these charges were fixed in money terms, and so long as he and his descendants paid this composite price of possession, the land was theirs to work and enjoy. In that secure state the *censier* remained until the French Revolution re-lieved him of the obligation to pay the price.

With his domain gone, the French landlord now became a *rentier.* His welfare depended on the amount of money rent he received, on its purchasing power, and on payments in kind which probably were not more than enough to meet the needs of his household for bread and wine. His receipts from his *censiers* were fixed. If prices went down his purchasing power increased; but if they rose, his income bought less and his standard of living fell. Unfortunately for him, they rose throughout western Europe, from about 1150 for over two centuries, and may have doubled during that period. The peasants benefited from this enhanced return for their produce, but the *rentier* was hurt. The evidence suggests that he fared badly in the long run, as men who live on rent and interest have done in other periods when their income either did not come in or lost its purchasing power under the weight of rising prices, currency depreciation, or mounting taxes.

Just as the price curve began to show signs of turning downward (after 1350) other troubles befell the *rentier*. The Black Death hit France severely. The Hundred Years' War destroyed population and property, led to frequent devaluations of the currency, and robbed the landlord of his chief claim to prestige or power when English archers toppled him and his great horse, a mingled heap of flesh and ironmongery, in the mud or dust of the battlefield. His king transferred some profitable judicial functions from the seigniorial to the royal court. His economic collapse was often tragic, his home was scoffed at as a *château de la misère*, and he was obliged to sell part or the whole of his estate to townsmen who were putting their wealth into land.

The English Domain Entrepreneurs. The English landlord wound up the Middle Ages in a plight which was not quite so sad, yet was one of gloomy contrast to the golden age enjoyed by his thirteenth-century forebears. During the twelfth century some manorial landlords had abandoned cultivation of the domain, had let the villagers add its arable strips to theirs, and consequently, since they had no further use for labor services, had "commuted" week and boon works for payments in money. In the thirteenth century, however, this tide turned. Labor services no longer declined but rather increased. The cultivation of the domain by its owner expanded, while the amount of land in peasant hands almost stood still. Professor Postan finds some such development on over 650 manors out of the 800 he has examined. The explanation seems to be that many landlords saw and seized the opportunities for increased profit offered by higher prices and flourishing trade. The thirteenth century was "an age of rising production, expanding settlement, technical improvements, the investment of capital, the application of a greater amount of labor to the same amount of land" (Postan).

Small farmers played their part in that advance. Many of them were already free to give their whole attention to it, and it may be that small or absentee estate owners were willing to let their tenants go ahead at full speed by releasing them from labor services. But some of the large landlords were far too wide awake to let slip the chance of enhancing their income by working their own lands. Like their class in earlier and later times, they threw themselves into the business of commercial farming with the utmost vigor. For their enterprise they needed as much labor as possible. They therefore were not merely likely to frown on any tenant who wished to commute his "works" but eager to cancel any commutation compacts which had been made in the past, and to increase their claims for labor from both villeins and freemen. They cut down the amount of land a villein held but did not reduce the amount of work he must do for it; they turned the required labor services from "days" into amounts of work, and the latter might take more than the old number of days to perform; they demanded work rather than money if they could choose between the two; and they revived old claims which had been allowed to lapse. Where the domain had been leased to tenants they took it back when leases expired, and added to it by cutting pieces out of the commons. Thus they got as much unpaid labor as they could exact, sometimes after hard tussles between "the will of the lord" and "the custom of the manor," and directed its use on the largest possible domain.

Great and small men threw themselves into the production of grain, cattle, dairy produce, and wool. The grain, cattle, and dairy produce were mostly consumed in England, though there might be a little export of them in good years; but the flocks of sheep supplied far more wool than could be spun and woven in village cottages or by urban textile workers, and a great part of the clip therefore went to feed the clothmaking industries of the Low Countries or Italy.

Some producers needed more land. Villagers obtained it by leasing part of the domain of unenterprising landlords or of the holdings of their fellows; or they rented a bit of waste or forest and improved it, a process known as *assarting*. "A busy land market was in operation, through the medium of the lord's court, for the sale, exchange, and lease of the villein holdings" (Levett). The prosperous farmer added to his acres, while the victim of debt, incompetence, or restlessness let some of his go. Landlords also wanted more land and got it in part by encroaching on the commons and wastes. The villagers might not like this, since it reduced the area available for their livestock; but if they were villeins their protest won little support from lawyers, crown, or legislature. The Statute of Merton (1235) said the lord could occupy waste land, provided he left enough for his *free* tenants; but it gave no protection to the unfree.

Some cultivators took steps to use their land more efficiently. If they could gather their plowland into a few compact blocks instead of having strips scattered widely over the fields, they would waste less time in moving from one patch to another, boundary disputes would end, and such processes as sowing or harvesting could be carried out more economically. By 1300 some groups of tenants had consolidated their arable holdings by agreement among themselves, and by similar pacts had cut into the commons to increase the area of plowland or meadow or to enclose pastures for the better handling of sheep. Landlords meanwhile had withdrawn their strips of arable domain from the village fields and welded them together. Thus the village map underwent some changes in the interests of improved or expanded production.

The Organization of Production. The organization of production for sustenance and market reached its highest level on the estates of the large landlords. Dukes, earls, bishops, and abbots owned lands scattered over a wide area in many counties. If these estates were not too far apart, each might be assigned the task for which it was best suited, either that of supplying food for the central household and the residents of the other manors or that of producing goods for market. Of the numerous manors owned by Crowland Abbey, some grew grain, others concentrated on livestock, and all sent their chief product to feed the abbey, to supply each other, or to market. In some years 10,000 bushels of wheat came to the central granary, along with 5,000 to 6,000 bushels of malt for the monks' ale and much other food for man, hog, or hen. The abbey could therefore devote its central farm to rearing cattle and sheep. In 1309–1310 the abbot sold over 9,000 fleeces of wool to Italian, Flemish, and German merchants, along with much livestock and cheese.

An even more elaborate organization prevailed on the properties, scattered over eight counties, of Canterbury Cathedral Priory. This abbey was near the London market and within easy reach of ports which traded with the continent. Four monks managed the estates as an integrated enterprise. Those which were near by supplied the abbey with food, while the remote ones earned revenue by producing for market. The flocks numbered nearly 14,000 sheep in 1330. Arable areas were enriched by the use of lime, and the grain yield per acre far exceeded that of less-nourished fields. Much capital was put into the land, an endless struggle was waged against sea and swamp by building embankments or draining marshes, and the reclaimed lands were leased to tenants. By this combination of specialized high farming, liberal use of capital, and rents from the newly won holdings, the abbey exploited its opportunities to the full. It was not alone, for we know of an earl whose flocks were as large as those of Canterbury, of another abbot who had 20,000 sheep, and of a bishop who had nearly 30,000.

The Decline of Domain Farming. The "golden age" of English domain farming lasted until the early fourteenth century. "The later fourteenth century, from about 1340, was the critical age, and the fifteenth century the age of stagnation" (Power). The floods and famines around 1320 clouded the sky. Then came the Black Death, the Hundred Years' War, and finally a civil war known as the War of the Roses (1455–1485). Prices fell, but hired labor became scarcer and grew more costly when wages rose after the Black Death. Taxes mounted to pay for war, and bore heavily on land as well as on such easily taxable products as wool. Manorial profits therefore declined and landlords lost their zest for farming. They abandoned the cultivation of their domains wholly or in part, leased them to the bailiff or the villagers, and sometimes supplied equipment, livestock, and seed for the first year. As the domain declined or disappeared the need for labor services did likewise, and commutation therefore became inevitable. By 1500 most English cultivators held their land on payment of money or produce.

With his domain disintegrated, the English landlord reached a position similar to that of his French counterpart. The rent payments from his villeins were fixed in amount; customary services in labor, money, and kind had been translated into money and kind, the terms had been entered in the manor court records, and when a copy of that entry was given to the tenant he became known as a copyholder. So long as he fulfilled the terms he was immovable, and the holding might pass from generation to generation, subject to payment of the succession fee (heriot and relief). The rent from leasehold tenants—which usually included that paid for assarted holdings, reclaimed land, or villein holdings which had been converted into leaseholds—could vary in amount, since the price might be changed when the lease was renewed. But in the leaner decades which came after 1340 it was not always possible to find new tenants; the landlord might be obliged to accept lower rents, and even then he was not always able to avoid having some holdings vacant.

The fifteenth century was therefore a relatively gloomy one for the English landlord. Sometimes he tried to supplement the shrunken income from his estate by squeezing what he could out of his surviving rights as lord, or by striving to become a local or national political boss, in order to lay hands on the rewards and spoils of office. He might support these efforts by keeping a body of armed retainers who bullied and battered like a modern gang. This political plundering helped to produce the Wars of the Roses, in which the nobles largely killed each other off. Much of their land passed by peaceful sale or violent transfer into other hands. By 1500 few landlords were direct descendants of the barons who had crossed the Channel with William the Conqueror in 1066.

In this development of a passive landlord class and a more independent peasantry, the church and monastic institutions lagged somewhat behind, yet moved in the same direction. Canterbury Cathedral Priory decided before 1400 to lease all its estates and henceforth lived on rents until it was dissolved in the sixteenth century. Its revenues remained at a high level for a long time, possibly because its tenants were kept busy supplying London's needs. But other religious estates were less happily located or less wisely managed. On the continent the same was true. The Cluniac order, founded in 910, came to grief eventually because its monks confined their manual labor to transcribing books and relied on fixed money rents which were inadequate in purchasing power by 1300. Exactions by pope or king cut into monastic gross revenues; there was some extravagant spending on buildings and plate, some rash investing and borrowing, occasional poor administration, and unwillingness to forgo the customary cake when there was money only for bread. Consequently many monasteries had suffered financial shipwreck long before the Reformation destroyed them.

The changes in rural life described above did not embrace the whole continent or even the whole of any country. Not all landlords burned with a desire to wring the last penny out of their estates. Most peasants may have been conservative, and the commercialization of agriculture was a slow and partial process except in favored areas. Open fields, extensive commons, wide wastes, fallow fields, and important fragments of lordly or landlordly power were widespread even as late as the eighteenth and nineteenth centuries. But the survivals cannot obscure the changes and disturbances which in many parts of central and western Europe had altered the relation between the lord and his land, between him and his tenants, between him and his ruler, or between his wants and his income.

The Medieval Frontier

In Chapter IV we saw how the wandering northern Europeans settled down in the places that seemed most favorable and from those bases soon began to go out to colonize new regions. This filling in of the empty spaces was stopped and partly undone by the turbulence of the eighth to tenth centuries; but it was soon resumed and generated great volume as well as momentum during the twelfth and thirteenth centuries. By the fourteenth century most of the areas capable of settlement had been filled up, and the movement subsided.

Sometimes the movement was a short one, to clear and occupy land on the fringe of the village, or to bring into use those expanses of swamp, moorland, or forest which lay between or on the rim of the settled regions. But the greatest migration went far. Its slogan was "Go east, young man!" and it carried western Europeans across Germany, beyond the Vistula, to the lands on the east coast of the Baltic Sea.

The motives that took men to the medieval frontier were as mixed as the men. On the one hand, kings and princes wanted more territory, lords sought estates, bishops saw new realms to convert, monks wished for land and solitude, merchants searched for goods and customers. On the other hand, the potential cultivators included dispossessed peasants, runaway serfs, debtors, younger sons to whom the family holding offered no future, refugees from justice, invasion, or civil war, adventurers and restless fellows. Some came from the Low Countries, crowded out by the rapid growth of population or washed out by the inroads of the North Sea. A few were transferred willy-nilly by their lord to help settle his new fief. More were attracted by offers of cheap land and by pictures of a land of Canaan flowing with mead and honey. One group of immigrants consisted of knights who went crusading south of the Baltic instead of east of the Mediterranean.

The monasteries were the earliest powerful force working on the frontier. Many Benedictine abbeys were posted out in the wilds, and in the seventh century they were dotted along the eastern edge of the Frankish kingdom. When Charlemagne drove the Saracens far back into Spain he handed much of the devastated Franco-

Spanish borderland to abbeys. The monks originally had no desire to attract settlers; they sought only to make secluded homes for themselves; but their wish to be left alone was not granted, for the laymen who came to live near them made the abbey a core of colonization and even of town-planting.

The Cistercians were more intrepid frontiersmen than their Benedictine predecessors. When they appeared in the early twelfth century the best areas had all been occupied. They therefore had to settle in remote or inferior places—the valleys and moors of northern England or Scotland, the fringe of wild Wales, the dreary, sandy stretches along the Bay of Biscay, or the racial frontier where Germans were steadily subjugating Slavs. Within fifty years they had founded over three hundred settlements. Much of the land was fit only for pasturage, and in Britain the Cistercians became the chief flockmasters; but they cultivated the soil assiduously wherever possible, and their granges, as their estates were often called, became highly productive. They drained, irrigated, studied the relation between the soil and the kind of trees that grew on it, and experimented in seed selection, vine grafting, and horse breeding. They taught tenants how to farm and attracted settlers by offers of cheap land. They dug minerals, produced salt, built mills, fostered the making of linen or woolen cloth, and traded widely. Eventually they grew avaricious and lazy, and ceased to justify their existence. But they had done a fine piece of pioneering work.

In France, Flanders, and Holland the areas devastated by man, the virgin forests, and the natural swamps or inundated lands received attention from all kinds of landowners after about 1050. Generous terms were offered to settlers, as "a peasant was a valuable property for whom lords quarreled" (Koebner). Those who came might be called *hospites* or *hôtes* (guests). At the least they were provided with a hut and a patch of garden land, and then set to work clearing a holding. What they cleared they were allowed to hold in hereditary possession, subject to payment of a fixed quitrent; or they were given half of it to keep rent-free; or they kept all of it but handed over half the produce to the landlord. There was no serfdom, no *corvée, taille,* aid, or military service. When the French king began to settle his empty lands in a large way, he outbid the terms which the church had offered to *hospites*. He announced that he was establishing a *ville neuve*—a new township or village, though he might hope it would grow into a town—and was embodying the settlers' individual and collective rights or privileges in a written document, a charter.

By such methods the empty spaces of France became settled during the eleventh to thirteenth centuries. Farther north in the Low Countries the job was begun about the same time but completed much earlier. In England there was less to be done because of the smaller area; but some lands were reclaimed from fresh or salt water, *vaccaries* (cattle holdings) and sheepfolds were carved out of wastes and forests, and when the Welsh had been subdued (by 1284) it became possible to exploit more thoroughly the rural resources along the western border of England.

The Drive to the East. It is possible that all this populating of patches in the west was actually more important than was the eastward march of the frontier. But the mixture of missionary work, conquest, migration, and colonization which went on beyond the Elbe was a more spectacular performance. Its starting point was a line from Hamburg to Venice. To the east lay the territory sparsely occupied in the north by Wends, Prussians, and other tribes of Slavs; in the middle, rather more fully and with a stronger feudal system, by Poles and Czechs, who also were Slavs; and in the south by Magyars. Slav farming technique was far inferior to that of the west, as for instance in the use of a very crude plow which merely scratched the surface; and there were vast areas of good farm land still under forests or in marshes which the Slavs did not know how to reclaim. Consequently the Slavs prevented their land from becoming overcrowded by exporting their children as slaves.

Into this region Germans were venturing long before the big push began. Merchants went seeking slaves, wax, furs, honey, and amber. Bishops and monks were invited to come by princes who had been converted to Christianity, while settlers were sought and welcomed by Slav rulers who recognized that the superior methods of the west would increase the productivity of their territories. Charlemagne pushed the bounds of his conquest, conversion, and colonization as far as modern Austria in the south and to the Elbe in the north; but that advance was checked by the Magyars, in places rolled back, and not heavily resumed until the twelfth century.

At each step, to the Elbe, the Oder, or the Vistula, German princes followed up their conquest of a region by establishing fortified centers whose name usually ended with *burg* (a fortress), e.g., Brandenburg. The country was cut up into marks, each under the control of a margrave. Archbishoprics and bishoprics were set up, abbeys were founded, nobles received large holdings, and the work of bringing in settlers began. Where the Slav princes and their people survived they were absorbed into the new order. They had to accept the new ruler, become Christian if they were not so already, and adopt the agricultural methods introduced from the west. There was no unnecessary extirpation of the native population, and no assumption that the only good Slav was a dead one. Consequently the Slav villages continued as they were, but with a German minority of lords, abbots, and immigrants setting a quicker pace on new roads to soil utilization.

The empty lands were a different story. If they were to be made productive, men who knew how to drain or deforest must be brought in to do most of the work with such Slav labor as could be collected, or to do all of it. This called for immigration on a larger scale. Some landlords therefore employed promoters (*locatores*) whose business was to select a suitable piece of land, divide it into farms, and then go to the Rhineland or the Low Countries in search of settlers. As a reward for success in such village-planting, the *locator* was to receive a large holding for himself, become the local judge, retain a large fraction of the emoluments of justice, operate the mill, and generally enjoy the rewards that came from his position as promoter and overseer. He was to promise liberal terms to settlers, such as personal freedom, no labor services, and a perpetual title to holdings on payment of an annual quitrent.

By such methods an archbishop of Bremen obtained hundreds of Low Countrymen to tackle the swamps around the lower Weser and a margrave of Brandenburg settled villages around his headquarters. Adolf, Count of Holstein, founder of Lübeck and one of the most energetic colonizers of the early twelfth century, sent his agents into Westphalia, Holland, and Flanders to "proclaim that all who were in want of land might come with their families and receive the best soil" in "a spacious country rich in crops, abounding in fish and flesh and exceedingly good pasturages." Henry the Lion, Duke of Saxony, who took Lübeck from Adolf in 1158, sought immigrants for that city and for large areas he had captured from the Wends. The response to his invitation was so embarrassingly large that he passed many of the newcomers on to Hungary, where they attacked the forests on the rim of the Danubian plain.

By the thirteenth century German influence had reached as far east as the lower Vistula. The Slavs proved fairly apt pupils, adopted the German iron plow, established villages under their own locators, and intermarried with their teachers. Cistercian abbeys were widely scattered in the forest belt, and the work of their lay brothers was supplemented by that of free Slav or German tenants. Beyond the bounds of German princely power, rulers in Poland, Bohemia, and Hungary welcomed the westerners, not merely to open up the forest frontier and create villages but also to develop the mining frontier which came into being with the discovery of metal deposits in the hills that bordered their lands.

As plain, marsh, and forest filled up, systematic settlement of villages was accompanied by systematic planting of towns. To attract merchants and artisans, liberal forms of municipal government were granted by the lordly promoters, with a constitution and code of laws copied word for word from those of some such well-known city as Lübeck or Magdeburg. These towns gathered up far more goods than had ever before come from the Slavs, helped Germans to oust Scandinavians from the Baltic trade, and served as stepping-stones to the great Russian fur fair at Novgorod.

In the thirteenth century the frontier crossed the Vistula and added East Prussia, Lithuania, Latvia, and Estonia to the German sphere of settlement and trade. The conquest of that region was the work of the Order of Teutonic Knights. This order sprang from an association formed by German crusaders at the seige of Acre (1191). When the Saracens proved too strong to be driven from the Holy Land the Teutonic Knights retreated to Venice. Then they moved inland to battle with infidel Tatars who were threatening Hungary. Then a Polish duke invited them to defend his land against attack by pagan Prussians. They consented, on terms which promised them half of what they conquered but which they quickly turned into a claim to full sovereign power.

Thus began more than half a century of conquest and of suppressing subsequent revolts (1230–1290). By 1280 colonization could be seriously undertaken. A hundred knightly families obtained estates, and about 1,200 villages were established. Those Prussians who had been rebellious were turned into serfs, but the rest remained free. The hope of importing large numbers of German settlers was not fully realized, for the supply of people willing to emigrate so far east soon ran out. Greater reliance therefore had to be placed on the natives, but enough Germans came to act as a strong leaven. The familiar story of drainage and forest clearance was repeated; the heavy plow, the three-field system, the water mill, the hereditary quitrent tenure, and village-planting by locators were introduced as they had been all the way across Germany. The yield of grain or animal products was far greater than the local population could consume, while the forests supplied lumber, potash, and furs. The country became a large exporter of grain and timber to Scandinavia, the Low Countries, and the British Isles. The Vistula basin took its place as one of northern Europe's granaries.

The Order of Teutonic Knights was generous in its grant of civic rights and issued nearly a hundred town charters. It improved roads and rivers and policed them. It had a keen eye for revenue; it collected much in land tax and rent, retained rights over fishing, hunting, mining, and milling, and either exploited them itself or charged a substantial royalty to concessionaires. As the produce received in payment of these various dues had to be sold, the order turned merchant and shipowner. It put its spare money to work by making loans, and gained the moneylender's usual reputation as a rapacious creditor.

After 1350 the eastward movement drew to a close on all parts of the frontier. The population of western and central Germany was being either absorbed by the cities or cut down by the Black Death, while the supply of available land was running low or was being taken up by native-born easterners. In 1410 the order was crushed by Poland at the Battle of Tannenberg. Its aggressive foreign policy had roused enmity on the borders; its commercial activity had alienated the Baltic merchant class; its charges had come to seem too heavy to the peasants; and the mercenary army on which it now relied was costly but unreliable. Out of its defeat it emerged with only East Prussia. There it carried on a little colonization in the forests, but the day of its greatness and of its service had ended long before it was dissolved in 1525.

Summary. The German migrations made a profound mark on the history of central Europe. They increased the population of sparsely inhabited regions, extended and improved cultivation, and brought a wider area into the circle of commerce. German technique lifted the level of agriculture and mining even in regions beyond the German political boundaries. The settler was induced to migrate by being offered terms far better than those of the cultivators in the old west; but the native peoples who had to be relied on for a considerable part of the pioneering work also gained an improvement in their status as well as in their living standards when the more efficient farming yielded its richer harvest. Landlords were concerned mostly with the income they received from their new estates and little in directing their cultivation; peasants therefore were free to do as they wished with their working days.

In the center of the continent, as in the west, the middle of the fourteenth century marks the end of expansion. What happened then is complicated and obscure, but its results seem to have been unhappy for the large landowners who had taken so much of the initiative in the frontier movement and presumably had seen their incomes increase from the enterprise. Now the increase ended. Prices fell between 1350 and 1450, which may mean that the expansion in production had been overdone. The whole movement must have involved a large outlay of capital, and many landlords had gone heavily into debt. If income was now shrinking the interest payments must have become oppressive, and even the capable Cistercians got into financial difficulties. Political developments played their part; there was much conflict, some anarchy, and many unstable situations. The Teutonic order was not the only medieval institution to be weakened; the old aristocracy and in some countries the church lost or were soon to lose their power, their income, and even their land. In their place when the dust clears we find a new landlord in possession. He may be a bourgeois, or a small country property holder who has prospered and risen, or a rough fellow who has fought on the right side. In Germany he may be called a *Junker*, in England a squire or country gentleman. But he is a new broom, and he may wish to sweep away many medieval cobwebs. What he does to his estate and its people we shall see later.

BIBLIOGRAPHY

The outstanding work is the first volume of the *Cambridge Economic History of Europe*, edited by J. H. Clapham and Eileen Power (1941). Its title is *The Agrarian Life of the Middle Ages*. It covers the whole continent from the late Roman Empire to the end of the Middle Ages.

For brief surveys of the whole continent, see:

Irvine, H. D., *Making of Rural Europe* (1923), chaps. 1–3.

Kulischer, J., *Allgemeine Wirtschaftsgeschichte* (1928–1929), vol. i, chaps. 8–16.

Pirenne, H., *Economic and Social History of Medieval Europe* (1937), chap. 3.

Power, Eileen, "Peasant Life and Rural Conditions," in *Cambridge Medieval History* (1932) vol. vii, chap. 24.

Thompson, J. W., *Economic and Social History of the Middle Ages* (1928), chaps. 20, 24, 27, 29.

For the rest, regional studies must be used. Only the more general ones are listed below, for the monograph literature is overwhelming. A good list of it will be found in the *Cambridge Economic History*.

ENGLAND

Ashley, W. J., *Economic Organization of England* (1914), chaps. 1, 3.

Bennett, H. S., *Life on the English Manor* (1937).

Bland, A. E., Brown, P. A., and Tawney, R. H., *English Economic History: Select Documents* (1914), part 1, sections 1, 3.

Coulton, G. C., *The Medieval Village* (1926).

Gras, N. S. B., *A History of Agriculture* (1925), chaps. 4, 5.

Gras, N. S. B., and Ethel, C., *Social and Economic History of an English Village* (1930).

Gray, H. L., *English Field Systems* (1915).

Homans, G. C., *English Villagers of the Thirteenth Century* (1941).

Hone, N. J., *The Manor and Manorial Records* (1925).

Lipson, E., *Introduction to the Economic History of England* (1915), vol. i, chaps. 1–4.

Orwin, C. S. and C. S., *The Open Fields* (1938).

Power, Eileen, *Medieval People* (1924), chap. 1.

Power, Eileen, *The Wool Trade in English Medieval History* (1941), chaps. 1, 2.

Prothero, R. E. (Lord Ernle), *English Farming, Past and Present* (1912), chaps. 1, 2.

Seebohm, M. E., *Evolution of the English Farm* (1927).

Smith, R. A. L., *Canterbury Cathedral Priory: A Study in Monastic Administration* (1943).

Students can get the flavor of manorial records from the books by Hone, Gras, or Bland, Brown, and Tawney listed above; also from *Translations and Reprints from the Original Sources of European History* (Univ. of Pennsylvania), vol. iii, No. 5, or from Cave and Coulson, *Source Book for Medieval Economic History* (1936), parts 1, 4.

FRANCE

Bloch, M., *Les caractères originaux de l'histoire rurale française* (1931), chaps. 1–3.

Coopland, G. W., *The Abbey of St. Bertin and Its Neighbourhood* (1914).

Sée, H., *Histoire économique de la France* (1939), part i, chap. 1; part ii, chap. 1.

GERMANY

Meitzen, A., *Siedelung und Agrarwesen der Westgermanen und Ostgermanen, der Kelten, Römer, Finnen und Slawen* (1895), especially the Atlas to vol. iii.

Thompson, J. W., *Feudal Germany* (1928), part ii.

ARTICLES

Beveridge, W. H., "The Yield and Price of Corn in the Middle Ages," *Econ. Hist.*, May, 1927.

Carston, F. L., "Slavs in Northeastern Germany," *Ec. H. R.*, 1941.

Kosminsky, E. A., "The Hundred Rolls," *Ec. H. R.*, January, 1931.

Kosminsky, E. A., "Services and Money Rents in the Thirteenth Century," *Ec. H. R.*, April, 1935.

Levett, E. A., "Financial Organization of the Manor," *Ec. H. R.*, January, 1927.

Lucas, H. S., "The Great European Famine 1315, 1316, 1317," *Speculum*, October, 1930.

Neilson, N., "English Manorial Forms," *Am. Hist. Rev.*, July, 1929.

Orwin, C. S., "Observations on the Open Fields," *Ec. H. R.*, May, 1938.

Postan, M. M., "The Chronology of Labour Services," *Royal Hist. Soc. Trans.*, 1937.

Postan, M. M., "The Fifteenth Century," *Ec. H. R.*, May, 1939.

Robbins, H., "A Comparison of the Effects of the Black Death on the Economic Organization of France and England," *J. Pol. Econ.*, August, 1928.

Rosenberg, H., "The Rise of the Junkers in Brandenburg-Prussia, 1410–1653," *Am. Hist. Rev.*, October, 1943.

Wretts-Smith, M., "Organization of Farming at Crowland Abbey," *J.E.B.H.*, November, 1931.

Encyclopaedia of the Social Sciences: Articles on Agriculture (Medieval), Agrarian Movements, Aids, Corvée, Entail, Feudalism, Land Tenure, Manorial System, Serfdom, Slavery, Village Community.

VII

MEDIEVAL INDUSTRY

When we turn from agriculture to industry and commerce, the medieval panorama becomes far less crowded. The number of men who made their living by manufacturing or by trading was much smaller than was that of those who lived on the yield from their work on the land, on the foods which they processed from their farm produce, and on the simple articles which they fashioned in their own homes out of some local supply of fiber (wool or flax), wood, clay, or possibly metal. Even the partly commercialized tenant farmer probably had little money left to spend on manufactured articles after he had paid his rent, repaid his debts, bought his livestock, and met the other expenses involved in operating his holding. If he had any spare cash, most of it was likely to be earmarked for acquiring more land or livestock. Usufacture was the normal approach to the villager's enjoyment of those goods which he was capable of making. In the picture of world industrial history it covers the greater part of the canvas.

The Limits of Usufacture. Yet medieval manorial records show clearly that the cultivator did not do everything for himself, and it is easy to see why. Even when manufacturing is what the word means—making by hand—four requirements may be essential, in addition to the raw material. The first is the manual skill in the use of tools and the knowledge of how to combine ingredients or how to treat them—baking, roasting, brewing, arranging, assembling, and so forth—in order to get a satisfactory product. The second is the equipment. Fine work can be done by a skilled person with a few such simple tools as the tailor's shears and needles, the leather-maker's half-dozen essential tools, or the carpenter's kit. But no villager could be expected to possess a supply of tools for several occupations, especially in an age when metals were scarce and costly. It is possible that every cottage had a spinning distaff but improbable that all had a loom; and some medieval industries used far more elaborate equipment than an amateur could afford. The third re-

130

quirement is power, which may be needed in quantities greater than can be drawn from human or animal muscles. The fourth is fuel, unnecessary for some occupations but vital to those which require the application of heat, call for a suitable hearth, and need a satisfactory container for the material.

When these essentials are listed, it becomes obvious that usufacture must be supplemented by drawing on the special or superior skill or equipment of others for certain processes or products. The special equipment might be the mill, with its great stones turned by wind and increasingly by water power; the oven, so constructed as to let the fire do its work without endangering the whole building; or the blacksmith's shop with its anvil, forge, and motley of tools. The superior skill was supplied by the miller, baker, smith, or by those who had been trained to use the hand tools they possessed. Consequently the manor court rolls record the deeds—and often the misdeeds—of men whose last names indicate their occupation: Faber, which later becomes Smith, Webster (Weaver), Lister (Dyer), Walker (Fuller), Carpenter, Cooper, Mason, Baker, Brewer, Taylor, and so forth down a long list of crafts.

Some of these men, such as the miller or smith, worked at the place where their equipment was, and customers brought materials to them for treatment. Others went to the place where the work was to be done, and might have to travel far to find enough customers to keep them fully employed. A wandering weaver, for instance, would come to a house which had prepared a quantity of woolen or linen yarn and possessed a hand loom; he wove the yarn into a better kind of cloth than the family knew how to make, passed on to other houses in the village, and then to the next community. Harness makers or shoemakers carried tools, thread, nails, buckles, bits, and special kinds of leather to supplement what the family had tanned or what had been made for it by the village tanner. Wool combers carried their combs and the charcoal stove in which to heat them. Such men worked on material belonging to their customers. They might work in the manor house as well as in the farmhouse. Like the peddler, they moved on a regular circuit.

In larger villages and towns the number of customers was great enough to allow some workers to confine their movements to a smaller area or to set up permanent workshops. They might still labor on materials brought to them, and in effect ran service stations. But it would be a natural step for an energetic craftsman to buy materials and make them into finished articles, either in response to an order or in the hope of finding a buyer. The front of his workshop became a store; he displayed his wares on a counter on the sidewalk or in a window; he sold in market place or fair, or peddled his products through the streets and countryside. Professor Gras suggests that this little industrial unit be called *retail handicraft*. It involved direct contact between craftsman and consumer, but the former sold the product of his equipment and skill, not merely the use of them. In practice he probably did both.

Retail handicraft remained an important part of industrial life until modern times, especially in industries supplying a purely local demand for food, clothing, buildings, and furniture. Tailors, shoemakers, butchers, bakers, and many others made or processed goods and sold them direct to customers. The unit of production was small; the craftsman used the labor of his family, but might employ a journeyman or two and be training an apprentice. His equipment was not costly, and if he did not need valuable raw materials or carry a large stock of finished articles his capital needs were small. Even if he possessed a superior kind of skill bordering on artistry, worked in costly materials, and made luxury goods for rich patrons, his customers might supply the raw materials, or he might be able to obtain them easily on credit from the merchant who imported them.

The Larger Industries. While many industries remained small scale, local, and retail in scope, a few reached larger proportions, became more elaborately organized, obtained some of their material from remote sources, and sold some of their products in distant markets. There was nothing new in this; it was what some Greek and Roman producers had done, and what some eastern Mediterranean industries continued to do. Constantinople in the tenth century had elaborate rules to govern the conduct of its jewelers, silk garment merchants, silk spinners, silk weavers, and perfume dealers, as well as the more humble candlemakers, soapmakers, leather cutters, bakers, joiners, plasterers, marble workers, locksmiths, and house painters. The Saracens transplanted skills in leather and metal working, dyeing, carpetmaking, and silk weaving from the Near East to Spain and Sicily. The church was a channel through which examples of fine work were spread over the west, and may have spread the makers as well as the products. The growing importance of the armored knight stimulated the enterprise of armorers, while the shift from wood to stone for building churches and castles called for great numbers of skilled masons.

Even without these influences from the east, the western peoples possessed enough skills to enable them to develop commercial manufactures where a supply of raw material and a market were available. The Low Countries and England, for example, had much wool and also deposits of the fuller's earth used for cleaning woolen cloth. Their people were making that cloth for export by the seventh or eighth century. Charlemagne sent a present of Flemish cloths to Haroun al Raschid in Bagdad about 800 A.D. In 796 he complained to the king of Mercia about a fraudulent reduction in the length of woolen cloaks he had bought from England, ending his letter with the request that the next batch be "made of the same pattern as used to come to us in olden times." In northern France and eastward through Germany flax was widely grown and served as the basis for a linen industry which sold its fabrics far afield. In eastern Belgium and other places where ore deposits were easily tapped artisans became widely known for their weapons, armor, and other metalware, e.g., in Dinant and Liége. Some convents sold the embroidery or cloth made by their nuns.

Influence of the Crusades on Industry. Industrial life was quickened in the north by the growth of population, towns, and trade, and by the eastward movement of settlers and traders. The immigrants and native people east of the Rhine or Elbe became better buyers of manufactured wares as they became sellers of primary produce, and the Hanseatic merchants whose trading territory eventually stretched from Lisbon to Novgorod handled industrial goods as well as raw materials and foodstuffs. In the south and west (including France), but also in the north to some degree, the crusades exerted a great influence on industry and commerce alike. Their effect on commerce will be examined in the next chapter. Here we need only consider that on the taste and therefore on the consumer demand of those warriors who had hitherto known only the relatively crude western way of life.

The crusaders went, saw, and were conquered by the dress, food, and dwellings of a people alongside whom they were rough backwoodsmen. They saw the luxury of the east as a whole, not as fragments in a wandering Syrian's pack; and they liked it. They bought pieces of silk, cotton, or fine woolen cloth and sent them home to their church or friends. They developed a taste for spices, sauces, rich dishes, and the sugar candies of Tyre and Bagdad. They became accustomed to rugs on the floor, tapestries on the wall, and the feel of underclothing next to the skin. They handled damask, brocade, fine armor, and swords such as few Christian workers could fashion. Sometimes they stayed in the east; but those who went home created a demand which stirred western traders to import eastern goods and stimulated western craftsman to produce wares which were like them.

How strong this urge to imitate was we have no way of knowing, but the improvement of old industries or methods and the development of new ones are very marked, especially in the luxury field, during the twelfth and thirteenth centuries. The silk manufacture planted in Sicily by the Saracens was expanded by their Norman conquerors in the twelfth century, and then spread to the mainland. Lucca and Naples were its early centers, and Lucca remained the most famous producer; but Florence, Genoa, and Venice also made silk fabrics which rivaled those imported from the east. The dye industry benefited from closer contact with Bagdad, the great market for colors from India and Persia, as well as from secret processes for dyemaking which Italians picked up from loquacious Levantines.

The Venetian glass industry, already well established by the eleventh century, was strengthened by the transplanting of skilled workers from Constantinople when that city was captured in the fourth crusade (1204), and thus became better able to serve both luxury and popular demands for vessels, mirrors, glass gems, and beads. So important did the industry become that its welfare was closely guarded by the state. The artisans were segregated on an island just outside the city, and anyone who tried to take the trade secrets elsewhere was threatened with death. As compensation the glassworker was highly paid, became by senatorial decree a gentleman and burgess, and was entitled to marry a woman of patrician blood. The industry did, nevertheless, spread to other parts of Italy and beyond, but Venetian glass remained for centuries a commodity of high repute and wide sale.

The crusades stimulated the making of armor and weapons. The high-grade work became concentrated in such centers as Brescia, Nuremberg, and Liége, and there was a great measure of specialization. A fourteenth-century Italian merchant bought his coats of mail in Milan or Nuremberg, his gold-handled swords in Florence or

Lyons, his blades in Milan, Toledo, Nuremberg, or Solingen, his spurs and leather trunks in Paris, and the cords for his crossbows in Hungary. Division of labor was evident in the Avignon firm which employed one man to make visors, another iron gauntlets, another brassards, and another spurs.

Contact with the east stirred the west to improve its domestic furnishings. As the rich laity and the church developed a desire for more decorative products in wood, metal, stone, fibers, and leather, the Low Countries, France, Italy, and the German towns built up the necessary skilled labor force. Flanders produced not merely good cloth but also elaborate tapestries and carpets. Lucca and Florence supplied taffeta, damask, brocade, and cloth of gold. Florence exported religious pictures, church ornaments, and costly cutlery. Paris laid the foundations of her subsequent reputation as the luxury workshop of Europe, with fine furniture, ornate armor, rich tapestries, and delicate jewelry among her specialties. No country sent so many men on the crusades as did France or felt so strongly the influence of those expeditions in changing the standard of living, increasing the variety of foods, enriching the wardrobe, and decorating the home.

The Textile Industries. Clothmaking was a widely spread usufacture, but it also became the most important industry working for local and distant markets, and the most highly organized. Its expansion was especially marked from the eleventh century, and was an important factor in the growth of towns, especially in Italy and the Low Countries. The silk branch of the industry was small, since the supply of raw material was scanty and the product was luxurious and costly. The linen branch was larger, for flax was grown on both northern and southern farms, and the product ranged from coarse to fine. But the woolen branch loomed largest in the picture, and its records have received most attention from scholars.

Flanders and Florence became the outstanding woolen cloth producers, but they never enjoyed a monopoly. The Flemish industry was probably the older. Its raw material was close at hand or could be drawn across the North Sea from Britain. Its labor supply was abundant, even when the soil of Flanders was employing all the people it could carry and after many Flemings had gone off to the eastern frontier. Its markets were found in north and south alike, for while Flemish cloths were selling in Scandinavia and Novgorod by 1100, they were also being sent to the Mediterranean by an overland route through eastern France to Genoa. Flemish merchants took them part of the way, to the Champagne fairs. There the pieces were sold to Italians who carried them to Genoa or Florence, where the cloth was dyed, finished, and then shipped to all parts of the Mediterranean, from northwest Africa to Cairo and Syria. By 1300 Flanders was dotted with important textile manufacturing towns— Arras, Courtrai, Malines, and a dozen others; but the chief ones were Ypres, Ghent, and the growing port of Bruges.

In Italy Florence took the lead. At first, like Genoa, she bought unfinished cloths from Italian or foreign weaving districts and put them through the many processes needed to give the fabric its final color and surface. Her cloth finishers were organized in a strong guild, the *Arte di Calimala,* which sought to advance the interest of an industry depending on foreign supplies and foreign markets. By the thirteenth century, however, more attention was being given to importing raw wool and to the production of fabrics in or around the city. This development seems to have been helped by the Humiliati, members of a religious order which was pledged to manual labor and carried out that vow by doing textile work. The Humiliati had attained great skill, a high degree of division of labor, and something like mass production of fine fabrics. They came to Florence in 1239 and helped to raise the efficiency of the whole industry. The clothmakers had their guild, the *Arte della Lana,* which regulated its members but also helped them to get their materials, to finish their goods, and to sell them.

According to Villani, who wrote a chronicle of Florence, the members of these two guilds in the early fourteenth century employed about thirty thousand people, who produced seventy to eighty thousand pieces yearly and imported at least ten thousand. Like their counterparts in Flanders they used only imported wool for their high-quality cloths, and drew it from England, Scotland, Spain, and Burgundy. Italian merchants frequented the wool fairs and penetrated to the farms or ranches where the wool was produced. Sometimes they bought the whole yield of monastic flocks, signed contracts to take the entire clip for as many as a dozen years at fixed prices, and even paid some of the purchase money in advance. During the thirteenth century Italians displaced Flemings as the chief exporters of English wool; but they in turn were ousted by English exporters during the fourteenth century.

Though overshadowed by these two great producers, other countries had their woolen manufacturers. The English made cloths of all qualities; the cheap ones went to northern markets, but the good ones fetched high prices in Italy. There were also substantial woolen industries in France and Spain.

Organization of the Textile Industry. The retail handicraft unit was quite inadequate for meeting the needs of the large cloth industries, or indeed of any industry which depended on distant supplies of raw material, on scattered or remote markets, on customers who would be slow in paying their debts, or on methods which required costly equipment or passed the material through a long series of processes. If the producer could not go far afield to get his wool and dyestuffs or sell his cloth, some middleman must do it for him. If the wool was costly, the cost of production heavy, and the payment long delayed, the small craftsman must let someone else make the outlay and wait for the money. The growth of luxury trades, of industries which served large or foreign markets, and of long-distance carriage of raw materials therefore placed an increasing number of men between the primary producer and the craftsman or between the craftsman and the ultimate consumer. When the artisan produced not for retail sale but for a merchant who accumulated stocks and sold them in larger quantities, he was what has been called a *wholesale handicraftsman.*

Middleman and craftsman might meet on terms of equality and independence. The latter could display his goods in an open market held on appointed days in some town and be free to sell to any trader who was satisfied with his quality and price. But this condition gave place in the export and luxury industries to a different relationship. The merchant might like some craftsman's work and therefore give him an order for a quantity of goods or take his whole output. He might offer to supply the raw material and even the implements, or to advance the money with which the manufacturer could buy material or pay wages. If he merely bought the goods the craftsman was still economically free; but the more the trader financed the producer, the greater was the latter's dependence on him and the nearer he drew to being in effect a wage earner. Some craftsmen sank into that condition through debt; some may have relied on the trader for their equipment and raw materials from the start of their working career. On the other hand, some craftsmen prospered, employed many journeymen, and rose to be traders, giving orders and putting material out to their less fortunate fellows.

This kind of development went farthest in the textile industries, partly because it was stimulated by a special technical consideration. Wool had to pass through a long series of processes between the day it was taken out of the sack in which it had come from the sheep farm and the time—possibly six months later—when the finished cloth was packed, ready for sale. "In Florence the process of cloth-making included about twenty-six different steps" (De Roover). If the cloth merchant was to be sure of getting the right kind of goods at the right time, production must be skillfully coordinated to keep the material flowing down the stream from one process to the next. A giant firm might control the whole stream, from buying wool in Spain or England to selling finished cloths in a remote market. This would, however, involve a heavy outlay of capital and a long wait before the sales returns were in with their evidence of profit or loss.

Giants were therefore rare, and most men were content with shorter ventures. For instance, the Florentine merchant, who sometimes was a weaver who had prospered and climbed, bought his wool from a merchant who had imported it. In his central warehouse the wool was sorted and then put out to be washed by a firm which specialized in that process. The material was returned to the warehouse, sprinkled with olive oil to make the fibers easier to work, and then put out to be spun into yarn by spinsters who worked in their homes. The yarn was gathered up, brought to the warehouse, wound on bobbins or made into warps, and then put out again to be made into cloth by domestic weavers. The piece was carried to the warehouse in a greasy, filthy, evil-smelling state, and must now be sent to be fulled (i.e., cleaned and shrunk) by some firm which had the requisite equipment and water supply. It was then put out to a firm specializing in dyeing, then to another which had the skilled workers and tools needed for giving it a finished appearance and for packing it neatly. Then its owner might sell it to some local merchant who took it to market, or he sent it to his partner or agent in a distant port.

Here indeed was need for control and coordination, for considerable skill in management, for the use of much capital in operations or in various kinds of equipment, and for sharp eyes—one to see that work was done according to specifications, the other to prevent outworkers from embezzling material entrusted to them. The variations on this general theme were countless. Sometimes the entrepreneur owned the fulling mill, dyeworks, and finishing shops; sometimes the wool or yarn was put out in a lump to some master spinner or master weaver who as contractor agreed to do the work at a fixed price and then employed people who worked for him at piece rates. Some domestic workers owned their equipment, but others rented them from the man at the head or from the contractor.

One feature, however, remained constant: for the tasks requiring the greatest amount of labor—spinning and weaving—it was more economical to put the material out to the workers' homes than to gather the workers into a central workshop. If power-driven machinery had been available in place of the distaff, spinning wheel, or hand loom, the situation might have been different; but we know of only one process—silk throwing—where such equipment was in use. This water-driven "throwing mill" was invented before 1272 by some one in Lucca. It dispensed with the labor of many manual workers and produced a high-grade silk thread. It could, however, be operated by a man and his family and therefore did not lead to any great congregation of workers. In the cloth-finishing processes labor was gathered together because of the use of machinery in fulling and of large vats and many chemicals in dyeing, or because much room and careful supervision in finishing were necessary. During the late twelfth century and throughout the thirteenth there was a widespread introduction of the fulling mill, in which wood hammers driven by a water wheel took the place of human hands and feet. But the basic processes of making yarn and converting it into cloth remained unmechanized and domestic until the eighteenth and nineteenth centuries.

In the Low Countries the making of cloth seems to have become dominated by large entrepreneurs even earlier than it did in Italy. In fact "it is the earliest example in European history of a 'great industry' in the modern sense, producing for a world market and organized on highly capitalistic lines, with its captains of industry, its minute division of labor and its urban proletariat" (Power). Merchants took steps to finance and organize the production of the goods they needed for market, or craftsmen prospered to the point where they were directing the labors of many employees.

One of these *drapiers*, the thirteenth-century Sire Jehan Boinebroke of Douai, obtained the cloths he exported by putting out material to master craftsmen and wage earners. Our knowledge of him consists chiefly of complaints, and may therefore be one-sided. He was charged with exploiting his workers to the utmost, defrauding them, paying in truck (goods) instead of money, ruthlessly suppressing any dissatisfaction they might express, and evicting them from their homes. What his reply or defense was we do not know; but we do know that the relations between the big merchant or producer and those who made his goods could be strained when he or they wished to be aggressive, when depression forced him to seek a cut in labor costs, when rising prices drove them to seek higher wages, and when war or external competition threatened the welfare of both parties. The big businessmen usually controlled the city government and used it to promote or defend their economic interests. This drove their workers to agitation for a share of civic power or to revolt against their political and economic masters. The annals of the great Italian and Belgian cities are sprinkled with the blood of such conflicts; sometimes the horny-handed and the "blue nails" won, more often their masters prevailed, but when the centuries of expansion came to an end both sides were the victims of social strife, of war disturbances, and of competition from other regions or countries.

Organization in Other Industries. The practice of putting out work and materials was not peculiar to the textile industry or to the Middle Ages. If a production line ended with the assembling of a number of parts, e.g., into a suit of armor or a set of harness, the material for each part was put out to be made by different workers, and the bits were then assembled in a central workshop. Putting out spread over industries in England, France, Germany, and Holland whenever they reached the stage of catering to large markets. The central figure might be a merchant who imported the material, such as Swedish steel. In England the dyer was sometimes the key figure, since most dye materials had to be brought from abroad. Dyers appear in at least one English town as "capitalist entrepreneurs, purchasing wool, having it washed and dyed . . . probably on their own premises, giving it out to carders and spinners, employing weavers and fullers throughout the town, under stringent supervision, at piece rates fixed by themselves, and marketing the finished cloths from their own stalls at the great East Anglian fairs of Boston, St. Ives, or Stamford" (Carus-Wilson). As we shall see later, this *putting-out system,* or *Verlagssystem* as the Germans call it, possessed great vitality up to the nineteenth century.

Mining showed as great diversity of organization as did manufacturing. Where minerals were found near the surface or in out-crops, little capital was needed, and the mining unit was small; German farmers in their spare time dug iron ore and smelted it with charcoal. Deeper deposits required larger outlays for the mine and for the smelting or refining equipment. A landlord might provide this capital, borrow it, or form a syndicate in which kings, nobles, clergy, and rich merchants would invest. Sometimes the right to mine would be leased, granted as a concession in return for some loan, or handed over as collateral security.

Mining therefore became a field for investment, and capital migrated from wealthy cities to the mountains and backwoods of central Europe, Sweden, or wherever the ore deposits were situated. Shares, or fractions of them, were bought and sold. We know of a transaction concerning one-eighth of a share in the mine at the Störa Kopparberg (the Great Copper Mountain) in Sweden. Most of the shares in that famous mine were owned by people who played no part in working it, including a bishop, a king, a royal official's wife, and the widow of a Lübeck merchant. Genoese financiers poured money into Polish salt mines, while Italian and German capital and German miners were to be found wherever there were minerals—which usually meant metals—to be exploited. The miners were hired workers, with fixed hours and wages and subject to severe discipline. Mining was thus another medieval occupation to possess such capitalistic features as a wage-earning class, costly equipment, large-scale production, and a constant need of more funds for development. In return it sometimes gave rich rewards to those who were willing to risk their money, and at the end of the Middle Ages such outstanding financiers as the Fuggers, the Welsers, and the Hochstetters had their thumbs deep in the mining pie.

Building was an industry apart. Its products were not usually for sale, and the consumer took the initiative in bringing them into being. The chief exception to this practice was the building of houses which could be rented to town dwellers. We know little about this important aspect of the physical growth of towns, but the church, local lay landlords, and merchants seem to have provided the capital and owned the houses. Where timber was abundant the buildings, even manor houses and churches, were built of wood, but clay, straw, reeds, and tiles played their part. In the older Mediterranean lands the early exhaustion of the forests and the risk of fire during the long dry summer led to the use of stone and bricks, and in northern Europe these materials became generally adopted for the larger buildings by about 1100 A.D.

Much building could be done by amateurs, with the aid of carpenter or thatcher, and participation in building or repairing houses might be part of a villager's labor services. But the great tasks were done for the crown, nobility, church, and towns in answer to the call for defense, luxury, piety, civic pride, or rivalry. Only the lay and ecclesiastical great possessed or could borrow the money needed to buy and transport the materials needed for cathedrals, courts, castles, city walls or halls, or to pay the large wages bills. An army of 400 masons, 1,000 laborers, and 230 other men was employed in building one Welsh castle, but there the work had to be completed in a hurry. Some tasks could be done more slowly; another Welsh castle took nearly 40 years to complete, and the nave of Westminster Abbey took 150 years.

The workers on large buildings were wage earners, who labored under the direction of some superintendent on plans prepared by an architect who was often the chief mason. Some of them remained in one spot for years, but others wandered around seeking work. Some were "impressed" and taken long distances when a king ordered his sheriffs to collect labor for a building project. The ruler's right to impress or draft has a long history and in the Middle Ages could be used to gather a labor force. When simple styles gave place to elaborately carved decorations in wood and stone, to painted or gilded walls and images, and to stained-glass windows, a whole range of higher skills was demanded. Most of the decorators worked on the spot, but the glass and the statues of saints might be made by urban craftsmen who worked on orders or made stock in anticipation of demand. We get a hint of mass production of standard patterns when an English maker of images had trouble in getting payment from an agent to whom he had delivered fifty-eight heads of John the Baptist.

Conclusion. Medieval manufacturing thus ranged from usufacture, usually aided by settled or migratory experts, through a long list of retail craftsmen who supplied the needs of their town or adjacent countryside, up to large firms which used considerable amounts of capital and employed many men and women either in the worker's own home or in some central shop. The long-range movements of customers and the migrations of skilled workers spread the demand for luxury goods and the ability to produce them over a wider area of Europe. But the demand for luxury goods was limited to royalty, nobility, church, and richer townsmen, and the production of the supply was therefore concentrated in a few regions which were favored by their access to raw materials, their location on the trade routes, their ample labor supply, the resourcefulness of their entrepreneurs, and congenial political conditions.

To complete the industrial picture, some account of the methods of raising the capital and of the regulation of industries by the town, guild, or state is needed. This must be postponed until we have examined medieval commercial activities.

BIBLIOGRAPHY

Boissonnade, P., *Life and Work in Medieval Europe* (Eng. trans., 1927).

Clapham, J. H., "Commerce and Industry in the Middle Ages," in *Cambridge Medieval History*, vol. vi, chap. 14.

Espinas, G., *La draperie dans la Flandre française au moyen age* (1923).

Gras, N. S. B., *Industrial Evolution* (1930), chaps. 1–4.

Lipson, E., *Economic History of England* (1915), vol. 1, chap. 9.

Passant, E. J., "The Effects of the Crusades upon Western Europe," in *Cambridge Medieval History*, vol. v, chap. 9.

Pirenne, H., *Medieval Cities* (Eng. trans., 1925).

Salzman, L. F., *English Industries in the Middle Ages* (1923).

Thompson, J. W., *Economic and Social History of Europe in the Later Middle Ages, 1300–1350* (1931), chaps, 7, 9, 10, 13, 17.

ARTICLES

Carus-Wilson, E. M., "An Industrial Revolution of the Thirteenth Century," *Ec. H. R.*, 1941.

Carus-Wilson, E. M., "The English Cloth Industry in the Twelfth and Thirteenth Centuries," *Ec. H. R.*, 1944.

De Roover, R., "A Florentine Firm of Cloth Manufacturers," *Speculum*, January, 1941.

Lane, F. C., "The Rope Factory . . . of Venice in the 15th and 16th Centuries," *J.E.B.H.*, August, 1932.

Larson, H. M., "A Medieval Swedish Mining Company," *J.E.B.H.*, November, 1930.

VIII

MEDIEVAL COMMERCE

Commercial developments and operations have constantly forced themselves into the preceding pictures of medieval agriculture and industry. Nevertheless, it is necessary to examine more systematically the men who made their living by trade, the commodities they handled, the routes they followed, the markets they served, and the way they organized and conducted their business.

Like agriculture and industry, commerce conformed to no one pattern. The exchange of goods rested on many kinds of personal division of labor or of regional specialization. It is highly probable that the local "neighborhood" trade among villagers and that between them and some near-by market town was quantitatively the most important. Yet many exchanges involved a longer journey: between coastal and inland areas, between regions which had minerals or forests and those which had none, between sub-arctic, temperate, and semi-tropical zones, between industrially advanced and backward communities, and even between industrially developed towns, since no one community could be good enough at making everything to be self-sufficing. Where the producer and consumer lived near each other, the trade might be handled by those farmers or artisans who produced the goods, as, for instance, in a village or small town or in the traffic between a town and its hinterland; but interurban, interregional, and intercontinental trade must be carried on by men who devoted much (or all) of their time to commerce.

It is with the longer-range trade rather than the local that this chapter is concerned. There was enough of it to be worth competing for, enough to interest rulers in its control and taxation, and enough to produce wealthy men, powerful associations, and rich cities. It can be divided into three main sections: (1) northern, (2) southern, and (3) exchange between north and south.

The Northern Trade Area. Although some of the commodities which the different parts of northern Europe exchanged were luxuries—for instance, wine and furs—most of them were raw ma-

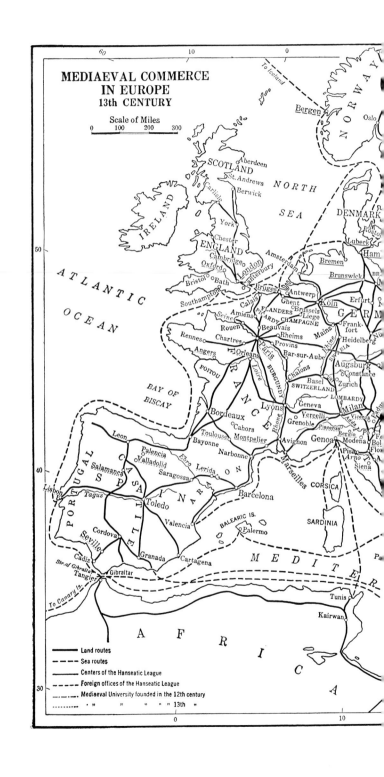

MEDIAEVAL COMMERCE IN EUROPE 13th CENTURY

Scale of Miles
0 100 200 300

Land routes
Sea routes
Centers of the Hanseatic League
Foreign offices of the Hanseatic League
Mediaeval University founded in the 12th century
"   "   "   "   "   "   13th   "

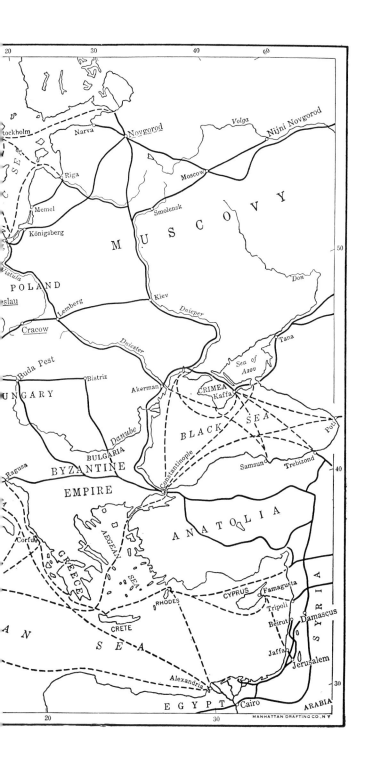

terials (copper, iron, tin, timber, hides, and wool) or necessary food-stuffs (fish, salt, beer, and grain). Weighty, bulky, and low in value, these products could not bear heavy freight charges; but since few producers or consumers were far from river or sea, water trans-portation could be widely used. The Scandinavians, and still more their German successors, designed roomy cargo boats with capacious holds. Freight costs were consequently not prohibitive.

Of the luxuries, wine was the chief. The main vineyards were in France south of the Loire (Guienne and Gascony) and in the Rhine and Moselle valleys. The French wines went largely from Bordeaux, La Rochelle, and Oléron to England, the Low Countries, and Scan-dinavia. The chief customers were kings, nobles, the church, and the richer townsmen. In 1242 Henry III of England bought about 360,000 gallons for the royal cellar, and at that time his country im-ported over 2,500,000 gallons yearly, which was more than a gallon per head of the population and about three times per head as much as in 1913. Wine was not too expensive to be afforded by the upper middle class, and the vintner came into prominence in the larger towns as purveyor to merchant and landlord.

The second luxury commodity was fur. It is a truism that where the settler appears the fur-bearing animals disappear. Consequently the clearing of the forests in western and central Europe made furs much more scarce. Traders therefore were obliged to depend in-creasingly on supplies from Scandinavia, Russia, and eventually Siberia. The great fair at Novgorod and the city of Kiev were the gathering points for Russian furs.

Of the northern trades, that in fish served most people. There were fast days all through the year, and Lent came at an appropri-ate time, when the store of salted meats laid in during the preceding autumn had run low. Fish therefore supplemented local food pro-duction and made fasting less unpleasant. The supply was abundant, for in the shallow northern seas stretching from the Bay of Biscay to the Baltic and the northern Atlantic as far as Newfoundland, fish of many kinds, from the sardine to the whale, were found. In the mid-dle of the North Sea the shallow water which covered the sandy Dogger Bank was one of the best fishing grounds. An even better one was the Sound, the narrow strait which led into the Baltic. Every year the herring shoals went there to spawn just off the Scania peninsula of southwest Sweden. From August to October they were crowded so thickly together that, according to a contemporary fish story, "you could cut them with a sword." During those months thousands of boats hauled in full nets, an army of workers cleaned, salted, and packed the catch, while merchants swarmed there to buy the fish in return for food, salt, nets, and barrels. A fourteenth-century observer declared that there were 45,000 boats at work and estimated the total labor force at 300,000. Though his figures are probably exaggerated, they indicate the great extent of this annual harvest of the sea. Some of the catch went a long way to market—even as far as Spain and Italy. Its transportation required a large fleet, and the more profitable part of the business lay in distributing rather than in catching.

The fishing industry needed much salt, whether the catch was sold wet or dried. Farmers also required salt for preserving meat, and the commodity must therefore be distributed over every area where people were living. It was obtained by evaporating sea water or the brine from salt springs or by mining rock-salt deposits. The most important producing areas were the Bay of Biscay coast and the springs of Lüneburg, just south of Hamburg. "Bay salt" was the cheapest in Europe for three reasons: there were rich salt deposits on the coast, there was plenty of warm wind to evaporate the sea water, and the salt could be carried cheaply as ballast in wine ships. Bay salt supplied English and Low Countries markets, and was carried to Scania to compete with the Lüneburg salt which had to be brought overland to Lübeck at relatively heavy freight rates. Other shores contributed to the salt supply; some inland springs and rock-salt deposits in Cheshire, Salzburg, and the Carpathians were exploited, and from these places an occasional place name gives us a clue to the paths along which the salt was carried in cartloads, horseloads, or manloads to the scattered multitude of consumers.

Seafaring people required shipbuilding materials, the growth of towns called for building lumber, while the trade in fish, wine, and beer created a need for barrels. These demands, when combined with the clearing of forests for new settlements, soon exhausted the local lumber supply in thickly populated regions. Then the forests of Norway or the Baltic lands became valuable. From them came tar, pitch, and timber for the shipyards; rafters, oak or pine boards for houses; and potash, which was extracted from wood ashes and used to make lye or soap for washing or bleaching. The Vistula was for a long time a great waterway for the transport of spruce and other woods from Prussia and Poland.

Sweden had copper and iron deposits as well as forests. The latter supplied the charcoal which was the only fuel used for smelting iron until the eighteenth century. By 1300 Sweden was winning that reputation as a producer of high-grade iron and steel which she has held ever since, while the copper mine of Störa Kopparberg had already begun to pour out a stream of metal that has not yet dried up. But Scandinavia had no monopoly of Europe's mineral supply. England contributed tin, lead, and a bit of coal, Belgium yielded copper and iron, Spain was still turning out her varied supply, while a boom in mining produced great quantities of silver, gold, and copper from the Bohemian hills after A.D. 1200.

There was much interregional trade in the common farm products. A country like Norway could not grow much grain and must import supplies. A crowded region like Flanders and Brabant relied on foreign farms for a substantial fraction of its food. On the other hand the new settlers south and east of the Baltic had a surplus of grain, and found markets for it in Norway or the Low Countries. In good years England might have some cereals to spare, and sent them to Gascony to pay for wine. The Hansards carried butter and cheese from one country to another. But the really large traffic in farm produce was limited to Spanish and English wool, French wine, and Baltic grain.

The Hanseatic Towns and League. Much of the long-range trade of the northern area had by 1300 passed into the hands of merchants who hailed from a hundred towns scattered between the Rhine and Reval. The towns which had easy access to the North Sea and to the settled river valleys of northwestern Europe were the first to become important. Cologne was especially favored by her location for contact with the industrial and commercial Low Countries, England, the eastern frontier, and the south. By A.D. 1000 the "men of the Emperor," chiefly Cologne merchants, were enjoying royal protection in London. By 1157 the group (or *hanse*) had a hall there. It opened its purse when Richard I came back bankrupt from the third crusade (1194). In return it was virtually exempted from customs levies and given the right to sell or buy in any English fair. Groups from other German towns, especially Bremen, Hamburg, and Lübeck, soon appeared in London, and by 1300 the traders from some sixty towns enjoyed common rights and a common residence. They lent money to kings and as security were given control of customs collection, of Cornish royal tin mines, and sometimes of the crown jewels. They won, or rather bought, preferential treatment over native traders; thus in 1347 they paid only 12*d.* on each cloth exported, while Englishmen paid 14*d.*, and others 33*d.* At times their ships carried three-fourths of the British wool exports and nearly all those of cloth. Their walled headquarters included a wharf on the Thames River bank, a hall, armory, houses, warehouses, and a *staalhof* or sample yard in which they displayed their wares. The term "steelyard" came to be applied to the whole settlement, and its occupants were popularly known as the Merchants of the Steelyard.

England was only one part of the Hansards' parish. Their ships went to Lisbon with fish, picked up Gascon wine and Bay salt, and brought them northward. They gained control of much Norwegian trade, thus spreading their western connections from the Bay through London and Bruges to Bergen. Meanwhile they went east, for, as we have seen, the eastward frontier movement was commercial as well as agricultural. When the settlers advanced beyond the Elbe, Hamburg at the mouth of that river began its career as one of Europe's great ports. When Lübeck was captured by Henry the Lion in 1158 it was soon filled with traders from Westphalia and the Rhineland. From that base merchants advanced to seek business on every island in the Baltic, at every river mouth on the coast, and at every commercially strategic point on the great plain. When Gothland was captured from the Scandinavians, Hansard merchants took over the old trade center of Wisby. Along the coast such Slav towns as Danzig were expanded, and by 1270 the line of German trading stations reached to Reval on the coast as well as to Novgorod in the eastern interior. Stockholm in Sweden, like Bergen in Norway, passed under Hansard political control.

While the hanses of merchants gained protection, preference, favors, or even dominance in the ports to which they went, their own home towns joined hands to clear the traffic lanes of dangers. One of these dangers was piracy, ever present or at least ever possible. Another was the Danish king, who controlled the Sound, collected dues from ships passing through that strait, and might wish to raise his charges to heights that seemed exorbitant. These twin menaces led Lübeck and other towns to seek safety in alliances after about 1220, at a time when inland cities were joining hands to protect their merchants who traveled on road or river. The striving for security on the way and for profitable conditions at the trading outposts reached its climax in the mid-fourteenth century. All hanses of merchants trading outside Germany were organized into a kind of super-hanse with headquarters on Gothland, and meanwhile the towns completed the building of the Hanseatic League about 1358. One of the League's first tasks was to crush Denmark. By the Treaty of Stralsund (1370) the Danish king was forced to give the victors two-thirds of the Sound dues for the next fifteen years, hand over some castles which defended the strait, grant the League veto power in the selection of the next monarch, and confer or confirm various privileges.

The League thus reached the summit of its power. Of the eighty coastal and inland member towns, Lübeck was the head. Its delegate presided over the diet which met at least once every three years to frame policy, decide questions of war and peace, consider problems of currency, shipping, and commercial law, or settle disputes. The League had no army or navy and no regular sources of revenue but had to rely on the ships, soldiers, and money of such towns as felt disposed to send them, or on emergency customs levies. Yet it wielded great power. The field of its operations lacked strong territorial rulers, except perhaps the Teutonic Knights, and since the Knights and the League had many common interests each helped the other, the Knights giving aid on land while the League rendered assistance by its ability to assert sea power. The League was therefore able to open doors for its own merchants and to close them to others. It could back the business activities of its traders by diplomacy, and diplomacy by force.

The Hansards' success was not, however, due merely to skill in wielding a big stick or in exacting a high price for aiding financially embarrassed rulers. It was also a reward for the efficiency with which they exchanged goods over a large trade area. They served the financial, commercial, and transportation needs of primary producing regions which as yet had few ships, an underdeveloped trading class, and little capital. The Hansards found markets for their produce and brought them in return the primary products or manufactured articles they needed. Cheap transportation was provided by the large cargo ship, the *kogge*, with its capacity of 1,500 to 2,000 tons burthen. Lighthouses, buoys, and trained pilots made navigation safer. A comprehensive body of maritime law was developed or copied from southern ports to govern relations between merchant, shipowner, captain, and crew, to fix responsibility for damage, to prevent overloading or undermanning, and to maintain discipline afloat. Capital and management were supplied for the development of mineral deposits. Finally, by focusing all their long-range traffic on the great Flemish port of Bruges, the Hansards enjoyed the benefits which that city offered as a halfway house between the Bay and the Baltic, as a market for the products of the Low Countries and the Rhineland, and as terminus of the journeys which Italian merchant ships began to make to northern Europe after 1300.

The Hansards built up a marked supremacy, but not a monopoly, in northern trade. Merchants of other lands had to walk humbly or warily in the Hanseatic trade preserve. If their king was strong enough to protect them by threatening to take an eye (or two eyes) for an eye if his subjects suffered harm at Hansard hands, they might get ahead unmolested. English traders, for example, penetrated the Baltic during the fourteenth century; they built up a flourishing exchange of English cloth for Prussian or Polish grain, hemp, and lumber, and their colony in Danzig had many of the features of a hanse. Other English merchants went to Norway and Iceland. So long as English kings backed these "adventurers," the Hansards had to be circumspect in their behavior and granted English merchants the same privileges as England gave them. But when, after about 1440, English politics lapsed into confusion and civil war, the Hansards violently drove the hapless Englishmen out of every northern market, from Danzig to Iceland.

The Southern Trade Area. Mediterranean trade was partly a matter of distributing goods obtained from Asia, but there was sufficient regional specialization around that sea to make certain areas stand out as suppliers of particular commodities. Spain had its primary staples (wool, wine, oil, sugar, iron, rice, fruits, and onions), its fine leatherwork, textiles, or hardware, and its dressed skins or furs of lamb, kid, hare, or rabbit, to which the Moors gave superior appearance and high-sounding names. The Barbary coast of North Africa yielded one of Europe's few decorative materials, coral. Behind that coast lay the desert; on its fringe sheep and goats were pastured, while across it from the south came slaves, ebony, ivory, ostrich feathers, and gold. Lombardy and Spain were famous for the horses needed as military mounts. Crete and Greece produced sweet wines and dried fruits. Cotton, which weavers were mixing with flax to make a light cloth called fustian, grew in Syria.

Alum for the dyer was drawn from Asia Minor, and Egypt was still a granary. The Black Sea yielded fish and led to gold, furs, and grain. The western Mediterranean contained tunny fish, Sicily had the sulphur needed for dusting vines, and the Adriatic was the chief southern source of salt. Finally, the leading towns had their manufactured specialties.

Yet all this exchange of southern produce seemed less important than that in oriental goods. European workshops had learned to make some articles so well that imports were no longer needed; but Europe had no deposits of precious stones and was barred by its climate from growing spices, drugs, certain dyes, cotton, or much silk. These things must be obtained from east of Suez, and the greatest of them was spices. What the herring did for northern commerce, spices did for southern; and when seventeenth-century Holland held the herring trade in one hand and the spice trade in the other its pockets bulged.

The medieval poor could not afford spices and relied on such local herbs as mint or sage to give taste to the flesh of elderly cattle, muscular hogs, and sinewy sheep. But the rich used spices lavishly on both salted and fresh viands. Medieval cookbooks had no room for foods served *au natural* or *au jus*. For example, ducklings and young rabbits were put into pasties and treated as follows: "Take plenty of good cinnamon, ginger, cloves, grain of Paradise, half a nutmeg, some mace and galingale, and [mix and beat] them well. Moisten with vinegar and verjuice [juice of unripe grapes]. When the pasty is almost cooked, pour the sauce therein and set in the oven to boil. In winter put in more ginger." Liquids were also spiced. The spice bill for Edward I's household in 1300 was at least $100,000 in modern money.

Commercial Effects of the Crusades. Asiatic goods reached the threshold of Europe along three main routes. The first came overland from China, Persia, or India, on long caravan trails to southern Russia or Asia Minor. There the ways fanned out: to Constantinople or the Mediterranean in the south; across Russia by the Varangian route to the Baltic in the north; or to Kiev and then westward through Poland and Bohemia or through Hungary and Austria to central Europe and the Rhineland. The second route came across or up the Tigris-Euphrates Valley and reached the Mediterranean on the coast of Syria. The third used the Indian Ocean and Red Sea and then made a short portage across the desert to the Nile and so to Alexandria. Transportation on the Asiatic part of the journey was in the hands of Arabs or other easterners, and the goods were then bought by Scandinavians for the Baltic trade, by Jews for the traffic across central Europe, and by Syrians or Byzantines for the Mediterranean markets. But even before the first crusade (1096) some Italian cities, especially Venice, were making contact with the termini of all the trade routes. They were carrying pilgrims to the Holy Land, trading with Constantinople, south Russia, Syria, and Egypt, accumulating ships, capital, and experience.

The crusades came as a heaven-sent opportunity to establish firmer footholds in the meeting places of East and West. The Italian cities were therefore willing to transport, provision, and finance the warriors—at a price. They stood ready to throw their armed galleys against coastal cities which happened to be important ports. If the warriors were to reap rewards by carving feudal estates or kingdoms out of the sacred soil, their bourgeois allies must have their share of the spoils guaranteed before they raised a sail or moved an oar. The spoils must include a part of the booty and possession of a section of each city. In that section there would be a church, market, oven, and warehouses; ships would unload and trade would be conducted duty free; the merchants would settle disputes in their own court, and no external tax collector would have power to levy imposts on their property.

Genoa was the first city to seize the opportunity. She helped besiege Antioch (1098) and in return got a church, a market, and thirty houses. This was only the beginning of Genoa's acquisitions. Pisa, Amalfi, Marseilles, Montpellier, and Barcelona received similar rewards for their services, but the largest beneficiary was Venice. Her financial strength was great, and she could hurl a fleet of 200 ships against any port. In return she secured a quarter of Jerusalem and of the great port of Acre, a third of Tyre and Ascalon, free trade throughout the kingdom of Jerusalem, exemption from sales taxes in ports and markets, and courts of her own in every city frequented by her merchants.

For nearly a century the crusaders and traders held most of their prizes. The movement had long since lost its religious character in the eyes of the fighting men, while in those of the cities it had never been anything but a commercial speculation. When the time came for the fourth crusade, Venice therefore had no scruples about turning the expedition into a trade war. She agreed to transport the crusaders to Syria or Egypt and provision them for a season; but they must pay their passage money and some other charges before sailing and give Venice half of their conquests. When they proved slow in paying, Dandolo, the old, blind, but wily doge, offered to cancel the debt if they would oblige Venice by capturing Zara, an Adriatic port which had long been a thorn in her side. They did so, moved on, and were then persuaded to change their objective to the capture of Constantinople, where Venetian traders were feeling the heat of Genoese and Pisan competition and the coolness of the emperor. The city was captured and pillaged in 1204, the emperor deposed, and the plunder divided. Venice got about three-eighths of the city, and the Genoese were evicted. She established a virtual monopoly of the trade of the Eastern Empire by securing control of the Bosporus and taking strategic islands, ports, market centers, and steppingstones. Since she already had a good footing in Egypt and was well established on the Syrian coast, she towered above all rivals as the greatest trader in Europe.

The infidel who studied this new style in crusading might well comment on the way Christians loved one another. Yet such actions were in keeping with the general tone of relations between the Mediterranean rivals in medieval times, as they had been in the days of ancient Greece. No Hanseatic League ever had a chance of coming into being in that sea of city-states. Conflicts were real trade wars, fought with diplomacy, alliances, armies, navies, and privateers. Amalfi was sacked by Pisa in 1135, and Pisa in turn was defeated in a naval battle by Genoa in 1284. Genoa did not become downhearted when she was evicted from Constantinople. In 1261 she fomented a revolution in that city, overthrew Venice's puppet emperor, broke her rival's grip on the Black Sea, and established herself as the favored trader, even the monopolist, in the imperial lands. The process of give and take continued, and the blows were often hard. But they were never fatal, for there was enough profit to permit an occasional absorption of heavy loss—so long as the Asiatic goods continued to come through.

Mediterranean Shipping. By 1200 the Mediterranean seaways were probably busier than they had ever been before. Professor Byrne has given us a vivid picture of Genoese medieval shipping. Much of it was coastal, for captains were still loath to get out of sight of land. By about 1150 conflict with the Moslems in the western Mediterranean had given place to a condition of relative peace, and trade around that half of the sea therefore expanded. But the east-ward journeys to the Levant, Egypt, and the Black Sea were far more important. Only one trip a year could be made to these remote regions, since much time was spent collecting cargo at each port of call, and in winter the ships must hibernate. For the expeditions great care had to be taken that vessels were seaworthy and were not overloaded or undermanned and, if the merchant passengers were fastidious, that no mules, horses, falcons, pilgrims, or other obnoxious companions were carried. Danger of attack from the land or on the sea caused ships to carry crossbows, lances, headpieces, and fighting men, and to sail in fleets of three to ten vessels convoyed by state galleys for at least part of the journey.

When the traders reached their destination they entered the Genoese *fondaco* where merchants and agents from Genoa lodged and traded under the rule of their own consul. They collected spices, perfumes, fabrics, alum, raw cotton, and female slaves. They sold the metals, furs, leather, lumber, wine, arms, woolen cloth of various qualities, and other acceptable European products, but often had to pay for some of their purchases in gold or silver.

In essentials this picture is true of the shipping of Venice, Pisa, Montpellier, Barcelona, and other ports. In the case of Venice the canvas would be larger and show the Senate regulating trade and traffic with great strictness while encouraging it with skill and en-ergy. Once a year from the twelfth to the eighteenth century the doge solemnly cast a wedding ring into the Adriatic. Every effort was made to keep the marriage monogamous, by insuring that Venetian ships were as good as possible, by beating down or captur-ing rival ports, by restricting or shutting out alien vessels, and by seeking preferential or exclusive favors from foreign rulers.

The cream of Venetian trade was the commerce in spices or other goods of small weight but high value, and it must be carefully car-ried in the best possible container. The state therefore built galleys in its own arsenal. They were long and narrow vessels, propelled by sails and oars, designed for speed and for fighting. The state also ran a rope factory to protect "the security of our galleys and ships and similarly of our sailors and capital." The actual operation of the state galleys was leased by auction to the highest bidder, but the government fixed the freight rates and saw to it that cargo space was made available to all traders instead of being monopolized by any great firm. The galleys carried a company of archers and sailed in fleets at times and on routes fixed by the Senate. By 1400 there were about twenty of these great ships, working on six regular services— to the Black Sea, Syria, Egypt, North Africa, Spain, and the North Sea.

The milk of Venetian, and indeed of all Mediterranean, trade was the traffic in bulkier cheap goods, such as cotton from Syria, alum from Asia Minor, wine, oil, grain, lumber, fish, and salt. These cargoes were carried in privately built ships which resembled the Hanseatic *kogge* in being roomy, broad of beam, and driven solely by sail. They were known as cogs, round ships, or unarmed ships. Their freight rates were low because they were much more cheaply operated than were the galleys; but they might be defenseless against attackers, even when they sailed in a convoy with the galleys. They did the bulk of Venice's fetching and carrying, but Senate decrees and war risks confined the spice and similar precious trades to the merchant warships.

While Venice and Genoa dominated the Mediterranean picture, other centers farther west grew in importance. In southern France Aigues-Mortes, Marseilles, Montpellier, and Narbonne shared in the general trade expansion, looking southward to North Africa and northward to the overland trade with the Low Countries, as well as eastward. In Spain the slow recapture of the country from the Moors led to the union of Aragon and Catalonia and to the emergence of a new commercial and political power in the Mediterranean. Italians conducted much of Spain's foreign trade, but in Barcelona a native trading class emerged which by 1300 was handling the wool and metals from the hinterland, trading with Africa and the Levant, going outside the Strait of Gibraltar, using well-developed banking institutions, and operating under a code of maritime law which was remarkably complete. Barcelona built up a Spanish empire in the western Mediterranean long before Columbus found one across the Atlantic.

Italians in Asia. The crusades placed Italian outposts on the coasts of the Black Sea and of the eastern Mediterranean. To those points most traders were willing to let Asiatics bring the goods from the Orient, but a few were not so content. Missionary zeal and commerce alike lured some Europeans to tread the trails or traverse the seas east of Suez to Persia, Arabia, India, the East Indies, and China. By 1300 the Franciscan friars had outposts at Zaitun on the China coast and at points in India or central Asia. Marco Polo was in Asia from 1271 to 1295, but he was a traveler, almost an emigrant, rather than a person seeking goods for the Venetian market. There were, however, some who went intending to return with oriental produce, and when a Florentine, Pegolotti, wrote a handbook on commercial practices in the early fourteenth century he included a detailed description of the road to China.

The amount of goods taken or brought back by Europeans can, however, never have been large. The southern route was almost entirely a waterway and therefore offered the best opportunity for the movement of large cargoes at low freight costs. In 1291, however, the pope forbade Christians to trade with Egypt and at about the same time the sultan of that country began a serious effort to keep Red Sea traffic as a preserve for his own people. The middle and northern roads were largely overland and therefore costly; but if Asiatic peoples and rulers were friendly it might be safe for Europeans to travel on them and pass the heavy freight bills on to the ultimate consumer. Until about 1340 there was enough friendship and safety to induce some Italians to settle in Persia, India, and even as far away as Zaitun, while others set out in small groups on round trips to India. But we know that one of these groups brought no bales back; its return cargo was chiefly a collection of pearls and of Indian gold currency, which indeed were goods of small bulk but great value.

By 1340 conditions in Asia had changed to anarchy, inhospitality, and violence. Order was eventually restored, but Europeans remained unwelcome, and the task of moving goods westward had to be left to Asiatic traders or transporters. Efforts to circumvent the Egyptian ban on access to the Red Sea were not very successful. Europeans therefore were compelled to wait for their goods on the threshold of the Orient, especially at Alexandria. They knew, of course, that all barriers could be by-passed if an all-water route were available. In 1291 two Genoese, the Vivaldi brothers, steered two ships out of the Strait of Gibraltar and turned south to seek that seaway. They vanished without trace, and two centuries elapsed before the route around the Cape of Good Hope was eventually discovered.

Trade Between Northern and Southern Europe. The third main division of medieval trade was that between the Mediterranean lands and the north. It was partly an exchange of the wares of two different climatic zones, partly an exchange of southern manufactures for northern primary products; but there was some passage southward of manufactured articles.

Until about 1300 traffic was almost entirely by land and river. The Varangian route through Russia felt the competition of western rivals even before it was damaged by the advance of the Tatars from Asia and the capture of Kiev in 1240. In central Europe the north-south roads from the upper Rhine or Danube used the Alpine passes to reach north Italy. Italians gradually let this trade with the lands east of the Rhine and north of the Brenner Pass go into the hands of German merchants. Venice evidently decided that sea traffic with the Near East was more profitable than land trade with the north. She therefore welcomed the Germans who came through the Brenner or other passes, provided the famous *fondaco dei Tedeschi* (German factory) to accommodate them, and allowed them to conduct their business under strict regulations to preserve order and prevent smuggling.

In the west the most famous trade route was that which started at Bruges, gathered up the produce of Flanders and northeast France as it ran south through Champagne and Burgundy, and descended the valley of the Saône and then of the Rhone to the Mediterranean coast. This "vertebral column of the land commerce of France through history" (Laurent) was traversed by merchants from both ends and both sides. Its meeting place for them was in the Champagne fairs. (See Chapter IX.) By the twelfth century we find Low Countries merchants collecting cloth in towns ranging alphabetically from Abbeville to Ypres and carrying it to Champagne. Every year six caravans left Genoa to buy that cloth in the six fairs. A less useful road crossed from the Bay of Biscay through Bordeaux and Toulouse to the Mediterranean at Narbonne, using rivers at each end, but with a land portage across the watershed until a canal was constructed in the seventeenth century.

Inland Transportation. Between the collapse of the Roman Empire and the eighteenth century good road making was almost a lost art. Abbeys, towns, and lords might improve a ford or build a bridge; a village could be stirred into action by mud and flood; and rulers who had cause to move about on business or from one hunting lodge to the next made spasmodic efforts to compel landlords and tenants to render the highways passable. In general, however, a road was a strip of land on which people had the right to travel, rather than an improved surface. Over the moors, through the passes or forests, or across the swamps it might be little more than a path. In easier country it was often so wide that a horseman could find some unbroken surface on which he could ride quickly, while cattle could wander along, finding some food as they moved; but wheeled vehicles found the going hard in wet weather.

On such roads the normal speed was the walking pace of man or animal; twenty miles was a good day's journey, and some daily "stages" were shorter. When news and mail had to be carried quickly, couriers might cover forty to fifty miles in a day, and some cities or large business firms ran regular fast services. A journey of a thousand miles from Calais to Rome took a relay of express riders twenty-seven days to complete in 1200, and when the arrears of a Scots king's ransom had to be rushed to London in 1375, the carrier averaged thirty-six miles a day. By the early fifteenth century a regular mail service carried letters from Bruges to Venice in about twenty-five days; but the Romans had been able to do the journey in about the same time a thousand years before. In the carriage of goods the packhorse or the two-wheeled wagon, moving at the easy pace of horse or oxen, set the speed and the day's journey. A drover who steered a small herd of cattle and a large flock of sheep along 130 miles of fairly level English highway in thirteen days in 1323 probably made a fast passage.

The shortcomings of the roads were in part counterbalanced by the widespread use of rivers. Most of the streams had some natural defect; the Rhone was too rough and fast, and like the Danube and Po had no good mouth; spring floods, summer low water, and winter ice impeded navigation; and there were many perpetual shallows, rocks, or rapids. But most waterways were capable of use, and some were improved, especially in the Low Countries, where they were linked by canals. Downstream traffic moved easily, but upstream movement was slow, since poles, oars, or simple sails were the only power available for combating the current. Professor Stenton finds that for English medieval travelers the waterways were never more than an occasional—and rather slow—supplement to the road system. In 1319 the English king invited the students of a Cambridge college to spend Christmas with him. Those who went by road took five days to travel 150 miles and reached the palace in time for the party, but those who went on a combined road and boat route spent nine days on the way and were three days late. On the continent and on large rivers water travel may have been more expeditious, but in all countries there was slow movement of cargo.

Safety was more important than speed, and the human enemies might be worse than the physical. Not all highway robbers and outlaws were as high principled or romantic as was Robin Hood. A twelfth-century guidebook warned pilgrims that one part of northern Spain was "inhabited by wild people," and the wild men were not confined to Spain or to the poor. When Henry IV restored peace to Germany in 1093 a chronicler described the effect in a paragraph which reveals how bad conditions could be: "And now the boatman on the river glided in safety by the dungeons of the robber barons who had hitherto fattened on his spoils; the roads were no longer infested by marauding bands; the forests gave no shelter to lurking brigands; the highways were open to the trader and the wayfarer to pass on their way in peace; and the professional depredators were themselves reduced to that beggary and penury which they had so long inflicted on others." In France kings tried to make nobles responsible for outrages committed on their estates. In England a statute (1285) demanded that the edges of highways connecting market towns be cleared, "so that there be neither dyke, tree, nor bush whereby a man may lurk to do hurt within 200 feet of either side of the way."

To the physical dangers of travel were added the financial burdens. The Romans had collected tolls from travelers and traders but had spent at least part of that revenue on the roads. Medieval kings, bishops, and lords continued to make the levy but spent little of it on roads, bridges, or river improvement. They imposed new tolls on the slightest pretext but did not repeal them when the emergency had passed. In 1369, for example, a new charge was imposed on goods carried on part of the River Loire. The money was needed to placate an English commander during that period in the Hundred Years' War, but the toll continued to be collected down to the time of the French Revolution.

Rivers were heavily dotted with toll stations. On the Rhine the number of them grew from nineteen in the twelfth century to more than sixty by 1400, and on the castle-strewn gorge between Bingen and Coblenz the traveler had scarcely left one pay station before the next one came in sight. It has been estimated that the levies paid on that part of the Rhine amounted to two-thirds the value of the cargo. It has also been suggested by Professor Heckscher that the river tolls drove traffic away from what was normally the cheaper form of transportation and forced traders to use roundabout, less satisfactory roads. The little we know about medieval freight charges shows that rates on land were heavy. An English abbey which obtained its stone from a quarry less than five miles away paid £104 for the material and £347 to those who carted it. Although this is not a fair illustration, it is an extreme instance of a general condition. Freight charges, when supplemented by tolls, made a wide gap between prices at the beginning and the end of a journey.

To protect themselves against physical attack and financial extortion, merchants banded together and traveled in armed companies, while the towns to which they belonged joined hands. The Hanseatic League was only the best known of many such defensive unions. In the mid-thirteenth century the League of the Rhine, comprising seventy towns, patrolled the roads and operated a fleet of armed boats on the main stream or its tributaries, from Cologne to Basel. Having suppressed marauders it then attacked oppressive toll collectors, and many a castle or pay station was destroyed. The Swiss towns opposed the levy of burdensome imposts on roads and at strategic points in the passes; in their case joint action led to permanent confederation and the birth of the Swiss nation. Even where the oppression was not acute, merchants worked hard to secure the reduction or abolition of tolls both in their own country and in foreign lands. If they were strong enough, or if the ruler held long-run views of enlightened self-interest, they might succeed—especially if they were able to offer an immediate grant of money to a harassed king or lord or were willing to pay a fixed sum each year as the price of the concession.

Sea Transportation. One would expect water transportation between the Mediterranean and the North Sea to have been more economical than land carriage; yet there was apparently little attempt to develop that route until the end of the thirteenth century. Even heavy raw materials like wool and metals went overland from England and the Low Countries to the south. Perhaps the volume of business did not justify the use of the sea; improvements in ship construction and in the use of sails may have been necessary; and the capital outlay on vessels may have been too large until city governments were willing to shoulder the burden. The journey was long; the route lay through two bottlenecks—the Strait of Gibraltar and the Straits of Dover—where attack by pirates was easy; and the

Bay of Biscay is often unkind even to those who cross it in a large modern liner.

At the end of the thirteenth century the sea route was opened. One decisive factor was the sudden deterioration of conditions along the route through Champagne. The counts of Champagne had pursued liberal policies toward those who went that way or used the fairs. But the county passed by marriage into the hands of the French king, who tried to solve his financial problems by increasing several charges, attacked his Jewish and Italian creditors, debased the currency, fought a long war with the Count of Flanders, and generally played havoc with the flourishing interchange between north and south. His action seems to have tipped the scales in favor of the sea route. In 1300 the first little fleet of Genoese galleys reached the English Channel. The Venetians met this move by establishing a rival service, and in 1314 their first galley arrived in Antwerp. From that time onward for two centuries fleets of heavily armed Genoese, Venetian, and Florentine vessels were sent each year. The Champagne fairs were ruined, and the "vertebral column" ceased to carry much through traffic.

The galleys ambled along the Spanish or North African coast, calling at several ports. They put into Lisbon, and then crossed the Bay of Biscay to the English Channel. There the fleet divided; some ships went to Southampton and London while the others sailed on to Bruges or Antwerp to meet the Hansard and Low Countries merchants. For a long time Bruges was the greatest port of northern Europe, but during the fourteenth century Antwerp began to steal up on it. (See Chapter XI.) In one of these two termini the Flanders galleys unloaded their silks, raisins, wines, spices, dyestuffs, and other Mediterranean or oriental wares; they took on linens or woolens, wool, and metal and then sailed to England to join their fellows who had been picking up wool, hides, tin, and cloth. The reunited fleet then returned to Italy, after an absence of at least a year.

Conclusion. Enough has been said to show how European trade extended its range during the second half of the Middle Ages. Its volume was small when compared with that of a modern age equipped with easy transportation. Insecurity marked it at many points because of the changeable moods and pressing financial needs of rulers, the seesaw of commercial rivalries, and the capricious opening or closing of markets. The eastern routes might be disturbed by movements of Asiatic peoples. The western highways might be blocked by war or harassed by the violence which ensued when peace turned soldiers adrift or destitution drove villagers to desperation. Yet despite what used to seem heartbreaking obstacles until twentieth-century war piled up still worse ones, merchants adventured their money, persons, and wares. Blissfully ignorant of the transportation facilities they lacked by being born five or six centuries too soon, they went afield or sent their goods. They developed forms of organization and practices which spanned long time and wide space, concentrated exchange on certain places and periods, minimized some risks or insured against them, mobilized capital in order to put spare funds to work, and evolved credit devices which served as an excellent lubricating oil in making the commercial machine work more smoothly. These aspects of commercial and financial organization or practice will be the subject of the next chapter.

BIBLIOGRAPHY

See end of Chapter IX.

IX

MEDIEVAL COMMERCIAL
AND FINANCIAL ORGANIZATION

Medieval commercial enterprises displayed a wide variety of sizes and patterns. At one extreme, the seller might be a little shopkeeper or a craftsman who sold his own products. At the other, he was a member of a firm engaged in large-scale long-distance commerce and banking, including high financial dealings with popes or kings. In between we find every conceivable kind and scale of business.

The Traveling Trader. Trader and traveler were often synonymous. Many a merchant took, rather than sent, his goods to market or went out to buy what he needed. He might be a humble peddler, carrying his wares on his back, on a packhorse, in a wagon or boat. His stock could consist of only one commodity, such as salt, or be a motley of small goods for all kinds and ages of buyers. One thirteenth-century French peddler announced that he had girdles, gloves, cords for viols, needles, thimbles, purses, veils, arrow points of iron, buckles, pins of brass and silver, kerchiefs of linen for young beaux and of hemp for clowns, rolling pins, brooches, cowbells, tablets and pens for clerks. For ladies' toilets he had razors, tweezers, mirrors, toothbrushes, toothpicks, combs, rouge, and powder. For boys there were spinning tops; for old women, paternosters; and for men he had dice, including "two which when thrown fall on the aces." Some peddlers prospered; one, an Englishman, made a fortune and then became a saint; another, an Icelander, rose to be a large landowner and founded a family so famous that one of the sagas records its deeds. But many peddlers earned reputations far from saintly or heroic and were more likely to be suspected of receiving stolen goods or of having killed and skinned any cat that was missing.

Higher in the scale came the traveling merchants who dealt in raw materials, food, livestock, manufactures, and eastern imports. They accompanied their goods, and armed groups of them, with a banner and a leader, were to be found traversing the roads, crossing the seas, passing from fair to fair, and sojourning in a *fondaco* in the distant cities to which they went. These men might move as in a groove between two or three places or in a wider but fixed circuit, as for instance the men of Cologne who frequented London or the Low Countrymen and Genoese who met at the Champagne fairs. But others, possibly younger and greatly daring, roved wider wherever a new market was opening up or an old one seemed to be worth invading. They were like the Persian merchant in the *Arabian Nights* who announced his intention to carry Persian sulphur to China, Chinese porcelain to Greece, Greek or Venetian brocade to India, Indian steel to Aleppo, Aleppo glassware to Yemen in Arabia, and striped fabrics of Yemen to Persia. Then, said he, "I will give up foreign commerce and settle myself in a warehouse."

The "Sedentary Merchant." If the Persian finally got his warehouse, he had many a European counterpart. To some traveling traders success (and advancing age) brought the decision to settle down in some town. There they could invest their wealth in urban or rural land, put it into goods which younger partners would take abroad, supply fractions of the capital needed for building ships, or make loans to traders, the town, the church, or the crown. But if they were not ready, able, or willing to retire into such investing idleness, they might continue their trading career from a city office and warehouse, and operate afield through partners, agents, or employees. They no longer spent a lot of their time sitting on a saddle; they now sat on a bench or buffet. Instead of tramping the dusty roads or fairgrounds, they walked the floors of their countinghouse, warehouse, and yard, the streets and squares where merchants congregated, and the way down to the wharf. They had become sedentary or resident merchants.

The merchant who managed a far-flung business from his city premises was not necessarily, however, a retired roamer. He might be a man who had built up a town business which eventually stretched its hands out to bring materials from afar, produced goods in quantities beyond local needs, and exported them. Whatever their origin, these city businessmen were the most important figures in commercial life until the nineteenth century.

Though the merchant ceased to travel, his goods could not become sedentary. The task of buying, selling, and moving them still had to be undertaken. In modern times the moving is done by "common carriers," of which the railroad is the best example; by ships, planes, or trucks which are "chartered" (i.e., leased) for a period or for a journey by the owner of the goods from the owner of the carrier; or by ships or trucks which belong to the owner of the cargo. Common carriers relieve merchants and producers of the need to sink large sums of capital in transportation facilities. There were some of them in ancient and medieval times. The Venetian state-owned galleys served as common carriers with space available for sale to all who desired it. Private shipowners and land carriers offered similar facilities; but much transportation had to rely on the shipper's ability to charter a vessel, to hire wagons and horses, or even to own what he needed. Only the largest merchants could fill a whole ship or would care to risk the loss of an entire cargo. Ship-owning or chartering would therefore call for joint action by a number of shippers.

For the sale of his goods or the purchase of supplies the stay-at-home merchant relied on partners, agents, or employees who traveled or lived abroad. He might entrust his goods to some merchant who was going to foreign ports or to the captain of the ship. He and his fellow exporters might employ a *supercargo*, who traveled on the vessel, sold the wares at various ports of call, spent the receipts on such goods as his patrons required, and received a salary or commission or both. But increasingly at points where the resident merchant hoped to do much business he used partners or agents who lived in the places where he wished to buy or sell.

The Partnership. Until the joint-stock company appeared in the seventeenth century the partnership was the usual device for uniting two or more persons in an enterprise which could not be done satisfactorily by the capital and labor of one person. Partnerships could be of many kinds, but three are most noticeable.

1. One partner contributed the capital, the other did the work. The former risked the loss of his funds; the latter bore the burden and fatigue of the journey, braved shipwreck, pirates, or highway robbers, and faced the risk of having no reward for his labor if the enterprise failed. If it succeeded, the investor received three-quarters of the profits, the trader one-fourth. This plan, as old as ancient Babylonia, was in common use in Italian cities by 1100. It was called a *commenda;* the investor commended his capital to the trader, usually for one voyage. He might commend funds to many traders, while each of them might take goods supplied him by many investors. The *commenda* thus offered an opportunity for a young

man who had just completed his period of training, but lacked capital, to start out on a business career.

2. The trader supplied part of the capital, usually a third. For his labor he received the regular quarter of the profits, and his capital entitled him to a third of what was left, which would be a quarter of the total profit. His combined reward was therefore half the yield of the venture. By the twelfth century this fifty-fifty arrangement was well known in Genoa and Venice. It was called a sea partnership (*societas maris*). The trader's capital might be money he had made in earlier *commenda* partnerships; the investor's capital could be the sum he had formerly commended plus the profits it had earned. If all went well the reward might be rich to both parties. We know of a series of three Genoese trading ventures in which the investing partner tripled his capital while the traveler, who had begun with nothing, emerged with a sum nearly three-fourths the size of the capital originally commended to him.

3. The *commenda* and *societas maris* were temporary and often small-scale compacts, easily made and duly ended. A larger and more lasting organization was erected when a small group of persons contributed their funds and labor to a "real partnership" (*vera societas*). The partners might be friends, or an older merchant might take younger men into his firm and sometimes, by marriage, into his family. They agreed to work together for a fixed number of years, often five, under conditions set down in a formal contract. Some partners stayed at home to operate the business at headquarters, others traveled or managed the foreign branches.

Of the "real partnerships" the most real, important, and durable were those which mobilized the capital and labor of a family. Recent research is emphasizing more and more the economic vitality and influence of the family, and it has been suggested that instead of talking about "individualism" we should speak of "familism." "In most societies, at most times, it has been the great family which by its wealth, power, prestige, and presumption of permanence has been the outstanding institution in private economic enterprise" (Lane). After carefully scrutinizing the Genoese at work, Professor Reynolds is impressed by "the great strength, in the lives of the thirteenth-century men who had such character and initiative as made them do things at all, of the family interest. To understand that a man of any importance thought above all of his family affairs—before politics, fighting or business—is a help in understanding how business itself operated." This "overriding interest of family" Reynolds finds not merely among the rich and great but "right down all the ranks of society to the hired journeymen, apprentices, and farm peasants. Family runs through business and out the other side into politics."

Some family firms supply the "big business" names of the Middle Ages, as they did later. In 1300 the Bardi firm contained fifteen members, of whom ten were members of the family, and in 1331 the latter owned thirty-seven of the fifty-eight shares into which the capital was divided. In Venice family partnerships were many, large, and enduring. In Genoa three brothers operated alum works in Asia Minor, owned some ships, leased others, and ran shipping services to every part of the Mediterranean.

These three types of partnerships merged into one another and developed every conceivable variation or extension. Sometimes a real partnership supplemented its capital by accepting investments, loans, or deposits at fixed rates of interest from outsiders. The funds put into business came from every kind of purse, large or small. Norwegian kings invested money in expeditions bound for Iceland and Britain, while their subjects provided sails, ropes, gear, oars, or bales of cargo to equip and stock the ship. Genoese noblemen, churchmen, widows, guardians of orphans, sailors, craftsmen, peasants, and shopkeepers risked their money in commercial ventures. A merchant of Venice was asked by his old nurse to invest some ducats she had saved. In England the dowries of brides might go to supply trading capital.

At times a venture used the funds of too many people to be described as a partnership. The shipbuilding industry, for example, called for large amounts of capital. Any group which decided to build a big vessel would invite friends to become owners of a share of fraction (locum) of the ship. Many people might thus hold a claim on the ship's earnings. These fractions could be subdivided, and a man who wished to minimize his risks would own fragments in many vessels rather than a large share in one or two.

The actual operation of large ships on long voyages offered another opportunity for pooling funds from many pockets. In Venice the state provided the capital for building the galleys but leased the vessels for each voyage to the highest bidder. He then had to provide money for outfitting them, for the food and wages of the crew, and for all the other expenses of a round trip that would, in the case of the Flanders galleys, take at least a year to complete. Meanwhile those who sent goods on the ships risked cargoes worth from a quarter to half a million ducats. The financing of ship operations and the provision of some cargo were therefore done by "joint ventures," in which many individuals or partnerships invested. A "company of the galley" was formed to supply running expenses, and the amount was frequently divided into twenty-four shares. Similarly, while many traders sent their own goods, some of them combined to supply part of the cargo. The master of the galley managed the operating funds, and the goods jointly bought were entrusted to some overseas agent or to a supercargo. When the galleys returned, the profits were shared out and the joint venture wound up its affairs.

Markets and Fairs. Much trade was conducted privately, as for example the purchase of wool in the west or of grain in the east, by merchants who went around the producing regions and bought the clip or the crop—sometimes long before the former had been shorn or the latter harvested. But we know most about the markets and fairs in which formal transactions took place in public. Both were held at a set time and place. Sellers knew that if they took their wares to the appointed spot on the proper day and hours, they would find buyers gathered there. In an age of small trade volume and slow transportation this knowledge saved time and travel. Both were controlled and protected by the landlord or city on whose ground they were held. Both had their rules, tolls, stall fees, and other charges; but both were free from some restrictions which towns imposed on ordinary retail trade in the interest of the local dealer.

The differences between them were of degree and kind. The typical market was a weekly gathering of people from an area so small that the country dwellers could come to town, do their selling and buying, and get home, all in one day. Most of the exchange may have been between producer and consumer, but the middleman crept in, purchasing goods which the district or town produced in quantities beyond local requirements. This was true of some industrial wares, e.g., cloth or metal goods, as well as farm produce. Since the area served was small, markets were thickly sprinkled over the country, sometimes so thickly that they competed with each other. When a medieval English lawyer suggested that they ought to be at least six and two-thirds miles apart, he gave a good indication of the limited range of the transactions.

If a town grew large a weekly market would be insufficient. Goods were offered two or three times a week; some hours on market days were earmarked for the sale of one article and the next period for that of another; special days or sites were set aside for the cattle market; or several market places were provided. The need to protect goods from bad weather led to the building of market halls. Such developments gave the large town an almost daily market of some kind; when supplemented by the growth of shops and of merchant warehouses they offered continuous opportunities for obtaining what the buyer desired.

The fair served a different purpose. Held yearly or half-yearly, often in a sleepy little town or on the outskirts of some large center, it might last several days or even some weeks. It attracted goods and traders from a wide area, and its business was wholesale rather than retail. Its original function may have been to provide facilities for the sale of a district's wool clip, surplus harvest, or livestock, but in some places it developed a national or even cosmopolitan fame and flavor.

Periodical gatherings of buyers and sellers had been well known to the ancient world. They were held on frontiers of city-states, at neutral points, or outside temples. The crowds which gathered for a religious festival provided a large body of customers, the gifts they gave the gods were sold, and divine protection hovered over trade as well as worship. As Christianity spread, the church fostered the growth of fairs and markets, placed a cross in the middle of the market place as a reminder that the peace of God rested on the trader and his wares, and received much income from tolls or stall fees, as well as from the sale of its own produce.

Lay lords were equally quick to recognize the benefits which trade gatherings would bring to their purses. The right of a lord to hold a market or fair on his land could be obtained only by a special grant from the crown. That right was eagerly sought. During the prosperous thirteenth century about 3,300 charters were issued giving English landlords authority to operate markets and forbidding the rise of near-by rivals whose competition might make them "tortious nuisances." On the continent the same development took place, and by 1300 every country was well equipped for exchange large or small, wholesale or retail, local or long distance.

In the market place the transactions between neighbors were easily regulated by local officials. (See Chapter X.) On the fairground the task of control was more difficult and the need for speedy settlement of disputes much greater. Men might be there from many parts of Europe. Sales of large quantities of goods were made, usually on credit; many different currencies were brought together; principals, agents, or partners bought, sold, borrowed, lent, repaid, and made contracts. If the fair was to function smoothly its owner must guarantee protection from violence and provide a court in which acceptable justice could be dispensed promptly. Mediterranean traders had a long legacy of customs and usages for dealing with commercial disputes. Northern merchants had worked out certain recognized rules of the game, and on such great interregional meeting grounds as the Champagne fairs these rules were fused in a code of merchant law. In England the fair court was known as the Pie-powder Court (from *pieds poudreux,* "dusty feet"). Traders came to it with the dust of the fairground thick on them, to state their case. Procedure was simple, red tape rare, judgment prompt, and execution immediate. All contracts, acknowledgments of debt, or promises to pay were officially sealed by the clerk of the fair and might be enforced for as long as thirty years.

Of the hundreds of fairs scattered over medieval Europe, many were known only locally but some won wide repute. That of St.-Denis near Paris went back to at least 629, and by the eighth century was frequented by northern merchants who went there to buy wine from the estates in the Seine valley. By the ninth century Novgorod was becoming well known as a fur fair. By 1100 Lombards were visiting Flemish fairs, and the Easter fair at Cologne was famous. The Christmas fair in Venice was marked by the offering of the new supply of spices which had left India with the favorable monsoon winds of the previous spring. In England four great wool fairs were eventually eclipsed by one at Sturbridge, near Cambridge. There for three weeks were gathered English wool or cloth merchants, Venetians and Genoese with oriental and Italian wares, Flemings with cloth and metal goods, Spaniards and Frenchmen with wine, Greeks with currants and raisins, and Hansards with fur, amber, and tar.

The Champagne Fairs. The most famous fairs were those of Champagne. Champagne was a fertile area east and southeast of Paris, on or near the upper reaches of half a dozen navigable rivers. Through it passed the overland north-south route. Its counts kept their territory free from war, pursued an intelligent policy of internal improvement, and preserved order on road and river. Fairs had been held there since the eighth or ninth century. By the twelfth century six annual fairs had become widely known; two at Troyes, two at Provins, one at Lagny, and one at Bar-sur-Aube. They were so timed and lasted so long that there was a fair in full swing somewhere in Champagne nearly all the months from January to October. The trade in cloth, skins, and furs was most important, but there was traffic in almost every other kind of European or Asiatic goods, down to pots, pans, and old clothes. On the fringe of the fairground, amusement or amazement was provided by jugglers, minstrels, wild-beast shows, acrobats, and human or animal freaks.

The Champagne fairs played an important part in the development of credit. Men bought goods and kings or lords bought or borrowed at one fair, making a promise to pay or repay at a later one. Their promise was recorded, and became known as the "fair letter" (*lettre de foire*). When the business of selling goods was ended, some time was spent in settling old debts and incurring new ones. In later fairs which grew up at Lyons and Geneva this business in credit seemed more important than that in goods. The Champagne fairs also developed "clearinghouse" characteristics. When a merchant in the closing days of a fair took stock of his position, he found that much money was due from others to him and much due by him to others. When all came to settle their crisscross of debits and credits, each might find there was little left over to be paid in coin or other kinds of money. Goods sold had paid for goods bought.

The golden age of the Champagne fairs ran from about 1150 to nearly 1300. Then came a sudden decline, caused in part by the disturbances (described in Chapter VIII) which followed the passage of the region into the hands of the French king. But economic factors also did some damage. As sea transportation developed between the Mediterranean and the North Sea, buyers and sellers gathered where the ships came in, especially in Bruges, now the meeting place of southern and northern sea lanes. The city and the Count of Flanders gave Italian traders the privileges they were accustomed to enjoy in foreign ports, protected them against arbitrary claims, fixed the tolls and port charges they were to pay, gave them the right to have a *fondaco* and a consul for the men from each city, and generally tempted them to make Bruges their Low Countries headquarters, as the Hansards were already doing.

Italian firms responded by ceasing to send representatives to Champagne and by settling agents or partners in Bruges. There they found all the facilities of a fair but in addition could transact business all the year round. Faced with the competition of these better trading methods and harassed by misrule, the Champagne fairs lost ground; but the need for fairs as concentration points for goods and traders did not vanish. When Antwerp displaced Bruges as northern commercial center in the fifteenth century, much of its business sprang from handling the wares which came to four large fairs held each year, and in eastern or central Europe the volume or character of trade was such that the fair remained the best place for transacting it for centuries to come. In the west, however, the fair was not enough. Regional and interregional commerce needed permanent bases, strategically situated on river, crossroads, estuary, or coast, permanently manned and in continuous operation. To such well-located towns goods, whether bought at fairs or privately from producers, could be gathered for export, and imports could come in bulk and then be distributed at leisure in smaller lots.

Commission Merchants. In such commercial centers the larger Italian and Hanseatic firms established branches in charge of a partner, a salaried manager, or an agent who was paid a commission on the goods he handled. In them also appeared many immigrant or native independent commission agents and merchants. These stood ready to sell goods consigned to them and to buy anything that a patron required, and charged a commission of 1 to 3 per cent. They served small and large consignors alike. A young Venetian, Andrea Barbarigo, who started his business career in 1418 with only 200 ducats and ended it with a comfortable sum of at least 10,000 ducats, did most of his business through such agents in Syria, Palestine, Spain, London, and Bruges.

The use of commission agents gave the consignor great flexibility and range of enterprise. He could send one kind of goods to a market one year and then switch to another place or commodity next year if the prospects seemed better. He could trade in as many towns and countries as he wished without leaving his own business premises or having to meet the overhead and operating costs of running branches of his own. The agent knew local conditions, and since he lived on his commission earnings he was likely to be energetic in discharging the tasks assigned to him. Sometimes he was too energetic and sold his patron's goods too cheaply or bought goods too dearly. At any rate, he was frequently scolded on those grounds, possibly justly but often on the sound working rule that it was bad form for a principal ever to express anything but dissatisfaction with the actions of his agent.

The advantages of the commission system were not gained without cost. Contact could be maintained only by voluminous correspondence. One Italian merchant, Datini of Prato, operated a business which touched all the Italian cities, Spain, France, Bruges, London, North Africa, and the Levant. He dealt in spices, arms and armor, cloth, religious pictures and ornaments, cotton veils, fruit, wool, handkerchiefs—anything, in fact, that promised a profit in an age when there was seldom enough business to make a man rich by handling only one commodity. From his numerous agents came 120,000 letters in fifty years, and it is safe to assume that he and his clerks wrote at least as many. The correspondents described conditions, reported good and untoward events, gave advice, sought instructions, and excused themselves from responsibility for bad bargains. On the strength of their information, which sometimes arrived too late, Datini must make his decisions, conscious that the news might be stale by the time it reached him or that it had been sent simultaneously to all his competitors. The sedentary merchant could not afford to have a sedentary mind or pen if he was to make money in a world of trade by remote control.

Medieval Money. The ancient European world was acquainted with the use of metal money, not merely in the Mediterranean lands but in the barbarian north and west as well. Gauls and Britons had gold coins before the Roman conquests; they even had skillful counterfeiters who coated copper disks with a film of gold. The Germanic peoples knew the precious metals both as medium of exchange and as measure of value. The earliest known Anglo-Saxon laws (about 700 A.D.) fixed fines for offenses: the penalty for striking off a man's nose was sixty shillings; that for killing a cat was fourpence. Payments to church, king, or to the tribute-imposing Vikings were made at least partly in money. When barter took place or when rent and other dues were paid in kind a money value was often attached to the goods. It is therefore incorrect to picture early medieval northern Europe as being in the grip of a "natural economy" in contrast to a later "money economy." The contrast was rather one of degree, of more or less use of money.

No coinage could be maintained without an adequate supply of precious metal. Central and western Europe had considerable mineral deposits of silver but little of gold. During the centuries following the collapse of the Roman Empire in the west the supply of gold seems to have been drained away into hoards, into church decorations and ornaments, or to the east. The minting of gold ceased, and the silver penny (*denarius*), or a German variant called the mark, became the standard coin. The Frankish king Pepin was minting pennies by 755, and similar coins were struck by English monarchs, archbishops of Cologne, and other owners of mints. For petty retail purchases the penny was too valuable, and was therefore cut into halves or even quarters—the latter known as a *quadrans* or a farthing. For large transactions the penny was too small; we know of one thirteenth-century payment made in 6,000 pennies and 12,000 halfpennies. Twelve pennies counted as a shilling (*solidus, sou*), and twenty shillings as a pound (*libra, livre*); but shillings and pounds were "money of account"; they were not actually minted.

The movements of gold within and without the Moslem world (see Chapter IV) were reflected in the history of gold currencies. Constantinople had a gold coin known as the *besant, bezant,* or *byzant,* while the Moslems produced one called the *dinar.* Each of these was acceptable in the backward west and north; in fact the dinar, rechristened the *mancus,* circulated and had by 800 become the unit of value for large transactions in that part of the continent. As more gold passed into the non-Moslem world, Kiev began to make its own gold coins in the tenth century; in the eleventh the Italian cities imitated the Sicilian gold coins and the Christian princes who had begun the recapture of Spain imitated the dinar; in the twelfth these rulers, along with some German emperors and bishops, began to make gold pennies. Finally, in the thirteenth century, the Italian cities were getting sufficient gold from the Moslem world or from Russia to permit them to mint gold coins of their own. Florence issued the florin in 1252; soon Venice produced the ducat, Spain the pistole, England the noble, France the louis d'or, and Germany the gulden. The leading currencies thus became bimetallic and the relative value of the two metals was officially fixed.

Maintaining a satisfactory coinage has rarely been an easy task, and medieval coins were defective for at least four reasons. In the first place, minting methods were simple, and skilled rogues could easily counterfeit or tamper with coins. Most penal codes condemned the false coiner to the loss of a hand, but some ordered him to be boiled alive. In the second place, too many kings, nobles, bishops, and cities possessed the right to issue coins. In late medieval Germany there were about six hundred money-makers; during the disintegration of the Frankish kingdom three hundred vassals claimed the right; in Italy each city had its own currency. England remained comparatively free from this evil and was the first country to centralize control of minting. The French kings tried to do likewise and by 1300 had reduced the number of currencies to about thirty. The German cities strove to conform to a common standard, but the general picture was one of great diversity. When money talked, it spoke as many languages as did the builders of the Tower of Babel.

In the third place, there was little stability in the precious metal content of the coin. To its owner the mint was a source of revenue. He charged a fee (*seigniorage*) for minting bullion or reminting old coins, and might claim the right to remint—or to raise the official value of existing coins—as often as he pleased. If the new coins contained less precious metal than the old ones, their value fell and prices rose. The increase in the price of *local* produce might not be in full inverse ratio to the decline in the quantity of silver in the coin, since the inertia of customary prices, consumers' resistance, and price regulation prevented a seller from doubling his prices if the silver in a penny was reduced by half. But goods brought from abroad might mount in cost in full proportion to the depreciation, because the foreign exchange value of a coin was determined by the amount of precious metal it contained.

In days of war and empty treasuries the temptation to make a little silver go a long way was irresistible. The progressive debasement of currencies became a normal part of public finance in an age that had no printing press to produce paper money, few emergency taxing devices, and no bond-selling "drives." One French king, John "the Good" (1350–1364) tinkered with his coins eighteen times in a single year to raise money for his bit of the Hundred Years' War. His English antagonist was much more restrained, but the silver content of the English shilling was reduced by stages from 250 grains in the thirteenth century to 166 in the mid-fifteenth. Depreciation of silver pennies eventually made their purchasing power so small that larger coins were needed, worth four, twelve, twenty-four, or more pence. These groats, gros, grossi, or "thick pennies" were in turn progressively debased. People therefore turned more eagerly to gold coins, only to see them depreciated during the fifteenth century. Medieval money refused to discharge the first duty of a standard of value: it would not stand still.

The fourth defect of medieval currency was the lack of a universally accepted ratio between the values of gold and silver. Each government fixed, and changed, its own figure. At the end of the fifteenth century, for instance, 10 units of gold were equal to 98 units of silver in Spain, 105 in Italy, 110 in France, and 111.5 in England. If a man took 98 units of silver from England to Spain he could exchange them for 10 units of gold, for which he could get 111.5 of silver when he returned to England. How much profit he had left when the round trip ticket and other costs had been paid for, we cannot say, but we know that Venetians exported silver to Spain and North Africa and obtained gold in return. If there was much of this kind of transaction or much payment of foreign debts in bullion, a country's money supply would be disturbed as the metal which was undervalued went to lands where its worth was greater.

Behind the whole monetary situation lay the comparative scarcity of precious metals in face of all the things they had to do. The yield from Spain, central Europe, Russia, Africa, and a few other places had to meet the demands of decoration, currency, hoarding, and shipment to the Levant. Barbarigo and his fellow Venetians shipped silver and gold in every vessel that went to Alexandria, Acre, or Beirut. In 1433 the cash carried by the eastbound galleys was probably worth nearly as much as all the other goods on board. Consequently countries which had no gold or silver mines might grow alarmed if the amount of specie that came in was less than what they needed to send out. At least seven times during the fifteenth century England forbade the export of gold and silver, controlled exchange transactions, and ordered foreign merchants to employ part of the receipts from the sale of their wares in the purchase of English goods. While these were emergency policies to meet critical conditions, they indicate a general attitude. Only mature economic centers which imported at least as much as they exported could regard precious metals with indifference as ordinary commodities which, like cloth or spices, were normal subjects of influx and outflow.

"Paper" Money. Medieval trade fortunately did not depend solely, or even perhaps chiefly, on payment in coin. In that respect it resembled modern trade, in which only retail purchases are made with metal disks while the larger dealings are settled by checks or

printed paper money. Medieval commerce made its own money. It devised (or inherited from the ancient world) various methods for making payment in a distant place or at some future date without much movement of coin. These methods were developed by merchants, money-changers, and bankers, and by the thirteenth century documents which contained an order to pay or a promise to pay bridged the gaps of time or space, served as media of exchange, and made possible both the elaborate use of credit and the expansion of banking.

Payment without much transfer of coin or bullion was effected in various ways:

1. In the Champagne fairs, as we have already seen, the clearinghouse settlements largely canceled out the obligations of men who were buyers and sellers alike. These settlements covered more than the actual business transacted in Champagne, for when loans or purchases were made elsewhere it was often agreed that the sums due be paid at some forthcoming Champagne meeting.

2. In commercial towns banks of deposit had appeared by 1200. Into them a man could put his money and have it placed to his credit. If later he wished to pay a debt he went to the bank and authorized the banker to give the money to the creditor or to transfer it to his account. Eventually he wrote his order to the banker, thus making out a check; but until the sixteenth century a signature on a check was rarely accepted unless the signer testified in person that it was genuine. The transfer of money from one account to another in this way economized the use of coin.

3. In the modern world a firm which exports goods frequently does not import any; but the medieval trader who took or sent out goods usually bought "returns" and therefore had little or no payment to collect or make in a far place. If he did owe money abroad he faced a transfer problem. He could buy the necessary foreign coins from a money-changer and ship them to his creditor; but the cost of freight and the risk of loss made that method unwise and led to the development of bills of exchange and drafts.

Since the bill of exchange is one of the most important documents in commercial history, an effort to understand its nature and use is desirable. It seems to have begun as an acknowledgment of a debt to a foreigner and a promise to pay in the foreigner's currency by a certain date. It might read and operate as follows: "I, A. B. [Genoese importer], have accepted from you, C. D. [Alexandrian exporter], goods of the value of *xyz* pounds of Genoese money, and I promise to pay to you in Alexandria, in bezants of Alexandria, *pq* bezants to the pound, before [a certain date]."

This bill was sent to C. D. He sold it for bezants to some Alexandrian importer (E. F.) who owed pounds to G. H., an exporter in Genoa. E. F. sent the bill to G. H., who presented it to A. B. and collected pounds. Thus two debts between two remote towns were settled with one document and two local transfers of money.

From this original form the bill of exchange gradually developed more complicated features and uses. It could be "drawn" by the seller on the buyer, in which case it was an order to pay. Its full use will be explained when we see it at work in later centuries. (See Chapter XVI.) Meanwhile the Genoese importer, A. B., could make his payment in another way. He paid his pounds to some local money-changer or merchant who had an agent in Alexandria. In return he received a draft ordering that agent to pay the required sum in bezants, sent this draft to his creditor, who presented it to the agent and obtained his money. But whatever the actual procedure, payment over long distances in foreign currencies was effected by the passage of documentary orders or promises to pay. The supply of currency in circulation was not reduced as it would have been if coins were idling away their time traveling to and fro.

One of the greatest medieval transfer tasks was that of getting to the pope the various payments collected in every country, from Poland and Hungary to Scandinavia, England, and Spain. Some of these payments were revenues from papal estates, some were levies paid on special occasions, some were income taxes. The transfer was made by using the business machinery of the Italian international merchant-bankers. These men received the money in the country of origin and used it to buy goods. In England they purchased wool, shipped it to Italy, and paid the pope what was due to him out of their Italian funds. The Knights Templars also served as transfer agents for all kinds of clients. Their militantly Christian order, founded in 1118 to fight the infidel and care for the sick, the pilgrim, or the poor, acquired properties in east and west alike, had treasuries in many capitals, and operated fleets. It was therefore able to transfer bullion or to sell letters of credit or drafts by which money paid into one "Temple" could be paid out in any other.

Credit and Banking. Medieval economic life was permeated with credit. Professor Postan has shown that an unbroken series of credit sales stretched from the English woolgrower to the Polish purchaser of Flemish cloth. "Cash on delivery" was relatively rare. Lending and borrowing were equally all-pervasive, and the debtor-creditor relationship was found in all classes, from peasant to pope. The loans were of all kinds—short, medium, and long term. There were "consumption loans," spent on food, clothing, comforts, or luxuries; and there were capital loans, used to finance production or trade.

The needs of borrowers were met by both amateur and professional lenders. The former entrusted their spare money to merchants, money-changers, bankers, craftsmen, and peasants. Monasteries and bishops lent their surplus income or accumulated treasure to peasants and nobles; the abbots of Flanders and Lorraine were probably the largest lenders in those regions till the twelfth century, and almost lost their amateur status. As security they took a mortgage on land, mills, or other income-producing gages, and their foreclosures when debtors defaulted added greatly to church property. In villages the priest sometimes made loans, and in the towns traders advanced money or materials to craftsmen.

Of the professionals, the pawnbroker tided people in all walks of life over a temporary shortage of funds by lending them money on the security of personal property, from jewels, furniture, or clothes to the craftsman's tools. He rendered a very necessary service, took considerable risks, had heavy overhead and operating expenses, and his interest rates—up to 40 per cent on small loans—were therefore high. Consequently he was as unpopular as he was indispensable. By the fourteenth century Italians were to be found as far from home as Bruges and London conducting pawnshops; but like the Jews who preceded them, they provided funds for consumption rather than for production and trade.

The more important lender was the banker. He reached the claim to that title along two roads. In the first case, he might originally or mainly be a money-changer, to whose *banca* (bench or table) people came when they wished to exchange local coins for foreign ones. He traded in bullion, and sometimes operated the local mint, thereby becoming the ruler's financial agent. He sold drafts and toured the fairs changing money. From these predominantly exchange functions he passed on to take deposits, allowed depositors to withdraw their money on giving proper notice, and used their money as well as his own to make loans. He was doing all these things in Genoa by 1200. His depositors were promised interest or even a share of any profit he made on their money, and he obviously therefore was expected to put it to use. He was thus discharging the banker's functions of deposit, transfer, and lending.

Meanwhile traders developed these same aspects of banking business as part of their work, and it is difficult to decide whether some of them were not more money merchants than dealers in goods. A firm rarely ceased to handle merchandise; even the Medici at their fifteenth-century height placed trade first and banking second. The two went hand in hand, spreading out over the Mediterranean and then to northern Europe. Bruges in its prime swarmed with branches of the Italian merchant-banking houses which dealt in bills of exchange and made loans to the neighboring princes, lords, and cities. Lombards ran its pawnshops, while its own citizens changed money, took deposits, transferred money from one man's account to that of another, and showed that they had learned the inner secret of banking by lending so heavily that they never had enough cash in reserve to meet all their liabilities to their depositors.

Public Finance. No matter how high he climbed, no merchant-banker could feel that he had reached the pinnacle unless he enjoyed the honor and profit—and shouldered the risks—of serving the financial needs of town, city, state, territorial ruler, or high ecclesiastic, including the pope. "If great bourgeois fortunes were made in trade, the greatest merchant fortunes were made in finance, and above all in state finance" (Power). Yet the long, dreary record shows that the higher the standing of the patron the more probable it was that the risk would sooner or later overwhelm the honor and profit in disastrous ruin. Those who financed towns and cities might be able to keep a grip on the reins; but the creditors of king or pope were exposed to the possibility—or even the certainty—that their debtor would use his sovereign or spiritual power to rid himself of his obligations when they became too heavy. Royal credit ratings were especially low.

The capital needs of towns and cities were greater than could be met out of revenue. Large sums were wanted for building walls or rebuilding them as the population grew dense inside them or too thick outside them, for harbors, waterworks in the Mediterranean centers, defense and war. Some Flemish towns spent at least four-fifths of their revenue on defense. Borrowing was therefore a normal civic practice. Sometimes a town offered the lender an annuity for the rest of his life and even for that of his heir as well. In Genoa,

Venice, and some other cities a syndicate was formed to make a loan. As security it was given power to collect some of the taxes, and from this revenue it paid the interest or repaid the principal to creditors. It gradually expanded its operations and privileges until eventually it became manager of the whole civic financial system and in addition ran a bank of deposit, loan, and transfer. The Bank of St. George in Genoa was the most famous of these debt-servicing institutions; but like those in Milan and Venice it was frequently so strained by the city's demands for funds or by shortage of revenue that it had to suspend payment.

Royal and Papal Financing. The greatest prizes and pitfalls were connected with three financial services required by kings and popes. (1) Revenues might need to be collected, transferred, safeguarded, and put to use till spending time came. (2) Revenues might need to be spent before they were collected; the money must therefore be borrowed for a short term and repaid when the taxes came in. (3) Normal revenues were quite inadequate in wartime and must be supplemented by loans. To meet short-term requirements the borrower gave some kind of bill which he promised to repay at an early date. For longer loans the crown might "farm" its sources of revenue or hand over the enjoyment of a piece of royal property. It received its loan or was paid a regular annual sum by the farmer and let the lender or farmer recoup himself by managing and taking the income from the property, by collecting some tax, or by operating some profitable monopoly.

In the west the Jews were the first medieval high financiers. Then the Templars were prominent in the twelfth and thirteenth centuries. In addition to their transfer services already described, their castles in various places and their Temples in Paris and London offered safe deposits for treasure. The one in Paris was the chief cashbox of the French king, while that in London collected, guarded, and administered the royal revenue. The pope borrowed from them; kings, princes, nobles, and ecclesiastics ran what were virtually current accounts and occasionally overdrew them. In 1307, however, the French monarch rid himself of his heavy debts by trumping up a charge of vice and black magic against the Templars. The order was destroyed, and its treasure was divided between the pope and the king.

By that time Italians had climbed into the places of financial power. Bankers of Siena and then of Florence collected, transmitted, guarded, and invested the papal income or lent money when it fell short. Firms rose and fell, won favor and lost it, but never lacked successors. In the fifteenth century the Medici had the business, but by 1500 papal patronage had shifted to an Augsburg firm, the Fuggers. In France the Florentines took the place vacated by the Templars. In England Italians were as deep in royal finance as in the wool trade. They supplied the sinews of war for the first two Edwards (1272–1327). Since they were bankers for Paris as well as Westminster, the outbreak of the Hundred Years' War in 1337 promised profit whichever side won. That promise proved illusory, and Florence learned again that he who sups with royalty needs a long spoon. By 1345 Edward III owed the Bardi and Peruzzi a very large sum. The repudiation of his debt in that year, coming on top of losses in France, Naples, and Flanders, spread panic and ruin throughout Florence. Perhaps the Peruzzi deserved that fate, for although the firm's capital was only 90,000 florins it had lent Edward 600,000 florins, and he was not the only borrower. The credit seems too foolishly large for the capital foundation, even in war-profiteering times.

Florentine finance reached its peak in the Medici family. By 1400 the combination of international banking, papal favor, and trade in wool, cloth, silk, leather, alum, furs, and spices was putting the firm ahead of most of its rivals. Those rivals had used their political power to oppress or suppress craftsmen and wage earners, but the Medici, by keeping out of politics, won a reputation as "friends of the people." When discontent provoked revolt, Cosimo de'Medici emerged (1434) as "the people's choice." For three generations a Medici ran the business and the city. The third of the line, Lorenzo the Magnificent (died 1492), scrapped the constitution, became in effect a prince, lavished wealth on art, architecture, and letters, and played a part in international politics. But he was more competent in politics than in business. The firm was shaken when governments in England and Burgundy repudiated debts and when the pope transferred his patronage to other houses. Lorenzo postponed ruin by mingling the assets of the city-state with his own liabilities, but when France invaded Italy in 1494 the Medici reign ended for a season, and the business went to pieces.

While Italy led in big business, merchant-banking, and state financing, she had no monopoly of these fields. North German funds fed the capital needs of the Baltic lands. South German merchant-bankers served princes, exploited mineral deposits, and cut deep into Italian preserves during the fifteenth century. In the Low Countries the Louchard and Crespin families were lending wealth made in trade to the princes, lords, and towns of their region long before the Italians came north.

In France the Manduel family loomed large during the thirteenth century, but the most famous merchant-financier was Jacques Cœur (1395–1456). Son of a furrier, Cœur became a goldsmith and director of the mint at Bourges. His fleet of ships, laden with cargo and pilgrims, plied between Montpellier and the Levant. He had over three hundred factors and agents working for him. He operated a silk mill, paper mill, dyeworks, as well as silver, copper, and lead mines. He lent heavily to royalty and nobility and for fifteen years was the king's treasurer and master of his mint. His spending was as lavish as his earning. He owned a palace, abundant plate, and twoscore estates; he built an annex to Bourges Cathedral, founded colleges and chapels in at least three cities, and patronized the arts. But royal disfavor and a multitude of enemies among the merchants and nobles led eventually to his downfall, imprisonment, and death in exile.

In England the collection and export of wool fostered the growth of a comfortably prosperous merchant class. When Edward III defaulted on his Italian debts he turned for aid to a small group of about thirty English merchants who had become rich enough out of early war contracts and speculative profiteering to serve his needs. Yet within a few years, by about 1350, these men had all burned their fingers; "bankruptcy, imprisonment and temporary or permanent ruin was the lot of many of them" (Power). The general story is thus the same in all countries. Merchants who confined their enterprise to the plain of ordinary commerce had abundant risks to face; but those who went on to scale high peaks by serving temporal or spiritual rulers usually discovered that mountain climbing was as fatal as it was fascinating. Yet there was never any lack of men willing to take the risk. Perhaps each new climber was convinced that in his case "things are going to be different."

The Jews. As western Europe developed its commercial and financial class the Jew fell into the background or out of the picture. In the early Middle Ages he had traversed the east-west land and sea routes. But on the Mediterranean he soon faced growing Italian competition, and by the twelfth century the names of old Syrian merchant families had almost disappeared from the records of Genoese trade. Meanwhile traffic on the overland route from Kiev across central Europe had to contend with the lower freight charges on goods carried westward by sea, and was then deprived of supplies by the invasion of south Russia. Middle Europe now got its oriental goods from Venice or Genoa.

The Jew began his financial work as money-changer and lender. In the tenth or eleventh century he was the chief lender in many countries. At the lowest he was a pawnbroker and old-clothes dealer; in the middle he lent to farmers and small landowners; at the top, one Christianized Jew was papal banker and founder of a line that included a pope and the wife of a Sicilian king. In Poland he was the money-maker, and coins carried inscriptions in Hebraic script. Since the Christian ban on usury did not apply to him, he could engage in financial activities which were in theory out of bounds to Gentiles. But the exercise of these activities stirred up the hatred of debtors, especially of small farmers and landowners when they saw their pledges sold or their lands foreclosed; the profits of his activities were likely to be regarded as borrowable or heavily taxable by the rulers under whose special protection the Jews lived; and the activities themselves were eventually invaded by men who found ways to circumvent the prohibition of usury. Wherever the Italian or German trader and lender went in, the Jew was soon placed on the defensive, and his position was weakened by the fact that he did little solid trade in commodities.

Hostility to Jews flared out of that dislike of infidels which was generated by the crusades. It was fed by the debtor's dislike of his creditor. It led to occasional outbursts of mob violence, and to official hostility when a ruler felt that he could do without the services which the Jews were rendering, when he wanted to repudiate a debt, or when popular clamor called for it. Philip Augustus expelled the Jews from his French royal domain in 1182, but they were allowed to return later on payment of heavier taxes. In 1306 Philip IV evicted them, repudiated his debts, and seized their property. They were readmitted subsequently, only to be expelled a third time somewhat later. England drove them out of the country in 1290, after they had been evicted from many towns and sucked so dry by forced loans or heavy taxation that they were no longer any use to the crown. In 1370 they were driven from the Low Countries. Many German towns expelled them during the Black Death on such charges as that of having poisoned the wells; but they were readmitted when the hysteria passed, for the towns needed the taxes they paid, while traders, lords, and princes wanted access to their purses. Yet there as elsewhere their social status and economic strength were impaired by racial animosity and the rise of Gentile rivals. In Spain the tolerance which had been shown them by the Moor vanished with him; persecution culminated in eviction in 1492.

Medieval Capitalism. The question "Was the medieval economy capitalistic?" has sometimes been hotly debated. The answer naturally depends on one's definition of capitalism and on possession of enough evidence to permit an informed verdict. The most obvious and literal definition is that propounded by Professor Gras: "To the historian, capitalism is simply a system of getting a living through the use or investment of capital." If this definition is accepted, then every historical period, and even every prehistoric age since man got his first tools, has been capitalistic. All economic systems have been capitalistic. They have differed from each other (1) in the relative importance of capital goods or funds, when compared with that of land, labor, or management; (2) in the fields of enterprise which attract or require large quantities of capital; and (3) in the way the capital is accumulated and managed. The periods studied so far in this book are marked by different kinds of capitalism, to which Gras applies such adjectives as "pre-business," "petty," and "mercantile," while the periods still to be examined are labeled "industrial," "financial," and "national."

This view of capitalism as something which has always been with us is too simple and colorless to satisfy some scholars and others who are interested in—or excited over—certain aspects of "modern" capitalism. To Werner Sombart, who spent most of his life (1863–1941) writing and rewriting a huge work on *Modern Capitalism,* any economic system is marked by three characteristics: its *spirit,* outlook, purposes, and motives; its *organization,* including the way the factors of production are put together; and its *technique,* methods, equipment, and knowledge. To Sombart the spirit of capitalism is a striving for profit without limit, regardless of social consequences and free from control by church, state, or any other restraining force. The organization must be relatively large scale, while the technique must show a readiness to make innovations, a zest for careful planning and intelligent direction, and a careful weighing of means and ends. Since the medieval economy seemed in Sombart's eyes to lack these features or at least to be deficient in them, it was precapitalistic or non-capitalistic, and could only be described rather lamely as handicraftism.

From the description of medieval conditions in this and preceding chapters it will be apparent that there was enough capitalism to fill Gras' categories of pre-business, petty, and mercantile, and that while much enterprise fitted Sombart's handicraft pattern some large sections of it could not be squeezed in. Many opportunities were being exploited by men who owned (or had access to) capital and whose actions were inspired by the desire for as much profit as they could get. "By the end of the eleventh century the part played by capitalists in the exchange both of goods and money was considerable" (Pirenne). By the twelfth century the Flemish and Italian cloth industries were "based upon a wage system and an elaborate division of labor . . . and run by big entrepreneurs for an international market. . . . International trade and international finance, based upon an elaborate credit system, animated by the unbounded desire for gain and capitalistic to the tips of its fingers, was already in existence in thirteenth century Italy" (Power). The letters of Datini and Barbarigo show these men weighing their decisions with the utmost care, seeking to cut a cost here or make an extra ducat there, looking for chances to buy in the cheapest market or by limiting competition to sell in a dear market, and shifting their interests to any point on the map where the prospect seemed brightest. The ledgers of fourteenth-century merchants show that these men were conducting complicated businesses with intelligence, foresight, and a detailed knowledge of their financial position. There was no lack of capitalistic spirit, organization, or technique in the management of the great estates during the thirteenth century.

It may be true that the acquisitive instincts of medieval men were overlaid with religious and other non-economic interests; but if we examine secular sources of information men's motives often seem material rather than spiritual. It may be that the spirit of gain was subjected to control and restraint—political, religious, and economic (see Chapter X)—but some of these could be evaded, were not easily enforced, and were relaxed when the need was great or the pressure strong. It may be that the most powerful brake on the development of medieval capitalism was the slow rate at which capital was accumulated. The low productivity of the main occupation, agriculture, made the building up of capital a slow process, all too often undone by famine, murrain, or war. Similarly the yield from handicrafts left little over when simple consumption needs had been met. But the practice of investing money in trading ventures or of depositing it with money-changers, bankers, or merchants mobilized for active service much spare wealth that might otherwise have been consumed or hoarded by its owners. Further, if the medieval supply of capital seems meager by modern standards, the need was much smaller. The modern demand for great sums of fixed capital in railroads, factory buildings, machinery, power plants, and harbors had not yet been born. Capital was needed chiefly for operations, to be turned over, to be cast on the waters in expectation of its return; and there seems to have been no serious lack of funds to meet that kind of need.

The important question therefore is not "Was the medieval economy capitalistic?" but "How large did the more advanced capitalistic enterprises loom in the whole picture?" No precise answer is possible since we lack materials for measurement. It is clear that they dominated the towns engaged in the great export trades, the industries which supplied the goods, and the rural areas which supplied the raw materials. The export trades were almost certainly a small part of the whole economy. Their influence may have acted like a small cake of yeast, but the cake was too small to leaven the entire bread supply. The most we can say, therefore, is that it took all shapes, sizes, and kinds of enterprise to supply medieval wants; no single one could do the whole job.

BIBLIOGRAPHY

GENERAL BOOKS

Boissonnade, P., *Life and Work in Medieval Europe* (Eng. trans., 1927).

Cave, R. C., and Coulson, H. H., *A Source Book for Medieval Economic History* (1936), part ii.

Clapham, J. H., "Commerce and Industry in the Middle Ages," in *Cambridge Medieval History*, vol. vi, chap. 14.

Day, C., *History of Commerce* (1907), chaps. 6–13.

Fayle, E. C., *Short History of the World's Shipping Industry* (1933), chaps. 2, 3.

Gras, N. S. B., *Business and Capitalism* (1939), chaps. 1–3.

Kulischer, J., *Allgemeine Wirtschaftsgeschichte* (1928–1929), vol. i, chaps. 17–29.

Pirenne, H., *Economic and Social History of Medieval Europe* (1937), chaps. 4, 5.
Pirenne, H., "Northern Towns and Their Commerce," in *Cambridge Medieval History*, vol. vi, chap. 15.
Sée, H., *Modern Capitalism* (Eng. trans., 1928), chaps. 1–3.
Sombart, W., *Der moderne Kapitalismus* (1922), vol. i, pp. 31–309.
Thompson, J. W., *Economic and Social History of Europe in the Middle Ages* (1928), chaps. 17, 23.
Thompson, J. W., *Economic and Social History of Europe in the Later Middle Ages* (1931), chaps. 4, 5, 7, 9, 18, 19.

SPECIAL SUBJECTS OR COUNTRIES

Ashley, W. J., *Economic Organization of England* (1914), chaps. 2, 4.
Beardwood, A., *Alien Merchants in England, 1350–1377* (1931).
Byrne, E. H., *Genoese Shipping in the 12th and 13th Centuries* (1930).
Doren, A., *Italienische Wirtschaftsgeschichte* (1934), vol. i.
Lane, F. C., *Andrea Barbarigo, Merchant of Venice, 1418–1449* (1944).
Laurent, H., *Un grand commerce d'export au moyen âge* (1935).
Lipson, E., *Economic History of England* (1915), vol. i, chap. 6.
Power, E., *Medieval People* (1924), chaps. 2, 4, 5, 6.
Power, E., *The Wool Trade in English Medieval History* (1941), chaps. 1, 3, 6.
Power, E., and Postan, M. M., *Studies in English Trade in the Fifteenth Century* (1933).
Salzman, L. F., *English Trade in the Middle Ages* (1931).
Sée, H., *Histoire économique de la France* (1939).
Usher, A. P., *Early History of Deposit Banking in Mediterranean Europe* (1943).

ARTICLES

Bloch, M., "Le problème de l'or au moyen âge," *Ann. d'hist. écon.*, January, 1933.
Brinkmann, C., "The Hanseatic League," *J.E.B.H.*, August, 1930.
Brun, A., "A Fourteenth Century Merchant of Italy," *J.E.B.H.*, May, 1930.
De Roover, R., "Money, Banking, and Credit in Medieval Bruges," *J. Ec. H.*, supplement, December, 1942.
De Roover, F. E., "Early Examples of Marine Insurance," *J. Ec. H.*, November, 1945.
Hartsough, M., "Treatise on Book-keeping under the Fuggers," *J.E.B.H.*, May, 1932.
Lane, F. C., "Family Partnerships and Joint Ventures in the Venetian Republic," *J. Ec. H.*, November, 1944.

Lopez, R. S., "European Merchants in the Medieval Indies," *J. Ec. H.*, November, 1943.

Pirenne, H., "The Stages in the Social History of Capitalism," *Am. Hist. R.*, April, 1914.

Pirenne, H., "The Place of the Netherlands in the Economic History of Medieval Europe," *Ec. H. R.*, January, 1929.

Postan, M. M., "Credit in Medieval Trade," *Ec. H. R.*, January, 1928.

Postan, M. M., "Medieval Capitalism" (a bibliographical article), *Ec. H. R.*, April, 1933.

Postan, M. M., "The Rise of Money Economy," *Ec. H. R.*, 1944.

Reynolds, R. L., "Genoese Trade in the Late Twelfth Century," *J.E.B.H.*, May, 1931.

Reynolds, R. L., "In Search of a Business Class in Thirteenth Century Genoa," *J. Ec. H.*, supplement, December, 1945.

Stenton, F. M., "The Road System in Medieval England," *Ec. H. R.*, November, 1936.

Strieder, J., "Origin and Evolution of Early European Capitalism," *J.E.B.H.*, November, 1929.

Usher, A. P., "The Origins of Banking: the Primitive Bank of Deposit, 1200–1600," *Ec. H. R.*, April, 1934.

Verlinden, C., "The Rise of Spanish Trade in the Middle Ages," *Ec. H. R.*, February, 1940.

Encyclopaedia of the Social Sciences. Articles on Banking (Commercial, to the close of the 18th century), Bardi, Bills of Exchange, Capitalism, Jacques Cœur, Coinage, Fairs, Hanseatic League, Judaism, Marine Insurance, Medici, Military Orders, Putting-out System.

X

THE REGULATION OF MEDIEVAL INDUSTRY AND COMMERCE

The medieval craftsman or trader carried on his work in a community which endeavored to help him at some points but to regulate him at others. Control came from four quarters—the church, the town, the guild, and the territorial ruler in countries where there was one. The records of aid and regulation are voluminous and yet defective. They tell what was decreed, whether it began with "Thou shalt" or "Thou shalt not." But often we do not know the motive behind a command, the general trend or particular circumstances which produced it, the extent to which it was obeyed or enforced, or the effects and consequences. Interpretation of the source materials is therefore often difficult.

The Church and Economic Life

"The power of the church in the medieval town was ever-present and all-pervasive. It operated through the ritual of the sacraments, the jurisdiction of the ecclesiastical courts, the charitable foundations of the orders, through the pictorial teaching on church walls and windows, open-air sermons, public inflictions of penance, the celebration of saints' festivals, and in many other ways. There can be no reasonable doubt that the social teachings of the church, along with its other doctrines, were by one means or another impressed upon every townsman, in so far as he was capable of understanding them" (Thrupp). Few of those social teachings had, however, materialized in concrete rules of conduct. Murder, theft, and a few other crimes were naturally on the black list; but the seven deadly sins—pride, covetousness, gluttony, lust, anger, envy, and sloth—were, like the seven principal virtues—faith, hope, charity, prudence, temperance, chastity, and fortitude—not always easily translated into terms of the workshop, market place, or fairground. The exhortation to "do unto others as ye would that they should do unto you" might avail little against the peasant's urge to get all he could or the trader's love of haggling to the very last penny. It might be possible to love one's neighbor as oneself, but how far did neighborliness extend? To members of another guild, to the poor within the walls, the villagers beyond them, or the "foreigner" from another town or country? The constant call for the subjection of the individual's interest to the common good was not accompanied by any "particularized definition of the common good, as the citizen should have conceived it" (Thrupp).

Usury. At only three economic points—lending, selling, and the use of property—did the church become specific. Its condemnation of usury, i.e., the charging of interest, was not original, for Aristotle and Judaism had urged that loans be free of charge. It thought of the lender as one who parted temporarily with money for which he had no immediate use, and of the borrower as a person in need. The loan should therefore be a neighborly act. To exploit a fellow Christian's necessity was a deadly sin. The devil would take the sinner's soul, the church brand him a heretic, and the king get his worldly goods.

The chief weakness of this attitude was its oversimplification of the position of both parties. On the one hand, it would be a rare situation for a man, especially a townsman, to have no possible use for his funds save that of an interest-free loan. On the other hand, need and misfortune were not the only forces that led men to borrow. When humble villagers and townsmen sought loans of grain, cattle, raw materials, clothes, furniture, or money, they might do so in order to tide over a bad season or other disaster; but they might be borrowing to bridge the perennial gap between sowing and reaping, to secure a stock of industrial raw materials, or to set up a farm or shop. The large borrowings of nobles, churchmen, towns, and rulers were often for unproductive purposes—to build walls or homes, wage war, pay ransom, provide a daughter's dowry, or buy luxuries; but some were used to finance domain farming, buy more land, or conduct some other form of enterprise. In between these loans to the poor and the titled rich lay the whole class of debts incurred by traders, industrial organizers, and bankers, who hoped to profit by the use of other men's money.

Faced with such varied conditions, neither church nor state could maintain a simple attitude of hostility. Each was itself a large borrower. Kings repudiated debts, but when they were incurring them they had to agree to pay a price. Not even the pope could borrow free of charge, and papal records show payments frankly called *usura*, sometimes at rates as high as 28 per cent. While, therefore, the church took the debtor's side and sought to hold the line, it was obliged to admit exceptions or allow bulges in that line at such points as the following: (1) When the lender accepted the risk of losing his money if the enterprise failed, interest was legitimate. (2) If repayment was not made when it was due, interest was a just compensation for the delay and a fitting penalty for the breach of promise. (3) If the lender surrendered an opportunity to use his money in a venture that might have yielded him profit, he was entitled to interest. In these and similar cases the stress was on the status of the lender, on loss and risk. Not till the fifteenth century do we find church fathers like Antonino, archbishop of the financial city of Florence, admitting that loan capital had something to do with the productivity of an enterprise and was therefore entitled to reward. His flock had known that for at least two centuries.

These ideas influenced legislation in many lands. In Denmark a thirteenth-century code said interest on delayed repayment was legal. In 1390 the London city authorities ruled that any man who lent "for certain without risk" but charged interest was a usurer. In 1485 the English parliament legalized interest on overdue loans. Eventually, however, usury came to mean the imposition of excessive rates. Meanwhile the church severely punished in its courts those "manifest," "public," "notorious usurers" who openly ran a business as moneylenders or pawnbrokers, and ordered them to make restitution to their victims. At first it also compelled the larger merchant-lenders who operated in private to make restitution if it discovered, when hearing confessions or making wills, that they had engaged in usurious dealings. The restitution might be made to those who had been wronged if their names were known; otherwise the money went to "the poor" or to the church. At least one thirteenth-century firm, the Peruzzi family, collected capital from each partner to add a special share to the firm's funds. The profits on this share were devoted to charitable uses and were regarded as restitution for any transactions which fell under the charge of usury. After about 1350, however, the church seems to have concerned itself chiefly with the "degraded manifest usurer-pawnbroker," and to have nearly exempted "the merchant and financier from the stigma of usury and from liability to crippling actions" (Nelson) in its courts. The merchant princes gave generously to the church; but their gifts and bequests were regarded as philanthropy rather than as restitution.

The Church and the Just Price. In selling, as in lending, greed was anathema. Some church writers inherited the ancient aristocratic contempt for the trader; others condemned some of his methods. To St. Thomas Aquinas (about 1250) trade was an undesirable calling, a badge of man's fall from grace; but since it was a necessary (or inevitable) evil, it might be tolerated if the seller was content with a *just price.* Let him be satisfied with a return which covered his material costs and paid him for his labor; let him meet the needs of a modest living standard and give any surplus to the poor; then his activities would be lawful and Christian. Other writers, more realistic, were willing to let weight be given to (1) losses due to misfortune or miscalculation, (2) scarcity or abundance, (3) the labor involved in conveying goods from producer to consumer, and (4) the need for different rewards according to the *conditio,* the social class to which the worker belonged. By the fifteenth century Antonino, the Florentine archbishop, was ready to admit that a just price should cover these items and also *industria,* by which he meant the zeal, enterprise, and business ability of the seller. But all writers agreed that justice was violated when any man monopolized the supply of a commodity and sought to extract exorbitant prices from the consumer.

TOWNS AND THE FOOD SUPPLY

The church's views on price coincided with those of lay rulers, for the protection of the urban consumer, especially of his food supply, was an important duty of town or state, or both. The larger the town the greater was its dependence on supplies from afar and its danger of starvation in an age of poor transportation. The greater also was the percentage of wage earners in its population and the menace of riots if food became scarce or prices went too high. Consequently "no city of that time could depend for its food on the free operation of the law of supply and demand" (Lane). Two courses were open. The town could build granaries and buy, import, store, and sell food. Or it could forbid exports, insist that no supplies in transit be allowed to leave the town until they had been offered for sale, and regulate the practices of dealers in victuals.

The cardinal trading sins were *forestalling,* which literally meant obtaining goods before they got on to the market stall by buying them outside market hours, outside the market place, or outside the town walls; *regrating,* or buying in bulk in order to sell retail; and *engrossing,* i.e., buying so heavily that the available supply was cornered and none was left for other dealers. All these malpractices must be checked. In addition, weights and measures must be inspected and the sale of unsatisfactory goods prevented.

Public provision of food and regulation of the trader went back to Egypt, Greece, and Rome. The ancient policies were copied by Constantinople. There the Prefect of the City watched over the victualing guilds, controlled exports and imports, supervised weights, measures, and coins, and generally protected consumers and the court. Butchers must wait until the livestock arrived to be sold in the market. Any pork dealer caught meeting the pig drovers outside the city or buying from them secretly inside it was to be shorn of hair and beard, flogged, and expelled from the trade—a punishment inflicted on other kinds of offenders. Cattle vendors must point out the defects in their beasts to potential customers. Prices or profit rates were fixed. The prefect announced the price of fish each morning after studying the fishmongers' guild report on the size of the previous night's catch. The price of a loaf of bread remained constant, but the weight was increased if grain prices fell and reduced if they rose. Hoarding was a serious offense.

Throughout the rest of medieval Europe similar policies prevailed. In Venice and Florence the public provision of grain and some other foods was a normal part of city government. In England state and town regulations worked hand in hand. By 1202 the king was fixing the price of bread, and an act passed in 1266 laid down the principles which guided local authorities for more than five centuries in their periodical issue of the "assize of bread and ale." The weight of the loaf was to fluctuate with the price of grain, but the price of ale was adjusted in keeping with that of the materials from which it was made. In years of famine or distress the central government might fix other prices, such as those of eggs and poultry. But in normal times Westminster left to the local authorities the work of regulating prices, of safeguarding quality, and of checking forestallers or engrossers.

Attempts to protect the quality of essential commodities also went back to the ancient world. Greece and Rome condemned the adulteration of flour and wine, and the medieval attack on fraud was conducted along the whole front. Manor courts enforced the assize of bread and ale, fining bakers who sold bad or short-weight loaves, butchers who sold "putrid and unwholesome flesh and likewise very dear," and brewers—or brewstresses, for usually they were women—who sold weak or bad beer or who "did not send for the ale-taster." In the towns civic laws, guild ordinances, or state decrees dealt with the grosser offenses. Paris forbade the adulteration of beer, the misrepresentation of wine, the artificial coloring of butter, and kindred frauds. In London the city punished those who sold bad bread by fining them, standing them in the pillory, or dragging them through the streets tied to a hurdle, with the offending loaves hung around their necks.

How far these efforts achieved their objective we cannot estimate, but it is probable that the control of bread prices was fairly effective. A study of one English town (Norwich) shows that punishment did not deter culprits from further misdeeds. That town's most fertile source of municipal income was the offending brewer, but fishmongers, poulterers, and other victualers were fined year after year for violating the assize. If they had suddenly become lawabiding the city might have faced bankruptcy. Other records show the same unrepentant persistence in forestalling, overcharging, and trade trickery. It may be as unfair to judge the Middle Ages by the police dockets as it would be to judge our own times, but it is clear that original sin was not completely cast out by all the exhortations and control. It is equally clear that no government could prevent wide fluctuations in prices when famine reduced the supply and war or other disturbances blocked the channels of trade. Florence tried to keep the price of grain within sight of 10/– per unit of measurement during the early fourteenth century; but during the famine of the late twenties the city had to pay 38/– and the price touched 50/– in 1329.

THE TOWN AND ITS GENERAL ECONOMY

In watching over the interests of consumers all towns faced a common problem. In furthering and regulating the general interests of industry and commerce, they all had a common outlook, which can be labeled "localism" or "particularism." Medieval society has been described by Professor Heckscher as a "peculiar blending" of universalism and particularism. On the one hand there were features of universal unity and of uniformity. The church gave spiritual unity to Christendom, with a common form of government, language, code of conduct, and canon law. The Holy Roman Empire tried to restore some of that political unity which the pagan Roman Empire had achieved. Kings and landlords who owned estates in many regions, traveled great distances, married foreign wives, and subscribed to chivalric standards common to the whole European knightly class had a wide outlook on the world. Merchants evolved common rules to govern their transactions with men in or from remote parts.

Yet life for most people was focused on the village or the town in which they lived. There was no sense of nationality. A man was a Parisian, not a Frenchman, a Venetian, but certainly not an Italian, and in a town ten or twenty miles from his own he was regarded as a "stranger" or "foreigner." Villages a few miles apart waged bitter, unending feuds. Between town and country there need be no affection. Central national governments did not exist in most parts of Europe. Where they did, as in France, their effective authority did not reach far and they must leave much power in the hands of feudal subordinates who were often insubordinate. Even England, with its small area and its easy communication by land or sea between the various regions, came only slowly to political unity; yet it was the first country to do so. In short, the center of interest was the village pump or the town market square, and the circle had a small radius.

Any wide view of harmony between the interests of different towns or areas was therefore unlikely. Rather each town's hand was against every other town and even against the surrounding countryside. The aim of every civic government and of every voluntary association within the town was to protect and promote the business of its own people. The policy of Venice has been described as one of "outspoken, consistent, municipal egoism" (Heckscher), and the description fits medieval towns in general—not to mention modern ones. On occasion towns might unite to meet a common menace, as did the Hanseatic and Rhineland cities; but separatism was more marked than solidarity. In an expanding economy such as that of the thirteenth century there was a desire to get the lion's share of the additional business. In the less profitable stationary period which followed there was a struggle to keep what one had. Urban policy was based on the premise and fact of interurban rivalry.

Towns sought to protect or advance their interests in a variety of ways. In the first place, each tried to control the economic life of the surrounding countryside, to compel the villagers to sell their produce only to the town, to buy the things they needed only from it, and even to refrain from carrying on any manufactures which competed with those of the town. In the second place, the stranger was subjected to restrictions, whether he came to pass through, to trade, or to settle. If he was passing through with goods, he might be obliged to offer them for sale for at least two or three days or to sell them to city merchants who would then carry them forward. If he came to trade he must not sell retail, or deal with other foreigners except through a citizen broker. If he wished to settle he must spend years—from ten to as many as twenty-five in Italy—before he could acquire the full rights that went with citizenship. In the third place, the town sought freedom from tolls and harbor dues abroad, tried to get its merchants' goods into market or port on payment of lower charges than were imposed on those of its rivals, and endeavored to secure privileges for its traders in foreign cities.

How effectively this policy of preference or exclusion was pursued, or how far it was successful, we have no way of measuring. Stronger cities were more likely to get what they wanted at home and abroad than weaker ones. Between towns of equal strength there could be either conflict or a recognition that mutual concessions, sometimes embodied in formal treaties, were the better policy. The fairs with their freedom from urban restrictions offered a large loophole for unfettered trade. A town which wished to grow or needed to regain population after it had been ravaged by war or plague would have to be generous in its admission of immigrant craftsmen or traders. Where registers of freemen have survived they reveal that men from other towns within the country and from those outside it did gain admission to citizenship. Professor Reynolds finds that in thirteenth-century Genoa there were hundreds of "significant and insignificant" people from other Italian cities, from France and even England visiting or residing, contributing "a very live element in Genoa's business world," practicing their industrial crafts, selling, renting, taking apprentices, and investing in overseas ventures, "quite as born Genoese did." But they paid extra taxes as foreigners or their position was defined by some treaty between Genoa and their native city. Genoa was no "wide open" town, free for all comers. Even Bruges, which threw its doors open to foreigners, reserved such important occupations as brokering and money-changing to its citizens. Charity was not the only thing to begin at home.

THE GUILDS

Much labor has been devoted to the study of medieval guilds, yet we still know little about how they came into being and are unable to answer many questions concerning their extent, powers, effectiveness, progress and decline, or the reasons for some of the things they tried to do. On three points, however, there is no doubt. In the first place, medieval man, like his ancestors and descendants, was a born "joiner." In the second place, no medieval political authority was for long indifferent to the existence of any voluntary association which grew sufficiently strong or important to be noticeable, usable, taxable, or dangerous. In the third place, there was a bridge between the guilds of Hellenistic or Roman days and those of the Middle Ages. The *collegia* of the Western Empire may have disappeared, though there is reason to believe that they continued in some Italian towns, especially Rome and Ravenna. The *collegia* of Rome set the pattern for the guilds of Constantinople.

Guilds in Constantinople. From *The Book of the Prefect*, a tenth-century compilation of orders, we get a vivid picture of the manner in which enterprise was regulated in the capital of the Eastern Empire. Some of the rules were probably made by the guilds and approved by the prefect, but others were imposed by him. The guild officials were responsible for their enforcement, the prefect's staff helped and supervised the officials, and the state punished offenders. Even if the guilds began as voluntary associations they were now part of an elaborate bureaucracy, units for taxation, and groups responsible for certain kinds of unpaid service.

The ambitious aim of the ordinances, according to the *Book*, was to insure "that the human race may be governed fittingly and no person may injure his fellow." There was a high degree of division of labor, and each man must keep within his own bounds. The weaver could not be a merchant, the spinner could sell only yarn. Victualers must not encroach on the preserves of the perfumer, soapmaker, linen merchant, tavern keeper, or butcher "even in the slightest degree," under pain of the customary flogging, shearing of locks and beard, loss of goods, and banishment.

Applicants for admission to a guild must give proof of skill and good character. The banker had to be vouched for by respected and honest men willing to guarantee that he would not pare, cut, or put false inscriptions on coins. The notary must pass a severe test "to ensure that he has a knowledge and understanding of the laws, that he excels in handwriting, and that he is not garrulous or insolent, and does not lead a corrupt life, but . . . is serious in his habits, guileless in his thoughts, eloquent, intelligent, a polished reader, and accurate in his diction. . . . He shall also have received a general education, so that he may not make mistakes in formulating his document and be guilty of errors in his reading." Even then he could not be admitted if there were already twenty-four notaries at work in the city, but must await a vacancy.

The guildsman's actions were carefully ordered. The tavern keeper must close his doors at 7 P.M., in order to prevent the "habitual daytime patrons, if they have the opportunity of returning at night, from leaving intoxicated and shamelessly engaging in fights, deeds of violence, and brawls." The goldsmith must work in a shop on the main thoroughfare, so that he might have less opportunity for furtive fraudulent workmanship. The metal worker who adulterated his material, like the banker who tampered with coins, was to have his hand cut off. Joiners, plasterers, painters, and others who took contracts must finish one job before beginning another. Builders must take care that the foundations of walls, domes, or vaults were solid, and if a structure collapsed within ten years, except through an act of God, it must be rebuilt free. When guildsmen depended on imported supplies each member must be able to get a share of the available goods. If, for example, a rich silk dealer brought in a large stock of foreign purchases, he must be ready to sell some of it to his poorer colleagues at a profit of not more than 8½ per cent.

Guilds in Western Europe. We know very little about guilds in the west before A.D. 1000. During the eleventh century the documents concerning towns become less scanty and guilds of traders or craftsmen are mentioned in them. Associations of merchants appear, uniting men in the towns in which they operate or in those to which they travel. The name may be *hansa, gilda mercatorum,* or *fraternitas mercatorum,* which we can translate as merchant guild. By 1050 the merchant guild of St. Omer was strong enough to have a guildhall and to be providing funds for paving the streets or building the walls. In 1060 Scandinavian traders had a guild at Utrecht. In Flanders and France merchants' associations were probably nu-

merous by 1100, and during the twelfth century the hanses of many
towns joined in wider fraternities to smooth the path to some common market, such as that from Flanders to England or that between
the textile towns and the Champagne fairs. During the twelfth century scores of charters were granted to merchant guilds in England.

Meanwhile the twelfth-century records tell of guilds of makers
and sellers of different kinds of goods. The weavers' guild of Mainz
is mentioned in 1099, that of Cologne in 1112, those of London and
other English towns by 1133. There are guilds of dyers and fullers
about the same time. Paris had five guilds working on leather by
1150. A century later the prefect of that city compiled a register of
the laws and customs of about a hundred guilds, and this number
was equaled or exceeded in London, Frankfurt, Lübeck, and other
towns where industry and commerce became many-sided. Florence,
Venice, and the Flemish towns were well supplied with the guilds
they needed. Some towns, industries, or distributing trades, especially in the French provinces, had no guilds until late in the Middle
Ages; but in most towns of central and western Europe they were
in existence by about 1300.

The aspirations and policies of guilds were influenced by the kind
of town in which they operated and the character of the occupation
which their members carried on. Medieval Europe had towns of all
sizes and kinds. If we omit the lonely giant, Constantinople, with its
estimated million inhabitants, they ranged from the "big four"—
Milan, Venice, Florence, and Paris, each with about (or at least)
100,000—down through middle-sized cities of 50,000 people such as
Genoa, Barcelona, Cologne, or London to smaller yet important industrial and commercial places like Bruges, Lübeck, Nuremberg, or
Ypres, and then to communities of a few thousand inhabitants.

The towns varied greatly in the character of their economic life,
ranging from far-flung commercial-industrial-financial activities to
predominantly local production and trade. Most of them belonged
to the latter rather than the former end of the range. Their businessmen comprised, as Professor Eileen Power puts it, "a *petite bourgeoisie* serving an inelastic town market and grouped into the professional associations proper to such a market." Their guildsmen
work "for a local urban market in which demand and supply are
alike known and inelastic. In such a town there is no room or need
for individual businesses to expand, and it must never be forgotten
that the majority of the towns of the middle ages were of this type.

The whole egalitarian social policy of urban governments and town crafts and the whole body of canonist doctrine on such subjects as usury, the just price, and the fair wage rest upon the fact that the typical *milieu* of the urban middle class is one in which individuals cannot extend their share in that market beyond a certain limit without impinging on the standard of life of other individuals."

Where a town or occupation expanded beyond service of local needs to that of an elastic outer market, the situation and problems which the guilds faced would change. The *organization* of enterprise became more complex, a *haute bourgeoisie* took charge of it, and the *associations* of those engaged in it might have different purposes. Actually in the larger towns both kinds of market existed. The tailors, builders, barbers, shoemakers, and storekeepers were still limited to serving local customers. But merchants, clothmakers, and metalworkers could cater for both the home and the foreign market.

The Merchant Guild. The merchant guild sought to protect and help its members in their home town, on their journeys, and at their destination. Since it had often played a prominent part in obtaining whatever municipal self-government the town enjoyed, its aims might coincide closely with the town policies which have already been described—exclusive or preferential privileges in the local market, lower tolls or freedom from them on the road, and satisfactory trading facilities in other market centers. While seeking to protect its members against outsiders, the guild protected them against each other. Unfair competitive methods were forbidden. Any guildsman who bought merchandise must share it with another member if the latter had been present when the transaction occurred and wished to have some of the goods. In this way the richer traders were prevented from monopolizing supplies and the poorer brethren could get quantities suitable to their needs. The guild sometimes chartered vessels to provide adequate transportation facilities to a fair or an important market. To prevent that market from being glutted it might impose a stint on the amount of goods each man could send.

The merchant guild reflected the economic character of the town. In a small community of only local importance it seems to have been a group of the miscellaneous traders who met the needs of the town and adjacent countryside. If, however, its members served a wider market, problems would arise in the course of securing supplies for export. The merchant guild then sought to strengthen its members' hands in their dealings with those who made the wares. If these makers were organized in craft guilds of their own, the merchant guild or the town government which the merchants controlled exercised authority over the craft guilds and either made the rules or claimed the right to veto them.

In the English provincial towns, for instance, the dyers became the organizers of cloth production and sellers of the finished pieces. They had no dyers' guild—perhaps because there were not enough of them in any of the towns—but were members of the merchant guild. That body claimed for them a monopoly of urban dyeing and a ban on country dyeing. It regulated the dyeing processes to prevent bad work and occasionally fined a member for using illegal materials or methods. But it also controlled the weaving and fulling guilds, forbade weavers to take their own cloths to the fair or to sell them to any foreigner, and generally strove to make the textile craftsmen subservient to the merchant guildsmen.

The merchant guild, like all other kinds, was a brotherhood. If a member was sick or fell on hard times it came to his aid. When he died it gave him a good funeral and cared for his widow and children. Brawlers and scandalmongers were punished, especially if they injured the reputation of the group by their misconduct away from home. When two Leicester merchant guildsmen resorted to blows at Boston fair, they were fined a barrel of beer, to be drunk by the other members. The brethren ate together on feast days and worshiped together in the church of their patron, St. Nicholas.

Craft Guilds. The merchant guild was probably an omnibus in which different kinds of traders could ride. In the craft guild membership was limited to those who practiced the same craft or process, made the same kind of product, or sold the same kind of commodity. Voluntary association on this narrower foundation might be stimulated by the fact that people of the same occupation often lived, worked, and sold in the same street or quarter, drank at the same inn, and worshiped in the same church. That church might encourage the formation of such groups. In Venice the early guilds met in the cloisters of an abbey, dined in the refectory, kept their archives and funds in the sacristy, had their altar in the church, and paid an annual fee to the abbot. In London the link between economics and religion was sometimes strong. For instance, the smiths quietly took an oath, with their hands on the Gospels, to defend one another in disputes with other citizens, to work only for members of the group, and to cease work when curfew sounded. They made a casket into which each member put a farthing a week to provide a wax taper in honor of the Blessed Mary and St. Landus and to build up a fund for the relief of smiths who fell into poverty. Anyone who violated his oath was taken before the archdeacon's court, and if he offended three times he was excommunicated.

In the creation of craft guilds, politics was as important as religion. In the first place, a ruler might confer monopolistic privileges on some group. In return the guild made an annual payment, thus becoming a taxpaying unit. In the second place, a ruler, especially a town government, might regulate an industry or trade by putting an official at its head or by calling together those who practiced it and asking or commanding them to form a guild. Often this step was taken when some trouble had occurred in an occupation. "Divers dissensions" among the London builders in 1356 led the mayor to summon delegates before him. They described their trade customs, a code of rules was drawn up, and within a few years a full-fledged guild was in being. But whatever its origin, the craft guild moved toward the status of "an industrial corporation enjoying the monopoly of practising a particular profession, in accordance with regulations sanctioned by public authority" (Pirenne).

Craft Guild Policies. Guild ordinances touched the guildsman's relations with fellow members, non-members, members of other guilds, future members, dependent workers, and consumers. The spirit that animated them was one of comprehensive protectiveness; the group was to be protected from competition or injury by outsiders, the individual member was to be protected from the destructive, unfair, or fraudulent competition of his brethren, while both he and the consumer were to be protected from defective workmanship and poor or dishonest products.

The relative importance of these aims probably varied from time to time. When things were going well the guild might be less concerned with seeking or safeguarding its monopoly, but when depression or danger appeared every possible device was adopted to maintain the group's welfare against all comers and to prevent any one member from getting too much of the business into his hands. Professor Postan has pointed out that many of the available guild records belong not so much to the expansive part of the Middle Ages as to the subsequent "phase of lost horizons." "The monopolies, the regulations, the rigid control of individual enterprise, the barriers to the entry of outsiders, and most of the other measures of restriction were produced, rather suddenly and rather recently, in response to the declining trade and falling prosperity." Yet enough is known about policies in the earlier centuries to show that seeking or tightening an exclusive privilege was normal guild strategy both early and late.

Monopoly. Monopoly of the local industry or segment of trade was sought as an aid to assured income and a prerequisite of effective regulation. Some of the earliest ordinances and charters suggest that guildsmen valued it so highly that they were willing to pay a substantial annual price for it. For instance, the London weavers' royal charter of 1155 fixed £12—enough to buy about 3,000 gallons of wine—as the annual tax cost of their monopoly. At least ten other English occupations had guilds which made similar payments to the king in that century. In Rouen (in 1189) no tanner could ply his craft without the guild's permission, no man could be a butcher in Paris (in 1182) unless the brethren approved, and similar rules applied in many other places or occupations.

These monopolies were not easily maintained. They had to be guarded against infringement by producers or traders within the town and by those who lived outside. The London weavers spent two centuries struggling to maintain their grip of the industry against the attacks of the city government or of the cloth merchants. In 1355 they were defeated when the city fathers decreed that any citizen could engage in any craft without joining the appropriate guild, provided he obeyed the guild's ordinances and submitted to inspection by its officials. In industries where the raw material, equipment, and skill were easily acquired, where the market was expanding, or where merchants had worked their way into the organization of production, it was easier to aspire to guild monopoly than to achieve or hold it.

Competition from outside the town could be hurtful if rivals in suburbs, small towns, or villages were able to pick up the necessary skill, yet paid lower rents, taxes, food prices, and wages and were free from guild restrictions. When hard times came in the fourteenth century, Belgian guildsmen supplemented their rules against rural clothmaking by sending out "regular armed expeditions . . . against the villages in the neighbourhood, and looms or fulling vats were broken or carried away" (Pirenne). In England the introduction of the fulling mill after 1200 created a serious problem for the textile towns and their tax-paying guilds. The new equipment was driven by water power; the mills must therefore be located upstream where waterfalls or rapids could be harnessed, but the old clothmaking towns were situated downstream, where the rivers were slow. The new machines did the job more cheaply with less labor, and the urban fullers who had used their hands or feet were at a serious competitive disadvantage. The presence of the mills stimulated clothmaking in the adjacent countryside. The business of the urban weavers and fullers was in consequence so seriously injured that they became unable to pay the annual guild dues to the crown. In their lamentations to the king they asserted that the number of weaver-guildsmen had fallen three-fourths since the days of full employment. They urged that something be done, that city-made cloths be forbidden to go to the mills for fulling, and that urban cloth producers be prevented from putting out their raw materials beyond the city gates. Sometimes their prayers were answered in part, but the results were disappointing. Weaving and fulling alike migrated. The guild monopoly had little to do with starting the exodus and could do less to check it.

Apprenticeship. While every craftsman or trader was expected to be in his guild or to be working with its permission, entry was not free or easy. An adult newcomer to town must prove that he had the necessary skill and character, find sponsors, and pay entrance fees. The young man who wished to enter the occupation must undergo a period of training as apprentice to some guildsman. In the "indenture" which set forth the relations between master and pupil, the youth promised to be industrious, honest, obedient, orderly, and loyal. His master's commands he would obey, his goods he would protect from theft, waste, or injury, his trade secrets he would keep. Taverns and gaming houses he would not frequent, matrimony he would not contract. He would not run away or be guilty of any "folly and jollity" that might injure his master. In return he was to be taught all that appertained to the art, craft, or mystery, to be fed, clothed, often lodged, and chastised when he deserved it.

Since the apprentice of today was the journeyman or master of tomorrow, the guild was interested in the number of pupils, the length and character of their studies, and their career when their technical education ended. The city also was interested, for unruly apprentices disturbed the public peace, apprenticeship was one way to gain the freedom of the city, and there were fees to be collected. Guild and town therefore regulated the age at which an apprentice could be taken, the length of his training, the number of pupils to each master, and the tuition costs.

The training period varied greatly according to the amount of skill required. In London it was from two to fifteen years, but gradually settled down to seven, and in 1563 that term was imposed by the state on the whole country. On the continent the youth worked for two to six years in his master's workshop, and then spent three to five postgraduate years as a journeyman in other towns obtaining further experience. The number of apprentices a master could take was usually limited, to insure that each pupil received adequate attention, to keep down the number of skilled workers seeking admission to the craft, and to obviate such unfair competition or defective work as would result if some masters were getting many goods made by immature or unpaid learners.

When the apprentice had "served his time" he might wish to become a master craftsman. If so, he went through certain procedures and paid for initiation as burgess and guildsman. His skill was tested, his workshop inspected, and he must prove that he had sufficient funds to make amends for any damage done to customers' goods. If he met all requirements he gained the right to practice his craft. Possibly he did so as a junior partner, and maybe a son-in-law, of some master craftsman. Not all ex-apprentices could take this step at once. The town might insist on a preliminary period of wage earning and travel. A wife with a dowry might be an indispensable economic asset not yet acquired. If capital was lacking, some time must be spent in earning and saving. But a journeyman's wages provided little surplus for savings, and some ex-apprentices never passed into the master class—possibly because they did not want to—but remained journeymen all their lives. As the Middle Ages drew to a close the barriers that must be surmounted to reach independent status seem to have risen higher, and it is probable that in earlier times the number of young men able or willing to become their own masters has been exaggerated.

The Regulation of Enterprise. The new master entered a world of disciplined production and sale. The rules reflect a mixture of motives; some spring from the guild's desire to insure good work and fair, equal, competitive conditions, while others suggest the community's desire to protect the consumer. Work on Sundays and saints' days was banned, to prevent the impious from making more money than the pious and to safeguard true religion. Night work was forbidden, because candlelight was too poor for accurate work and the noise disturbed sleepers. Bad workmanship was attacked by every guild and town. Penalties were prescribed, for example, for the weaver who put faulty material into his piece, the fuller who lost or damaged a customer's fabric, the tailor who pawned cloth intrusted to him, the butcher who mixed tallow with lard or sold dead dog or cat, and the jeweler who used colored glass. Work must not be done in chambers, cellars, or back rooms, but "only in halls and shops next the road in sight of the people," so that the officers of the guild could examine the work in progress at any time. Punishment ranged from confiscation of the faulty wares, a fine, or scolding to destruction of the worker's equipment, a period in the pillory, and eviction from the craft.

Many ordinances sought to secure fair play and equal competitive conditions between rivals. Masters must not try to steal one another's workmen or customers or strive to gain an advantage in securing raw materials. Goods must not be hawked through the streets, but be offered only in shop or market. At St. Omer the seller was forbidden to attract attention by blowing his nose or sneezing when customers were around. The boatman bringing beer to Bruges must not display any signboards singing the praises of his cargo. The professional ethics of medical and legal practitioners are a survival (or revival) of these rules against blatant solicitation or advertisement.

Restrictions on the number of apprentices, journeymen, and implements or on the quantity of goods produced might spring from a lasting desire to let all share in a limited local market; or they may have been the product of a period of depression. The same desire might cause guilds to frown on innovations or inventions which helped one master to increase production or reduce costs but threatened to disorganize the established way of doing things and injure the rest of the guildmen. An invention which could be afforded by all masters might be welcomed, as when the weavers of Speyer accepted the spinning wheel in 1297. How far guild opposition actually retarded technical advances we cannot say, but the attitude certainly was cautious and suspicious. The ideal was "stability of conditions in a stable industrial organization" (Pirenne), "order rather than progress, stability rather than expansion" (Lipson). "Free competition," if such an idea was conceived, seemed to be a dangerous disruptive notion, the enemy of the existing order.

The guild fixed minimum prices and maximum wages, but in the former task it would be subject to a civic or state veto. In 1298 the London city fathers sent the coopers to jail for having raised the price of barrel hoops. In the same year they denounced the carpenters for gathering together in a "parliament" and binding themselves "by corporal oath not to observe a certain ordinance made by the mayor and aldermen touching their craft and their daily wages." The regulation of wages by guild, city, or state became important during and after the Black Death, when the surviving wage earners took advantage of their scarcity value to ask for higher pay. The English king in 1349 and parliament in 1351 tried to force people to work at the wage level prevailing before the pestilence, and half a dozen laws were passed during the next 150 years to check demands for "outrageous and excessive hire." Guilds and towns supplemented the state's action. In France a royal ordinance of 1351 limited the increase in wages and prices in the Paris region to one-third. In Castile the legislature fixed maximum wages in 1351. In no country were these efforts successful; some increases in rates had to be allowed, and wage earners continued to ask for more. The hours of labor were regulated, and absenteeism was fought by the guild, with civic or state support. All the hours of daylight must be used. This meant a working day from 4 or 5 A.M. to 7 or 8 P.M. in summer, and from dawn to dusk in winter.

Social Activities. The craft guild had its important social aspects, and religion, mutual aid, amusement, or politics sometimes seemed more important than business. The brethren were exhorted to "be loving and gentle and friendly one to another," to eschew quarrels, refrain from slander, and abstain from calling each other liars. If a member got into legal trouble or became sick, the guild aided him. At his death it gave him a decent burial and devoted some thought to the welfare of his dependents. Since towns had high death rates at all times and were severe sufferers when the plague came, the sickness and death benefits must have been very important. Often the guild had a livery, a common type of dress to be worn at such functions as processions, banquets, and masses. Nearly every guild had its patron saint, chapel, altar, or at least a candle burning in a church. In some English towns the guilds were responsible for the presentation of the Corpus Christi plays, a series of tableaux or scenes depicting human history from the Creation to the Day of Judgment, performed on Corpus Christi Day on movable platforms at different points in the town.

Guilds in the Later Middle Ages and After. In many occupations or countries guilds retained or even tightened their hold as the Middle Ages drew to a close and in the centuries that followed. This was due in part to the grip they had on the city government or the support they received from the state. In France the crown, striving to strengthen its power over the feudal nobility and towns, saw in the guilds a useful instrument for controlling industry and collecting revenue. It therefore favored them, made membership compulsory, established guilds in the many towns which lacked them, but regulated and taxed them vigorously. In Germany guilds used their control of the town to safeguard their position. In London citizenship was confined to the members of about ninety guilds, and in many English provincial towns the guilds had much to do with municipal affairs.

Economic factors helped many guilds to retain their vitality. The local urban market remained the only one available for many producers and traders long after the Middle Ages ended. Since the character and organization of enterprise remained unchanged, the associations of entrepreneurs could carry on their work, holding more tightly than ever to their privileges during the lean periods as well as during the centuries of stability or growth which followed. Like privileged groups in all times and places, they tended to become exclusive clubs. Entry became less easy. In England some of the richer London guilds strengthened their monopoly by securing charters of incorporation from the crown.

When we pass from the *petite bourgeoisie* with its inelastic local market to the *haute bourgeoisie* serving larger elastic domestic or foreign markets, the story is similar at some points but very different at others. In the export trades association among merchants might still be essential to safety and success. When, for example, English cloth exporters set out in the late fifteenth century to reestablish themselves on the continent in the face of fierce Hansard opposition, their only hope of getting a footing lay in standing and working together, seeking to create what was virtually a *hanse*. The result was the "regulated company," which carried the principle of regulated monopolized trade on into the early modern world. (See Chapters XV, XVI.)

The differences in the story sprang from the character of the organization in the great industries. There the crucial problem was the relationship between the merchants or great industrialists who bought the goods or organized their production and those who performed the manufacturing processes. The former might be members of a merchant guild, as in provincial England; or they were in a powerful "major" guild of their own, such as the Florentine clothworkers' *Arte della Lana*. In any case they and their guilds ran the city government and used it to control the craftsmen's "minor" guilds as well as the wage earners. Between merchant, master, and wage earner there was plenty of room for conflict of interests. Wage earners organized journeymen's guilds, struck to gain higher wages when prices rose or labor was scarce, and resisted wage cuts when times were bad. Merchants might seek, or be forced by depressed conditions, to lower the price they offered for work or goods, and masters found themselves between the upper millstone of these reduced payments and the nether one of journeymen's refusal to share in the loss.

The great industries and the towns in which they had grown up therefore witnessed many storms during the fourteenth and fifteenth centuries. Italian, Belgian, and Rhineland master craftsmen and wage earners attacked their merchant-rulers, demanding a share in city government or even full control. For a time the producing guilds triumphed over the traders, but once they were in power, the victors broke up into fierce factions, each seeking its own narrow advantage. Weavers fought fullers, wage earners quarreled with masters, and merchants were humiliated. Eventually the craft guilds lost their political grasp, and civic control passed back into plutocratic hands or forward into those of some dictator like a Medici or a territorial ruler like the Duke of Burgundy. But in the meantime the merchants had deserted the turbulent towns as sources of supply, and encouraged production in small towns or villages where guild rules were unknown and costs were lower. The old industries emigrated from their urban homes to more hospitable regions, and the new industries that were emerging during the late Middle Ages usually grew up in places which had no medieval industrial history. Craft guilds suffered as the members found their occupations gone. Towns which had produced large quantities of goods, many rich men, and some great buildings lost the first two and had little more than the third to remind them of their former prestige.

Given the character and organization of the great industries, these conflicts and consequences were perhaps inevitable. In part they were symptoms of the strains to which those parts of the European economy were increasingly subjected when the long secular trend of expansion gave place to at least a century of fixed or shrinking opportunity. Postan's study of England and Pirenne's examination of western continental Europe reach the same conclusion. The parts of the picture they have painted reveal "an age of recession, arrested economic development and declining national income" (Postan). The great industries, like the great farms and ranches, felt the pinch. The entrepreneur tried to adjust matters at the expense of his producers; the latter sought to defend their standard of living at the expense of him and of everybody else except their own craft or process. The friction generated much heat, but little light or power.

Yet the closing years of one era are usually the beginning of a new one. Some developments in politics, religion, and economics, already under way during the fifteenth century, were destined to give new stimulus and character to the early modern world which was just around the corner.

BIBLIOGRAPHY

Cave, R. C., and Coulson, H. H., *A Source Book for Medieval Economic History* (1936), pp. 169–182, 193–259.

Consitt, F., *The London Weavers' Company* (1933).

Dempsey, Bernard W., *Interest and Usury* (1943).

Gras, N. S. B., *Industrial Evolution* (1930), chap. 5.

Gross, C., *The Gild Merchant* (1890).

Hauser, H., *Travailleurs et marchands dans l'ancienne France* (1920).

Kramer, S., *The English Craft Gilds: Studies in their Progress and Decline* (1927).

Lipson, E., *Economic History of England,* vol. i (1915), chaps. 6–8; vol. iii (1931), chap. 5.

Pirenne, H., *Economic and Social History of Medieval Europe* (1937), chaps. 2, 6, 7.

Saint Léon, M., *Histoire des corporations et métiers* (1923).

Salzman, L. F., *English Industries in the Middle Ages* (1923), chap. 11.

Salzman, L. F., *English Trade in the Middle Ages* (1931), chaps. 4–6.

Thompson, J. W., *Economic and Social History of the Middle Ages* (1928), chap. 28.

Thompson, J. W., *Economic and Social History of Europe in the Later Middle Ages* (1931), chap. 17.

Unwin, G., *The Gilds and Companies of London* (1908).

Unwin, G., *Studies in Economic History* (1927), part ii, essays 1, 2.

ARTICLES

Boak, A. E. R., "The Book of the Prefect," *J.E.B.H.*, August, 1929.

Carus-Wilson, E. M., see articles cited in Bibliography of Chapter VII.

Evans, A., "The Problem of Control in Medieval Industry," *Pol. Sc. Q.*, December, 1921.

Meyer, E. F., "English Craft Gilds and Borough Governments in the Later Middle Ages," *Colorado University Studies,* February, 1929; February, 1930.

Nelson, B. N., "The Usurer and the Merchant Prince," *J. Ec. H.*, supplement, 1947.

Thrupp, S., "Social Control in the Medieval Town," *J. Ec. H.*, supplement, 1941.

Thrupp, S., "Medieval Gilds Reconsidered," *J. Ec. H.*, November, 1942.

Encyclopaedia of the Social Sciences: Articles on Apprenticeship, Aquinas, Guilds, Journeymen's Societies, Just Price, Usury.

XI

THE MAKING OF EARLY MODERN EUROPE

The five centuries which separate the Middle Ages from our own day can be divided into two main periods—early modern and modern—with the eighteenth century as a very broad boundary line. The first period retained many features that were medieval, for complete breaks are rare in economic history, or in history generally. At the same time it developed characteristics which have led historians to speak of it as the period of "the commercial revolution" as distinct from "the industrial revolution" which came later; as "the age of mercantilism" in contrast to the subsequent age of free enterprise and trade; and as the era of "early capitalism" which grew during the nineteenth century to high, full, adult, or mature capitalism. Each label has its merits, but no one of them suffices to unlock the doors to an understanding of the reactions which took place between physical resources, technologies, and social institutions between 1450 and 1750. The present chapter will therefore be devoted to an examination of the general economic features of the period and of the environment in which men carried on their work.

Population. Though reliable figures are very scanty, it seems evident that Europe's population increased considerably between 1450 and 1750. The increase was not continuous or general, and probably did not become marked until after 1650 or even after 1700. There were many plagues and famines, and although the former were not as serious as the Black Death, famine might cause widespread death from starvation. There were many wars, some fought with prolonged ferocity, especially when rebellion or religious differences embittered the struggle. The Thirty Years' War (1618–1648) is said to have reduced the population of the German states from over 20,000,000 to less than 14,000,000, but the latter figure is probably too low. After 1650, however, the wars were less destructive, and some countries were spared their ravages. Throughout the period high birth rates were countered by high death rates, especially of infants and of mothers at childbirth; medicine and surgery were still

213

crude, public health advanced little beyond rudimentary water supplies and quarantine precautions, and there were such special causes
of high mortality as summer epidemics in towns and scurvy or shipwreck among sailors.

In these circumstances the population history of different parts of
Europe varied greatly. England had by 1600 more than regained
its losses, and during the next 150 years the population nearly doubled. The number of people in France oscillated violently about the
20,000,000 mark from the fourteenth century to the early eighteenth,
and then grew rapidly to about 25,000,000 in 1750. The population
of Spain rose during the "golden age" of her imperial expansion in
the sixteenth century but declined during the seventeenth, while
that of Portugal was weakened in quantity and quality by the drainage of men for the ships and armies that were needed for her eastern empire. Holland and Scandinavia probably resembled England
in their vital statistics. Germany's population rose until the mid-
sixteenth century, was cut down during the long war after 1618, and
recovered slowly when peace came. For Europe as a whole Willcox
estimates a total of 100,000,000 people in 1650 and of 140,000,000
in 1750. By the latter date some countries could regard a growing
population as a normal phenomenon; but rapid growth did not become common to all Europe until the nineteenth century.

Occupations. The occupations Europeans pursued showed some
shift in relative importance. Agriculture remained the main field of
employment, and most of it was subsistence farming with methods
of tillage or animal husbandry that showed little change. But the
needs of capital cities, especially Paris and London with populations
eventually approaching the half-million mark, of provincial towns,
industries, ships, and larger armies all helped to carry farther and
wider that demand for food and raw materials which had been so
insistent in medieval Italy and the Low Countries. Where this call
of the market was heard and could be answered because of improved mercantile or transportation facilities, agriculture became
more commercial, greater attention was given to cash crops, some
improvement was made in the treatment of the soil, and the area of
wild land was reduced. There was, however, no spectacular frontier
movement comparable to that which had swept eastward in the
Middle Ages and no such fundamental change in methods as came
in the modern period.

In industry the old staple woolen and linen manufactures resumed their expansion and added new kinds of fabrics, such as light worsteds and fustian (a mixture of linen and cotton yarns). The invention of the knitting frame (about 1600) made possible the production of stockings on a relatively large scale. There was a greater use of more vivid dyes and a higher skill in weaving patterns into tapestries and silk cloth or in printing them on the surface of linens or cottons. The supply of raw cotton increased with the expansion of trade with the Levant, the discovery of the ocean route to Asia, and the spread of production in the West Indies. The supply of raw silk mounted when the output of Italy was supplemented by imports from the Orient. The slave trade and America offered new markets for fabrics ranging from the cheapest to the best, while kings, princes, and aristocrats encouraged the introduction or expansion of luxury textile manufactures.

More important than the textile developments were those in the extraction and use of minerals. Improvements in the equipment or methods of mining, smelting, and refining metals caused an expansion in the supply of silver, copper, lead, tin, zinc, and iron, a greater output of such alloys as bronze, brass, and pewter, a highly developed metal-goods industry of vast variety, a raid on the forests to obtain fuel, and a consequent ability to meet the demand for metal weapons as well as for civilian goods. Where coal was available and cheap it supplemented or displaced wood as fuel in many industries which needed much heat, such as brewing and distilling, evaporating brine, or producing glass, bricks, pottery, alum, soap, and paper—all of them industries which grew in importance during the period. As shipbuilding expanded, the cutting and shaping of lumber and the production of pitch, tar, and other naval stores were stimulated, both in northern Europe and in North America. The development of the Newfoundland cod fisheries brought new business to the salt industry, while many commodities that were imported from America created new processing industries, such as the manufacture of tobacco and the refining of sugar. European industry thus became more competent in more fields.

In spite of these substantial advances in agriculture and industry, the center of interest is nevertheless in commercial developments. Traders now distributed a greater variety of goods in larger volume, not only over the markets of Europe but in smaller measure over the islands and coast lines of other continents. They handled the increasing quantity of oriental produce that reached Europe, bartered miscellaneous wares for slaves in Africa, and distributed commodities that came from the Americas. To finance this European and Greater European commerce they elaborated the older types of business firm and when necessary supplemented them by using joint-stock accumulations of capital. To obtain the kind of wares they needed they sometimes financed or even initiated and supervised industrial production. They wrestled with more complex banking and currency problems, improved their coastal and ocean shipping services, and developed more comprehensive forms of insurance. Favorable location, political changes, and aggressive efficiency helped new trading centers to advance at the expense of the medieval leaders. Government policies sometimes sought to foster domestic trade, stimulate foreign commerce, and preserve for the parent land and its colonies the benefits of empire. In a variety of ways, therefore, it is the enterprise of the commercial class that gives the early modern period its chief economic characteristics.

That enterprise operated in an environment which had changed considerably since the great economic advance of the thirteenth century and continued to do so. The changes were associated with the Renaissance, the Reformation, the rise of large territorial states, and the maritime discoveries. These intellectual, religious, political, and geographical developments had far-reaching economic consequences.

Economic Aspects of the Renaissance. One manifestation of the Renaissance was a growing interest in the physical world, which paved the way for the researches in physics and other fields during the seventeenth century. The men whose names stand high on the roll of early modern science were usually far from being cloistered students. They were men of affairs, interested in both the "pure" and the "applied" significance of the problems they sought to solve. Leonardo da Vinci (1452–1519) was artist, architect, poet, musician, sculptor, civil and military engineer. He observed and designed improvements on the industrial equipment of his day; he dreamed of a flying machine that would bring him fame and of a needle-polishing machine that would earn him a fortune; he filled notebooks with sketches of spinning machines, power looms, roller bearings, universal joints, gears, lathes, screw cutters, turbines, and a steam cannon.

Increasingly during the next two centuries men wrestled with the problems of "natural philosophy," not merely, as one Englishman wrote in 1648, for "the great delight and pleasure" of the work itself but because "there is also much real benefit to be learned" by men concerned with the technical aspects of production. Mining, metallurgy, ship construction and operation, building, painting, dyeing, the processing or finishing industries, and agriculture all could ask questions. It might be profitable as well as interesting to search for an answer by experiment, observation, trial and error.

Another manifestation of the Renaissance was the growth of new tastes, desire for comfort, and even love of ostentation among the rich. A new elegance replaced simpler medieval standards in south and north alike. Medieval man had devoted much of his spare income and labor to building cathedrals, churches, abbeys, and castles. Early modern man may have felt there was no need for more of these structures and had other possible attractive uses for his wealth. He therefore built palaces, town houses, and country mansions with chimneys, glass windows, elaborately patterned ceilings, tapestries or paintings on the walls, books from the new printing presses on his shelves, ornate furniture, and well-kept gardens. His clothing became as decorative as his surroundings, and his leisure time was spent in pursuits that were often sumptuous, sensuous, and expensive.

The satisfaction of these wants called for highly skilled craftsmen, artists, and architects. The Mediterranean cities already had a fair supply of such workers and quickly increased their number. The northern countries were not so well staffed, except in a few such points as making tapestries; but they imported the new luxuries from the south, persuaded Italian craftsmen to migrate northward, and strove to develop their own production of silks, fine glass, cloth of gold, and other essentials of lavish living.

Economic Effects of the Reformation. The Reformation did not cut deeply into all parts of Europe. Its direct lasting effects were confined to Scandinavia, Holland, much of Germany, parts of France and Switzerland, Great Britain, and the northeast corner of Ireland. In these lands, housing perhaps a quarter of Europe's population, the influence of the religious upheaval was profound. In the first place there was a great distribution of property and income. In England the abbeys were dissolved (1536 and 1539). Their buildings, lands, and plate fell into the hands of the crown, which gave, leased, or sold some of them at once, tried to keep the rest as an addition to the royal domain, but was gradually obliged to sell most of it in order to meet the costs of government. Much of the property of the regular church, along with that of religious guilds or that held by craft guilds for religious purposes, was confiscated by the king or the towns. It has been estimated that a third of the total national wealth of England thus changed hands.

Many monastic landlords had not been in a healthy financial condition or an enterprising frame of mind. Some of the new owners regarded their property as a speculation in real estate, at least one town sold the church plate and jewels to pave its streets, and some abbey buildings were turned into manufacturing workshops. But many of the new landlords vigorously developed their estates, tapped the mineral deposits, and strove to produce more income than the monks had ever dreamed of desiring. In north Germany the princes who broke away from the church despoiled it, and in Sweden Gustavus Vasa took the ecclesiastical lands. The breach with Rome ended the remittance of income to the pope.

In the second place the Reformation accentuated intolerance on both sides, provoked persecution, led to civil or interstate war, and caused much involuntary emigration. Even before the great schism appeared, Spain completed its purification of the country by expelling Moslems and Jews in 1492, and the Jews were later evicted from Portugal. Catholics fled from Protestant lands when their position became intolerable, but the greatest movement was that of Protestant refugees from France, the present-day Belgium, and other Catholic lands to England, Scotland, Holland, the Rhineland, the Protestant Swiss cantons, and the Hanseatic towns. Their welcome was cordial at first, because of their faith and often because they brought industrial skills which their hosts lacked. But sometimes the official creed of their new home changed back from Protestant to Catholic, from Lutheran to Calvinist (or vice versa); occasionally they roused the enmity of native vested interests; and in such cases they had to move on. They fared best in England and Holland. In the former they made notable contributions to industry, while the flight of craftsmen, merchants, and money dealers from Antwerp and the southern Low Countries into the northern provinces during the long struggle with Spain (1566–1648) helped to make Holland the leading commercial power in Europe.

In France civil war ended with a verdict in favor of Catholicism, but the Protestants (Huguenots), mostly artisans or traders, were conceded civil, religious, and political rights in the Edict of Nantes

(1598). This edict was, however, revoked in 1685, thus forcing many of them to seek homes in the British Isles, Germany, Holland, and North America. In Protestant lands the new order proved to be highly divisible; an official church might be established, but people who were dissatisfied with some aspect of its organization or teachings broke off into new sects. In England these "non-conformists" or "dissenters" suffered economic and political disabilities, while on the continent life was often made uncomfortable for those who insisted on deserting the new official line in order to draw one of their own. Tolerance was a plant of very slow growth, and the disabilities were at times sufficiently irksome to induce or force some men to emigrate.

The influence of the Reformation on economic behavior, on codes of conduct, and on the laws governing economic life is hard to measure. Protestants repudiated the authority of the church and claimed the right to let their individual consciences be their guide, with the teachings of the Bible as a guide to conscience. Yet they were by no means unitedly in favor of scrapping the old rules with the old ruler. Luther condemned usury, middlemen, bankers, and luxury with the fervor of a medieval priest or of a peasant in debt, and called on the civil rulers to restrain or prohibit them. Calvin talked more like "a man of affairs, who assumed, as the starting point of his social theory, capital, credit, large scale enterprise, and other institutions" (Tawney) of the urban commercial society he knew so well in Geneva. In his eyes it was as just to charge a moderate rate for a loan to a potentially profitable enterprise as it was to collect rent from land; but it was "evil and foul" to wring heavy interest from the needs of poor peasants or craftsmen.

In this view, as in those concerning prices and trade in general, Calvin did not differ much from late medieval writers or from the Jesuit economic moralists of the sixteenth century. Protestant governments usually dealt with such matters by fixing maximum interest rates, by providing public pawnshops for poor borrowers, and by continuing to control food prices or restrain forestallers; but in these policies they acted in the same traditional way as did their Catholic contemporaries.

Protestantism was even less specific than Catholicism in translating Christianity into a code of economic and social commandments. Its emphasis was largely on personal character and piety. When it searched for the essentials of good personal character and conduct it discovered them in those high ideals which the medieval church had espoused in its finest hours. Protestant moralists found nothing wrong, but rather everything that was admirable, in the monastic or priestly rules of hard work, prayer, and abstinence. The wrong lay firstly in the church's lapse from those rules into worldliness, laxity, idleness, and luxury, and secondly in the churchman's assumption that his vocation was the only one acceptable in God's sight.

Calvin, like Luther, denied this assumption and insisted that every occupation, however humble, could be a vocation, a "calling," worthy of its full reward in this world and the next, *provided* it was practiced in accordance with the stern discipline of the monastic rule. The man who brought to any task the qualities of industriousness, thrift, sobriety, honesty, and abstinence, and in addition prayed and went to church regularly, promoted the glory of God as greatly as did any priest or monk. According to Calvin, he also proved that he was a member of that small "elect" company predestined by God for eternal salvation. If, meanwhile, his labors yielded a goodly income, if asceticism forbade him to waste his substance in riotous living and thus accumulated capital in his hands, he did no wrong. The really deadly sins were sloth, luxury, and self-indulgence, as expressed in the wearing of gaudy clothes or jewelry, dancing, attending plays on secular subjects, gambling, getting drunk, or stopping away from work when one was not ill. The elect might shun these sins naturally and voluntarily, but the rest of the population must be kept by law from committing them and be made good by the strictest regulation of its working hours and still more of its leisure.

The Calvinist view of life and work, and the puritanical outlook that closely resembled it or sprang from it, were stimulating or comforting to any trader, craftsman, or farmer who needed stimulus or comfort. Laymen who had been working hard in the service of mammon but had doubted whether their aims and methods harmonized with Christian standards now learned that they had been serving God as well. Calvin had dignified their occupation, removed any inferiority complex they might have, challenged them to fulfill their lay stewardship with stern self-discipline, and given moral sanction both to worldly success and to at least some of the qualities which they knew were essential to its achievement.

This "Protestant ethic," as Max Weber called it, was in part the product of the growing commercial element in central and western European society. It can be regarded as a devout serious-minded townsman's revision and restatement of a code of Christian conduct which had been devised for an earlier rural feudal-clerical society. With the commercial class gaining strength it was perhaps inevitable that when the church came under critical fire some such revision should be made to harmonize Christianity and commerce.

How far the Protestant ethic in turn gave a distinctive character to the spirit of economic enterprise in Protestant countries is still an unsettled—and probably unsettleable—question. As we saw in Chapter IX, there was plenty of capitalistic organization, technique, and spirit in the Middle Ages, and a good deal more of it by 1500. It may be true that this spirit "found in certain aspects of later Puritanism a tonic which braced its energies and fortified its already vigorous temper" (Tawney). But Puritanism was not the only tonic. An equally potent one was the wide range of new opportunities which were opening up to sixteenth- and seventeenth-century Europeans. If these were to be seized, if the necessary capital was to be accumulated and success to be achieved, men of any sect must venture greatly, work hard, and save rigorously. The overseas opportunities were greatest to those who lived in the relatively poor, thinly populated, but geographically well-located British Isles, northern France, and Holland. It was this new chance, quite as much as a reformed ethic, that stimulated the boundless effort and laid down the exacting rules of the game.

The Reformation had little effect on the economic or social policies of governments. It is true that towns and states were obliged to give increased attention to the care of the orphan, widow, unemployed, sick, aged, destitute, and lazy when the charitable activities of the monasteries and guilds were curtailed or stopped. "Poor relief" soon became a public obligation, administered by lay officials and financed by taxes. Yet Catholic countries also were compelled to regard the problem of pauperism as too large to be handled solely by the church. Of legislation controlling economic enterprise there was, as we shall see later, a comprehensive abundance, but the motives behind it were as thoroughly secular in Catholic France as in Protestant England. In general, the influence of religion over politics and over political economy grew weaker in all countries.

The Rise of National States. The emergence of national states, governed by rulers who exercised sway over large areas, was perhaps the most important political development of the early modern period. On the one hand the universalism of the Middle Ages lost strength when the unity of western Christendom was shattered by the Reformation and as the Holy Roman Empire failed increasingly to maintain a measure of control over the hundreds of states of various sizes in central Europe. On the other hand the local particularism of the Middle Ages was weakened by the persistent and sometimes forcible efforts of rulers to get into their own hands the powers which had been wielded by feudal lords and the towns. This development was most evident in England, France, Spain, Portugal, and later in Sweden. Some states came into being by evicting a foreign ruler, as when the seven Dutch provinces established their joint independence of Spain or when Gustavus Vasa freed Sweden from Denmark. War widened a king's territory, for instance, in Russia and Austria; sometimes a marriage produced the same result bloodlessly; a genealogical table might reveal that the ruler of one state was the next king of another; and full organic union took place by mutual consent between England and Scotland in 1707. Only Italy and Germany stood apart from this process and remained divided into many political units. Elsewhere Europe passed under the control of centralized national governments, each with a legislature or royal lawgiver, a corps of officials, courts capable of overriding local dispensers of justice, an army of professional soldiers, and a treasury with a large gaping mouth.

The national state was usually autocratic. Its ruler was, or at least tried to be, absolute master rather than servant of his "subjects." His disposition might be benevolent, his aim the promotion or protection of their welfare. But as a political entrepreneur he had his own objectives, wants, sense of values, and methods, or, to apply Sombart's terms, his own organization, technique, and spirit, and to these the economy must both contribute and be subordinated. His wants might include large palaces, luxurious court life, more territory, a holy war against Protestantism or Catholicism or the Turk, the feeding of a personal grudge against another ruler, or a general desire to be a larger frog in a pond where competition was keen.

To the satisfaction of such wants he might feel it was worth while devoting wealth without too much thought of the cost. Louis XI, like many other kings, "would never surrender a political advantage for an economic benefit" (Strayer). Philip II of Spain was ever ready to squander in a holy war the wealth which flowed from his American empire. Louis XIV cared nought for the fact that his determination to extirpate the Huguenots meant the destruction or flight of one of the most skilled and industrious fractions of his people. If the landed nobles still possessed any power to influence the crown, their own standards of value might make them approve the kind of things their ruler wished to do. The church raised few or no objections; rather did such eminent ecclesiastics as Cardinal Richelieu shape and serve the political ambitions of their royal masters. The bourgeoisie might be consulted and some of its members be appointed to high or low office; but it was regarded as an inferior section of society, and its wishes were likely to be granted only insofar as they seemed to coincide with the interests of the state.

Only in Holland and later in England was the commercial middle class strong enough to influence statecraft. Since Dutch independence was won by the joint efforts of the landed aristocracy, the merchants, and the ship-operating population, the last two groups were never socially or politically inferior to the first. In the late eighteenth century a Frenchman described the position as follows: "In no other country is the profession of commerce so esteemed as in Holland. The merchant there is honored and regarded as a member of a class which is the strongest pillar of the republic. The road to honors and to the highest dignity in the state is open to him. He can marry into the patrician families which are in possession of the most distinguished offices of the Republic and which do not disdain to be in business themselves or to train their children for such a career. In England," where the power of the crown was increasingly subjected to control by a parliament which reflected the wishes of land and trade, "they have almost the same attitude toward commerce as in Holland; but in France, Spain, Portugal, and Germany there persists a barbarous prejudice against this profession, which partly destroys the good effects of the encouragements accorded by the state to those who practise it."

Even in Holland and Britain, as elsewhere, the mass of the population had little or no political influence. It might be protected by an absolute monarch against innovations which threatened to disturb the settled order, such as the introduction of machinery, the export of food, the enclosure of common lands, the eviction of tenants, or a serious increase in rents. If the problem of pauperism, famine, or unemployment became acute, something would be done in an attempt to prevent suffering from leading to violence. In general, however, the masses had no way of expressing themselves except by riots which rarely produced the desired effect.

The State and the Economy. In the chapters which follow we shall see the state trying to do things *to* the economy and *for* the economy by laws, decrees, or administrative practices. If all these efforts, spread over two or three centuries, are raked together, they make an imposing heap of government intervention and control which can fittingly be called *étatisme* (a good French word) or *statism* (an ugly English translation). Scarcely any aspect of economic affairs was immune from attention. The purpose of that attention varied greatly. Sometimes it was a desire to unify the nation economically as it had been politically, by introducing standard weights and measures, establishing one currency for the whole country, removing internal tolls and tariffs which impeded the movement of goods from one region to another, improving the roads on a national plan or linking the rivers together with canals, and imposing uniform regulations on industry or commerce in place of the varied ones which had been developed by local guilds or towns.

At other times the state was concerned with pulling the economy and itself out of the chaos and ruin into which war or depression had plunged it, by reviving agriculture, restoring wasted farms, stimulating industry and commerce, seeking colonial expansion, and repairing the currency or overhauling the tax system. Most of the items that go to make up *étatisme* were, in fact, attempts to recover from hard times, to cope with the aftermath of war, or to replenish an empty treasury.

Many policies tried to use economic means to increase the state's ability to hold its own in the quarrelsome family of nations and to strengthen its capacity for withstanding or striking blows in the hurly-burly of diplomacy and war. If a ruler was to keep what he had, take what he wished from others, recuperate from the last war and prepare for the next one, his country's economy must be sufficiently diversified and developed to supply all that was needed. He must have within easy reach the appropriate necessaries for war, especially munitions, ships, sailors, soldiers, and money. To be sure of these he must protect any industries which had already been developed, foster the introduction and growth of those which were lacking, build up a merchant marine, and develop foreign commerce in such a way that traders sold more goods abroad than they bought, thus causing a stream of precious metals to flow inward in payment for the surplus exports. If such policies weakened the economy of a potential enemy, this "preparedness" program would be doubly effective.

Governments were therefore greatly preoccupied with the inadequately developed state of their people's industry, commerce, and shipping. When Adam Smith surveyed the policies of the sixteenth to eighteenth centuries he coined the term *mercantile system* to describe the efforts "to enrich a great nation rather by trade and manufactures than by the improvement and cultivation of land, rather by the industry of the towns than by that of the country." This term, or its variant, *mercantilism,* has become firmly rooted in the vocabulary to identify the policies by which the early modern state tried to create a reservoir of economic resources, to stimulate a variety of occupations, to reduce dependence on the industries, ships, or traders of other countries, to build up a large national income, and thus create a fiscal counterpart to a politically powerful state.

How needful that strength was is evident when we recall that during the sixteenth century there was fighting nearly every year in some part of Europe; that the next century enjoyed only seven calendar years of peace; and that England was at war, mostly with France, during 84 of the 165 years between 1650 and 1815. The conflicts varied greatly in range and intensity, and few, if any, of them can be compared with the two great struggles of the twentieth century. Religious factors became less potent causes of war after 1650; but personal or dynastic ambition played a larger part, France's growing might cast a constant shadow over her neighbors, and economic issues caused more discord. Holland stood ready to fight if her shipping and trade were threatened, and the French minister Colbert welcomed a war with her in the hope that it would ruin her economically. Developments in the New World threw new bones of contention into the ring, especially when the French, British, and Dutch joined the Spaniards and Portuguese in empire building; but a purely colonial question was not likely to provoke war unless there was some European issue at stake as well. While economic factors might have little to do with starting many wars, economic benefits were usually among the spoils claimed by the victor.

The burden of war costs was increased by rising prices during the sixteenth century, by developments in the equipment and methods of land conflict, and by the fact that the antagonists often were able to use navies. The soldier was usually a mercenary who had to be provided with arms, food, and pay. Gunpowder, cannon, and muskets were expensive, and the size of armies grew rapidly as we approach and pass 1700. The advantage given the offensive by the coming of firearms was met eventually by building fortresses such as those which France erected from the Alps to the North Sea. Maritime nations began to build navies, and by 1780 some of the three hundred vessels in the British fleet were carrying as many as a hundred guns.

State Revenues. To meet their growing military and civilian expenditures, the national governments of the sixteenth century still relied largely on the revenue system of a feudal state. As medieval society added towns and trade to its rural economy, rulers had managed to supplement their incomes from land and feudal dues by taxing townsmen, commerce, and personal property. Now still more money must be squeezed out of old sources of revenue and new ones must be discovered. Taxes were heaped on sales, on exports, and increasingly on imports. Titles were sold, and people who became rich were forced to buy them. Monopolies of some branch of industry or trade were sold at a good price. Regulations which on the surface seemed to aim at raising the level of economic morality turn out on closer inspection to be devices for taxing craftsmen or traders "under the more or less false pretence of guiding industry along the right lines" (Heckscher). Hopes of freeing domestic trade from internal tolls or customs dues faded because the state could not dispense for a moment with the revenue from such levies. Crown properties were squeezed hard to yield more income and some of them had to be sold. On the continent the royal claim to ownership of salt and mineral deposits was asserted with greater vigor. In Sweden Gustavus Vasa not merely appropriated all the uncultivated land but embarked on trading enterprises of many kinds in order to earn profits as a universal provider. Metal currencies were depreciated and by 1700 government paper money was being printed.

Even the most comprehensive money-raising policies could not meet the combined cost of luxury and pugnacity. Loans must be raised in war years, but sometimes in days of peace as well, to supplement revenue or anticipate its receipt. Kings sent their servants, cap in hand, to the great loan markets, there to incur debts which frequently grew so large that partial or complete default was inevitable. Spain defaulted at least six times between 1554 and 1647, and thereby wrecked the Fuggers. Henry II of France evaded his obligations in the 1550's and converted his short-term debts into perpetual *rentes*. The Thirty Years' War drove German princes to break their bonds and their bondholders. The popes, who were paying out half their income in interest after 1580, often forced creditors to accept reduced interest rates or principal sums. As old lenders abroad were ruined new ones were sought at home, and might be tempted by a high interest rate or by a trading monopoly or the right to set up a bank. Compulsory loans might be demanded if voluntary ones were not forthcoming: Colbert seized the deposits in the French savings banks; Charles I in 1640 took the treasure which citizens had sent to the mint to be made into coins and released it only when its owners agreed to lend him money. In 1672 his son, Charles II, defaulted on an interest payment to London goldsmith-bankers. He was in good company, for French ministers habitually got out of tight corners by repudiating some debts, scaling others down, and lowering the interest rate on the remainder. Colbert began his career as chief minister by such a drastic reduction of interest and principal (1661 and 1664) that he seems to have eased the treasury of about two-thirds of its annual obligation.

During the eighteenth century wars became much more costly, the debt piled up more rapidly, but its capricious handling by declarations of partial bankruptcy became less common. In Britain the growing power of parliament after 1688 reduced the financial liberty of the crown, converted the debt from a royal to a *national* debt, and led to an improvement in the tax system. In periods of peace there was some effort to reduce the debt, but the achievement was puny when compared with the additions made by five wars between 1700 and 1783. Those conflicts raised the debt from about £16,000,000 to £240,000,000. In France the debt rose in about the same proportion, i.e., fifteenfold, during those years, in spite of the slashing away in 1715 of half the loans incurred for the War of the Spanish Succession. After that piece of surgery there was no further serious operation. Consequently the burden of interest became crushing and helped to precipitate the French Revolution.

The Economy and the State. The picture painted above emphasizes the way in which the state used economic means to promote its own political ends. There is, however, another side to it, in which we see individuals, groups, regions, and classes using political means to secure profitable economic ends. Of the items which went to make up mercantilist policies and ideas, some may have originated with rulers, ministers, or "bald-headed men in [government] offices, with strong class prejudices, an inclination to magnify their own authority, and a comprehensive ignorance of the lives of nine-tenths of those over whom it [was] exercised" (Tawney). But many items sprang from below, were urged on the state by some interested person or group, and were then imposed from above. In Holland and England policy tended more and more to reflect the wishes of the trading class or of sections and individuals in it; but even in Spain, France, and elsewhere economic interests could sometimes stimulate and steer state action.

Merchants, shipowners, manufacturers, or landlords were skilled in the arts of persuasion. They appealed to patriotic, religious, or social ideals and prejudices; they pointed out that their proposals would further the national welfare or swell the king's income; they exploited the growing antipathy toward the foreigner; they lobbied at court or in the legislature, published pamphlets, circulated petitions, held meetings, bribed courtiers, sent gifts to the king, and offered to share their profits with him. So long as kings wielded great power monetary inducements or appeals to royal interests were most commonly used; but where parliaments became strong, lobbying, bribery, printed pressure, and support of a political party became popular means to the desired end.

Whatever the method pursued, the aim was usually to gain some profitable favor, privilege, protection, or monopoly at the expense of rivals at home or abroad, of other interests or sections of the community, or of the consumer. Professor Unwin once suggested that nine-tenths of the inventive ingenuity of the seventeenth century was engaged, not in exploiting the powers of nature, but "in the endeavor to manipulate the powers of the state and the wealth of the community for the benefits of individuals." Adam Smith was equally caustic in his conclusion that "the sneaking arts of underling tradesmen are thus erected into political maxims for the conduct of a great empire," and in his verdict that the restrictions which various interests succeeded in imposing on colonial trade were projects "extremely fit for a nation whose government is influenced by shopkeepers." Yet it is doubtful whether any person or interest was averse to the idea that the state was an institution whose aid was welcome in the production of income.

Empire States. The states on Europe's western fringe became empire builders. Apart from powerful political and religious considerations, colonies offered opportunities for the sale of European wares, the securing of materials which the mother country did not produce, the investment of capital, the reaping of profits from trading and shipping, and the migration of such people as a country was willing to let go overseas. To stimulate these developments and keep the rewards inside the empire was a new task for statesmen.

We must not, however, exaggerate the importance of the colonial opportunities or of the imperial policies. While the discovery of ocean routes and continents added new fields for enterprise to the old ones, the quantity of capital, labor, ships, and commodities (apart from Spanish American silver and gold) was a small fraction of the whole European economy. There were limits to the total amount of trade that could profitably be done with the Orient or with Africa, and the New World was not one of unbounded attraction to investors, traders, or emigrants. Economic activity remained overwhelmingly European in its range; interregional trade in the eighteenth century was still chiefly an exchange of European products, as outside Great Britain it still is. Like the two or three highly capitalistic industries of the Middle Ages, the new overseas undertakings acted as yeast, leavening a lot of bread in the west, but their influence did not extend to the whole of Europe.

BIBLIOGRAPHY

Cheyney, E. P., *The Dawn of a New Era, 1250–1453* (1936).

Clark, G. N., *The Seventeenth Century* (1929), chaps. 1, 11, 12.

Clough, S. B., and Cole, C. W., *Economic History of Europe* (1941), chaps. 6, 7.

Ehrenberg, R., *Capital and Finance in the Age of the Renaissance* (Eng. trans., 1928), book i, Introduction.

Heckscher, E. F., *Mercantilism* (Eng. trans., 1935), vol. i.

Klarwill, V., *The Fugger News Letters* (Eng. trans., 1924).

Kulischer, J., *Allgemeine Wirtschaftsgeschichte* (1928–1929), vol. ii, chaps. 1, 2.

Nussbaum, F. L., *A History of the Economic Institutions of Modern Europe* (1933), part iii.

Renard, G., and Weulersse, G., *Life and Work in Modern Europe* (Eng. trans. 1926), Introduction.

Robertson, H. M., *Aspects of the Rise of Economic Individualism* (1933).

Sée, H., *Modern Capitalism* (Eng. trans., 1928), chaps. 3, 4.

Sombart, W., *Der moderne Kapitalismus* (1922), vol. ii.

Tawney, R. H., Introduction to Wilson's *Discourse upon Usury* (*1572*).

Tawney, R. H., *Religion and the Rise of Capitalism* (1926; Pelican American edition, 1947).

Weber, Max, *The Protestant Ethic and the Spirit of Capitalism* (Eng. trans., 1930).

ARTICLES

Clark, G. N., "Trade War and War Trade, 1701–1713," *Ec. H. R.*, January, 1928.

Fischoff, E., "The Protestant Ethic and the Spirit of Capitalism; the History of a Controversy," *Social Research*, February, 1944.

Hamilton, E. J., "Origin and Growth of the National Debt," *Am. Ec. R.*, May, 1947.

Hauser, H., "The European Financial Crisis of 1559," *J.E.B.H.*, February, 1930.

Heaton, H., "Heckscher on Mercantilism," *J. Pol. Ec.*, June, 1937.

Nussbaum, F. L., "The Economic History of Renaissance Europe," *J. Mod. H.*, December, 1941.

Strieder, J., "Origin and Evolution of Early European Capitalism," *J.E.B.H.*, November, 1929.

Encyclopaedia of the Social Sciences: Articles on Jesuits, Mercantilism, Mercenary Troops, Puritanism, Reformation, Renaissance.

XII

ECONOMIC EXPANSION IN EUROPE
AND BEYOND, 1450–1600

The Middle Ages ended in economic stagnation at many points. Population had been reduced, the volume of production and trade no longer grew as it had done in preceding centuries, and there seemed to be no new channels into which enterprise could flow. Then about 1450 the curves began to move upward in one country or occupation after another, and in spite of violent fluctuations or interruptions the general trend continued in that direction until about 1550, with the maritime discoveries gradually exerting their influence after 1500. In the fifties the advance was sharply checked by religious wars, the decline in mid-European mining, the extension of Turkish conquests in the Balkans and Hungary, and widespread royal defaults on debts. The rest of the century was disturbed and depressed in many respects, with a definite decline of prosperity in Germany and severe damage wrought on the industry and commerce of the Low Countries during the revolt against Spain. By 1600, when the clouds lifted, the shape of things to come was fairly clear: the New World had revealed some of its treasures; Spain and Portugal had become important because of the overseas empires they had staked out but were not equipped for active participation in European trade; the Italian cities were well located for trade through the Mediterranean but not for ocean traffic; Holland, England, and France were well placed for combining European and transoceanic commerce; and the Dutch were already started on the road to becoming the world's leading carrier and middleman. In the present chapter the economic revival in Europe and the first phases of the expansion of Europe overseas will be examined.

Economic Recovery After 1450. The factors responsible for a change in economic trends are rarely easy to discover, and this is true of the turning of the tide in the second half of the fifteenth century. The maritime discoveries cannot be given the credit, as they did not reveal their big secrets until the last years of the century and their effects were slow in being felt on any large scale. The impetus probably came from important inventions or innovations in Europe itself. The great advance in the production of metals got under way about 1450, especially in some German states, Bohemia, and Hungary. A new method of separating silver and copper when they were found in the same ore made possible the treatment of large deposits which had formerly been intractable. Water wheels came into widespread use; they worked pumps which extracted the water from mines, operated bellows that blew a strong blast of air through furnaces to aid combustion of the fuel and smelting of the metal, moved great hammers which crushed the ore or pounded the metal into desired shapes, and pulled containers full of minerals up the mine shaft. Trucks on rollers ran on wooden tracts, making it easier to move heavy loads underground or on the surface.

Armed with this equipment, miners worked on newly found ore deposits and brought deserted mines back to life again. The output of silver may have increased fivefold between 1450 and 1530. The new process swelled the yield of copper and therefore expanded the production of bronze (copper and tin) which was now being called (and used as) gun metal. Larger supplies of zinc became available, thus increasing the supply of brass (copper and zinc) for firearms. The new blast furnaces produced more iron of better quality.

The same period witnessed an expansion in clothmaking, both of the old fabrics and still more of new kinds, weights, qualities, and patterns of linen, woolens, worsteds, fustians, tapestries, velvets, and silks. In England the ground lost by the old towns was more than regained by production in rural areas and villages. The export trade, after standing still during most of the fifteenth century, got back to its fourteenth-century peak by 1500, and during the next fifty years the shipments of cloth from London nearly trebled. In the Low Countries a similar expansion occurred on both sides of the Rhine estuary. New producing areas came to the front; one place, Hondschoote, near Dunkirk, rose from being a mere village and by 1500 had 12,000 workers producing 100,000 pieces of light worsted cloth yearly. Other centers increased their output of tapestries, decorated with pictures depicting episodes in the life of Venus, Aeneas, or Jupiter, to cover the walls or drape the doors of rich men's houses. The production of fustians became a large industry in southern Germany; by importing cotton from the Levant and by directing the manufacture and sale of these durable combinations of linen and cotton the Fuggers and others laid the foundation of their great fortunes, and then built the first floor with profits drawn from the metal industry.

Many other items can be added to the list of late fifteenth-century advances. The first heavy use of cannon and small firearms in 1495 implied an earlier development of the armament industry and of the production of gunpowder. The printing press, practicable by 1450, was rapidly put to work; in 1500 one Nuremberg printer had two-score presses with a hundred employees, and it has been estimated that quite ten thousand editions had been produced by that year. The ending of the Hundred Years' War in 1453 allowed France to turn more of her energy to internal recovery and to building up her foreign trade, especially in the eastern Mediterranean. The end of the Wars of the Roses in 1485 gave England peace at last under a ruler who was strong enough to look after her merchants abroad and restore order at home.

Antwerp. Finally, the late fifteenth century saw Antwerp almost complete its rise to the position of being the commercial metropolis of Europe. Even in the fourteenth century it was exploiting its location at the mouth of the Scheldt to challenge Bruges as center of northern commerce. There was easy access by water to the sea, to the industrial areas of the Scheldt Valley, to the towns of a later Holland, and to the lower Rhine. There was also a good overland road to Cologne, from which point a combination of river, cart, and pack-horse transportation led southward to the Alpine passes and Italy. This route from the North Sea to the Mediterranean was by 1500 so well organized that a postal courier could traverse it in two weeks, and merchandise did so in about two months. Goods moved over it more quickly than they could go by sea, were more likely to arrive safely and punctually, and could be carried at most times of the year; yet the freight costs were little or no higher than those charged by ships.

Antwerp's own policies and those of her political overlords were almost as beneficial as was her location. When she built her second *bourse* (1531) to house the money-marketing business, she inscribed over its entrance the words, "For the use of the merchants of all nations and tongues." This welcoming of foreigners by the offer of liberal trading facilities had long been her policy. Consequently the Hansards came there early. The English took their cloths there when the Hansards drove them out of every other northern port except Bruges. The Italians moved in, as did south Germans, Portuguese, Spaniards, Frenchmen, Scandinavians, and Dutch. At four fairs held each year or by private purchase the cloths of adjacent countries were bought for shipment to Italy, there to be sold or re-exported to the Levant. In return spices, silks, fine oriental or Italian fabrics, fruit, metals, and other wares came north. The trade in bills of exchange, royal loans, and insurance grew large. Industries arose to print books, finish cloth, process such imported materials as sugar, and paint pictures for the export trade.

Antwerp thus had become a vast, complex, and highly sensitive market before Columbus crossed the Atlantic or a Portuguese ship reached India. It was not the only city to reflect the quickening commerce and finance of Europe. Relative newcomers such as Lyons, Geneva, Augsburg, Amsterdam, and in a smaller way Lisbon, London, and Bristol were growing in economic stature. The European economy was on the march once more, before the discoveries came to accelerate its pace.

THE EXPANSION OF EUROPE

Medieval Europe was hemmed in by barriers on every side. On the north were the arctic wastes. To the south, beyond the Moslem fringe of North Africa, stretched the Sahara desert, a thousand miles wide. Caravans crossed it, bringing slaves, ivory, and the gold which Europeans needed for their currency or for buying oriental goods in the Levant. The only way to circumvent it was down the inhospitable west coast, through treacherous seas and strong currents. To the west was the Atlantic. Across its northern part were stepping-stones—the Shetlands, Faroes, Iceland, Greenland, and Labrador or Newfoundland—separated from each other by five to eight hundred miles of ocean that was often rough, cold, and fogbound. In the central Atlantic the Madeira, Canary, and Cape Verde island groups rose out of the shallow ocean some distance from the African coast, and a long submerged mountain chain thrust a few peaks above the water at the Azores, nearly a thousand miles west of Lisbon but more than a thousand from Newfoundland.

To the east lay a continent of actual or potential invaders rather than one to be invaded. Asia's rulers and people were sometimes friendly but more often hostile to any European who wished to fetch his own goods from the Orient, and when they grew restless they might hear the age-old call to ride westward into Europe. On the two chief overland routes, from China and from the Persian Gulf, transportation and transshipment costs, middlemen's profits, and the risk of political levies or physical harm ran high. The seaway through the Red Sea was cheaper, but access to it was barred by the sultan's refusal to let Europeans cross Egypt, and at Alexandria or Cairo, where east met west, the market was occasionally disturbed by his monopoly of the sale of oriental wares and his attempt to charge extortionate prices for them.

In the breaking or surmounting of all these barriers (except that of the arctic) the leading medieval traders and shippers played little part. For a time it seemed possible that the Genoese, who were particularly interested in the western Mediterranean, might be pioneers in finding out what lay beyond the Strait of Gibraltar. In 1162 they were trading along the Atlantic coast of Morocco; in 1270 they rediscovered the Canary Islands, and in 1291 the Vivaldi brothers left Genoa on their ill-fated attempt to circumnavigate Africa. But, like Italians in general, the Genoese evidently felt no overwhelming urge to persist or to pour out their capital in the search for a new way to the oriental source of their supplies. They preferred to wrestle with rivals from other Mediterranean cities in the Levantine ports and to drive the best bargain they could with the sultan. If any of them did go searching it was as servants in the Portuguese, Spanish, French, and English ventures which produced the double achievement of finding the ocean route to Asia and of stumbling unexpectedly on new continents across the Atlantic.

It was natural that these ventures should be undertaken by westerners. Such ports as Lisbon, Cadiz, Bristol, and those of Normandy or Brittany looked out onto at least a semicircle of ocean. Their mariners and merchants could profit more by exploiting that ocean than by competing with Hansards in the North Sea or with Italians in the Mediterranean. These men knew the northern Atlantic and the fishing regions around Iceland fairly well. By 1350 the Azores were marked on some maps, so it seemed a reasonable assumption that farther west there might be more such islands, and beyond them Japan and China with their limitless wealth. It was also reasonable to suppose that if one worked down the African coast one might hope to pick up some slaves, ivory, and gold dust. Finally, since it was believed that there was a way around Africa to Asia, the only questions—admittedly big ones—to be answered concerned the length of the journey, the obstacles to be surmounted on the way, and consequently the extent to which an ocean route could compete with the old ones for the oriental trade.

There is much scattered evidence that western mariners were pushing far out into the north and central Atlantic during the fourteenth and fifteenth centuries, fishing, trading, or seeking islands. Their ships became more oceanworthy as the design of the hull and the supply or pattern of sails improved. The compass, in use since at least the twelfth century, told them which way they were going. The quadrant or astrolabe gave them their latitude by letting them measure the elevation of the sun or the north star; but accurate measurement was impossible except on rare occasions when the vessel was perfectly steady. Knowledge of winds and currents, improvements in steering equipment, ability to tack in contrary winds, and skill in "dead reckoning" the speed of the vessel all increased the navigator's power to go where he wished and fortified his hope of getting back home.

In the northern Atlantic these small-scale operations by private individuals or groups might result in immediate profit and ultimately in important discoveries; but the searches across the central Atlantic and along the African coast called for government sponsorship and financial support. Portugal's rulers supplied these requisites for almost a century of patient and frequently interrupted exploration. Prince Henry the Navigator earned the title bestowed on him by nineteenth-century historians by his systematic promotion of oceanic ventures. At Sagres, on the southwest tip of Portugal (and of Europe), he established a maritime research institute, with shipyard, observatory, and school for the study of navigation. He gathered in pilots, astronomers, cartographers, maps, books, and instruments, studied hulls and sails, listened to the reports of returned travelers, and in 1418 sent out the first of a long series of expeditions, some of them westward into the open Atlantic but most of them down the coast of Africa.

His chief aim was to expand Christendom and wage a holy war against Islam. The crusading spirit, virtually dead in most of Europe, was kept alive in Portugal and Spain by the long battle to expel the Moor from the peninsula and by his presence across the narrow strait in North Africa. By the time of Henry's birth (1394) a new Moslem wave, that of the Ottoman Turks, had swept over Asia Minor to engulf much of the Balkan peninsula. Before Henry's death (1460) Constantinople had been captured (in 1453), the crescent had replaced the cross over southeastern Europe, and soon the whole Danube Valley was to be threatened as far as the gates of Vienna.

Against this menace to the Christian world Henry and his successors hoped to launch a flank or rear attack. To do this they must join forces with Prester John, a legendary valiant scourger of Moslems and other infidels, whose kingdom, after having floated round most parts of Asia, was now believed to be in Abyssinia, at the mountainous source of the Nile and stretching down to the Red Sea. Since Prester John's warriors were said to be as countless as grains of sand on the seashore, an alliance of his army with Portuguese land and sea forces might overwhelm Moors, Arabs, and Turks in an attack from the south; it would destroy their merchantmen and navy in the Red Sea and Indian Ocean; and as material reward it would transfer the trade between the Orient and Europe from Arabs —and therefore from Italians—into Portuguese hands.

To find the way to Prester John was the prerequisite to this final glorious chapter in the history of the crusades. On that long way there were converts to be won, a holy war to be waged, and trading opportunities to be seized. The Madeiras, reached by the first expedition, were soon dotted with sugar plantations or vineyards. When the desert shores of the African bulge gave place to fertile inhabited coastlands, the cargoes that were secured yielded rich profits in Lisbon. These profits roused Castilian traders and their ruler to challenge the lucrative monopoly that Portugal was erecting, but the pope checked this Spanish threat by confirming Portugal's sole possession of what she held and also of whatever else she might find "as far as the Indies."

Henry died in 1460, but his work went on. By 1470 the coast of the Gulf of Guinea had been fully explored and as a trade area became an end in itself. Fortified posts were established, and almost every year saw merchantmen arrive, laden with cloth, caps, bells, basins, beads, horses, and wheat, which were bartered for ivory, slaves, gold dust, and some pepper which was inferior to the Asiatic product in spite of its hot taste. In 1471 the equator was crossed; but the shore line, which for more than a thousand miles had been running eastward, thus raising hopes it would continue to do so "as far as the Indies," had turned southward and did not change its direction for about 3,000 miles. It was also yielding fewer rich cargoes.

These twin disappointments were enough to break the heart of any explorer or trader. Back in Lisbon men wondered whether it would not have been better and shorter to seek a way to Asia across the Atlantic. Yet the search for Prester John and "the Indies" went on, and in a valiant effort to find them Bartholomew Diaz went so far that in 1488 he rounded the Cape of Good Hope. Ten years later Vasco da Gama reached Calicut in India, announcing he had come "in search of Christians and spices." From that advanced base the hunt for the Abyssinian ally could be conducted with more hope of success, and the diversion of trade from the ancient routes was now geographically possible.

Discovery of the Americas. Columbus talked of making converts, securing the gold, pearls, and spices of the Orient, and using part of this fortune to equip an army that would free Jerusalem from the Turk. He also hoped to find Prester John. But, having been on at least one of the Portuguese African trips, he seems to have decided that the better way to the treasure chest lay westward across the central Atlantic. It took him nearly a decade to find a patron willing to provide the funds he needed on the terms he laid down. The West Indies he found on his first two journeys (1492, 1493) were a disappointment to both himself and his sponsor, and it was left for others to reveal, by discovering the mainland, what a rich dividend Spain had received on its small reluctant investment.

While Columbus was pleading for a chance to make his grand gamble, events were coming to a head in the North Atlantic. The lands discovered by the Vikings in the ninth and tenth centuries had never been forgotten. Norway regarded them as part of its realm, and though settlements on Greenland had "gone native," Iceland and the shallow waters which comprise the northern ocean were often visited by ships from western Europe. During the early fifteenth century fishermen and traders from Bristol and other English ports made annual trips to Iceland. The traders took English food and manufactured goods, with Portuguese salt as ballast. These they exchanged for fish, which they carried to Portugal, and returned home with a cargo of wine, oil, and salt.

These activities injured the Hansards' traffic from Bergen and led the Germans to demand that the king of Denmark, who also ruled Norway, close Iceland to English traders. This ban, accepted by weak English kings and enforced by Hansard violence, stopped the trade for a time, but in 1490 Henry VII was strong enough to secure a treaty sanctioning the traffic for seven years. The men of Bristol used this period of grace to supply Iceland and to explore beyond.

In 1494 Cabot, a Venetian mariner living in Bristol, seems to have reached Newfoundland. There are claims that the Portuguese had been there in 1452 but kept the visit secret; also that a Danish-Portuguese expedition had gone so far in 1474. In 1497 Cabot went on a publicly authorized journey, and as he completed the round trip in three months, bringing back a detailed report on the fishing opportunities of the region, it seems probable that he had been to familiar lands or waters.

Columbus and Cabot discovered only islands, but exploration during the three subsequent decades revealed the coastal character-istics of much of the American mainland. After the circumnavigation of the globe by Magellan's expedition (1519–1522) the rest of the story was largely a matter of filling in details. By 1600 the shape of the world's land masses could be drawn with reasonable accuracy except at two points—the shores of the Arctic Ocean and of Aus-tralia. The search for a northwest passage round the top of America to Asia did not penetrate beyond Hudson Bay (discovered in 1609), and that for a northeast passage along the rim of Russia and Siberia virtually ended at Archangel. Many Europeans sighted or touched the Australian coast during the seventeenth century, but usually from the north or west. They therefore struck the worthless regions, and found only sandy waterless wastes, stunted trees, a strange beast with a long jump, and natives "the miserablest in the world." Not till 1770 did Captain James Cook discover the more fertile east coast, and the whole shore of the continent was not charted until the early nineteenth century.

Overland Expansion to the East. Europe's southeastern frontier was pushed in by the Turks, but farther north the boundary was pushed out to embrace a broad belt of Siberia. This expansion began in earnest about 1550, after a state based on Moscow had broken the Tatar barrier to the east and gained control as far as the Urals and the Caspian Sea. While political ambition played its part, eco-nomic stimulus was given by the approaching exhaustion of Euro-pean Russia's fur supply. The dash across Asia was completed when Russian explorers sighted the Pacific in 1640. Effective occupation took far longer, but since it was done by soldiers, officials, and traders, leaving the natives to do most of the fur collecting, the number of Russian migrants need not be large. Politics and eco-nomics were always closely intertwined, for the czar dominated the fur trade. He received pelts as tribute from the natives, as tithe from trappers, or by purchase. Consequently he was by far the greatest dealer in Siberian furs and had a double interest in the extension of his empire and his business.

Economic Effects of the Discoveries. The maritime discoveries produced at least half a dozen long-run economic consequences. (1) Greatly increased quantities of known produce and supplies of new commodities were drawn from the outer continents. (2) European goods, especially manufactured articles, found wider markets. (3) Europeans emigrated and settled in relatively large numbers in America, supplementing their own labor by drawing slaves in from Africa. In crowded tropical Asia there was room for only a few European traders or officials, and in Africa the soil and climate attracted very few settlers. (4) Trade and settlement offered new fields for the investment of capital. (5) Ocean transportation and intercontinental commerce opened new avenues for profit in building and operating ships, as well as in processing the colonial raw materials. (6) Administrative posts at home or overseas in the employ of governments or trading companies provided jobs ranging from the lowliest to the most lofty and lucrative.

It was, however, a long time before all these effects were full-grown. The short-run consequences, as seen during the sixteenth century, were evident chiefly in the use of the new way to the Orient, in the beginnings of the slave trade and cod fisheries, but most of all in the influx of precious metals from Spanish America.

The Oriental Trade. Along the new ocean route goods taken aboard at an Asiatic port could be carried to western Europe undisturbed by transshipments, portages, tumult on land, or sultans' imposts. A single ship could deliver a large cargo; in 1582, for instance, one Portuguese vessel reached Lisbon with 375 tons of pepper and cloves, "much cinnamon and other spices." These advantages were not, however, as overwhelming as they seemed. The new journey was longer in miles than the old ones: the distance from Calicut round the Cape to Lisbon was 9,000 miles, while that from Calicut through the Red Sea to Venice was less than 5,000 miles. The danger of shipwreck or of deterioration of the cargo was very great on the longer route. The Arabs had a well-established trading organization for handling and shipping produce, and any newcomer was bound to be a long time in building one that would be as good. Finally, Lisbon was not well located for serving as an *entrepôt,* to which goods could come in bulk and then be distributed over Europe in smaller lots. Little is known of the relative total transportation costs on the two routes, but it is possible that in the sixteenth century the all-ocean way had only scanty advantage over its rival.

The issue was not destined to be settled by economic factors alone, with victory going to the competitor who could supply Europe with spices at the lowest price. Portugal went east as crusader and trader, determined to get a monopoly of the westward flow of goods and also to wage the holy war on new battlefields. To establish the monopoly she must gain control of the producing regions and exporting harbors, close the entrances to the Persian Gulf and Red Sea,

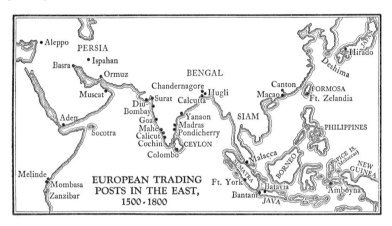

EUROPEAN TRADING
POSTS IN THE EAST,
1500-1800

and wipe out any Arab or Egyptian ships that came in sight. For the crusade she must provide a considerable army and navy for combined operations and draw on Abyssinia for material and men.

For about two decades she acted with vigor. In 1502 Vasco da Gama broke up Arab-Egyptian shipping so thoroughly that in 1504 scarcely any spices reached the Levantine ports or Mediterranean Europe. From 1506 to 1516 Albuquerque, commander of the fleet and after 1509 governor general of the Portuguese Indies, was untiring, aggressive, and triumphant. He captured Ormuz in 1507, thus blockading the Persian Gulf. He strung a chain of outposts from East Africa to China. He laid plans to capture Aden, establish a base inside the Red Sea, burn the Egyptian navy in harbor, and destroy the Moslem holy city of Mecca. He even suggested that engineers be brought from Europe to divert the upper Nile from its course, thus turning Egypt into a desert.

Though Albuquerque died before he could seal up the Red Sea, he did reduce and render fitful the traffic from India and points east to Alexandria and Aleppo. Portugal became for a time the leading, and in some years the only, recipient of East Indian produce. Her ships, laden with some European goods and well stocked with gold from Africa, went out regularly, returning to Lisbon with cargoes that were sent on to Antwerp to be sold. The king claimed a royal monopoly of the trade in pepper, his factors and agents tried to keep the price as high as possible, and he seemed to be richly rewarded for the enterprise of his ancestors. It is probable, however, that much of the royal profit was swallowed up in the cost of sustaining the forces needed in the Orient to suppress rivals. It is certain that those rivals were not permanently or completely suppressed. The Turks, who had gone on from capturing Constantinople in 1453 to conquer Syria in 1516 and Egypt in 1517, were eager to revive the old trade routes because of the revenue to be collected from them. Their eagerness was shared by the Venetians, by the French, who were competing more and more with the Italians in the Levant, and by the Arabs.

After about 1520 the Portuguese blockade grew weaker, the administration became incompetent or corrupt, the Red Sea could not be closed tight, and Arab bribes brought freedom from restraint. By 1540 at latest, goods were flowing once more in considerable volume through Aleppo and Alexandria to Venice, Ragusa, Marseilles, and other ports. Professor Lane estimates that by 1560 Venice was receiving more pepper than she had done before the trade was interrupted; that shipments through the Red Sea equaled and sometimes exceeded the Lisbon imports; and that the European consumption of pepper increased greatly—perhaps even doubled—between 1500 and 1560. It has been suggested that Portugal's appropriation of the African gold supply had reduced the Italians' ability to pay for what they wanted in the Levant. If that diversion of precious metal was a serious blow, the damage was repaired by the mounting supplies of silver coming from mid-European mines and then by the influx from America.

When force failed to kill competition, the new route lost much of its attraction. Some Portuguese even urged that a bargain be struck with the Turk in order to allow the spices to come up the Red Sea instead of going round the Cape. The cost of seeking monopoly was high to the Portuguese; the cost of defying it was also high; hence neither side may have gained much profit. The consumer apparently did not benefit by getting his supplies any more cheaply; spice prices in Antwerp fluctuated violently but in general rose at least as much as did those of other commodities.

It is thus evident that the discovery of the Cape route caused no immediate fundamental change in the trading relations of Asia and Europe. When, however, the Dutch and the English entered the Indian Ocean about 1600, Venetians, Arabs, and Portuguese were gradually pushed aside. The Dutch were as aggressive, forceful, and monopoly-minded as was Albuquerque in his prime, but the secret of their success probably lay more in the combined efficiency of their shipping, commercial, and financial methods. With their triumph, the spice traffic through the Mediterranean sank at last into unimportance.

The Orient gradually added other commodities to Europe's commerce and consumable goods. Cotton fabrics of all kinds from the cheapest to the most costly, porcelain, indigo, tea, drugs, raw silk and silk cloth, saltpeter, metalwares and metals came in considerable quantities. The development of the trade in these articles did not, however, become noteworthy until the Dutch and English went east to fetch them. (See Chapters XIV, XV.)

African Produce. Africa revealed no surprises as its coast line became better known, and its importance was dwarfed when Asia became an attainable terminus. In the last quarter of the sixteenth century, when the Portuguese East Indies were yielding the king a gross annual revenue of 2,000,000 crusados, the whole West African empire was giving him less than 300,000. Abyssinia proved worthless; its military strength was so feeble that the Portuguese had to help defend the country against its neighbors, and its Christianity turned out to be so stubbornly heretical that missionaries had to be sent there in a vain effort to inculcate orthodoxy. Meanwhile, French, English, and Dutch traders invaded Portugal's African preserves. They competed with her for the precious metal that came down from alluvial mines to the Gold Coast and for the elephants' tusks that reached the Ivory Coast; but their chief interest was soon concentrated on the wares of the Slave Coast.

The Slave Trade. Negro slaves had been used in ancient and medieval southern Europe, but the West Indies and the warmer parts of the American mainland offered a larger market than had ever existed before. American natives who were not killed might be forced into virtual or real slavery, but since there were not enough of them, especially for regions which developed plantation economies, workers must be imported. When the original practice of landing a party to kidnap Africans became unproductive, a regular triangular traffic developed. European ships went to the Gulf of Guinea laden with such trade goods as experience had shown to be acceptable in barter. After much haggling with the dealers, the price of a slave was decided; on one occasion a woman changed hands for a gallon of brandy, six bars of iron, two small guns, a keg of gunpowder, and two strings of beads, while a man cost eight guns, a wicker-covered bottle, two cases of spirits, and twenty-eight cotton sheets. When the hold had been filled, usually with at least two hundred slaves, the ship sailed westward, lost from 10 to 25 per cent of its cargo from disease, and disposed of the remainder to island or mainland dealers and planters. The vessel then took on a cargo of American produce, often including precious metal, and returned to its European home port.

Spanish America and Portuguese Brazil were the chief markets for the "black ivory" until the French, English, and Dutch plantations added greatly to the demand during the seventeenth and eighteenth centuries. The Portuguese held the sources of supply by virtue of exploration, on the strength of papal awards, and under the terms of a treaty of 1494 which gave Spain all lands west of a certain line but recognized Portugal's sole interest in those east of it. By this division of territory Spain was mistress of the Americas except Brazil. Brazil, Africa, and the East Indies were Portugal's preserve. Spain made the importation of slaves into her colonies a state monopoly but farmed the business out to licensed Spanish merchants who obtained slaves from the Portuguese and shipped them westward. After Portugal was annexed by Spain (1580) an *asiento* (contract, agreement) handed the traffic over to Lisbon traders in return for a fixed share of the profits.

The Portuguese were not strong enough to prevent English, Dutch, or French traders from getting slaves out of Africa or smuggling them into Spanish America. In 1701 Louis XIV forced Spain to transfer the *asiento* into French hands, but in 1713, as part of the spoils of victory in the War of the Spanish Succession, England took it from France and kept it till 1750. This legal trade in slaves supplied a smoke screen for the smuggling of other goods into the Spanish colonies. Yet it was less important than was the slave traffic which developed with the spread of plantations in the French, Dutch, and English possessions. The *asiento* granted permission to import 4,800 slaves yearly, but the total annual traffic sometimes amounted to 100,000 slaves during the eighteenth century.

The slave trade thus became an integral part of economic life on both sides of the Atlantic. Many European industries made the goods needed for barter or processed the colonial produce for which the slaves were exchanged. Ports like Bristol, Liverpool, Amsterdam, and Nantes grew larger because of their share of a business regarded as full of risks, potentially profitable, and quite respectable. One French trader, who evidently believed in the sacred rights of man, christened his slave ships *Voltaire, Rousseau,* and *The Social Contract.* Ship captains knew that their cargo was too valuable to be treated with unnecessary harshness, and the death rate in the hold was often no higher than among the crew. It has been estimated that in three centuries Africa contributed about 20,000,000 persons to the American labor supply.

American Produce. Europe knew what Asia and Africa had to offer, but what would America yield to those whose path to the riches of Cathay she so rudely barred? The answer eventually proved to be, "Everything, and in abundance." All the six opportunities listed above—for securing supplies of familiar and strange goods, for markets, migration, investment, profitable commerce and shipping, and government jobs—existed in the Americas. The catalogue of natural resources included fish in the waters before the coast was reached, furs, lumber, new commodities like tobacco, cocoa, corn, and potatoes, cotton such as Europeans already knew, dyewoods and such furniture timber as mahogany, drugs, edible beasts and birds, pearls, diamonds, and the two precious metals with which imagination paved the streets of distant places. There was room for the cultivation of staple products and plenty of grazing land. And this treasure house lay beyond an ocean that could be crossed westward in two months or less—a French ship went from Le Havre to the St. Lawrence in eighteen days in 1608—and eastward in at most five or six weeks.

Fish. For the first hundred years, however, the only American commodities to make much impression on European commerce were silver and gold, but there was a good beginning of the traffic in codfish and tobacco. The Banks of Newfoundland attracted fishers from France, Portugal, Spain, and England. Since these men operated far from their home base and markets, the catch must be preserved with the aid of salt. The cost of salt was therefore an important factor in determining the methods used, the nature of the product, and the chances of success in a highly competitive occupation. The French had the cheapest salt, the Portuguese ran them a close second, Spain lagged a bit behind, but the English had to import most of their supply from France or Portugal and its higher cost put them at a disadvantage.

The French were therefore the first to make a success of fishing on the Banks. They caught the big fish out there, cleaned and salted them on board ship, and took the catch home, still wet. This method was extravagant of salt, but the product was more palatable than dried cod and was bought by wealthy Parisians during Lent. A more economical method was to take the cod ashore and dry it, using less salt but more wind and sunshine. This the French gradually did, establishing drying stations on Newfoundland and on the shores of the St. Lawrence Gulf and of the present Canadian maritime provinces. The dried cod was sold to poorer Frenchmen or sent to Spanish and Mediterranean markets. The English had to make their dear salt go as far as possible, and therefore concentrated on drying fish. By 1600 the Spanish and Portuguese were being squeezed out of the industry, leaving the French and English to compete with each other and among themselves. Shore settlements multiplied, the West Indies gradually became a market for the "refuse" fish which was fed to slaves, and the industry became an important angle in the triangular, rectangular, or polygonal trade of the Atlantic region. (See Chapters XIV, XV.)

Tobacco. When Nature distributed her flora she gave Europe nothing fit to smoke. Tobacco, consumed by natives from the St. Lawrence to the Argentine, was therefore quite new to the white man. Sailors took leaf and seed back to Spain, and from that base the habit and the plant spread relentlessly as far east as Turkey. When Jean Nicot, French ambassador to Portugal, sent seeds from Lisbon to France, the plants which grew from them were christened *Nicotiana.* Raleigh introduced smoking to English court society, and by 1600 men of fashion smoked at bear- or bull-baitings, in the theater, and at home.

Like most new pleasurable commodities, tobacco roused bitter controversy between its devotees and those who on moral, physiological, or economic grounds disliked it. The former claimed that

"the soveraine weed, divine tobacco" possessed unbounded medici-
nal virtues as antiseptic, disinfectant, and cure for everything from
snakebite to toothache. The opponents called it "hellish, devilish,
and damned." They attacked the "filthy stinking habit" which made
bodies, rooms, dishes, and air evil smelling, led men to ape the
"barbarous and beastly manners of the wild, godless, and slavish
Indians," ruined them body and soul, and took money out of the
country or sent it up in smoke. Governments tried to stop or restrain
the use of tobacco. The pope threatened to excommunicate those
who took snuff in church. France decreed that purchasers must have
a physician's prescription and buy the medicine only at apothecaries'
stores. The czar ordered that first offenders be whipped, second
offenders be executed, and snuff takers have their noses cut off.
Turkey decreed the death penalty.

All such repressions failed to achieve their purpose, and governments became less hostile when they discovered that smoking
addicts were willing to pay high taxes. Richelieu detested tobacco
but welcomed the revenue it yielded. Venice in 1659 set up a
tobacco monopoly. England changed her tune when Virginia,
struggling for life as an infant colony, found that it could grow the
plant and thus provide a staple export, a source of revenue, and a
commodity which up to that time had been virtually a monopoly
of the Spanish colonies. From that point onward, England shaped
much of her early colonial policy in terms of tobacco. (See Chapter
XV.)

American Treasure. America revealed its store of precious metals
within a few years of its discovery. Much metal was already above
ground and was promptly acquired by the Spaniards as booty or
by barter. The *conquistadores* felt that their hazardous military
ventures were well repaid when in Peru they saw 1,300,000 ounces
of gold all in one heap and the king offered them a roomful of gold
as ransom. His subjects had life-size golden statues of trees, birds,
women, and wild animals dotted about their gardens, households,
or temples; utensils were of gold, and slabs of silver served as dining
tables. Here indeed was El Dorado.

The visible treasure was a trifle compared with that still underground. Natives, colonists, and German miners revealed rich deposits, a new method of extracting silver by amalgamation with
mercury was perfected about 1550, and by a happy coincidence
Peruvian supplies of mercury were discovered. In 1545 the Potosí

silver field in Bolivia was discovered and the fields of Zacatecas and Guanajuato in Mexico were soon attacked. The last of these was richest, but Potosí, being more easily pronounced, became a synonym for fabulous wealth. The output rose to its high peak about 1600, and though Potosí then showed signs of petering out, the yield elsewhere remained high until about 1630. After that date production ebbed rapidly and remained relatively low until a new silver boom began in Mexico about 1750.

Spain's rulers made elaborate plans to insure that they received their full share of the new riches. Mining was done by private enterprise, but all bullion must be delivered to royal assay offices. There it was cast into bars or plates, and a *quint*—usually a fifth, but sometimes less—was claimed by the crown as royalty. Then much, but by no means all of it, was dispatched to Spain. That which remained circulated in the colonies as currency, supported a rich upper class, and paid for the erection of churches and palaces. Some treasure was smuggled out of Latin America to the West Indies, despite the risk of drastic punishment if one were caught exporting it without permission. But a great part of it did go to Spain. The graph on p. 249 shows the value officially imported by that country. The receipts of the first four decades were largely loot, first from the West Indies, after 1520 from Mexico, and after 1530 from Peru. The later imports reflect the great expansion in mining after mid-century, reach their peak in the 1590's, and then decline.

Many early treasure-carrying ships were attacked by pirates or privateers. The danger of piracy led by 1565 to the organization of merchant fleets, which left Spain twice a year convoyed by warships. These *flotas* transferred the metal without much loss; on only two occasions, in 1628 and 1656, did the Dutch or English divert any large part of it from its destination. That destination was Seville. There the House of Trade (*Casa de Contratación*), which controlled the trade with America, received and distributed the bullion. Some of it—the *quint*—passed into the royal treasury; some had been sent by colonists to their relatives in the homeland; the rest went to pay merchants for the provisions and manufactured articles they had sent to the colonies.

Having reached Seville in safety, much of the treasure soon departed from Spain. A large part of the king's share was often earmarked in advance to pay interest or principal to his German and Italian creditors. Some of it was used to meet the wages and other costs of armies fighting Spain's battles in the Low Countries or elsewhere. The bullion might be handed over in Seville to the representatives of the Fuggers, Welsers, and other bankers, or be shipped to Antwerp, now a greater financial center than ever before. But after 1560 the revolt in the Low Countries and English piratical raids on Spanish ships passing through the English Channel

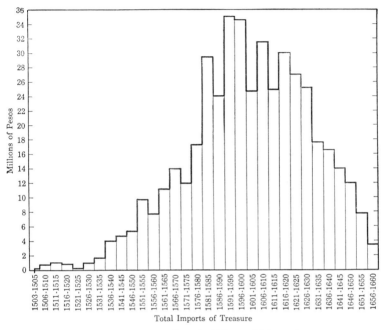

Total Imports of Treasure

SPANISH IMPORTS OF TREASURE

(From Earl J. Hamilton, *American Treasure and the Price Revolution in Spain, 1501–1650,* Harvard University Press, 1934.)

diverted the flow of metal from Antwerp to Genoa, thereby strengthening the already powerful banking group in that city at the expense of the Germans who had formerly financed Spain so heavily. Meanwhile much of the privately owned imports also left Spain. It went to France, England, Holland, Italy, and Portugal to pay for the fish, manufactured goods, or spices which were needed by Spain or her colonies. In these ways American treasure was spread over Europe.

Between 1521 and 1660 about 18,000 tons of silver and 200 tons of gold entered Spain through official channels from America. These

amounts seem small when compared with modern outputs and reserves; the total figure for gold is less than that of South African
production in many a single year during the twentieth century. But
they made a vast addition to sixteenth-century Europe's stock of
precious metal. They were supplemented by silver production in
central Europe, though this fell off rapidly after about 1550. Russia
added to the gold stock, especially after the czar gained control of
the Ural mountains, and by 1584 German and English miners were
directing the labors of 15,000 workers. West Africa continued to
send some gold.

Treasure and the Price Level. Perhaps the most important economic effect of the new metal was a long, large rise in the general
level of prices. Price movements in the sixteenth century, as in all
centuries, were influenced by many factors. In the first place, there
were short-run oscillations, caused by plenty or famine, as, for
instance, when very bad harvests in 1554 and 1555 quadrupled the
price of wheat in England; by news of the outbreak or end of a war,
as when expectation of peace between Venice and the Turks in
1540 pushed up the price in Antwerp of those cloths which were
popular in the Turkish Empire and at the same time lowered the
price of spices because it was assumed that Venice would soon be
able to pick up supplies in Aleppo and Alexandria once more and
thus compete with Lisbon; and by a host of other facts, rumors, and
speculations. War could also influence some prices by creating a
sudden demand, cutting off supplies, or closing markets.

In the second place, price movements were caused by alterations
in the precious-metal content or the official value of coins. In England Henry VIII and his successor tampered with the currency so
seriously that the silver which had been in one penny in 1520 was
spread into three by 1546 and into six by 1551. Prices did not move
in proportion, but in the last years of this "great debasement" they
were more than double those prevailing a decade earlier. Currency
manipulation was not always due to dire royal need. Some of it
was an attempt to prevent the value of silver coins from declining
in terms of gold coins when silver, flowing into Europe in greater
volume than did gold, fell in relative purchasing value. In 1527 and
again in 1539 Charles V, who was both king of Spain and Holy
Roman Emperor, tried to raise the value of silver coins by reducing
the official value of gold ones about 10 per cent. On each occasion
this step created great confusion, caused gold to run away to coun-

tries where its value had not been cut down, and provoked a collapse of markets and prices in Antwerp.

In the third place, some commodities rose in price for reasons of their own. The growing demand for charcoal denuded forest regions near the spot where the fuel was used, raised its price, and forced consumers to abandon their fires, import charcoal from distant places, or turn to coal. The sixfold growth of London's population between 1540 and 1640 probably pushed the prices of building materials and rents abnormally higher, as well as those of goods which had to be brought long distances to fill the city's other needs.

Finally, there was a long upward movement caused by the influx of treasure. As precious metal grew more abundant it became less precious, and more of it had to be given in exchange for a unit of goods. Central Europe had learned this fact after 1450, as its silver output increased and business generally recovered. Then Spain quickly felt the effect of her great importations, and soon the rest of Europe was in the throes of a "price revolution." Professor Hamilton finds that Spanish prices in a currency which remained uncorrupted were about 3.4 times as high in the decade 1601–1610 as they had been a century before. In France prices in silver were 2.2 times as high in the last quarter of the sixteenth century as in the first, but in debased coins they were considerably higher. In Leyden, the Dutch textile town, they rose 300 per cent between 1520 and 1580 and were still going up in 1620. English food prices rose 64 per cent between 1500 and 1540, and doubled again during the next decade of depreciation. Elizabeth reformed the coinage in 1560–1561 and checked any further increase through debasement, but the country shared in the general upward movement, and in 1600 goods cost 2.6 times as much silver as in 1500. In Alsace prices doubled during the sixteenth century, in Italy they nearly doubled, and in Sweden they had more than doubled by 1620. The graph for wheat prices (p. 252) shows a rise from an index number of less that 25 before 1550 to one above 75 around 1600 and above 100 during the war-full second quarter of the seventeenth century. Thus throughout central and western Europe things in general cost two to three times as much in 1600 as they had in 1500.

Price increases were at times so large and so rapid that they roused widespread discontent, especially among those whose income from rent, wages, or interest stood still or rose less slowly than did the price curve. As in all such periods, everybody blamed everybody else, and all kinds of remedies were proposed. Farmers were accused of withholding produce from the market, and they in turn blamed the covetous middleman. The exporter was charged with creating domestic scarcity by shipping too much abroad. The merchant was pilloried as a forestaller, and the usurer received the traditional condemnation.

More thoughtful observers felt that the cause lay elsewhere than in these forms of individual or class greed. One Frenchman, Malestroit, argued that the purchasing power of an ounce of silver had

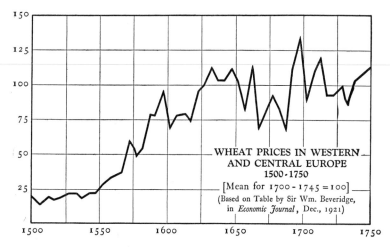

WHEAT PRICES IN WESTERN
AND CENTRAL EUROPE
1500-1750
[Mean for 1700 - 1745 = 100]
(Based on Table by Sir Wm. Beveridge,
in *Economic Journal*, Dec., 1921)

not changed at all for decades or even centuries. The whole reason for higher prices lay in the lowered silver content of coins. To a few men this debasement was not a complete explanation; it must be supplemented, or even supplanted, by a recognition of the vital connection between mounting prices and the influx of precious metal. A French scholar and lawyer, Jean Bodin, replied to Malestroit by insisting that the "principal and almost only cause" of increased prices was "the abundance of gold and silver, which to-day is greater than at any time in the past four hundred years." Bodin was not the first or the only man of his time to say this; nor did he see the whole problem, but left some aspects to be explored by later exponents of what we now call the quantity theory of money. Neither he nor Malestroit exerted any practical influence on currency controllers. Manipulation of the coinage was too well established as an emergency fiscal measure to be abandoned; and as for the American treasure, every country was eager to welcome it, no matter what its effect on prices.

Yet every government had to take notice of the discontent and "do something." Spain fixed legal maximum prices, France pegged prices and wages, but in neither country were the effects satisfactory. In England the uprush of prices around 1550 led to more price fixing, more severe restrictions on middlemen, more careful definition of forestalling, regrating, and engrossing, and even to the exclusion of traders from some branches of commerce. These measures accomplished little or nothing.

A more realistic policy was that of providing for adjustments to the changing price level. English landlords had tried to protect themselves when prices soared by changing the terms of any leases which came up for renewal. Some had insisted that the tenant pay part of his rent in produce at fixed prices or pay a sum of money which was equal to the prevailing market price of a certain amount of grain. In 1576 parliament passed a Rent Act, under which a landlord could claim that one-third of the money rent due to him be paid in wheat or malt, the value of which was fixed at about the price which had prevailed in 1550. His rent thus brought him a better supply of food and drink than if he had received it all in cash and had then been obliged to pay market prices for his supplies.

England also tried to provide for the adjustment of wages to changing living costs. Parliament in 1563 admitted that maximum wage rates fixed in various earlier laws were "in divers places too small and not answerable to this time, respecting the advancement of prices of all things." It therefore abolished the old maxima and ordered the justices of the peace, who were the local magistrates in each county, to review the wages question every Easter. They were to call before them "such grave and discreet persons as they shall think meet," confer with them "respecting the plenty or scarcity of the time, and other circumstances necessary to be considered," and then "rate and appoint" wages for the next year. In this way it was hoped a figure would be fixed which would "yield unto the hired laborer, both in the time of plenty and in the time of scarcity, a convenient proportion of wages." Wages would presumably go up or down as prices rose and fell.

The practice did not quite coincide with the presumption. The justices were usually landowners, their interests may have been with the wage payer rather than the receiver, their natural inclination was to reissue the same figures year after year, they had no satis-factory price statistics available and no adequate administrative machinery to see that the law was obeyed. In general the rates they fixed lagged far behind price movements, as wages usually do in all times and countries. If the rates they "assessed" and those actu-ally paid coincided, the result was a decline in the real wages and living standards of the worker who depended solely or chiefly on his wages. There is evidence, however, that sometimes the wages paid were higher than the justices' rate. Many workmen received board or bed and board as part of the remuneration. While urban wage earners may have had little time or opportunity to cultivate a piece of land, rural workers would have a garden plot or grazing rights from which they could obtain some of their food. Finally, there were large new developments in English industry between 1540 and 1640; it is possible that these increased the demand for labor and the pay that workers received.

A tentative conclusion would be that English real wages fell heavily during the years of debasement and rapid price increases—say from 1520 to 1560—but regained some of the lost ground during later decades. In Spain the available figures suggest that wages lagged behind prices during most of the sixteenth century but caught up with them by 1600. In Leyden the rapid expansion of the textile industry allowed wages to more than keep up with prices, and the same may have been true in other growing occupations.

On the land the effect of the price revolution depended on the position of the landlord. High prices stimulated the landlords of northeast Germany and Poland to push ahead with grain produc-tion and to depress the farmers on their estates into the condition of servile workers on large domain holdings. In France many land-lords, still *rentiers*, could do little to increase the income they drew from their tenants. In England some landowners were in a similar helpless position, since their tenants held their lands on rents which were unchangeable. But many of them had sufficient freedom of action to permit the collection of more income either in rents or in the more profitable use of their land. (See Chapter XV.)

While some classes or groups suffered from the rising price curve, others benefited. The independent craftsman or small master might be able to pass on his higher costs. The farmer would not be af-fected in so far as he was self-sufficing; he would gain from higher prices if he produced for market, but might lose some of that gain if his rent was adjustable; and it might now be worth his while to work the soil more intensively or to put common and waste lands to better use. The industrial employer gained wherever the gap between the value of his hired labor and the price he paid for it widened, but the extent to which this situation prevailed cannot be decided. The merchant profited by the greater volume of goods now entering the market, by the demand for commodities for America and the Orient, by the increased opportunities for speculation, as well as by the rising prices.

The expansion of the supply of precious metal had other effects on European economic life, on commercial expansion, and on adolescent capitalism. More currency was available for cash transactions, for building up bank deposits, or for accumulating personal funds which could be hoarded or invested. As Europe now had a larger supply of metal that could be used to pay Orientals for their wares, trade with the East expanded. The wealth that Spanish kings drew from El Dorado stimulated them to ambitious policies which were as costly as they were disastrous. It also roused in other countries an envious determination to lay hands on some of that wealth or to go out and seek new treasure grounds. The desire to obtain, conserve, and increase the supply of precious metals colored economic discussions and influenced commercial policies at many points during the seventeenth and eighteenth centuries.

BIBLIOGRAPHY

Abbott, W. C., *The Expansion of Europe* (1925), vol. i.

Beazley, C. R., *Prince Henry the Navigator* (1904).

Blake, J. W., *European Beginnings in West Africa, 1454–1578* (1937).

Clough, S. B., and Cole, C. W., *Economic History of Europe* (1941), chap. 5.

Edler, Florence, "The Van Der Molen, Commission Merchants of Antwerp: Trade with Italy, 1538–1544," in Cate, J. L., and Anderson, Eugene, *Medieval and Historiographical Essays in Honor of James Westfall Thompson* (1938).

Fayle, C. E., *Short History of the World's Shipping Industry* (1933), chap. 4.

Hamilton, E. J., *American Treasure and the Price Revolution in Spain, 1501–1650* (1934).

Haring, C. H., *Trade and Navigation between Spain and the Indies in the Time of the Hapsburgs* (1918).

Hauser, H. (ed.), *La vie chère au xvie siècle: la réponse de Jean Bodin à M. de Malestroit, 1568* (1932).

Innis, H. A., *The Cod Fisheries: The History of an International Economy* (1940), chaps. 1–6.

MacInnes, C. M., *The Early English Tobacco Trade* (1926).

Moore, G. A. (translator), *The Response of Jean Bodin to M. de Malestroit* (1947).

Morison, S. E., *Admiral of the Ocean Sea* (1942), chaps. 1–10.

Power, E., and Postan, M. M., *Studies in English Trade in the Fifteenth Century* (1933).

Prestage, E., *The Portuguese Pioneers* (1934).

Sanceau, E., *The Land of Prester John* (1944).

An international study of price history was begun in 1929 and most of the volumes have now been published. For their titles, consult a library card catalog under the names of Beveridge, W. H. (England), Elsas, M. J. (Germany), Hamilton, E. J. (Spain), Hauser, H. (France), and Posthumus, N. F. (Holland).

ARTICLES

Hamilton, E. J., "American Treasure and the Rise of Capitalism, 1500–1700," *Economica*, November, 1929.

Lane, F. C., "The Mediterranean Spice Trade," *Am. H. R.*, April, 1940.

Martin, G., "Commercial Relations between Nantes and the American Colonies," *J.E.B.H.*, August, 1932.

Nef, John U., "Prices and Industrial Capitalism in France and England, 1540–1640," *Ec. H. R.*, May, 1937.

Nef, John U., "Industrial Europe at the Time of the Reformation," *J. Pol. Ec.*, February and April, 1941.

Nowell, C. E., "The Columbus Question," *Am. Hist. R.*, July, 1939.

Rive, A., "The Consumption of Tobacco since 1600," *Ec. Hist.*, January, 1926.

Encyclopaedia of the Social Sciences: Articles on *Asiento*, Bodin, Mining, Plantation, Plantation Wares, Slavery.

XIII

ECONOMIC DEVELOPMENTS IN CONTINENTAL EUROPE, 1500–1750: I. THE HANSE TOWNS, ITALY, PORTUGAL, SPAIN

The spotlights of early modern economic history shift their beams from the medieval Italian, German, and Belgian centers and play on other regions. Portugal and Spain attract attention by leading the way to the riches of the new world, thus acquiring an income and importance far greater than they could ever have wrung from the exploitation of their own resources. But their grasp proved shorter than their reach; they dissipated much of the new wealth in unproductive political spending; their homelands were unable to supply many of the goods and services needed by their colonies; and their part in European commerce was passive rather than active.

Holland first and foremost, England later, and France in a smaller degree combined exploitation of the outer continents with the development of their own industrial and agricultural resources and with active participation in European trade. Their foundation and much of the superstructure were local, regional, or interregional. Their merchants and ships served the producers and consumers of their own lands, linked together the various sections of northern Europe, strengthened the maritime bonds between the Mediterranean and the north, and reached into central and eastern Europe to bring the products of those land masses down to the sea. Their chief concern was with supplying some of the needs and marketing the exportable produce of Germans, Russians, Scandinavians, Poles, Spaniards, Portuguese, or Turks, as well as with the home market. But to this domestic trade and intracontinental traffic they added a top layer of distant intercontinental commerce. Their enterprise was three-decker. They had three strings to their bow.

This concentration of the light on the western empire builders is, of course, somewhat unfair to the rest of the continent. It may be true that some parts of Europe had no economic history, lacked easy means of transportation to the outside world, saw no noteworthy developments in industry or commerce, but lived a humdrum life of usuculture and usufacture, with just enough trade to meet local needs and enough well-developed crafts to supply the wants of court or aristocracy. But this secluded self-sufficiency was far from general, especially when we approach and enter the eighteenth century. If any region had some rich natural resource, the local ruler or landlords might be eager to develop the production of cash crops, lumber, or metals for near or remote markets; western traders and ships came as close as they were permitted in order to buy, sell, and carry; immigrant workers might be welcomed to introduce their methods of processing or manufacturing; and kings or princes, such as those of Prussia or Russia, strove to modernize the economy of their realms by stimulating some industries or fostering some trades. Meanwhile the Italian cities, the towns which lay on the road and river trade routes of central Europe, and the Hansard centers lost some of their old importance, but they certainly did not die.

In this chapter the fate of the medieval leaders will first be examined, and we shall then see what Portugal and Spain made of their opportunities.

THE HANSEATIC TOWNS

The success of the Hanseatic traders had been the product of three ingredients: (1) the opportunities provided by the eastward-moving frontier; (2) efficient trading and shipping services for handling a wide range of commodities in a market stretching from Spain to the Baltic lands; (3) political and fighting strength, based on united action and the support of the Teutonic Knights, in dealing with economically backward or politically weak countries. That strength had won for them a more favored position in foreign ports and markets than was enjoyed by other foreigners or even by native traders.

By 1350 the frontier had ceased to move. In 1410 Poland smashed the Knights in battle. Strong states such as Poland, Brandenburg, Sweden, Denmark, England, and Russia gradually covered much of northern Europe and gave their own traders support by depriving the Hansard of his privileged position or by demanding easier access for their subjects to some of his markets. Thus the Duke of Burgundy relieved the Dutch in 1501 from an old obligation to buy lumber, tar, grain, and other products at Bruges—which had meant that they must purchase them from the Hansards. He thereby gave them official encouragement to go to Scandinavia and the Baltic and buy what they needed from the country of origin. English merchants, who had felt the German fury during the fifteenth century, took the offensive during the sixteenth, and in 1598 persuaded Elizabeth to close the Hansards' London headquarters, the Steelyard. Gustavus Vasa loosened their hold on Sweden, the czar evicted them from Novgorod (1494). Denmark welcomed westerners, since they loosened the Hanseatic trade monopoly of her territory and the passage of their ships into the Baltic increased her revenue from the Sound dues. Sweden closed the Gulf of Riga, thus blocking an important route to Russian furs and other products. In this new era of territorial states a league of towns was too weak to be effective.

Economic factors played a more important part in damaging the League and the trade of its members. The Dutch outdid the Hansards by the quality of their carrying and trading services in the North and Baltic seas. The fish took a hand in the struggle when the herring shoal, which for centuries had spawned off the Scania peninsula, began to go elsewhere in the early sixteenth century. Nature took a hand by choking with sand the entrance to the harbor of Bruges. The shift of oriental trade from Italy to Amsterdam and London after 1600 deprived some German inland towns of their overland transit and distributing business. Meanwhile the forces that had pulled the towns together were not strong enough to prevail against rivalry between them. Leipzig displaced Lübeck as fur market. Cologne occasionally broke away from the League and tried at least once to cut all the other towns out of the English trade. Hamburg in 1567 offered an open door to English cloth merchants at a time when the League was under fierce attack in London.

The League waged a fierce but losing fight against these heavy odds. Its last diet met in 1669. By that time Dutch competition and the ravages of the Thirty Years' War had reduced many towns to insignificance. But some of them lived on and grew, nourished by the export trade in grain, lumber, flax, hemp, leather, linens, beeswax, and honey from the German or Polish hinterland and the importing of British cloth, French wine, Mediterranean fruits, and colonial produce. Danzig was Europe's leading grain port. In the eighteenth century it counted 125 brick warehouses, capable of storing 100,000 tons of wheat or rye brought down the Vistula. In a good year at least a thousand vessels entered the harbor to pick up cargoes of grain, potash, and planks or other shapes of pine, fir, and oak. Stettin gathered in similar products from the Oder Valley, along with much of the linen cloth for which Silesia was especially famous; and every other Baltic port was an outlet for the produce of the lands south or east of that sea.

Lübeck went farther, by collecting all kinds of hides and skins and building up a great output of morocco and shoe leather. Hamburg served the growing Brandenburg-Prussian market which centered on Berlin as well as that of the states of the Holy Roman Empire. Down the Elbe or from the Baltic ports she drew great quantities of linen cloth, which she bleached and decorated with patterns. By the mid-eighteenth century Hamburg offered perhaps the widest variety of linens for sale in Europe. She was also weaving velvets, silks, brocades, and cottons, refining sugar, manufacturing tobacco, tanning hides, and making copperware. The Bank of Hamburg, founded in 1619, ranked second only to the Bank of Amsterdam.

THE ITALIAN CITIES

The decline of the Italian cities from their medieval preeminence as merchants, shippers, manufacturers, and financiers did not happen overnight. The spice trade recovered from Portuguese interference and was healthy until the early seventeenth century. The overland routes to India and China never quite lost their use for goods or people in a hurry, and there was some trade to be done with the Turkish Empire round the eastern Mediterranean or with such lands beyond as Arabia or Persia. For that trade, however, the Italians had to fight hard. The Turks not merely evicted them from some of their trading colonies in the Levant but welcomed, or at least tolerated, French, Dutch, and English merchants in their ports. In 1536 a Franco-Turkish treaty gave Frenchmen extraterritorial privileges in those harbors and made France the protector of all Catholics in the Near East. Marseilles flourished on the Levantine trade; when it received spice cargoes from Alexandria there were worried looks on the faces of Venetians and of the Portuguese in the factory in Antwerp. Englishmen were well established by 1600 in Constantinople, Smyrna, and Aleppo, as also were the Dutch. They were soon to work their way into some of the ports of the central

and western Mediterranean and even into the Italian ports, especially into Leghorn, where traders of all nations were assured of a
welcome and freedom of action.

Faced with such competitors and frequently involved in wars
with the Turk, Venice was handicapped by the lack of a supply of
oak for her shipbuilders. Her famous medieval galleys had been
rendered obsolete by the development of new types of vessels,
equipped with better sails and armed with cannon or muskets. The
near-by forests from which she had obtained ship timber had all
been cut down, and she therefore lacked the cheap material needed
for building a more efficient merchant fleet. By 1600 she was being
forced to buy her big vessels in Holland, the country that was just
stepping out to gain control of the oriental trade which for centuries had been the core of the Venetian economy.

As trade with the Far East passed into western hands, the Italian
cities depended more on their manufacturing industries and financial operations. Their fine wares stood supreme for a long time in
luxury markets at home and abroad; even in the eighteenth century
their silks, velvets, embroideries, lace, cloth of gold, gloves, stockings, Venetian glass, linen, and soap ranked high, if not highest, in
favor. Other countries had, however, picked up some of Italy's industrial secrets and equipment, had closed the doors to some of her
goods but left them open to admit her emigrating craftsmen, and
bought more of her raw silk but less of her fabrics. She was now
only one of many luxury workshops in Europe.

As financiers Italians were important until about 1650. After 1550
the Genoese displaced German firms in the service of the Spanish
crown, received the king's share of the American treasure, and managed the payment of war expenses. Florentines were the leading
figures in French high finance. From Paris or Lyons Italians or men
of Italian stock born in France spread their agencies over northern
Europe. One of them, Burlamachi, settled in London in 1605, became agent for the English government, and on one occasion
pawned the crown jewels in Amsterdam. These dealings with rulers sometimes led to partial or total loss of interest or principal; the
flow of profits from commerce into finance tended to diminish; and
when the imports of American treasure declined seriously after 1630
Italian bankers felt the effect of the impoverishment of Spain.

These recessions in commerce, shipping, manufactures, and finance still left Italy with a considerable amount of varied enter-

prise. Trade with the Levant, with the rest of the Mediterranean coast, and with the lands beyond the Alpine passes in central Europe was substantial. To the reexport of Levantine goods and the export of Italian manufactures was added that of raw silk, alum, marble, sulphur, and oil needed by woolworkers. While trading and banking profits had shrunk, a new source of income was found in supplying goods and services to the growing tourist traffic. In general, however, western and northern Europe had learned how to dispense with Italy's services, as it had with those of the Hansards.

PORTUGAL

Portugal was a poor country which by pioneering, spending, and working hard acquired a large empire. The size of her material reward depended on her ability to make the most of the new opportunities in Asia, Africa, and Brazil. As we have already seen, she threw herself with vigor into the task of seizing the oriental trade. The energy displayed by the crown was evidently equaled by that of civilians, for a German observer in India reported in 1580 that "the Portuguese here are even more diligent than the people of Lisbon." There was also considerable diligence in the slave trade, in the development of Brazilian sugar plantations during the seventeenth century, and in gold mining and diamond production during the eighteenth.

The country was, however, too small or ill equipped to meet all the demands of conquest, commerce, and colonization. In the first place, her population in 1500 is estimated at only 2,000,000, a figure which left little reserve for emigration or for manning merchantmen, warships, and colonial armies. The loss of life by shipwreck, disease, and war created a serious labor problem; according to one estimate the population dropped nearly half during the sixteenth century, and there was some introduction of African slaves to help work the farms of Portugal. In the second place, her own natural resources were limited. The staple products—wool, wine, fruit, salt, oil, and cork—did not provide either suitable cargoes for export to the colonies or raw materials for industries which could supply such cargoes. Portugal never developed any staple manufacturing occupations, but leaned on other countries for the cloth, hardware, and other articles needed by herself and her dependencies. A primary producing nation is not a very good center for an empire.

In the third place, Portugal lacked adequate capital and a good location. The former forced her to rely heavily on foreign financiers for funds to equip her oriental ventures. Though the spice trade was a royal monopoly, south Germans and Italians supplied much of the capital needed by the crown and played a large part in the trade in other commodities. Lisbon's location was so remote from the populous regions of Europe that the colonial imports must be transferred from the large ocean-going ships to smaller craft which carried them on to the Antwerp market. This traffic between Lisbon and Antwerp was conducted largely in foreign ships. Thus freight earnings, interest, and profits slipped at many points out of Portuguese hands. Much income that did go into the royal treasury was poured out again immediately to defray the costs of a lavish court, maintain the defenses of the empire, or wage more crusades against the Moor in North Africa.

Finally, Portugal was not strong enough to protect her whole empire or even herself. Spain annexed her in 1580, thus making Lisbon an enemy port to the Dutch rebels and to the English, who were soon at war with Spain. Portuguese interests in Asia and Africa could now be attacked in the cause of patriotism and profit alike. The process of evicting Portugal from the Far East was slow, difficult, and never complete; but when she finally regained her independence (about 1660), her overseas possessions had shrunk to Macao in China, Goa and a few other points in India, some posts in Africa, and Brazil. The oriental bases were of considerable trading worth, the African holdings supplied some slaves, and Brazil's value increased greatly when gold and diamonds were discovered there about 1700. Lisbon continued to be an important terminus of the ocean trade routes. But the economy remained unchanged. The colonial produce (including now the gold) and the homeland's raw materials were exchanged in Lisbon and Oporto for the cloth and other manufactured goods of Britain, Holland, and France, for English wheat and Newfoundland dried cod. In that exchange the British played the leading part after 1700. Portugal had, in effect, become a British colony. (See Chapter XV.)

Spain

By conquest, marriage, and discovery the Spanish Empire that reached its height in the reign of Philip II (1556–1598) was vast in size and resources. When Ferdinand and Isabella wed (1469) they united the central pastoral plateau of Castile with the eastern agricultural, industrial, and commercial regions of Aragon. Moorish Granada in the south was captured in 1492, and Portugal was absorbed in 1580. Thus the whole peninsula was unified. Outside Spain, Philip's realm included the territories of Milan, Naples, and Sicily, with their banking, industry, and agriculture. In the north it embraced the Netherlands—the old industrial regions of Flanders and Brabant, the great market of Antwerp, and the rapidly growing shipping, manufacturing, and trading towns of a later Holland. For a moment, when Queen Mary married Philip, it included England. Beyond Europe Philip ruled bits of North Africa, the Spanish American possessions, and those which fell into his hands with Portugal. He had a large army, a proud navy, great prestige until the English and Dutch shook it, and a religious fervor which made him regard himself as the arch-enemy of all heretics or infidels and as "the junior partner of Almighty God."

Much of this huge aggregation came quickly just before and after 1500 to a country which had modest resources, considerable aptitude in their exploitation, but some marked geographical and human handicaps. The physical shortcomings included great expanses of bleak plateau and rough mountain, a sparse rainfall, wide extremes of climate, and impassable barriers to inland transportation. The human limitations were strong sectional and racial divisions, patriotisms, and animosities, accentuated by the geographical barriers and by religious differences between Christian, Jew, and Moor; a society which placed land, the church, and crusading high on the list of values but put commerce and manual labor low down; an underdeveloped trading class except in Barcelona, and consequently a great reliance on Italians for much of the country's foreign commerce. Spain was highly feudal, militant, and clerical, but only slightly bourgeois.

The greater part of the country was mountain or plateau, fit only for pasturage. On it grazed millions of merino sheep, whose fine wool had long enjoyed a high reputation. Spain had a monopoly of this wool, and forbade the export of merino stock till the late eighteenth century. Other animal products, including the hides of cattle and goats, provided materials for the Moorish leather industries. The pastoral areas were owned chiefly by large lay or spiritual landlords. To protect their flocks and pastures the ranchers formed an association, known as the *Mesta,* which operated for four centuries after 1350 as a guild, with a council, officials, court, and a large measure of political power and royal favor. One of its main tasks was to facilitate the migration of the sheep from southern to northern pastures each spring and the return in the fall. The broad path along which the flocks moved must be kept clear of farms, inclosures, and fences, agricultural encroachment must be resisted, and the grazing area must be increased wherever possible. Royal support insured and expanded these facilities. The merino was king.

The eastern and southern coastal belt had soil, climate, and water supply suitable for the intensive and often irrigated cultivation of grain, vines, olives, fruits, rice, sugar, and silk. Here, as at some points in the interior, industry and trade created busy towns. The skill of Moors and Jews built up textile, hardware, and leather industries. Barcelona had won an important place in the traffic along the Mediterranean to the Levant, and by the fifteenth century ranked almost alongside the Italian commercial leaders. From the Atlantic coast and Bay of Biscay ports Spanish iron, wine, and wool went north to England, Bruges, and Antwerp.

Spain in 1500 housed about seven million people. To their ruler was now added sway over other parts of Europe and over the transatlantic empire. The first effect was to give a powerful stimulus to the Spanish economy. The second was to involve the country in diplomatic, religious, and dynastic disputes, and consequently in military or naval enterprises which swallowed up much of the new revenue from America and the old yield from Spain. The government lived at least up to its means; but while those means declined after 1600 the cost of trying to maintain Spain's position as the greatest power in Europe remained high.

The colonial demand for consumers' goods or capital equipment and the income which flowed into the royal treasury or the merchants' pockets expanded most forms of Spanish production. "Industry and commerce were geared to [the] steady and increasing stream of commerce" (Hamilton). Manufacturing centers like Toledo or Segovia and ports like Seville or Cadiz almost doubled their population in sixty years. Ships suitable for ocean crossings were built or bought, and by 1580 the Spanish merchant marine had become the second largest in Europe. The colonial church and government, erected on a large scale, needed great supplies from home. Spaniards emigrated to the colonies or went off fighting on foreign battlefields, yet the country's population increased by about 15 per cent during the sixteenth century.

This period of expansion and prosperity came to an end during the last years of that century. After 1600 agriculture, industry, and commerce declined fast and far. The merchant fleet dwindled three-fourths in a century, the shipyards lapsed into idleness, the industrial cities shrank—some of them to half their former size—and the total population fell about a quarter between 1600 and 1700. By the eighteenth century poverty was so widespread that water, it was said, had become the national drink. As the economic decline was paralleled by Spain's descent from a first- to a second-class power, the water tasted bitter.

The economic and political causes of this relapse are closely intertwined. The eviction of Jews and Moors was not a cause, for it happened too early, in 1492. The expulsion of Christianized Moors (Moriscos) in 1609 apparently did little or no economic harm. Emigration, the fleets, the army, and the missionary organizations took men—the cream and the scum—out of the country, while the church and the monasteries took them out of economic and matrimonial life. The sum total of these human leakages may have been large, but severe plagues around 1600 and 1650 were probably more serious in reducing the population. Attacks on the growth of church lands and complaints concerning the excessive number of monks indicate that some observers felt the church was absorbing too much of the national resources and dividend or that men and money might have been put to more productive use.

More disastrous than any such factors was the heavy burden imposed on the empire's wealth by an ambitious foreign policy, by the attempt to protect true religion against Moslem and Protestant alike, by long wars, and by a large court. The costs of royal consumption and conflict could not be met solely by quints and other colonial contributions; domestic taxes must be increased and large loans raised. In 1596, 1607, 1627, and 1647 the treasury was bankrupt. In 1639 the royal credit was so low that no one in Seville would advance money in anticipation of the arrival of the American treasure ships at less than 70 per cent discount. Merchants at times refused to supply goods to the palace until some of the outstanding bills were paid, and courtiers went from house to house begging alms for the king. Old taxes were raised or new ones imposed on goods produced at home, on exports and imports. The *alcabala,* a sales tax, went as high as 15 or 20 per cent.

Chronic inability to make ends meet led to debasement of the currency after 1598. "Philip II opposed unsound money no less tenaciously than he fought the cults of Luther and Mohamed" (Hamilton), but his successor, Philip III (1598–1621), found the budget unbalanced and the revenue all earmarked for creditors. He therefore debased the *vellon* currency, which was made of silver and copper and used for retail transactions, by extracting its silver, and then doubled the face value of each coin. His successor, Philip IV (1621–1665), had to cope with a revival of the conflict with the successfully rebellious Dutch, with the Thirty Years' War, revolts in Spain, Italy, and Portugal, pestilence, falling tax yields, and a marked decline in the receipts of bullion. He alternated policies of reckless inflation and penitent deflation; the former caused prices to skyrocket, the latter tumbled them down. These fluctuations "upset calculations, stifled initiative, impeded the vigorous conduct of business enterprise, and wreaked havoc upon the economic life of Spain" (Hamilton).

The final, and possibly the chief, cause of Spain's descent was the decline in the income she drew from the Americas. We can divide that income into five parts: the quint and other royal revenues from the colonies; interest on capital invested overseas; the net earnings from shipping services; profits made on goods sent to America and on produce obtained therefrom; and profits on commodities produced in Spain for export. During the seventeenth century the output of precious metals declined, and the quint fell with it. Of the interest sent to Spanish investors we know little, but it is doubtful whether the amount was large. The three other items are best examined as part of the story of colonial trade and policy.

Spain and America. Spain was the first modern state with a colonial problem to face and a policy to frame. There was little precedent to guide her except the traditional desire of all powers, civic or national, to keep every possible benefit for their own enjoyment and the feudal assumption that anything found overseas which did not already belong to a Christian prince became the personal property of the ruler whose flag was hoisted over it. The control of commerce and the colonies was soon in the hands of three bodies: (1) The Council of the Indies framed and administered policy. (2) The *Casa de Contratación* (House of Trade) established at Seville in 1503 kept watch over imperial economic developments, issued licenses to merchants, emigrants, and prospectors, dispatched the fleets, collected customs, and received the treasure. (3) The Merchant Guild of Seville regulated and helped traders, arbitrated disputes between them, served as their mouthpiece in dealings with the *Casa* or the Council, and raised funds for convoys or government loans.

These three institutions wielded great power. The first two, at least, were diligent and conscientious in their efforts to order colonial society and trade wisely, to promote material welfare, protect the natives, and prevent wealth from flowing into non-Spanish hands. Their achievements were substantial. Their difficulties sprang partly from their attempt to regulate the details of colonial life from the home country in an age of slow communication —"remote control" requires electricity; partly from the fact that colonists always develop interests and attitudes which conflict with those of their distant rulers; partly because home and colonial officials of all ranks and grades were often corruptible; and partly because the commercial policy they had to administer was unenforceable in full.

Commercial Policy. For a brief period the commercial policy was fairly liberal. Charles V (1516–1556) opened the American door to traders or immigrants from any part of his wide European dominions. He thus put the Spaniard in competition with Italian, German, and Low Countries rivals. His successor, Philip II, beset by enemies without and Dutch rebels within his realm, closed and bolted the door by initiating a policy of "Spanish America for the Spaniards." No goods could enter the colonies from foreign ports or in foreign ships. For safety's sake, all vessels must shuttle between Seville or (later) Cadiz and four American ports, to which goods were convoyed in two fleets each year, there to be sold in great fairs and then sent overland or in coastal ships to their final destination. Only Spaniards who held a license from the *Casa de Contratación* could trade with the colonies, paying heavy export and import duties. The returning fleets must head for Seville or Cadiz, where their cargoes were taxed and unloaded under strict supervision. Any colonist who trafficked with foreigners without special permission faced the risk of the death penalty; any foreigner caught trying to enter a colonial market was executed or sentenced to hard labor for life in a mine; and smugglers of bullion were sent to the galleys or into exile.

Only one provision was lacking to make the imperial exclusiveness complete: the rules did not say that only Spanish goods were to travel west, for Spain could not possibly supply all that she or her colonists needed. In the Middle Ages she had imported much from

Italy, France, and the Low Countries; now her expanding output could not keep pace with the American demand; and since the advance in Spanish prices was earlier, more rapid, and greater than that in other countries it is possible that her export industries were handicapped in competition with their foreign rivals. Consequently many of the goods which went to America were foreign products. A recent study suggests that nearly a third of the silver reaching Spain about 1600 went on to France to pay for goods imported from that country and reexported to America. During the next century French, Dutch, and English wares formed a large part of the cargoes sent to the colonies.

Foreigners did much of that sending, in spite of the rule that only licensed Spaniards could traffic with the overseas possessions. In her hours of weakness or defeat Spain signed treaties which not merely recognized the acquisition by other countries of American islands or mainland regions but also granted trading privileges, extraterritorial rights, and favorable tariffs to Dutch, English, and French merchants who settled in her home ports. These men entered into partnership with Spaniards, who often contributed no more than their name to the firm; but under that name it was possible to get a licence for shipping goods to the colonies. In 1691, according to one estimate, nine-tenths of the exports carried by the fleets belonged to firms which were really foreign. There was nothing unusual in this practice; it was a common device wherever a government tried to confine trade to its own subjects, and it made foreign capital available if the native supply was scanty.

Illicit Colonial Trade. Although some foreigners were content to trade through Spain with America, others were as eager to deal directly with the colonies as some colonists were to establish direct contact with them. Spanish Americans had many inducements to buy and sell outside the law. They got their goods and slaves more cheaply if no duties had to be paid or if imports came straight to them instead of on the roundabout route from northern Europe through Spain to the fairs and then to them. Miners obtained a better net return for their bullion if they did not have to send it to the assay office and pay the quint; it was better to sell to a foreigner for 85 than to get 100 at the office and then be obliged to hand 20 over to the king.

Foreigners wished not merely to sell in a market which for a long time was far greater than was that offered by their own colonies but also to obtain some products in greater quantities than were likely to reach Cadiz in Spain's inadequate supply of ocean ships. Everybody wanted to lay hands on the coins or the material from which they were made. Europeans needed them for shipment to the Orient; West Indian planters needed them for the purchase of slaves, provisions, and manufactured goods; and English mainland colonists must have them if they were to have any coins in circulation or pay for all the things they drew from England. Spanish America also had the dyewoods required by the expanding textile industries of northwestern Europe, some drugs that had become popular with doctors, and some hides that were welcomed by a continent which had not yet discovered how to produce enough feed to sustain increasing herds of cattle.

Foreigners therefore refused to be shut out of Spanish America. A few of them went as pirates in peacetime or privateers in wartime. Raids on the treasure fleets were infrequent, and piracy was more spectacular than substantial. The bankrupt Frenchman who set out "like an honest man," haunted the Pacific coast from 1684–1688, plundered towns and ships, and returned with enough gold, pearls, and dollars to satisfy his creditors may look good in a technicolor movie, as do the buccaneers who operated from such Caribbean bases as the island of Tortuga. But illicit trade was far more important than were these robberies, and became easier as foreign nations secured islands in the Caribbean or colonies on the mainland during the seventeenth century.

From such bases as Dutch Curaçao or St. Eustatius, British Jamaica or Barbados, and French Martinique, vessels went to Spanish colonial shores. Sometimes they hovered off the coast and slipped their cargoes ashore furtively or transferred them to the boats of colonial buyers. Often they sailed into port and bribed the local officials into collaboration. At times they enjoyed the informal aid of their own country's warships. The Spanish *guarda costas* (coast guards) were unpaid, but received a share of what they captured. Hence their conduct was unpredictable; they might accept a big bribe and let a vessel go, but often they seized whatever came their way, whether the ship was seeking port legally or otherwise, and every Spanish fleet returned to Cadiz bearing a batch of foreigners who had been captured by them. Spanish colonial ships joined in the illicit traffic, brought dollars, drugs, dyewoods, and hides to foreign American ports, and then made their way home heavy laden.

With the Spanish, Dutch, French, and English islands so close to each other and so near to the mainlands, neither Spain nor any other power could hope to preserve its imperial trading monopoly intact. When the Spanish fleet arrived in western waters in 1662, it found the fairs so fully stocked with smuggled goods that much of its cargo had to be taken back to Cadiz; yet at that date the non-Spanish footholds in America were pitifully small in comparison with what they were to become during the next hundred years.

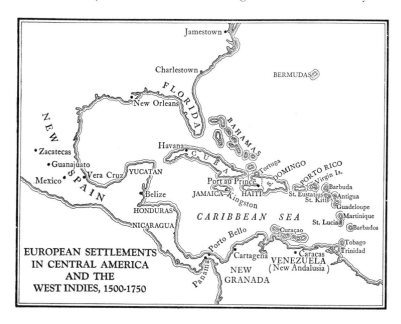

EUROPEAN SETTLEMENTS
IN CENTRAL AMERICA
AND THE
WEST INDIES, 1500-1750

Spain could no more suppress the direct traffic with her colonies than she could keep foreigners out of the legal trade through Spain. She kept her colonies by reluctantly allowing foreigners to trade with them; consequently by the end of the seventeenth century she had sunk into a sort of economic vassalage to her northern commercial neighbors.

Her own foreign trade was largely a matter of exchanging wool, wines, fruit, oil, silks, and linens made in the still flourishing region around Barcelona, native base metals and imported precious ones for the wheat of northern Europe, the fish of the North Sea and northwest Atlantic, and the manufactures of Holland, of France, but increasingly of England. By 1750 England was her best customer, the English controlled the largest wholesale houses in Spain, and British or Dutch ships carried most of the thousand cargoes that annually entered Cadiz except those few—less than a hundred—which came over the Atlantic imperial ferry. In rare moments of indignation against this apparent servitude, Spanish rulers resolved to build their own industries, provide their own capital, revive their merchant marine, run their own commerce, and stamp out smuggling. There was no lack of plans but a fatal shortage of nearly all the material and human resources needed for the task. The one thing that was abundant was a supply of rulers whose incompetence, temperament, standards of value, and even mental derangement made it certain that such dreams would not come true.

ANTWERP

Antwerp reached its commercial and financial pinnacle when the traffic from the outer continents was added to that of Europe. Twice a year the Portuguese king forwarded the spices received in Lisbon, to be disposed of by his factor in Antwerp; in July, 1538, for instance, a fleet of 130 small vessels delivered over 1,200 tons of pepper, nutmegs, cinnamon, and cloves. The ships which came from Spain bringing wool and wine now began also to carry silver and gold, destined to pay for goods needed by the colonies or to repay the debts of Charles V. The addition of these new branches of business to the old ones expanded not merely the trade in commodities but also the traffic in bills of exchange and in public or private borrowing. Loans were raised by kings, princes, and towns. As ocean transportation grew more important, marine insurance developed in volume and complexity.

The needs of commerce and finance attracted capital from all parts of central and western Europe and from men in all walks of life. The merchant-bankers who floated the large loans took deposits from or sold bonds to small investors. Groups of merchants pooled their own funds, or those they could borrow, to buy the whole incoming supply of such a commodity as pepper, and the making or breaking of these "corners" caused prices to rise or fall rapidly. Speculation of every conceivable kind was carried on by men who gambled on the prospects of peace or war, of political changes, of harvests being good or bad, of spice and treasure ships coming in or failing to arrive, or on what some astrologer had told them. The air was filled with rumors, scares, and advice to investors; with the bellowing of "bulls" who bought what they could not pay for, hoping to sell again at a higher price before they had to make payment; with the growling of "bears" who sold what they did not possess but hoped to be able to buy at a lower price before delivery day came; with schemes to defraud simpletons and plans to make easy millions.

This hectic, excitable community, this "seat of unbridled capitalism" (Sée), was bound to have its "fat years and lean years; years in which the pulse of business activities beat feverishly fast and others in which it was deathly slow" (Edler). It was also doomed to be the victim of disastrous politics. The break in the general upward trend during the 1550's hurt it. The revolt of the Low Countries against Philip II wounded it repeatedly and at last fatally. One of the first events in that revolt was religious disorder in Antwerp in 1566. This caused many leading bankers to emigrate. In 1576 the city was sacked by Spanish troops and in 1583 by French soldiers. Two years later, when it was captured by Spain, all Protestants who had not fled were expelled. Meanwhile the tumult in the industrial hinterland drove still more people north of the Rhine estuary; English pirates had rendered the Bay of Biscay and the English Channel unsafe for the Spanish wool and silver ships since about 1570; and when they were joined by the revolting Dutch "sea beggars" the seaways to Antwerp became impassable.

Antwerp's boom period thus came to a sad end. Its financial work moved elsewhere, especially to Genoa and Amsterdam; the English cloths went to Holland and Hamburg, the Dutch seized the oriental trade, sugar refining and printing were transferred to Rotterdam and London, and in 1598 Philip II excluded Antwerp merchants from direct trade with the Spanish or Portuguese colonies. When the Dutch and Spanish made a truce in 1609 the former controlled all the channels from the sea to Antwerp. For nearly two centuries these were kept closed as a deliberate part of Dutch policy, and Antwerp virtually vanished as a port.

With the eclipse of Antwerp and the beginnings of Spain's decline the center of interest moves to Holland, France, and England, the pacemakers of the seventeenth and eighteenth centuries. Their stories will occupy the next two chapters.

BIBLIOGRAPHY

See end of Chapter XIV.

XIV

ECONOMIC DEVELOPMENTS IN CONTINENTAL EUROPE, 1500–1750: II. HOLLAND AND FRANCE

The Dutch Republic

In the Middle Ages the region now known officially as the Netherlands and unofficially as Holland was a small, unattractive expanse of lowland, water, sand, and silt, dotted with a few fishing, shipping, and manufacturing villages. Its people farmed whatever land they could keep dry and made good woolen or linen cloth, and Amsterdam was a port of minor repute and a member of the Hanse in 1358. These conditions were in marked contrast with those of the highly industrialized and commercial areas south of the Rhine delta. Yet by 1650 Holland had become the chief carrying, trading, and financial nation in Europe, ranked first in some industries, dominated the oriental trade, conducted much of the slave traffic, and was a thorn in the side of every other western power.

The steps to that position involved the exploitation of water rather than of land. Rivers and canals made inland transportation easy and cheap; the Rhine, Meuse, and Scheldt rivers, which produced the estuary on Holland's southern border, gave access to busy rural and urban producing areas upstream; the North Sea was a fishery, a route to the coasts of northern and western Europe, and the doorway to the Atlantic. To seize these opportunities afloat was far more remunerative than wrestling with poor soil; yet the soil also was called on to contribute its quota to the national income.

The first noteworthy step was the extension of herring fishing far out into the North Sea, especially to the Dogger Bank off the shores of northern England. For this work the Dutch developed large boats of twenty to thirty tons, known as *busses* and carrying ten to fifteen men. They were thus able to use more and larger nets and to salt the fish on board instead of having to hurry it ashore for treatment. They also discovered an improved method of curing herrings which made the fish more palatable. The *busses* were first used about 1400, and by 1620 about two thousand of them were at work. The distribution of the catch, especially in southern Europe, employed a large fleet and opened the way for the carriage of more costly goods as well as the picking up of return cargoes. The herring fisheries were often called "the Dutch gold mine," a mine that never petered out. Whale fisheries, developed off Greenland or in other northern waters during the seventeenth century, proved to be a profitable silver mine.

The second step was the extension of coastal trade to Scandinavia and the Baltic lands. Every blow struck at the Hansards helped the Dutch, for though Denmark, Sweden, and Norway strove to get rid of the Germans they lacked the stature to step into Hanseatic shoes. The Dutch gained the lion's share of the trade in Baltic grain and lumber, controlled and financed the Swedish copper industry, and obtained access to Norway when Bergen was opened to them in 1524. Norway was almost as important a catch as were the herrings, for she supplied the cheap timber and naval stores which were the raw materials of Holland's vast merchant fleet.

Dutch Shipbuilding. The third step, though perhaps it should be listed as the second, was the development of a shipbuilding industry superior to that of any other country. The superiority was due to three factors. (1) Raw materials were bought in bulk for cash at low prices; Dutchmen paid less for Norwegian masts and boards landed in Holland than did builders in Norway. (2) In constructing the vessels there was some standardization of design, parts, and building methods. The *busses* were all very much alike, while the *fluitschip* (flyboat) which served as cargo vessel in European waters was designed on simple lines—long and broad, flat-bottomed, round-ended, and capacious. Such ships were put together by methods which faintly foreshadowed the modern assembly line. The use of such labor-saving machines as wind-driven sawmills and the organization of the shipyards, especially at Saardam, made it possible to produce ships quickly at low labor cost. (3) The builder was able to borrow money at a much lower rate than his foreign rival. Shipbuilding and owning attracted plenty of loan or share capital; even peasants and artisans were part-owners of vessels.

Shipbuilding became an export industry. By 1600 Venetians were buying Dutch vessels of more than seven hundred tons. In the seventeenth century Holland constructed the French East India Company's ships, sold flyboats, *busses,* and colliers to England, and provided merchantmen for Spain's colonial fleet. Colbert tempted Dutch workmen to come and energize the French shipyards. Peter the Great went to Amsterdam and Saardam to study shipbuilding, invited Dutchmen to Russia to build and operate his first warships, and chose one of them to be his first admiral.

The Carrying Trade. Cheap building and cheap operation went hand in hand. Since the *fluitschips* were easily handled, they needed only half as many sailors as were used on French or English vessels. The wide range of Dutch trade allowed ships' supplies to be purchased where they were cheapest. Consequently Dutch freight rates were usually said to be a third or a half less than those of other shippers. Rivals tried to destroy this advantage by charging higher port dues or shutting Dutch vessels out of certain routes, especially in coastal trade or to the colonies. The exclusion was rarely complete, and when Holland was neutral belligerents were glad to use her ships.

The fourth step was therefore the development of a sea-carrying traffic which ranged from Archangel in the arctic or from the most remote Baltic ports all the way round to Aleppo and Smyrna in the eastern Mediterranean. The Dutch conveyed grain from Danzig to Spain and Italy, Scandinavian lumber, copper, and iron to many countries, fish to the Catholic south, English woolens, German linens, and French wines or brandy to most markets. The cargoes brought from the south included Levantine silks, Mediterranean fruits or wine, Spanish wool, Bay salt, and American produce picked up in Lisbon or Cadiz. In this far-flung freight service Holland's position on the continent supplemented her central location on the sea routes. She was able to draw in, by river or road, the produce of Belgium and of the Rhine valley and its hinterland, and consequently was the sea carrier of such commodities as German wine and linens or Belgian lace, tapestries, cloths, and hardware. Dutch boats could navigate the Rhine as far upstream as Cologne; their cargoes were either sold there or sent on still farther in smaller craft or by wagon to the great fairs of Leipzig and Frankfort-on-Main.

In many of these freight movements a Dutchman owned the goods or was the commission merchant entrusted with their purchase or sale. If he was the latter, he might advance the consignor a fraction—half or three quarters—of the expected market value of the shipment, and when a sale took place he deducted the amount of the advance and the interest on it, as well as his commission, from the sum received. But he usually preferred to buy the imports, especially when they had to pass through a finishing or refining process before they were sold. Some of the great quantities of English woolens which he bought needed to be dyed and finished before he shipped them to buyers on the continent or outside Europe. He received German linens, whitened them at the famous bleaching works in Haarlem, and sold them abroad. Similarly with sugar, diamonds, tobacco, cocoa, and other commodities: Holland was the "staple" through which they passed, and something happened to them on the way.

The Dutch Empire. The fifth step was taken when the revolt against Spain embarked the seven northern provinces on a colonial career. Like the English they had been searching vainly for a northeast or northwest passage to the Orient, but now they could defy Spain and her vassal Portugal by sailing round the Cape of Good Hope. Between 1595 and 1601 at least fifteen fleets set out for the spice lands. Of eight ships that sailed in the spring of 1598 four were back by July, 1599, and could boast that "never have the Portuguese accomplished such a journey." In 1602 the Dutch East India Company was set up, uniting the groups which had nursed the infant trade. Its charter, granted for twenty-one years but periodically renewed, gave it a monopoly of Dutch oriental trade, with sovereign power to make war and peace, found colonies, build forts, maintain an army and navy, and do whatever seemed necessary for the extension of its power and profit.

That extension was effected by a combination of trading, fighting, and establishing control over native peoples. The Portuguese must be ousted by open force, for the Dutch had no more love of free competition than had their predecessors. The English, who had gone east about the same time as the Dutch, must also be checked. The struggle with them must be under cover and unofficial, since the two countries were at peace, except for brief intervals; but Jan Pieterzoon Coen, governor in the East Indies till 1629, made the English traders' lot most unhappy, and in 1623 put a band of them to death at Amboina.

By 1680 the Dutch had made the spice regions of the Malay Peninsula and Archipelago their own preserve and even the native traders had been eliminated. They held Ceylon and points on the shores of India, of the Persian Gulf, and of the Red Sea. They were stationed in Canton and had a trading colony on the island of

Deshima in Nagasaki Bay, and when in 1638 all Europeans were ordered to leave Japan the Dutch alone were given permission to stay.

The Company exploited its monopoly of Malaya to the full. As the only buyer it fixed the price the growers received at a figure no higher than would insure the production of the limited supply of spices that Europe could consume at the high prices which the Dutch sought to maintain. If the harvest threatened to become too large, plantations were destroyed. The homebound fleet left Asia about Christmas each year, laden with Japanese copper, silk, and porcelain, Chinese silks, green tea, pottery, tin, lacquerware, and wallpaper, Indian cottons, pepper, silks, and saltpeter, Persian carpets and fine cloths, Java or Arabian coffee, and Malay tin as well as the spices. The ships called at Mauritius and Cape Town, two way stations which had been settled to provide fresh food and water for the East Indiamen. When they reached home in early summer the Company disposed of the cargoes with great care. It sought to make the maximum profit on the sale of any goods it monopolized, such as high-grade cinnamon, cloves, and nutmegs, and held the price of these spices pegged high for many decades. It never exposed more goods for sale than it thought it could sell, even though this might call for the tipping of some goods into the sea. Profits fluctuated violently between 15 and 75 per cent in the early years, and on many occasions during the seventeenth century no dividends were distributed. After 1700 rates ran as high as 40 per cent in boom periods, but usually ranged between 12½ and 25 per cent. Even at these lower figures the shares were in great demand and sometimes sold at four or more times their face value. At that price a 12½-percent dividend yielded only about 3 per cent on the money paid by an investor for a share.

In North America Dutch ventures were less important. Little effort was made to settle colonists in the New Netherlands along the Hudson River. Fort Orange (Albany) and New Amsterdam (New York) were founded between 1614 and 1626 as fur trading posts, and the latter also served as a base for developing shipping services in the Newfoundland cod, Virginia tobacco, and West Indian tobacco or sugar trades. In spite of the annexation of the Swedish colonies of New Jersey and Delaware and of some aggressive attention to New England, the Dutch hold on North America was so weak that it was easily broken by the English in 1664.

In South America and the West Indies the Dutch did better. When their war with Spain broke out again in 1621, the West India Company was organized to merge all groups interested in transatlantic trade. It sent out hundreds of armed merchantmen who helped the fleet to harass the Spanish navy, seize the treasure *flota* of 1628, capture merchantships, defy Spain's restrictions on foreign traders, and annex much of Brazil. Curaçao and two other islands, all a stone's throw from the Venezuelan coast, were captured in 1634 and quickly became busy bases for illicit traffic, especially in slaves. Farther northeast, St. Eustatius was annexed for the same purpose. It lay near the Spanish, French, and English islands which were being rapidly developed. The Dutch stood ready to finance the planters and carry their produce to market. Neither British nor French merchants or shippers could offer so good a service, and it took a long time for them and their governments to pry the Dutch loose from the strong grasp they had gained on the island economies. Brazil was regained by Portugal, but Dutch Guiana was retained and became a large producer of coffee, sugar, cacao, and cotton. Finally, the Company had the West African coast in its parish, and from posts dotted there it gathered many slaves. Apart, however, from the rich pickings of the war years (1621–1648), the profits of the West India Company were never as great as those made in the Orient. Dividends were usually only 3 to 5 per cent, and in many years there were none.

This commerce with three distant continents, interwoven with the larger traffic nearer home, made the Dutch the owners of nearly half of Europe's shipping tonnage, "the Carryers of the World, the middle Persons in Trade, the Factors and Brokers of Europe . . . they buy to sell again, take in to send out; and the Greatest Part of their vast Commerce consists in being supply'd from all parts of the World, that they may supply all the World again" (Defoe). To complete their equipment for this work they became important industrialists and great bankers.

Industries. Some industries made the goods that Dutch consumers required, such as cloth, and exported any surplus. Others sprang from the country's *entrepôt* trade; they processed and finished the products which flowed into Holland in bulk and which were then reexported in smaller parcels to buyers in scattered markets. They reveal three common characteristics—dependence on special skill, on imported materials, and on the use of labor-saving devices.

The native supply of skill was supplemented by that of voluntary immigrants and of refugees who were attracted by the religious tolerance of their new rulers. The fury in the Spanish Netherlands drove countless *émigrés* northward. Huguenots came before the Edict of Nantes and after its revocation; the Thirty Years' War sent many Germans down the Rhine; religious discontent brought some people from England; and Jews who flocked in from Spain or Portugal were given civil rights in 1593. These newcomers strengthened many industries. Men from Hondschoote and other Flemish textile centers helped to quadruple the population of Leyden and lift its output from 27,000 pieces of cloth in 1584 to 110,000 in 1619. Belgian or French experts entered the bleaching industry of Haarlem and made Amsterdam famous as a producer of silks. Sugar refining expanded in Rotterdam and Amsterdam when the Antwerp refineries were ruined. Diamond cutting, which had emigrated from Venice to Antwerp, moved on to Amsterdam and has stayed there. Foreigners contributed some of the skill and precision needed for grinding lenses, making microscopes, producing pendulum clocks, supplying ships' instruments, and printing maps, charts, or books.

Virtually every industry worked on or with materials brought from abroad, for Dutch farms supplied only a small amount of tobacco, flax, wool, and madder. Imported raw tobacco, sugar, cotton, silk, cacao, metals, hides, and lumber were turned into finished products. Imported cloths were carried through the final processes of bleaching, dyeing, or printing, and the chemicals required for this work were drawn from India, America, or the Baltic lands. The eighteenth-century tobacco manufacturer might get his leaf from Holland, Russia, Hungary, Germany, Virginia, Havana, or Brazil; the dyer drew his alum from Italy, Smyrna, England, or Denmark; the silk weaver's fibers came from Italy, the Levant, India, or China; the copper worker had a choice of metal from Sweden or Japan; and the hides which went into a tannery might have come from the Argentine, Mexico, Poland, Denmark, or Ireland. If fuel was used it might be Norwegian firewood or English coal.

The use of labor-saving devices and the harnessing of power were widespread. The paper mills which fed the largest printing industry in Europe were located in northern Holland, where water power was available for driving the machines. Wind supplied power for many kinds of work, such as sawing lumber into boards, turning millstones, working fulling hammers, grinding various materials, as well as pumping water. The textile industry used a loom which wove several strands of ribbon and a machine which printed patterns on linens or cottons. A country with so many enterprises and a total population of only about 2,500,000 persons must make its labor count as much as possible in shipyard and workshop.

Agriculture. In agriculture economy of land was more important even than economy of labor. Forty per cent of Holland is below sea level, and in the seventeenth century some of this 40 per cent was actually under water. The three main tasks were to prevent further flooding, reclaim some submerged areas, and extract the greatest quantity of food from every acre by methods which were often horticultural rather than agricultural. There was little sense in growing grains, for these could be obtained cheaply from the Baltic ports. There was no room for fallow and no profit in poor livestock. The hoe was kept busy, manure was plentifully applied, vegetables, root crops, and artificial grasses gave a large yield per acre of food for man or beast, and high-grade cattle were virtually hand-fed instead of being turned adrift to hunt for their meals. Regions around towns were covered with truck gardens. To the cultivation of useful foods was added that of ornamental shrubs or flowers, of which the tulip was the most valued. Dutch agriculture served as a model for progressive landlords and farmers in other countries during the eighteenth century, and Dutch engineers were sought wherever a drainage problem had to be solved. Yet in 1800 a third of Holland was still sandy waste, and some large reclamation tasks, especially the drainage of the Zuyder Zee, remained.

Amsterdam. Amsterdam was by 1700 "the staple market about which international trade and finance revolved" (Wilson). Virtually all the industrial activities described above were carried on in or around the city. The harbor was capable of holding four thousand vessels, but its entrance was too shallow to admit large craft. The Bourse, large enough to accommodate five thousand traders, offered a range of commodities as wide as Dutch commerce itself. By 1585 the weekly list of "prices current" gave the price at which over 200 kinds of goods had been sold, and a century later it contained nearly 500 items. The Bourse also became Europe's chief money and stock market. The formation of the East India Company stimulated the sale of stocks. Gradually the shares of other companies, including such foreign ones as the English East India Company or the Bank of England, came into the market, as did the bonds of Dutch political units and eventually of some foreign governments.

Since the prices of stocks and bonds were far from stable, speculation in securities became almost as common as in commodities. In that kind of operation, Amsterdam had little to learn from modern London or Wall Street, for in the 1630's it was swept by a speculative mania which foreshadowed in almost every detail the stock market booms and bursts of the nineteenth or twentieth century. Prices rose gently at first, chiefly in dealings between professionals, but as the upswing became apparent outsiders entered the market. Soon all sorts of amateurs, from intellectuals to laborers, were buying, paying for their purchases with savings, cows, land, houses, furniture, or anything else that could be turned into cash. Rumors raged, prices soared—some of them more than twentyfold—and vast paper profits were made overnight. By 1636 the market was a madhouse; in February, 1637, it was a ruin. The only consolation left to the losers was the knowledge that they could plant, or possibly eat, that which had cost them so dearly; for the subject of the speculation had been tulip bulbs.

As a loan and capital market Amsterdam served its own citizens and government and also those of other countries. For Dutch borrowers there was abundant money available at rates which seemed incredibly low to envious foreigners. The East India Company floated bond issues at 3½ per cent, reputable merchants could borrow at that rate, and there was much provision of credit on mortgages to landlords. When London or Paris failed to raise the capital needed for some venture, aid was usually sought in Amsterdam. Loans to the Dutch government began when the rebel leaders needed money for the struggle with Spain, and were made later for wars with England and France. During the eighteenth century loans to foreign rulers became important. Hence, as Strieder says, the Bourse was a great reservoir which replenished the empty coffers of half Europe and provided rich Dutchmen and foreign owners of money with a field for profitable investment in colonial or European enterprise.

The Bank of Amsterdam. Founded in 1609 and modeled on the Rialto Bank of Venice, the Bank of Amsterdam was the first institution of its kind north of the Alps. Its sole business was to receive deposits and transfer money from one person's account to that of another. A merchant deposited such coin, bullion, and bills of exchange as came into his hands. The coins might be domestic or foreign, heavy or light, of various mintages with differing precious-metal contents. The bank valued the deposit in terms of the quantity of precious metal it contained and credited its owner with so many units of its own "bank money," the florin. Thus x grains of silver equaled one bank florin, a good French louis d'or was worth ten florins, and so forth. The depositor could then draw on the florins which stood to his credit to pay his debt to others; but as his creditors would have accounts with the bank the payment involved merely a book transfer.

The bank was not supposed to lend money; hence it could make no profit, and must charge a fee for its deposit, transfer, or exchange services. It did not, however, like to watch others earning income by lending. It therefore made loans to the city government or the East India Company and financed a municipal pawnshop. Its chief service remained, however, that of making commercial payment easy for its two thousand clients.

From her far-flung, diversified, and closely interwoven enterprises Holland drew a substantial income. Upper- and middle-class Dutchmen lived in solid comfort. They were interested in science and art, but the art of a Protestant society did not depict saints or the Virgin. Instead it took the secular life as its theme and found fitting subjects in trim landscapes, streets, courtyards, kitchens, taprooms, and docks, or in portraits of bankers, cloth hall syndics, and women peeling apples. The subject might be as prosaic as a herring *buss,* but the execution was as skilled and competent as was the cultivation of a tulip or the cutting of a diamond.

The Passing of Dutch Supremacy. During the eighteenth century Holland lost her economic preeminence, partly because she slipped back or stood still, but chiefly because others overtook her, copied her technique, and dispensed with her goods, services, ships, or funds. Lack of raw material prevented her from establishing a position as the permanent source of supply of any commodity. Her dependence on importing, processing, and exporting made her vulnerable if countries which supplied her or bought from her became industrially mature or politically unfriendly. Others could learn how to build and operate ships, banking skill was no Dutch monopoly, and people who dealt with one another through a Dutch middleman might decide to establish direct contact. Consequently the combination of advantages which the Dutch had enjoyed was broken up at one point after another, and Holland contributed to the disintegration by making one or two blunders or by being rigid of outlook in a changing world.

These developments become apparent after about 1730. The loss of carrying, *entrepôt*, and processing business is well illustrated in the growing direct exchange of English woolens for German linens. The English finished their own cloths and then took them to Hamburg, now grown into a great bleaching, dyeing, and printing center for linens gathered in from all the German and Baltic lands. Similar direct connections grew stronger between England and Russia, while Hamburg began to displace Amsterdam as the destination for ships bearing French wine or sugar and cargoes from Lisbon or Cadiz. Furthermore, the ships which traversed these routes belonged increasingly to one of the countries engaged in the exchange. England, the German ports, France, and the Scandinavian lands developed their own merchant marines. By 1780, therefore, it was estimated that the Dutch carrying trade in European waters had fallen off by at least half since 1700. Of the vessels entering Danzig during the 1770's only 30 per cent flew the Dutch flag; 25 per cent were Swedish ships, while the others belonged to Lübeck, Danzig, England, or Denmark. By that time England had far outstripped Holland in the foreign trade and shipping of Russia.

Dutch processing and manufacturing industries were hit hard by this loss of trade and traffic. They were hurt still more by the growth of protected and subsidized foreign manufactures, such as the Irish and Scots linen, the Russian tobacco, and the French or English silk industries; by the fact that rising taxes had pushed the cost of materials, of living, and of labor much higher than it was in other countries; and by the refusal of the Dutch government to impose protective tariffs on imported manufactured goods for fear of hurting the country's export-import economy. Dutch industrialists not merely lost their foreign markets; they also saw cheap foreign wares come in, paying low duties, to compete with their own products in their own market. At sea the old supremacy in herring and whale fishing was challenged, and only about two hundred herring *busses* were now at work. The whaling industry was injured by competition from Scandinavia and old or New England.

As opportunities for selling, making, and carrying declined or stood still in a century of expanding world commerce, Dutchmen turned increasingly to serving clients as commission merchants and to financial operations. Since they had more capital than could be employed profitably at home, they sent much of it abroad. They financed the new direct trade, especially that with the Baltic. Those who bought in that area had to pay cash, part of it when they sent the order and the rest when the goods were dispatched. Those who sold goods to Baltic importers had to grant credit for nine, twelve, or even eighteen months. The Dutch bridged with their funds the gap between the buyer's payment and the receipt of his goods, as well as that between the western seller's shipping of his wares and his receipt of payment for them. When, for instance, a Frenchman sent an order to St. Petersburg, he instructed his agent there to draw bills on an Amsterdam firm in order to get the money needed for executing the order. The Frenchman had, of course, already made arrangements with the Dutchman to accept such bills in return for interest on the money advanced and a small commission charge. He might also have agreed that the same firm should insure the cargo, charter shipping space, pay the freight and the Sound dues, and generally finance the whole transaction. Meanwhile, an Englishman who sent goods to a Russian buyer might be paid immediately by a Dutchman who later collected the purchase price from the importer, plus interest and commission.

Much Dutch capital was thus used to lubricate trade which no longer went near Holland. Much was also put into mortgages to landlords or short-term loans to farmers in Europe, some went to finance West Indian plantations, and a lot was used for investment or speculation in company stocks and government bonds. In the mid-eighteenth century Dutchmen held a third of the shares in the Bank of England and in the British East India Company, as well as a large slice of the British national debt.

Investment in that debt seemed good politics and better business. During the seventeenth century Anglo-Dutch commercial rivalry had led to at least two wars, but between 1689 and 1713 the two countries joined forces to thwart the ambition of France, the greatest land power in Europe as well as a menace at sea. After 1713 Holland, weakened and debt-laden by these wars, abandoned all thought of being a big power, let her army and navy deteriorate, and became a neutral in the Anglo-French struggle. Her financiers were, however, ready to back the British. Britain's fiscal system was much sounder than France's, yet there was enough uncertainty in international affairs to make her bonds fluctuate violently in price and consequently provoke speculation which might win quick profits but burned many fingers when the market broke in 1763 and 1773. There were also close personal business ties between London and Amsterdam. Dutch buyers therefore snapped up British bonds, but carefully avoided loans to France. By 1776 the British national debt had risen from £50,000,000 in 1740 to nearly £140,000,000, and Dutchmen held about £60,000,000 of it.

When France intervened in the American Revolution the Dutch changed their minds. Britain appeared doomed to fall under the blows of opponents on both sides of the Atlantic. Her debt was so large that bankruptcy seemed inevitable, while France had reformed her finances so much that her credit rating stood high. Dutchmen therefore made loans to France and America, but not to England, and friction over neutral shipping rights aligned Holland as a belligerent with her new debtors. Unfortunately for her, it was France that emerged bankrupt. Britain tottered and fell in America but not in Europe; her financial resources were discovered to be so good that she could stand on her own feet.

Holland's inaccurate forecasting cost her dearly. Her French investments became worthless after 1789. She lost ships and American colonies during the war with England (1780–1783) and thus was hurt at two of her remaining strong points—her trade in oriental goods and in American produce. When she passed under French control (1794–1815) she lost still more vessels and as many of her colonies as the British cared to take. In those turbulent decades her two great pillars, the East India Company and the Bank of Amsterdam, broke and fell. The Company had long been shaking under the stress of war and mismanagement, while competition from rival companies or from the clandestine trade of its own employees had pared down the profits on oriental imports. It ceased to pay dividends in 1783, and when the end came in 1798 its assets were worth only one-eighth of the liabilities, which amounted to at least $50,-000,000. In its fall it pulled down the Bank, which had lent heavily to the Company and had already been bankrupt in 1781.

When the war clouds cleared in 1815 Holland found she had saved some capital from the wreckage, and all her colonies were restored to her except Ceylon and South Africa. These assets, combined with her location and her skill in seafaring, commerce, and finance, helped to repair her damaged fortune. But in a world where coal, iron, and cotton were more important than herrings, linen, sugar, and spices, her place was no longer in the center of the world economy or even of that of northwestern Europe.

The Dutch story was that of a tiny, poor country whose people must earn their livelihood by exploiting the sea, foreign trade, and their own wits. The French story is that of a large land (200,000 square miles), most of it capable of some use. Over the six hundred miles from north to south the climatic range from temperate seasons to Mediterranean warmth made possible the growth of a wide variety of produce, starting with all kinds of grains and grapes and spreading out to include vegetables and apples in the north, olives and oranges in the south. There was feed for all sorts of animals, even for silkworms and edible snails; there were large forests, vast salt deposits, ores of iron, zinc, and lead, and some coal. France thus had most of the requisites for self-contained material welfare. She needed little from the outside world except tropical products, and a large foreign trade was not essential.

Her size is, however, likely to be as deceptive to us as it was to her early modern rulers. France was far from being really united politically and still farther from being one great domestic market. A large land area needs cheap, good means of transportation if the special products of different districts are to be exchanged. Two large river systems—the Seine and the Loire—provided natural or improvable waterways for much of France's share of the great European plain, and especially for the region of which Paris was the center. In the southwest the Garonne stretched more than halfway from the Bay of Biscay to the Mediterranean. From that sea the Rhone-Saône valley supplied a natural route nearly all the way up to the fertile Seine Valley and the north. But the Rhone was too swift to be navigable, and the other rivers, even when combined with the mediocre or poor roads, were not strong enough to bind France together in a national economy. Meanwhile the French coasts looked out over the sea to foreign lands which were nearer and more accessible than were other French coasts or the interior of the country. It might be more profitable for the people of the maritime provinces to seek markets in Italy, Spain, England, or the Low Countries than in the heart of France. Trade barriers, the legacy of medieval political localism, were not all removed when the country became united. Internal customs tariffs, local weights and measures, and legal or administrative differences were not swept away until the French Revolution, and effective economic unity had to wait for the coming of the railroad.

In area and population France was the largest European state west of Russia until the German Empire was founded in 1871. In the early modern period she housed at least as many people as lived in the Low Countries, British Isles, and Iberian Peninsula all put together. Her rulers therefore felt the urge to pursue ambitious policies, seeking to give the king absolute sovereignty over his realm, make France the leading power in Europe, and carve out an empire overseas. To realize these aims they felt they should stimulate and steer economic developments in directions that would add to France's power, prestige, wealth, and prosperity. They must establish national regulation in place of old feudal or municipal controls; encourage kinds of enterprise that flourished in other countries but seemed in danger of being neglected in France; wage economic warfare in the intervals between outbursts of the other kind, in order to win a place in foreign trade, shipping, and colonization; and repair the physical or financial ravages of war.

This economic *étatisme* ran through the whole period, reaching its peak in the policies which Colbert pursued from 1661 to 1683. Alongside it ran the state's insatiable need for revenue. That revenue was raised by a tax system which virtually defied all efforts to reform its two most unsatisfactory characteristics. In the first place the chief direct tax, the *taille*, was levied on personal and real property. But nobles, ecclesiastics, some officials, and some cities were exempt from payment of *taille*, as they also were from some *aides*, which were sales taxes levied on drinks, fish, livestock, wood and some other commodities. Since the state was debarred from taxing such a large slice of its subjects' property and income, it had to place heavier burdens on the middle class and poor. In the second place, the collection of *aides* and of the *gabelle* (salt tax), as well as the operation of the tobacco monopoly, was in the hands of tax farmers, who took far more from their victims than they had agreed to pay the state. Financing the government might therefore offer a more profitable and secure form of enterprise and investment than did agriculture, industry, or commerce. Consequently French productivity was impaired by the diversion of private income from potential use as capital into the coffers of the state or of the tax farmers, and by the preference which men with money showed for dealing in public finance.

This "constant haemorrhage of capital, which removed it from business as soon as it had been created" (Hauser) provided a marked contrast between French conditions and those prevailing in Holland and England. The contrast was intensified by French standards of prestige. Business was looked down upon as a debased occupation; to be bourgeois was to be boorish. Hence the ambition of many businessmen was to make enough money to permit them to purchase an estate, to buy the title, social prestige, and sure income that came with some government post, or even to do both. Other able men regarded the church and the army as the most attractive vocations. Meanwhile, many landlords had little interest in their estates except as sources of income from rent and dues. The combined result of these influences was to channel energy, ability, and wealth away from economic activities into ways of life which appeared more honorable, secure, or socially acceptable.

General Development of the French Economy. In periods of peace and good crops France could support a population which fluctuated around a figure of 20,000,000 persons from the fourteenth century to the early eighteenth. When such favorable conditions prevailed it rose rapidly, but bad harvests, often amounting to dire famine, caused acute crises and very heavy death rates, while frequent civil or foreign wars brought human suffering, economic destruction or dislocation, and financial chaos.

From such a tragic period France began to recover when the Hundred Years' War ended in 1453 with the final eviction of the English. The attack on swamps, moors, and areas that had relapsed into forest or waste was resumed, domestic trade flowed more freely, old fairs were revived or new ones founded, and foreign trade increased, especially in the Mediterranean under the energetic enterprise of such men as Jacques Cœur. Louis XI (1461–1483) encouraged the merchant class because he needed its support in his struggle to establish control over the aristocracy, and his schemes for stimulating industry and trade have led historians to call him "the father of French mercantilism." Frenchmen shared in the general European upward trend from 1450 to 1550, sending out transoceanic exploring, fishing, trading, or piratical expeditions, feeling the stimulus of rising prices, supplying some of the goods that new-rich Spain and Portugal needed for themselves or their colonies, and cultivating Renaissance standards of luxury.

After 1550 the European economic crisis and religious strife undid much of this advance. Civil war between Catholic and Huguenot filled most of the years 1562–1598 and left parts of France in ruins. During the thirteen years of peace that followed, private enterprise regained some lost ground, while Henry IV (1598–1610) and his ministers Sully and Laffemas worked hard to repair the finances, foster rural recovery, nurse industries, improve internal transportation, expand the merchant marine, and give thought to America. Again France shared in the wave of prosperity that swept western Europe during the early years of the seventeenth century.

Henry was assassinated in 1610, and much of the next half-century was disturbed by civil conflict, the Thirty Years' War, a fight with Spain, and the depression which descended on western Europe when the boom burst about 1616. From these troubles the French monarchy came out master of the nobles and towns, supreme in Europe, and with a better foothold in America. But the cost was heavy, French industry, trade, and shipping had shrunk, and the next twenty-three years were filled with Colbert's efforts at fiscal repair, industrial development, and the building up of foreign trade, a merchant fleet, and a navy. His plans, however, included an attempt to hurt the Dutch by doubling the tariff, impeding their shipping, and provoking a war. In that war (1672–1678) most of his favorite projects were wrecked, others failed for lack of funds or profits, and the rest were slow in achieving much success.

In 1685 Louis XIV revoked the Edict of Nantes and threatened Huguenots with imprisonment and confiscation of property if they persisted in their faith. Some accepted conversion, more or less sincerely, but many left the country. The loss of skilled artisans and energetic traders almost entirely depopulated some communities, reduced the size and wealth of others, and contributed to the three decades of depression that gripped the French economy until 1713. Other factors played their part. Colbertism "degenerated into a meddling tyranny over industries, an obstacle to progress and trade" (Hauser). French diplomacy provoked a new crop of wars, with England, Holland, Scandinavia, Prussia, and the Holy Roman Empire as antagonists. From them France emerged in 1713 shaken in prestige, bankrupt, with her plans for controlling the Spanish Empire thwarted, and with England in possession of Hudson Bay, New-foundland, Acadia, and the Asiento.

Again the task of reconstruction and economic expansion was taken up, this time in a peace which endured for the unusually long period of nearly three decades. It got off to a bad start, thanks to a grandiose scheme hatched by the Scotsman John Law for painlessly producing prosperity. (See Chapter XVI.) Law's projects provoked an outburst of paper-money inflation and stock speculation which crashed in 1720. When the debris had been removed, solid achievement began to be made in every direction—at home, in Europe, Africa, India, and the West Indies. Deadly famines were rare; the population, spared the *"massacres sociaux"* and *"sacrifices humains"* (Labrousse) of earlier food disasters, grew to 25,000,000 in a few decades. Rising prices for wheat and wine made farming prosperous; industries expanded and trade boomed.

War with Britain ruffled the forties. Then in the mid-fifties France's rulers felt strong enough to demand, as the price of continued peace, that London concede to them the heart of North America, a dominant position in India, and overwhelming supremacy in the slave trade. Britain rejected this demand, and in the Seven Years' War (1756–1763), a struggle terribly costly to both belligerents, France was defeated, losing Canada and retreating in India. Peace brought a breathing spell for drastic fiscal reform, but the temptation to seek revenge on Britain by aiding the American revolutionaries proved irresistible. Intervention was invaluable to America but by increasing the national debt by one-third it proved ruinous to France. It given just at a time when the long period of prosperity and expansion was drawing to a close. Prices fell—that of wine by half—and the depression in agriculture spread to industry and commerce. The burden of "the American debt," general economic *malaise*, and a ruined harvest in 1788 provided an ominous overture for the French Revolution.

Agriculture. Of the three sources of France's national income, agriculture was by far the greatest. While much of it was usuculture, there were two major commercial staples—wine and grain—and such minor ones as brandy, flax, hemp, olive oil, wool, silk, and animal products. Wine was produced in most provinces. It ranged from the *vin ordinaire* drunk by the poorer classes to the fine qualities which were in great demand at home and throughout northern Europe. Even a small grower might produce more wine than he could consume; consequently the condition of the domestic and foreign market and the price level determined the welfare of many cultivators. Political events sometimes interfered with exports, as when war with the Dutch prevented the enemy from carrying supplies from Bordeaux and other ports to northern European consumers, or when Anglo-French friction led London in 1703 to tax French wines more heavily than Portuguese vintages. French brandy was also in great demand throughout Europe; the value exported was sometimes a third that of the wine shipments.

Grain growing for market was less general than was commercial production of wine. The small farmer had little left for sale after he had put aside a fifth of his crop for next year's seed, paid any dues that must be delivered in kind, and provided for his family needs. The market was therefore fed by the larger farmers. It was chiefly an internal market, influenced by problems of transportation and of policy. Policy was dominated by grim memories of the fatal effect of periodical famines, especially on the towns and cities. Exports of grain were forbidden except in very good seasons, and in lean years provinces which had any surplus used their power to prevent it from going to famine areas. It is possible that France could not have built up a regular export trade in competition with the cheaper lands and serf labor of the Baltic granaries. At any rate, she did not attempt to do so; she therefore had relatively little to spare in good years and in poor seasons endured scarcity. The grain trade was ill organized except for feeding Paris; in very good years wheat might be ruined for lack of adequate storehouses, and inland transportation was so costly that it was cheaper and more profitable for southern growers to send their grain to Spain or Italy and for northern farmers to ship it to England or Holland than to deliver it in the middle of France.

In France as elsewhere the "price revolution" hurt those landlords who depended chiefly on fixed money rents for their income. Some seigneurs had to tighten their belts and starve on their estates; some sold their land to a bourgeois buyer and went off to seek a government job; but others, especially the new landowners, tried to wring more income from their tenants or from working the land themselves. They restored the domain where they could. If any holding fell vacant they changed the dues from fixed money payments to fixed shares of the produce or to short leases. They increased the fine paid when a farm changed hands. They lent money to tenants, and foreclosed if the borrower defaulted; or they supplied the cash when a village lacked money for payment of its taxes, and took in exchange part or all of the common land or rights. Some of them announced, after taking the advice of their lawyers, that common property rights did not exist, and that the community enjoyed the use of common lands only at the seigneur's pleasure.

These efforts to enhance income had uneven results. To them were opposed the tenacity of the villagers and the general hostility of the crown. The intendants, who were the king's provincial representatives, tried to check the landlords' encroachments and to protect peasants against the more obvious attacks. The tenants therefore held their ground without any serious challenge to their way of life and work until the landlords became really progressive or aggressive after about 1750. (See Chapter XIX.)

Industry and Commerce. Medieval France had practiced the usual kinds of handicraft production of necessaries, comforts, and some luxuries for the maker's use or for sale. The market for most industrial products was largely domestic, served by countless small-scale producers. Only in the northeast was the textile industry, like that of Flanders and Brabant next door, organized to serve a large foreign demand. France's chief exports were wine, salt, and cloth; her imports included Italian or Levantine wares, the cream of her foreign trade was in Italian or Hansard hands, and Italians were her chief financiers.

To early modern French rulers this dependence on others was deplorable. France must remedy it, establish those industries she lacked, make the weapons she needed for wars that were now being fought with guns, foster the growth of a trading class, and build up a merchant marine in her own shipyards. Thus would she cease paying what looked like tribute to foreigners. She would also stop the drain of precious metals out of the country and cause treasure to flow inward as foreigners paid for French goods with silver or gold. In terms of power politics every addition to her economic armory would weaken possible enemies. In terms of public finance it would provide new sources for taxes and loans. In terms of royal power, the king would have available the resources and support of a bourgeois class; this was far safer than having to depend on a rural society whose income was already heavily taxed and whose landlords might resist the crown's march to power.

From at least the mid-fifteenth century such aims and arguments had led to action. Louis XI and his successor welcomed shipbuilders and silk weavers from Italy, brought miners, metalworkers and printers from Germany, and imposed prohibitive import duties to foster the growth of the silk industry. Henry IV did almost everything, from trying to acclimatize silkworms in the cool north to hiring or subsidizing immigrant makers of Venetian glass, Persian rugs, Turkish carpets, Flemish tapestries, and other furniture or apparel for the court and aristocracy. Rivers, roads, postal services, weights and measures, shipbuilding, standards of workmanship, fairs, trading companies, colonies, all received attention.

Colbert. Colbert gathered up all the schemes and expedients of his predecessors for a grand, prolonged attempt to build a completely self-sufficing national economy. A little early business experience and a long career in state departments concerned with war and diplomacy were his qualifications for assuming control in 1661 of manufactures, commerce, finance, and well-nigh everything else —except war and diplomacy. He took office in the depths of depression, post-war fiscal chaos, and a frightful famine. Some industries were very sick, foreign trade and shipping were in Dutch hands, the treasury was empty, and two harvests had been bad.

To cope with such conditions Colbert brought tireless energy, a passion for order and detail, a belief that political persuasion or pressure could move mountains, and a dogged tenacity which kept him running in all directions simultaneously for over two decades. His outlook was frankly static and selfish: he regarded the total amount of money, manufactures, ships, and trade in the world as fixed, and he intended to get a larger share of it for France. This was to be done by replacing imports with French products and by elbowing foreign merchants and vessels out of journeys which began or ended in French ports. Millions of livres, he believed, would thus be kept from going out of the kingdom, such as the five millions shipped abroad yearly to buy metals, the four millions paid the Dutch for naval stores, or the million spent in Venice for mirrors. If his victims resisted these my-gain-your-loss policies he was ready to turn an economic war into a shooting war. His emphasis was chiefly on commerce and manufactures. He regarded them as "the fertile sources of the prosperity of the kingdom," as superior to agriculture, since they were subject neither to the seasons nor to the inconsistencies of the weather, and also as the weaker parts of the country's economic armor. Consequently, though he was in charge of the richest agricultural country in Europe, he did very little for cultivators. In a recent exhaustive description of his policies, less than 40 out of 850 pages deal with his rural program.

Colbert's methods fall under four headings: encouragement, regulation, protection, and company promotion. To foster the industries he wanted, he offered every conceivable encouragement. He ordered ambassadors and consuls abroad to become labor recruiting agents, operating underground since most states forbade their skilled workers to emigrate. He offered all kinds of honors and monetary rewards to Dutch shipbuilders and cloth finishers, Swedish miners and foundrymen, Venetian makers of lace or mirrors, German tin-plate workers and other experts. He topped his favors to a Swedish tar maker by finding him a French wife and providing her with the necessary dowry.

His inducements to immigrant or native industrialists included monopolies, prizes, titles of nobility, pensions, freedom from guild rules or taxes or militia duty, contributions of capital or workshop space or equipment, loans free of interest, lower tariffs on imported raw material and higher ones on manufactured goods. If these baits failed to catch the fish, he tried to force people to start industries or supply capital, and ordered towns or provinces to grant privileges or contribute cash. Sometimes he hunted out existing producers and urged them to expand their output. Often they hunted him out and got support, a monopoly, and funds. He took over the small Gobelin tapestry workshop set up by Flemish immigrants sixty years before and expanded it as a state enterprise to produce large quantities of tapestries, furniture, cloth, and jewelry.

With encouragement went regulation. The new industries and their older brothers must refrain from tricks of the trade, inferior or dishonest workmanship, and the use of poor materials or methods. By giving high quality they would win markets at home and abroad. Traditionally it was the business of the guilds, the towns, and later the state to guard working standards; but guilds were not numerous in France (outside Paris), and kings who wished to use them as regulators or as sources of revenue had in 1581 and 1597 ordered a nation-wide system to be set up—without much effect. Colbert revived this policy, ordered guilds to be formed for occupations which lacked them, and commanded all merchants and craftsmen to become members. He overhauled the guilds' ordinances and supplemented those of the textile industry with royal regulations which set forth in detail the kinds of cloth that could (or could not) be made, the processes and materials that were required (or forbidden), and many other technical instructions. He drew up a Code of Commerce to regulate trading methods and practices. The guild and royal rules were to be enforced by guild officials, special state inspectors, and the local authorities.

In using the guilds Colbert had a dual aim. He was quite as much interested in the new revenue he could extract from them as in the work of their members. Guildsmen must pay for their monopoly, for confirmation of their ordinances, for entrance to membership, and for other privileges. "Industrial control thus stood revealed as naked fiscalism," as "a kind of indirect taxation, taxing the consumers through the monopolistic artisans" (Heckscher). "The crown sold the right to work" (Sée).

Colbert gave protection to French industry by raising import duties a little in 1664 and then at least doubled those on manufactured goods in 1667. This was a hard blow at English, Belgian, and German wares, but its chief purpose was to hurt the Dutch, whose many-sided efficiency stirred Colbert to envy, hatred, malice, and economic war on every front. The Dutch threatened and finally took retaliatory steps, whereupon France gleefully started actual war in 1672 without bothering to declare it. The early campaigns went so well that Colbert dreamed of annexing Holland and of transferring much of her trade to French hands; but when the struggle ended in 1678 the Dutch had proved so formidable that he was forced to abandon his high tariff and restore the rates of 1664. The war he had provoked and welcomed wrecked his most important schemes; it used up money that had been earmarked for financing industries, injured trade and shipping, upset his plans for fiscal reform, and ruined his tariff. It also showed the rest of Europe that France was not invincible. On a smaller scale the high tariff provoked retaliation by Spain, German and Italian states, and England.

Colbert's efforts produced a motley of successes and failures. His one certain accomplishment was building up "the greatest industry in France"—that of "supplying the wants of the king and his court" (Cole). To this task he devoted vast sums of money, financing operations and then buying the products. He thereby strengthened France's position as heir or rival to Italy in the production and export of luxuries. "The French gobelins and furniture stuffs, the much sought after, beautifully woven materials, hosiery, ribbons, and lace with silk, silver and gold threads, mirrors and porcelains and many other products were received all over Europe with envy and admiration and imitated everywhere" (Heckscher). In these industries competition was not present and price was not an important factor; the same was true of Colbert's fairly successful cannon and sailcloth works, and in the naval shipyards where the state was the chief or only customer.

Outside these projects, which were virtually government usufactures, the score ranged from a few partial successes down to abject failures. Colbert's encouragement seems to have helped to develop the production of some goods which had formerly been imported, such as fine woolens, stockings, and serges, and to have expanded or improved the making of some already familiar commodities, such as linens. He may thus have increased the share which France contributed to meeting its own demands and reduced imports somewhat. But mediocre successes and complete failures take up the greater part of the record, even in such a case as the making of tin plate, which he was determined to establish "at whatever price it may cost." Inadequate capital, unforeseen management difficulties, popular hostility to some monopolies, foreign competition, and personal roguery upset the best-laid plans; even his Swedish tar maker played him false by decamping with the cash but leaving wife and children behind. No fostered industry made much impression in foreign markets, and none was healthy during the three decades of depression that followed Colbert's death. The marked industrial advance which came after 1713 suggests that peace and the growth of the colonial markets were more important stimulants than was ambitious state planning.

Internal Trade. The promotion of commerce formed part of every installment of *étatisme*. Two obvious steps were necessary to stimulate internal trade, but neither of them was financially feasible. The first was the removal or reduction of the many tolls that had to be paid on road or river and of the customs duties which were levied when goods entered "the five big farms" from the other provinces. The "five big farms" comprised a customs area which included most of northern France; the rest of the country, containing five-eighths of its area, consisted of "provinces reputed foreign" or "provinces effectively foreign." Goods passing from these provinces into the "five big farms" paid the same duties as if they had come from outside

France, and goods moving in the opposite direction paid export duties. The tariff rates were complicated, and when combined with the tolls and the freight charges they made the price of inland transportation very heavy. Salt quintupled in cost by traveling 260 miles on the Loire and passing about 50 toll stations. Yet the claims of the tollgatherers were so strong and the fiscal needs of the crown so urgent that it was almost impossible to lighten these burdens on movement. In 1664 Colbert simplified but could not remove the tariff around the five big farms; he abolished some tolls which were being illegally levied, but a multitude remained until the Revolution swept them away.

The second necessary stimulus to domestic trade was improvement of the means of transportation. Such work has, however, been costly of labor and capital in all times and places. Local labor was drafted for repairing roads; landlords could be ordered to keep the highways through their estates clear and passable; and individuals or groups might be induced to construct a bridge or improve a stretch of river by allowing them to charge tolls for its use. These patchwork efforts were unlikely to produce a satisfactory system; the state must supplement them in the interest of trade, travel, and troop movements; but the state seldom had adequate funds to spare. Henry IV spent a million livres a year on highways, but his successors lacked the interest or the money, and even Colbert never provided more than 600,000 livres in any one year.

Only when the long peace and recovery came after 1713 was a real road program begun. To supply the labor the royal claim to *corvée* was extended by ordering every peasant residing near a main road to work one month each year for the state. This heavy demand was resisted, sometimes riotously; it was not always enforced, and some of its results were poor. Turgot abolished it in 1776 in the belief that hired labor, paid wages out of tax funds, would be cheaper and more efficient. This time the taxpayers objected, and a modified *corvée* was reintroduced. On the eve of the Revolution 7,000,000 livres was being spent annually, and France at last secured 25,000 miles of the best main highways in Europe.

River improvements were also costly, and canals still more so. The former were left largely to private individuals, and a canal linking the Loire with a tributary of the Seine was constructed by the duc d'Orléans on terms which yielded a good return in tolls and freight earnings on the capital he had invested. But for France's most famous project, the Canal of the Two Seas, the crown had to provide nearly half of the 17,000,000 livres spent on the work, the provincial authorities contributed a third, and Riquet, a landowner who initiated the plan, emptied his pockets to find the remainder. This canal, connecting the Garonne with the Mediterranean, was finished in 1681. Its channel, 180 miles long, was carried at one point over a watershed 600 feet above sea level, a brilliant engineering feat. Its freight rates were about a quarter those charged for land carriage, and it proved useful to local traders. But the vision of vast cargoes floating across southern France instead of tossing and trailing round Spain, thus pouring revenue into the pockets of the French king and Riquet instead of into those of the Barbary pirates or the Spanish ports, proved to be an idle dream; very little through traffic used it. In the eighteenth century less ambitious but more useful projects were completed. By 1760 northeastern France and the adjacent Low Countries were covered by a network of improved rivers and canals.

Foreign Trade. In its wine, brandy, salt, wheat, linens, luxury goods, and later its Newfoundland cod and West Indian sugar, France had commodities for which there was no lack of markets abroad. In the Middle Ages the French, English, and Hansards traded from the north and west coast harbors. The Hundred Years' War curtailed their activities, but when peace came such ports as Rouen, St. Malo, Dieppe, Nantes, and Bordeaux sent vessels into north European waters as well as across the Atlantic. Marseilles rose to prominence in the Levantine trade, taking advantage of the extraterritorial rights accorded Frenchmen by the Franco-Turkish treaty of 1536. Nearer home there was Spain, a growing market as American treasure made it richer, and able to pay its bills with wool or precious metals; Antwerp, the place where everything could be bought and sold; and England, ready to take what France had to send in return for tin, iron, hardware, wool, and woolens.

The conflicts between 1550 and 1650 checked this advance. Meanwhile the Dutch got into full stride and by 1660 were conducting much of France's foreign trade, carrying her exports, imports, and coastal cargoes, and doing everything in the French West Indies except grow the sugar. That their services were conveying French produce into every near or remote market mattered nothing; in the eyes of French nationalists they were plundering the country of 4,000,000 livres a year in freight charges alone, and sucking the precious metal out as fast as it came in from Spain.

Colbert resolved to liberate French shipping and foreign commerce from this thralldom. Shipping was to be helped by charging higher port duties on foreign than on French vessels, by inviting Dutch shipbuilders to work in French yards, and by giving bounties to Frenchmen who built ships or sent them on long journeys. France's share in foreign trading was to be enlarged by establishing state-subsidized companies. The Company of the North (1669) was to invade Holland's Scandinavian preserves, exchanging wine, salt, and brandy for naval stores and lumber. The Levant Company (1670) would push the sale of French woolens in the Turkish Empire in face of Dutch and English rivals. The East India Company (1664) was expected to break into the oriental triopoly enjoyed by the Dutch, English, and Portuguese. The West India Company (1664) was to help Colbert in his effort to loosen the Dutch grip on the sugar islands, while the Senegal Company (1673) would break the Hollander's hold on the slave trade.

There was nothing new in these companies, for similar ones had been formed in earlier decades. There was novelty in the vigor with which Colbert brought them into being, the substantial subscriptions of capital made by king and court, and the browbeating or blackmail used to induce skeptical merchants in Paris or the ports to buy stock. There was nothing new in the companies' fate. They all failed to make profits for their stockholders, to build up a large or lasting business, or to divert much trade and carriage from the Dutch. They were casualties of the Franco-Dutch war.

The French Empire. During the early sixteenth century Frenchmen roved in all directions—to Brazil, the East Indies, the Slave Coast, the Banks, the St. Lawrence, and the waters off Florida through which Spanish treasure ships traveled unconvoyed on their way home. The merchants of Rouen planned a company for trade with the East Indies and organized a colonial exhibition with a model of a Brazilian village and fifty natives as its highlights. Yet in 1600 France's only remote activities were codfishing, a little smuggling or lawful traffic with Latin America, and the tiny beginnings of fur trading up the St. Lawrence.

Throughout the next century the cod were important. From "wet salting" the catch for the rich man's table, French fishermen went on to produce cheaper dried fish for southern Europe and the West Indian slaves. This step required land bases, but since the English had occupied the best sites on Newfoundland the French set up only one there, at Placentia, and mostly settled farther west on the St. Lawrence Gulf or in Acadia.

The fur trade received attention after 1599 when two Havre sea dogs were given a monopoly of the business on condition that they take out fifty colonists each year. This grant passed from one group to another until in 1627 Richelieu handed the control and trade of Canada to the Company of the Hundred Associates. Like its predecessors this company took out no more settlers than were needed to grow food for its agents. On the westward journey its vessels were too full of trade goods and provisions to have space for settlers and their effects. There was no need even for many fur traders in the early days, since the Hurons brought the pelts down to Montreal (founded in 1642) and bartered them there. Consequently, when New France was transferred from the Company to the state in 1663 it had only about a hundred farms and 2,500 white people.

By that time the Hurons had been stopped from coming down the river by having their trade routes (or their scalps) cut by the Iroquois. Competition from Dutch and English traders from Albany or Boston and still more from English buyers at Hudson Bay soon became severe. The French therefore were compelled to go west for their furs, and pushed to the head of the Great Lakes, the prairies, and the Mississippi. This long journey raised costs enormously, for the trader had to carry his own food and trade goods far upcountry and convey his purchases back. In addition, his government must give an expensive hand, building forts, providing presents to keep the natives friendly, and generally pursuing a policy aimed at dominating the whole continent west of the Appalachians. As a step in empire building this cost might be worth paying—if the plan succeeded; but it was a large sum to pay for beaver skins which were used chiefly for making men's hats. The price received for the pelts in Europe might not even meet the *commercial* costs of getting them, especially if the fashion in hats changed or the fur market was overstocked. As a business venture the fur trade was not important; the average annual export between 1730 and 1755 was only seventy-five tons of beaver.

Apart from that trade, New France was a string of mildly feudal seigniories and farms along the banks of the St. Lawrence. The farmers fed themselves, the officials, church, army, and fur traders but were unable to play their dual role in the French imperial plan. By that plan they were, firstly, to supply the French West Indies with the provisions and lumber needed there; Placentia would send all the fish required, and the island planters would concentrate on producing sugar or coffee for shipment to France. This task was too great for the St. Lawrence settlements. They were too far away from the islands, up a gulf and river made impassable by ice every long winter. Their soil and climate were too poor to attract many immigrants or yield much exportable surplus. Secondly, Canada was the forward base in the struggle for an inland empire; but she was neither manned nor financed adequately for that assignment. When the British took possession in 1763 the colony contained only 70,000 French Canadians. The foothold on Newfoundland had been lost in 1713, as had all hope of ousting the British from the Hudson Bay region. By 1763 two tiny islands and some fishing rights in the St. Lawrence Gulf were all that was left to France in North America.

The Sugar Bowl. In the Caribbean the French were far more successful. They secured Martinique, Guadeloupe, Haiti, and a dozen smaller islands. Sugar plantations multiplied on them after 1640, and at first the Dutch were their chief buyers, shippers, refiners, and suppliers of capital or slaves. Colbert resolved to confine the trade to French ships and home ports and to concentrate the refining in French hands. His West India Company failed to achieve these objectives in its brief profitless career (1664–1674), but Frenchmen did gradually gain most of the business. In the eighteenth century the islands expanded their production so greatly that they became Europe's largest sugar provider as well as exporter of much tobacco, coffee, cacao, indigo, rice, and cotton.

When the islands were captured by the British fleet during the Seven Years' War, strategic considerations suggested that they be kept. But the British West Indian interests did not wish to have them inside the British Empire lest their produce, grown at lower cost and sold at lower prices, injure the market monopolized by the dearer sugar from the British plantations. This argument prevailed; France lost Canada but was allowed to keep her sugar bowl. On the eve of the Revolution traffic between France and her West Indies was ten times that of 1713 and accounted for about a fourth of France's external trade.

In Africa and Asia France made little progress until the eighteenth century. The West Indian expansion stimulated French slaving from Africa, and a revitalized East India Company made great headway in India. Dupleix, who became commander of the Company's outposts in 1741, set out to curb and even to oust the rival English company. The times were turbulent, for the Mogul Empire which had kept India in some sort of unity and order had recently broken up, and adventurers who were scrambling for the pieces welcomed the aid of any European, especially if he knew how to organize armies, instill discipline, and operate cannon. Dupleix ingratiated himself with some of the new princes, aided them or became their ally, gathered military and naval forces, and by 1750 had gained much power, largely at the expense of the British. During the early fifties as many as thirty French ships were visiting India each year. But the British soon turned the tables on Dupleix; in 1754 his masters recalled him because his expensive policies were swallowing up the profits from trade; and during the Seven Years' War France's interests were trimmed down to a few trading posts.

Eighteenth-Century Progress. The growth of the West Indian plantations, the enterprise of the East India Company, and the fairly steady traffic in furs contributed to that general expansion which began with the recovery from Law's collapse and continued till the seventies. Marseilles, Bordeaux, Nantes, Rouen, and smaller ports were quickened by receiving, processing, and distributing the rising influx of colonial or oriental produce and by the production or collection of goods needed for the slave trade, the islands, the fur traders, and India. Colonial demands stimulated industries which supplied the outward cargoes. West Indian cotton fed a virtually new textile industry in Normandy, while some of the other colonial imports were reexported, along with domestic produce, to Spain, Holland, Hamburg, and the Baltic. Though smugglers leave no trade statistics, there was probably a growing clandestine exchange of wines, brandy, and silks for wool across the English Channel. According to the best available figures, French external trade more than trebled between 1716 and the 1770's.

This growth reacted on the country's industry and domestic trade. The luxury industries continued to flourish, but the more important developments were in heavy industries such as iron and coal, and in those which made cheaper cloths, hardware, and glassware. French products thus became *articles de luxe et de nécessité*. The state encouraged these newer enterprises. It recognized that some of the strength of the British enemy lay in the possession of industries that France lacked, and therefore advanced capital more freely than in the past, welcomed British inventors, technicians, and capitalists, and urged its officials to promote the introduction of new machines or processes into mines, workshops, and metal plants. French science grew lusty and French inventors had many important new ideas. Roads and waterways received serious attention, a Bourse was established in Paris, and France's backward banking system grew less inadequate. Peace allowed some taxes to be lifted from industry. Finally, some landlords began to be seriously interested in the agricultural experiments and better farming which were engaging the attention of their English counterparts by 1750.

From these landlords, from some members of the middle class, and from the thinkers the demand was increasingly voiced for less state regulation of the grain trade, of industry, and of commerce. The newer industries were fairly free from the guild and royal controls which still, on paper at least, ruled the older occupations. Even these controls became weaker, and the guilds were "already at the point of death" (Hauser) when Turgot in 1776 gave men freedom to work at any occupation they chose, to practice more than one trade, to use whatever equipment or technique seemed best, and to employ as many workers as they desired. Colbertism, with its concept of order in a static economy, was being at least partly submerged by the rising tide.

The long upward swing did not end with the Revolution. Rather it was the ending of the prosperous decades that helped to cause the Revolution. The tide turned about 1778 and ebbed for over a decade. Falling prices injured farmers, especially wine producers, and made them dislike the landlords to whom they had to pay rent or dues and the government to which they had to pay taxes from their shrunken income. Merchants, burdened with high taxes on their depleted profits, criticized the government for piling up debts by its American adventure and then for incurring still more by borrowing money for public works in the hope of relieving unemployment and restoring prosperity. Some manufacturers hated the Anglo-French trade treaty of 1786 which, by reducing tariffs, had exposed them to keen competition from British wares. Wage earners in town and country alike felt the effect of hard times on employment and wages. The bad harvest of 1788 raised the cost of food, a bitterly cold winter in 1788–1789 raised that of fuel, thereby reducing the amount of income left for purchase of industrial goods. When, therefore, national bankruptcy forced Louis XVI to call the Estates-General into session in 1789 for the purpose of putting the finances in order, economic conditions helped to convert what began as a measure of reform into a revolution.

BIBLIOGRAPHY

GENERAL

Clark, G. N., *The Seventeenth Century* (1929), chaps. 1–4, 11, 12.
Cole, C. W., and Clough, S. B., *Economic History of Europe* (1941), pp. 158–173, 196–223, 233–242, 318–343.
Kulischer, J., *Allgemeine Wirtschaftsgeschichte* (1928–1929), vol. ii, chaps. 5, 6, 16, 20.
Newton, A. P., *European Nations in the West Indies, 1493–1688* (1933).
Pares, R., "Economic Factors in the History of Empire," *Ec. H. R.*, May, 1937.
Renard, G., and Weulersse, G., *Life and Work in Modern Europe* (1926), chaps. 1–4.
Sée, H., *Modern Capitalism* (1928), chaps. 4–7.

PORTUGAL AND SPAIN

Chang T'Ien-Tse, *Sino-Portuguese Trade from 1514 to 1644* (1933).
Chapman, C. E., *Colonial Hispanic America* (1933), chap. 9.
Christelow, A., "Economic Backgrounds of the Anglo-Spanish War of 1762," *J. Mod. Hist.*, March, 1946.
Hamilton, E. J., *War and Prices in Spain, 1651–1800* (1948).
Hamilton, E. J., "The Decline of Spain," *Ec. H. R.*, May, 1938.
Haring, C. H., *Trade and Navigation between Spain and the Indies in the Time of the Hapsburgs* (1918).
Klein, J., *The Mesta, 1273–1836* (1920).
McLachlan, Jean O., *Trade and Peace with Old Spain, 1667–1750* (1940).
Prestage, E., *The Portuguese Pioneers* (1933).
Trend, J. B., *The Civilization of Spain* (1944).

HOLLAND

Baasch, E., *Hollandische Wirtschaftsgeschichte* (1927).
Barbour, Violet, "Dutch and English Merchant Shipping in the Seventeenth Century," *Ec. H. R.*, January, 1930.
Furnivall, J. S., *Netherlands India* (1939).
Hyma, A., *The Dutch in the Far East* (1942).
Posthumus, N. W., *Inquiry into the History of Prices in Holland*, vol. i (1946), Introduction.
Posthumus, N. W., "The Tulip Mania in Holland in the Years 1636 and 1637," *J.E.B.H.*, May, 1929.

Wilson, C. H., "The Economic Decline of the Netherlands," *Ec. H. R.*, May, 1939.

Wilson, C. H., *Anglo-Dutch Commerce and Finance in the Eighteenth Century* (1941).

FRANCE

Bloch, M., *Les caractères originaux de l'histoire rurale française* (1931).

Cole, C. W., *Colbert and a Century of French Mercantilism* (1939).

Gandilhon, R., *Politique économique de Louis XI* (1940).

Gershoy, L., *From Despotism to Revolution, 1763–1789* (1944).

Hauser, H., "The Characteristic Features of French Economic History from the Middle of the Sixteenth to the Middle of the Eighteenth Century," *Ec. H. R.*, October, 1933.

Labrousse, C. E., *La crise de l'économie française à la fin de l'ancien régime* (1944).

Nef, J. U., *Industry and Government in France and England, 1540–1640* (1940).

Sée, H., *La vie économique et les classes sociales en France au xviiie siècle* (1924).

Sée, H., *L'evolution commerciale et industrielle de la France sous l'ancien régime* (1925).

Sée, H., *La France économique et sociale au xviiie siècle* (1925).

Sée, H., *Histoire économique de la France: le moyen age et l'ancien régime* (1939), parts iii–vi.

Vignols, L., "Early French Colonial Policy," *J.E.B.H.*, November, 1929.

Young, Arthur, *Travels in France in 1787, 1788, and 1789.*

XV

ENGLAND, 1500–1750

Tucked away in the top left-hand corner of the map of Europe, fifteenth-century England was an unimportant, unfortunate country. Having lost all its French possessions except Calais by 1450, it then passed through three decades of civil strife. Its population had been reduced by famine and plague to possibly 2,000,000 persons in 1400. Wool exports declined, cloth exports stood still, and traders were driven out of northern markets by the Hansards. Agricultural profits had fallen so low that great landowners abandoned commercial farming and leased their domains. Tenants were scarce, some land was unoccupied, and the attack on wastes had ceased. Domestic commerce might still give a comfortable income to those traders and craftsmen who could protect their local market by guild restraints, and the wage earner may have benefited from the failure of wages to fall with prices. London, Bristol, and the rural textile areas were fairly active, but for landlords, wool exporters, the church, and the politicians the century was gloomy.

This picture contrasts strongly with that of the mid-eighteenth century. By 1750 the population had almost trebled and was growing quickly. Commercial agriculture covered much of the country, some grain was being exported, but wool was kept at home by law for use in a cloth industry that was now the largest in Europe. The production of metal goods was highly developed, and coal fired a wide range of industries. British merchants, using British ships, were firmly established in most European ports, in the oriental and African trades, and in every kind of traffic with the Americas. Emigration and conquest had created an empire with thirty transatlantic colonies. London was within a short step of displacing Amsterdam as the world's financial and commercial center.

The English Environment. Many factors combined to provide a favorable environment for the varied and balanced enterprise of these three centuries. England's area (50,000 square miles) was a quarter that of France, but four times that of Holland. Hence there was enough land to meet all the needs—except for wine and semi-tropical fruits—of four to six million consumers and leave some grain over for export. Even the worst regions were fit for sheep. Forests, though not lacking, could not bear too heavy raids by the shipbuilder, house carpenter, or charcoal burner. Ore deposits were sufficient to meet early modern demands, and coal was abundant. Consequently the raw materials were available for many kinds of industry. Transportation by river boats and coastal vessels gave access to most areas, and there were no serious natural obstacles to the use of roads.

England's location for northern European commerce was not quite as good as that of Holland, since the North Sea separated her from the delta leading to the Low Countries and the Rhineland. This disadvantage, however, was a low price to pay for the security which England enjoyed by being part of an island. She need not spend money on a large defensive army. Freedom from invasion let her industries carry on throughout the longest war, kept her countryside and towns from being ravaged, made the tone of life and government civilian rather than military, and permitted con-troversies to be waged without fear of intervention. For trade with southern Europe and the other continents her location was even better than that of Holland, provided that Ireland did not pass into the hands of any power that would use it as a base for attacking her in the rear or for menacing her sea lanes to the Atlantic. Her southern and western ports had quick access to the open ocean, and even such east-coast ports as London or Hull were better situated than was Amsterdam or Hamburg.

Finally, the political environment became increasingly favorable to economic enterprise. The loss of her possessions in France made England politically as well as geographically insular. Henceforth her foreign policy was not concerned with costly attempts to hold or win territory on the continent but with maintaining her own security and later her expansion overseas in face of the might of Spain and France. This policy, resting on sea power, did not absorb a large part of the country's income until conflict with France pro-duced what has been called "the Second Hundred Years' War" (1689–1815).

Constitutional developments eventually placed the government in the hands of the landed and mercantile classes. When the old feudal nobility largely killed itself off in the Wars of the Roses, the first Tudor monarch (Henry VII, 1485–1509) filled the vacuum with a strong central government which restored order at home and repaired English prestige abroad. Although he and his successors were disposed to be absolute rulers, they could not ignore the wishes of their chief subjects, do without their aid in administering local and central affairs, or dispense with their consent, expressed in parliament, when important decisions had to be made or more funds were needed. When differences of opinion became acute, especially after the Tudors gave place to the Stuarts in 1603, the subjects' capacity for restraining the king's will grew stronger. It was embodied in statute laws which parliament passed, in common-law principles which judges expounded, and in the reluctance of the local justices of the peace, usually country landlords, to enforce vigorously any laws which they or their neighbors disliked. It kept taxes low, beheaded Charles I in 1649, put Charles II on the throne in 1660, and deposed James II in 1688.

In the end parliament became the supreme power in the realm. Landlords were sufficiently strongly represented in it to shape agricultural policy. Merchants grew more influential as members of the House of Commons or through the pressure they could exert from outside. Consequently industrial and commercial policy, which before the Civil War "had been a policy imposed by the government on business interests . . . became to an increasing degree a policy imposed by business interests on the government" (Tawney). That imposition was made all the easier by the fact that the political capital, Westminster, lay immediately west of the commercial city of London, the country's chief port, market, and countinghouse. A merchant in a French port was a hundred to five hundred miles away from Paris when he had a grievance to voice or a proposal to make; but a Londoner had only to go two miles up the Thames to reach the government offices or houses of parliament. The contacts between land and commerce or finance were almost as close through investment, intermarriage, the entry of landlords' younger sons into business, and the purchase of estates by successful traders.

The English story can be examined under four headings: the growth of commercial agriculture, the spread of industries, the expansion of home and foreign trade, and the building of an empire.

AGRICULTURE

Agriculture was pulled out of its late medieval doldrums by the expansion of three markets. The first was London, which grew from 60,000 consumers in 1540 to more than 300,000 in 1640 and to at least 700,000 by 1750. To feed it, produce flowed in from every part of England, Wales, and later Scotland. The second was the woolen industry, which expanded greatly after 1500, thereby stimulating a demand for wool. The third was the continent, to which England became a minor grain exporter during the seventeenth century.

The first two demands were felt during the sixteenth century, which was also the period of the price revolution and the transfer of monastic lands. Rising prices bore heavily on those landlords whose tenants paid rents which had been fixed by custom or copyhold and which could not be changed for many years or generations. These *rentiers* saw the purchasing power of their incomes fall; yet the cost of maintaining their great households rose, especially if they felt impelled to keep up with the luxurious fashions that were spreading from southern Europe to the north. They squirmed all possible ways to increase receipts from their lands or tenants. Some married rich merchants' daughters, sought places on the government pay or pension roll, and cut down their domestic staffs. But only the most resourceful were able to avoid a tightening of the belt, and schools or colleges which had allowed their farm rents to become rigid suffered acute financial distress.

Not all landlords were restricted to this passive role of *rentier*. Some, perhaps most of them, managed to get rid of their customary tenants, to raise the rents of leasehold farms three to sixfold in half a century, and to do what they wished with much of their estates. They re-created or expanded their domains, cleared wastes, cut down trees, and tapped deposits of iron ore, coal, or stone. Their energy was matched by that of some wide-awake farmers.

While part of the rural revival was the work of peers and other large landowners, the outstanding figures were the squire and the yeoman. The squire was a country gentleman who ranked below the peer in status and acreage. He might be a merchant or lawyer who had bought an estate, or a small landowner who had extended his property, especially when the crown sold the ex-monastic lands in order to make the budget less unbalanced. Between 1558 and 1640 English rulers parted with land worth over £4,000,000, and most of it was bought by the local gentry. Of more than 3,000 manors examined by Professor Tawney, squires owned 80 per cent in 1640, peers had less than 7 per cent, and the crown had only 2 per cent. The king of England now owned very little of England, and the squire had become the backbone of English rural life. He might farm all the estate himself but more usually divided his interests between working some domain and collecting rent from tenants.

The yeoman was a large farmer who owned or rented as much as 200 acres of plowland or 600 acres in grazing regions. He was the country boy who made good in the country by practicing all the virtues lauded by Calvin. Hard-working, thrifty, land-hungry, he picked up a bit more land whenever he could, until his farm became so large that he must hire labor to help him run it. He therefore differed in scale of operations from the "husbandman" or the continental peasant, who had only enough land to keep his family busy. One of his class, Robert Loder, kept an account book from 1610 to 1620. It shows him tilling 130 acres in open arable fields, feeding cattle in enclosed pastures or on the open common, holding some meadow, and cultivating four orchards. He experimented ceaselessly, kept careful records, and debated the relative merits of growing more wheat or more barley, of using different kinds of manure, and of paying day or week or piece wages. To him farming was a business, which he strove to make as profitable as possible by using his capital and intelligence. Since he harvested 25 to 35 bushels of wheat per acre in an age when the yield is usually estimated to have been about 12 bushels, his efforts were evidently well rewarded.

Growing markets, rising prices, and new men were bound to disturb methods and conditions which had prevailed during the preceding century of stagnation. Yeomen and landlords alike took steps to put land to the most profitable use. They consolidated their scattered arable strips into compact plowfields and inclosed part of the commons, wastes, woodlands, and even bits of highway to provide additional cultivable acres, larger meadows, or better pastures. They thus devoted much capital and labor to the task of pulling more of the countryside out of that wild natural condition in which so much of it had remained throughout earlier centuries. They turned grainfields into sheepwalks if the net return promised to be higher; but for this conversion the landlord got most of the blame. He was bitterly accused of evicting tenants, throwing their holdings together, inclosing commons, and turning his estate into a sheep farm. Sermons, pamphlets, and poems denounced "the cruel inclosers," and regretted that "the simple and gentle sheep, of all creatures the most harmless, are now become so ravenous that they begin to devour men, waste fields, depopulate houses and whole townships." Riots and revolts broke out at times. The Tudors were so afraid that inclosures might provoke a serious peasant uprising that a series of laws was passed forbidding the conversion of arable land into pasture, the erection of hedges or fences, and the possession of more than two farms or 2,000 sheep.

The effect of this opposition was apparently slight; administrative machinery was weak and the laws were easily evaded. It seems evident, however, that the area affected by this inclosure movement was much smaller than the uproar would suggest; that only 500,000 acres were inclosed between 1400 and 1650, many of them in regions that were poor arable country; that there was less illegal eviction of tenants than oppression within the law; and that yeomen were as active in the movement as were the landlords. Not all the inclosed land became sheepwalks; much of it remained under the plow or was used as dairy farm, vegetable garden, and orchard. Finally, a great amount of tilled land remained in open fields, even until the eighteenth century.

During the seventeenth century inclosure continued more quietly, often by agreement among the interested parties. Some landlords and farmers experimented, introduced new crops, tools, and methods from France or Holland, sowed clover to improve grasslands, and gave a little attention to the potato and turnip as foods for man and beast. Reclamation of swamps began on a grand scale when in 1630 a group of English and Dutch capitalists engaged Vermuyden, a Dutch expert, to drain 400,000 acres in the low-lying eastern counties. The costs were heavy, the opposition of the fishing and duck-hunting natives was persistent, winter floods were hard to combat, and success was only partial. By 1750 nearly 750,000 acres —about one-fortieth of the whole country—had been drained; but the task was not finished until a century later.

One consequence of these developments was a great increase in the production of wheat. This enabled more people to eat white bread instead of that made from rye, oats, or barley, and provided a surplus for sale to Holland, Spain, and Portugal. Exports of grain had formerly been permitted only in years when abundant harvests

pushed the price below a low price fixed by law. After 1600, however, grain growing expanded under the stimulus of London's needs
and of a great rise in prices caused by disturbances in the Baltic
lands during the Thirty Years' War. A class of merchants emerged
to organize the domestic and foreign trade.

When peace returned to England and the continent in 1648 the
price index for wheat, which had climbed from about 75 to 110
during the long war, fell heavily and remained down, except in
times of famine or of the Franco-Dutch war, for three decades. (See
graph on p. 252.) English landlords and farmers therefore sought
relief, encouragement, and stability from parliament. Several Corn
Laws—"corn" is English for wheat and other grains—were passed
between 1660 and 1689. They allowed exports, no matter what the
domestic price, but could suspend them in time of scarcity; they
abolished free imports and set up a sliding scale by which foreign
grain paid a high customs duty if the domestic price was low but
only a small one if it went high; and they gave a bounty on exported
corn if the price dropped below a certain remunerative level.

The effect of these laws has been hotly debated without reaching
a unanimous verdict. The provisions favored the producer rather
than the consumer, as farm relief and encouragement measures have
done in all countries and periods. They assured the farmer a good
return by giving him the export bounty when prices were low, and
some landlords were therefore possibly able to raise rents. These
benefits were largely counteracted by the higher taxes, especially
on income from rents, which were imposed when the wars with
France began in 1689. The consumer was promised some protection by the sliding scale of duties, by suspension of exports in bad
years, and by the likelihood that if farmers normally set out to produce for both home and foreign markets the crop in lean years
would be larger than if they had planted only enough to meet
domestic demands.

Until about 1760 famines were rare, good seasons frequent, and
prices relatively low and stable. Grain exports averaged over 4,000,-
000 bushels a year, and imports were negligible. Yet in spite of the
Corn Laws the general tone of agriculture became less bracing than
it had been before 1660. Prices had ceased to rise, some of them fell,
but taxes and interest rates went up. Squires and yeomen saw their
rewards shrink or even vanish. Land passed out of the hands of the
less successful into those of large owners who drew their income

chiefly from political office or into those of a new crop of land buyers composed of rich lawyers, army contractors, high army officers, and leading politicians. These men were not "improvers." Engrossed in the political and social whirl of London, they bought or increased their estates—and sometimes erected vast mansions on them—for social prestige or political power, and were satisfied with a steady income from rents. A class of *rentiers* once more displaced many of the earlier breed of entrepreneurs.

INDUSTRIES

The outstanding industrial feature of early modern England was the diversification of manufactures. To the old staple, woolen cloth-making, was added a long list of light consumers' goods and "heavy" industries. Professor Nef has shown that these developments were so far-reaching between 1540 and 1640 that they constituted an "industrial revolution." The new products were often cheap enough to be afforded by the middle class and the not-quite-poor; they were useful rather than ornamental, necessaries and comforts rather than luxuries, window glass rather than goblets. But after 1700 great strides were made in catering for the rich, and by 1750 English manufacturers were not merely first in the "masses" market but were running some continental luxury producers a close race.

Textile Industries. Medieval England had made both high-grade and cheap woolens for home and foreign markets. Though wool was grown and manufacture carried on in most counties, East Anglia, west Yorkshire, and the region behind Bristol in the southwest were by 1500 the outstanding producing areas. The industry had spread to farms and villages where the cost of living was low, the supply of female spinners plentiful, guild regulation absent, and the water or water power good. Protestant refugees from the Low Countries introduced lighter kinds of cloth, popularly known as " the new draperies."

Much of the industry's market was foreign, and it therefore shared Europe's alternations of good and hard times. The boom which developed after 1500 trebled the exports from London, chiefly to Antwerp; but the European crisis of the fifties, the ruining of Antwerp, and the French religious wars made the rest of the century a period of stagnation. After 1600 the industry shared in the prosperity that swept Europe for over a decade. Its boom days ended when a scheme hatched by a London alderman, Cockayne, for finishing and dyeing pieces in England instead of in Holland succeeded only in dislocating the trade (1614–1617). The shrinkage of the central European market with the outbreak of the Thirty Years' War (1618) was a still more severe blow. Recovery came in that market with peace, but meanwhile some exporters had sought relief by pushing the sale of new kinds of cloth in France, Portugal, Spain, the Levant, and the outer continents. Consequently English woolens were known in virtually every part of Europe, in Latin America, the English colonies, and the Near and Far East.

The industry was regarded by the state as a prime national asset and by boosters as "the richest and most valuable manufacture in the world" (Defoe), worth more to England than were the mines of America to the king of Spain. For its sake farmers were forbidden to export wool, heavy duties were imposed on foreign fabrics, the use of cottons was checked, colonists were ordered not to make woolens for export, textile workers were not allowed to emigrate, and corpses must be wrapped in woolen shrouds. Countless laws sought to stamp out tricks of the trade, maintain quality, and thus prevent foreign customers from complaining that the cloths were cheap but nasty. Diplomacy tried to open new markets or ward off higher tariffs. This solicitude can be explained by the fact that woolen cloth accounted for nearly half the country's total exports in 1700, that in 1760 more than a third of it went to the British American colonies, and that the woolen interests had powerful spokesmen inside and outside parliament—though not powerful enough to insure that the various laws were vigorously enforced.

By 1700 those interests were looking with anxious eyes on two new rivals. English merchants who pushed into the Levant trade after 1580 brought raw cotton back, secured linen yarn from Ireland, and employed Lancashire workers to make fustian, with a linen warp and cotton weft. This light cheap fabric won favor at home, on the Slave Coast, and in the plantations. Meanwhile the East India Company imported cotton cloths, some of them plain but many covered with colorful printed patterns. These also became widely popular. Defoe declared (about 1710) that they had "crept into our houses, our closets and bedchambers; curtains, cushions, chairs, and at last the beds themselves were nothing but calicoes and India stuffs." Clothing and undergarments could be made of them, though fashionable young men still preferred linen shirts.

This double invasion angered the woolen producers and merchants. They denounced the cottons as "tawdry, pie-spotted, flabby, ragged, low priced, made by a parcel of heathens and pagans that worship the Devil and work for ½d. a day." Parliament dutifully stopped the entry of patterned pieces (1700); then, when the Company brought in plain fabrics and printed designs on them in England, the *use* of all printed cottons was forbidden (1721). Fustians were, however, exempt from this ban, so Lancashire continued to build up its new industry. Liverpool merchants financed it, supplied it with cotton from the Levant or West Indies, sold its wares, and paved the way for the production of all-cotton cloth that came with the invention of spinning machines after 1760 and the spread of cotton cultivation in the southern United States.

Of other textile industries, knitting was revolutionized by William Lee's invention in 1589 of a complicated "frame" which knit stockings far more quickly than they could be made with needles. The silk industry received a valuable addition to its skilled labor force with the arrival of thousands of Huguenot weavers after the revocation of the Edict of Nantes; its equipment was improved when designs of a secret silk-throwing machine were smuggled out of Italy in 1718 and used for the construction of great complicated water-driven "throwers" which reduced the cost and time of one important process; and its market was expanded by banning the entry of French silks and giving a bounty on the export of English pieces. By 1760 silks came second to woolens on the textile list. Much linen was also made in England, Ireland, and Scotland.

Mining and Metallurgy. In the mid-sixteenth century the great attack on mineral deposits spread from central Europe to England. The country had iron, zinc, copper, lead, and tin ores. On the continent all mineral deposits belonged to the crown, and this "regalian right" was stoutly maintained; but in England it was pared down to gold and silver (of which there was virtually none) by a judicial decision of 1568 and a law of 1688. Landlords therefore owned the base metals and coal under their estates and had a strong inducement to extract them or to lease the deposits and collect royalties from mine operators. English, German, and Dutch capital combined to finance extraction and refining. Hundreds of German technicians and skilled workers were brought over; in 1642 a colony of 4,000 foreigners was mining and smelting copper at Keswick in the northwestern mountains. Continental drainage methods, refining processes, power-driven hammers, wire-drawing machines, and other devices were introduced along a metal belt which stretched from Cornwall through Wales to the north. The output of tin, copper, zinc, and of their alloys, especially brass, increased greatly; but the more ambitious schemes failed to produce the profits which had been expected.

Iron. Some English iron deposits had been worked since pre-Roman days, but the output from primitive smelters was small and poor. In the sixteenth century the blast furnace was introduced; a water wheel operated bellows which blew air through the furnace, thus making the smelting more thorough and yielding iron of better quality. When a monastic estate in the Weald (i.e., the forest) of Sussex passed into the hands of the Sidneys, a forge and a furnace were erected in the abbey buildings, skilled labor was brought from the continent, and a famous gun-casting industry was born. Its products, ranging from little weapons weighing two pounds to cannon which weighed four tons, were sold all over Europe.

Sidney's example was followed wherever ore and streams were found close together. The charcoal, of which about two tons were needed to smelt one ton of ore, was obtained from trees cut within a radius of five to ten miles from the furnace. Cut-over land might yield a second growth within fifteen or twenty years, and a furnace which commanded a wide expanse of woodland could therefore operate for many decades, provided it kept its output related to the local fuel supply. If it did not exercise that restraint, it was eventually obliged to close down or bring its charcoal in from afar at heavy freight costs. In the Weald ironworks charcoal accounted for 50 per cent of total expenses in 1550, but deforestation raised it to a ruinous 80 per cent by 1750. The ceiling for English iron production was thus fixed, at a level too low to meet all requirements, by the limited supply and cost of fuel. Some iron had to be imported from Sweden or Russia, and a bit from North America. Men tried to use coal, but the metal picked up impurities from the coal while ridding itself of those in the ore. Though coke was being made from coal by 1650, a hundred years elapsed before its successful use in blast furnaces freed the iron industry from bondage to charcoal.

Coal. Coal was known and used a little in medieval England. It was washed up from submarine outcrops and picked up on the northeast coast—hence its name, "sea coal"; or it was dug from hillsides and shallow pits. By 1600 firewood had become so dear that coal was being used by brewers, distillers, salt producers, brick or glass makers, and many other manufacturers who needed a lot of heat. In 1550 the output was perhaps 200,000 tons, but in 1700 it was nearly 3,000,000 tons. While some of it was burned by industries located alongside the mine, much of it went long distances by sea or river. In 1700 Newcastle was sending 1,250,000 tons yearly to London, Holland, France, and Hamburg; large sums of capital were invested in mines, ships, or merchants' stocks; and agreements between producers or distributors restricted output or controlled prices. Yet so little was coal known outside Britain that a French treatise on commerce published in 1781 felt it necessary to inform readers that "coal is an inflammable substance."

On the basis of coal and of domestic or imported metals England became Europe's leading producer of many kinds of metal goods. Sheffield concentrated on cutlery and other steelware, but Birmingham made almost every kind of small article from every kind of metal—knives, guns, swords, locks, snuffboxes, buttons, buckles, and other things needed for apparel, home, army, or farm. Of the goods made by these two towns the French treatise mentioned above declared: "They are without doubt the best made, the finest, and the most perfect known in the world."

In addition to the textile, mining, and metal industries there were others, such as glassmaking, paper manufactures, printing, tanning, brewing, and distilling. In 1722 the brewers produced thirty-six gallons of beer per head of the whole population, and the distillers added a gallon of gin. Many industries grew up outside the medieval centers of population and were therefore free from guild control; some were too young to be subject to policies of state regulation which were imposed by the Tudors but fell into abeyance after 1640; and most of them showed a marked interest in improving equipment and methods, especially as we approach or pass 1700. German technique had been absorbed in the sixteenth century, Huguenot skills in the late seventeenth, and this learning of lessons from abroad continued in the eighteenth. Meanwhile native ingenuity contributed new tools or machines to "abridge labor," reduce costs, improve quality, overcome the fact that wages were higher than on the continent, and thus attract buyers with every weight of purse. By 1700 an Englishman was at least half justified in boasting, "Our artisans [are] universally allow'd the best upon

Earth for Improvements." By 1760 the boast was on the point of being fully justified.

COMMERCE

The growth of London, of commercial agriculture, and of the provincial industries was closely interwoven with an expansion of domestic and overseas trade. Marketing facilities improved in every way. Fairs continued to be centers for the sale of livestock and seasonal farm produce. Some weekly or twice-weekly markets acquired importance as places where merchants and small industrial producers could meet. The grain and provision trades needed many wholesale or retail dealers, as for instance those who gathered up the 4,000,000 bushels of grain exported annually, probably an equal amount for feeding London, and the 33,000,000 bushels of malt which were used by the country's brewers in 1722. Furs, tea, indigo, tobacco, and other imports from remote regions were sold by public auction. The Royal Exchange, built in 1566, served as London's Bourse. Peddlers hawked their wares through the streets or the countryside, while in the large towns retail stores overflowed from the market squares into residential districts, so that a pickle shop operated next door to the London home of a duke. Middlemen increased in numbers faster than did the population and overcame the medieval distrust of their calling. A London directory for 1677 listed nearly two thousand merchants engaged in foreign trade.

Transportation. Like France, England had to wait until the eighteenth century for the construction methods and capital needed for making good highways, fully navigable rivers, and canals. In 1555 each parish was ordered by law to draft all householders for four (later six) days' work on the local roads each year. This plan relied on amateur supervision and provided no funds for materials; the "statute laborers" did little more than fill holes or ruts with earth. After 1660 tolls began to be charged on some highways; thus part of the burden of maintenance was transferred to those who used the road. But this plan and principle did not become general until the next century. Travel on wheels or on horseback remained slow. A proposal made about 1665 for an improved postal service was based on the use of horses which would travel about five miles an hour; but its author admitted that "probably the same may better bee performed by men exercis'd in it, by reason footmen can go where horses cannot" (Petty). Movement was hazardous in winter,

and freight charges were high. Yet the roads were used; manufactured goods, grain, wool, cattle, even geese and ducks went
along them where there was no other way.

Often there was another way, the river or the sea. No part of the
small country was far from fresh or salt water. The chief rivers
started far inland and had large estuaries. Their courses might be
broken by natural or man-made obstacles, and improvement was
sometimes opposed on the ground that it would expose local producers or traders to competition from outside. But they flowed
through fertile territory, mining regions, or manufacturing areas,
and the goods which traversed them soon reached a port from which
a ship could carry them along the coast or abroad. River and coastal
traffic therefore grew large, especially when the length of navigable
waterways was doubled between 1660 and 1750 with funds raised
by groups of landlords, merchants, and manufacturers.

Domestic trade was not impeded, as in France, by interprovincial
tariffs. National unity produced internal free trade, and when Scotland united with England and Wales in 1707 Great Britain became
the largest customs-free area in Europe. Union opened the small
Scotch market to English traders and gave northern England freedom from the age-long nuisance of border raids. In return Scotland
gained free access to England and her colonies. To Glasgow the
traffic in tobacco, sugar, rum, and textiles proved a well of wealth.
To Scotsmen in general, whether selling cattle or seeking a career,
was revealed "the noblest prospect which a Scotchman ever sees—
the high road that leads him to England" (Dr. Johnson). The
southbound traffic on that road soon became, and has remained,
heavy.

External Commerce. English overseas trade reflected the changes
in agriculture and industry as well as the country's growing stake in
remote continents. Wool, the chief medieval export, had almost disappeared from the list long before its shipment was banned in 1660.
Now the country imported wool for some of its cloths. Woolens, a
poor second on the medieval list, now ranked far ahead of such
commodities as metals, hardware, leather goods, wheat, coal, and
beer. To these domestic exports was gradually added the reexport
of that part of Asiatic or transatlantic produce for which Britain
became *entrepôt*. On the import side were the wines, fruits, oil,
merino wool, and cotton of southern Europe, the lumber, iron, copper, flax, hemp, and naval stores of northern and Baltic Europe,

some manufactured specialties from Italy, France, or Germany, and the cargoes from the Orient and America. The core of English foreign trade was thus an exchange of the products of native skill on native materials for the staple surpluses from forest, vineyard, mine, and farm of several continental regions. It was a more solid core than that of Holland, which depended on imported material and on *entrepôt* characteristics which could be duplicated or dispensed with, or than that of France, in which luxury goods formed so large a part of the exports.

London. London was the hub of foreign as well as domestic trade. In 1600 it handled nearly three-fourths of the cloth shipments; in 1700 it dispatched four-fifths of all exports and owned two-fifths of the country's merchant tonnage; in 1750, 75 per cent of the shipping entering British ports anchored in the Thames, over two-thirds of it bringing goods from the outports. Many interacting factors produced this preeminence. All main roads and the longest river led to London. Most of the population and of the fertile land were in central or southeastern England. The Thames was deep enough to let the largest ships come up to London Bridge and the customs-house; and its estuary was nearer to the Low Countries, the economic heart of the continent, than was any rival gateway to the sea. To these geographical advantages were added those which came from the presence of the government next door and from the constant influx of ambitious young men, eager to make a fortune in the big city.

London was therefore "capital, metropolis, port and entrepot, all in one" (Westerfield). It offered the best shipping services to many foreign ports and secured the best naval convoys to waft them on their way. Coastal vessels which brought London its food and fuel delivered goods to be exported; cloths came by road from the west and north. Its commercial, credit, insurance, and banking facilities were far more highly developed than those of the outports. The big trading companies had their headquarters there. The Bank of England, founded in 1694 to serve the government's needs, also met those of London merchants. London merchants exploited fully the advantages which their location, resources, and political influence gave them. They showed initiative in seeking out new fields for enterprise, such as Russia, the Levant, the Orient, and North America. At the same time they were aggressive in trying to restrict or evict such foreign trading rivals as the Hansards, and to secure for their own trading companies the exclusive control of both new and old branches of commerce. Sometimes, especially in Elizabethan and early Stuart times, they got what they sought, usually because they could pay for it.

The provincial traders were, however, far from helpless. They avoided being swallowed by "the great whale," developed direct connections with some markets, evaded the monopolies by "interloping," and eventually helped to break most of them down by parliamentary action in the late seventeenth century. Of the outports Bristol was the chief. It took advantage of its location to trade down the eastern edge of the Atlantic as far as the Slave Coast and also to cross that ocean. Its hinterland produced all kinds of exportable commodities—cloth, hardware, iron, coal, salt, lead, glass, and so forth—and its imports made it a great tobacco manufacturer. Newcastle based its trade on coal and salt, Hull exported Sheffield cutlery and Yorkshire cloth, but the rapid rise of Liverpool did not come until after about 1750.

English foreign trade was conducted mostly and increasingly by English traders. They had handled most of the medieval wool, cloth, and wine trade; only in dealings with the remote Baltic and Mediterranean in the bleak fifteenth century had the Hansards or Italians been predominant. Now these foreigners slipped into the background but by no means disappeared; they were gradually joined by Dutchmen, Portuguese, Spaniards, and others who settled in London or some provincial center, buying and selling goods for their home firm or serving as agents. Meanwhile English merchants resorted to every kind of trading method: they bought or sold on commission for continental or colonial patrons; they shipped goods or imported them through continental agents or factors; they went out or sent out partners, agents, or factors to ports as far apart as Archangel and Aleppo.

English merchants were not entitled to go to some markets unless they were members of the company which held by charter a monopoly of trade with a particular region. The "regulated company" arranged for fleets of convoyed ships to carry their goods, protected them from harm abroad, limited the amount of wares they could offer for sale, supported their claims as creditors, enforced their obligations as debtors, made them responsible for the quality of the articles they sold, and watched over their morals and manners. Only members of the Merchant Adventurers' Company could send cloth to any market between the mouth of the Somme (in northeast France) and the tip of Denmark. The Eastland Company (formed in 1579) monopolized trade with Scandinavia, Poland, and the east coast of the Baltic. Trade with Russia was confined to members or agents of the Muscovy Company (1555), and that with the Turkish Empire was reserved for the Levant Company (1581). In these last two, as in a series of African companies, members sometimes traded on their own account, as the Merchant Adventurers and Eastlanders always did; but in other periods they put their capital into a joint-stock fund and entrusted the business to paid servants. The East India Company (1600) and the Hudson's Bay Company (1670) used the latter method from the start.

The company members called themselves "fair traders," and claimed that foreign trade could not be conducted wisely except by a responsible, disciplined group. This claim is questioned by modern scholars, who have decided that the Merchant Adventurers were a strong and unscrupulous monopoly, "an intolerable compound of bully and humbug" (Tawney), more concerned with restricting trade than with expanding it. The outsiders called themselves "free traders," resented exclusion from any market that promised profit, invaded the companies' preserves, and attacked the monopolists. In 1689 or soon afterwards they persuaded parliament to allow anyone to sell cloth in the Adventurers' territory and to reduce the entrance fees and qualifications of the other regulated companies, leaving only the East India and Hudson's Bay companies in full possession of their respective domains. Nearly all channels of trade were thus thrown open; even the East India trade could be tapped if one obtained a license from the Company.

English merchants or agents had by 1750 established themselves in most European ports. In the Baltic they made headway against Dutch competition, especially after 1700. They became so numerous in Gothenburg (Sweden) that the town was sometimes called "Little London." Traffic with Russia had begun in 1553 when a London group sent three ships in search of a northeast passage to the Orient. When the sole surviving vessel reached Archangel its commander went overland to Moscow and won the czar's permission to trade. The Muscovy Company was promptly formed (1555), and the czar granted it freedom from taxation as well as extraterritorial rights. It did not find a northeast passage; its dream of a large overland traffic across Russia to Persia and India never came true; and it was crowded out of the Archangel trade by the Dutch during the seventeenth century. When, however, Peter the Great opened his window on the Baltic by building St. Petersburg in 1703, Anglo-Russian trade expanded greatly. It was helped by the fact that while the Company's original trading privileges were protected by treaty, no other foreign group had received such a special or generous grant. Consequently the English were able to safeguard their civil rights and business dealings far better than could any of their rivals. This was an invaluable asset, since Russian commercial methods, customs administration, and judicial procedures were so different from those of the west that, in the words of a French writer, the trade of St. Petersburg was "a labyrinth in which it is hard for a stranger to keep hold of the thread that might guide him through it." By 1750 the British held first place in that city's foreign commerce, supplied a third of the imports, bought three-fourths of the exports, and owned nearly half the ships that entered the harbor.

In the North Sea area, Hamburg succeeded Antwerp after 1564 as the center of the Merchant Adventurers' activities. When trade was thrown open in 1689, more Britons went there, to Bremen, and to inland market centers. In return, Germans settled in England. One of them, John Baring, emigrated from Bremen in 1717 to enter the West of England cloth trade; his sons built up the famous international banking firm of Baring Brothers. Anglo-Dutch trade stimulated a similar two-way migration; by the early eighteenth century there was a large Dutch colony in London, while of the Britons who went to Holland two firms—the Hopes and the Cliffords—became widely known merchant-bankers.

Anglo-French trade was all too often the victim of politics, especially when Colbert raised his tariff in 1667 and England soon afterwards became France's rival instead of her protégé. The ban on wool exports, largely an anti-French measure, was followed by one on the import of French silks and by high duties on French wines. At the end of the War of the Spanish Succession (1713) the treaty makers agreed that trade barriers were to be lowered, but English textile interests opposed this proposal so violently that it was abandoned, and no mutual reduction of tariffs was effected until 1786. Smuggling therefore flourished, but regular trade was hindered. French wine, once "the common draught of every tavern," almost vanished from the import list, and when "a lady applys to her mercer for a French silk, he is not so great a fool to deny her, but shows her an English pattern for a French, and generally satisfies her with the name instead of the thing."

Spain and Portugal were fertile fields for English traders. Commercial treaties signed between 1654 and 1670 gave them generous extraterritorial rights to live and trade under conditions more favorable than those enjoyed by French rivals. Portugal even granted the right to trade through Lisbon with Brazil or to live out there. By 1660 there were sixty English firms in Lisbon. Their business was shaken when England placed heavy duties on Portuguese wines and sugar, and Portugal retaliated by banning the import of English cloths. This blow hurt so much that in 1703 the Methuen Treaty was negotiated, admitting the wines at two-thirds the duty levied on French ones and reopening the ports to English fabrics.

Anglo-Portuguese trade flourished during the next half-century. British merchants living in their "factory" in Lisbon or Oporto supplied wheat, fish, and cloth to Portugal and her empire, in exchange for port wine, wool, oil, and the gold that was coming in ever rising volume from Brazil. To foreign observers this trade seemed one of the main reasons for Britain's rise to commercial preeminence. To Pombal, who became dictator after the terrible Lisbon earthquake of 1755, it was the badge of servitude; but his Colbertian efforts to develop industry and a native trading class did more harm to British interests than good to Portugal's economy.

Since at least 1550 Englishmen had been living in Seville or Cadiz, trading with Spain and its colonies. Their trade rested on the solid need of each country for the other's produce. But some of their fellow countrymen were anxious to ship goods direct from England to Spanish America, and to do it legally instead of having to play hide-and-seek with the *guarda costas*. When, therefore, the slave Asiento was transferred to the English South Sea Company in 1713, its provisions were expanded to permit one ship to take a cargo of English goods each year to the Spanish possessions. The terms were shockingly abused by the Company's officials for their own personal gain. The annual ship seemed to have almost unlimited cargo capacity, and slave vessels took in unlawful goods, often worth more than the slaves. Sometimes their sailors were blackened and dressed as slaves, and when they got ashore they unloaded the cargo. Complaisance was bought with bribes that went as high as the pocket of the minister in charge of the colonies. This traffic injured Spain's merchants and treasury. She tried to stop it, if necessary with force;

but when a trader called Jenkins lost an ear, English mob hysteria forced London to declare war on Spain in 1739. In 1750 the Asiento was terminated, but smuggling continued. In 1762 the Spanish king decided he could smash British commercial power by joining France in the Seven Years' War—at a time when France had already lost that war. The small benefits that came from direct trade with the colonies thus caused friction that provoked two Anglo-Spanish wars.

In the medieval Mediterranean English traders were rarely seen; but by 1580 they were taking cloth, lead, tin, and herrings to North Africa, Italy, and the Turkish Empire. The Levant Company (1581) failed to develop trade overland with India; but its factories at Smyrna and Aleppo served as bases for barter with the people of western Asia, exchanging woolens for Persian silks, carpets, drugs, and cotton for Lancashire. Nearer home, Leghorn became a popular port for picking up Mediterranean produce.

Shipping. From at least medieval times native ships shared with foreign vessels in carrying English external trade. At times the state took steps to protect them, partly on the ground that the merchant marine provided ships and sailors for the navy. In 1381 English traders were forbidden by law to ship their wares on foreign vessels and in 1488 were told not to import French wine or woad in them. This method seems to have achieved little; sometimes it provoked retaliation, and often there were not enough English ships available. In 1559 it was abandoned in favor of a policy of encouragement: goods carried in English ships paid lower duties than did those in foreign holds, home-built ships were given bounties, and attempts were made to foster that "nursery for seamen," the fishing fleet, even by ordering people to eat fish on certain days though they were no longer Catholics.

In spite of such measures, it was not easy to build and operate ships in competition with the Dutch herring-*busses* and flyboats. England's growing scarcity of ship timber was accentuated by the navy's demand for oak; such naval stores as tar had to be imported from Sweden or Finland; and English ships therefore cost more to build than did those of Holland. As colonial trade developed, the Dutch invaded the carrying business from Virginia, the West Indies, and the codfisheries. Then during the Civil War (1642–1648) they strengthened their hold on English trade in every direction—coastal, continental, transatlantic, and oriental.

When peace faced the country with the task of repairing its damaged economy, the East India and other interests urged that steps be taken to expel the Dutch ships. Their proposal, embodied in the Navigation Law of 1651, was amplified in 1660, 1662, 1664, 1673, and later dates into a comprehensive control of trade and navigation covering every part of the world. The shipping clauses of these navigation laws contained four provisions: (1) Foreign vessels were excluded from colonial ports, and trade between England and her possessions or between the colonies was reserved for English or colonial ships, with predominantly English or colonial crews. If any precedent was needed for such restrictions, the Dutch provided it by keeping their colonial ports closed, as did the French, Spanish, and Portuguese. (2) Goods entering England or her colonies from non-English parts of Asia, Africa, and America must come in English or colonial vessels. (3) Goods reaching England from Europe must come in English ships, or in those of the country which produced the goods or of the country from which they were usually shipped. (4) Coastal traffic was closed to foreign vessels.

The Navigation Laws may have been provoked by depression, but they remained on the statute book until 1849. They subordinated commerce to shipping by depriving the English trader of the cheap Dutch services from, and therefore to, some parts of Europe. Yet they impeded the production of English ships capable of taking the place of the Dutch vessels, since shipbuilding materials now had to be imported in Scandinavian or English ships, and the price of an English-built ship was therefore increased. They cut the Dutch out of the carriage of goods to England from the Baltic and southern Europe, but English vessels were not able quickly to fill the vacuum, especially in the Baltic. Actually the blow at the Dutch was not as heavy as it sounded. They could still bring to England the goods for which their country was the normal outlet; this included the produce of the Rhineland and other parts of inland Europe. Dutch firms had branch houses in England, to which they transferred some ships, and these operated inside the law. When the Dutch were neutral in Anglo-French wars their ships were sought as eagerly by the English as by the French.

On the sea lanes to India and the colonies the laws were effective. The East India Company soon won back its trade. Transatlantic shipping benefited by the eviction of the Dutch from their New Amsterdam base of operations in 1664 and by the ability of New England to build good cheap ships which operated under colonial

owners or were sold in England after two or three voyages for about
£400 apiece. By 1775, it is estimated, almost a third of the British
merchant marine had been built in colonial yards. Long before that
time English traders had strengthened their positions in the Baltic,
buying lumber and naval stores in the north and purchasing all the
oak that was offered in Danzig. In the long run, and at a price we
have no way of measuring, England got her large merchant marine.
In the 1660's the ratio of English to foreign tonnage leaving London
was about 2 to 1—a figure which suggests that the Dutch by no
means monopolized the carrying trade. In 1688 the ratio for all England was 2 to 1. By 1750 the outbound tonnage had trebled, and the
ratio was now 10 to 1.

Imperial Economic Developments

Apart from Cabot, English mariners played no part in the major
explorations, and there is little evidence of their roaming far afield
until after 1550. Then the expeditions became more numerous. Some
sought a northeast passage to Cathay, as for instance that which
got to Archangel in 1553; some looked for a northwest passage, as
did Frobisher in 1576, but he found only some stone which turned
out not to be precious ore. Others invaded the preserves of Spain
and Portugal; Hawkins made three slaving journeys (1562–1568)
and was finally violently ejected; Drake sailed for the South Seas in
1577, plundered two treasure vessels, circumnavigated the globe,
and returned home in 1580 with his sole surviving ship ballasted
with bullion; and pirates or privateers preyed on Spanish and Portuguese victims wherever they found them. Fishing boats went to the
Banks, trading vessels to Africa, and the prospects of oriental trade
were explored. Finally, Gilbert in Newfoundland (1578–1583) and
Raleigh in Virginia (1580–1595) tried to plant settlements, both in
the hope of finding precious metals.

Merchants, shipowners, landlords, and sometimes Queen Elizabeth and her courtiers contributed funds to finance these expeditions. Yet apart from Drake's booty and that of lesser sea robbers,
the rewards were very disappointing. No treasure lands or passages
were discovered, no colonies lived. Consequently, in the first place,
a perpetually penniless government was not likely to spend money
developing wooded wildernesses; it gave its blessing and a charter
to any subjects who cared to test their luck, but there was no royal

initiative or investment in the creation of the British Empire. In the second place, traders who wished to tap oriental trade must sail round Africa, braving the opposition of Portugal and of her new master, Spain. In the third place, the failures of Gilbert and Raleigh underlined lessons already learned in attempts to plant colonies as part of the sixteenth-century reconquest of Ireland. Most of these projects were wrecked on the rocks of finance. The promoter's estimate of the minimum time and maximum capital needed for bringing the enterprise to the self-supporting and profit-yielding stage was always belied by unexpected delays or expenditures, trouble with the natives, unsuitable settlers, the refusal of disgruntled investors to complete payment on their shares, and the lack of prompt "returns" of Irish produce that could be sold to provide the dividends which had been promised.

The East India Company. By 1600, therefore, there was costly experience to warn people against expecting quick or rich rewards from planting colonies. Thanks, however, to the defeat of the Spanish Armada in 1588 and the success of the early Dutch trips to the Orient, a trading venture round the Cape of Good Hope did look safe and profitable. In 1600 Elizabeth granted a charter to "The Governor and Company of Merchants of London trading in the East Indies." It conferred a fifteen years' monopoly of English trade in the Indian and Pacific oceans. By 1615 twelve voyages had been organized—some of them yielding over 200 per cent profit—and a score of trading posts set up in India, Malaya, and Japan. During the next sixty years the Company also traded with Persia and got a foothold at Canton in China; but the Japanese evicted it from their land, the Dutch drove it from the Spice Islands, and its interest was therefore concentrated on Canton and India.

In India stormy episodes with native princes or traders and with European competitors called for skillful diplomacy, bribes, forts, and fighting. Unlike its Dutch rival, the Company got no support from the state; in fact, it was often in as great trouble in London as in India, had difficulty in getting its charter renewed, and at times faced English rival groups which had been granted power to trade in Asia. It had to provide its own defenses but naturally tried to keep expenditure on these uneconomic items as low as possible. When, however, the French threat developed under Dupleix and the breakup of the Mogul Empire led to anarchy, the trading company had either to become a political, military, and naval power or to face extinction. Its army under Clive captured Bengal in 1757, and soon it was, in effect, ruler of 30,000,000 people.

The Company's trade was chiefly an exchange of American precious metals for Asiatic produce. As Europe still produced few goods that Orientals desired, the value of the silver and gold taken eastward was usually two or three times that of the cloth, base metals, coral, and a few odds and ends. Critics denounced this kind of trade as a cardinal sin; it "carried away the Treasure of Europe to enrich the heathen" (Defoe). The Company retorted that it brought back cargoes worth much more than its total exports, sold a large part of them abroad, and thus eventually returned far more specie to England than it had taken out. It insisted that without silver it could not compete with its "never-to-be-reconciled enimys," the Dutch and French, since "the natives will not trade their pepper for goods." It tried to create an oriental demand for British wares, but had little success until about 1800, when Lancashire, with its new machines and abundant American cotton, produced cheap fabrics that found a vast market in Asia.

The Company's imports at first were chiefly spices. By the eighteenth century, however, the demand for spices was declining, possibly because of the increased supply of sugar. The import list was now headed by those cotton and silk cloths which so disturbed English woolen producers. Though parliament banned the entry of printed cottons, and then forbade their use, the Company could sell plain cottons in England and ship "prints" to foreign markets. Second on the list came the leaf for "that excellent and by all Physicians approved China Drink called by the Chineans 'Tcha,' by other nations 'Tay,' alias 'Tea.'" The rest of the imports consisted of pepper, coffee, drugs, raw silk, porcelain, and saltpeter as ballast.

The Company loomed large in the British foreign-trade picture; during the first half of the eighteenth century it handled possibly a sixth of that trade. It had its good and bad times, its monopoly was frequently attacked, but it stood its ground. Its stockholders were influential, its cheap or free loans and annual tribute to the state were large, and its value in the struggle with France became greater. Not till 1813 was trade with India thrown open to all comers, while that with China remained closed till 1834. Its stocks were desirable investments and good subjects for speculation. A lowly place on its Indian pay roll gave opportunities for spare-time earnings; a high position offered the chance for acquiring a large fortune —and the certainty of ruined health.

America. Lacking the stimulus of precious-metal deposits or the aid of a substantial supply of native laborers and customers, English transatlantic enterprises proceeded more slowly than did those in Latin America, faced greater initial difficulties, and required more input of men and money. The outcome was a motley of activities of every kind except ranching and mining; of fur-trading outposts, fishing bases, West Indian and tidewater mainland plantations which produced the semi-tropical or tropical commodities that England needed, and Temperate Zone colonies which had little to offer her but found customers among the planters, fishermen, and southern Europeans for their foodstuffs, lumber, and shipping services. The story of these developments is relevant to this book only insofar as it affected the economic life of the British Isles in particular and of Europe in general.

Fish. The first successful enterprise across the Atlantic was cod-fishing. Between 1550 and 1600 English fishermen attained a position of major importance in Newfoundland waters. Merchants of Devon and Cornwall dispatched fleets to the Banks each year. The catch was lightly salted and dried ashore, and the ships went back to sell it, chiefly in southern Europe. Then settled fishing bases grew up in Newfoundland and New England after 1600, and the market widened with the spread of the island plantations. The "merchantable" cod was exchanged in Spain or Portugal for wine, wool, fruits, silver, and gold; the "refuse" fish went to feed West Indian slaves and was paid for in produce and Spanish treasure. Thus "cod from Newfoundland was the lever by which [England] wrested her share of the riches of the New World from Spain" (Innis). English, Newfoundland, and New England fishers competed with each other as well as with the French. They were helped by the cheapening of salt production in England, also by the fortunes of war, which drove the French out of Newfoundland in 1713 and from all her other bases except two small islands in 1763. They could therefore sell cod at a lower price than did the French, and the chief markets passed almost entirely into their hands.

Fur. Of the four gateways into North America the French used the St. Lawrence and later the mouth of the Mississippi, while the English acquired the Hudson River and Hudson Bay. The river was already a fur trader's route to the interior when it was taken from the Dutch in 1664. The bay was No Man's Water until, in the 1660's, two Frenchmen crossed the "fur forest" north of the Great Lakes to reach it. They failed to convince their own rulers of the value of the all-sea route between the bay and Europe but roused the enthusiasm of one or two New Englanders, who in turn found willing listeners in London. A group consisting more of imperially minded lords and leading politicians than of merchants financed the founding of the Hudson's Bay Company in 1670. The impulse was adventure, curiosity—there was still a chance that minerals or the northwest passage might be found—and the desire to outdistance the French.

That desire was fulfilled; the bay proved to be the cheapest approach from Europe to the fur forest, and the French were forced in 1713 to recognize the Company's title to the region. The Company had many lean years and made only moderate profits, and the scale of its business, like that of other fur-trading areas, was not large. The value of the pelts received by England from all North America never reached £25,000 a year until the Canadian supplies were added in 1763. From 1722 to 1775 furs accounted for less than 3 per cent of the mainland exports to England and to less than 0.5 per cent of all British imports. The trade was economically insignificant to Britain as it was to France. Its importance lay in the part it played in the struggle for the heart of the continent.

Colonies of Settlement. During the seventeenth century nine English settlements were made along the Atlantic coast of North America; two more (Connecticut and Rhode Island) were offshoots of Massachusetts, and two (New Holland and Delaware) were taken from the Dutch, who in turn had taken Delaware from the Swedes. Of the nine, three were promoted and financed by joint-stock companies, the remainder by private proprietors. The most important of the former was the product of a wave of prosperity, "an all-pervading smell of money" (Tawney), and an enthusiasm for projects of all kinds that swept London in the early seventeenth century. The Virginia Company, formed in 1606, hoped that its establishment of trading connections with the American seaboard would induce settlers to go out on their own initiative and at their own expense. Its investors were assured that they would receive good dividends when the first expedition, sent out in 1607 to seek a passage "to the other sea," search for minerals, and trade with the natives, sent back its returns in goods.

When the ships came back almost empty, many investors fell away. Those who remained gradually realized that there could be little commerce without colonization and that far more capital and immigrants would be required for the latter before there was any prospect of profit from the former. In all, £200,000 was eventually spent, about 5,000 persons were transported to Virginia, and the arrival in London (1613) of the first shipment of tobacco raised hopes that a staple exportable commodity could be produced. The hope proved to be justified; yet when the Company was dissolved in 1624, victim of Indian raids and disease abroad, of internal brawls at home, and of the depression that followed the boom, the colony had only about a thousand inhabitants and the stockholders had lost virtually all their investment.

Those who financed other settlements fared little better on either side of the Atlantic. Under royal pressure the City of London agreed in 1610 to invest £20,000 in colonizing Londonderry in Ireland, but actually spent £60,000 and lost most of it. The backers of the Pilgrim Fathers' Plymouth Plantation (1620) recovered only a third of their capital, and the founders of the Massachusetts Bay Company (1629) escaped loss only because they migrated to the colony and received their reward in land. After that date company colonization passed completely out of favor. In the proprietary colonies, such as Maryland (1634) or Pennsylvania (1682), the promoters were less interested in immediate income than in planting a community with some distinctive religious or political flavor. Their receipts from land sales or from the dues which they were entitled to collect built no fortunes.

As Spain's ability to dominate the West Indian region grew weaker, England secured about a dozen islands or tiny archipelagoes which were then developed by private proprietors. Barbados, first settled in 1628, was so healthy, flat, and fertile that by 1675 its population was calculated to comprise at least 50,000 whites and 80,000 slaves. Jamaica, taken from Spain in 1655, came to rank first as producer, slave market, pirates' nest, focal point for traffic with Spanish America, distributing center for British goods, and channel through which treasure flowed to the mainland colonies or England. The great expansion of plantation production during the eighteenth century increased the demand for slaves; the demand was accentuated by losses suffered in occasional hurricanes or slave revolts, and by the need for replacements—calculated at over 5 per cent yearly in Jamaica—to provide for ordinary "wear and tear" of the labor force. It was met from British fortified trading stations on the African coast. During the century 1680–1786 it is estimated that over 2,000,000 slaves were carried to the British colonies, in addition to those delivered to Spanish America under the Asiento and to the plantations of other countries.

The Colonial Market. Early advocates of colonization prophesied that a great demand for English manufactures would be found among the natives or be created by settlers. The natives proved to be disappointing, in spite of their acquired taste for rum and guns, but the settlers did provide a growing market. Between 1660 and 1775 the mainland population increased at an average rate of one-third per decade. By 1775 there were at least 2,500,000 white people living between the St. Lawrence and Georgia, a considerable number in the West Indies, and a large army of slaves. Though usufacture and local handicraftsmen met the needs of most households and communities, there was a sufficient body of buyers to make a valuable addition to the demand for the products of all the staple English industries. In 1700 shipments to the colonies comprised 15 per cent of English exports, but by 1775 they accounted for 33 per cent, and had increased sixfold in volume. Some merchants and manufacturers devoted almost all their energies to supplying America. The westbound cargoes included cloths and clothes of all kinds and qualities, guns, hardware, glass, paint, pottery, playing cards, bottled beer, books, sealing wax, slippers, and snuff. Coal miners and salt producers increasingly provided the ballast. Southbound cargoes consisted of the goods made for the slave trade, which was thus a further colonial stimulus to English industries.

Occasionally some manufacturers, such as the makers of woolens, beaver felt hats, and hardware, grew worried when they heard that colonial craftsmen were producing these goods for sale, and persuaded parliament to check the export of colonially made woolens (1699) or hats (1732) and to prevent the erection of any more mills to slit or roll iron into forms suitable for fabrication into ironware (1750). Such restraints, imposed at the request and for the benefit of one vested or desirable interest at the expense of another, were part of every country's domestic or imperial policy. They were paralleled by the ban on English wool exports for the benefit of the textile industry and on tobacco growing by English farmers for the benefit of American planters, or, in our own day, by the restrictions on margarine for the sake of dairy farmers. They were justified on the ground of regional specialization, expressed in an assertion (1699) that "the intent in settling our plantations in America [was] that the people there should be employed in such things as are not the product of this kingdom." Actually they were panicky products of selfish group pressure in time of depression, unimportant, ineffectual, and unenforceable. The colonies had no adequate wool supply for making good cloth, hats continued to be made so long as fur was available, and the colonial production of iron goods did not interfere with the large importation of such articles from Britain.

Colonial Produce. As producers of commodities that England lacked or that could be resold in continental Europe, the West Indies and the southern mainland colonies ranked highest. Further, their concentration on the production of exportable staples—tobacco, sugar, coffee, rice, indigo, and cotton—made them rely on Britain and the middle or northern mainland colonies for ships, commission merchants, loan capital, foodstuffs, manufactured goods, lumber, and supplies of slaves; and the exports which paid for these goods or services did not compete with any products of the mother country, but rather freed her from dependence on foreign supplies. The middle and northern colonies had little, apart from ships, that England needed. Their temperate-climate farm produce was not wanted; the furs were not important, transatlantic freight costs were too high to allow American lumber to compete with Baltic supplies, and an attempt (1705) to stimulate production of naval stores, masts, hemp for ropes, and flax for sailcloth by offering bounties on such goods sent to England had slight effect.

As buyers and sellers the West Indies and the southern mainland colonies were therefore the most valuable part of the overseas empire. In 1700 English exports to the middle and north were worth only one-third of those to the south, and in 1767 only two-thirds. In each of these years the southern exports to Britain were three times as valuable as those from farther north. As for the West Indies, Jamaica in 1767 imported more British goods than did Virginia and Maryland, the two best mainland buyers, and the islands as a whole bought half as much as did all the continental colonies.

Colonial Trade and Trade Routes. Apart from the early tobacco trade, the Hudson Bay traffic, and some of that in slaves, British transatlantic trade was free from company control, open to all subjects of the crown; "free enterprise" and "rugged individualism" began at Land's End. The trade routes along which goods traveled were determined chiefly by commercial considerations, partly by regulations incorporated in the Navigation Laws, and in slight measure by the unwillingness of Spain and France to permit foreign ships and certain cargoes to enter their home or colonial ports in competition with the products or ships of their own empires.

We have already seen how the shipping clauses of the Navigation Laws fostered the English and colonial merchant marines by shutting Dutch vessels—those "eternal prowlers for gain"—out of the imperial carrying trade. The laws also contained clauses which aimed at making England rather than Holland the market for colonial products, the *entrepôt* through which they passed to continental European consumers, and the gathering point for most European goods destined for the colonies. To realize the last aim, such goods were ordered to come to England and then to cross the Atlantic in English or colonial ships; the other two were to be achieved by listing certain "enumerated" colonial products which could be sent only to other colonies or to England. The mother country would thus be sure of getting supplies and be released from dependence on foreign producers. In return the products were admitted free or paid such low duties that they enjoyed a monopoly of the English market, especially for tobacco and sugar. English rather than Dutch traders would earn the reward for processing and handling any colonial wares that were sold on the continent. The English treasury, rather than the Dutch, would receive the duty on imports— even though part or all of it was refunded (as a "drawback") on any colonial goods that were re-exported.

This routing of colonial cargoes was largely limited to produce which came naturally to northwestern Europe. The market for sugar, tobacco, cotton, dyewoods, and indigo was chiefly in that region, and some northern merchant must handle the products for the planter. Hence there was a strong case—as well as abundant historical precedent—for deciding that the merchant be a national rather than a foreigner, a friend rather than a foe who was ruthless in asserting his economic strength and imperial exclusiveness, a taxpayer who helped to pay for the navy which protected the colonist and provided the convoys for his cargoes. Where, however, the trade did not directly affect northwestern Europe there was freedom of movement. Fish, rum, and grain were not "enumerated" until 1766 and could go to any port that would admit them; even then they could be taken direct to southern Europe. New England could ship lumber direct with the fish, as Pennsylvania could with its wheat or flour; then the vessels could bring back salt and wine from southern lands or islands, even though that opened the door to smuggling from continental Europe.

Inside these rules, or outside them wherever they were felt to be restrictive, many trade channels were cut. The broadest and deepest was the direct exchange of English goods for colonial staples. A ship would leave England, bound for a colonial port or for the wharves of the tidewater tobacco planters. There it unloaded the varied wares which had been ordered by planters or merchants or were being consigned by English exporters to their agents. Then it sailed back home with a cargo of produce consigned to a British merchant. By the mid-eighteenth century some of these "regular traders" were making two round trips a year. The British merchant sold the goods on commission, bought and dispatched the articles asked for by his colonial patrons, and advanced money to them for land buying, capital improvements, the purchase of slaves, operating costs, or consumption needs. The improving commercial and financial equipment of London enabled him to give as efficient service as could be found in Amsterdam, including the growing direct contact with most parts of Europe. As British industries achieved quality as well as variety, he had at hand the best sources of supply for most manufactured goods that the colonists required. His capital and credit resources were usually stretched to the full in handling the business of his clients, and he had to be on the alert to see that their colonial legislatures did not pass laws which would depreciate the value of the currency in which they paid their debts or render worthless the security for his loans; for "the colonies did all that debtor communities can do to frustrate their creditors" (Pares).

This direct exchange of English goods for colonial produce was the most important part of imperial trade. In 1769, for instance, the thirteen mainland colonies sent over 50 per cent of their *recorded* exports to Great Britain, and received 60 per cent of their recorded imports from that country. Direct trade was a prominent feature of English traffic with the West Indies, the only feature of the small Hudson Bay business, and virtually the only kind between the St. Lawrence and Europe under French or British rule. It did not, however, cover the whole picture, for the obvious reason that, while all the colonies needed British manufactured goods, they also needed some things that Britain could not supply, they produced commodities for which she was not a market, or they had a surplus left over when the Empire's demands had been met. Consequently other trade routes, often triangular or more roundabout, were followed; some missed England, others were intercolonial, and some included foreign ports. If we take a map of the Atlantic, mark three regions—Newfoundland, the mainland coast, and the West Indies—on its western edge, mark three others—the British Isles, the Iberian Peninsula, and West Africa—on the eastern edge, and then draw lines joining each point of this hexagon to the other five, the result is a fairly good map of the ocean lanes which British or colonial vessels traversed.

The route might go from a British port with barter goods to Africa, to the West Indies with slaves, and back home with plantation produce and treasure. It might run round one of the two fish triangles—England–Newfoundland–West Indies–England, or England–Newfoundland–southern Europe–England. After 1660 more and more trips originated in American northern and middle ports. These ports had few local supplies suitable for England, but from sea, forest, and farm they could procure cargoes acceptable to the other four angles of the hexagon. They could build serviceable cheap ships in which to carry them, and the Navigation Laws, combined with the eviction of the Dutch from New Holland, removed a formidable competitor from some routes. New Englanders caught fish offshore or on the Banks; their lumber was wanted in the islands for buildings and for the universally necessary barrel; they gathered up such provisions as New England farms had to spare; and from West Indian molasses they made rum that was welcome on the Banks—where men found the fishing intolerable without strong drink—and in the African slave market. Meanwhile the middle colonies, particularly Pennsylvania, expanded their output of farm produce, especially of wheat, after about 1700.

These commodities furnished cargoes for far-flung carrying trade and commerce. The simplest—and possibly the largest—traffic was the direct exchange of lumber, barrel heads and staves, foodstuffs, and animals for West Indian produce (including molasses), specie, and British manufactures which could be bought in the islands. An easy triangle carried food and rum to Newfoundland, fish to the Indies, and an island cargo back home. More ambitious Boston venturers took food and rum to Newfoundland, fish to southern Europe, wine and precious metal to England, and there either sold ship as well as cargo or came home laden with manufactured goods and possibly some passengers. Philadelphians took wheat instead of fish to southern Europe. Some Americans entered the slave trade, carrying rum to Africa, slaves to the Indies, and island produce back home.

Thus the "aggressive commercialism" (Innis) and cheap general utility ships of New Englanders, Philadelphians, and New Yorkers developed a many-sided commerce on what is often called the herring pond but ought to be called the cod pond. They supplied the needs of fishermen, plantation workers, and southern Europeans, tapped Latin American treasure, and at some point gained purchasing power to spend on British manufactured wares. When the Navigation Laws or any other laws favored their enterprise they took full advantage of them; if the regulatory shoe pinched they had little difficulty in taking it off. Smuggling was "a venial sin" (Lipson), law enforcement was lax, and detection was unlikely. How extensive the illicit trade was we have no idea. Professor Kirkland suggests that the acts controlling trade and navigation were "not extensively violated" for the simple reason that they "coincided with the natural conditions of trade"; Professor C. M. Andrews doubts whether they "ever were a serious menace to colonial development," and it is noteworthy that they were not included in the exhaustive list of grievances enumerated in the Declaration of Independence.

When the Revolution gave thirteen of the thirty colonies freedom to map their own economic course, the only apparent immediate effect was a decline in the percentage of United States produce going to the British Isles—from 50 per cent in 1769 to 35 in 1790. Most of the tobacco continued to go there, but the total shipments declined. By 1810 cotton had displaced tobacco as the leading export, and Liverpool was the destination of the overwhelming part of it. Hence the United States was soon shipping a greater fraction of her exports to the British Isles than in colonial days. Meanwhile the new freedom to import from any part of the world had little effect. In 1790 nearly nine-tenths of the manufactured goods reaching the United States came from British ports, and as late as 1860, 77 per cent of all the imports from Europe came from them.

The possession of colonies and the policies controlling them helped to develop England's carrying trade, merchant class, and export manufactures. Possession and the character of British industries would under any circumstances have caused these developments, and the influence of policy was one of degree rather than kind. No other policy was historically possible and no policy—or empire—was without its price. If a few Londoners and provincials made fortunes, the whole country paid for them in the taxes which provided bounties on some colonial exports, in the higher prices at which tobacco and sugar were sold in the protected British market, and in the growing expenditure on a navy to protect the Empire's ships or on an army to defend dangerous frontiers. Until the Seven Years' War (1756–1763) Englishmen bore these defense and other burdens in full, without question. Then, having spent over £100,-000,000 on a war in which the fate of the whole Empire was at stake, they asked that the burden be shared, but discovered that it could not.

What continental Europeans thought about the impact of the British colonies on Europe was well expressed by a Frenchman in 1781. "The inhabitants of North America have always been free to send their produce directly into the countries of Europe in which they thought they could sell them to the best advantage; and this commerce has become so extensive that it has already done infinite harm to the trade of many people in northern Europe who have been accustomed from time immemorial to supply Central Europe [i.e., Germany, the British Isles, France, Italy, Spain, and Portugal] with many commodities which Americans are able to furnish more cheaply than can any European nation."[1]

BIBLIOGRAPHY

GENERAL

Ashley, W. J., *Economic Organization of England* (1912), chaps. 3–6.
Clark, G. N., *The Wealth of England from 1496 to 1760* (1946).
Dietz, F. C., *An Economic History of England* (1942), chaps. 7–15.
Lipson, E., *Economic History of England* (1931), vol. i, chaps. 4, 10; vol. ii, chaps. 2, 3; vol. iii, chap. 4.

SPECIAL SUBJECTS

Andrews, C. M., "The Acts of Trade," in *Cambridge History of the British Empire*, vol. i, chap. 9.

[1] *Traité général du commerce*, by Samuel Ricard, revised and considerably augmented by "Mr. de M°°" and published in Amsterdam, 1781.

Barnes, D. G., *History of the English Corn Laws, 1660–1846* (1930).

Beer, G. L., *British Colonial Policy, 1754–1765* (1922).

Beer, G. L., *Origins of the British Colonial System, 1576–1660* (1922).

Campbell, M., *The English Yeoman under Elizabeth and the Early Stuarts* (1942).

Clark, G. N., *Science and Social Welfare in the Age of Newton* (1938).

Court, W. H. B., *The Rise of the Midland Industries, 1600–1838* (1938).

Curtler, W. H., *The Enclosure and Redistribution of Our Land* (1920).

Ernle, Lord, *English Farming, Past and Present* (1912), chaps. 3–6.

Foster, W., *England's Quest of Eastern Trade* (1933).

Fussell, G. E. (ed.), *Robert Loder's Farm Accounts* (1936).

Gipson, L. H., *The British Empire before the American Revolution* (1936–   ). See table of contents of each volume.

Harper, L. A., *The English Navigation Laws* (1939).

Knorr, K. E., *British Colonial Theories, 1570–1850* (1944).

Lawson, M. G., *Fur: A Study in English Mercantilism* (1943), chap. 2.

McLachlan, Jean O., *Trade and Peace with Old Spain, 1667–1750* (1940).

Morse, H. B., *Chronicles of the East India Company Trading to China, 1635–1834* (1926).

Nef, J. U., *Rise of the British Coal Industry* (1932).

Nef, J. U., *Industry and Government in France and England, 1540–1640* (1940).

Pares, R., *War and Trade in the West Indies* (1936).

Power, E., and Postan, M. M., *Studies in English Trade in the Fifteenth Century* (1933).

Rees, J. H., "Mercantilism and the Colonies," in *Cambridge History of the British Empire*, vol. i, chap. 20.

Scott, W. R., *The Constitution and Finance of English, Scottish, and Irish Joint-Stock Companies in 1720* (1910), vol. ii.

Tawney, R. H., *The Agrarian Problem in the Sixteenth Century* (1912).

Tawney, R. H., and Power, E., *Tudor Economic Documents* (1925).

Unwin, G., *Studies in Economic History* (1927), part ii, chaps. 5, 8, 9, 11.

Westerfield, R. B., *Middlemen in English Business, 1660–1760* (1915).

Wright, C. W., *Economic History of the United States* (1941), chaps. 4, 8, 11.

ARTICLES

Donnan, E., "Eighteenth-Century English Merchants," *J.E.B.H.*, November, 1931.

Fisher, F. J., "The Development of the London Food Market," *Ec. H. R.*, April, 1935.

Fisher, F. J., "Commercial Trends and Policy in Sixteenth Century England," *Ec. H. R.*, November, 1940.

Habakkuk, H. J., "English Landownership, 1680–1740," *Ec. H. R.*, February, 1940.

Kingsford, C. L., "Beginnings of English Maritime Enterprise," *History*, July, 1928.

Lennard, R., "English Agriculture under Charles II," *Ec. H. R.*, October, 1932.

Nef, J. U., "The Progress of Technology and the Growth of Large-Scale Industry in Great Britain, 1540–1640," *Ec. H. R.*, October, 1934.

Pares, R., "The Economic Factors in the History of the Empire," *Ec. H. R.*, May, 1937.

Stone, L., "State Control in Sixteenth Century England," *Ec. H. R.*, 1947.

Tawney, R. H., "The Rise of the Gentry," *Ec. H. R.*, 1941.

XVI

INDUSTRIAL AND COMMERCIAL ORGANIZATION, 1500–1750

Much of the description of medieval organization given in Chapters VII–IX could be repeated here as a picture of the structure of early modern industry, commerce, and finance. Production for the maker's use (usufacture) or by small craftsmen remained the broad basis of industrial work. Fairs and public markets were important meeting places for buyer and seller. The one-man or family firm and the partnership continued to conduct most of Europe's business. Yet the expansion of relatively new industries, the improvements in equipment, the growth in the volume of trade, and the lengthening of the traffic lanes had their effect. They caused a growing amount of manufacturing to be conducted by men who gathered large numbers of producers into central workplaces or collected large quantities of their products through elaborate putting-out systems; they brought together a few considerable sums of capital to finance joint-stock companies; and they called forth better marketing and banking services.

THE ORGANIZATION OF PRODUCTION

The persistence of usufacture can be understood if we remember that Europe was overwhelmingly agricultural, that many farmers —especially small ones—had little to sell, that their purchasing power was therefore low, and that making things at home was a normal part of workaday life. Some raw materials were at hand, some equipment was simple, and there was spare time when night or winter put an end to outdoor work. Hence the family made many of the things it needed, aided by village or wandering craftsmen. Though most German rural households spun and wove linen, less than a third of the looms in Prussia as late as 1843 belonged to professional weavers. An English observer reported in 1797 that in the northern parts of his country "almost every article of dress worn by

343

farmers, mechanics, and labourers is manufactured at home, shoes and hats excepted. . . . There are many respectable [i.e., middle class] persons at this day who never wore a bought pair of stockings, coat, or waistcoat in their lives." Great country mansions maintained their own staffs of industrial workers, and the diary of a French countess in 1700 shows her supervising the labors of resident or visiting clothmakers, garmentworkers, builders, wigmakers, and others. Many of the skilled craftsmen brought into France by Colbert or into other European courts were primarily engaged in what might be called royal or state usufacture.

Independent small-scale handicraft production of goods for sale was also widespread. The family was the firm, and if more labor was needed it was obtained by training an apprentice or employing one or two journeymen. Prussian statistics for 1816 suggest that there were only fifty-six apprentices and journeymen for every hundred masters. The goods were sold direct to consumer or merchant in shop, market place, or public hall. Many independent craftsmen were townsmen, but some were country dwellers who combined industry with work on a piece of land. A classic instance of the latter was furnished by the Yorkshire woolen cloth industry carried on by thousands of "clothiers" in farmhouses and village homes in the valleys or on the hillsides southwest of Leeds. The clothier bought raw materials in small parcels at a near-by market town. With the help of his family and possibly an apprentice or wage earner he made one or two pieces of cloth each week, sold the product to a merchant or factor in the weekly or semi-weekly market, purchased a fresh supply of wool, and went back home to repeat the process. Sometimes he worked to order and sold his cloth privately; but he was a free agent, with a well-organized public market in which he could sell to the merchant who offered the best price. A few acres of land or some common rights provided opportunities for gardening, cultivation, and grazing. His implements cost little: one clothier's inventory, dated 1779, valued the total textile equipment at less than £10, which was equal to the combined value of the "spangled cow" in the barn, the clock in the hall, and "one large bibell" in the parlor.

Similar instances could be drawn from most countries. In Belgium, for example, villagers made unbleached linen pieces and took them to such weekly markets as that held in Ghent every Friday. In each case the same characteristics were apparent: a small amount of capital, inexpensive equipment, easy access to raw materials, a product of fairly simple pattern that could be made in a few days, and ready facilities for its prompt sale for cash. A writer in 1747 estimated the "sums necessary to set up as master" in each of the hundreds of London occupations. He listed more than forty which could be begun with £20 or less, ninety with £50, and seventy-five with £100. In towns, especially on the continent, guild restrictions might still make it difficult for a man to launch his own little enterprise, but in rural regions there was opportunity for those who possessed the requisite skill, determination, energy, and small capital.

Yet the future did not lie with the little fellow. During the Middle Ages one or two industries, especially the export branch of cloth production, had become dependent on large industrial entrepreneurs or merchants for capital, direction, and marketing. By 1750 this condition was much more common; it was evident in the widespread putting out of material and the gathering in of relatively large numbers of persons to work under the employer's supervision.

These developments were the result of at least three factors. The first was commercial. The task of supplying some markets called for a knowledge of consumers' needs and fashions, for capital, enterprise, and possibly for a skill that the small craftsman did not possess. The markets were far away; or they were large and required great quantities of standardized goods for armies, cities, and plantations; or they were luxury markets, needing wares that were made of expensive materials, that took a long time to make, and that were often not paid for until a still longer time had elapsed. Further, some goods were new, or new to Europe, e.g., cottons, printed books, and fine pottery; if they were to be supplied, someone who had capital and was willing to take risks must organize production. Finally, the merchant who relied on the public market could not be sure of getting the kind or quantity of goods he desired, and in good times competition with his rivals would enhance the price he had to pay. If he interested himself in production, he could specify quantities, qualities, and patterns, obtain supplies at or near the cost of production, and eliminate some profits that otherwise went to retailers of raw materials or to producers.

The second factor was technological. Methods of production influenced the organization of an industry. Much medieval mining and smelting was done by one or two men, often farmers, in a small pit or forge; but the methods of the fifteenth and later centuries required large fixed capital outlays and a considerable labor force. Even where no improvement was made in plant or processes, division of labor might allow cheaper or better production than was possible when one man did many tasks, and that division could be best developed by a large entrepreneur.

The third factor was personal. In any industry or form of organization that was free from strong restraint, some men advanced while others stood still or slipped back. Unusual skill, energy, initiative, a fortunate marriage, or some other asset helped a craftsman here and there to rise above his fellows, to take on more journeymen, put out much material, and spend his time directing production and selling a large output. His neighbors called him a self-made man, his tombstone might describe him as "merchant," but we can call him a manufacturer-merchant. In the same way some traders grew rich by trading, and while some of them developed banking or shipowning as a second interest others turned to financing or organizing the production of the goods they sold, thus becoming merchant-manufacturers.

The Putting-Out System. Illustrations of the play and product of these factors can be picked from most parts of Europe after 1500, but most easily after 1700. Let us look first at the industries in which producers continued to be chiefly domestic workers, doing their jobs in their homes or small workshops. Of the countless instances only a few need be given. In Lyons, in the 1780's, 48 silk merchants gave out materials to over 800 master craftsmen, and in Nantes 2,000 masters were in the service of about 200 merchants. In Germany some handicraftsmen, grouped in their guilds, remained strong and independent in urban occupations until the nineteenth century, but many town industries and most rural ones became organized in some form of *Verlagssystem* (putting-out system). The Fuggers got the metals they wanted by putting out working capital and equipment to over a hundred small groups of silver miners, bought their product, and deducted the amount advanced or charged interest on it. Flax was put out to be spun and woven over a wide area of Silesia, while articles of wood, metal, leather, or fiber were made by peasant families in their spare time or in the winter months and delivered by them to the *Verleger* or his local agent.

In England many of the industries which rose to prominence after

1500 did so outside the old towns and were developed by merchants who supplied working capital, materials, or even tools in order to be sure of getting the goods they wished to sell. The traders of Hull imported Swedish or Russian iron and steel, sold it on long credit to the cutlery makers of Sheffield, then bought and exported the product. Liverpool merchants imported flax and cotton and put them out to be made into fustians. Some Yorkshire clothiers became middle-sized or large employers of outworkers, while in East Anglia and the West of England the typical clothier was the man who bought wool in bulk, put it out to an army of domestic workers, and sold a large quantity of cloth. In the eighteenth century two Lancashire cotton merchant-manufacturers gave out material to 600 looms and 3,000 workers, and a Manchester producer of ribbons, tapes, and similar smallwares employed a hundred domestic looms. In Birmingham countless small producers made different metal articles or did different processes; the connecting link was the *factor*, who supplied material and sometimes tools, made weekly advances of money, gathered in the products and sold them, probably to some merchant who had ordered them.

The English hosiery industry supplied a good illustration of the transition from urban handicraft to rural putting-out. When the knitting frame came into use after 1600 London became a great producer, consumer, and exporter of knitwear. After 1650, however, knitting was taken up in the midland counties. There was plenty of good wool here, rents, taxes, prices, and wages were low, but the chief market, the capital, and the merchant were over a hundred miles away, in London.

To link maker and merchant a far-flung putting-out system developed, with the hosier as its central figure. He received orders and patterns from London, procured supplies of yarn from dealers, and in some central town gave out the material every Saturday to knitters who took it to their homes, sometimes ten to fifteen miles away. There the children wound the yarn on bobbins, the master and his apprentice worked at the frame, and the wife sewed up the seams at the back or foot of the stocking. On Saturday the week's work was taken to the hosier, payment received, and a new supply of yarn obtained. The hosier also gave yarn and large orders to a bagman, who distributed them to scattered farms or remote villages where people knitted in their spare moments. In the towns and larger villages a third method of production developed, based on division of labor. One home worker made stocking legs and took them to the hosier's warehouse, where they were put out to another worker who added tops and feet, while in the warehouse itself women seamed and embroidered. Some knitters owned their expensive frames, but many rented them from the hosier, or from men who had put capital into frames, at a charge which absorbed as much as one-sixth of their week's earnings.

The essential features of the putting-out system can now be summarized. The entrepreneur put capital into industry in order to get the goods he wanted. At the least he supplied material to men who had their own equipment and regarded themselves as independent master craftsmen; at the most he supplied everything, and his workers received only wages. He drew on the full-time labor of town craftsmen and on the full- or part-time work of widely scattered country folk. In theory his workers were "self-directing," subject to no discipline except that of making a livelihood, and free to work for anyone they wished unless they were tied by debt to one patron —a very common condition. The system permitted a high degree of division of labor, and there was no technical limit to the number of workers a man could gather into his labor force.

The question naturally arises, Why did not entrepreneurs gather the producers in, rather than putting the material out? The answer is that some did, some did not, and some both put out and gathered in. Putting out had many defects. Much time was wasted conveying material to and from the home. What was saved in low wages was partly lost in time or transportation costs, though if the time was the worker's the employer need not complain. Production might be held up if material did not flow smoothly from one process to the next, as when the weaver waited for his yarn from the spinners or the knitter of tops found the hosier had run out of leg pieces. Standards of workmanship were not easily maintained, goods might not be delivered on time, and embezzlement or theft of material by workers or distributors was a widespread sin. If work was done in a central workshop many of these defects would disappear. Loafing and theft could be checked, standards maintained, division of labor developed, and the capital invested in material would not eat its heart out in interest charges while goods were meandering along the highways and byways at less than three miles an hour.

These advantages would, however, have to be dearly bought. The cost of a building to house many workers would be great, especially if it had to be large enough to accommodate the women and children who had helped to do the work at home. In a town the ground rent would be high. Equipment must be provided, and if there was no adequate local labor force cottages must be erected to attract workers from a distance. Few organizers of production had money to spare for such fixed capital outlays. They needed their funds for working capital in an age when there was a long lapse of time between buying raw materials and getting paid for the finished product. Further, if the equipment was the same as that used in the home, its output would be increased only in so far as the disciplined regular toil of a supervised employee displaced the irregular labor of an outworker. But foremen would be needed to maintain discipline, and that would add to the wages bill. Finally, many domestic workers resented any attempt to draw them from home. There they could enlist the aid of the whole family. They were free to work or play when they pleased. To obey the summons of a factory bell was loathsome. A big workshop would be too much like the workhouse, that grim building in which local authorities made paupers work for their sustenance. When factories did begin to sprinkle the countryside, many domestic workers refused to enter them or to allow their children to take jobs in these industrial bastilles.

The margin of advantage was therefore too slight to tip the scales in favor of the congregation of workers in industries which were traditionally domestic. On rare occasions the building problem was solved, as when the dissolution of the English monasteries rendered many edifices vacant. At least one large clothier filled every available corner of an abbey with looms and even turned the church into a weaving shed. But the experiment does not seem to have been a lasting success, and in any case the supply of monasteries was quickly exhausted. During the eighteenth century some of the new and expanding French industries combined gathering in and putting out on a large scale. In Orléans a hosiery firm assembled 800 knitters and had 2,000 workers outside; at Nantes great workshops were built to make wares for the slave trade; but in general, where the same equipment and processes could be used at home as in the large shops, the domestic worker held his ground.

Centralized Production. The great majority of early modern industrial workers "laboured in their homes, in town cellars or garrets, or in village cottages. But that majority was by no means so overwhelming as has been supposed" (Nef). If there was a putting-out system, there was also a gathering-in system. Its basis was more technological than economic; men were gathered together mostly to do work which could not be done at home. The mining and metallurgical industries supply the most obvious illustrations, often on a large scale. One silver mine in the Tyrol had nearly 7,000 workers in the seventeenth century. The mining and smelting works at Keswick in northern England had over 4,000 foreign employees in 1642. While many coalpits were worked by a handful of men as late as 1800, Professor Nef estimates that half the English coal miners in 1700 labored in groups of a hundred or more men, and that some mines had 500 to 1,000 workers. At Anzin, the French coal-mining center, one firm had 1,500 employees in 1756 and 4,000 in 1789.

Where the conversion of metals into wares required little equipment but much skill, the small domestic producer prevailed, e.g., in Birmingham and such German tool and cutlery centers as Solingen. But if a big job had to be done, such as casting cannon or other heavy pieces, if water power could be used to drive machines, or if all processes from smelting to the making of finished goods were carried on by one firm, large units emerged. One of the most famous of these was built up by Polhem at Stiernsund in Sweden about 1700. Polhem was an enthusiast for machines, power, division of labor, and consequent reduction of costs. He believed that "nothing increases demand so much as low prices" and that the way to lower prices was through the use of "machines and appliances which will diminish the amount or intensity of heavy manual work." He copied equipment he had seen elsewhere or invented his own, and drove it by water power. He used machines to cut bars, slit nailrods, roll iron into sheets, cut cogwheels, hammer pans, shape tinware, and make all kinds of household appliances, plowshares, and clock parts. Each of his hundred workmen was trained for a special process, and their almost automatic movements probably suggested those that a machine could perform.

The nature of the product or the improvements in equipment brought workers together in other industries. The great arsenal of medieval Venice, which had employed more than a thousand workers to build galleys and make rope, sails, or masts, had smaller descendants in the shipyards of France, Holland, and England. Calico printing required large workrooms, much dye, and many printing blocks. Sugar refining, distilling, and the production of soap, salt, beer, paper, gunpowder, or glass needed fairly large sums of capital for buildings, vats, pans, and fuel and were carried on by teams of wage earners. Brewing remained chiefly a domestic or small-scale occupation, but in the seventeenth century some large producers arose to supply big towns, win popularity for certain brands, and quench the thirst of Englishmen or Germans overseas. Thrale, Dr. Johnson's friend and patron, was a large London brewer, who paid his superintendent £500 a year. When he died, the brewery, which Johnson described as "not a parcel of boilers and vats, but the potentiality of growing rich beyond the dreams of avarice," was sold for £135,000.

In the French glass industry most shops were small, employing not more than fifteen men; but one firm, the Royal Plate Glass Company, which was organized in 1665 as part of Colbert's program of industrialization, began with two hundred workers and by 1750 employed a thousand men in walled factories that were guarded like a fortress. Other state-aided and subsidized manufactures also ran to great size, and some kinds of arms were produced in large volume under state ownership or favor in France, in the Prussia of Frederick the Great, and in the Russia of Peter the Great.

The Status of Labor. Much of the industrial organization described above rested on a basis of open or veiled wage labor. The man who owned his equipment and worked on his own material for an open market was economically independent; but most other workers depended chiefly on the day or piece wages they earned. If they lived in rural areas they could supplement their earnings by drawing some produce from the soil, but those who dwelt in the larger towns had to rely mostly on the price they obtained for their labor. In town and country alike their welfare depended largely on the rate of payment and on the regularity of employment.

The rate of payment might be fixed by custom, but custom was now rubbed threadbare and had scarcely ever prevailed in the newer occupations. The rate might be fixed by the state, as under the English law of 1563, but by 1650 that law was becoming inoperative. We know too little about actual wage rates or receipts to be able to make generalizations, even for one country. Apparently spinning, which was a by-occupation for some but a livelihood for others, and which was easily learned, was poorly paid; but crafts which were highly skilled, into which entry was difficult, or in which workers easily banded together received relatively high wages When hosiers first put out goods in the midland counties they paid the rates current in London, but gradually whittled them down. In the French glass industry apprentices received a third of the master's piece rate and women half as much. There, as in many other employments, the workers were given board and lodging in addition to their money wages. There was no close relationship between wages and prices. Wages lagged behind prices during the sixteenth century, then caught up with them, especially when prices leveled off during the seventeenth. During the first half of the eighteenth century wage rates went up somewhat, while prices stood still or even declined; but after 1750 prices mounted again and most wages trailed behind.

The regularity of employment was influenced by many factors. In some parts of Europe the state demanded that workers be hired for a year, and in such skilled industries as plate-glass making they might be tied by a written contract for three to five years in order to insure that they did not take their skill elsewhere. In England, France, and Holland a worker must have a testimonial or clearance papers from his old empoyer before he could seek a new one. All such rules were, however, more applicable to urban wage earners, to those who worked on the employer's premises, and to farm labor than to rural outworkers.

Whether he worked at home or in a mine, smelter, or central workshop, the employee had his periods of enforced leisure. Bad weather held up the arrival of material, goods which were to be bleached or dried outdoors remained damp or yellow when the sun failed to shine, and some industries had to close down in winter. More serious than the seasonal fluctuations were those caused by the expansion or contraction, often sudden, of the market. War, peace, famine, a new foreign tariff or prohibition, or the collapse of some speculative boom could quickly spread gloom. Famine threw the whole economy out of gear by raising prices of food so high that there was little purchasing power left for buying other commodities. But whatever the cause, unemployment was a recurrent and familiar feature of early modern life.

We may soon be able to draw a graph of business fluctuations back to at least 1500. Already much is known about such periods of depression as that which injured the continental mining and English textile industries in the mid-sixteenth century. The depression which followed the early seventeenth-century boom was so long and acute that in 1622 an English royal commission was appointed to ascertain why "trade in general is so far out of frame that the merchants and clothiers are greatly discouraged, so that great numbers of people employed by them . . . want work." Or again much is known about the post-war difficulties of 1713 and 1763; about the troubles which came in 1772–1773 when speculation in Amsterdam and London blew prosperity to pieces, and when American resentment shut British goods out of the colonial market. John Wesley wrote of the consequences in 1775: "Trade is exceedingly decayed and thousands of people are quite unemployed. Some I know of have perished for want of bread; others I have seen walking up and down like shadows."

Labor Associations. Given a class of permanent wage earners and groups of men working together in one spot, labor organization and occasional clashes of interest or will between employer and employee were inevitable. Journeymen's societies or *compagnonnages* (*compagnon* = journeyman) were the natural counterpart to guilds of masters in occupations where the journeyman had little hope of attaining economic independence. They looked and talked like guilds, guarded standards of training and workmanship, cared for the sick and bereaved, fostered a fraternal spirit, and had their elaborate mystic initiations. In Germany and France local groups were linked in a loose federation, and the wandering journeyman was cared for by his brethren in the towns he visited. Sometimes masters and men joined hands against the common enemy—the merchant who tried to cut the price he paid the master for goods. More frequently the men locked horns with their employers in bitter fights concerning hours, wages, or the number of apprentices. Employees in the French glass factories grew increasingly restless during the eighteenth century, and in 1711 workers in a number of Normandy factories decided to strike for a 66-per-cent increase in wages and a closed shop.

In England combinations of wage earners appear after 1660, though there had been journeymen's guilds in the fifteenth century. They were strongest in London and in those parts of the textile industry which were most capitalistic (such as the west of England) or which congregated workers to dye and finish cloths. Even when there was no permanent organization, wage earners sometimes gathered together, fought their battle, and then dispersed. "Industrial strife was often as acute in the eighteenth as in the nineteenth century" (Lipson).

In all countries the state tried to suppress this incipient labor movement. Associations were declared illegal or were regarded as lawful only so long as they did nothing to improve or protect the wages contract. In Holland the ban simply drove them underground, and in 1692 men who attended illegal assemblies were threatened with capital punishment. In France a long series of decrees, stretching from at least 1539 to 1789, declared combinations to be unlawful. In England a law of 1548 condemned those who made any agreement on wages or prices, while the common law frowned on combinations, conspiracies, or any other action in restraint of trade. Parliament at various times (in 1721, 1726, 1749, and 1773) was provoked by labor unrest to pass repressive laws. At the same time it tried to safeguard workers' interests by reviving the assessment of wages by local justices. The attempt at repression, like that at revival, achieved little.

•Working Conditions. Industry, like agriculture, called on the whole available labor supply, from the young to the aged. Child labor was normal and as old as labor itself, in the fields, in the industrial pursuits of the home, in workshop or mine, and in crawling up chimneys to sweep them. Defoe almost gloated over the fact that in the textile industry a child of four or five years could, if well brought up, "earn its own bread." One of the virtues claimed in 1678 for a new spinning device was that with it "a child of three or four years may do as much as a child seven or eight years old." In mining districts boys and girls went with their parent (or parents, for often the mother also went) to work at the pit mouth or underground. In Aachen (Aix-la-Chapelle) children of seven to twelve years shaped the heads of needles and punched holes in them, since these operations required very good eyesight.

Women worked before and after marriage. They had their place in domestic industry, in workshop and mine, on the wharves where fish were cleaned, in the farmyard and dairy as well as in the fields. When they received wages, the rate was low, much lower than that of men doing the same work. In the words of a Lancashire spinster, "The pay is not much, but it helps to boil the pot."

Hours of labor, unchanged from medieval times, stretched from dawn to dusk, and even longer if artificial light was available. In London the usual hours in workshops were from 6 A.M. to 8 P.M., but the domestic worker who was master of his own time might be at his bench by 5 A.M. and stay there till 8 or 9 P.M. if the task had to be finished by delivery day. How often he interrupted his work we cannot say. Lack of material might stop him; gardening, agriculture, harvest work, fishing, and drinking might break the tedium, and the complaints that he alternated between idleness and feverish endeavor cannot all be dismissed as untrue. In some continuous processes, as for instance where a furnace had to be kept going, the seven-day week was general.

Some industrial processes carried great hazards of accident and occupational disease. Mining had scarcely begun to wrestle with the problems of ventilation or prevention of explosions. Glaziers suffered from "the Palsey," pewterers became paralyzed, and refiners needed strong lungs. Wool combers worked in an atmosphere charged with fumes from their charcoal stoves, while most domestic workers labored, slept, and ate in air full of industrial fluff, dust, or odors. Many tasks were physically strenuous, since all the power came from the worker's muscles, and were monotonous repetitions of one or two movements. There might be abundant glamour of high craftsmanship in the artistic occupations, but little of it in weaving, spinning, making nails or chain links, or hewing coal in a mine almost innocent of drainage or ventilation.

Since much manual labor depended on the skill, knowledge, and judgment of the worker, training was often still necessary. Formal apprenticeship survived, and was demanded by custom, guild decrees, or the state. The English parliament in 1563 forbade any person to "set up, occupy, use or exercize any craft, mistery, or occupation now used or occupied within the realm" unless he had "been brought up therein seven years at the least as apprentice." This provision remained on the statute book until 1814, but by 1700 at latest it was being ignored or whittled away by amendment or judicial rulings, and apprenticeship was therefore largely a matter of local practice and trade custom. Industries in which skill or knowledge came from long training continued to insist on apprenticeship. Any youth who wished to enter wholesale, foreign, or even some retail trades would be formally indentured and trained in the office, shop, warehouse, and "field work," going with his master round the markets and visiting London or foreign parts. Apprenticeship was still the gateway to freedom of some cities and to a master's rank in guilds or companies, while some labor unions were strong enough by the eighteenth century to keep out the un-indentured worker.

By that century, however, some occupations called for little or no special skill, others could be learned in a few months or a year or two, and those which were not practiced in England in 1563 were exempted from the law by the phrase "now used or occupied." A book on vocational guidance published in 1747 urged parents not to indenture their children unless they had enough money for setting them up as masters later on, and reported that in many occupations apprentices were rarely or never taken. When machines began seriously to invade the manual occupations, hand workers appealed to the state for protection and asked that the apprenticeship law be enforced. Yet many who made this plea had not been legally trained.

The Unit of Enterprise

Medieval enterprise was in the hands of one-man or family firms, of partnerships, and of groups of investors who entrusted the conduct of their business to a manager. These units were capable of conducting most of the business of the early modern period, but the need for long-term investment of great sums of capital brought the last of them to maturity in the joint-stock company with permanent capital and transferable stock.

Medieval business organization reached high-water mark in such Italian family firms as that of the Medici of Florence. At its peak the Medici father and sons controlled a trading-banking house and three cloth establishments in their home city, had eight trading and banking branches scattered from London and Bruges to Venice and Rome, handled the papal finances, and were deeply involved in loans to rulers—though they always insisted that their trading business was more important than their banking. They provided most of the capital for all these operations, but supplemented it by taking into partnership men who could invest some capital and in addition possessed such ability that they could be put in charge of one of the enterprises. They also accepted deposits—on which interest was paid but so camouflaged as not to seem usurious—from anyone who cared to lend them money for a fixed period. But although the Medici thus depended on outsiders to manage their businesses for them and to provide much of the funds, the head of the family laid down the general policies that were to be pursued and kept the branch managing partners under as strict control as was possible in an age of slow communication. Professor de Roover suggests that the collapse of the firm in 1494 was due in part (*a*) to the weakening of central control over the actions of the men on the circumference and (*b*) to the fact that, rather than refuse the deposits which rich people wished to make with them, they "succumbed to the temptation of seeking an outlet for surplus cash in making dangerous loans to princes."

The Fuggers. The family firm found a congenial home in southern Germany and produced one of the most famous firms of all time in the Fuggers. The Fugger success story begins when Hans, a master linen-weaver, left his Swabian village for Augsburg in 1380. There he made a fortune in the fustian trade. His son, Jacob I, made yet more money, still out of cloth. The third generation did better still, for its head, Jacob II, served his apprenticeship in Venice, learned the trading and accounting methods of that metropolis, and imbibed some of its ambitious spirit. When urged to take life more easily and enjoy his vast fortune, he replied that he wished to go on making profit as long as he could.

That wish sought fulfillment in three main ways. In the first place, Jacob added silks and velvets, spices, metals, and jewels to the linens and fustians which had been the staple commodities of earlier days. For selling these goods he created an "empire of counting houses and merchandise depots," a set of fifteenth-century chain stores in all the great cities of central and western Europe. In the second place, he went into the metal trade. Princes were in the habit of claiming the right to buy the entire mineral output of their territories at less than market prices, and when in financial need they would lease this right to the highest bidder. As Jacob was often that bidder, he gained control of the output of silver, copper, and iron in the Hapsburg lands of central Europe and of silver and mercury in Spain. From buying and selling metals to mining and refining them was an easy step. Mines were bought or financed, new equipment was installed, mines, foundries, and smelters were brought under single ownership, and compacts made with rivals, especially the Welsers, brought the supply of some metals under nearly monopoly control.

In the third place, the Fugger firm became the giant in public and private finance. It dealt in foreign exchange, lent money to private or royal borrowers, handled the papal revenues, and by its bribes influenced the election of two popes. For the Hapsburgs it would do almost anything—at a price usually paid or secured by metal concessions. Its loan of half a million gold florins provided the bribes that secured the choice of Charles V as Holy Roman Emperor (1519), and when Charles was slow in repaying the debt, Jacob wrote him, bluntly reminding him that "it is well known that Your Majesty without me might not have acquired the imperial crown."

When Jacob II died (1525) the firm was the wealthiest in Europe. Its capital had grown fortyfold and was more than doubled during the next twenty years. But the loans to the Hapsburgs were absorbing a dangerously large part of it, and the fourth generation—an Anton, not a Jacob—lacked the business skill of the third. When Spain and France defaulted on debts in 1557 the Fuggers were hard hit. In the following decades loan after loan turned bad, and by 1607 the firm was bankrupt.

The structure of this amazing business was that of a patriarchally governed family group which supplemented its own funds by accepting deposits. Much that was lent to governments or put into mining belonged to others, from princes to peasants. The firm was less eager to rely on outside funds than were some of its rivals, yet its failure ruined so many depositors that Augsburg had to build a larger debtors' prison.

With the collapse of the Fuggers and the declining importance of their competitors the day of the great international family firms came to an end, at least for the time being; but the family continued to be the business unit on a smaller scale in every land. Grandfather, father, sons, and sons-in-law might work together; the elder generation often managed affairs at headquarters while the younger members took to the road, crossed the seas, or operated foreign branches. Usually a document recorded the contribution of capital and of work each member was to make, the rate of interest he was to receive on the former and the share of profit he was to get for the latter. The family firm thus gave itself the formal pattern of a partnership, and perhaps a name—"Smith and Sons," "Brown, Brown, and Brown," or "Jones Brothers."

Partnerships. The partnership in its various forms (described in Chapter IX) satisfied many business needs of early modern Europe and of the new wider world. It might be formed for a project or for a period. America offered novel opportunities for project partnerships. One was seized by Velasquez and Cortes; each man supplied half the capital for the conquest of Mexico, participated in the campaign, and got half the spoils. Pizarro and Diego de Almagro lacked funds for their attack on Peru, so they invited a rich Spanish cleric to join them. He provided 20,000 pesos, they pledged themselves to do the fighting, and the plunder was to be shared equally among the three of them. To bind this compact they took mass together, each receiving a third of the wafer.

As conquest gave place to trade, Spanish merchants explored the market by using *commenda* partnerships. The merchant provided the capital; the active partner took goods to America, sold them, returned with bullion or other produce, and received his quarter of the profits if there were any. Gradually, however, trade settled into the hands of partnerships which lasted for a number of years. One member went to live in the colonies to buy and sell for the firm and to handle consignments for its clients. On such resident overseas partners and commission merchants Europeans came increasingly to rely for the management of their trade in the American colonies.

The partnership for a period was a more solid affair than that for a project. It was intended to endure for a certain length of time, usually three to seven years, and if successful it might be renewed. It conducted a mercantile, industrial, banking, or shipping enterprise, incurred debts and granted credit, sometimes on a large scale. If it became insolvent, who was responsible for satisfying the creditors? Some partners had run the business—to ruin—and contributed to its capital fund. They obviously must accept *unlimited* liability and hand over all they possessed to pay the firm's debts. But other partners might have supplied only funds and have played no part in management. Were they to be put in the same parlous position as the active partners, or should their liability be limited to the loss of the money they had invested? English law made all partners equally subject to unlimited liability. On the continent, however, especially in France, partnerships came to be divided into two classes: if all members were active the firm was a *société en nom collectif*, and all must accept unlimited liability; but if some merely commended their money to the care of the firm the organization was known as a *société en commandite*, and its inactive partners were liable to lose only their investment. This distinction was transferred overseas, and is therefore still found in Louisiana and Quebec, former French colonies; in the rest of North America the English general rule of unlimited liability prevails.

Companies. In earlier chapters we saw the formation of companies and examined their work. Here we are concerned with their structure, status, and financial organization. Legally the essential characteristic of a company was its possession of a corporate personality, conferred upon it by the state through the grant of charter or other official act. The company could make rules and enforce them, it could sue and be sued, and its life might last as long as its charter continued to be renewed. The Hudson's Bay Company, chartered in 1670, is still alive, and the Bank of England celebrated its 250th birthday in 1944. A partnership had no legal personality, each of its members must sue or be sued separately, and although it could be renewed if its members desired, it was automatically dissolved if one of them died or became bankrupt.

Companies were of two main kinds—regulated and joint stock. The former was the less important and seems to have been little used outside England. It was a "fellowship" or "society" to foster, protect, and govern its members' exclusive enjoyment of some branch of foreign trade. It was an association of men, not an accumulation of capital. As Wheeler, secretary of the Merchant Adventurers' Company, said in 1601, it had "no banke nor common stocke, nor common factour to buy and sell for the whole companie, but every man tradeth apart and particularlie with his own stocke and with his factour or servaunt," making his own profit or suffering his own loss, but enjoying the benefits secured and submitting to the regulations imposed by the company. Its field was intracontinental rather than intercontinental trade. The member could go out with goods, transact business, and return home in a fairly short time. The link between ownership and use of capital was strong; the owner might fare better by running his own business than by putting his funds in a joint-stock venture; and if he failed he had only himself to blame. When, therefore, some companies, such as the Russia and Levant companies, which began with "one stocke and purse for all," became dissatisfied with the results, they converted themselves to the regulated type in which "every man ran his own venture."

Joint-Stock Companies. The joint-stock company was an association of capital. It raised a fund to be administered by appointed or elected officers for the development of some branch of production, trade, or finance. The investors might be many or few, some of them had no knowledge of the business, their contribution might be small or large. Eventually the unit of investment became a certain amount of money, ownership of those units became transferable, and shares could pass from hand to hand without disturbing the financial structure or the operations of the company. The early directors might be men who had promoted the project, obtained the charter (with its grant of a monopoly of the chosen field), and undertaken the sometimes arduous task of persuading people to invest funds. Their successors were selected by the stockholders on the ground of their repute as competent businessmen or of their political and social prestige.

There was nothing new in the collection of capital from many purses and its administration by managers. As we saw in Chapter IX, medieval investors owned fractions of boats; the financing of Venetian ship operations and the provision of outward cargoes were undertaken by "joint ventures"; and groups of men provided the loans needed by such cities as Genoa or the capital required for the mines and refineries of central Europe and Sweden. The sixteenth century offered new inducements to pool funds for such projects as exploiting English metal deposits, trading, raiding, and exploring. In 1553 a group of London capitalists raised £6,000 in shares of £25 each "for the discovery of the northern parts of the world." Hawkins' slave journeys, Frobisher's search for the northwest passage, and Drake's raid in Spanish-American waters were financed by groups of aristocratic or mercantile investors. Queen Elizabeth occasionally contributed capital, and urged others who "might be willing to venter sumwhat in the voiadge" to take shares of £100 each in Frobisher's project. The colonizing schemes in Ireland and those of Gilbert and Raleigh in North America were dependent on support from many sponsors and failed partly because it was not adequately forthcoming. The joint-stock method was applied to trade with Russia and the Levant. Similar enterprises were undertaken in France and Holland.

Very few of these speculative leaps in the dark gratified their investors. Drake's journey of 1577–1580 was an outstanding success. It cost only £5,000 to equip, but his return cargo of Spanish treasure was worth £1,500,000. The queen received £250,000 of it—no wonder she knighted Drake—and the other sponsors drew 4,600 per cent profit. But most of the other projects were disappointing in their results. The Anglo-German metal enterprises failed to earn large rewards; the colonization schemes collapsed dismally; the

Levant Company, which had been richly capitalized in 1581 out of Drake's plunder, found business so poor that in the nineties it distributed the funds that remained and became a regulated company.

The East India Companies. Meanwhile Holland had found what was for two centuries to be the main field for successful joint-stock enterprise. During the 1590's a dozen groups of investors financed journeys to the East Indies. Though some of them prospered, the competition between them raised the buying price of spices out there and lowered the sale price at home; the rivals seemed more interested in injuring one another than in presenting a common front to the enemy, Spain; and there was no regulated company to restrain them. In 1602, therefore, the government amalgamated them in the United East India Company. The capital was provided by groups in six towns or provinces. Each of these six "chambers" had its own directors, equipped its own ships, supplied its own cargoes, and received its own goods from the Orient. The central body exercised only general control, especially of affairs in the Far East. The charter declared that investors had the right to withdraw their capital from the Company at the end of each decade, but when the first decade was closing the directors repudiated this provision. They pointed out that some of the funds, sunk in forts, ships, and arms, could not be reconverted into cash. They suggested that dissatisfied stockholders get their money back by selling their shares, since there were plenty of people eager to buy them. Consequently there was never any disbursement of capital. The Company had a permanent joint stock from the beginning.

The English East India Company obtained its charter on the last day of 1600. Nearly 220 "adventurers" were named in that document, which established a form of government almost identical with that of a regulated company. Yet in spite of the scanty success of joint-stock trading in Russia and the Levant it was recognized that the Indian Ocean was too remote to be visited by a flock of regulated individual merchants and must be approached by "a joint and united stock." Nearly sixty years elapsed before that stock became a permanent fund. Until 1613 each of the twelve voyages was financed by a separate contribution from those members who felt disposed to participate. When the ships came home and the books were made up, the sponsors were to get back their capital, plus whatever profit had been made.

This method produced confusion in bookkeeping. The accounts

of one journey had not been wound up when the next one left, the ships might not even be back, and investors were therefore invited to allow what was going to come to them from the last trip to be invested in the next one or the next but one. For instance, all the stock in the first voyage (1601) was transferred to the second (1604), that of the third (1607) to the fifth (1609), and the eleventh (1612) was financed by using a quarter of the return from the third (1607). To overcome this confusion, the "First Joint Stock" (1613) was raised to cover four voyages and the "Second Joint Stock" (1617) financed seven "adventures." During the next two decades, however, the Company encountered such difficulties with the Dutch, with its own king, and with English rivals that its life was precarious, and some single trips were again financed. Yet the need for forts and other protective equipment in Asia called for the sinking of money in what was called "dead stock" for "defence of the trade," as distinct from "quick stock." The strength of the Dutch rival seemed to spring from its permanent capital fund.

In 1657 the Company issued an invitation to investors, promising that at the end of seven years the assets would be valued. Any member could then withdraw his share and let his place be taken by someone else. During the seven years some good dividends were paid, and when they expired the assets were found to be so valuable that few stockholders wished to withdraw. In effect, therefore, the Company had got its permanent capital; members henceforth received only dividends, and those who wished to sell their stock had no difficulty in finding buyers.

Outside the oriental trade, joint-stock enterprise wrote a poor record. The Dutch West India Company was established (1621) to fight Spain rather than to conduct trade, and its profits came more from plunder than from commerce. The Virginia Company was a costly disappointment. The thirty or more companies founded by Colbert and his predecessors achieved little except the eating up of French funds. Prussia founded African and East India companies in the 1680's, but neither of them succeeded. The Hudson's Bay Company's career grew more precarious as French hostility was intensified, and during the war of 1702–1713 it tried to avert disaster by starting an insurance business in London.

During the last decade of the seventeenth century and the first two decades of the eighteenth, company promotion took on a new lease of life in new directions. Companies were formed in England to improve rivers, supply water to cities, make glass or paper or silk cloth, operate banks (especially the Bank of England, founded in 1694), sell insurance, develop mines, catch fish, and salvage, at a profit of 10,000 per cent, the treasure from a ship sunk forty years before in the Spanish Main. Meanwhile the struggle between France and her enemies after 1689 created acute problems of war finance and, after 1713, of coping with vast war debts.

Prostrated by bank failures, insolvencies, industrial stagnation, agricultural distress, and social unrest, France turned for salvation to a Scots immigrant, John Law. Law was a man of "fertile brain, magnetic personality, persuasive tongue, . . . adventurer, projector, gambler, monetary theorist, statesman, and financial wizard" (Hamilton). He established the *Banque Générale* (1716), organized the Company of the West (1717), raised much capital, and secured title to Louisiana. Then he gathered in the monopoly of the tobacco trade, the African slave trade, the East India Company, the Mint, the collection of taxes, and control of the country's finances, and offered to convert from short to long term the vast public debt of 1,500,000,000 livres. For a time it seemed certain that whatever he touched would turn into gold—or into the notes which his bank, deserting its early conservative caution, poured out to finance these many projects. Consequently the demand for the shares of his Company of the West became so intense that the market price rose from 500 to 18,000 livres. The note inflation stimulated business and pushed up the price level of commodities at least 100 per cent. Then in 1720 all the bubbles burst; the price of the Company's stock collapsed, the overissue of notes wrecked the Bank, and commodity prices fell fast and far. The blow to French banking development was severe, and joint-stock companies fell into bad repute.

In England they fell into worse repute. There the South Sea Company, founded in 1711 for "trading to the South Seas and other parts of America and for encouraging the Fishing," took over £10,000,000 of short-term national debt from the state's creditors, paying them in cash or in its own stock and converting the debt into a long-term obligation. On it the government paid interest, and in addition gave the Company the Asiento and a monopoly of British trade in the South Seas. In 1719 the Company offered to take over still more debt in return for more monopolies. When this offer was accepted, the Company's prospects for great profit looked so good that a boom in its shares developed. The price rose from 126 in late 1719 to 1,050 in mid-1720. All other stocks, old and new, behaved in like manner. Many new companies were floated; some of them were reputable, but others propounded fraudulent, fantastic schemes for earning great dividends by such operations as trading in human hair, making square cannon balls, marketing an air pump for the brain, or perfecting a wheel for perpetual motion. Change Alley, the stock market of the day, became a "roaring Hell-porch of insane and dishonest speculators," to which all classes of people swarmed, "some to undo and some to be undone."

In September, 1720, the crash came. From the wreckage the South Sea Company emerged alive, but many companies disappeared, and the stain made on joint stock during those mad years was not washed off for a long time. Parliament passed the "Bubble Act" (1720) which declared that only companies formed by charter or by a private act of parliament were legal. To secure this official sanction was a slow, costly proceeding. When large sums of capital were needed later for making a turnpike road or cutting a canal, parliament would pass the necessary law establishing a turnpike trust that could borrow money or a canal company that could sell stock. But others forms of enterprise had difficulty in securing a legal personality. Some of them operated without it as unincorporated firms but used the capital structure and methods of joint-stock companies, with the aid of lawyers who discovered ways of getting round the Bubble Act.

On the continent the prosperous decades which came after about 1730 produced some trading and industrial companies. A few were privately sponsored, as, for instance, the Swedish East India Company, formed in 1731 by an Anglo-Swedish group to bring oriental produce to Europe in competition with the older companies, or the Danish General Commercial Company, founded in 1747 in the fond hope of making Copenhagen the *entrepôt* for trade between the north of Europe and the rest of the continent. Other companies were sponsored by rulers eager to develop their country's commercial or industrial equipment. Austria acquired several of them, to refine sugar at Fiume or to carry the produce of Austria, Hungary, and Bohemia through Fiume or Trieste to Mediterranean markets. In Portugal Pombal set up companies whose task was to oust British traders and manufactured goods. In Prussia Frederick the

Great established a company to develop direct trade and shipping with foreign countries, gave it a monopoly of the importation of salt and the trade in wax, and took 2,100 of its 2,400 shares.

Few of these companies scored even small successes. Economic organization on the continent, as in England, remained predominantly personal rather than corporate. Its outstanding figures were not company directors or managers but individuals. The private firm was more versatile and could undertake a greater variety of activities than was possible for a company established for one special purpose. It could have one or many strings to its bow—trading on its own account or as commission merchant, dealing in one commodity or many, exporting or importing or both, entering into short or long partnerships, buying in open markets or putting out material, chartering ships or becoming part-owner of vessels, consigning goods to whatever markets were attractive, dealing wholesale or retail or both, engaging in banking, or doing whatever at the moment seemed profitable. The company was confined to the tracks it had laid down; but to the individual most roads were open, and he could blaze paths of his own across open country or through primeval forests. Wherever he went he could travel light; no great amount of capital had to be sunk in plant. In comparison with him, the company was a minor specialized part of the economy, and an "investment counselor" in the seventeenth or eighteenth century would have been hard pressed to find a well-diversified list of stocks to recommend to a client who wished to invest his funds safely but profitably.

CURRENCY AND BANKING

The Coinage. The best that can be said of Europe's currencies is that they were better in the eighteenth century than they had been in the fifteenth, that much of the improvement had come since 1650 or 1700, and that they were still far from adequate to meet certain needs. The practice of debasing coins by reducing their precious-metal content or "crying up" their face value in time of financial stress came to an end in England when Elizabeth in 1561 recalled the base coins issued by her three predecessors. From that time onward there was virtually no tampering with the silver coins, and changes in the content or value of gold coins were largely due to variations in the relative market prices of gold and silver, since the country was on a bimetallic standard. On the continent Spain suffered from wild variations between depreciation and restoration during the first half of the seventeenth century and did not gain stability until after 1700. France, having experienced nearly 300 alterations of its currency between 1300 and 1700, went through 42 more during the war and post-war difficulties of 1700–1716. She did, however, establish a new standard in 1726 and succeed in keeping it almost unchanged until the Revolution. Holland and Italy were countries of currency calm.

Coinmaking was a primitive and costly process until at least 1650. The old method of putting a blank disk between two dies and then hitting the upper one with a hammer was replaced about 1650 by the use of a screw press, but two strong men were needed to operate the press. Output per man or per press was low. The making of a gold coin might cost 5 per cent of its face value, that of a silver piece 25 per cent, and that of copper coins was relatively so high that mints rarely had time or desire to make them. All kinds of coins were easily counterfeited, the gold and silver ones were clipped and filed, or holes were bored in them from the edge and the cavity was filled with base metal. In 1695 the English Exchequer found that a large collection of coins it received weighed about half their official weight, thanks to maltreatment or to ordinary wear and tear. By 1650 a machine was available for milling the edge of the disk, but a skilled scoundrel could still give the coin a new milled edge after he had clipped or filed it. No merchant would think of operating a countinghouse or going on a trading trip without a small balance which he used for weighing questionable coins.

An important event in currency history was the abolition by England in 1666 and by France in 1679 of the practice of making money by making money. The seigniorage charge, which mints had levied on those persons who brought bullion to be minted or old coins to be reminted, was abolished, and in England the cost of the "free minting" was to be borne henceforth by levying a duty on imported alcoholic liquors. It was, however, a long time before some rulers abandoned the right to the income they had been accustomed to collect from seigniorage. It was also a long time before any government made provision for regularly withdrawing old, worn coins from circulation and replacing them with new ones. Consequently even the best currencies suffered from an inadequate supply of coins and from wide circulation of overworn ones. In remote rural areas coins were rarely seen even in the eighteenth century, and barter was a normal form of petty trade. In important towns the scarcity of small change and the virtual absence of copper coins led some retailers to issue their own *token* coins, made of lead or other cheap metal. In 1610 about three thousand London wine dealers, tapsters, bakers, and others had tokens in circulation within the area they served, and this practice continued until at least 1800. Private enterprise also tried to compensate for state lack of enterprise by producing counterfeit copper coins or "lead half-pennies coppered over." It was estimated in 1753 that half the copper coins in circulation in England were illegal products. The famine of copper coins was not broken until just before 1800 when a steam engine was introduced to supply power for operating coinmaking machines.

Early modern statesmen seemed less concerned over the quality of their currency than over the quantity inside their borders of the bullion from which it was made. Some of them talked as if they thought wealth and precious metals were synonymous, with the latter as "the only true and productive form of wealth" (Cole). Others were content to regard gold and silver as two among many forms, but as the most desirable, tangible, and liquid form for both public and private use. Precious metal was the sinews of war, the best kind of capital for loan or investment, the stimulant of trade, the payer of all debts, the substance with which taxes were paid, and a hoardable material which moth and rust could not corrupt. The more a country had of it, the stronger and better off it was—and no country would admit that it had enough.

The question therefore arose, How could a country which lacked domestic or colonial sources of supply get and keep enough? Apart from occasional captures of treasure ships, a nation's supply was determined by the amount which merchants brought in as a result of foreign trading activities, less the amount they took out. The imports were universally acceptable; the exports evoked hostility which might originally be instinctive but soon became buttressed by many arguments. Some men, "bullionists," urged that the precious metals be regarded as "contraband merchandise" (Colbert) and that their export be banned save in very exceptional cases. Others agreed that an increase rather than a decrease in the national supply was essential; but they urged that it be acquired by control of foreign trade rather than of the metals. If that trade was "so wisely managed" that more goods were sold abroad than were bought, the imports would pay for only part of the exports, and the "overplus," "remayne," "overvallue," or "favorable balance" (as it was finally called) must be paid for by an import of treasure. In such trade it might be wise to allow the export of gold or silver to Asia if the goods which came back and were sold in Europe, America, or Africa brought in more treasure than had originally gone far east.

Into the jungle of this controversy we need not penetrate. The bullionist's position was untenable in full unless he was willing to shut his countrymen out of the oriental and Levantine trade. The balancers had a better case, but it was weakened by the lack of any statistical service that could discover the value of exports and imports, even for any one foreign country, and consequently no subtraction sum could be done to ascertain whether the balance was favorable in any or all directions. England in 1696 appointed an "inspector-general of exports and imports" whose task was to supply such figures. But his commodity quantities were unreliable, since he could not include smuggled goods; his values were not based on invoices; many of the entries made by merchants were incorrect; and he had no way of ascertaining the value of such "invisible exports" as were made when shipping services were rendered to foreigners and colonists or such "invisible imports" as had to be paid for when Englishmen used foreign ships to carry their goods. He could not give "even an approximate estimate of the real general balance of trade" (Clark), yet his figures were by far the best produced by any European government, and some governments produced none.

The solicitude for treasure led every government to impose restraints on movements of bullion or coin. The Dutch were the least restrictive; like the Venetians they came to regard the precious metals as commodities of commerce, they were rarely short of supplies, and they never banned the export of coin; but they did forbid the export of bullion until 1647. In England the East India Company was given special permission to export treasure, but general freedom to export bullion or foreign coins was not provided by law until 1663, and the export of English coins was banned until 1819. Colbert was a fervent bullionist, determined to enforce the ban on exports of treasure. He rejoiced when metal flowed in from Spain; he tried to stop the taking of it to the Levant and other regions; yet he was compelled to permit his East India Company to carry it to the Orient, and when in 1662 Louis XIV bought Dunkirk from Charles II of England for 5,000,000 livres in hard cash, Colbert had to let nearly fifty carts carry the chests full of coins to Calais for ship-ment to London.

Spain and Portugal, the main ports of entry for American treasure, kept up a front of forbidding its export except under license, but the ban was almost completely ineffective. British and Dutch ships were by treaty immune from inspection and loaded the metallic part of their cargoes after dark. A regular weekly packet boat from England to Lisbon carried little but mail and metal back home, and when-ever a British warship put into Lisbon the sailors called on the British merchants there and returned to their vessel with small bags of coin or bullion fastened to strings which were slung round their shoulders in such a way as to be concealed by their outer garments. By 1750 half the gold leaving Lisbon found its way to England. Few early modern laws were more generally evaded than those which tried to control the movement of precious metals from one country to the others.

There was, however, one fact or factor which did exert a powerful control. Most countries still had bimetallic currencies. Each fixed the relative official value of silver and gold, and there was no inter-national agreement on that ratio. Meanwhile the relative market value of the two metals varied as one became more or less plentiful than the other. Since it was well-nigh impossible for governments to revise their official ratio to keep abreast of these market changes, one of the metals might become undervalued in terms of the other or in terms of its value in another land. England, for example, was prone to undervalue silver. That metal therefore tended to dis-appear from circulation. Merchants who brought silver into the country would not take it to the Mint if they got there only five shillings out of each ounce but could get 3 per cent more from a goldsmith or an East India Company buyer. Silver coins, especially new full-weight ones, would be melted down, since the silver in them was worth more than their face value. Silver was shipped off to pay debts, to buy Asiatic produce, or to be exchanged in London or Cadiz for gold, which was brought back to London, coined at the Mint, and then exchanged for more silver coins for export to buy more gold. This development during the eighteenth century pro-duced such a scarcity of silver coins and such an abundance of gold in England that in 1774 the first step was taken toward the abandon-ment of bimetallism and the establishment of a monometallic gold standard. (See Chapter XXIV.)

Commercial Paper. The early modern business world, even more than the medieval, made its own medium of exchange, on pieces of paper. Trade, whether conducted at a fair, a weekly market, or in private, was on a credit basis. The buyer might give a promissory note which he would honor two, three, six, or more months hence; or the seller might make out an order to pay at the appointed time, thus producing a bill of exchange.

Since the latter became the more usual procedure, let us examine an imaginary instance. The seller of cloth (A) to a London merchant (B) drew a bill on B, ordering him to pay by a certain date to A (or to C, from whom A had bought wool or dyestuffs). He sent this bill to B, who wrote "Accepted" and his signature on the face of it and returned it to A. Then several things might happen. (1) A kept the bill till it matured if it was payable to himself, and collected the money on pay day. (2) He sent it to C if it was drawn in C's favor, and C collected his debt at the appointed time. (3) A or C might wish to turn the bill into cash at once, and therefore sold it to another person at a discount, leaving him to collect it in full at maturity. If the discounter gave £99 for it, and received £100 from B when the bill matured, the difference was interest. (4) Some neighbor of A or C (let us call him D) might owe money in London; he therefore bought the bill from A or C and sent it to his creditor, who would then collect his money from B, while A or C had got his money from D. (5) A or C might *indorse* the bill by writing his name on the back of it and then use it to pay some creditor, who in turn might indorse and pass it on again, so that a bill might pass through many hands, gathering indorsements and paying more debts, before the time came for it to mature and be paid by B. If B failed to pay, then the indorsers were in turn liable, from A downward. A bill thus "backed" was a fairly safe negotiable instrument, possessing a great deal of that fundamental asset of currency, i.e., acceptability.

The bill just described is that of the eighteenth century. It differed from its medieval ancestor chiefly in being more easily negotiable and discountable. The financial transactions of the late medieval and sixteenth-century fairs had developed the rules of the game; by 1600 the courts or laws of Genoa and Naples laid down rules to make negotiability legal; Holland agreed that a bill indorsed by the person to whom the money was to be paid was good about 1650, and England did so about 1700.

Given that boon of negotiability, the use of bills in domestic and foreign trade grew very large. In centers like Amsterdam, Hamburg, and London, as also in large provincial towns, goldsmiths, private bankers, and merchants or others with spare funds would discount good bills and then sell them or collect the cash on settlement day. Merchants who did a large business in distant lands became well known out there; hence a colonist who bought goods in Europe would ask one of them to "accept" and pay for him the bill drawn by the seller, would pay him a small commission for the service, and would recompense him out of the proceeds of sales of the colonist's produce. A central or southern European who wished to buy goods in the Baltic would first arrange with an Amsterdam firm to accept and pay the bills which he would then instruct the Baltic vendor to draw on it. When an order for cloth went from Boston or Philadelphia to an English merchant, it would be accompanied by the request, "Please draw on Mr. So and So, my correspondent in London." Provincial merchants had their accepting agents in the commercial capital; their creditors were told to draw on these agents and their debtors were ordered to pay to them what was owed. During the eighteenth century the "bill on London" not merely was the most common form of commercial paper in English home and imperial trade but advanced rapidly to rival the "bill on Amsterdam."

Banking. The services which banks render are usually classified under four headings: (1) They receive deposits which they must return to the owner on demand or after an agreed length of time. (2) They transfer money from one depositor's account on his written order to another person or another person's account. (3) They lend money to public or private borrowers on some form of security. (4) Until the nineteenth century some of them issued their own notes, but the power of note issue has now been concentrated in the hands of a central bank. Deposit, transfer, loans, and issue are the functions of a full-fledged banking system. Let us see how far they developed during the early modern period.

Banking in Southern Europe. By 1500 there were public or private banks in most trade centers. All accepted deposits which could be withdrawn by their owner or be transferred to another person, in some places by the use of checks. All made loans; the public banks set up in Barcelona, Valencia, Genoa, and a few other towns could lend only to the city governments; the smaller private banks lent to traders, shipowners, landlords, and clergy; the big merchant-banking houses also financed princes, kings, and popes.

Since many private bankers were still more merchant than banker, they put some of the money entrusted to them into their own trade or into partnerships. "These investments were the greatest single source of weakness to the banking houses of the early period" (Usher), for economic crises wrecked many merchant houses, the banks they ran, and the families whose money they were holding. Venice was greatly worried by bank failures during the sixteenth century. It appointed commissioners to watch the banks, forbade the use of checks, and adopted other safety devices. In 1587, after debating the abolition of all private banks, it decided to establish a public bank which would be made really safe by being forbidden to lend money to anybody. The Bank of the Rialto (1587) and the later Giro Bank (1619) received deposits, effected transfers, but made no loans. Milan established a similar bank in 1593, while Sicily and Catalonia opened banks like that which had been set up in Barcelona in 1401 to receive deposits, transfer money, and make loans to the city. The whole field of private loans was thus left untouched by these public banks.

Banking in Northwestern Europe. Northwestern banking developments resembled those of the south but went farther. The Banks of Amsterdam (1609), of Hamburg (1619), and of Nuremberg (1621) were copies of the deposit-exchange banks of Venice and Milan. The ban imposed on loans was evaded, quietly in Amsterdam and by establishing a loan bank alongside the Hamburg bank; but in neither case was much lent to a government. Consequently in the north, even more than in the south, there was a large area to be covered by private bankers in meeting (1) the needs of those who wished to find a safe place and an interest-yielding depository for their spare money and (2) the demands of public and private borrowers for loans.

These needs and demands were met by many kinds of people. In France the tax farmer would pay interest on deposits. Holland swarmed with merchant-bankers, who used deposits along with their own funds to lend money by discounting, accepting, making advances on consignments, or participating in loans to governments. In England merchants would pay interest on money which they could use in their own businesses, in traffic in bills, or in loans to the state. The broker welcomed deposits to help him in pawnbroking, billbroking, or dealing in bullion. The scrivener, who wrote mortgages and contracts, was often entrusted with money by clients and asked to find a borrower.

None of these was a full-fledged banker, and it was the goldsmiths who finally gave London its private banks. By 1660 they were displacing the scriveners as handlers of other people's money. Their strong rooms became safe deposits for their clients' cash and other valuables. On the cash they were by the 1660's paying 6 per cent interest. They gave its owner a receipt stating how much he had deposited, and then recorded on the back of it the amounts he withdrew, thus producing a primitive passbook. They allowed him to write orders to pay part of his money to others, thus bringing the check into use. Sometimes they gave him a note when he made his deposit, on which they promised to pay him (or another person named by him) the sum mentioned on it when it was presented to them. This promise to pay on demand a specified sum in cash was a bank note. As such notes circulated but were rarely presented, the goldsmith's coin supply tended to mount with the increase in deposits, or at least was replenished by new deposits as old ones were withdrawn. Thus he discharged three of the four functions— deposit, transfer, and note issue.

On the basis of the cash in hand the goldsmith discharged the fourth, by making loans to traders or the government. The loan might be in coin or in his own bank notes; it was usually made for a short term by discounting a bill of exchange which would mature in a few weeks or an Exchequer "tally," i.e., a government promise to repay a debt with interest in the near future. If the loans had all been for commerce the goldsmith's record might have been almost spotless, but the crown still ran true to tradition. In 1672 the Exchequer "stopped" payment of interest (10 per cent) or redemption of short-term debts owed to the goldsmiths. The latter were severely shaken, and some of them never quite recovered; but the episode "barely checked the growth of private banking" (Clapham). It did, however, shake the credit of the government. Charles and his successor James had to borrow from Louis XIV to make ends meet.

The Bank of England. In 1688 parliament ejected James and placed a Dutchman on the throne, and in 1689 England was at war with France. As the problems of war finance became acute, scores of suggestions were made for solving them. One of these was propounded by William Paterson, a Scot who had been in America and was now a large London dealer in colonial produce. He suggested that the government borrow £1,000,000 *in perpetuity* at 6 per cent, and give the lenders the right to establish a bank. Parliament liked the idea of a loan which would never have to be repaid, and in 1694 passed a law providing that the "Recompenses and Advantages" of any group that provided £1,200,000 should be 8 per cent interest and permission to incorporate itself as Governor and Company of the Bank of England.

The capital was fully subscribed in twelve days; within another month the loan was flowing into the Exchequer, and within five more months the whole sum had been placed in the government's hands. By 1760 the original loan had multiplied tenfold as a result of wars and state emergencies, but the interest on it had fallen to 3 per cent. The Bank served the state and most of its departments, handling the raising of loans, the sale of lotteries and annuities, the business in short-term borrowing, and the payment of interest. By 1781 the prime minister could describe it as "a part of the constitution." But alongside its public functions it gradually developed those of a bank serving the needs of London commerce. It dealt in bullion, discounted bills for almost every kind of manufacturer or merchant, and lent money to the East India, South Sea, and Hudson's Bay companies; and some London bankers used its deposit, transfer, and lending services. Its notes became a useful addition to the country's currency and were usually in high repute.

In banking history the importance of the Bank of England lies in the successful union of all the functions—deposit, transfer, loan, and issue—in one institution and in the Bank's ability to serve the state and the business world without losing its head either literally or metaphorically. It was copied on the continent but without much success. Excessive demands by the state and the overissue of notes spoiled the career of Law's bank, a Danish bank lasted only from 1736 to 1757, while others which began to use notes had to learn, at great cost, the danger of overproduction. The Bank of Amsterdam and the Bank of Hamburg came to grief through unwise lending to one or two large clients.

As part of the reward for its service to the state, the Bank of England gained the usual monopoly conferred on early modern companies. It was to be the only incorporated bank in the country; parliament would charter no rival banks, and no private bank could be run by a partnership of more than six persons. Since the Bank did only a small part of the commercial banking of London and virtually none in the rest of the country, the bulk of English banking was therefore carried on after 1694, as before, by private bankers who were descendants of the goldsmiths or by merchants, shopkeepers, manufacturers, and even farmers who developed banking as a side line and who might eventually come to regard it as their main enterprise. A *Bankers' Who's Who* of 1800 would have told of banks founded by a grain merchant in Edinburgh, a Quaker worsted manufacturer in Norwich, an ironmaster in Birmingham, a grocer in Leeds, a tea dealer in Manchester, and so on. It would have listed Francis and John Baring, heads of the largest merchant-banking house in Europe and descendants of the German immigrant who had made good in the West of England cloth trade. But under the name of Smith it would have said, "See *Debrett's Peerage*"; for one Smith, a Nottingham mercer, had started a bank before 1700, and his grandson, after twenty-five years of profitable parliamentary and financial work, had in 1797 become Lord Carrington, to the dismay of George III (who disliked Smith's connection with countinghouses) and the disgust of Arthur Young (who disliked his abandonment of family prayers when he became a peer).

In other countries public banks, of which there were by 1700 over a score, were usually limited in scope to deposit and transfer functions or to serving the state. The private banker held most of the commercial field. In Amsterdam the Hope firm, founded by a Scot in the seventeenth century, was known wherever white men bought or sold. In France Law's failure made people afraid of bank notes, and no serious effort was made until 1776 to start a bank of issue. Merchant-bankers in the ports gathered money from all parts of the country to finance production or trade with Spain, Africa, and the West Indies. The tax farmers absorbed many people's savings, while many Parisian private bankers financed men who bought produce from or advanced money to the peasants of southern Europe. But French banking organization remained weak, and when France sent money to help the American revolutionaries in 1778 she had to use the banking machinery of Amsterdam to get it across the Atlantic.

The banks described above rendered service to business units which, according to the standards of the period, were middle-sized or large. By 1750 loans could be obtained in Holland or England at 3, 4, or 5 per cent, except in times of crisis or heavy government borrowing. The Bank of England lent money or discounted bills at 4 or

5 per cent. This rate contrasted strongly with the 8 to 12 per cent charged on the Antwerp Bourse in the sixteenth century, or with the 6 per cent which the London goldsmiths paid about 1670 on the deposits which they then lent to the king at 10 per cent. The small borrower was helped in some degree by civic, religious, or private pawnshops, by advances from the merchant for whom he worked, or by loans from moneylenders. The price he paid for this accommodation was still high, in spite of usury laws which limited the rate of interest. In the peasant regions of France, Italy, and Spain the borrower agreed to repay his debt after the next harvest by handing over produce valued at a specified price. Since this price was usually well below that at which the produce would sell even if the harvest was abundant, the lender was sure of a modest return of 10 to 50 per cent, and might make as much as 80 or 100 per cent if prices ran high. The provision of cheap rural credit for Europe's largest occupation was one of the problems awaiting solution in the nineteenth century.

BIBLIOGRAPHY

Clapham, Sir John, *The Bank of England: A History* (1943), vol. i, chaps. 1–3.

Corti, Count, *Rise of the House of Rothschild* (Eng. trans., 1928), chap. 1.

Day, C., *History of Commerce* (1907), chaps. 16, 17.

Ehrenberg, R., *Capital and Finance in the Age of the Renaissance* (Eng. trans., 1928).

Feaveryear, A. E., *The Pound Sterling: a History of English Money* (1931).

Gras, N. S. B., *Business and Capitalism* (1939), chaps. 3, 4.

Heaton, H., *Yorkshire Woollen and Worsted Industries* (1920), chaps. 3, 5, 9, 11.

Heckscher, E. F., *Mercantilism* (Eng. trans., 1935), chap. 7.

Kulischer, J. M., *Allgemeine Wirtschaftsgeschichte* (1928–1929), vol. ii, chaps. 9–13, 18–25.

Lipson, E., *Economic History of England* (1931), vol. ii, chaps. 1, 2.

Nef, J. U., *Rise of the British Coal Industry* (1932), part iv.

Nussbaum, F. L., *History of the Economic Institutions of Modern Europe* (1933), part iii, chaps. 1–5.

Renard, G., and Weulersse, G., *Life and Work in Modern Europe, Fifteenth to Eighteenth Centuries* (Eng. trans., 1926). See especially "Conclusion."

Richards, R. D., *The Early History of Banking in England* (1929).

Scott, W. R., *Constitution and Finance of English, Scottish, and Irish Joint-stock Companies to 1720* (1910–12).

Sombart, W., *Der moderne Kapitalismus* (1922), vol. ii.

Strieder, J., *Jacob Fugger the Rich* (Eng. trans., 1932).

Tawney, R. H., Introduction to Thomas Wilson's *Discourse on Usury* (1924).

Unwin, G., *Studies in Economic History* (1927), part ii, chaps. 5, 7, 8, 11.

Usher, A. P., *Early History of Deposit Banking in Mediterranean Europe* (1943).

Van Dillen, J. G. (ed.), *History of the Principal Public Banks* (1934).

Westerfield, R. B., *Middlemen in English Business, 1660–1760* (1915).

ARTICLES

Barbour, V., "Marine Risks and Insurance in the Seventeenth Century," *J.E.B.H.*, August, 1929.

Carus-Wilson, E. M., "Origins and Early Development of the Merchant Adventurers' Organisation in London," *Ec. H. R.*, April, 1933.

Clark, Dorothy K., "Edward Backwell as Royal Agent," *Ec. H. R.*, November, 1938.

De Roover, R., three articles on the Medici Bank in *J. Ec. Hist.*, May and November, 1946, and May, 1947.

Gilboy, E. W., "Wages in Eighteenth Century England," *J.E.B.H.*, August, 1930.

Hamilton, E. J., "Prices and Wages in Southern France under John Law's System," *Ec. Hist.*, February, 1937.

Judges, A. V., "The Origins of English Banking," *History*, July, 1931.

Kulischer, J. M., "La grande industrie au xvii⁰ et xviii⁰ siècles," *Ann. d'hist. écon.*, January, 1931.

Lipson, E., "England in the Age of Mercantilism," *J.E.B.H.*, August, 1932.

Nef, J. U., "Dominance of the Trader in the English Coal Industry in the Seventeenth Century," *J.E.B.H.*, May, 1933.

Nef, J. U., "Industrial Europe at the Time of the Reformation," *J. Pol. Ec.*, February and April, 1941.

Nelson, E. G., "The English Framework-knitting Industry," *J.E.B.H.*, May, 1930.

Sayous, A. E., "Partnerships in the Trade between Spain and America," *J.E.B.H.*, February, 1929.

Scoville, W., "The French Glass Industry," *J. Mod. Hist.*, December, 1943.

Tawney, R. H., "Modern Capitalism: a Bibliography," *Ec. H. R.*, October, 1933.

Viner, J., "English Theories of Foreign Trade before Adam Smith," *J.P.E.*, June and August, 1930.

Encyclopaedia of the Social Sciences: Articles on Balance of Trade, Banking, Bill of Exchange, Bubbles, Bullionists, Capitalism, Companies, Fuggers, Gresham's Law, Journeymen's Societies, John Law, Thomas Mun, Negotiable Instruments, Partnerships, Pawnshops, Putting-out System.

XVII

ECONOMIC CHARACTERISTICS OF THE PAST TWO CENTURIES

The remaining chapters of this book are concerned with economic developments since about the middle of the eighteenth century. The three outstanding features of the period have been a great increase in population, a marked advance in the ability to exploit natural resources, and a growth in mobility. Between the three there was close connection; around them as cause or consequence most of the other features of the period revolve.

Population. The growth of population took place at a rate unknown in any earlier period. Beginning in some countries during the first half of the eighteenth century, it reached its highest point— 1.14 per cent per annum for the whole continent—between 1900 and 1914. Estimates and census returns run as follows:

Year	European Population	Increase During Half-Century
1750	140,000,000	. . . . . .
1800	188,000,000	36 per cent
1850	266,000,000	40 " "
1900	401,000,000	50 " "
1939	540,000,000	35 " " in 39 years

In spite of the emigration of possibly 55,000,000 Europeans, there were nearly four times as many people inhabiting the continent in 1939 as in 1750, and they accounted for a quarter of the world's total population.

The causes of this unprecedented growth were medical and economic. There was little or no apparent increase in the birth rate, but a long series of improvements in public and private health made possible a reduction of the death rate by preventing or curing disease and saving life at every stage from birth through infancy to maturity. In the eighteenth century vaccination began to be prac-

380

ticed in a few places, the segregation of infected persons became a little better, some towns improved their water supplies or cleaned their streets of a bit more refuse, while physicians, surgeons, and apothecaries gained in knowledge and skill. In the first half of the nineteenth century the rapid growth of industrial and commercial towns challenged humanitarians, doctors, and governments alike to a battle against dirt, filth, and foul water, then against germs, and finally, when the study of bacteriology matured, to an attack on bacteria. Typhoid, cholera, dysentery, diphtheria, scarlet fever, and even tuberculosis gradually lost their old terror, and meanwhile antiseptics revolutionized surgery and obstetrics.

By the early twentieth century the advance on all medical fronts had helped to cut the death rate in northwestern Europe to half the figure for 1800 (i.e., from at least 30 per 1,000 persons to about 15), though it still ran as high as 24 in southern Europe and 30 in eastern Europe. The infant mortality rate (of children under one year old) declined later than did that for older persons, but eventually fell far in northwestern Europe. In England and Wales it was 153 for every 1,000 babies born in 1850; by 1900 it had dropped to 120 and by 1930 to about 65. In the south and east it was still very high but beginning to drop.

Productivity. While sickness lost many of its terrors, starvation lost more of them. Alongside greater chances of survival came increased means of subsistence, in terms of food, clothing, shelter, and other necessaries for the poor, with comforts and luxuries for the middle class and the rich. By 1900 famine was a word of no meaning to most of Europe west of Russia. A dietitian—if there had been any at that date—would have discovered much malnutrition throughout the poorer sections of the population, but even there the supply of food was better and better-balanced all the year round than it had been two or three generations before. It took two world wars to remind Europe through undernourishment that abundance was not a birthright.

The increase in all means of subsistence was the result of a great increase in productivity, i.e., in the physical output per worker per working hour (or other period of time); in the yield per unit of land; or in the contribution per unit of capital. This enhanced productivity was in turn the outcome of two developments: new or improved techniques for the use of resources and new or improved organization and conduct of enterprise.

Technology. The changes in technique included (1) the designing of better tools and still more the invention of machines; (2) the widespread use of new kinds of power, especially steam; (3) the ability to extract and use metals in cheap abundance; (4) the use of coal as fuel and later, in a smaller measure, of oil; (5) the accumulation of a body of knowledge which in its lower levels we can fitly describe as "know-how," in its higher reaches as scientific data and principles capable of economic application. In the fields of production these five aids—machinery, power, metals, coal, and science—changed the way in which much work was done, reduced the cost and increased the volume of output, released production from limits imposed by the available supply of human skill or strength, brought new industries and occupations into being (e.g., mechanical engineering and the electrical industries), made possible the production of goods hitherto unknown (e.g., rayon or plastics), gave new uses to old materials (e.g., by getting sugar from beets or paper from wood), turned waste products into by-products, and increased the farmer's yield from his land and livestock.

In the field of transportation the railroad, steamship, motor vehicle, and airplane—all of them power-driven machines—reduced barriers of space, cost, and time, allowed remote places and the interiors of large land masses to send their goods to distant consumers, made possible the carriage of cheap, bulky raw materials, minerals, foodstuffs, and manufactured articles halfway round the world, and moved people at speeds that would have seemed astronomical rather than terrestrial two centuries ago. Communication was revolutionized when fast, cheap mail services, the mass-produced newspaper, the telegraph, telephone, and radio carried information quickly to faraway places, knitting the world together into something approaching one market for the great staple commodities. Commerce expanded, permeating more and more of every country's economy as improved transportation brought buyers within easier reach of producers, and linking Europe with the rest of the world for the purchase and sale of common necessaries needed by the masses. The volume of goods moved and sold increased far more than did the population; the value of international trade, for example, grew twentyfold during a period which saw the population double.

Every part of Europe sooner or later brought this developing technique to bear on whatever physical resources it possessed. A new discovery or invention might convert an apparently useless bit of nature into an exploitable resource, as for example when it became possible to extract aluminum from certain clays, when waterfalls could be harnessed to produce electricity, or when iron ores heretofore useless for making steel because they contained phosphorus were subjected to a new treatment which removed that element. In some regions the application of the new technique was held back by

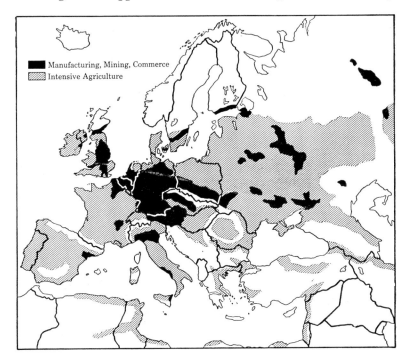

Industrial Europe and Agricultural Europe

conservatism, ignorance, unfavorable political or social conditions, lack of capital or satisfactory labor, or inability to reach a sufficiently large market because of defective means of transportation. Much Russian agriculture, for example, was still primitive in 1900, and that country's coal-beds had only just begun to be vigorously tapped.

"The Two Europes." Without coal and iron no country could develop the new type of industrialism to the full. Consequently the uneven distribution of these minerals divided the continent into two fairly distinct regions which have been called "Industrial Europe" and "Agricultural Europe." The former began geographically and in large measure chronologically on the coal fields of Wales, Scotland, and England, crossed the North Sea, and stretched eight hundred miles through northeastern France, Belgium, and southern Holland to Germany, where the strongholds were in the Ruhr Valley, Saxony, and Silesia. In the twentieth century Russia developed its own industrial belt, running northward from the coal fields of the southern Ukraine to those near Moscow and to Leningrad. Activity was most intense wherever coal and iron deposits were found close enough together to permit the development of "heavy industries" —producing iron and steel and products which required considerable quantities of those metals; where raw materials, such as cotton or wool, could be brought to the coal and made into lighter consumers' goods; and where coal could be moved cheaply to some point at which raw materials, labor, and markets were available.

Industrial Europe was predominantly urban. Towns of all sizes dotted it, sometimes separated by intensively cultivated farms and truck gardens, but in other places crowded so close together that it was hard to see, through the smoke from countless factory chimneys, where one ended and another began. In the most industrialized countries, such as Belgium and England, the population by 1930 averaged more than 700 persons to the square mile. Each census revealed that a growing percentage of the population was town- or city-dwelling; by 1920 the figure had risen above 60 in Germany and reached 80 in England and Wales. The fraction engaged in agriculture declined to a third or quarter of the "gainfully occupied" workers, and in England to less than a tenth; but that engaged in mining and manufacturing rose to two-fifths or even a half, that employed in trade and transportation was about a fifth, and the remainder was accounted for by the large number of professional, government, and personal services and servants that a modern urban-industrial-commercial society requires.

Agricultural Europe contained a larger area and more people than did Industrial Europe. In addition to the farming regions of the latter (including much of France, Germany, and Great Britain), it embraced Ireland, Scandinavia (especially Denmark), the Iberian and Italian peninsulas, and the region east of a line drawn from Finland to Sicily. In these lands some special factor, such as hydroelectricity in northern Italy or Spain or Sweden, oil in Rumania, cheap labor, a pocket of special skill or inventive ability, a high tariff, or a planned drive such as the Soviet Union's Five-Year Plans, might break the rural horizon with manufacturing plants; but, with the exception of Russia, lack of the right resources bar the transfer of any country from the agricultural to the industrial column and prohibit any great change in the predominantly rural and farming nature of the economy. Agricultural Europe's main task and opportunity was to feed itself and produce surplus cash crops or animal products for Industrial Europe.

Economic Organization. The advances in equipment and technical knowledge reacted on the organization and conduct of most forms of enterprise. The entrepreneur was confronted by the challenge to adopt the technological innovations if he was not to be left behind, and by new, larger, and more complex problems of management and policy. In the first place he needed more capital, both fixed and operating. In agriculture, peasant farming prevailed over most of Europe, with the peasant and his family supplying the chief ingredient, labor. Although he was characteristically conservative, he was obliged to spend some money on fixed improvements, machinery, better livestock, fertilizers, etc. if he was to keep his hold on the markets he served. In England and some continental areas the "high farming" technique adopted by big landlords and middle-sized or large farmers required an outlay of much capital for inclosures, reclamation of wastes, drainage, and other improvements as well as for farm operations. In industry even the early machines, containers, steam engines, and buildings cost far more than the simpler equipment they displaced and absorbed considerable sums of working capital for fuel, raw materials, and wages. In later industrial developments, such as steelmaking, steamship building, or the production of electrical appliances or automobiles, the capital requirements were still larger. Transportation was, however, the hungriest enterprise. The initial cost of making canals, roads, railroad tracks, rolling stock, steamships, docks, stations, freight yards, planes, and airports was enormous, while the operating expenses were great. In merchandising, the large warehouse, the department store, the long lines of smaller shops in main—and therefore high-rental—streets, the stocks of goods they carried, and the many pages of newspapers which they filled with advertisements were all indications of the great sum of capital involved in putting goods within reach of the consumer.

The economy thus became far more capitalistic in every branch— agriculture, industry, commerce, transportation, and banking. Even the professions needed more capital equipment for the lawyer's or doctor's office and the school; and the most laissez-faire state had to invest much money in post office, highway, military, naval, and public health facilities.

In the second place, the economies of operation tended in many occupations to increase with the size of the firm up to a fairly high point, and favored the employer who gathered in his workers rather than the one who put out his material. We shall see later with what tenacity small units survived in agriculture, in retail distribution, and in industries which produced unstandardized goods or rendered purely local services. Further, there was still plenty of room for such one-man, family, or partnership firms as could accumulate sufficient capital or obtain enough credit to start on a small scale in the hope of growing middle-sized or large. But in certain fields the need for gathering funds into large permanent heaps was present from the beginning (e.g., canals and railroads), giving greater scope to the joint-stock company and placing an expanding part of enterprise under its control. Consequently the standard type of unit in industry, transportation, and finance became that in which captains of industry, colonels of commerce, and brigadiers of banking ran firms financed with their own capital, with borrowed money, or with that of stockholders. They used comparatively costly plants and employed on their premises large numbers of wage or salary earners who owned no part of the business but were dependent for their livelihood on the sale of their labor.

In such large units the role of the entrepreneur assumed great importance and responsibility. His work has recently been analyzed by Professor Arthur H. Cole as that of "innovation, management, and adjustment to external conditions" in at least half a dozen directions. He must determine the firm's "business objectives" and change them when necessary or desirable; develop and maintain its organization, including efficient relations with his subordinates and employees; secure adequate funds and keep the confidence of those who supplied them; acquire efficient equipment and renew or revise it when it was wearing out or becoming obsolete; develop markets for the product; and, if it seemed desirable, try to maintain good relations with public authorities and with society at large.

In all these directions there was great opportunity for success and great risk of failure. Possibly never before in history had the openings for profitable enterprise been so vast and varied as they were in the nineteenth century. The old fields of commerce and finance offered richer pastures than ever as the volume of trade expanded by leaps and bounds, as the public and private needs for capital in the Old and New Worlds became insatiate, and as buyers or sellers could be reached at the uttermost corners or the innermost recesses of all the continents. To these old areas of enterprise were added the virtually new ones of manufacturing in its new dress and dwelling place, mass mining, metallurgy, the capital goods industries, and transportation by common carriers. The old ways of seeking profit were supplemented by new ones in a stream that never ceased to flow.

The century of great opportunity was, however, also the century of great risk. At all times the entrepreneur could make wrong decisions or be incompetent, overoptimistic, or overpessimistic. He might misread the present and make poor forecasts of the future. Methods which had brought success might be retained too long, a firm's arteries might harden, changes be "too little and too late." Rarely did any firm enjoy a long monopoly of its market, for the old guild and state restrictions had disappeared and free choice of occupation or enterprise had become public policy in most parts of Europe, except for such public utilities as streetcars and gas or electric supplies. The producer of a new popular pattern, product, or service quickly had rivals on his trail, and any patent machine, process, or commodity that he possessed could be copied by his competitors after a certain number of years. His profits as innovator were soon pared down by imitators, of whom the flock might be so great that profits became meager for all.

The boon of free competition could thus become a menace, especially when the business cycle turned inevitably downward at least once a decade, when the field became overcrowded, or when the profitable innovations of one generation, such as the canal, cheap iron, or clipper ship, were confronted by those of the next in the form of the railroad, cheap steel, or the steamship. Consequently the temperature chart of profit fluctuated greatly, the mortality rate of enterprise was high, and the average expectation of life was short —certainly far shorter than threescore years and ten. The struggle to survive expressed itself in many ways. Sometimes it led to a change in the character of the product, as when some western European farmers, faced with fierce competition from the cheap grain of Russia and the New World after 1870, switched their attention chiefly to the care of dairy and beef cattle, of pigs and poultry. Sometimes survival was sought by gathering rivals together in cartels which limited the competition by fixing minimum prices, limiting output, or sharing out the market. In every country the state was urged to help by providing tariff protection against foreign rivals.

Labor. By the early twentieth century about four-fifths of the "gainfully occupied" population of such industrially advanced countries as Britain and Germany consisted of wage or salary earners who worked on their employers' premises, usually in some commercial center or in industrial towns and large villages. The assemblage of employees, urban work and residence, and dependence on wages were not new, but they now became predominant characteristics of industrial society. They therefore raised new problems, or accentuated old ones, concerning wages, hours, working conditions, the employment of women and children, the loss of income through unemployment or sickness or accident or old age, the cost of living, the supply of houses, and the provision of a healthier working and living environment. Of these problems the most immediate ones—wages, hours, and working conditions—became the subject of collective bargaining as labor unions were formed and grew in strength. But these and the other problems all found their way sooner or later into the politics of every industrial state. They led to vigorous campaigns for economic and social reform, to propaganda and popular pleading, and to the creation of parties which sought chiefly the wage earner's support. Criticism of the treatment meted out to "labor" by "capital," condemnation of the system under which the wage earner worked, and dissatisfaction with the share he received of the wealth he helped to produce were the starting points of most schemes for the revolutionary reconstruction of society as a socialist or communist commonwealth.

The State and Economic Life. The relations between the modern state and the economy were no less intimate than in earlier periods; but the nature of both state and economy was different in many respects. The movement toward large territorial states advanced farther with the unification of Italy (1870), the federation of about two dozen states in the German Empire (1871), and the spread of the Austro-Hungarian and Russian empires. These four countries, along with the United Kingdom and France, ranked as "great powers" because of their population, area, resources, and fighting strength. Among them they housed 390,000,000 of Europe's 460,-

000,000 people in 1914. Their overseas empires contained another 500,000,000 (chiefly in the British Empire), and their home and overseas population therefore comprised more than half the people of the world. Well below them was one middle-sized state, Spain (20,000,000 people), eleven small ones with populations ranging from 8,000,000 down to 2,000,000, and a few tiny units.

The economic policies which these states pursued to aid, protect, regulate, tax, and supplement or supplant the enterprise of their citizens were influenced by the character of the government, the play and clash of interests and ideas, and the turn of events—especially unpleasant ones. The character of the government reflected, often imperfectly as in a curved mirror, the economic features and social pattern of the country. Where agriculture and large estates were predominant, political power remained in the hands of an autocratic monarch, a landed aristocracy, and the church. But wherever industry, commerce, and towns developed or land passed into the hands of peasant proprietors, the old order was obliged, usually reluctantly under pressure from strong agitation or even revolution, to let merchants, manufacturers, farmers, and then wage earners share in the government. That share, often set forth in the clauses of a written constitution, involved (a) a vote for at least one of the two legislative houses and the distribution of seats in that house according to the distribution of population, a feature which made the legislature "representative," and (b) control of the executive by the legislature, with the former "responsible" to the latter and dependent on a majority vote for approval of its proposals or actions.

Representative government usually came in at least two installments, with the middle class enfranchised first—in England in 1832, in some other countries by 1850—the wage earners later, and finally the women after 1914. By that date Britain and the continental western states from France to Scandinavia, along with Switzerland and Italy, had republican or limited monarchical systems which were responsible and representative. The German Empire was representative but not responsible; the kaiser and the landed aristocracy, assisted by some business leaders, ran the executive, the army, and foreign affairs without too much regard for the votes of the legislature. Revolution won a legislature for Russia in 1905, but neither was it fully representative nor did it control the czar and his ministers. In most other parts of Europe the crown and the landlords might not have yielded even so much of their power, but they were under increasing pressure to do so.

The spread of representative government and the consequent increase in the importance of political parties allowed economic groups, regions, and classes to voice their wishes in a more direct manner than the older methods of petition, agitation, or violence. Their spokesmen might win seats in the legislature. The newspapers, which increased in number and circulation during the nineteenth century and found more readers as education spread from the middle class to the poor, gave publicity to their views. Rival parties might woo them by incorporating their proposals in platforms, by promising to cure their ills, or by offering them good things of which they had never thought. If they were dissatisfied with the older parties they might organize one of their own, a decision responsible for the rise of labor and socialist parties in the late nineteenth century. The task of the legislator, the judge, and still more the administrator, grew in weight and complexity as the state strove to serve the interests of different sections of the nation, to embody in policy and practice new ideas that had won sufficient favor, and to wrestle with new problems as they emerged in a changing society.

It was a many-sided task. In point of time the first aspect was the removal of institutions or controls which had become obsolete or objectionable. Serfdom, guild or company monopolies, state regulation of industry or wages or prices, interprovincial tariffs, restrictions on the export of grain in France or of wool in England, bans on the importation or use of cottons, tax farming, and other aspects of the medieval or mercantilist legacy were targets for criticism after about 1750. Some of the critics were intelligent, informed onlookers like Adam Smith, who analyzed the state policies and found most of them lacking in economic common sense. Others were landlords, merchants, or manufacturers who found them impediments to the advancement of their enterprises. The French Revolution gave the critics power to sweep away those parts of the old order that they disliked, and the sweeping continued when French armies invaded neighboring states. In Britain the industrial regulations—of wages, apprenticeship, clothmaking, etc.—were formally repealed during the first half of the nineteenth century, but most of them had been ineffective for a long time; the restraints on foreign or imperial trade and the Navigation Laws were relaxed or removed piecemeal during the second quarter of that century.

By 1850 the dismantling of the machinery of early modern state control was almost completed in northwestern Europe. Individuals had been given freedom to practice whatever occupation they wished in whatever way seemed best to them; to go where they desired at home or abroad; and to buy or sell in whatever market best suited their purpose, free from price regulation and confronted in foreign trade by tariff barriers which had been removed almost entirely in British ports and were much lower than formerly in those of most continental countries. An age of free enterprise, of *laissez faire*, and of relatively free trade had been inaugurated.

The modern government could not, however, be merely a liberator or abdicator, with "Anarchy plus a police constable, a sailor, and a soldier" as its motto. If the newer breeds of landlord, farmer, manufacturer, and merchant were eager for it to abandon its old tasks, there were plenty of new ones for it to do. It must create conditions favorable for enterprise equipped with the new techniques; frame laws which made the formation of joint-stock companies easy and kept paper currencies sound; provide a good postal service, build railroads and improve waterways if the traffic was not sufficiently large to induce private investors to undertake such work; and keep taxes as low as possible. If newborn industries needed still more favorable conditions for growth the state would help them by providing tariff protection or giving them bounties, and if old occupations experienced harassing competition from younger foreign rivals the same help might be forthcoming. The period in which free-trade arguments received a kindly hearing was brief— from about 1840 to 1870.

The regulations which were swept away had been appropriate to the old social order or economic organization. As the new order and organization took shape the need for new regulations became apparent. The most obvious illustration was the growing concern with the conditions under which children, women, and then men worked in factories, mines, ships, or stores, and later with the wage earner's lack of income when sickness, accident, old age, or unemployment deprived him of the ability to sell his labor. The motives behind the movement toward comprehensive labor legislation were mixed. In the early days the voice of humanitarianism, which became audible in the late eighteenth century and gained in strength during most of the nineteenth, condemned conditions of "child slavery" as strenuously as it was condemning Negro slavery and produced an early example of those popular agitations outside and inside the legislature which characterize modern public life. Party politics played a part, as when Bismarck strove to win wage earners away from the growing Socialist party by giving them a wide range of social insurance benefits. Finally, the sheer pressure of facts, such as widespread unemployment in times of depression, forced governments to "do something." But whatever the motive, the provision of favorable conditions for employees became as important a function of government as was that of providing favorable conditions for entrepreneurs.

Regulation became necessary in most other fields. Joint-stock companies were subjected to certain rules in the interest of their creditors and their stockholders. Railroads became enterprises of "general interest" when they gained a virtual monopoly of inland transportation, and their passenger or freight rates began to be subjected to control. Regulations to insure the sale of pure food in full weight or measure protected the consumer. The powers and limitations of labor unions might need to be defined, unqualified persons might be forbidden to practice certain professions, and during the depressed 1930's many schemes were devised to control the marketing of farm produce and restore the price level. Thus in field after field individuals were legally free to undertake whatever enterprise they wished but in the interest of the nation, consumers, employees, other entrepreneurs, or even of themselves were subject to regulation of the way they conducted it. Before they began their enterprise the state had a word to say, for the introduction of compulsory education—beneficial though it might be—up to a prescribed age was a regulation of the individual's activities such as no earlier period had thought of imposing—or could have afforded. And in the enjoyment of the reward for their labors the state played a part by import or excise taxes which reduced the quantity of goods that could be purchased, by income taxes which after 1900 began to be steeply graduated, and by death duties which took a big bite out of large real or personal estates.

By 1914, therefore, the state in the economically advanced countries of western Europe was deeply immersed in a variety of activities—aiding, regulating, undertaking some enterprises, providing certain amenities which had come to be regarded as essential parts of a nation's life, and generally functioning as a social and economic service state. Each innovation had been the subject of long political controversy, bitterly opposed and sometimes delayed by those whose incomes seemed threatened. The basic concepts of private property and enterprise had not been attacked, but only the way in which they were enjoyed or exercised. The growing socialist movement was urging the transfer from private to public ownership of the means of production, distribution, and exchange. But its methods were strictly parliamentary; it hoped to effect the transformation by converting electors to the socialist cause, gaining majority control of the government, and legislating socialism into being —a hope which seemed very remote. Only in countries where such conversion or control was impossible because of lack of the parliamentary form of government (Russia, Spain, or Hungary) or where representative politics were grubby or corrupt (as in France and Italy) did suggestions for a short cut by revolution or a general strike find favor—and there was little reason to take the malcontents seriously.

Voluntary Associations. The state was not the only instrument to which men turned in their desire to defend themselves, improve their well-being, or solve their problems. Modern man was quite as much a social animal or organizer of voluntary associations as was his medieval ancestor. His material interests, sometimes tinged with a more idealistic hue, led him to devise or develop producers' cooperative societies to help him get his loans, purchases, processing, or sales services more cheaply; consumers' cooperatives to supply him with the goods he needed without profit; health insurance clubs into which he would pay contributions when well and then draw benefits in money or free medical attention when sick; labor unions to guard his interests as wage earner or employers' unions to guard against labor unions; professional associations to maintain and raise standards of training and maintain ethical codes; and countless organized groups composed of men engaged in the same kind of business enterprise. He would be a rare person who by 1914 was not a member of some such group, benefiting by its work and accepting its restraints.

The Standard of Living. The material welfare of the modern world was therefore determined by the efficiency with which private enterprise applied the new techniques, by the character of state aid and regulation, and by the influence exerted by voluntary associations. Until 1914 these forces caused a general lifting of the standard of living over the greater part of the western world. The increased yield from European agriculture and industry and the tapping of the virgin resources of the New World made this possible. Lower prices permitted luxuries to become comforts or even necessaries, and the money left over when food supplies had been obtained went to buy more clothing or furniture, better housing accommodation, or means of pleasure and recreation. Poverty still remained a big black mark on society, and production was insufficient to give every European the income needed for enjoying the living standard of the better-paid artisan. But poverty was less dire than it had been a century before. If the rich had become richer, the poor had grown less poor. The improving public and private health facilities reduced the loss of income and man power caused by sickness and unsanitary surroundings. The state social services provided benefits for which the poor did not pay more than a fraction of the cost, and were in effect a transfer of income through taxation from the middle and richer classes.

The increased volume of income was obtained with a smaller expenditure of labor time. It became possible now to reduce the hours of all industrial workers toward the eight-hour day, to free many married women from industrial or mining work, and to dispense with child labor. The exclusion of children from factory or mine, though sought on humanitarian grounds, was possible only because the new mechanical equipment and the productivity of industry allowed producers to supply the market's needs without the aid of tiny fingers. No earlier century was rich enough to be able to regard childhood as a period of play and education, free from the necessity of adding to the family income.

These gains in material welfare were not uniformly spread, did not come in a steady stream, and were not obtained free. Often they had to be fought for. Sometimes one class paid heavily for the benefits obtained by others, as when the cheap food from Russia and the New World after 1870 was a boon to the wage earner but a bane to many western farmers. The advance of the machine in old industries destroyed the livelihood of manual workers. Further, the standard of living was subject to the fluctuations in the business curve, and the wage earner who spent fifty years offering his labor for sale found a scarcity of buyers during at least five depressions in that half-century. If at the end of that period he could still make a sale he was often more fortunate than his first employer, for the insecurity of labor was paralleled by insecurity for capital and enterprise.

On the eve of World War I that insecurity seemed to be diminishing. The study of business cycles was leading banks to cooperate in pursuing credit policies which might apply the brake to overaccelerating booms, eliminate the violent crises and panics in which those booms had usually ended, and diminish the severity of the subsequent depressions. At the same time schemes which insured workers against complete loss of income because of sickness, accident, or old age were spreading from Germany to other countries, and in 1911 Britain led the way in introducing insurance against lack of income from ordinary unemployment. The future, therefore, looked more secure thanks to the combination of voluntary precautionary steps by business itself and the widening concern of the state for social and economic welfare.

The Twentieth Century. That future proved to be far from secure, for the twentieth century struck three shattering blows—two titanic wars and one unprecedented depression—at the economy and the polity which the nineteenth century had so energetically erected. Interest in the state as an instrument of social and economic reform had obscured in many people's minds the fact that governments had foreign policies as well as domestic, soldiers as well as factory inspectors, and diplomats who studied maps as well as agricultural experts who studied manures. This mental lapse was understandable, for though the nineteenth century witnessed some wars—such as that which Prussia waged against Austria in 1866 or against France in 1870–1871—they were short, involved only two or three powers, and did not seriously ripple the waters. There was no general or protracted conflict comparable to those of 1702–1713, 1756–1763, or 1792–1815, for the simple reason that there was no nation strong enough on land and sea, in industrial development or in financial resources, to challenge Britain. The nineteenth century, which really began in 1815 and ended in 1914, has been labeled the Hundred Years' Peace or the *Pax Britannica.* The British navy commanded the oceans and could block any colonial expansion of which it disapproved in South America, Africa, Asia, or the Pacific. British diplomacy, money, materials, warships, and if necessary soldiers could be swung to the support of any European power that was seriously threatened by another one, especially if the threat seemed to endanger Britain's island security or her lines of communication with her imperial and foreign markets.

Germany, by her unification, her conquest of Alsace-Lorraine, her rapid growth in population, her quick maturing as manufacturer, foreign trader, and shipowner, her alliance with Austria-Hungary and Italy, and finally her building of a navy, eventually faced Britain with a challenger on land and sea. It also put a first-class power in the heart of Europe, eager to expand economically and, if the chance came, politically, to the east and southeast, in regions where Britain had vital interests and Russia had ambitions. While, therefore, Europe was undergoing after 1900 one of its greatest advances in economic welfare, in growth of population, and in social legislation, the stage was being set for World War I.

That war (1914–1918) was less destructive of civilian life and property than was its successor, but the military losses were probably greater. The long conflict did, however, seriously strain and dislocate the belligerents' economies and polities. It broke them both down in Russia and delivered them into the hands of the Communists, who embarked on the arduous task of rebuilding them on a new revolutionary pattern. It broke them both up in Danubia when the Austro-Hungarian Empire fell apart. It broke some of the ties of trade between Industrial and Agricultural Europe as well as between Industrial Europe and the outer world. It deprived Germany of her chief iron ore deposits, her ships and colonies. It sank much of Britain's merchant marine, swallowed up some of her overseas investments, and weakened her export trade. It dislocated costs and prices, damaged domestic currencies, threw international exchange rates awry, and created vast debt obligations. It raised the standard of living of some ill-paid workers but lowered that of the middle class and the old rich. War accustomed many men to the use of force and to a belief in its usefulness in solving the domestic or international problems which the post-war world had to face.

Those problems baffled the wits and resourcefulness of old governments and still more of the new ones which had come into being. By the late twenties some of them seemed to have been solved, some of the damage had been repaired, production and trade were recovering, currencies were becoming stable, and there were even patches of prosperity to be seen. Then the second severe blow was struck, and the depression which began in 1929 deepened relentlessly for about three years. No country escaped its impoverishing ravages, its severe unemployment, and its low prices. Every government was driven to drastic measures in an attempt to stop the rot, relieve suffering, and promote recovery. Despair opened the door to dictatorship in Germany and strengthened the grip of that form of government in Italy and other parts of the continent. The dictators' policies involved territorial expansion, feverish rearmament, and war.

World War II was destructive of everything, but its novel features were the onslaught on civilians and on the fixed plant of production or transportation. An earthbound economy had become vulnerable to airborne attack; its destruction was at least as important as was that of enemy forces. The battle was therefore in large part one between civilian production and aerial destruction. The loss of life from bombing and the demolition of industrial establishments or transportation facilities slowed the economic wheels, brought some of them to a standstill, and smashed others entirely.

When peace came, much of the physical plant which had been erected by the capital and labor of at least a hundred years needed repairing or completely rebuilding if even the necessaries of life were to be made available. The task called for a young Hercules. Instead it had to be faced by a war-weary Europe that was short of everything—food, labor, raw materials, coal, ships, trains, homes, foreign exchange to pay for imports, confidence in the future, and youth. For it was a middle-aged and aging Europe. Two wars had decimated two generations of young manhood; the inter-war period had witnessed such a marked reduction in the birth rate that the days of rapidly growing population had ended in the west—but not in the east. The statistical stars in their courses had for at least two decades been forecasting an inevitable passage through a brief period of stationary population to one of declining numbers, with an increasing percentage of the people in the upper age brackets. The first of these stages was expected in France by the late thirties and in England, Germany, and most other western countries by the mid-forties. It is safe to assume that the war made its arrival certain.

Post-war Europe therefore faced the task of repairing its badly damaged fabric with a reduced and older labor force. In addition its physical resources—minerals and soil fertility, for example—had been badly depleted by the war. Finally, its polity was more divided than ever, as the conflict of ideas, wills, and interests between east and west came out into the open. The inability of the victors to agree on a permanent settlement of the German and Austrian questions held up plans for the economic restoration of these lands. The passage of eastern countries inside the Russian sphere of control impeded trade between them and the west. The conflict between Communist parties and their rivals in Italy and France dissipated in political schism and struggle much energy badly needed for economic salvage work. The maintenance of large armies of occupation continued to be costly and to keep men away from their former civilian jobs. Hence many factors combined to make recovery from the ravages of war both slow and difficult, and even to make the extent of possible recovery uncertain.

The Chronology of the Period. In the following chapters we shall examine the development of the general characteristics set forth above. That development is so continuous from the eighteenth century to at least the tragic tumults of the twentieth that no particular events, years, or even decades provide satisfactory dividing lines. A good case can be made out for breaking the span of two centuries in the middle, with the years around 1850 serving as an observation post from which the achievements of the preceding hundred years can be surveyed. By that time the general pattern of the modern economy, polity, and society had been worked out in Britain. Important inventions and discoveries made during the last half of the eighteenth century were extended and improved after 1800. By 1850 machine production had established itself in most industries; steam power was being used not only by manufacturers and miners but also by the new railroads and steamships; coal mining was going deeper to supply the ever expanding demand for its product; cheap iron was being produced in a volume that rose about 6 per cent each year. Agriculture had learned new methods, secured labor-saving equipment, discovered the value of chemical fertilizers, and redrawn the village map. The factory system had been built up by industrial entrepreneurs, largely with their own funds, while other capital needs could now be met more easily, thanks to the passage of laws which simplified the formation of joint-stock companies. Banks were building up adequate reserves as the recent gold discoveries in California and Australia poured precious metal into their vaults, and meanwhile the fear that they might print too many notes had been reduced by state regulation of the note issue.

By mid-century, commerce had got rid of its domestic and

some of its external restraints. Peace had freed the seas of the menace of privateering, given navies more time to spare for suppressing piracy, and demobilized the mercantilist policies which for so long had assumed that commerce was only war fought with trade weapons. Britain had thrown its ports open to the foodstuffs, raw materials, manufactured articles, and ships of all nations, and free-trade ideas were gaining some favor in other lands. Labor problems had been faced: factory laws were on the statute book, inspectors were enforcing them, unions had groped through trial and error to a form of organization which proved workable, and consumers' cooperation had been born. The middle class had secured the vote and wage earners were clamoring for it. Organized popular propaganda had become part of public life and violence had ceased to be a form of political argument in Britain, but not on the continent.

Most of these economic advances had taken place on British soil, but by 1850 they were being increasingly transplanted to the continent. In 1851 Englishmen traveled by rail from the far corners of their land, at a special excursion fare of about a penny (two cents) for seven miles, to see the industrial marvels that had been gathered into the Great Exhibition, a vast edifice of iron and glass in Hyde Park, London. Yet perhaps 1856 is a more noteworthy date than 1851, for in that year Bessemer announced his method for making steel cheaply in large quantities and Perkin produced a mauve dye from coal tar. These two events foreshadowed the great advances during the next half-century in steel production and industrial chemistry. They were supplemented by many others; some were new arrivals, such as electricity, petroleum, and rubber; others were improvements on the technology, organization, or business methods of the preceding period.

Industrial Europe now spread over the continental coal and iron fields. There were great exhibitions in Paris in 1855 and 1867, in Vienna in 1873; but the greatest industrialization took place in Germany—which never staged an exhibition—creating keen competition for Britain in some fields and establishing German supremacy in others. The European railroad network was completed, not merely linking town and country but tying the whole continent together. The steamship extended its range from the North Atlantic to cover all parts of the world, taking out European emigrants and manufactured goods and bringing the cheap farm produce of the outer continents to compete with the output of European farms. The last quarter of the nineteenth century was therefore marked by keen rivalry in all kinds of enterprise, by falling prices and meager profits, by attempts to ward off or diminish the force of the blows, and by an intensification of economic nationalism which produced a new wave of protectionist policy and empire building.

By 1900 the competition was abating, the necessary adjustments had been made, prices were rising, and most forms of business were becoming profitable. But the spread of industrialism on the continent had brought a labor movement into being there. It had to fight fiercely to gain recognition of its organizations by employers or by the state, and in addition its program often had a strong socialistic tinge. The rising cost of living left wages lagging behind. In spite, therefore, of great advances in social legislation in some lands, labor was restive and aggressive, and the ordinary political methods of securing reform seemed inadequate for getting some of the things some of its younger leaders were demanding. The First World War came upon a continent that seemed to be girding itself for a class struggle and hearing strident voices attacking the state, private property, and "the capitalistic system."

Most of these developments after mid-century were largely continuations, intensifications, or diffusions over a wider area of movements well under way before 1850. The period up to 1914 will therefore be treated as one, but the reader can with advantage keep in mind the characteristic features of each half. The years since 1914 have, however, witnessed marked changes in many of the trends which made the nineteenth century believe in "progress." A mid-Victorian would be grievously distressed by the end of the rapid growth of population, of production, and of international trade, by the serious shrinkage of some natural resources, the instability of currencies, the extreme forms of economic nationalism, the swollen power of the state, the suppression of the individual and restriction of his free enterprise, and the resort to force rather than to argument to advance (or defend) a cause. Meanwhile the far-reaching exploitation of large natural and human resources by state enterprise in the Soviet Union since 1920 has created a new challenging kind of economy and polity. Finally, the impact of a mature, rather than a "colonial frontier" United States economy on Europe has been felt only since 1914. Some aspects of the story since that date therefore call for treatment in chapters of their own.

BIBLIOGRAPHY

Bowden, W., Karpovich, M., and Usher, A. P., *An Economic History of Europe since 1750* (1937), chap. 1.

Carr-Saunders, A. M., *World Population; Past Growth and Present Trends* (1936).

Clapham, J. H., "Economic Change," *Cambridge Modern History,* vol. x, chap. 23.

Cole, A. H., "An Approach to the Study of Entrepreneurship," *J. Ec. H.,* supplement, 1946.

Delaisi, F., *Les deux Europes* (1929).

Knowles, L. C. A., *The Industrial and Commercial Revolutions in Great Britain during the Nineteenth Century* (1921), part i.

Nussbaum, F. L., *History of the Economic Institutions of Modern Europe* (1933), part iv, chap. 1.

Polanyi, K., *The Great Transformation* (1944).

XVIII

MODERN EUROPEAN AGRICULTURE:
PART I. BRITISH AGRICULTURE

Since agriculture is still Europe's largest occupation, its development during the last two centuries may justly claim attention before we turn to examine those other forms of enterprise which made Industrial Europe. The story reveals the following main features:

1. The increased commercialization of agriculture, greater attention to cash crops and animals for market, and a growing concern with questions of price, cost, and competition.

2. Changes in farming technique, leading to better utilization of the soil, improvements in animal husbandry, new crops, and the provision of more feed for livestock. These steps were often prefaced by the abolition of such village open fields and common pasture rights as still survived and the division of the land into individual farms, each run by its occupant according to his own plans and ability.

3. The reorganization of rural society. In England the trend was completed toward the large estate, cut up into substantial farms which were worked by tenants with the aid of hired labor. On the continent serfdom was abolished. When this happened, the emancipating state made provisions by which the liberated peasant could become owner of all his holding by compensating his landlord in a series of money payments, or could retain part of it by surrendering the rest. In France the landlord did not actually get his money; in Russia he did, because the state undertook the financing of the transaction; in Prussia the larger peasant surrendered part of his land, but the lowliest freedmen emerged landless. Much of Europe thus became a region of peasant proprietors. Landlords, the church, and the crown still retained large tracts of land, but their estates declined in size or number as governments peacefully helped peasants to buy them after 1900 or forcibly seized them during the postwar turmoil after 1918. Apart from Great Britain, Spain, eastern

Germany, southern Italy, and Hungary, the day of the great estate came to an end.

4. The emergence of problems peculiar to a peasant economy in a world of commercial farming. The peasant's holding was small and grew smaller as population increased, especially if the law insisted that it be divided more or less equally among all the heirs. Improved cultivation or concentration on certain crops or animals might wring an adequate living out of fewer acres, while birth control, migration to the cities, and emigration to America or Siberia could relieve the pressure on the limited amount of land. The peasants of western Europe discovered ways of making their holdings productive enough to carry the load imposed on them, and in France and Ireland birth control limited the load. Cooperative societies helped them to overcome the disadvantages of small-scale production; supplied them cheaply with credit, seed, implements and other things they needed; packed, processed, transported, and sold their product, and generally gave their enterprise an efficiency comparable to the best that could be found in industry or transportation. But in many parts of central, eastern and southern Europe population outstripped productivity, and peasant holdings became too small either for efficient operation or for filling the larder. It was easier to demand more land from the remaining large estates than to find the capital or spread the knowledge that might increase the output per acre. Poverty and peasantry were therefore synonymous.

Until about 1850 the center of interest in agricultural change was in Great Britain. The continent had by then altered its *agrarian* structure by abolishing serfdom, except in Russia and Rumania, and these countries took the step in 1861 and 1864 respectively. Liberation had little immediate effect on *agricultural* developments. There were few important innovations or changes in methods, and commercial farming did not expand greatly until the railroad provided access to market for regions that were not well served by rivers or canals. When a continental enthusiast for progress sought ideas or precedents, it was usually to England that he turned. The English story will therefore be told first.

The English Countryside about 1700. In Chapter XV we noted the growth of commercial farming during Tudor and Stuart times, the expansion of grain exports, the inclosure of some land, the evidence of some interest in experiment and improvement, the decline in profits under the burden of high interest rates and taxes during the wars with France (1689–1713), and the passage of much land into the hands of large owners who were more interested in political life and its rewards than in improving their estates.

In 1696 Gregory King estimated that 10,000,000 acres, a quarter of England and Wales, were waste. Most of this territory lay west of a line drawn from Berwick due south to Dorset, a region of moor, hill, and mountain; some of it was in the low-lying eastern districts, covered with sand hills or exposed to risk of perennial flood. Between these two areas lay the broad central belt of better land, dotted with villages three or four miles apart and devoted to a combination (in varying proportions) of grain growing and animal husbandry, largely on open fields and common pastures. In spite of the work of earlier inclosers, half the parishes and cultivated land of the country were still "open" in 1700.

In this middle belt the farmer had arable strips in the plowfields, a claim to a share of the hay from the meadow, perhaps a piece of pasture inclosed by hedge or fence, and the various common rights, such as we saw he enjoyed in medieval times. Although there had been some consolidation of arable strips into compact blocks—an improvement recognized as desirable by progressive farmers and landlords—"fragmentation" was still widespread. We know, for instance, of one villager who held 80 acres in 164 pieces; another had 166 acres in 217, a third 2 acres in 6 lots, and a very little fellow had 1 acre in 8 fragments. A village priest held 132 acres in 124 pieces in 53 different places in 7 fields. Cultivation was still on a two- or three-field rotation, one stage of which was fallow, controlled by the village group. A farmer could plant what he wished—grains, peas, or roots—but his strips must be harvested by a certain date so that the field could be thrown open for grazing and must be left fallow when that point in the rotation was reached.

Livestock were fed during the summer on the commons and wastes, on the stubble after harvest, and in the meadow after the hay had been cut. There is evidence of inclosed pastures in some villages, but the task of turning a piece of wild land into a field of rich grass was rendered difficult by the scarcity of good grass seed and of manure. "To make a pasture breaks a man" was a farmer's adage indicating that the venture was slow and laborious. If the cattle had to be kept indoors during the winter they ate straw and the hay from the meadow. There is little evidence that arable land could be spared for growing feed. As in medieval times, lack of winter fodder forced the farmer to kill or sell such animals as he could not carry through till spring. Consequently the number of livestock stood still or grew slowly, the supply of manure and of draft animals did not increase, the land was insufficiently nourished, the area under cultivation could not be expanded, the growing of forage crops could not be seriously undertaken. The circle was still vicious and unbroken.

Cultivation was greedy of time and labor. Two men, one boy, six horses, and a heavy plow might spend a day turning one acre of heavy soil. The fallow had to be plowed and harrowed, even though it was not to be planted, in order to destroy weeds, "rest the land," and let it replenish its supply of nitrates—though no one knew this chemical fact until long afterwards. Seed was sown broadcast, and the birds devoured much of it before it could be covered. Even when it began to be drilled and buried more promptly the English farmer described the process in an adage which ran:

> Sow four grains in a row,
> One for the pigeon, one for the crow,
> One to rot and one to grow.

The crop rarely yielded more than five or six times the amount of seed used. It was harvested with sickles or scythes and threshed with flails.

To the advocate of better farming the open village and its methods seemed utterly bad and were condemned in such language as is commonly used on sin and gin. Some of the admitted defects were unavoidable so long as open fields and common rights prevailed; others were curable only as knowledge of better methods spread and was applied, and were to be found on inclosed farms as well as on open fields. The strip system wasted land in roads and footpaths. It wasted time in getting men, implements, and teams from one strip to another or from the village to the more distant fields. The commons were often overstocked in spite of the "stint" which tried to limit the number of animals a man could put on them. Breeding was likely to be "the haphazard union of nobody's son with everybody's daughter" (Ernle), and cattle diseases were hard to combat when all the animals were jumbled together. The wastes were sometimes smothered with inedible growths. The yield of meat and wool was small, beasts which had to roam far afield for their food were lean

and long of limb, and "the roast beef of old England" was probably
tough.

A more serious potential defect was the barrier to individual
initiative and innovation, whether the individual was farmer or
landlord. The farmer could not experiment too much with his plowland, as for instance by planting as well as tilling his fallow or by
turning some of it into pasture for a few years. The common rights
of his fellows to graze their animals on his stubble or fallow and on
his share of the meadow after the hay had been cut stood in the
way. He and other substantial farmers might agree that it was desirable to abolish these common pasturage rights; but every village
contained many small farmers or laborers who drew little income
from crops and who therefore depended vitally on the opening up
of the large area of meadow and arable fields in due season for the
sustenance of their livestock.

To any landlord who was seriously interested in the income he
received in rents, there were two objectionable features in the open
village. In the first place, the unimproved commons and wastes
might be capable of being made more productive, but only after
they had been divided up and subjected to a considerable expenditure of capital and labor. He was legally entitled to do this to his
wastelands, provided he left enough grazing facilities for his tenants; but a total attack on all the wastes and common pastures
would be so costly and provoke so much opposition that it was a
task not lightly to be undertaken.

In the second place, the landlord's freedom to reorganize his
estate, in order to make it more productive of goods and rent, was
restricted by the terms on which some farmers held their lands.
Some of them were freeholders, owners of their acres and common
rights; others were copyholders, virtually perpetual tenants, or
leaseholders "for lives" who could not be displaced until the last
of the "lives" had expired, even though (until about 1700) they
were in arrears with their rent. If such men were opposed to change,
the only course was to buy them out or secure parliamentary power
to overrule them—each a costly procedure.

Modern scholars are more disposed to say a kind word for the old
order than were its contemporary critics. C. S. Orwin, an eminent
agricultural economist, finds that the open-field system was an ingenious, efficient way of meeting the villagers' needs in the circumstances and with the technique available. Professor Usher points

out that the strictures on fallowing and other practices "involve much exaggeration," since fallowing was essential until "the introduction of commercial fertilizers [after 1840] enabled the farmer to develop his fertility program by systematic importation." The farmer was neither an ignoramus nor a fool. He preferred tried and trusted methods to newfangled notions which often were found to be ill-informed or foolish. But if the pressure of demand became too great to be met in old ways; if the prospect of income grew brighter for landlord or farmer; if knowledge of more productive methods was made available; if the capital needed for improvement or reorganization was forthcoming; and if a way was found to overcome conservative opposition, then the structure and methods of village life were doomed to drastic transformation. The eighteenth century supplied all these things. Let us look first at the knowledge.

The Search for Improvement. Between the introduction of printing and 1700 more than a hundred English books or pamphlets on rural problems and practices were published. Many of them described methods, often those used by advanced native or continental cultivators, which would yield readers greater pleasure and profit from their lands. The royal road to profit was *improvement*. Those who would travel on it must do two things. Firstly, they must improve their farming methods by such innovations as drilling seed instead of broadcasting it, use more manure, plant turnips and clover in the fallows, and transfer the potato—still suspect as a food —from the garden to the field. Secondly, they—and "they" usually meant landlords—must put their estates to better use: bring heaths and moors under cultivation, drain swamps, sweep away open fields, abolish grazing rights on arable and meadow, divide up the commons; then, when the estates had been converted into compact separate farms, preferably large ones, they must encourage tenants to improve their holdings by giving them long leases and promising to compensate them for any capital or labor they sank in such work.

The seventeenth century was richer in proposals than performance, though there was some movement on each of the two lines which the writers recommended. The next century was rich in technical experiments. We pass from the one to the other in the person of Jethro Tull (1674–1741). Tull is noteworthy for three reasons. In the first place, he was a landowner, a member of the class which was the driving force both in seeking for better methods and in changing the village map. There were "spirited farmers" willing to try new ways, but the pioneer work was done chiefly by landlords. They had the funds to foot the bill for trial and error, they could borrow money for permanent improvements more easily than could the farmer, their very livelihood was not at stake, and their enterprise might yield rich reward in increased rents. Their contacts with other areas or countries gave them a width of interest that the farmer lacked, while their political power was a guarantee that parliament would aid rather than hinder their plans.

In the second place, Tull got his inspiration by watching Frenchmen at work in their vineyards. Other landlords picked up ideas in the same way—one, for instance, as a political exile, another during a sojourn as ambassador in Holland. The British agricultural advance owed much to foreign methods and seeds—"Spanish clover, Burgundian and French grasses, the horse hoe of Languedoc, and the French method of cultivating turnips in fields" (Gras)—and when the movement gathered momentum the continent was scoured to find plants or animals that would flourish under British skies. But imitation soon passed over into innovation. By untiring experiment and consequently by making important additions to agricultural knowledge the British gave the continent far more than they had taken.

In the third place, Tull, like all other improvers, had to fight the conservatism of his laborers and tenants, and to realize how great the *vis inertiae* of a countryside can be.

Ill health turned Tull from law and politics to the land. Observation of French vignerons plying the hoe and plow around their vines gave him his clue: perhaps the secret of success was to keep the irons in the soil, to till incessantly, fight weeds, and prevent the earth from becoming hard. He therefore plowed his land very thoroughly, drilled wheat seed in rows some distance apart, and hoed between the rows as long as the plants permitted. In 1701 he invented a drill and in 1714 a horse hoe. He grew grain on the same patch of land for thirteen years, got heavier crops than did his broadcasting neighbors, but with far less seed and no manure. Late in life (1731) he expounded his theory and practice in a book. This was unfortunate, for though his facts could not be challenged, his theories, especially about the harmfulness of manure, seemed ridiculous to well-informed readers, while his drill and hoe were unsatisfactory or cumbrous. Scoffers made merry at his expense, but here and there a landlord in England, an author in France, or an agricultural society in Scotland found guidance in his pages.

The center of interest shifts from a sickly squire to one who, in the words of Arthur Young, "quitted all the power and lustre of a Court for the amusements of agriculture." Viscount Charles Townshend (1674–1738) was born to rule. He rose to the very top of the political ladder. Then, when he lost the prime-ministership in 1730, he retired to his estate in Norfolk, not to sulk in his tent but to spend the rest of his life wrestling with wastes, rabbits, and stubborn tenants. Much of his land was a sorry panorama of swamp or sand on which a few sheep found starvation rations and "two rabbits struggled for every blade of grass." Townshend had seen such territory in Holland turned into fertile fields, set out to do likewise, and succeeded. He dressed the sandy expanses with marl (a mixture of clay and lime) and turned them into soil. He also experimented with a four-course rotation of wheat, turnips, barley, and clover, thus producing human and animal food in alternate years and abolishing the fallow season. He drilled and hoed, planted trees, inclosed wastes, and welded small holdings into larger farms which he let on long leases.

Townshend thus provided two important innovations. The cultivation of sandy soils was demonstrated to Englishmen. More important still, the production of fodder could become an integral part of arable farming. The cultivation of turnips and clover not merely put the fallow to use but actually benefited the soil as much as did fallow tillage, since hoeing the turnip field killed the weeds and the clover transferred nitrogen from the air to the soil. Meanwhile the new feed crops allowed animals to be carried through the winter; the circle became beneficial. What corn is to North American animals, the turnip became to English livestock, and the man who first vigorously cultivated it comes down to us as "Turnip Townshend." He had his immediate reward in a larger income from his estate.

Tull and Townshend pointed the way to feeding more animals but did not face the task of breeding better ones. That problem was not seriously attacked until the second half of the century. Here and there a landlord built up a good flock or herd, but the aim differed from that of today. Sheep were valued chiefly for their wool and manure, cattle as milkers or draft animals rather than as butchers' victims. Between 1760 and 1790 Robert Bakewell changed the whole outlook. Improved roads and waterways were bringing the growing population and the grazier nearer together and opening up a larger market for meat and milk—a fact reflected in the rising prices of meat and dairy produce. At the same time the way to obtain more feed was becoming widely known, and it is possible that the horse was displacing the cow as draft animal. Bakewell therefore set out to develop breeds in which bone and sinew were less important than prime cuts. He chose his animals carefully, inbred judiciously, and produced greatly improved types of cattle and sheep. He kept his methods secret and charged such high prices that jesters said "his animals were too dear to buy and too fat to eat." But his work and that of other men revolutionized animal husbandry, giving the world such famous breeds as Shorthorn, Hereford, and Devon cattle, Berkshire hogs and Leicester sheep.

The "new husbandry" spread slowly at first. Townshend's farmers were loath to spend time, labor, and money on drilling seed or hoeing turnips. The chief converts were found among the landlords, and the indifference of the big politically-minded estate owners toward improvement gave place to an interest which by 1750 had become a fashion, almost a craze. Walpole is said to have read the reports from his bailiff before he looked at the day's state papers. Royalty indorsed the cult; George III turned part of his Windsor estate into a farm, trudged round it in heavy boots, and liked to be called "the farmer king." Copying Townshend, Coke of Holkham (1752–1842) transformed his sand hills, marshes, and rabbit warrens into a model estate by doing all the latest things—spending much money, encouraging his tenants with prizes, good buildings, and long leases—and converted his annual sheepshearing into a mixture of house party, short-course summer school, and agricultural show. The Duke of Bedford copied Coke but had larger parties. In Scotland landlords experimented with Polish oats and Siberian barley, and grew turnips—which at first they ate as dessert.

This interest in improvement gradually infected most sections of society. Burke discussed cabbages and pigs almost as earnestly as he did the grievances of American colonies. When Arthur Young rambled round the country about 1770 he found enterprising farmers everywhere, including one who was famous for his turnip slicer, his drain-digging machine, his thresher, and his belief that electricity would stimulate the growth of crops. Agricultural societies offered prizes and medals, tested new implements, obtained land for experimental plots, published accounts of new things, organized agricultural shows, and sent out questionnaires.

The new methods found their greatest publicity expert in Arthur Young (1741–1820). Young failed dismally on three farms, partly because he knew nothing about the work and partly because he wasted his substance on experiments. Then he embarked on a career as one of the most voluminous and influential agricultural writers of all time. He conceived the idea of making a series of long observation tours—a plan rendered more attractive by the fact that a nagging wife made home life unbearable. He toured England and Ireland, made three trips to France, and went as far as Italy. Each tour became the subject of one to four volumes. In vigorous prose he described and praised the work of the progressive landlords or farmers. He pilloried swamps, wastes, commons, open fields, fallows, small farms, short leases, broadcast crops, and unhoed fields. He urged that the countryside be covered with large inclosed farms, well improved and equipped, and let on long leases to tenants who understood high farming.

His industry was amazing. In three years he produced sixteen volumes. In the eighties he began to edit and write much of the *Annals of Agriculture*, which ran to forty-five volumes. In 1793 he became secretary of the Board of Agriculture and thus gained more scope for travel, writing, and contacts with the high or mighty. His books were translated into foreign tongues; learned societies in Germany, France, Italy, and Russia bestowed honors on him; Washington wrote seeking his advice about implements, Lafayette asked him for a landscape gardener, Catherine the Great sent young men to sit at his feet, and Alexander invited him to make a series of Russian agricultural tours. George III carried the latest issue of the *Annals* in his coach and Napoleon in Elba belatedly read his *Travels in France.*

The Stimulus to Improvement. The eighteenth century was thus marked, in a measure far exceeding its predecessor, by a belief in what Young called his only fixed principle, "the principle of change." Until about 1760 it was not a response to any urgent need for change, for there was apparently little pressure of demand that could not be met in the old ways. England not only was able to feed herself but exported some grain, and wheat was cheaper than it had been during the seventeenth century. The early urge to better farming or extension of acreage cannot be found in the lure of high prices or the stress of scarcity. It may have been due to the desire to reduce production costs, and it certainly reflected the landlords' wish to make worthless lands yield produce and rents. It was also part of that general quickening of the scientific mind which characterized the century. The joy of experiment, of achievement, and of a richer rent roll was a satisfying reward, and meanwhile possibilities were uncovered for wider exploitation when the need came.

That need came after 1760. The population of England and Wales had grown about a quarter between 1700 and 1760; it rose a third (2,000,000) during the next forty years. The birth rate was as high as it had ever been, and the death rate had begun to fall about 1730. The decline was slow until about 1780, and when Johnson consoled Boswell for the loss of a child he reminded him that "to keep three out of four is more than your share. Mrs. Thrale [wife of a rich brewer] has but four out of eleven." But it was sure, thanks to improving sanitation, better medical knowledge and practice, improved food supplies, a decline in urban gin drinking, and "the increasing concern with personal hygiene which was characteristic of the eighteenth century" (Shryock). As industrial changes attracted much of the increased population to the manufacturing and commercial towns, the need for bread, milk, meat, and wool rose accordingly. Transportation facilities were being improved rapidly, linking town and country more closely.

While demand was being stimulated, a period of bad weather injured supply. Between 1765 and 1792 there were only two really bountiful harvests and fourteen poor ones. The average price of wheat from 1716 to 1765 had been 35/– a quarter (eight bushels), but for the next three decades it was 51/–, 43/–, and 47/– respectively. As much wheat was imported as was exported, and after 1792 exports vanished, never to return. England was now pressed hard to provide her own breadstuffs. The danger of this situation was made manifest when the war with France began (1793). For over twenty years imports of continental grain were uncertain, American farms were far away, and the homeland must carry the load. Again nature was harsh, for between 1793 and 1814 there were fourteen poor seasons, of which seven were shockingly bad. Every available acre must be put to work, every belt tightened. Countless emergency measures were passed to forbid the making of starch, hair powder, and spirits from grain or potatoes, or the sale of fresh bread. Wartime depreciation of the paper currency and poor crops combined to raise the average wheat price from 47/– per quarter in the pre-war decade to 93/– for the years 1805–1814; but in the worst year it rose to 126/6, which we can think of as nearly $4 a bushel in a period when few wage earners received $5 a week.

The stimulus of rising prices was thus felt from about 1760 onward and became powerful during the war decades. Rents could be raised, land sold at high prices, and poor soil tilled at a profit. A country parson looking over his congregation one Sunday morning in 1796 noticed a farmer's wife wearing a black veil and commented, "Times must be good for farmers when their wives can dress in such style." According to William Cobbett, war prosperity converted the farmer into an obnoxious *nouveau riche* who crammed his house with "pianos, sofas, and all sorts of fooleries," rode a fox-hunting horse, served wine at his table, and seemed not to resent his wife's use of cosmetics or his sons' imitation of the fashions and behavior of young squires or lords. Cobbett was a journalist given to colorful exaggeration; but his picture is probably substantially accurate.

Inclosure: The Last Phase. Growing demand, wartime needs, and the new husbandry combined to accelerate the work of sweeping away open fields and common pastures from those regions where they still survived. Much—perhaps most—inclosure was effected by agreement among those whose claims and interests were involved. Some landlords inclosed after buying up freeholders' farms which were mixed with their own or buying out the interests of their long-term tenants, a practice which in the early eighteenth century had almost reached "the magnitude of a campaign" (Habakkuk) on some large estates. Where agreement was impossible or the cost of removing obstructions too great, landlords turned increasingly to parliament for aid. Parliament was in part a landlords' and merchants' club, full of enthusiasts for high farming. If a petition, asking for legislative permission to inclose some land and signed by owners of a substantial majority of the value of "estates, rights, interests and properties" of a district, was submitted to it, an inclosure act was usually, but not invariably, assured of passage.

This act appointed commissioners who examined all claims, decided how much land—usually one-seventh—was to be given to the church in commutation of tithes, earmarked land for charitable purposes, laid out the roads, and then redistributed the remainder "in such quantities as the commissioners shall adjudge and deem to be a full compensation and satisfaction." The act might deal only with the striped arable fields, which were said to be "inconveniently situated" and "incapable of considerable improvement in their present state." It might apply only to the common pastures and wastes, declaring that "the said commons (which by experience are found to be bad pasturage for sheep by rotting them in wet seasons) should be divided." Or it might make a complete sweep, abolish open fields, commons, meadows, and wastes, and replace the diverse rights of each claimant with one piece of land.

The number of inclosure acts passed between 1700 and 1760 averaged about four a year. Between 1760 and 1792 the average was over forty. During the war it rose to eighty, but after 1815 inclosure slackened its pace, partly because of rural depression but chiefly because most of the land had been dealt with. By 1845 the movement was almost completed; about 4,000 acts had been passed, affecting over 6,000,000 acres, or a fifth of the country. The area inclosed by agreement was apparently far larger, perhaps twice as great. After 1845 the fragments were dealt with. By 1900 an open field or common pasture was a curiosity, the land had been divided into compact farms and fields, and the 2,000,000 acres of common or wasteland that remained were regarded as worthless until two world wars forced some of them into use.

From patient research the economic and social consequences of this last chapter in inclosure history are gradually becoming clear. The first result was the putting of a considerable area of wild, unimproved land to better use. Each acre of former common or waste could now be subjected to such treatment as its occupier or his landlord thought best, and that treatment usually began with a vigorous effort to raise the productivity of the soil. During the war years the effort was sometimes overdone, and much land that had been plowed up ceased to be profitable when peace brought an end to high prices. Inclosure of the open fields was not always followed by better tillage; yet it did often serve as a prelude to improved methods and output. The nation as a whole gained from the increased productivity which inclosure made possible.

The second result was an increase in the number of middle-sized and large tenant farms. Such farms already occupied a great part of the uninclosed areas and were becoming more numerous. Successful farmers enlarged their holdings and landlords regarded the ideal estate as "one tenanted by large farmers holding 200 acres or more, paying their rents regularly and keeping the holdings in repair" (Habakkuk). Meanwhile the amount of land in the hands of small farmers, equivalents of the continental peasant, seems to have been declining, as was also the percentage of farmers who owned their land or held it on long secure leases or copyhold tenure. In sixty unclosed parishes studied by Professor Lavrovsky, less than a quarter of the land was *owned* by those who worked on it; about 10 per cent of them *occupied* 75 per cent of it; hence the remaining 90 per cent of the villagers held only 25 per cent of the land in holdings of a few acres apiece or they had none at all.

Inclosure hastened the spread of large farm units. The acts authorizing it provided that copyholders and freeholders must receive land proportionate to the size of their former holdings, but that all leases were void, subject to compensation of the tenant. If therefore the landlord believed that "poverty and ignorance are the ordinary inhabitants of the small farm," he carved the land that came into his hands into large units, which he allotted to the best farmers available. In that allotment the former holders of a few acres were likely to be left out in the cold.

So also was the laborer. He had supplemented his wages by grazing such few livestock as he could acquire on the commons and possibly by cultivating a plot of garden or fragment of the open fields. Sometimes his "right" to graze was found by the commissioner to be invalid, a usurpation or trespass. If it was valid, the scrap of land he was offered in its stead might be too small to supply what the commons and wastes had afforded him, and he was tempted to take a lump sum of money instead. In general he lost access to any land and became entirely dependent on his wages. Arthur Young, arch-advocate of inclosure, admitted later that "by nineteen inclosure bills in twenty [the poor] are injured, in some grossly injured." Recent research shows that he did not overstate the case; that "in every way inclosures tended to divorce the poor from the soil" (Johnson); and that while the material injury inflicted by the loss of commons and pastures was great, "still more serious was the moral damage" (Ernle).

Landlords, freeholders, copyholders, and favored tenants benefited from inclosure, but they had to pay the price. There were fees and expenses to be paid to parliamentary officials, lawyers, commissioners, surveyors, and valuators. Roads and fences had to be provided and new farmhouses and barns must be built if the farmer was to live on his land. Those who owned their new holdings must defray their own costs, usually by going into debt, while the tenant must compensate the landlord for his outlay by paying higher rents. Hence agriculture became more heavily capitalized, partly through inclosure and partly because of the increased equipment and operating costs of the new husbandry.

Rising prices after 1760 made the carriage of these financial burdens fairly easy, and after 1793 farming became geared to high war costs and prices. Cultivation was extended to inferior soils, land was bought at high prices, long leases at heavy rents were cheerfully assumed, and the number of operating owners increased as tenants purchased their holdings. If farmers bought pianos and their wives bought veils, Coke of Holkham could take satisfaction from the knowledge that his energy and investment, supplemented by the war, had raised the annual rents of his estate from £2,000 in 1776 to £20,000 in 1816.

Agricultural Advance After 1815. The good times ended when peace came in 1815, bringing a decline in prices but no comparable fall in costs. From a famine peak of 15/10 ($3.90) a bushel in 1812 wheat fell to 8/2 ($1.96) in 1815 and averaged 8/9 ($2.10) for the first post-war decade. The landed interests secured protection from imports when the Corn Law of 1815 forbade the entry of wheat if the domestic price fell below 10/- ($2.50) a bushel; but in spite of this bit of farm relief the price went down. Meanwhile wages, rents, interest rates, and national or local taxes, which had all risen during the war years, could not easily be lowered. Farmers who concentrated on wheat felt the depression most severely; poor land went back to grass or scrub, mortgages were foreclosed, landlords were obliged to reduce rents in order to retain tenants, and two hundred country banks failed in fifteen years.

The distress was not, however, general or protracted. Imports of food were small until mid-century, and the farmer had a virtual monopoly of a market which rose from 14,000,000 consumers (United Kingdom) in 1801 to 21,000,000 in 1821 and to 27,000,000 in 1841. He gave less attention to inclosing and cultivating heavy clay lands which required "five or six ploughings, five or six harrowings and rollings" (Fussell) before they were fit for seeding, and turned to lighter soils which could be sown after only one plowing. Factories rather than blacksmiths produced better implements. The seed drill became more widely used as its efficiency improved—a hundred years after Tull had sung its praises. A Scot found a new way to drain land, and someone invented a machine which made drain-pipes cheaply (1844). Some farmers used steam engines to haul plows, and the steam-driven threshing machine reduced the man power needed for that process. Experiments with harvesters were ceaseless, but a successful machine attracted little attention until it was improved in America and returned to England to be displayed at the Great Exhibition of 1851.

By 1840 the readjustment from a war economy to peacetime con-ditions had been completed, sometimes painfully, and the improve-ments started by the eighteenth century had been fully incorporated into agricultural practice. At that moment a new approach to better farming was revealed by the chemist. Even in the seventeenth cen-tury men had asked, "What is the food of plants?" but their answers were all guesswork. By 1800 some people were suspecting that chemistry might solve the riddle. In 1802 Humphry Davy, a young London scientist, gave (and later published) a course of lectures on the connection between chemistry and plant physiology. During the next four decades men in Sweden, Switzerland, Germany, and France conducted experiments in field and laboratory. Boussin-gault's field work in France made him the "founder of modern ag-ricultural science" (Fussell), while in Germany Justus von Liebig provided a landmark in the progress from empirical rules to scien-tific principles when, in 1840, he published the results of his labora-tory researches in a volume entitled *Organic Chemistry in Its Appli-cations to Agriculture and Physiology.* Liebig's thesis was that plants contained certain chemicals; the carbon and nitrogen they had drawn from the air; the minerals, such as phosphorus and potash, from the earth. Soil was not just so much undifferentiated dirt, but a chemical complex. It might originally be devoid or by cropping be depleted of the essentials of plant nutrition. By applying the right kind and quantity of fertilizer the defect could be repaired and the exhaustion prevented.

Some of Liebig's views were challenged and corrected by others. Boussingault showed that plants did not get enough nitrogen from the air, but must draw some from the soil. One of Liebig's admirers, Lawes (a young English landlord), and one of his pupils, Gilbert, established in 1843 the famous experimental farm at Rothamsted and began investigations which not merely amended Liebig's conclusions at many points but broadened greatly the field of knowledge by researches which are still being conducted today. In the eighties the bacteriologists revealed that the soil, in addition to being a chemical storehouse, was also the abode of bacteria whose activities influenced the growth of plants. But the earlier chemical discoveries were important enough in themselves to start the intelligent use of animal and chemical fertilizers. The search for the latter ranged over the whole earth, even to battlefields in quest of bones. Bone dust, nitrates from Chile, guano from Peru, potash from German mines, phosphates from North Africa or from phosphoric iron ore all were applied to the soil of Europe to supplement the supply of animal manure. Their use abolished the need for fallow and built up fertility in grass and arable lands alike.

Armed with drains, machines, and fertilizers, English agriculture began after 1840 to enjoy a silver age and then a golden age. Good roads and canals were supplemented by railroads after 1830, the industrial areas were getting more crowded, and the import of foreign foodstuffs, though growing, was still small. In 1846 the Corn Laws, which had been amended and made less prohibitive, were repealed and grain was admitted duty free. The consumers of food defeated the producers; the manufacturers and merchants, aided by a potato famine in Ireland, beat the landlords. The latter predicted speedy ruin when their protection vanished, but foreign competition did not become acute until after 1870, and British farming entered the best two decades in its whole history. The improvements came to a head and the result was regarded enviously by foreigners as a model of perfection. Wheat prices were good, wool had doubled in price in twenty-five years, and the urban demand for meat and dairy produce was excellent. Prosperity enveloped both the landlord and his tenant farmers; even hired laborers were stirred to seek a better share of the general well-being.

The Land System. In that flourishing quarter-century the land system also reached the peak of its development as a trinity of large landlord, tenant farmer, and landless laborer. In 1873 over half of England and Wales was owned by 2,250 persons in estates which ranged from 1,000 acres upward and averaged 7,300 acres apiece. Political power, social prestige, and good rentals in prosperous years made land as desirable an investment as it had been in medieval and Tudor times, though the growth of the industrial and commercial classes had reduced the political power. Arthur Young rented a farm from a landlord who had been butler to a duke, a neighboring estate had recently been bought by a brandy merchant, and Young scoffed at the pagodas and temples erected as country houses by "some oilman who builds on the solid foundation of pickles and herring." The nineteenth-century merchant, banker, and manufacturer was as eager as his predecessors to acquire broad acres.

Once an estate had been acquired, family pride decreed that it should be made larger whenever possible, but its division or sale was an unforgivable sin. Division was prevented by the practice of primogeniture—inheritance by the eldest son. He in turn was protected from temptation to sell any part of his heritage by being obliged, on reaching manhood, to "entail" it, i.e., settle it on the next generation, usually not yet born. When his father died he took possession, but only as life tenant. He enjoyed the income, but the estate belonged to his son, who in due course entailed it to the next heir. Entail and primogeniture passed the estate down unimpaired, unless some disaster forced the life tenant and the heir to agree to let part of it go. In hard times this rigidity was a disadvantage, since it shackled the landlord to an unprofitable form of property. There were plenty of hard times ahead.

Apart from the "home farm," descendant of the much larger domain, the estate was not cultivated by its owner but leased to tenants. In 1910 tenants tilled seven-eights of the farms and 90 per cent of the land; the percentage of owning operators was far below that on the continent or in North America, and the figure had been falling for probably two centuries. The landlord-tenant relationship was capable of every gradation from harmony to hostility, according to the qualities of heart and mind of the two parties, local custom, the terms of the lease, the rulings of common law, the later provisions of statute law, and variations in rural prosperity.

Three aspects were of special importance: the length of the lease, the amount of the rent, and the source from which capital was to be drawn for improvements. In the inclosure days long leases had often been granted, especially when a farm contained much unimproved soil; but when land had been broken in, the contract was made for a shorter period, usually for one year. The lease stated the amount of rent that was to be paid—a fixed sum, not a share of the product. It laid down the use to which the land was to be put, and imposed restraints on the farmer in order to maintain the fertility of the soil and protect the farm from deterioration or damage. It might provide that the landlord would undertake certain fixed improvements, and that if the tenant devoted his own time and money to making specified improvements he was to receive compensation for them when he quit the farm; but this latter provision was limited to leases granted by the more enlightened landlords and was far from being a general practice. Hence the farmer might find his tenure insecure, his eviction possible or his rent raised at the year's end, and his outlay on improvements lost.

On the best estates these risks were small, and in 1875 the first of a series of laws was passed to remove them. The tenant's right to compensation for improvements was recognized first; then came protection from (or compensation for) eviction at the end of his lease "without good and sufficient cause," safeguards against increased rents, and freedom to crop his land and sell his produce as he wished, but with the stipulation that the landlord could claim compensation for any damage the tenant had done to the farm's fertility. The state thus stepped into the rural field as it had into the industrial; it imposed on backward landlords the conditions which were voluntarily granted by enlightened ones; it placed the tenant in as good a position as if he were the owner yet at the same time safeguarded the interests of the landlord and afforded effective protection against the "mining" of the soil. Under such circumstances many families have held their farms for decades, even generations, on a year-to-year lease. The average occupation has been about fifteen years, which is longer than that of the North American owner-farmer.

From 1851 to 1871 there were about 250,000 farmers and nearly a million hired laborers; the ratio was about 1 to 4. Since over 40 per cent of the farmers operated family farms and many others hired only one or two workers, the largest units might employ a dozen or more men and women. In such cases the farmer was a "clean boots" rather than a "dirty boots" entrepreneur, concerned with direction, management, and marketing. He belonged to a rural upper middle class, his wife did only the pleasanter domestic and farm chores, and he was usually a solid pillar of church and Conservative party.

The laborer was the third person of the rural trinity. The loss of the commons made him dependent on his wages, while the passage of spinning and other domestic industrial pursuits into factories might deprive his wife of her money earnings. His wages were low, except where proximity to manufacturing areas compelled the farmer to pay better rates in order to prevent laborers from going to the towns. His hours were long; his house might be picturesque but was poor. If he was ambitious he migrated to town or emigrated, though some laborers of marked tenacity and ability stepped up to become small farmers. At rare intervals unemployment, a threat of lower wages, dislike of a new machine, or the voice of a trade-union charmer gathered laborers together to smash threshers, burn haystacks, or join a union; but lack of energy, education, or class consciousness prevented farm hands from doing much to protect or advance their welfare. British agriculture in its palmy days "gave returns sufficient to reward adequately all the parties to production. It was the maldistribution of profits, rather than any lack of them, which led to the change for the worse in the lot of so many of the laboring class" (Orwin).

The Agricultural Depression. The palmy days and the golden age ended quite suddenly, and the period 1875–1896 was for western European farmers in general, but for British ones in particular, a time of gloom. The price level, which had risen rapidly and far after the gold discoveries in California and Australia (about 1850), remained high until about 1873. Then came a long, severe descent which lasted for over twenty years. Just as the decline began, English agriculture was stricken by a number of bad seasons—a tragedy of rain and mud, of rotting crops and dying animals, or of drought and parched earth. Between 1874 and 1882 only two good crops were reaped, and that of the blackest year (1879) was about half that of the good year, 1874.

Western Europeans were inured to climatic vagaries, and farmers had counterbalanced short crops with high prices. But this time it was different. The bread which Europe had been casting on the water in the form of emigrants and capital now came back on an ever rising tide of foodstuffs. In 1850 three-fourths of Britain's wheat imports came from the Baltic or Black Sea ports, and only one-eighth (5,000,000 bushels) from North America. By 1870 the imports had almost doubled; they supplied about half the country's flour, and nearly half of them (34,000,000 bushels) came from America. By 1880 imports had nearly doubled again, but transatlantic supplies had almost trebled (92,000,000 bushels) and accounted for three-quarters of the imports.

These figures were an echo of the rapid expansion of settlement, production, and railroads that followed the Civil War. Free home-steads, the steel plow, spring wheat, the binder, and the new kind of flour mill all facilitated the spread of prairie wheat fields. Elevators, bulk handling, grading, and cutthroat competition between railroads and lake carriers reduced the cost of hauling grain from Chicago to New York from about 33 cents in 1870 to 14 cents in 1881. When the grain reached the coast it found the old sailing ship and the new steamship fighting each other for freight. In 1874 the cost of sending a bushel of wheat across the Atlantic was 20 cents; by 1904 it was 2 cents. Grain exchanges, the telegraph, and the ocean cable knit the world into one market, and a world price took the place of a British or European level. That price seems to have been influenced chiefly by the state of the grain crops in Rumania and Russia, but developments there combined with those in the New World to depress it. Wheat sold in North American ports for $1.47 in 1871; by 1882 it was down to $1.18 and in 1885 to 86 cents.

Wheat was the first and worst but not the only villain of the piece. Lard, bacon, and pickled beef or pork had been sent from America to Europe before 1850; the export of live cattle began about 1870; but that of goods from packing plants, canneries, and dairy factories now became more important. Nor was the United States the only disturber of rural peace. Eastern Canada built up its farm exports, and by 1883 the railroad was opening up Manitoba; but the flow of Canadian prairie grain across the Atlantic was not great until after 1900. Australia added wheat to wool exports after 1860. The refrigerated ship appeared in the early eighties, but two decades elapsed before great quantities of beef, mutton, butter, and fruits could be shipped from the southern hemisphere across the equator and arrive in edible condition in northwestern Europe. Nearer home, Russia and Rumania increased their outpouring of grain at a rapid rate after 1870, and while Russia's rye went chiefly to continental markets her wheat exports to Britain in some years rose to 40,000,000 bushels, placing her second only to the United States.

This revolution in food supplies pleased the consumer. As the general price level sank 40 per cent between 1873 and 1896, food became plentiful and cheap. Violent fluctuations of supply and price were now a thing of the past, for if Europe's harvest was bad that of America might be good. Bread absorbed a smaller part of the wage earner's income, money was released for other purchases, and the standard of living rose. The "hungry forties" and the old fear of famine were forgotten. The British housewife put a girdle round the earth every time she filled her shopping basket. The manufacturer rejoiced, for cheap raw materials helped him to keep his prices low, cheap food kept his workers from seeking higher wages, and swollen imports created a demand for more manufactured exports. The investor was happy, for this influx of produce from the New World paid the interest or dividends on the capital he had been pouring overseas since 1815 in an ever widening stream.

To the farmer the influx was a tragedy. If he had concentrated on grain he was hit first and hardest. An efficient British farmer using good land could make ends meet if the price of wheat did not go below 6/- ($1.50) a bushel; but a poor farmer on poor land would need more. In 1878 the price sank below that figure, and after hovering for four years around 5/9 began a bumpy decline to a low point of 2/2 (53 cents) one day in 1894. The price of other foods, such as meat and dairy produce, fell less and later, but had dropped 20 to 30 per cent by 1893, while that of wool was cut in half.

In varying degrees every country in northwestern Europe felt the effect of this invasion from Russia and the New World, and reacted to it in one of two ways. The agricultural classes in France and Germany were politically strong enough to secure tariff protection, but in Great Britain wage earners and their employers were too powerful to permit any return of "taxes on food." The ports therefore remained wide open to the farmers of all lands. Certain concessions were given to farmers and landlords; local taxes were eased and freight rates lowered. But this relief reduced costs very little, and agriculture was left to sink or swim as best it could in the new currents of international trade.

Where the current was fiercest—in the wheat market—many farmers sank. Whole farms were abandoned; submarginal land reverted to grass, weeds, and thistles; the arable area fell a quarter and the wheat area a half between 1875 and 1894. Landlords had to absorb the financial shock by remitting or reducing rents, farm the land themselves for lack of tenants, or use it for sport. The capital value of land dropped from £2,000,000,000 to about half that sum. The number of farm laborers declined from nearly 1,000,000 to just over 600,000 during a period which saw the total population rise by 11,000,000.

The successful swimmers were those whose products were less

exposed to competition from the low-cost overseas supplies or who switched their interest toward such products. British agriculture changed its direction or emphasis, abandoned the least defensible parts of the home market, and let the country rely on imports for four out of every five bushels of the wheat it consumed. In 1907 it was estimated that 20,000,000 acres of land abroad were growing wheat for British consumers, and that an equally large expanse was supplying them with half their meat and much of their dairy produce. A quarter of the wheat, corn, barley, and oats that entered international trade went to Britain, as did virtually all the bacon, mutton, and lamb. Most of the farm exports of Australia, New Zealand, and Canada went there, along with 95 per cent of Denmark's butter, the larger part of the Argentine's beef, and most of Ireland's butter and bacon. The country produced about £170,000,000 worth of the foodstuffs it needed, imported about £200,000,000 worth from the temperate zone, and had become "a nation of self-suppliers for the week-end only" (Middleton).

Having surrendered some of his market, the British farmer nursed that part in which competition was lighter, i.e., in perishable goods and high-quality produce. Cheaper bread left consumers with more money for milk, meat, butter, fruit, eggs, and vegetables. As the price of sugar fell more than half between 1880 and 1900, the consumption of jam expanded greatly, causing a demand for fruit and other ingredients. The stricken wheatlands of East Anglia were taken over by Scotsmen, who were used to mixed farming, who had their race's genius for handling cattle, and who carefully improved their pastures to produce butter and milk for London or pedigree stock for export to all parts of the world. Since the New World sent cheap animal feed as well as human food, the cost of keeping livestock was reduced. Labor costs were pared by hiring fewer men, and smaller farms, worked chiefly or solely by the family, became more common.

The pains of readjustment were eased when the price curve turned upward in 1896 and mounted about a third in less than twenty years. On the eve of the First World War the rural sky was clearing, quiet unexcited prosperity prevailed, and a new equilibrium seemed to have been reached, disturbed only by consumers' complaints about the high cost of living. Vast food imports were accepted as inevitable, since 120,000 square miles could not possibly feed 45,000,000 people, and as desirable, since they helped to provide the highest standard of living in Europe. In 1913 the ships brought in wheat and flour to supply bread for forty-two weeks out of the fifty-two; also for every man, woman, and child they delivered 170 pounds of sugar, 65 pounds of meat, 23 of potatoes, 20 of butter or cheese, 7 of tea, but only 10 ounces of coffee.

The continuance of this heavy reliance on overseas farmers depended on two conditions—the *physical* ability to bring the food into port, and the *economic* ability to pay for it by exporting goods, shipping, or other services and by spending the income which Britons received from their overseas investments. Two world wars and depression in between impaired both these abilities. During the first war the submarine and the naval or military diversion of merchant ships reduced considerably the influx of food—wheat by a fifth, beef and sugar a third, mutton and butter a half, eggs and apples three-quarters. Farmers were urged to plow more land and offered guaranteed minimum prices till 1922; laborers were guaranteed a minimum wage, but runaway prices and rents were checked by fixing the former and restraining landlords from raising the latter at their pleasure, as they could do during the Napoleonic War. Tractors, large implements, and the labor of war prisoners, interned aliens, and women volunteers helped to increase the cultivated acreage by nearly two million acres, to raise the wheat yield from ten weeks' supply to sixteen, and generally to wring about one-quarter more produce from the soil. The wolf was driven from the door, but only as far as the sidewalk.

When the war ended he vanished and was quickly forgotten. There were no Corn Laws this time, and the guaranteed minimum price was abolished. The flow of food from overseas was resumed, prices fell, and the farmer reverted to his pre-war place, filling only special shelves in the national larder. A subsidy began to be paid in 1925 to encourage him to grow sugar beets, and improvements in canning methods induced him to produce more fruit or vegetables for the canneries. The sugar subsidy was, however, as far as he could persuade the government to go in giving aid. Politically and economically he was a small minority, for agriculture employed only about 7 per cent of the working population. Most Englishmen looked upon the countryside as a place to walk or ride in on Sunday, a vista of possible golf courses and sites for commuters' dwellings, or just a stretch of land separating one town from the next. They regarded the late war as a regrettable accident into which Europe had slipped, but one not likely to be repeated. And they took it for granted that the country would continue to be economically able to pay for that two-thirds of its food which it imported.

As the depression of 1929 deepened into crisis the country discovered it could not pay for all its imports—food, raw materials, and manufactured goods. Its exports of goods, its shipping earnings, and the income from overseas investments were not enough to meet the bill. (See Chapter XXIX.) The farmer's plea for protection was now supplemented by cries for the protection of industry. In 1931 free trade was abandoned and agriculture again became a ward of the state. Wheatgrowers were guaranteed a minimum return of 45/- a quarter ($1.35 a bushel); the difference between the market price they received and this figure was met by a subsidy financed by a levy on flour. Other foods were taxed if they came from foreign lands but continued to enter duty free from the dominions. Meat and some other imports were restricted quantitatively by fixing the quota that could be sent from different countries. Marketing schemes were devised to control the sale of some domestic and imported products. Subsidies increased in size and number.

These piecemeal expedients may have raised the farmer's income but they did not reduce the country's dependence on overseas supplies. In 1939 Britain was producing no more than a third of the food she consumed, and imported about half a ton of food or feed per head of the population. The cultivated area was down to 13,-000,000 acres, the lowest figure in her modern history. The number of livestock was higher than ever before, but a third of their feed was imported. Economic ability to pay for all this food as well as for raw materials and manufactured imports was precarious in the years just before 1939 and it vanished when war came. So also did some of the physical ability to bring the goods in.

The years 1939–1945 therefore witnessed a drastic reduction of imports and a strenuous effort to increase rural production. The influx of food for humans was reduced a third, and such commodities as rice, fruits, and vegetables almost disappeared from the import list. The entry of animal feed dwindled from over 5,000,000 tons to a mere trickle, with the result that underfed cattle yielded less milk and the number of sheep, hogs, and hens fell sharply. Emphasis was placed on producing wheat, potatoes, sugar beets, and vegetables; the plowed area was increased by over 60 per cent, in spite of the demand for land for camps and airfields. The use of tractors and machines grew greatly, drainage schemes were pushed to completion, farmers whose methods were judged inefficient were forced to mend their ways, and 1,500,000 garden plots were tilled by civilians in their spare time.

These efforts enabled the country to increase the output of human food by at least 70 per cent, to meet about 70 per cent of its strictly and austerely rationed requirements, and to supply some of the needs of allied armies camped on British soil. But it was still necessary to import a quarter of a ton of food per head of the population, and these 11,500,000 tons (1943) could not be paid for by exports of goods or services. Shipments of gold, the sale of foreign securities, borrowing, and Lend-Lease solved or shelved the problem of payment, but when peace came a grim situation had to be faced. The old buying power had been badly depleted. Foreign markets had been sacrificed, the merchant marine had been damaged, and the surviving ships could not quickly be released for civilian service. The overseas securities had been sold and a former creditor nation had become a heavily laden debtor. Loans from the United States and Canada did not last long. A feverish drive to rebuild the export trade moved too slowly toward its goal. Rationing was made even more severe than during the war years.

Post-war Britain therefore faced three stark facts. (1) The country could not fully feed its 47,000,000 people from its own soil, but must import a portion of what it needed. (2) The task of obtaining, through exports of goods and services, sufficient foreign exchange to pay for that portion was going to be hard and the sum made available was unlikely to grow large enough to pay for food imports comparable in volume to those of former days. (3) British farmers would therefore have to be called on to produce still more; but they could not possibly fill all the gap created by the loss of external purchasing power, and the living standards of the whole nation must suffer accordingly.

BIBLIOGRAPHY

See end of Chapter XX.

XIX

MODERN EUROPEAN AGRICULTURE: PART II. FRANCE AND GERMANY

The Continental Countryside in the Eighteenth Century. Continental agriculture in 1750 was seen at its best in Holland, Belgium, the region around Paris, the Rhine Valley and the Po Valley in north Italy. These densely populated areas had long ago evolved, under the stimulus of urban or export demand, such features as water control, rotations free from fallow, careful methods of tending livestock, and intensive tillage of vineyards or gardens. Foreign markets were served by the French, Rhineland, Iberian, and Italian vignerons, the sheep ranchers of Spain, and the grain growers of the southeast Baltic lands and Sicily.

Outside these regions, production was chiefly usuculture. There had been some attacks on wild lands, some consolidation and inclosure during the centuries, but striped or irregular-shaped open fields, common pastures, wastes, and forests made up much of the landscape from northeastern France to the Ural mountains. In southern Sweden a score of farmers occupied five to six thousand strips, some so narrow that one could not turn a vehicle on them without trespassing. In Spain a farmer might have 16 acres in 120 plots scattered within a radius of three miles, while some of a Russian peasant's strips might be three to ten miles from his home. Two- or three-field rotation prevailed, as did village control of the farmer's calendar and common grazing rights on pastures, in the forest, on the meadow after haymaking (*vaine pâture*) or on the arable fields after harvest. Equipment and methods were primitive. Arthur Young saw French farmers in 1788 threshing their wheat by driving horses or mules over the sheaves and then throwing the trodden grain into the air to allow the wind to blow away the chaff. Wood plows were in widespread use in eastern Europe, as well as farther west, even in the early twentieth century.

In examining the rural economy, two questions are important: What was the relationship between the peasant and his landlord, and who was the entrepreneur? At the one extreme, especially in France and western Germany, the landlord was a passive *rentier*, while the peasant, now a free tenant or subject only to certain payments and surviving feudal obligations, was the entrepreneur. At the other extreme, particularly in Europe east of the Elbe, southern Italy, and the Iberian Peninsula, the landlord operated his large domain for the sustenance of his household and for market, demanded labor services from his serfs, and in return allowed them to spend the rest of their time cultivating the remainder of the estate to supply their own wants.

In France the land belonged to the crown, church, nobility, and wealthy townsmen. About a third of it was occupied by *censiers*, perpetual hereditary tenants comparable to English copyholders, who could bequeath or sell their holdings as they wished. They paid the seignior an annual *cens*, fixed long ago as a sum of money and now a mere mite in terms of purchasing power; they made other periodical or special payments, often in kind; they must still use such *banalités* as the landlord's oven or wine press. In addition to these claims on their income they rendered tithe to the church, paid *taille* to the crown, and were liable for *corvée* on the roads. With the remaining land the landlords could do as they wished. They rarely wished to cultivate it themselves, but used some for hunting or pleasure parks and leased the rest to tenant farmers, *métayers*, or *censiers* who needed more land. The tenant farmer often had a large holding which he worked commercially with a considerable labor force; but the *métayer's* holding was usually small, the landlord took half the produce, and the cultivator's share was scarcely enough for his sustenance. In this respect he was not alone, for the great majority of French farms were too small to provide an adequate income and many country dwellers had no land at all. When in the eighteenth century population began to grow rapidly, land hunger became acute and the common rights were such an important supplementary source of livelihood that any attempt to abolish them encountered fierce resistance.

In western and southwestern Germany conditions resembled those of France. Small farmers tilled most of the land, paying dues in kind, labor, or money—the *Zins* was the equivalent of the *cens*. These were rather more onerous than in France, and while some men had become perpetual tenants others enjoyed less secure tenure. Many holdings, even when supplemented by common rights,

were too small to furnish enough income, and the villagers therefore practiced handicrafts for sale or as workers in the putting-out
system in order to keep the pot boiling.

East of the Elbe conditions were different. Political and economic
factors combined with the character of the soil to make the landlord the dominating figure. The ruler's need to rely on local landlords for such services as fighting, tax collecting, and the administration of justice produced conditions similar to those in medieval
France or England. Meanwhile the rising grain prices of the sixteenth century and the expansion of Dutch trade in the Baltic stimulated landlords to produce wheat or rye on a large scale. They increased the size of their domains by reclaiming more waste and by
reducing the size or number of tenant holdings. They claimed more
of the peasant's time, pushed him into serfdom, and forbade him to
leave home.

The eastern estates thus became virtually *latifundia* fringed with
sufficient servile holdings to provide labor and teams of draft animals. The work of the landholding serfs was supplemented by that
of landless laborers and by domestic workers bound to the lord's
house—children must work, if required, for some years as domestic
servants in that house. After harvest great barges, manned by a
score or more of peasants and commanded by a representative of
the landlord, descended the Vistula or some other river that flowed
to a Baltic port. There the grain was sold, and a cargo of wine,
brandy, and other goods was taken back upstream. The large shipments of grain (or livestock) did not reflect the richness of the soil,
for much of the land south or east of the Baltic was poor sandy
stuff, calling for considerable labor and capital if it was to be made
or kept fertile. They were made possible by exploiting a rural population which contemporary western Europeans called slaves and
which ate little of the grain it produced. In eastern Germany, Poland, and Russia some landlords developed industries or tapped
mineral and forest resources, and called on their bondsmen to provide the necessary labor for workshop, mine, forge, or sawmill.

Between these two extremes of deeply rooted peasant cultivation
and large landlord enterprise every possible condition could be
found. In Denmark, for example, the landlords resembled their
Baltic counterparts in their zeal for commercial farming. They withdrew the domain arable strips from the open fields and consolidated
them in compact blocks for more efficient operation; but when some
of them tried also to absorb their tenants' holdings as well they were

stopped by royal veto (1682, 1725, and 1769), and Denmark thus saved its small farmers. In Prussia, France, and Austria the royal power was similarly used to protect the peasant from encroachment on his land or common rights, partly in order to prevent rural unrest and also to keep the political power of the aristocracy on a leash. In central Germany (Thuringia) the domains were so small that one day's work a week and two days at harvest sufficed to deal with them. Most of the labor dues were boon works, for which the laborers were so lavishly recompensed with food and drink that in one place they resisted all attempts to abolish them until 1852.

The continent's varied agrarian society was liable to be strained and disturbed in any one of a number of ways. On the one hand the peasant was not likely to undertake innovations or improvements. Professor Hauser once enumerated the characteristics of the French peasant as slowness, love of routine, individualism, obstinacy, avidity for work, passion for acquiring land, and a spirit of economy and resistance. A fellow countryman (Professor Bloch) regarded the peasant's tenacious conservatism as the fruit of long resistance to new ideas and attacks. These descriptions would fit European peasants as a whole. From such men, short of capital, rarely exposed to new ideas, and eager to put their scanty savings into a hoard or a new piece of land, no enthusiasm for new equipment or methods could be expected. If they wanted a change, it would be the removal of the obligations they owed to lord, state, or church and, better still, the acquisition of more land from the carving up of any existing great estates or large farms. Conversely, there were two changes they did not want: an increase in those obligations and a reduction in the amount of land they held or in the common rights they enjoyed.

Interest in Rural Improvement. On the other hand, the landlord, whether *rentier* or entrepreneur, did become interested in changes in agrarian organization and agricultural practice, especially after about 1750. So also did the state. Virtually every ruler imported merino sheep from Spain, toyed with the idea of abolishing serfdom, and in Austria, Prussia, Denmark, and Savoy took at least one or two steps in that direction, chiefly on their own domain lands. Frederick the Great drained large swamps, dredged rivers, made roads, gave land to ex-soldiers after the Seven Years' War, and generally tried to repair the rural ravages of that conflict.

While western "benevolent despots" sought to improve their old kingdoms, eastern rulers gave attention to the new lands which had come into their possession. The expulsion of the Turks from the Danube Valley gave the Hapsburgs a vast area in Hungary to settle, first with ranchers and then, when the richness of the prairie soil was revealed, with grain growers and vignerons. Farther south the liberation of Rumania opened a similar fertile granary, but a still larger territory fell into Russia's hands when Turks and Tatars were finally driven from the Ukraine and the lands north of the Black Sea. The development of this area by granting huge land areas to the nobility, by encouraging the settlement of immigrants from as far away as France, Germany, or England, and by transplanting serfs from the north made the colonization of this "New Russia" an event comparable to the eastward movement of the thirteenth century or to the American westward movement of the nineteenth.

The royal interest in improvement and expansion was shared by many great landlords. Some of it was native-born, but much of it was imported from England and suffered from the sea passage. Some of it was dilettante, a new game of playing milkmaid, the latest craze, a relief, as Voltaire said in 1750, from an overdose of poetry, tragedies, comedies, operas, novels, romantic histories, and moral reflections still more romantic. But in spots it went deeper. French, Prussian, and Russian landlords formed societies to study English ideas and methods. Some of them experimented with crops and cattle. Scientists such as Linnaeus in Sweden and Parmentier in France tried to give reasoned answers to such questions as "Is the potato a desirable food?" In Germany a doctor, Albrecht Thaer (1752–1828), expounded the virtues of English agriculture in the University of Berlin, and poured out the results of his own experiments in books which earned him a statue in Berlin and wide repute as the Arthur Young of Germany.

By the seventies there was widespread belief in high places that the land could be made more productive and profitable if open fields and common rights were replaced by individual farms. There was also a less widespread conviction that serfdom must go. How these beliefs were translated into works can best be seen by examining the agricultural development of the leading countries.

FRANCE

To any French landlord who had adopted the new faith, two courses were open. (1) He might collect all dues to which he was entitled, raising those which were not fixed and reviving claims that had lapsed. (2) He might try to abolish the villagers' common right to graze cattle on the meadow after the first (or even the second) crop of hay had been cut (*vaine pâture*); to annul the similar right over the arable land after harvest; and to divide the commons and wastes, claiming a third of them as his property, thus securing possession of land which he could divide into new large farms. He did both these things. He had been endeavoring to do the latter in some areas since the sixteenth century, with considerable success in the west and south; but elsewhere the opposition of the peasants or of the government had been too strong. After 1750 the state was converted from opposition to encouragement; between 1760 and 1780 decrees authorized the abolition of *vaine pâture*, permitted the partition of commons, and encouraged the attack on wastes by exempting improved land from taxation for a decade.

How far these attempts to increase efficiency and income were carried it is hard to say, but it is improbable that they went very far. Lack of capital prevented some landlords from drastic action, the *censiers* were hard to move, and the small cultivators and landless laborers opposed any steps which reduced the pasturage available for their livestock. The opposition may have been slight during the prosperous decades; but when the tide turned in the seventies, crumbling prices and paring the profits of grain growers and vignerons, indignation grew intense against the landlord, the large farmer, and the king, who seemed to have deserted his people.

The Revolution and the Land. The assembling of the Estates-General in May, 1789, and the attack on the Bastille in July stirred the peasants to reiterate forcefully the grievances and wishes to which they had already given expression. They wanted three things: (1) a check on the landlord's recent encroachments—"the feudal reaction," as it has been called—and the limitation or reduction of his claims; (2) more land, to be obtained from the crown or church estates and the large farms; (3) a ban on inclosures and the guarantee of pasturage rights. Attacks on *châteaux* and the burning of records containing details of peasant obligations forced the National Assembly to consider rural discontent, and the discussion, taking a melodramatically unexpected turn, ended in an all-night session (August 4–5) with a string of resolutions to destroy the feudal regime, abolish personal serfdom, deprive the lord of his hunting and game privileges, strip him of judicial power, stop the payment of tithes to the church, have a medal struck, and sing a *Te Deum* in

Notre Dame Cathedral to celebrate the end of feudal privilege.

In a calmer aftermath the necessary laws were passed. The landlord lost the income he had collected as local judge, but the *cens* and other payments which could be regarded as rent were to continue unless the peasant cared to end them by paying the landlord a sum equal to twenty or twenty-five times the annual dues. The *censier,* however, having heard that the feudal system was abolished, refused to pay rent or redemption money, and during the dark days of invasion and internal strife in 1793 he was officially excused from all payment of any kind. He emerged a proprietor in fee simple; the first of his three demands had been more than amply granted.

The second was not so satisfactorily met. When the church lands, along with those of the crown and of the *émigrés,* passed into the hands of the state, the government sold them by auction in order to obtain revenue. The largest purchasers were the men with money—the middle class, landlords who wished to add to their estates, speculators, large farmers, and prosperous peasants. Nobles who did not leave the country retained their property; many *émigrés* bought back their own estates by getting friends or agents to bid for them; and at least half the church lands were never sold. Some petty proprietors did get land; they pooled their money to make a joint purchase, or a large buyer cut up his purchase and sold it in pieces; but there was no large-scale transfer to the peasantry and no clean sweep of the great estates.

The third demand, for protection of grazing rights, was coolly received. The legislative assemblies believed in individual freedom and regarded the old order as barbarous. In 1791 proprietors were given the right to work their lands as they pleased, and inclosure was authorized, subject to fair treatment for all claimants. Pasture rights were restricted by decreeing that meadows should not become open grazing land until the second hay crop had been cut. These decisions resembled those of the prerevolutionary rulers; although they did not abolish common rights, they made no serious effort to strengthen or reestablish them. In practice, however, they made little difference to land utilization, for the powers they granted were exercised very slowly. The peasant's conservatism, the absence of any such autocrat as an English landlord or inclosure commissioner, and the lack of any such pressure on production as the war imposed on the British countryside all combined to prevent the

French inclosure movement from proceeding at more than a snail's pace until railroads and growing markets gave cultivators an incentive to change their methods or increase their output. That incentive was not felt till the second or even the third quarter of the nineteenth century.

The Revolution abolished entail and primogeniture and made compulsory the already widespread practice of dividing property equally. The *Code Napoléon* modified that rule a little: if there was only one child the father could bequeath half his property as he wished; if there were two children he could dispose freely of one-third, and if there were three or more the fraction was a quarter. The rest must be equally divided.

The outcome of the Revolution was thus not revolutionary; it modified rather than transformed rural society. The *censier* shed his liabilities to lord and landlord, but little new land came to him or to the landless laborer. Far from being an unqualified victory for

Size of Holding	Number of Holdings	Percentage of Total Number	Percentage of Total Area
Less than 2.5 acres	2,088,000	38	25.6
2.5 to 25 acres	2,524,000	46	25.6
25 to 100 acres	746,000	13.5	29.6
100 to 250 acres	118,000	2	44.8
Above 250 acres	30,000	.5	44.8

the peasants, the Revolution ended in a compromise of doubtful advantage to most of them. "What they gained is perhaps more difficult to discover than what they did not" (Lefebvre); but at least they fared better than did the English small farmer or laborer. During the nineteenth century peasant proprietorship gained ground, and in 1914 two-thirds of the soil, comprising four-fifths of the holdings, was tilled by its owners. Tenants and *métayers* cultivated the remainder. Some of the former held large farms comparable to those in England, but the preponderance of small holdings in 1908 is revealed by the following table. In that year France, with an area of about 200,000 square miles, had about 5,500,000 farm units, or nearly as many as had the United States.

The small size of over four-fifths of the holdings was a result of the things grown, of the system of inheritance, and of a scarcity of hired help. An area of three or four acres was not small if used as a vineyard or vegetable garden, while a holding that was statistically large might not be really big if used as pasture or grainfield. Equal division of property tended to subdivide holdings every generation, and if families were large the share of each heir would eventually become too small, even if supplemented by the *dot* of his wife, to provide a living. Birth control checked this development after about 1870. The French population has virtually stood still for seven decades, and during much of that time the attraction of the towns drew so many young men and women from the villages that an original surplus of rural labor was converted into a scarcity.

Agricultural Progress. In 1852 a Frenchman could write, "A thirteenth-century peasant would visit many of our farms without much astonishment" (Delisle). Little had happened since 1789 (or 1815) to stir the peasants from their traditional ways. After 1850 movement was more perceptible. The railroad came, and "five years of a railroad in France produced more tangible results than fifty years of emancipation" (Clapham), by bringing the farmer and the growing industrial towns into closer contact. Rural credit facilities made cheaper loans available. Farm implements and steam engines were made or imported, 27,000,000 acres of wasteland were reclaimed between 1840 and 1890, inclosures multiplied and fallows disappeared as chemical fertilizers freed the farmer from dependence on his dung heap, breaking the old relationship between *blé et bête* (grain and beast). The wheat acreage rose 35 per cent and the output 47 per cent between the thirties and the seventies. Wheat became the staple food in place of rye or buckwheat.

The grain exports of Russia and America threatened France as they did England; but there were more votes in the French rural ballot boxes, industry did not tower above agriculture, and the manufacturers were not free traders. The tariff was therefore raised on factory and farm products alike. This substantial protection—7 francs a quintal (36 United States cents a bushel)—kept French wheat prices from dropping more than 28 per cent, against a British fall of 50 per cent. The farmer let some land go back to grass and improved the cultivation of the better soils, thus raising total production 20 per cent and the yield per acre 23 per cent in thirty years. His yield per acre (19.4 bushels) was nearly twice that of a century before, but only half that garnered by the high farmers of Belgium and Denmark. He tilled far less intensively than they did, used less fertilizer, and put less capital into modern equipment. Yet in 1912 he grew over 300,000,000 bushels of wheat or nearly half as much as did the United States; he ranked second to Russia as European grain grower, and his countrymen were the greatest wheat consumers in the world, disposing of about eight bushels per head each year.

With those eight bushels they consumed at least thirty gallons of wine. For every five acres growing wheat in 1870, there were two under vines, scattered over 67 of the 86 *départements* and tilled by about 1,500,000 vignerons. In the list of exports wine came second to textiles. Production was damaged by pests twice during the century. In the fifties a fungus called oïdium reduced the vintage by two-thirds in five years. A sulphur spray brought salvation, but the phylloxera, a green fly which ravaged the vineyards in the sixties and seventies, was not so easily conquered. Between 1875 and 1879 two-thirds of the vines were injured or ruined, and the crop fell by 70 per cent. Eventually roots which resisted phylloxera were imported from America, and French vines were grafted on them. By 1900 the pest had been eradicated and production rose toward its old volume. Demand had, however, adjusted itself to the diminished supply; some Frenchmen had learned to tolerate other kinds of drink; Italy, Russia, and the United States had increased their tariffs; new areas were producing wine; and people who in French eyes looked insane were crusading against alcohol. Wine prices therefore fell low and were not fully restored by reducing production. After 1918 shrunken demand from prohibition America and impoverished Europe damaged the market once more; production in the late twenties was no greater than on the eve of World War I, and the thirties were lean years for all kinds of cultivators.

Most other French farm products were those suited to peasant enterprise. The potato and sugar beet were relatively new, and both called for much labor on a small piece of land, as did also dairy produce, fruit, eggs, and vegetables. All found growing markets in urban centers at home or across the English Channel at seasons when the harsher British climate made production impossible. In silk production France never became more than a poor second to Italy; her output was badly injured by disease among silkworms just after 1850, and recovery was impeded by the influx of cheap silk from China and Japan. But her wool production had benefited greatly from the enthusiasm for importing merino sheep about 1760; by 1900 she ranked third in Europe (after Russia and Great Britain) in the quantity of wool produced but rivaled Great Britain in the quality of the fleece.

Effects of World War I. The First World War hit French agriculture hard. About 7,000,000 acres—mostly thickly settled—were in the battle zone, and a third of them were badly damaged. Of 8,500,000 land workers about 5,000,000 went into the army. The military demand for horses removed much power from farms, supplies of chemical fertilizer from Germany were cut off, and the area under cultivation fell heavily. Restoration and recovery were, however, rapid, and production was back by 1925 to its 1913 level.

This quick convalescence did not conceal disquieting tendencies which were present before 1914 but had been accentuated by the conflict. Out of war the country came stricken in man power, for over a million rural workers had been killed or incapacitated; out of victory had come a new impetus to industrialization; but there was no stimulus to raise the birth rate. Town and country competed for the shrunken labor supply, and the town won. Between 1921 and 1926 nearly a tenth of the agricultural workers left the farm. The rural population declined from 22,000,000 in 1911 to less than 21,000,000 in 1926 and to 20,000,000 in 1936. By the last date only 49 per cent of the population resided in communities of less than 2,000 persons. The farm laborer's place was taken in part by Italians, Poles, Spaniards, or Belgians, and by 1929 one in every twenty of the "active rural population" was a foreigner. Lack of labor led to the conversion of some arable lands to pasture, to the subdivision and sale of large farms, and to further use of machinery. But on the peasant holdings, especially those which consisted of scattered patches, the use of machinery was impossible and the cost too great; there was no substitute for human labor. Meanwhile some products faced market difficulties. Silk was meeting the competition of rayon; foreign wine drinkers had reduced their purchases; sugar and wheat were headed for the price collapse of 1929.

When that collapse came the state rushed to the farmer's aid by raising tariffs and imposing quota limits on imports. These steps sheltered the farmer against the full force of ruinous prices. In July, 1931, wheat sold in protectionist France at $2.00 a bushel, or three times its price in free-trade England, a fact which stimulated farmers to grow more wheat than their country needed and to dump it on a glutted world market, while depriving their own countrymen of the benefits of cheap food. This, like other steps, was no cure for depression, and French agriculture shared the economic *malaise* which gripped France up to the outbreak of World War II.

That war caused heavy destruction of farm property in the fighting areas, but its chief effect may prove to have been the accelerated diminution of the labor supply. The absence of large numbers of French prisoners from the country for five years caused the birth rate to fall still lower. An aging and declining rural population faced the task of carrying on the work with few labor-saving devices.

GERMANY

The End of Serfdom. Some German landlords and public administrators gave heed to the ideas that were being voiced in England and France after 1750. But though there was much talk there was little action until a strong wind swept in from the west, bringing the French occupation of western Germany after 1793 and the later crushing defeat of the Prussians at Jena (1806). In the occupied areas the French abolished serfdom; but they did not blot out the landlord's claims to rent from his perpetual or shorter-term tenants, and when they left in 1814 these claims remained virtually intact. During the next thirty years some peasants tried to buy freedom from their obligations, but with little effect until 1848.

The revolutions of that year were started by city workers and middle-class Liberals, but the peasants joined them, for the collapse of credit and the failure of the potato crop in the preceding years had made them desperate. Rulers saw that if they placated the peasants the revolution would be fatally split, and hurriedly took steps to reform the land system. The peasant was to become completely free of his lord and yet keep the whole of his holding, paying compensation in a long series of small installments. This plan got off to a bad start, as cholera, war, and ruined harvests dogged the years 1848–1853. Thousands of peasants, unable to make their payments, surrendered or sold their holdings and emigrated to America. Others survived and eventually emerged owners of their land, so that western and southwestern Germany became one of the peasant proprietor strongholds of Europe.

In Prussia defeat by Napoleon convinced the rulers that a drastic reorganization of military, social, and economic conditions was necessary. Stein, who took charge of the government in 1807, had a library rich in English authors, had apparently read Smith's *Wealth of Nations* at least two or three times, and knew all the arguments in favor of economic freedom. He had also decided that France's military strength came from a liberated peasantry, while Prussia's weakness lay in the lack of patriotic fire in an army of privileged nobles and unfree soldiery. His Edict of Emancipation (October, 1807) therefore announced a comprehensive list of new freedoms. It destroyed the peculiar caste system which forbade noble, townsman, or peasant to do tasks that belonged to the other two classes, and declared that all men were free to choose whatever occupation they wished. It removed restraints on the buying or selling of land between classes and permitted the breaking of entail. It abolished personal serfdom: "From Martinmas, 1810, there shall be only free persons." Thus the army would consist henceforth of "the people in arms," citizens rather than serfs.

The Edict made virtually no change in the terms on which the peasant held his land. He was still a tenant, paying the old dues in labor, kind, or money. This matter was dealt with, after Stein's dismissal, by his successor, Hardenberg. A decree of 1811 provided that peasants with hereditary tenures—the equivalents of the *censiers*—were to pay a sum equal to twenty-five years' rent to obtain title to their full holdings, or surrender a third of their land to compensate the landlord for his surrender of the other two-thirds; those with non-hereditary tenures were to relinquish half. This provision was not easily administered, and in addition was unpopular with the landlords. They had visions of losing the labor services of their tenants and of seeing their domestic and landless ex-serfs drift away. They fought a delaying action with considerable success and averted or postponed developments unpleasant to themselves.

The end of a complicated, slow-moving story was not reached until after mid-century. Only the larger peasants emerged with much land after parting with a third, many medium and small holdings passed into the landlords' hands, and domestic servants and landless laborers remained virtually bound to their jobs until about 1850. The price paid in land or money for emancipation "left great masses of peasants either landless or with so little land as to leave them only the choice between labouring on the estates and more substantial peasant holdings or seeking the industrial labour market of the towns" (Brinkmann).

Large and Small Holdings. These agrarian developments in east and west were not rapid. They were almost finished by 1871, but some Saxon peasants did not make the final redemption payment until 1907. Their chief result was to make Germany "a country of free landowning peasants and powerful cultivating squires" (Clapham). In 1907, 93 per cent of the farms, covering 82 per cent of the agricultural area, were owned by their cultivators. Of the two main types, the peasants were predominant west of the Elbe, while the politically powerful cultivating squires (often called Junkers) or nobility held sway over the lands east of the Elbe, especially along the Baltic coastal plain. The following table and the map on page 442 indicate the distribution:

PERCENTAGE OF CULTIVATED LAND IN HOLDINGS

	Up to 12½ ac.	*12½–50 ac.*	*50–250 ac.*	*Over 250 ac.*
West of Elbe	22	40	30	8
East of Elbe	8.5	22.7	28.5	40.3
All Germany	15.8	32.7	29.3	22.2

West of the Elbe 62 per cent of the area was in farms of not more than 50 acres, and 40 per cent was in those units of 12½ to 50 acres that could be regarded as large enough to yield a family income. Such units covered a third of the cultivated area of the whole country; they grew in number as the nineteenth century drew to its close, and in 1907 over a million of them occupied 25,000,000 acres.

The last column and the map show most vividly the contrast between southwest and northeast or north. The terms of emancipation, the retention of judicial power, the poor quality of the soil (calling for considerable expenditure if it was to be improved), and the concentration on sheep or rye all played into the Junkers' hands. The large estates were operated by their owners or by managers who increasingly had been formally trained for the work, with local hired labor. After 1870 the lure of the New World or of the new industrial Germany pulled laborers away in such large numbers as to create a serious problem. To solve it, landlords welcomed immigrants from Poland and Russia. Many came for the season, even for the harvest, but some stayed. In 1912 over 500,000 foreigners were engaged on German soil.

Eighteenth-century rural reformers recognized that the abolition of common pasture rights, the division of commons, and the consolidation of scattered holdings were desirable preludes to agricultural improvement. A long series of edicts ranging from 1771 to 1872 laid down what might be done, prescribed the procedure to be followed, and, on paper at least, showed a more tender regard for the welfare of the little fellow than was the case in England. The movement was slow, took place chiefly during the nineteenth century, and affected the east more than it did the west. Common rights were abolished over nearly 40,000,000 acres between 1820 and 1870. Between 1870 and 1911 nearly 50,000,000 acres, owned by 2,500,000 persons, were consolidated in Prussia alone. Yet in 1908 nearly half the total area of farm and forest in that state was little changed,

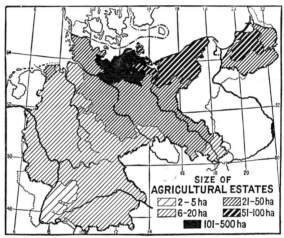

(From Bowman's *The New World.* Copyright, 1928, by World Book Company, Yonkers-on-Hudson, New York.)

while in the west about half the tilled land still lay in scattered strips, and an airplane photograph of a central German village would have served as an excellent illustration for a description of a medieval open-field manor. After 1918 governments encouraged the consolidation of parcels of land which were dispersed or were uneconomic in size or shape. By 1929, 8,000,000 acres had been rearranged, but 6,000,000 remained. The results suggested that production costs had been reduced by a quarter while output had increased by a third.

Agricultural Development. During the first half of the nineteenth century the stimuli to German agricultural expansion were as much external as domestic. The high prices of the Napoleonic War years stirred eastern landowners to extend their fields, reclaim, deforest, and borrow money for improvements. Peace brought a painful deflation of prices and profits, which ruined many Junkers; four-fifths of them lost part or all of their estates. But this unhappy phase soon gave place to one marked by expanding foreign and home markets, especially for grain, wool, sugar, and potatoes.

Of the four products, wool, sugar, and potatoes were relative newcomers to Germany. While America fed Europe's growing demand for cotton, that for wool was met by a great increase and improvement of flocks in Europe and then by the spread of sheep-grazing in the antipodes. Improvement was the result of the dispersion of Spanish merinos during the last third of the eighteenth century. Monarchs interested in agricultural advance obtained sheep, by gift or purchase, from the Spanish court. In France the Rambouillet merino, bred on the farm of Louis XVI, revolutionized French flocks. In Germany the Elector of Saxony imported and popularized the breed, and soon Saxon wool was so good that Spanish breeders were buying Saxon rams. Other states followed Saxony's lead, Junkers built up large flocks, and after peace came in 1815 the expansion was rapid. In Prussia alone the flocks grew from 8,000,000 in 1816 to 17,000,000 in 1837. Buyers from all parts of Europe attended the wool fairs at Stettin, Breslau, Berlin, and other places. Exports to Great Britain jumped from 5,000,000 pounds in 1820 to 32,000,000 in 1836. Germany ousted Spain from its position as the world's leading producer of fine wool and held that place until dethroned by Australia after 1850.

Beet Sugar. In 1747 a German chemist discovered sugar in beets. In 1797 a Silesian, Achard, set up a factory and published a book telling how to increase the sugar content of the root and to extract it more cheaply. Little notice was taken of him, in spite of Napoleon's enthusiasm for beet cultivation as a counterstroke to the British control of the sea routes to the West Indian sugar bowl. After 1815 production began in earnest and by 1836 a third of the sugar used in France was obtained from beets. In Germany Junkers and smaller farmers assiduously cultivated the new crop as part of a three- or four-field rotation. Russia, Bohemia, Belgium, and other countries followed suit, with the result that by 1850 the European annual output of sugar was 200,000 tons. While this was only about one-sixth of the world production of cane sugar, it was already two-thirds as much as Europe had been importing from the Americas in the late eighteenth century; and as slavery had been abolished in the West Indies by 1850 the cane-sugar producers had been weakened in their ability to withstand the competition of their upstart rival.

By 1890 the world, which meant chiefly Europe, produced 3,700,000 tons of beet sugar, or three-fifths of the total sugar supply. By 1910 the figure was 8,600,000 tons, and the fraction was still nearly three-fifths. While the area planted with beets had expanded rapidly, technical improvements had increased the sugar content of the root from 7 to about 20 per cent, and also the ability to extract more of it in the factory. Germany led in beet production, growing a third of the world's crop in 1914; Russia and Austria-Hungary were rivals for second place, and the fourth area stretched from Paris to Holland. As the supply mounted the price fell, an early modern luxury became a modern necessary of life, and the masses were able to develop a sweet tooth. Beet-sugar producers squeezed the West Indian cane growers out of the European market, and then went on to compete with each other. When production in most countries expanded beyond domestic needs the competition became intense, especially for markets in countries which grew little or no beet. In that battle the growers clamored for state aid and caused the fingers of continental statesmen to become sticky. Each country raised tariffs high against foreign supplies but gave a bounty on its own production or exports. This policy expanded production still further, presented non-producing countries like the United Kingdom, Italy, the United States, and India with cheap sugar, but forced consumers in the beet-growing countries to pay a high price for their own sugar and the bounty as well.

This international philanthropy ended in 1902. Concerned over the damage which subsidized beet sugar had inflicted on her West Indian colonies, Britain threatened to impose duties on bounty-fed sugar unless the bounties were abandoned. As a result of the Spanish-American War, the United States had become interested in the welfare of cane growers in the Philippines, Puerto Rico, and Cuba, and imposed duties to offset the bounties. In 1902, therefore, the Brussels Sugar Convention was signed. The producing countries agreed to abolish bounties and to impose only low duties. The importers promised to ban or tax heavily any sugar from countries which refused to toe the line. Cane sugar could now compete with its rival on equal terms and its output rose three-fourths in the next eleven years. But beet production rose two-thirds in the same period, despite the loss of bounties. Consequently the prospect of overproduction, surplus stocks, and ruinous prices was grim in 1914.

While war and revolution played havoc with European beet fields, high prices stimulated a vast expansion of cane growing, especially in Cuba and Java. When peace came the beet fields were quickly restored and expanded, the Brussels Convention was scrapped, tariffs went high, and one of the chief markets for exports, Great Britain, encouraged its farmers to start growing beets by providing both a tariff and a bounty on production. The world output of sugar rose from less than 15,000,000 tons in 1913 to over 25,000,000 in 1930. A sugar crisis was almost the first phase of the wider one which emerged in 1929. Prices went low, tariffs and quotas blocked trade channels. In 1931 the harassed producers of both kinds of sugar signed a second Brussels Convention, in which they agreed to limit or reduce their output and also to restrict their exports for five years.

The Potato. Until about 1750 most Europeans regarded the potato as poisonous. Only after that date did cultivation become at all widespread, first in Ireland and Prussia but later over the whole of the European plain. By 1914 the potato crop had climbed to second place (next to the grains) as human food for northern Europe; the continent grew nine-tenths of the world's supply, half of it in Germany and Russia. The yield per acre was four to six times that of wheat. Cultivation was continuous and intensive and could therefore be carried on by a peasantry accustomed to applying much labor to little land. The potato combined with the grains to supply a large part—perhaps half—of the calories consumed by human beings; it fed hogs and served as raw material for making alcohol.

The Domestic Market. In 1871, when the Empire was founded, Germany housed 41,000,000 people, against only 25,000,000 in 1815. River and rail were tying the country together; the *Zollverein* (customs union) of 1834 had removed interstate tariff barriers; and the trend toward industrialization had been strong since about 1840. The domestic market for farm produce had therefore expanded greatly. After 1871 the growth of population and industry was still more rapid. Hence the manufacturing towns needed more and more food, but the farmer could supply it only by intensifying the improvement and treatment of the soil at a considerable cost. At the same time the towns attracted labor from the countryside, thus raising the wages which the Junkers had to pay, and attracted peasants' children, thus reducing the supply of unpaid labor on which family farming everywhere depends.

German agriculture was thus becoming subject to higher costs of production when the tide of cheap produce swept in. The competition struck chiefly from the east. Since two-thirds of the population ate rye bread the worst enemy was Russian rye, which entered Germany in rapidly rising volume during the seventies. Meanwhile wheat came from Russia, Rumania, Hungary, or America; some meat arrived from America; and Australian wool not merely pushed German exporters out of their foreign markets but entered their home ports as well. Laden with high costs and heavy mortgages, the Junkers bore the brunt of the invasion and took steps to check it. If their outer market for grain and wool was gone, at least they would strive to keep the home one intact. They skillfully won the political support of the peasants by talking of the need for a united front of all agriculturists against "big business," bankers, and food importers; at the same time they joined hands with the iron and other manufacturers whose business had been depressed since the boom days of the early seventies; and they persuaded Bismarck to join them in abandoning the free-trade attitude which had been his and theirs in the days when they were great exporters.

The tariff of 1879 gave moderate protection all round. A small duty (6½ United States cents a bushel) was imposed on grain, but was raised by 1887 to 35 cents. American pork was excluded on the alleged ground that it was not processed with sufficient care to guarantee its freedom from disease. Railroad rates on grain were reduced, taxes on land or on the income from it were kept low, and bounties were given to beet-sugar growers. This policy benefited the Junkers most. It did not completely protect them from the effects of the agricultural onslaught, for the Berlin price of grains was higher than that in London only by the amount of the tariff; but the fall was only 20 per cent on wheat and 12 per cent on rye. Farmers in general did not have to abandon any part of their home market as their British counterparts had done. But their prices did go down, their occupation was relatively stagnant and depressed, and the tariff prevented them from obtaining the cheap feed which British and Danish farmers were using for building up their animal husbandry. Germans therefore moved far less than did Britons from a cereal-potato diet to a more varied mixture containing considerable quantities of animal products, vegetables, fruits, and oils.

When prices turned upward in the mid-nineties agriculture responded to the stimulus with a marked improvement in land utilization and a great increase in productivity. The harvests in 1913 were nearly double those of 1890, though the labor force was little larger. This advance was due in large part to more intensive cultivation, the greater use of fertilizers, and the maturing of agricultural cooperation. The use of chemical fertilizer was vitally important because of the poor quality of much German soil, and especially the deficiency of nitrogen, potassium, and phosphorus. Guano from Peru and Chile contained all three chemicals. Chile had the only known supply of nitrates, and in 1913 Germany was buying a third of its export. But potassium salts were found at home—in Stassfurt in 1852 and later in Alsace and other regions. Phosphorus was known to be present in the iron ore of Lorraine, and when in 1878 a process was discovered by which this ore could be converted into steel, a growing supply of phosphorus became available for fertilizer. By that time ammonium sulphate (containing nitrogen) had become a by-product of the coke ovens and coal-gas plants, and in 1913 the first German factory was set up to perform the miracle of taking nitrogen from the air and "fixing" it in a chemical fertilizer.

From these varied sources German soil drew nourishment. Of potash the country had a world monopoly till she lost Alsace in 1919, and used half of her output at home. She tapped phosphate deposits in North Africa or on islands in the South Pacific to supplement the yield from her steelworks.

Cooperative Credit. Agriculture needs financial fertilizer as well as chemical. Rarely does a rural entrepreneur possess sufficient money of his own to defray the cost of buying, improving, equipping, and operating his land. The cost of all these tasks tended to increase during the nineteenth century, but the banking system, wrapped up in its service to industry or commerce, gave scant attention to the need for rural credit, especially the need of the small farmer. He had to rely on the storekeeper or produce merchant or go to the professional moneylender. He paid such high interest rates that it was often impossible to keep abreast of those charges. He was born in debt, lived in debt, and died in debt. The savage attacks on Jewish and other usurers sprang from the bitter hatred felt by hopeless debtors toward creditors who were as necessary as they were inexorable.

Germany was the first country to find a way out of this credit morass, and the two methods evolved there were copied throughout Europe, the Orient, and the United States. The first method was

tried in 1770 by a group of Junkers who were trying to lift themselves out of distress after the Seven Years' War and then to raise
more loans for extending their production of grain and livestock.
Lenders were unwilling to meet their request for funds except at
high rates, for land was an uncertain security and mortgage deeds
were not always easily salable. On the suggestion of a Berlin merchant, the state authorized an experiment. Let the borrowers form
an association which would raise money by selling bonds and lend
it to the members. The first *Landschaft* (Land Mortgage Credit
Association) was formed in 1770 and was soon imitated. Its bonds
were backed by all the property of all the members; it lent mem-
ber-borrowers up to two-thirds the value of their property, insisted
that they repay the loan by installments, disciplined them, and might
even take over the administration of their estates. The government
in turn supervised the group and appointed the higher officials.
These precautions made the bonds almost gilt-edged securities
which never lacked buyers. The interest rate on them was low (3 or
4 per cent), and the borrower got his loan at a little above that
figure. The system spread from large landlords to smaller farmers
and to other countries. When in 1913 an American commission
visited Europe to study rural credit, the land mortgage bond was
hailed by one pilgrim as the greatest discovery since 1492 and was
adopted (1916 and 1923) as a means for raising funds by the Federal Farm Loan system.

The second German solution of the rural credit problem was the
Raiffeisen cooperative bank. In 1848 Frederick Raiffeisen, burgo-
master of a group of Rhine villages, observed the petty, costly scale
of peasant borrowing and the tragedy enacted when a usurer gob-
bled up the meager assets of his debtor. With capital wrung from
philanthropists he set up a very successful loan society (1849). Then
in 1862 he persuaded the villagers of Anhausen to form a cooperative bank, in which the people of the district could deposit their
savings and from which the local farmers could borrow. By 1905
about 13,000 of these banks were at work. Each member contributed
only ten marks ($2.50) of share capital; but he also accepted un-
limited liability and put all his property behind the bank as a guarantee of its solvency. Each bank was small, the village was its
parish, and it was operated cheaply and simply, with the accountant,
usually the schoolmaster or priest, as its only paid official. It received deposits and considered applications for credit. Its decision

depended on the applicant's personal character, his project, and his ability as a farmer. If he passed this triple test, he obtained his loan at about 4 or 5 per cent. If the bank's funds were exhausted, it could draw on a central bank, and after 1895 a government bank made additional money available at 3 per cent.

The Raiffeisen principles worked with remarkable success. Unlimited liability proved a sound foundation, the borrower's personal reputation and ability were good security, and operation on a nonprofit basis, largely by honorary officials, permitted a low interest rate. Around the central task of making loans other services, such as purchasing supplies or processing local produce, were gathered. By 1910 Germany had 17,000 credit banks of the Raiffeisen or similar pattern, with 1,500,000 members, an annual turnover of nearly $1,500,000,000, and a record of only nineteen failures since 1896. After the First World War, inflation wiped out the value of the mark and hence of their deposits and loans; but the work was resumed when stability returned, and by 1930 about 4,000,000 members were enrolled in more than 36,000 little banks. By adding the purchasing, processing, and selling societies to this number, an indefatigable arithmetician discovered that Germany in 1930 had one rural cooperative society for every 1,594 inhabitants and for every 1,760 acres of farmland.

Effects of World War I. In 1913 Germany produced no more than two-thirds of her food and fodder requirements, importing the other third. Yet she apparently had no blueprints prepared for dealing with the food problem if war came. Her strategists expected a short war, won in a few weeks or months, as had happened when she fought Austria and France half a century before. When this expectation was upset her agriculture was put to an increasingly severe test. The seas and Russian plains were cut off, and supplies of food, feed, raw materials, and fertilizers were thereby denied her. The withdrawal of manpower and horses hurt peasant cultivation. The soil was not adequately dressed and the extraction of nitrogen from the air had not developed far enough to repair the damage. Productivity fell and livestock declined in number. Rationing became more and more severe, substitute foods were sought, meatless days were decreed, and agriculturists were subjected increasingly to regulation. Nothing could, however, check the deterioration caused by the lack of labor, fertilizer, and equipment.

The peace settlement of 1919 transferred a fifth of Germany's rye lands and a smaller fraction of the wheat, barley, and oats fields to Poland, France, Belgium, or Denmark. The potash and phosphoric fertilizers of Alsace-Lorraine went to France. Germany lost about one-eighth of her rural productive capacity. She now had to import rye from the east and fertilizer from the west, paying for them from an export trade which was not easily rebuilt. The first five post-war years were difficult, but by 1924 restoration and reorganization of the German economy were getting under way. In that rebuilding there was much serious, high-sounding talk about "rationalization." A new heaven and a better earth were to be made by the rational overhauling of equipment, organization, and practice. For agriculture this meant machines and power, improved breeds and seeds, the study of marketing methods and the careful keeping of farm accounts.

Rationalization, like inclosure, costs money. Inflation of the currency had blotted out old debts, but it had also obliterated the funds from which new ones could be incurred. America and Britain stepped in to provide the money at high interest rates, and Germany succumbed to the temptation to borrow for every conceivable purpose, public or private, urban or rural. When prices fell in 1929 this load of new debt became crushing. As ever, the price and debt crisis was worst along the "rye belt" of the north and northeast, still predominantly a region of Junkers' large estates in spite of some attempt to "resettle" the area with smaller farmers. The Brüning government tried to relieve the distress; the tariff was increased, prices were pegged above the general market level, and interest rates on mortgages were lowered. In a world gone all awry, these efforts had little effect. The Junkers were neither saved nor satisfied, and when Brüning decided to speed up the "resettlement" of their bankrupt estates they took steps which led to his overthrow in May, 1932. Within eight months the Nazis were in the saddle, to ride complete state control toward the goal of self-sufficiency at all costs. (See Chapter XXIX.)

BIBLIOGRAPHY

See end of Chapter XX.

XX

MODERN EUROPEAN AGRICULTURE:
PART III. AGRICULTURAL EUROPE

Of the twenty-seven countries in Europe in 1939, only eight—Germany, the United Kingdom, France, Belgium, Holland, Austria, Switzerland, and Czechoslovakia—qualified as industrial nations by virtue of the fact that one-third or more of their people were engaged in manufacturing pursuits and that industry was the largest occupational group. In the remaining nineteen agriculture came first, employing about 40 per cent of the working population in Sweden and Denmark, 50 to 60 per cent in Italy, Hungary, Spain, and Portugal, and 80 per cent or more in the Balkans and Russia.

Eleven of the thirteen countries which lay east of Germany were in 1939 estimated to be self-sufficing in food or were net exporters of a surplus. Of the fourteen western lands, only Denmark was a net exporter; the rest depended in varying degrees on food imports to supplement their own farm produce. These imports were obtained partly from Agricultural Europe—grain from the eastern belt, fruits and oil and rice from the south, dairy and other animal products from Denmark, Holland, and Ireland. But in addition to these intra-European food shipments, estimated at 9,000,000 tons in the 1930's, Europe drew on other continents for possibly 40,000,000 tons of human food and animal feed, divided equally between these two categories and also equally between the British Isles and the continent.

Differences in soil, climate, markets, and history make it impossible to describe in brief general terms the developments in Agricultural Europe. All countries experienced a substantial growth of population, with the consequent pressure on the available supply of land and the challenge to render the soil more productive, to emigrate, or to starve. All felt the pull from subsistence to commercial farming, and seized the opportunity to develop special lines of production, so that Spain eventually exported more onions than wool, Rumanians exported wheat but ate corn bread, Denmark exported

451

butter and ate margarine. Only the largest of them could hope to benefit much by surrounding their home markets with tariff walls; the smaller ones must adapt themselves as best they could to changes in market competitive conditions. Most of them were inhabited by peasant tenants or owners, who must work out methods of coping with the problems of capital, credit, producing, processing, and marketing if they were to survive in a world of changing technique and unstable prices. In a few of them large entrepreneurs prevailed and the rural proletariat which they employed was eventually infected by the social and economic ideas popular among urban wage earners.

Denmark. One of the most important developments of the last century has been the expansion of the dairy industry and the spread throughout the temperate zones of the practice of eating butter with bread. Lacking feed for cattle, Mediterranean Europe has always used olive oil or goat's milk. But when northern Europe overcame its shortage of feed, the building up of dairy herds and the large-scale marketing of milk, cheese, and butter became possible. In butter production and marketing Denmark did the pioneer work, and quickly found followers on both sides of the Atlantic and of the equator.

Much of Denmark's soil is "poor sand-riddled stuff" (Haggard) and the country's climate is little better. Its peasants retained their land, by buying it, when they gained their freedom, and secured their full share when inclosure of commons took place. The landlord was not allowed to expand his domain, and the fusion of holdings was forbidden. By 1880 most of the country was held by farmers who owned an average of seventy acres apiece, but there were some larger estates—relics of the domains—and many cottagers' small plots. Since 1900 lands belonging to the state, church, and some large landowners have been parceled out, and the country today contains about 100,000 full farms (of which five-sixths are freehold), 100,000 part-time holdings, and a handful of old estates.

Large landlords and peasants alike exported grain and meat, chiefly to England. In the 1860's and 1870's the price of butter rose, while that of grain stood still and then began its rapid fall. The landlords therefore turned to dairy farming, and the smaller men were already following their example when the Russo-American grain invasion took place. "Arable dairying" became the rule; the soil was given a liberal supply of fertilizer and assiduously cultivated to provide fodder roots, grain, and grass. These were supplemented by the cheap feed, especially corn and oilseed, from overseas, and were fed to dairy cattle in rich fields during the summer but in barns during the seven bleak winter months. The cream, separated from the milk by the use of the De Laval separator (invented in 1879), was made into butter in dairies which assumed the character of a factory. The buttermilk was fed to hogs, thus permitting a large output of good bacon; and since the Englishman who bought the bacon ate eggs with it 365 times a year, hens were worth keeping and feeding on the cheap imported grain.

Although the landlords were the innovators in production and the ordinary commercial houses built up the early export trade, the smaller farmers not only proved to be good imitators but also did their own innovating by developing cooperation at every point. The first cooperative dairy appeared in 1882, the first bacon factory in 1887, and by 1909, 3,600 societies were at work. The capital was subscribed by the members, and when it had received its fixed rate of interest any surplus that remained was distributed in proportion to the amount of business each member had done with the society or the quantity of milk, hogs, or eggs he had sent in to be processed, packed, or sold. The society rendered these services on a scale and at a standard of quality which he could not maintain on his farm and soon did them better than did the large landlords or private firms. Cooperatives handled over three-fourths of the buttermaking and bacon curing, and substantial fractions of the export trade. They bought feed and fertilizer in bulk and provided cheap loans for their members. They thus mobilized funds from many small purses to give the producer the benefits of large-scale buying of the materials he needed, large-scale processing and sale of his produce, and loan capital at low cost. Cooperation became part of the Danish atmosphere.

If cooperation was the nitrogen, education was the oxygen. In the fifties and sixties, when the peasant and political outlook was rather gray, Bishop Grundtvig and Kristen Kold, son of a shoemaker, began to organize "people's high schools." By 1885 over a hundred existed, with 10,000 students. To them young men went in winter and young women in summer. Their work was not vocational or technical, but cultural and civic. In them the young Dane got an interest in life at large, a pride in his place in society, and an enthusiasm for his class and country. The spirit that gave stimulus, leadership, and morale to the agricultural transformation was distilled in those schools.

As a food factory Denmark became very efficient. Its cows and pigs, of which there were 85 and 80 respectively for every hundred human inhabitants, were well bred and well fed. The yield of milk per beast in 1939 was over 800 gallons a year, and the yield of butterfat rose nearly fourfold in fifty years. The hogs were veritable epicures, fed on skim milk and barley to produce high-grade bacon, pork, and ham, and to be ready for the British market after six months on that diet. The excellent uniform quality of the product and the ability to deliver fresh goods all year round made the country an ideal source of supply. Exports of butter, bacon, and eggs grew from 32,000,000 crowns in the early eighties to 300,000,000 in 1913 and to 750,000,000 in 1928. Virtually all the bacon was exported, as was 90 per cent of the butter; the Danes ate four pounds of margarine for every one pound of their own butter. The United Kingdom was the chief customer, in the 1920's taking almost all the bacon, two-thirds of the butter, and five-sixths of the eggs. Germany was a poor second best. The tariff and quota measures taken by these two countries after 1929 to protect their farmers and the preference given by Britain to the dairymen in her dominions therefore injured Denmark. Her exports of butter and bacon declined, production was reduced, and her own people ate more butter. In September, 1939, war virtually cut off her access to the British market, and in April, 1940, she passed under German control. Loss of overseas supplies of feed forced her to reduce the number of livestock and to feed the remainder more sparsely, with the result that there was a great decline in the milk yield per beast.

Holland. The cult of the cow, the pig, and the hen spread to most other countries with varying degrees of fervor. Russia and Germany, by virtue of their great size, had most cattle and the largest output of butter, eggs, and pork products; but Holland came closest to Denmark in the density of animal population, the quality of livestock, the use of imported feed, and the high percentage of the product exported. Her dairy interest was divided between butter, cheese, and condensed milk; in 1928, 70 per cent of the cheese and 55 per cent of the butter were sent abroad. Meanwhile her older horticultural industry expanded under the stimulus of foreign demand, the area devoted to bulbs rose from 700 acres in 1850 to

12,000 in 1930, and gardeners supplied a fifth of the country's rural exports.

Holland's agriculture was, as ever, that of a small crowded country. Over half the 220,000 full-time holdings ranged from 2½ to 12½ acres. Reclamation of flooded land or sandy waste was vigorous in periods of good prices, and the coming of the steam engine made possible the use of far more powerful pumps than could be driven by windmills. In the twentieth century the state took steps to rearrange holdings where the law requiring equal inheritance had caused excessive subdivision of land. In one case, 795 morsels were redivided into 26 farms. In 1918 parliament decided to launch its greatest battle against the sea—the reclamation of the Zuider Zee. Victory would add a tenth to the cultivable area of the country and provide room for 300,000 people. In 1932 the massive sea dike across the mouth was completed and the piecemeal work of pumping out the sea water, of controlling river inflows, and of desalting the reclaimed soil went on throughout the thirties.

During the German occupation (1940–1945) the lack of imported food and feed reduced the quantity and quality of the dairy herds and caused pastures to be plowed up for cropping. Allied bombing in 1944 destroyed the dikes protecting Walcheren island in the southwest, but the damage was fairly quickly repaired. The retreating Germans took many dairy cattle with them and slaughtered or shipped the hogs and hens. Holland therefore emerged from the war with only about two-thirds her former number of livestock and with some districts stripped of animals. At the same time the systematic destruction or looting of industrial plants, harbors, and rolling stock had brought the whole economy to a standstill.

Ireland. Ireland benefited almost as much as did Denmark from the growing British market for animal products, but only after passing through a long period of tribulation. Lack of minerals prevented her from developing factory industries. Abundant moisture made her an "emerald" pasture but rendered grain growing somewhat hazardous. Conquest imposed an alien landlord class on the country. In Ulster tenants and owners were of English or Scots origin, the relations between them were fairly harmonious, and the "Ulster tenant right" gave the cultivator secure tenure as well as compensation for improvements or freedom to sell them to his successor. Elsewhere the tenant was Irish, vanquished, Catholic; the landlord

English, victor, Protestant. Often the latter was an absentee, who left the management of his estate to a bailiff or leased it in one or two large blocks to middlemen, who in turn leased it to cultivators in small pieces, on short leases or leases at will. The landlord or middleman was rarely willing (or able) to spend money on improvements; he might let the bare land, leaving the tenant to provide everything else; yet if the demand for land was intense a peasant might find, after he had brought his patch of bog or hill into fair cultivation, that his rent was to be raised or his tenancy terminated without compensation.

The demand did become intense during the latter part of the eighteenth century and the early decades of the nineteenth. Markets for grain, wool, butter, and meat expanded, especially in Portugal and Britain, while more flax was needed to feed the thriving linen industry. Meanwhile the spread of potato growing gave a subsistence crop to a population that rose, despite much emigration to England, Scotland, and North America, from an estimated 4,000,000 in 1781 to a census count of 8,200,000 in 1841. In that year Ireland carried 252 people to the square mile, against 274 in much more highly industrialized England and Wales and only 164 in France. Competition for land therefore became keen, rents were stretched on the rack, and holdings became smaller; in 1841 more than half of them occupied five acres or less. Those who tended them often had virtually no capital beyond a spade. They subsisted on potatoes and paid their rent with whatever other crop or animal products they could raise. If the potato crop failed they would have no food.

That dire disaster came in 1845, when blight destroyed half the potatoes. Next year's crop was worse, and on top of starvation came typhus. The death roll was heavy, and those who could get aboard a ship scurried away from the stricken land. In 1846, 100,000 persons left for North America alone, while countless others crossed the Irish Sea. The tide ran high for decades; not till the nineties did the transatlantic exodus fall below 50,000 a year. By 1911 the island housed only 4,400,000 people, a drop of 47 per cent in seventy years. There had been nothing like this dispersion before, certainly not in modern times.

As population fell, the land famine lifted somewhat and holdings became larger. But rents were still high; capital and security of tenure were lacking. The countryside was the scene of guerrilla warfare, bailiffs were shot, and the English language gained a new word when some evicted tenants persuaded their neighbors to break off all relations with their landlord, Captain Boycott. By 1870, therefore, the British government was forced to recognize that the Irish problem could not be left to solve itself by the operation of the inexorable law of supply and demand. The first step protected the tenant, as laws of 1870 and 1881 gave him "the three F's"—fair rent, fixity of tenure, and free sale. The fair rent was to be fixed by a land court if landlord and tenant failed to agree, and was to remain unchanged for fifteen years. Fixity of tenure was assured by banning eviction except for non-payment of rent. Free sale gave the tenant the right to sell the unexhausted value of his own improvements to his landlord or successor. This "Magna Carta of the Irish peasant" had some beneficial effects but came a generation too late. The rents, first fixed in 1881, were to run unchanged till 1896; but as prices fell a third during that period the fair rent became a grievous burden.

The second step helped the peasant to become a proprietor. In 1885 the British government began to advance money to tenants who wished to buy holdings, and allowed forty-nine years for the loan to be amortized. Later acts made more loans, gave an outright subsidy of £10,000,000, built houses, and set up boards to aid those who wished to move from "congested districts" to sparsely peopled areas. Circumstances favored this policy, for education, cooperation, and rising prices increased the farmer's desire to own land and his ability to pay the installments. By 1916, 375,000 tenants out of 500,000 had begun to buy; the area transferred—10,000,000 acres—comprised half the country and two-thirds of the area fit for farming. In the next decade the work was completed, and a nation of tenants was thus transformed into one of owners.

Land reform alone did not make good farmers. A country lacking capital and knowledge of modern methods was still overcrowded even with only 5,000,000 people (1891). Cultivation and animal husbandry were vastly inferior to those of England or the North Sea lands, and men were still wrestling with soil so poor that "the bones of the earth were everywhere sticking through its skin" (George Russell). Into this land of little promise came Horace Plunkett, with his gospel of education and cooperation and his slogan, "Better farming, better business, better living." In 1894 he established the Irish Agricultural Organization Society to promote cooperative societies. Within a decade eight hundred societies had been formed, and by 1917 over 110,000 farmers were members. The government helped by establishing a Department of Agriculture and Technical Education (1899), which set up colleges and demonstration farms, sent out itinerant teachers, and offered prizes or subsidies.

Revolution and civil war ravaged Ireland between 1916 and 1923. Farm property was destroyed, land went out of cultivation, herds were decimated, and the quality as well as the quantity of production suffered. When peace came, bringing self-government but dividing the island, the new rulers in Dublin and Belfast and the cooperatives strove to repair the damage and to raise standards. Both were colossal tasks, for in serving his only big market—Great Britain—the Irish farmer still lagged far behind his Dutch, Danish, and dominion rivals. He also was still the victim of politics. When Dublin in 1932 decided not to remit to London the installments collected from farmers under the land-purchase scheme, London placed a heavy duty on Irish goods, and the tariff war which continued till 1938 did him more harm than good. Neutrality during World War II was no unmixed blessing, for although the British market remained open to the Irish farmer's exports the shortage of shipping cut off most of his imports. Meanwhile during the first half of the twentieth century he has learned how to prevent the land from becoming overcrowded. In spite of the limits imposed on immigration by the United States and the great decline in emigration, Ireland contained very few more inhabitants in 1939 than in 1900.

Mediterranean Agriculture. The Mediterranean lands witnessed no such shifts or innovations in production as did the northern countries. Growing domestic populations increased the call for the old staples—wheat, wine, fruits, and oil—while the temperate zone's demand for oranges, lemons, grapefruit, dried or fresh grapes, figs, dates, wine, silk, rice, and olive oil created a northward flow of traffic which is estimated to have amounted to at least 1,600,000 tons a year in the 1930's.

Agrarian society differed little from that of earlier centuries. Land was held in large estates by rulers, nobles, the church, or rich townsmen. In regions of intensive and irrigated cultivation it was usually tilled in small—often too small—holdings by tenants, who in 1750 might still carry some feudal obligations but either enjoyed hereditary possession and paid fixed dues or worked on a sharecropping arrangement. Where intensive operation was impossible, as for instance in the grain or cattle regions of southern Italy and Sicily or the mountainous interior of Spain, *latifundia* persisted, managed by the landlord or his representative. The labor force was supplied by a few resident employees or small peasants and a legion of laborers who were hired for the season (ranging from 90 to 150 days) and then returned to their homes in rural towns or large villages to exist as best they could till next season.

Italy. The wave of agrarian and agricultural reform did not penetrate deep into southern Europe. It exerted its chief influence in northern Italy. There the king of Sardinia freed the peasants of Savoy from personal serfdom by decrees of 1762, 1771, and 1778. Bonaparte abolished more aspects of feudalism, and some church lands were sold, most of them to rich townsmen. As the movement toward Italian independence and unity gained strength, many of its leaders were convinced that English agricultural practices, industrial equipment, railroads, and parliamentary forms pointed the road the country should tread. Cavour, for example, put money into the technical improvement of his commercially farmed estate and also into mills equipped with English machines. Young nobles returned from English tours full of enthusiasm for the ways of work and government they had observed, and by the forties north Italian rulers were alive to the need for change. Some of these enthusiasms were brought to earth, especially on the moist or irrigated Lombard plain. Silk production expanded, and the soil was fully exploited by planting wheat, flax, or vines in between the mulberry trees on which the silkworms fed. Italy became Europe's chief silk producer and second largest vigneron, had olive oil to spare for export, and until 1910 grew enough wheat to supply her own needs.

While substantial farms and small *mezzadria* (sharecropping) holdings were intermingled in the north, the latter type was deeply rooted by history and topography in the hilly lands of Tuscany and Umbria. "No country is greedier in the demand which it makes upon labor. Without the constant care of peasants responsible for a small area of land—tending the surface of the soil, strengthening the terraces, looking to the ditches, repairing assiduously the ravages of sun and rain—the hills of central Italy would sink into a state of arid desolation. The land is in a sense greedy also of capital. The vines, most sensitive of economic plants, must every year be sprayed with sulphur dust or sulphate of lime; the soil, not naturally fertile, calls for a constant application of manures, while every system of *petite* culture demands a large outlay for dwelling houses and farm buildings" (Hancock).

In the *mezzadria* contract the landlord provided the land, buildings, and heavier implements, was responsible for the general upkeep, and paid the taxes. The peasant provided the family labor—sometimes that of three generations—and the smaller implements. The produce was shared, usually equally between the two parties, but tradition decreed that the peasant's livelihood was the first charge on it, so that he got his larder stocked in lean years before any division took place. Some landlords tried to teach their tenants better methods, helped them to fight pests, and effected great improvements without changing the terms of the compact. Many did nothing, others sought to increase their share of the produce from half to two-thirds, especially when easier access to growing markets gave farming a more commercial flavor. This effort stirred up unrest. Unions of *mezzadristi* emerged, as did unions of landlords, each claiming two-thirds of the crop, and collective bargaining rarely ran smoothly. After 1918 the tenants won better terms and the cultivator kept a larger fraction of the yield or paid a fixed rent. But these gains were more than undone when the Fascist policy of the twenties and thirties destroyed unions or rendered them impotent, at the same time strengthening the hands of the landlord and subjecting the peasants to the control of the local political boss.

In the south the gangs of laborers who worked on the *latifundia* were often restless, revolting against the leader who signed the contract for their employment and against the landlord with whom he made it. After 1900, when unions were legalized, labor organizations became more responsible, negotiated with employers, and took contracts to supply labor. In the general turmoil after 1918 the cry, "The land for the peasants" often meant "Land for the laborers." It gathered urgency because one important source of income had been almost cut off. The immigration restrictions imposed by the United States in 1917 and later years prevented many Italians from going to that country, for the season or for a few years, earning some dollars, and then either bringing them back or remitting them to the folks at home.

To meet that cry and at the same time provide food for a growing population, Italy gave some attention to land reclamation. The Campagna marshes had been attacked as early as 1878, and after

1900 the drainage of mosquito-infested swamps, flood control, irrigation, and reforestation were undertaken. War interrupted the work, but the Fascists resumed some of it after they gained power in 1922. The most spectacular achievement was the reclamation of the Pontine Marshes just south of Rome. Yet this costly project provided only 2,500 new farms, and contributed little to winning that "battle of wheat" which began in 1925 as an attempt to reduce the country's dependence on imports for much of its staple breadstuff. In 1922–1924 half the wheat consumed was imported, but between 1924 and 1931 the tariff was raised five times, to nearly $1.00 a bushel, and farmers were told how to improve their methods of growing it. The yield was substantially increased; the consumer was penalized to subsidize the production of wheat at high cost; but self-sufficiency was not attained. Italian soil was inadequate in quantity or quality to meet the food requirements of over 40,000,000 people. The desert colonies of Africa could not fill the gap, while exports of farm specialties or factory goods, earnings of emigrants, and the spendings of tourists scarcely sufficed to provide enough funds to pay for what must be imported. Yet a second-class economy was called on by Mussolini to support an ambitious foreign policy in the attempt to make Italy a first-class power.

Spain. Of agricultural and agrarian change there was little in Spain till the twentieth century. The outstanding features remained unaltered: Large estates prevailed, worked in the center and south as great units, producing one staple commodity—wheat, grapes, olives, or wool—with a legion of laborers, but in the north divided into very small, scattered sharecropping holdings. The wages of the seasonal laborers and the shares of the croppers were unbelievably small, even by southern European standards, and had to be supplemented by other work wherever it could be found, including South America, or by remittances from relatives over there.

Defeat in the Spanish-American War jolted the government out of some of its torpor. The growth of mining and manufacturing created middle and industrial wage-earning classes with reformist or radical outlooks. World War I brought neutral Spain great prosperity, while peace brought recession, unrest, and repression. There was talk of schemes of "inner colonization" which would settle landless laborers on state lands, and some landlords took such steps on their own properties. The republican revolution of 1931 was bent on changes of every kind and hue; but its law of agrarian reform

(1932), which was intended to break up *latifundia,* never had a chance of being put into effect, and the counterrevolution, led by General Franco, which began in 1936 wrecked all prospect of even moderate land reforms.

Austria-Hungary and the Balkans. The Austro-Hungarian Empire gave political and economic unity to an area of 250,000 square miles inhabited in 1914 by over 50,000,000 people. The political unity was resented by the 30,000,000 nationality-conscious Czechs, Slovaks, Poles, Rumanians, Serbs, Croats, Italians, and others who were subject to the rule of 12,000,000 Austrians and 10,000,000 Hungarians, and the "ramshackle" empire fell apart under the strain of war and defeat in 1918. The economic unity rested on the Danube and its tributaries, on a good railroad system, on the commercial and financial services of Vienna, and consequently on the ability of each region to concentrate on the development of its special natural resources, to sell its product in a large domestic market, or to export what it could. Austria proper, a land of hills and alps, bothered little with crops, but much with livestock, with the exploitation of her metal ores and forests, and with manufactures of many kinds. Bohemia was more favored for growing sugar beets and grain crops, and coal deposits made her industrial as well as agricultural. Hungary was the granary, part of that great grassy plain which also covered Rumania and southwest Russia and which, when plowed up, proved to be rich arable soil.

The breaking of the Danubian prairie was stimulated when foreign markets were made accessible by the opening of the Black Sea to navigation, the improvement of the Danube waterway, and the coming of railroads. In 1829 Turkey was compelled to open the Bosporus and Dardanelles to merchantmen of all powers at peace with her, and the Black Sea thus ceased to be a Turkish lake. In 1856 navigation of the Danube was made free to ships of all nations, and an international commission was set up to improve the stream, give it a satisfactory mouth, and regulate its traffic. Railroads were built from the river to the plains, and the work of converting much of Hungary and Rumania from ranches into large grain farms began. By 1900 Hungary was the world's third largest wheat exporter; Budapest was a great milling center, and its replacement of millstones by rollers had revolutionized both the making of flour and the kind of grain that could be milled. Rumania began the nineteenth century with 90 per cent of its farm land under grass but ended it with 85 per cent under the plow. Maize (Indian corn) flourished better than wheat in the long hot Danubian summer, but the natives ate the former and exported the latter.

World War I smashed the Austro-Hungarian Empire, and the peace settlement accepted the breakage as both inevitable and desirable. Austria lost two-thirds of its territory, and Hungary shriveled to less than a third of its former area. Some of the richest farm, forest, and mineral land went into Czechoslovakia, Italy, Serbia, Rumania, or Poland. Tariff walls built by its new rulers fenced off those lost lands, cutting across the old lines of internal free trade. Austrian ironworks must now import their coal from the former Bohemia, consumers must import their sugar, dairy produce, and grain, and Austria must strive to grow things for which she was not well fitted. Although the merits of liberation of unfree nationalities might be unquestionable, the breakup of a great free-trade area did considerable injury to all the dismembered parts. A new or readjusted economy had not been worked out by any of them when the depression of 1929 wrecked their prices and the export markets on which most of them had to depend. Their dependence on Germany as the chief foreign customer combined with their political and military weakness to make them easy prey for Nazi ambitions.

The agrarian history of the region reveals every degree, method, and result of emancipation. The ex-serf in Austria became a peasant-proprietor. In Hungary the land was kept and farmed by large owners, and their employment of over 4,000,000 hired laborers (1910) placed Hungary second only to Italy (which had 4,500,000) as the stronghold of the rural proletariat. In the central and western Balkans, where the rugged topography gave little scope for tillage, villagers combined individual cultivation of small plots with common use of the rest of the land for grazing sheep, goats, and hogs. They paid tribute, usually a fraction of the produce, to some Turkish lord, and when he was evicted during the nineteenth century the peasants usually took the land for themselves.

On the richer Rumanian plains the story was different. The native king and his feudal landlords (*boyars*) had been left in power by the Turks, subject to payment of tribute. When the Turk departed they were still there. As the opportunities for commercial grain growing increased, the boyars raided their peasants' land and labor in order to expand their own domains and output. Revolts ensued. In 1864 a liberal-minded king abolished serfdom, decreed that peasants should retain land in proportion to the number of oxen they owned, but ordered them to compensate their landlords for the loss of the land and feudal dues. The upshot of this plan was that the landlords got most of the land; some peasants were ready to sell their holdings, while others were unable to pay the installments, especially when grain prices fell after 1875. By 1905 three-eighths of the arable land was in estates of 1,250 acres, which were operated as heavily capitalized large grain farms; few peasants had enough land for a livelihood, and many had none at all.

RUSSIA

In 1800 about 40,000,000 people lived under the rule of the czar. Very few of them were in the arctic north or in remote Siberia, and few lived in the forests or poor pastures that lay north or east of a line running from St. Petersburg (now Leningrad) to Moscow and then southeastward. This line served as one boundary of populated Russia. The other boundaries had been pushed outward by conquest during the eighteenth century to embrace Finland and the east coast of the Baltic, to take bites in the three partitions of Poland, and to reach the north shore of the Black Sea, the Caucasus region, the Caspian Sea, and the steppes beyond. As we have already seen, the task of filling up these southern empty spaces produced great waves of mass colonization and immigration, which in due course resulted in a rising tide of production and export of grain.

Of the 40,000,000 Russians, about one-tenth belonged to the 14,000 noble landowning families, the church, and the small but growing middle class. Some of the rest were free farmers, but most were crown peasants who resided on the state lands and were technically personally free, or were serfs on the estates of the nobles and subject to about as complete a form of serfdom as had existed in any country at any time. Perhaps a million of them were "household" serfs; an unknown number worked in mines, metal-refining plants, or industrial workshops; the overwhelming majority divided their time between cultivating their landlord's domain and tilling their own share of the village land.

Over most of Russia the serf was not so much an individual as a member of a village community (*mir*). The village council shared out the arable fields in strips among the families, either according to "mouths" (in which case each child counted as one) or according to "souls," of which a child had officially only a fraction. Redistribution took place every few years (six to thirteen) in order to take account of changes in population. The village also controlled farming practices and regulated rotation.

Emancipation. Though emancipation found advocates even before 1800, and though serf revolts or abolitionist propaganda disturbed the calm, little happened until the disastrous Crimean War (1854–1856), with its revelation of incompetence and corruption, convinced the czar that many reforms were necessary. The Edict of Emancipation (1861) liberated the serf from his lord but did not liberate the land from him. He, or rather the *mir*, retained about half of it. The *mir* could rent or buy it; in the latter case the government paid the owner in bonds, and the *mir* became responsible for collecting the money to repay the government in installments spread over forty-nine years. These provisions were the result of a compromise between the opposition of the landlords and the determination of the government. The Edict was verbose, full of qualifying clauses and exceptions; many nobles continued to oppose it, officials could not always avoid injustice or blunder, and valuation was full of pitfalls. Consequently the task of administering an edict affecting 40,000,000 serfs and 350,000,000 acres proved difficult. Yet by 1880, 85 per cent of the peasants had begun to buy, and in 1881 purchase was made compulsory, but at reduced prices.

Emancipation could not liberate the peasant from simple arithmetic. As the population increased 80 per cent in forty years there was a diminishing share of land for him. In 1861 the average holding was about eleven acres, but by 1900 it had dropped to seven. While quantity fell, quality did not rise, for even if knowledge concerning better farming methods was available and acceptable to the whole *mir*, the necessary capital was lacking and the annual installment hindered its accumulation. That installment put the peasant into a new bondage—to the market and price system. In the past he had paid rent for his land by working on the domain. Now he must produce sufficient cash crops to provide the money for the redemption payment and also for direct or indirect taxes. Those taxes grew more burdensome because the government was spending vast sums of money, especially during the nineties, to build railroads and subsidize the growth of industries. Money was borrowed from abroad, and such borrowing raised the annual interest charge that the central government must be able to pay abroad. Grain was forced into the export market, there to compete with that of America and other parts at ever falling prices, in order to secure foreign credits with which to pay creditors or buy capital goods. The subsidies to the protected industries were lavish. The cash for all these needs was wrung chiefly from the peasant. Consequently there might be little product left over for the family's cabbage soup and black bread, and in famine years there was little for market or for food.

The first four decades of emancipation were therefore painful for the ex-serf. The number of farms possessing two horses declined, that of farms with one horse or none rose. Russia entered the twentieth century with its rural problem more acute than ever. Millions of peasants were land-hungry, food-hungry, and in arrears with their installments. The Revolution of 1905, though chiefly an urban revolt, won them some concessions. Their remaining installments were canceled, and large areas of state or crown land were thrown open for sale. One reform went deeper: it aimed at emancipating the peasant from the *mir*, now regarded as a breeding ground for discontent, and making him a free individual proprietor. Stolypin, who became prime minister in 1906, felt that the dissolution of the *mir* was good anti-revolutionary tactics and sound reform strategy. It would remove both a forum for malcontents and a barrier to the building up of an enterprising but politically conservative peasant class. He therefore decreed that any villager could withdraw his holding into a separate farm and that the whole village could liquidate itself as land controller by a majority vote.

By 1916, 40 per cent of the holdings had been withdrawn and 10 per cent of them consolidated, chiefly by dissolution of *mirs*. Some men sold their land when they got it, and went off to the cities or emigrated. Others bought land and built up farms, some of them so large that hired labor was necessary. Meanwhile the general atmosphere was more stimulating. The central and local governments became more helpful to the farmers. A State Land Bank aided in the purchase of crown lands and also of so much of the remaining nobles' estates that by 1914 four-fifths of the arable land in European Russia was peasant property. Agricultural cooperation spread quickly; by 1913 there were 13,000 societies with over 8,000,000 members, some of them lending money at rates far below those charged by usurers. The use of modern farm implements increased, Danish ideas about cattle breeding and feeding found favor, harvests were good, grain production and exports reached record figures, and prices were rising. The expansion of industrial centers provided larger domestic markets, and the Trans-Siberian Railroad, begun in 1891, opened up a great new field for colonization, to which nearly half a million farming families flocked between 1906 and 1915. Thus there was evidence of rural improvement on every hand. The construction of railroads and the growth of manufactures were also relatively rapid, while the Duma (legislature), established after the revolution of 1905, was gaining experience, influence, and ability to serve as critic or guide to the ministry.

These developments had not, however, gone far enough to enable the country to bear to the end the strain of such a war as came in 1914. When Russia broke down in 1917, the cause was not so much military losses—though they were tragically heavy—or the collapse of the economy. Production had been surprisingly well maintained in spite of the withdrawal of possibly 15,000,000 men and the closing of land routes and seaways to all places except Siberia. It was the glaring ineptitude and incorrigible rottenness of the czar's autocratic administration that caused revolt. The first episode fittingly was a demonstration in Petrograd (now Leningrad) against the muddled failure of the authorities to distribute the substantial supply of food that was in the city and the revolt of the troops who were called out to shoot the demonstrators. Once started, there was no stopping the mass uprising. The Provisional Government which took control faced an impossible triple task—trying to build up a new administrative system, to initiate reforms in every direction, and to restore production and morale so that the country could keep in the war. It failed in all of them. War-weary armies defied their officers and melted away; workers seized factories and ejected their owners or managers; peasants snatched the land, livestock, and personal property of anyone who was not a peasant. It was anarchy without a police constable, and when the Bolshevik party in November, 1917, boarded the ship of state it found itself on a rudderless derelict.

Communist Land Policy. The Bolsheviks, or Communists as they soon came to be called, were Marxian socialists. Their theory, evolved in terms of the industrial capitalism of western Europe, envisaged society as engaged in a titanic class struggle between "bourgeoisie" and "proletariat." The former owned all the means of production in great heaps that were becoming larger and fewer; they employed the propertyless proletariat, and they controlled the

whole machinery of government. To win the class struggle three
steps were necessary: (1) The bourgeoisie must be deprived of its
political power and a "dictatorship of the proletariat" be established. (2) The property of the bourgeoisie must be "expropriated"
and the whole concept of private property be discarded. (3) The
socialized economy would then be run by a society which now
contained only one class, for the benefit of all.

For Russia this picture was a distorted caricature, or worse. The
bourgeoisie was still small in industry and banking, the state owned
the railroads, and the government was certainly not bourgeois. In
the chief field of Russian property and enterprise, the landlord was
vanishing and *latifundia* were rare. The peasant could scarcely be
called bourgeois unless one stretched the term to include anyone
who owned a machine, bought or leased more land, and employed
hired labor; but the label pinned on him was *kulak*. The peasant
could scarcely be called a proletarian except insofar as his inadequate holding or lack of any land obliged him to eke out his income
or earn all of it as a hired laborer. In his desire to stick to what land
he had and to get more he was a thoroughgoing individualist. The
new rulers therefore had in (and on) their hands a society with
very little bourgeoisie or proletariat, but with countless family
farmers who could not be made to fit into the socialist scheme
without drastic treatment by a surgeon and a psychiatrist.

When the Bolsheviks established their dictatorship, the few non-
proletarians had been deprived of their political power and their
property. Factory workers, peasants, and returning soldiers had
made a clean sweep of the latter, especially on the land. All that the
new rulers need do—or could do—was to declare that the seized
estates were abolished without compensation and authorize a partition which had already taken place. The peasant holdings thus
grew in number from 15,000,000 to 25,000,000; but they expanded
only 60,000,000 acres, which gives an average of only six acres
apiece to the new ones even if all the filched territory fell into the
hands of landless men.

The peasants now held 96 per cent of the land. But did they *own*
it, and could they do as they liked with its product? To both parts
of the question the answer must be "No." For, in the first place, to
tolerate peasant ownership would mean accepting the continuance
of private property in the only field where there was much of it,
and in one where the owner was notoriously tenacious and con-

servative. In the second place, the peasant must provide food for the starving towns and for the Red Army, which had been organized to resist Allied intervention and wage civil war with anti-Bolshevik Russians. Private property in land was therefore formally "abolished once and forever." Land was declared to be held in trust; it could not be bought, sold, leased, or bequeathed. Its possessor was a public servant and must hold no more acres than he could work without hired labor. From his product he must take only "according to his needs"—an orthodox socialist phrase—and deliver all the surplus to the state. In return the state would supply him with the manufactured goods and services he required.

This policy had disastrous consequences on the already low level of production. It fixed, very low, the amount the peasant could keep for himself, no matter how hard he worked. Worse still, the manufactured goods and services were not forthcoming. Industry was in ruins, the marketing machinery had been destroyed, and the inflated paper currency was worthless. Hence the peasants either produced no surplus or concealed and bartered it in the black market. The government sent troops to punish the non-deliverers and to seize grain, and sometimes they took the farmer's seed. The cultivated area diminished, drought took a hand, famine and plague were widespread. By 1921 the situation was desperate. The peasants were in passive or active revolt, and a change in policy was urgently necessary.

The only possible change was to retreat on the rural front. In the New Economic Policy (NEP) of 1921, the hated requisition of surpluses was abandoned. Instead of keeping a fixed quantity of produce and handing all the rest to the state, the peasant now handed the fixed quantity—a tax in kind—to the state and was then free to consume or sell the rest in the restored domestic market. He did not get legal title as owner of his land, but was given power to lease it, rent land from others, bequeath his holding to his son, and hire labor. He thus acquired the status of a perpetual tenant and regained some of the individual freedom of enterprise he had been acquiring before 1917. He responded as he had done in earlier days. He got his cooperative society to work again, expanded his output, and if he was a good farmer he once more became a *kulak*. Having won one victory over his new masters, he worked for more. He criticized the disparity between the low price he received in markets still virtually controlled by the state and the high price he had to pay for the scanty supply of inferior factory goods. He wanted a free market, a reduction of the tax in kind, and freedom to pick his own political delegates instead of having to choose them from a list limited to the party faithful. He was not afraid to show that he had a powerful weapon in his hands—his ability to withhold food supplies from the towns.

The peasant problem therefore had to be faced by the government when its struggle for sheer survival was over. By 1926 production had reached its pre-war level in industry and agriculture. The peasant was responsible for the latter, since attempts to run former royal estates as great "Soviet farms" or to cultivate them by groups (*artels*) of landless laborers had yielded poor results. The policy makers were in a quandary. Was Russia to lapse into the hands of a peasant class which was showing bourgeois capitalistic traits in its striving for property, profit, and political power, or was the course to be set toward communism in agriculture as well as in industry? After fierce doctrinal disputes between right, center, and left, with bitter personal conflicts between Trotsky and Stalin, the decision was reached in late 1927 to embark on the first Five-Year Plan, aiming at a great expansion of state manufacturing industry and simultaneously at the collectivization of agriculture.

Collectivization had two aspects. In the first place, despite lack of success with state farms, more and bigger ones (up to 300,000 acres) were to be established. They would be run by managers, employ armies of laborers, and be well equipped with tractors, giant plows, and combine-harvesters. About 5,000 of these farms were organized, but their record was unsatisfactory and their importance declined during the late thirties. In the second place, villagers were to merge their holdings, implements, animals, seed, and farm buildings in one great farm unit (*kolkhoz*) and operate it collectively, working in brigades under brigadiers, each with its assigned task, and all subject to a local official who in turn was responsible to higher authorities. Great emphasis was placed on the use of tractors and machines to displace the wood plows, scythes, sickles, and flails that were still standard equipment for a great part of agriculture. The machines were to be obtained from motor tractor stations which were to be dotted about the countryside. In return for this aid and for manufactured goods the kolkhoz would hand over its surplus produce to the state.

This revolutionary plan, breaking almost every village egg to make a giant omelet, was introduced with fanatical, ferocious zeal and resisted with equal but futile stubbornness. The kulaks, nearly a million in all, naturally resisted most since they had most to lose. They were promptly "liquidated"—dispossessed of all they owned, sent to concentration camps in the northern woods and wastes, or killed. The middle and smaller peasants were "faced with the choice" of toeing the line or of being subjected to heavy taxes, restrictions on the sale of their produce, and other discriminations. They usually submitted, and collectivization triumphed.

In the process there were heavy losses and some concessions. Peasants ate or sold their livestock rather than put them into the pool, with the result that flocks and herds were decimated. Liquidation of the kulaks and slaughter of the animals coincided with three bad harvests (1931–1933), and the loss of life from famine has been estimated at 5,000,000 people. Though the drive for collectivization went on, concessions and stimuli gradually supplemented force. In 1932 the state's claim to the surplus was replaced by that to a share —nearly 20 per cent of the product. The tractor service station claimed nearly another 20 per cent, taxes and seed reserves had to be provided for, and the remainder, estimated at between 40 and 50 per cent of the collective product, was then to be shared among the producers according to the number of days each person had worked and the different values attached to various kinds of day labor. Incentives were offered to stimulate effort, and in 1940 an experimental offering of bonuses for increased production proved so successful that the practice was applied widely. Early attempts to deprive the peasant of ownership of his house and bit of garden were abandoned, and he was given freedom to sell the produce of that garden in "free markets" not dominated by government buyers and price fixing. By paying differential wage rates, by tolerating the private garden plot, and by permitting uncontrolled private trade in the yield from that plot the state gave the individual a little scope for personal effort and profit.

By 1940 individual farms were rare. The change from small-scale peasant to large-scale operation had been completed. The use of farm machinery had expanded greatly, the small plots or narrow strips of arable had been merged in great fields, to which men and women marched to labor. Private property was now limited to small tools, the farm-home and garden. The work was done by what we can regard as a system of sharecropping, with the state as landowner, provider of heavy equipment, and tax imposer taking about half the product, and with the laborer supplementing his share of the other half by his side earnings. The weakest feature of the new order was its handling of livestock, partly because of the early slaughters and partly because that kind of work is not capable of mass mechanical operations. The areas under the new plows rose slowly until the late thirties; then it increased considerably, and the wheat crop in 1940 was 80 per cent above that of 1913. The kolkhozes fed the industrial towns which grew rapidly under the series of Five-Year Plans. They were not called on to take the peasant's place as a great exporter of farm products, or if they were they never reached the figures of the years before 1914. Whether they gave their members a better standard of living than had prevailed in those years we have no way of measuring. But their chief achievements were (1) to provide food and raw materials for the rapid drive toward industrialization without which Russia could not have withstood the German onslaught of 1941–1943, and (2) to provide the same produce during the war in spite of the loss of the country's richest provinces. Whether a peasant economy and a capitalistic industrial system would have been capable of these accomplishments, and at what price, we also have no way of deciding.

"The Green Revolution." On the western fringe of the red revolution in Russia there occurred a contemporaneous "green revolution." From Finland to Greece the large estate was attacked by men who had no land or wanted more, and by political leaders who were seeking their support. There were plenty of objects for this attack. A third of the arable land of Hungary was in estates of more than 3,000 acres, and three of them covered half a million acres in all. About 1,730 men—mostly German-Austrians—possessed nearly 30 per cent of Bohemia, while a million peasants in that country had less than five acres apiece. Two hundred families owned 58 per cent of the land in Estonia, 31 per cent of Russian Poland belonged to less than 1 per cent of the population, and half Latvia was in 1,300 estates. Finland, Serbia, Rumania, and Lithuania all had similar targets at which peasant, laborer, or politician could shoot.

War made land redistribution a matter of practical politics for several reasons. (1) The peasant, as food producer or soldier, must be induced to fight, farm, and fast by promises of land as a reward. Defeat, demobilization, blockade, the collapse of currencies, and the misery of towns made his position stronger. Sometimes he formed his own political party, sometimes he let other parties woo him, but he was never shy about naming his price. He wanted more land. (2) The returning soldier must be cared for. (3) The six new states born of the war had to formulate policies to shape their economic and social structure, and that structure was predominantly rural. (4) Many governments acquired crown, state, church, or monastic property or land which had been taken by a foreign aristocracy when it conquered the country. Reconstruction in central and eastern Europe therefore meant land reform, just as farther west it meant the salvaging of industry, commerce, and currency.

The methods adopted ranged from a limited respect for property rights to a disregard little different from the Russian point of view. Estates belonging to the church, crown, or alien nobles were taken over entirely. Other landowners were allowed to keep a certain area, ranging from 250 acres in Latvia to 1,250 in Rumania. Compensation might be promised, though Latvia took the land by one law and forgot to pass a second one providing the funds. Valuation was low and payment rarely adequate: Bulgaria paid half the market price; Czechoslovakia paid the pre-war value, but in depreciated currency; Estonia paid in bonds bearing a very low interest rate. In Germany, Austria, and Hungary, where the program was reformist rather than revolutionary, owners received kinder treatment. Hungary imposed a capital levy payable in land on large estates, and got much property in that way. In distributing the land, claims were received from men who had no holdings or whose farms were too small. The land was not a free gift; the peasant must pay the state, in installments, sufficient money to cover the cost of compensation and distribution.

Some of these plans were carried out with unwise haste or hate, others with considerable care. Although the result was a substantial transfer of territory, the amount available proved much smaller than enthusiasts had expected. In Czechoslovakia, the big estates covered 10,000,000 acres. Of these, only 3,000,000 were cultivable, and a quarter of them had to be left in the hands of their owners. By 1929, 1,900,000 acres had been transferred to 500,000 purchasing peasants and only 400,000 acres were left. Of the 7,000,000 acres of forest lands the owners kept about a quarter, and only a quarter of the remainder had passed to the village communes by 1929. The Czechoslovak government lent small holders money for equipment, improved rural education, established people's high schools, sent out traveling teachers, and accomplished the transition more successfully than did any other country.

In Latvia nearly 100,000 holdings had been created or enlarged by 1928, and the peasants held 80 per cent of the land, in place of 40 per cent in 1914. Danish experts were engaged, cooperation took root, and this former grainfield gained fame as a butter exporter. In Finland 100,000 new holdings appeared, as did large numbers in Estonia and Lithuania. Greece carved 145,000 holdings out of church, state, and private lands. Rumania did the largest job of all, for by 1927 nearly 1,400,000 claims had been met, 9,000,-000 acres had been made into peasant holdings, 2,500,000 acres had been labeled grazing commons, and 1,200,000 acres had been proclaimed public forests. Only 10 per cent of the country was now in estates of more than 250 acres. In Germany most of the Junkers managed to keep their estates intact. In Austria reform was limited to land which had been turned from peasant farms to sporting reserves since 1870. In Hungary only about a twentieth of the land was redistributed, and the country remained an "island of *latifundia* in a green sea of agrarian reform."

The whole movement, breaking up or paring down about 35,000 estates, was inspired by political and social rather than economic motives. Land was handed not to those who could make the best use of it but to those who had least. The size of holdings was fixed with a view, not to sound farming, but to the satisfaction of the greatest possible number of claims. There was little preliminary thought about "the economics of the agricultural industry" (Mitrany). Some unexpected, unwelcome consequences were therefore soon evident.

In the first place, the new owners had little or no capital. Their government had to borrow money, at relatively high interest rates from Sweden or America, to compensate the landlords and provide the peasant with fixed and operating capital. These debts became burdensome to peasant and government alike when prices sagged in 1929. In the second place, many holdings were still too small, given existing methods, equipment, or failure to consolidate scattered patches of land. Yet methods changed slowly, consolidation lagged, and governments even had to check some peasants from further fragmentation. In the third place, the disappearance of the large estate ended the demand for hired laborers, but not all the former hired men got land. They were now jobless as well as landless. Finally, when large estate farms were cut up, land was often withdrawn from the production of some staple marketable crop and turned to uses more suitable to the needs, ability, and resources of the smaller cultivator. The peasant gave more attention to filling his larder than to cash crops, and this may have raised his standard of living. Yet he could not retreat too far from the market, for he must procure money to pay his interest and installments and buy what he needed.

In the Baltic lands he sought that money less in the grain market than the old landowners had done, and turned to the Danish type of farming with such vigor that in 1929 the four countries—Finland, Latvia, Estonia, and Lithuania—exported more butter than did Holland, almost twice as much as did Ireland, and a third as much as did Denmark. In Czechoslovakia he turned to sugar beets and livestock. In Rumania his only possible cash crop was wheat, as it had been in the days of the great estates; but he grew it far less efficiently than had been done then, and its grade was so low that the label "Of Danubian Origin" began to acquire a "derogatory meaning in the international [grain] trade" (Mitrany).

Whatever he produced, he had to look to Industrial Europe for much of his market. The welfare of over 100,000,000 people living in the belt from Finland to Greece, bounded by Russia on the east and by the Baltic, Germany, Austria, and the Adriatic on the west, depended on what the west would buy and the price it would pay. Parts of that market had been lost during the years of war, revolution, and land reform. The greatest loss had been the wheat market. In 1909–1913 Industrial Europe bought nearly half its wheat imports from Russia and Danubia, the remainder from the New World and India. From 1915 to 1924 no Rumanian wheat entered a British port, and Russia had very little wheat, rye, or anything else to spare. Danubia slowly crept back into the market, but Russia remained outside. Hence during the years 1924–1929 the New World supplied 94 per cent of the export trade in wheat. In 1927 Industrial Europe imported 660,000,000 bushels, but only 20,000,000 of them came from the eastern granary, and much of that was poor quality. Since Italy, Germany, and France were already raising their tariffs against wheat or other cereals, the European grain grower experienced difficult times before the crash in prices came in 1929.

The tariffs, quotas, and other impediments imposed during the next four years made the times harder still. Eastern growers frantically gathered together to seek salvation, but neither their plans for restricting exports nor their proposal that Industrial Europe should give preference to their produce had any hope of acceptance. While Europe as a whole cut its wheat imports nearly in half, no country was inclined to be more kindly disposed toward its agricultural neighbor than it was to distant continents. Consequently there was no cure for ruinous grain prices. The dairy farmer was in little better plight; his foreign markets were barred or restricted, and the export price of his product dropped nearly three-quarters. Beet sugar fell into the quagmire of excess production of beet and cane product. No commodity, in fact, seemed to find a welcome in a foreign port.

When the long, dreary night ended, the landscape had changed. Not only had the depression left a legacy of restraints on international trade in foodstuffs, it had also strengthened or created dictatorships, including a powerful one in the heart of Europe. Germany was the natural market for much of the farm produce of the lands that lay east or south. Her drive for *autarky* (self-sufficiency) before and after 1933 did not greatly increase her agricultural production or reduce substantially her imports. She needed to buy some foods and many raw materials abroad, but her ability to pay for them was checked by reduced ability to sell her manufactured goods in highly protected or restricted markets in western Europe or overseas. On the other hand, much of Agricultural Europe, especially Danubia, was in desperate need of larger export markets, and these were not to be found in Britain, France, or Russia. To sell to Germany was better than not selling at all. For Germany to buy, on terms which she could lay down because she had no competitor, was both good business and sound strategy. Hence the Danubian lands and some in the Baltic and Balkans were economically dependent on Germany long before they were politically subject to her.

BIBLIOGRAPHY

GENERAL

Bogardus, J. F., *Europe: A Geographical Survey* (1934), chap. 6, and agricultural sections in description of each country.

Bowden, W., Karpovich, M., and Usher, A. P., *An Economic History of Europe* (1937), chaps. 3, 8, 13, 28, 29, 34, 38, and Bibliography.

Bowman, I., *The New World: Problems in Political Geography* (1928).

Gras, N. S. B., *History of Agriculture* (1925), chaps. 7–10.

Irvine, H. D., *The Making of Rural Europe* (1923).

Jonasson, Olaf, "The Agricultural Regions of Europe," *Econ. Geog.*, October, 1925, and January, 1926.

Sée, H., *Esquisse d'une histoire du régime agraire en Europe aux xviiie–xixe siècles* (1921).

Sorokin, P., Zimmerman, C., and Galpin, C. J., *A Systematic Source Book in Rural Sociology* (1930), vol. i.

Encyclopaedia of the Social Sciences: See list of titles under Agriculture and Cooperation in vol. xv, pp. 548 and 550.

ENGLAND

Ashley, W. J., *Economic Organisation of England* (1915), chap. 6.

Bland, Brown, and Tawney, *English Economic History: Select Documents* (1914), part iii, section 2.

Brodrick, G. L., *English Land and English Landlords* (1881).

Clapham, J. H., *Economic History of Modern Britain* (1926, 1932, 1938), vol. i, chaps. 4, 11; vol. ii, chap. 7; vol. iii, chap. 2.

Curtler, W. H. R., *The Enclosure and Redistribution of Our Land* (1920).

Davies, E., "The Small Landowner, 1780–1832," *Ec. H. R.*, 1927.

Fay, C. R., *Great Britain from Adam Smith to the Present Day* (1932), chap. 12.

Fussell, G. E., "English Agriculture from Cobbett to Caird, 1830–1880," *Ec. H. R.*, 1945.

Fussell, G. E., and Compton, M., "Agricultural Adjustment after the Napoleonic Wars," *Ec. Hist.*, 1939.

Gonner, E. C. K., *Common Land and Inclosure* (1912).

Gras, N. S. B. and E. C., *Social and Economic History of an English Village* (1930). See especially the Enclosure Act of 1794.

Habakkuk, H. J., "English Landlordship, 1680–1740," *Ec. H. R.*, 1940.

Hammond, J. L. and B., *The Village Labourer, 1760–1832* (1911).

Hammond, R. J., "British Food Supplies, 1914–1939," *Ec. H. R.*, 1946.

Hasbach, W., *History of the English Agricultural Labourer* (1909).

Heaton, H., *The British Way to Recovery* (1934), chap. 5.

Lavrovsky, V. M., *Parliamentary Enclosure of the Common Fields in England, 1793–1815* (in Russian, 1940). See the review of this book in *Ec. H. R.*, 1942.

Mantoux, P., *The Industrial Revolution in the Eighteenth Century* (Eng. trans., 1928), part i, chap. 3.

Marshall, T. H., "Jethro Tull and the New Husbandry," *Ec. H. R.*, 1929.

Middleton, T. H., *Food Production in War* (1923).

Orwin, C. S., chapter on "Agriculture" in Turberville, A. S. (ed.), *Johnson's England* (1932), vol. i.

Prothero, R. E. (Lord Ernle), *English Farming, Past and Present* (1927), chaps. 14, 17–19.

Young, Arthur, *Autobiography*. Also any of his Tours.

FRANCE

Augé-Laribé, M., *L'évolution de la France agricole* (1912).

Augé-Laribé, M., *L'agriculture pendant la guerre* (1925).

Bloch, M., *Les caractères originaux de l'histoire rurale française* (1931), chap. 6.

Clapham, J. H., *Economic Development of France and Germany, 1815–1914* (1923), chaps. 1, 8.

Déléage, A., "La vaine pâture en France," *Rev. d'hist. mod.*, September–October, 1931.

Labrousse, C. E., *La crise de l'économie française à la fin de l'ancien régime* (1944).

Lefebvre, G., "La place de la révolution dans l'histoire agraire de France," *Ann. d'hist. écon.*, October, 1929.

Loutchisky, J., *L'état des classes agricoles en France à la veille de la révolution* (1911).

Marion, M., *La vente des biens nationaux* (1908).

Ogburn, W. F., and Jaffé, W., *The Economic Development of Post-War France* (1929).

Sée, H., *Economic and Social Conditions in France in the Eighteenth Century* (Eng. trans., 1927).

Young, A., *Travels in France, 1787, 1788, 1789.*

GERMANY

Brinkmann, C., "The Place of Germany in the Economic History of the Nineteenth Century," *Ec. H. R.*, April, 1933.

Buchenberger, A., *Agrarwesen und Agrarpolitik* (new ed., 1914).

Clapham, J. H., *Economic Development of France and Germany, 1815–1914* (1923), chaps. 2, 9.

Dawson, W. H., *Evolution of Modern Germany* (1908), chaps. 12–15.

Ford, G. S., *Stein and the Era of Reform* (1922).

Gerschenkron, A., *Bread and Democracy in Germany* (1943).

Knapp, G. F., *Die Bauernbefreiung und der Ursprung der Landarbeiter* (2nd ed., 1927).

Middleton, T. H., *Recent Developments in German Agriculture* (1916).

Skalweit, A. K. F., *Agrarpolitik* (1924).

Stein, R., *Die Umwandlung der Agrarverfassung Ostpreussens* (1918).

Von Walterhausen, Sartorius A., *Deutsche Wirtschaftsgeschichte, 1815–1914* (1920).

OTHER COUNTRIES (IN ORDER OF TREATMENT)

Jones, H., *Modern Denmark* (1927).

Scheffler, K., *Holland: the Land and the People* (1932).

Rowntree, B. S., *Land and Labor in Belgium* (1910).

Plunkett, H., *Ireland in the New Century* (1905).

Pomfret, J. E., *The Struggle for Land in Ireland, 1800–1923* (1930).

Basch, A., *The Danube Basin* (1943).

Newbigin, M. I., *Southern Europe* (1932).

Hancock, W. K., "Italian Métayage," *Ec. Hist.*, January, 1928.

Morgan, O. S. (ed.), *Agricultural Systems of Middle Europe* (1933).

Antsiferov, A. N., and others, *Russian Agriculture during the War* (1930).

Baykov, A., *The Development of the Soviet Economic System* (1946), chaps. 2, 8, 12, 17.

Pokrovsky, M. N., *Brief History of Russia* (Eng. trans., 1934), vol. ii.

INTER-WAR DEVELOPMENTS

The Agricultural Crisis (League of Nations, Econ. and Fin. Section, 1931).

Delaisi, F., *Les deux Europes* (1929).

Mitrany, D., *The Land and the Peasant in Rumania* (1930).

World Agriculture (Royal Institute of International Affairs, 1933).

COOPERATION

Faber, H., *Cooperation in Danish Agriculture* (1918).

Fay, C. R., *Cooperation at Home and Abroad* (1920).

XXI

EUROPEAN INDUSTRIAL DEVELOPMENTS
SINCE 1700

When the industrial history of the last two centuries first began to
be studied, certain developments which took place in England during the latter part of the eighteenth century seemed to have been
so unexpected, rapid, dramatic, and disruptive that the term "Industrial Revolution" was applied to them. Later research has dras-
tically modified that first impression. We now know that the technological changes after 1760 were "the completion of tendencies which
had been significantly evident since Leonardo da Vinci" (Usher);
that the "developments which took place in the reign of George III
[1760–1820] must . . . be regarded as the quickening of an age-
long evolutionary process, rather than as a violent break with the
past and a fresh beginning" (Redford); and that it is misleading to
apply the word "revolution" to changes which had been in preparation for two centuries before 1760 and then took another century at least to work themselves out.

The technical industrial changes of the eighteenth century did
not come suddenly out of a clear sky. The seventeenth century had
its inquisitive minds, stirred to invention by such stimuli as economics, war, medicine, art, religion, or the disinterested search for
truth. Science grew in knowledge and stature. Some of its devotees
disliked Petty's suggestion (1680) that they ought to "principally
aim at such experiments or observations as might prove to be of
great and immediate use"; but "pure" scientific discoveries concerning the vacuum and atmospheric pressure quickly proved helpful to men who were seeking better pumps for waterworks or mines.
Meanwhile discoveries, inventions, and improvements were made
by industrialists in quantities that were far from insignificant during
the sixteenth and seventeenth centuries. The methods of making
glass, clocks, chemicals, and munitions advanced. Metal refining,
knitting, cloth finishing, ribbon weaving, woodcutting, printing,

shipbuilding, and other occupations found new or better equipment. The harnessing of animal, wind, or water power became more common, the industrial use of coal grew, and steam power was on the threshold by 1700.

These instances may seem to make a meager total when compared with those of later centuries. There were powerful obstacles to advance; some of them were technical, such as the lack of a good cylinder-boring machine until about 1775, but others were human. Popular or state opposition was easily aroused against any invention that threatened to injure some strong vested interest, or to reduce the demand for labor and thus cause more people to need poor relief. At various times mobs destroyed sawmills, ribbon looms, and knitting frames. Guilds condemned equipment or methods that gave one member an advantage over his fellows. The city of Danzig forbade the use of a loom which wove several strands of ribbon, and suffocated its inventor (1586). Charles I of England ordered the destruction of a needle-making machine (1623) and banned the casting of brass buckles (1632) on the ground that six casters would endanger the livelihood of six hundred guildsmen who were making buckles in the old way. These actions voiced the belief that change was not desirable if it disturbed the established order. They were most common when trade was depressed or when the economy was relatively stagnant, as it seems to have been during much of the period between about 1660 and 1720. In such conditions protection against innovation seemed highly necessary. To use terms popular in our day, "full employment" must be insured in a "static economy."

How effective the hostile decrees were, or whether they were even generally and continuously enforced, we have no way of knowing. But we may suspect that here, as in other aspects of *étatisme*, administration lagged far behind legislation. In any case, conditions and attitudes change as we get well into the eighteenth century. The change in conditions was marked by the growth of population on both sides of the English Channel after about 1730, and by that of domestic and foreign trade during the long upward swing which Britain and France alike experienced. Such figures as are available suggest that French external trade increased about fivefold in value between 1715 and 1787, while the volume of British overseas trade doubled between 1720 and 1760 and doubled again by 1795. Statistics of cloth and coal production, of coastal shipping, of improved rivers, turnpike highways, and new canals all tell the same tale, as does abundant evidence of a substantial expansion in the domestic market and of a rising price level after about 1750. On the continent the industrial expansion in France was apparently paralleled by the growth of manufactures in the German states, Belgium, Spain, Switzerland, and Russia. By the third quarter of the century the European economy had become expansive.

This change in conditions was accompanied by a change in attitudes, both governmental and popular. "The restrictive paternalism of the state and the obstructiveness of the guilds" (Clark) were weakening by 1700 in England and by 1750 in France. In the latter country monopolies for the production of glassware and coal were revoked or disregarded. The tax on industrial capital and profits was greatly reduced; ministers and officials "all worked to introduce new machinery, new kinds of furnaces, and new chemical processes into mining and manufacturing" (Nef); capital was provided for new enterprises, foreign technicians and capitalists were welcomed, scientists were held in great honor, and English inventors who had been stoned at home were showered with hospitality.

In Britain the Statute of Monopolies, which had been passed in 1624 to prevent the crown from capriciously giving monopolies to favorites or selling them in order to raise money, assumed a new significance. It had exempted from its ban any grant of a "patent of monopoly" to the "first inventor" of any new manufacture, whether his "invention" was merely an industry, process, or piece of equipment already known abroad or something he had "invented" in the modern meaning of the word. Few such patents had been granted before 1700, but by 1750 the number issued annually was about eight, and it reached nearly fifty in the 1780's. Parliament made a special grant of one (1718) to Lombe, who introduced the water-driven silk-throwing machine from Italy; and when, fourteen years later, he tried to get it renewed, he was given £14,000 instead. In 1775 parliament extended James Watt's steam-engine patent, due to expire in 1783, until 1800. It also tried to insure that the country get the sole benefit of its inventions by passing laws in rapid succession—five of them between 1773 and 1786—to prevent the export of machines, models, or drawings. These laws, like others forbidding the emigration of skilled artisans, were not easily enforced.

Popular interest in industrial improvement resembled the wave of curiosity and zest for experiment that we saw sweeping agriculture. Societies were set up to foster technical progress. In London the Society for the Encouragement of Arts, Manufactures, and Commerce was even wider than its name. Founded in 1754, it offered money, medals, and other rewards for specified achievements, built up a museum of machines and models, and circulated its publications widely. In English provincial towns such as Birmingham or Manchester and in such continental cities as Paris or Hamburg similar societies were at work. America had its counterpart in the Society for Promoting and Propagating Useful Knowledge.

Meanwhile, as individuals or as members of learned societies, the scientists of all nations were in touch with each other, developing a "remarkable *esprit de corps*" strengthened by "frequent personal relations" (Pace), such as those which made Benjamin Franklin a well-known figure among the scholars of many lands. The scientists were also getting into closer touch with industry and agriculture, for their knowledge of physics and chemistry was now reaching a point where it could answer some technical questions. Arthur Young submitted his soil problems to the chemist, Priestley. Scheele found chlorine in 1774, and Berthollet discovered in 1785 that it would bleach fibers, reducing that process from months to days or even hours. Matthew Boulton, one of the leading British industrialists after 1760, counted among his intimate friends such men as a former professor of mathematics and natural philosophy in Virginia, Franklin, Roebuck (a pioneer industrial chemist), Priestley, James Watt, and Josiah Wedgwood, whose researches in industrial chemistry solved some of the problems surrounding the making of good pottery and won him election as a Fellow of the Royal Society.

The decades after 1750 were thus marked by a quickening spirit of inquiry and search for new things. Magazines, encyclopedias, dictionaries, and yearbooks chronicled new machines and methods. The first balloon flight in 1783 created a temporary but enthusiastic "air-mindedness." Men played with the idea of a submarine, of a horseless carriage, and of a ship without sails. Clockmakers designed elaborate mechanical figures, including a robot that played chess. All things seemed possible: One genius took out a patent for "a perpetual power" that was to drive everything; another announced the creation of a "composition for shaving without the use of razor, soap, or water."

The Inventor's Problem. Against this background of an expanding economy, a favorable political attitude, and a stimulating intellectual environment, we can now examine the problems which in·

dividual inventors sought to solve. They were of many kinds. Some of them came from the interplay of supply and demand. On the one hand, a growing demand for a commodity strained the existing organization and equipment of an industry, called for larger or quicker production, and stimulated the search for machines that would allow more work to be done by each person. Demand thus provoked changes in the methods of supply. On the other hand, a producer might see a great slumbering demand waiting to be awakened if goods formerly sold to a few at high prices could be produced in quantity and sold to the multitude at low ones. Supply would thus create a virtually new demand, whether for cheap crockery or hardware in the eighteenth century or for cheap bicycles, automobiles, or radios in later generations.

Some of the earliest problems actually to receive attention were those which checked the expansion or even threatened the existence of mines and ironworks. The mine manager had to find better ways of fighting the water that flooded deep seams and of ridding the underground of poisonous or explosive gases. Until he found them his mine could never be more than a shallow pit with a short watery or fiery life, and vast mineral deposits would lie untapped. The ironmaster's enterprise was debarred from expansion and faced with extinction unless he could find a substitute for charcoal. In such cases dire necessity was the mother of inventions which turned the tide in what threatened to be a losing battle.

Many inventors sought to "abridge labor," dispense with skilled workers, counteract the lack of them, permit the use of children, or overcome the advantage which producers in other countries enjoyed because their wage rates were lower. In 1770 a Scots papermaker claimed that his new rag-cutting machine did more work than eight men had formerly done. In 1760 the London Society of Arts offered a prize for a spinning machine, on the ground that "manufacturers of woollen, linen, and cotton find it extremely difficult in the summer season, when the spinners are at harvest work, to procure a sufficient number of hands." Four years later it gave this prize "for a masterly improvement in the spinning wheel, by which a child can do double the business that even a grown person can with the common wheel." Campbell in 1747 reported that London watchmakers had invented engines for cutting the teeth of cogwheels, thus reducing "the expense of workmanship and time to a trifle in comparison to what it was before and [bringing] the work to such an exactness that no hand can imitate it." He also described the setting up by paint shops of horse mills "to grind the colors and sell them to noblemen and gentlemen ready mixed at a low price, and by the help of a few printed directions a house may be painted by any common labourer" at one-third of the cost in former days when skilled painters mixed their own material by hand. Finally, it was frequently asserted that machines were needed to enable English goods to compete with the products of much-lower-paid continental wage earners.

Some of the growing army of inventors and improvers of other men's inventions are known, but many who made important contributions are not. Some were small craftsmen or master manufacturers who by accident, inspiration, or the play of a fertile mind "hit upon" a new device or fundamentally improved an old one. A few were onlookers who strayed into the company of problems that practical men said were insoluble, and brought a fresh mind to the task. Edmund Cartwright, the first designer of a power loom, was a country parson. He had never seen a loom, had never turned his mind to any mechanical problem—beyond the writing of eighteenth-century poetry—until he heard some hardheaded Lancashire manufacturers say that a power loom was urgently needed but could not be made. Eli Whitney, prospective schoolteacher, heard southern cotton planters declare that "if a machine could be invented which would clean the cotton with expedition, it would be a great thing both to the country and to the inventor." But they were as empty of hope and ideas as the Lancashiremen had been, and it was left to Whitney to solve their problem.

The outsider grew in importance during the nineteenth century, but he was usually a professional inventor or a pure scientist. The former explored unknown fields for the monetary reward. The latter might be little concerned with the practical application of his discoveries, but the industrial world was not for long indifferent to him. Sometimes it took up his findings, sometimes it laid its problems at his door, as for instance when an epidemic of explosions drove mineowners to Davy's laboratory in 1815 with a plea that he devise a safe miner's lamp. As the nineteenth century progressed, physics or chemistry gave birth to new industries and helped old ones to understand the nature of the materials they were using. In the twentieth century the birth rate and the understanding have increased greatly.

The Spread of Machine Production. By 1700 the use of machines was widespread and in some cases had long been common for such heavy tasks as fulling cloth, grinding grain and some industrial raw materials, sawing lumber, slitting iron sheets into nailrods, crushing ore, and hammering large pieces of metal; also in a smaller degree for work of a lighter, more delicate nature, such as stamping coins, turning wood or soft metals, making clock parts, knitting, and printing. For the heavy work the power was supplied by water, wind, or animals, for the lighter tasks by water, animals, or human muscles. Yet many processes were still manual in 1700, depending on the worker's skill and strength in his use of such simple tools or equipment as hammer, saw, spinning wheel, hand loom, needle, shears, or file. The file was "the chief and ultimate instrument of precision in the heavy metal trades" (Usher), and shears with blades nearly two feet long were the only implements available for cropping the surface of woolen cloth.

Machines in the Metal Goods Industries. Throughout the first half, as well as the second, of the eighteenth century, new machines appeared in both heavy and light industries. Campbell's account (1747) of London occupations tells not merely of the paint-mixing mill and the watchmakers' engine but also of machines which had recently displaced the punch and hammer for making seals or medals, thereby reducing the price of some products from 42/– apiece to 4/– a dozen; of flatting mills which had relieved goldsmiths and tinmen of the burdensome task of beating their ingots into sheets; and of other innovations. Ten years later (1757) Josiah Tucker extolled the uncommon dexterity of English mine operators and metallurgists "in their Contrivance of the mechanic Powers," their use of cranes, horse engines, water wheels, steam engines, inclined planes, and mills for making rods, plates, or wire. He also reported that in the metalware industries of Birmingham and Sheffield "almost every Master Manufacturer hath a new Invention of his own, and is daily improving on those of others," with the result that Birmingham products were "so exceedingly cheap as to astonish all Europe" and that a stalwartly Protestant region could make crucifixes for Catholic lands at a wholesale price as low as 7½d. (15 cents) a dozen.

During subsequent decades the technical advance in this industry becomes associated with the name of Matthew Boulton. Boulton in 1762 built a factory which soon employed more than 600 workers.

He installed a steam engine to supplement the two water wheels which supplied power for rollers, polishing or grinding machines, and various sorts of lathes. From making buckles, steel jewelry, and buttons (at prices ranging from 3d. to 140 guineas [$735] a gross) he went on to produce artistic Sheffield or silver plate. Then he developed and sold Watt's steam engines, and finally designed a coinmaking machine, driven by steam power, which solved the problem of providing a cheap copper currency. Lesser men were equally energetic and resourceful. Consequently it was possible for a Frenchman to write in 1780 that "in spite of the dearness of living and wages, generally much greater in England than in France; in spite of the English customs duties on foreign iron and steel; in spite of the costs of transportation into France via Hamburg and other ports [during a period when the two countries were at war]; in spite of the French customs duties on the goods as German hardware; in spite of all these things, [English metal goods] enjoy preference in France over the products of all other manufacturers of the same articles."

Machines in the Pottery Industry. While the men of Birmingham were using machines to help them supply the world with good cheap metalwares, another group living fifty miles to the northwest, in Staffordshire, was using them to help develop an industry which gave the world good cheap pottery. Early modern Europe had learned some of the secrets of making the beautiful chinaware which the East India companies brought from the Orient. Princes financed porcelain workshops in Dresden, St. Petersburg, Sèvres, and elsewhere to supply court or aristocracy, while Italian, Dutch, and Huguenot craftsmen made wares for less exalted customers. But most of these products were costly and ornamental rather than useful. For eating and drinking the well-to-do used pewter, copper, silver, glass, or gold vessels; the poor had wooden plates, leather mugs, or poorly glazed pottery which was the crude product of peasant handicraft.

From about 1700 onward some Staffordshire potters strove to raise their occupation above that peasant level. They introduced the potter's wheel and other pieces of equipment or methods from the continent. They obtained better clay and flint stones from Cornwall or other south coast points than could be procured locally. They used water wheels or windmills to turn machines which ground and mixed their ingredients; but as these supplies of power were fitful or soon became inadequate the potters were the first manufacturers to install Watt's steam engine after it became available (1776). The engines not merely did the heavy grinding and mixing work but also turned potters' wheels and later operated presses that squeezed clay into molds in which cheap pottery was given its shape.

Josiah Wedgwood (1730–1795) was one of the leaders in revolutionizing the production and sale of pottery. Perceiving that there were two markets to be served, he divided his plant into "Useful" and "Ornamental" units. In the former he made "such vessels as are made use of at meals," including those now in growing demand because of the rapid spread of tea drinking. In the latter he made cameos, vases, bowls, and other articles for personal or domestic decoration; but his chief interest was in the large-scale production of useful articles. In his factory at Burslem (1759) and then in one he built at Etruria (1769) he experimented ceaselessly with clays, glazes, colors, ovens, and temperature control. He invented or improved tools, lathes, and other pieces of equipment. He bought three steam engines and used their power wherever it could be applied for light and heavy work. Since quality was as important as quantity, he employed artists, ransacked the relics and records of the ancient world for classical designs, and tried to turn "dilatory and drunken idle worthless workmen" into skilled operatives. Since he brought much of his materials from the south coast, two hundred miles away or more, and sold his wares in a wide market, he was an enthusiast for navigable rivers, canals, and turnpike highways. He studied marketing as keenly as he did manufacturing, sent out illustrated advertisements, established a London showroom, and traded directly with almost every country. His ornamental products were bought by royalty and nobility. His useful wares found their most famous customer when Catherine the Great ordered a dinner and tea service of 952 pieces, each carrying a different English scene. His plainer cream-colored plates, cups, and teapots became part of the equipment of countless humbler homes.

Others followed closely on Wedgwood's heels or were alongside him. By their scientific approach, quest for quality, use of factory methods, and business energy they merited the description carved on Wedgwood's tombstone: they transformed "a rude and inconsiderable manufacture into an elegant art and an important part of national commerce." In the early nineteenth century a traveler could report that "from Paris to Petersburg, from Amsterdam to the farthest point of Sweden, and from Dunkirk to the extremity of the south of France, one is served at every inn upon English ware. Spain, Portugal, and Italy are supplied with it, and vessels are loaded with it for both the Indies and the continent of America." By 1830 over £500,000 of pottery was exported yearly, over half of it to the United States. After 1850 machinery encroached further on those processes which had remained in the hands of the skilled craftsman or artist. As it did so, and as other countries developed large-scale production, the price of crockery fell still farther, eating and drinking became more hygienic, pewter and plate passed into the antique shop, and washing dishes became a heavy domestic chore.

Machines in the Textile Industry. After praising the inventive producers of metal and metalwares, Tucker remarked that "as to Machines in the Woollen and Stuff Way, nothing very considerable hath been of late attempted, owing in a great Measure to the mistaken Notions of the infatuated Populace, who, not being able to see farther than the first Link of the Chain, consider all such Inventions as taking the Bread out of their Mouths; and therefore never fail to break out into Riots and Insurrections whenever such Things are proposed." There was some truth in this description of the textile workers' turbulent hostility to innovation. Clothmakers were familiar with unemployment caused by wars, tariffs, and depression. They feared that labor-saving machines would cause what a later age called "technological unemployment," and no one could foresee any such great increase in the supply of raw wool or cotton as would be needed to maintain full employment if machines invaded the industry.

Yet the industry had its problems and some men were searching for ways of solving them. At almost any point in the movement of material from the bale to the finished piece, the traffic might be held up by a lack of spinners, weavers, or finishers; but the worst jam came where yarn makers and weavers met. One cotton loom used up the product of four spinners, but a woolen weaver kept ten persons busy preparing yarn. For every additional weaver employed, many more hands must be found. Spinners rarely lacked work, but weavers were frequently idle for want of yarn. In the knitting industry the frame workers could obtain enough silk yarn after

Lombe introduced the silk-throwing machine in 1718, but makers of woolen or cotton hose were often held up by lack of yarn of the desired quality.

In 1733 John Kay, a Lancashire loom builder with a gift for invention, patented his flying shuttle. It was cigar shaped, fitted with tiny wheels, and could be knocked across the loom instead of being thrown from hand to hand. Weaving could now be done more quickly, and only one person (instead of two) was needed to produce a wide cloth. The invention roused the weavers' wrath, Kay was forced to go into hiding, and eventually he fled to France. The shuttle was only slowly adopted in England, and was scarcely known in the United States as late as 1810; there may have been some technical reason for this, but in any case quicker weaving was worth little until yarn was forthcoming in greater abundance.

That abundance came through a series of inventions which increased the quantity and improved the quality of yarn. In 1733 Paul (son of a French refugee) and Wyatt (an inventive-minded carpenter) began to try spinning yarn for knitters by the use of rollers. In 1741 they set up a little mill, but their effort was unsuccessful, and roller spinning had to wait till Richard Arkwright, a Lancashire barber with little inventive ability but much business capacity, took up their idea, improved it, obtained a patent in 1769, and established a mill driven by waterpower in 1771. His "water frame" produced fine strong yarn, suitable for cotton stockings or cloth. At almost the same moment (1770) Hargreaves, a Lancashire weaver, patented his spinning jenny, on which one person could spin eight, then sixteen, and finally over a hundred threads of yarn at once. It was an inexpensive, simple device; it could be worked by hand in the home, and therefore increased the supply of yarn without requiring any outlay in mills or power; but the yarn it made was rather weak. In 1779 Crompton, a Lancashire jenny spinner, combined features of the water frame and of the jenny in a hybrid appropriately called a mule, which made a large quantity of fine strong yarn. The mule was gradually improved, and adapted to water power; by about 1830 it had become automatic in its operation.

With these and other machines at work in cottages and mills, the yarn famine quickly ended, only to give place to one of weavers. Irish emigrants swarmed into Scotland and northern England to join the expanding army of hand-loom workers. Mechanics strove to apply power to the loom, but the technical problems were only slowly solved. The power loom did not seriously threaten the hand loom in the cotton industry until about 1830 and in the woolen industry until almost 1870.

Other textile processes were mechanized at various times between 1780 and 1860. In 1784 a copperplate printer patented a machine which printed patterns on the surface of cottons or linens by the use of rollers, as in the modern printing press. During the next decade some New Englanders applied the principle of the modern lawn mower to the work of cropping the surface of woolen cloth. In 1804 Jacquard brought to a head the efforts of many predecessors to adapt the hand loom for weaving patterned fabrics. Wool combing proved almost as difficult to mechanize as did weaving, but by 1860 its problems had been solved. The scarcity of wool in the early nineteenth century led to the designing of machines which salvaged the fibers from rags and cast-off clothing and allowed them to be remanufactured into cloth that became known as "shoddy."

The textile machines quickly increased the output per worker and reduced the cost of production. Between 1779 and 1812 the cost of making cotton yarn dropped nine-tenths. The mule's fine cheap yarn "brought to the masses of the people better goods than even the rich had been able to afford in the earlier period" (Usher), and in addition provided Europe at last with a commodity which could be shipped in vast quantities to the Orient. When the power loom became efficient, women displaced men as weavers, and one of them could look after two, three, or four looms. Her main task was to stop the loom when the shuttle was empty, put in a full one, start the loom again, and watch for broken threads. In 1894 Northrop produced an automatic loom which changed the shuttle mechanically without halting the work, but stopped of its own accord if any thread broke. A weaver could supervise many more such looms. They were best fitted for weaving plain cheap fabrics and therefore found favor in the factories of the American south and in Japan; but they were less satisfactory for finer grades of work and were therefore much less popular in Europe.

In the woolen industry, machines had by 1800 reduced by four-fifths the number of workers needed to turn a bale of wool into yarn. By 1840 the labor cost of making the best cloth had fallen at least half, though weaving was still done by hand. In 1770 the wages bill might be two to five times tthe cost of the wool, but by 1830 labor, maintenance, and capital charges combined seem to have cost far less than did the raw material.

Machines in Other Industries. Most other industries became mechanized during the nineteenth century. By 1830 Frenchmen and Englishmen were designing machines that would imitate the movements of a seamstress in pushing a needle all the way through cloth; but American inventors, trying to reproduce mechanically the stitch used in sewing mailbags, evolved a more satisfactory machine in Howe's model (1846). The new device became the instrument for converting cheap cottons, woolens, and shoddy into garments for the masses. In the fifties a stronger machine was designed for sewing together the upper parts of shoes. Supplemented later by American machines for cutting, nailing, and finishing, it displaced the old shoemaker with his knives, lasts, awls, hammer, and mouthful of nails.

The growth of towns and factories called for large supplies of building materials. Machines for making bricks were designed in England and America soon after 1800, but woodworking machines were produced in America to meet the demands of builders of wooden houses and overcome the scarcity or high cost of skilled labor. An English observer in 1853 was surprised to find New England factories equipped with machines built specially for planing wood or cutting joints for doors, window frames, and stairs. In the furniture trades he found every process, "from sawing to sandpapering," done mechanically. These methods were transferred to the Baltic countries which produced lumber for the housebuilders and to the furniture factories of western Europe, thus providing cheaper homes and furniture. Into those homes after 1850 came a gradually increasing supply of machine-processed groceries. Large-scale production of such commodities was possible only when cheap transportation and the spread of advertising opened up a wide market, allowing the biscuits, candies, cocoa, jams, flour, or soap of some large firm to be sold over a whole nation and even abroad. The production of cheap tinned steel sheets in Wales by 1880 and the American invention of machines to make glass bottles and jars about 1900 provided an ample supply of cheap cans or glass containers for foodstuffs.

The group of keyboard machines was the product of European and American inventors. By 1875 serviceable typewriters were available; the first adding machine appeared in 1888; and the printing industry got its first linotype in 1884. That industry had applied steam to work its presses in 1814. Then improved papermaking machines helped to reduce the cost of newsprint after 1830, at a time when the cylindrical press was speeding up the printing of newspapers and the telegraph was supplying them with news more quickly. As the public's reading appetite grew, the supply of rags for papermaking became inadequate, but during the sixties wood provided a cheaper raw material, and the price of wood-pulp newsprint dropped from 12 cents a pound in 1872 to less than 2 cents in 1900. By 1914 most European newspapers were sold for one or two cents apiece and good reprints of recent books for 12 to 24 cents.

Mechanical Engineering. While machinery conquered old industries it also made possible the creation of new ones. The bicycle, automobile, and electrical equipment industries were three of its numerous offspring, born in the late nineteenth century or early twentieth. But of the newcomers the first-born was the industry that made the machines which made the machines which made the goods that consumers required. For constructing a water wheel or windmill, hand loom, jenny, or early mule, few metal parts were needed, and the builder was little more than a skilled carpenter. It soon became evident, however, that equipment driven at a rapid pace must have many parts of brass or iron; that cogwheels and bearings could not be left to grind themselves into a neat fit through noisy friction but must be made according to precise specifications; and that steam engines could not be efficient unless pistons fit cylinders all through the stroke. Watch or clock makers had developed machines to produce smoothly working complicated mechanisms, and the makers of small wood or metal goods devised lathes, drills, and other mechanical aids to accuracy. But the production of large metal pieces was done by casting the material in a mold and then giving it final shape by grinding or filing. Such methods were so defective that a cylinder made for Watt by the best workmen available in Glasgow varied by three-eighths of an inch in diameter, and Smeaton, a famous engineer, gloomily informed Watt that "neither tools nor workmen existed that could manufacture so complex a machine [as his engine] with sufficient precision."

The way to precision was to clamp both cutting tool and material firmly in a machine; then the tool could be adjusted and guided to do its work—grinding, boring, slotting, drilling, turning, or cutting. The development of such machine tools was the work of many men between 1770 and 1840. In 1774 John Wilkinson, who was so "iron mad" that he built an iron barge, an iron bridge, and an iron coffin (for himself), made a greatly improved borer for cannon and in 1776 used it to supply Watt's engines with cylinders which did "not err the thickness of an old shilling" in diameter. At last cylinders could be cylindrical. In 1794 Joseph Bramah, a jack-of-all-trades inventor, and his ally, Henry Maudslay, designed an all-metal lathe with the cutting tool held in a slide rest. Maudsley made the lathe capable of adjustment to the thousandth part of an inch and designed screw-cutting, planing, and other machines. During the next fifty years engine builders and machine makers improved their equipment, and by 1850 mechanical engineering had a full kit of machine tools. Within a decade it was to begin to have an abundant supply of cheap steel and of lubricating oil.

The steel came after Bessemer's invention of the converter (1856), the oil with the tapping of the Pennsylvania fields in 1859 and of the Russian fields on the shores of the Caspian Sea a little later. Till that time all kinds of animal or vegetable oils had been used. Olive oil lubricated delicate machinery, tallow, neat's-foot, and whale oil served heavier machines, and the bearings of railroad axles had been greased with a mixture of palm oil, tallow, and lye. Hence the extraction of oil from petroleum was a great boon to all who built or used machines. Now friction could be reduced and movement at greater speeds permitted. Oil and steel opened a virtually new chapter for the engineer and paved the way for mass production.

Power. Most of the eighteenth-century inventions relied at first on the old sources of power—treadles, handwheels, treadmills, donkeys, cows, Newfoundland dogs, or water. Of these, water was by far the most important, especially where heavy work had to be done. Since its use was largely limited to the banks of streams in hilly regions where the water was moving fairly rapidly toward a lower level, the supply of mill sites was soon exhausted by the spread of spinning or other mills. When the "thirsty season" of frost or drought came, the water wheel had to stop.

The Steam Engine. Steam was known to the ancient world as a power which opened temple doors or performed other miracles for the edification of the faithful and the confusion of skeptics. Leonardo da Vinci thought about its possible uses, and some of his early seventeenth-century Italian successors conducted experiments.

Long before 1700 scientists knew that atmosphere had weight and that if steam was condensed in a closed vessel a vacuum was created. Pepys in 1663 found Charles II "laughing mightily" at the Fellows of the Royal Society for "spending their time only in weighing of ayre"; but men who had to raise water for domestic or urban use or to fight floods in mines soon began to apply this knowledge to the solution of their problems.

One of the latter, Newcomen, was eager to improve the pumping equipment in Cornish tin and copper mines. He discussed the matter with Hooke, the physicist, examined some existing primitive engines, and by 1705 had made an engine model of his own. His fundamental idea was to put a vertical piston and cylinder at the end of a pump handle. The pump plunger was a little heavier than the piston; the former therefore descended of its own accord, lifting the latter. As it did so, Newcomen passed steam into the cylinder, and then condensed it by injecting a spray of cold water. As a vacuum was thus created, the weight of the atmosphere pushed the piston down, and the plunger was raised, bringing water in its train.

Newcomen's engine became popular as it was improved. By 1720 it was being adopted throughout the mining industry, and in 1769 Smeaton counted a hundred engines at work in the north of England coal fields alone. It was also adopted by the heavy industries to pump water up to a reservoir, from which it flowed over the wheel that worked grinding mills or operated the bellows that blew air through blast furnaces. The water wheel was thereby made more efficient. Some Newcomen engines were monsters; one of them had a cylinder six feet in diameter, its piston stroke was over ten feet, it was rated at 76 H.P., and it was said to "have the force to raise, at a stroke, above 307 hundred-weight of water." Even the smaller ones were more powerful than most water wheels. True, they moved slowly—about ten to fifteen strokes a minute; they were liable to be plagued with "constant disorder"; and the cooling of the cylinder for each stroke meant a great waste of heat. This last defect was serious in the Cornish mines, since coal had to be carried there from distant fields; but at pit heads the waste was not important, and Newcomen engines were therefore in use on the coal fields as late as 1830, three decades after Watt's patent had expired. Where, then, lies the importance and fame of Watt?

Partly in his nationality, for he was a Scot. His first patent was for "a new method of lessening the Consumption of Steam and Fuel in Fire Engines." As scientific instrument-maker for Glasgow University, he repaired a model of a Newcomen engine (1763). While doing so he realized the shocking waste of good heat, wondered how it could be saved, and in 1765 found an answer while walking one "fine Sabbath afternoon" across the Glasgow golf links. If condensation could take place in a separate vessel (a condenser), the cylinder would not have to be alternately heated and cooled, and many sixpences could be cut off the fuel bill.

Had Watt stopped at that point he would merely have improved the old engine and reduced the cost of pumping water by about two-thirds—in the case of one mine the amount of coal consumed dropped from nearly eleven tons to nearly five. But he went farther during the early eighties; he fed steam into each end of the cylinder to push the piston back and forth, thus changing the engine from an atmospheric to a steam engine which "worked" on each stroke; and in 1782 he added a crank and flywheel which provided rotary motion to turn shafts and drive machines.

Watt took out his first patent in 1769. Roebuck, head of the near-by Carron ironworks and cannon foundry, tried to give substance to his ideas with crude tools and unskilled workers. When Roebuck went bankrupt in 1773, one of his creditors was Matthew Boulton, whose metalware factory in Soho, near Birmingham, now employed over 600 workers. Boulton needed more power than his two water wheels could supply. His "love of a money-getting ingenious project" was stirred by Watt's engine, and he glimpsed a vision of Soho serving "all the world with engines of all sizes." He therefore let Roebuck pay his debt by handing over Watt, took the Scot to Soho (1774), and secured from parliament an extension of the patent till 1800.

By the time it expired, the partnership of Boulton and Watt had made the patented parts and installed them in nearly 500 engines. Boulton's own skilled artisans, Wilkinson's well-bored cylinders, and the engineers who went out from Soho to erect the engines had supplied power, first to coal and copper mines, then to the potters, to flour mills, ironworks, textile factories, and to six continental buyers. The average strength was only 16 H.P., the steam pressure was low, and mountainous engines brought forth only mouselike power. After 1800 keen competition between Soho and its rivals brought great improvements; higher pressures were developed and methods of transmitting power from engine to machine were made less cumbersome. From mines and industries steam quickly passed on to serve transportation; a Watt engine propelled the *Clermont* up the Hudson in 1807, and by that date men were experimenting with engines mounted on wheels. While water power continued to be used wherever it was available, industry was no longer tied to the river banks. It could now be located wherever raw materials and coal were most economically obtainable. In addition, its supply of power was freed from limitations of climate, rainfall, or the strength of human and animal muscles.

Electric Power. In 1831 Faraday showed how electricity could be produced mechanically, but no dynamo capable of prolonged operation was available until 1873. For another quarter-century, because the producing unit was small, the cost of generation high, and the range of transmission short, the use of electricity was limited chiefly to illumination or street traction. Parsons' steam turbine, invented in 1884, provided a better engine for turning larger dynamos in central power plants, but the difficulties of transmission and the cost of electrical appliances declined slowly. Until at least 1900 the only cheap electricity was that produced by generators turned by falling water, especially in the Alpine regions of southeastern France and northern Italy. In the late sixties a Grenoble papermaker, Bergès, had steered the water that tumbled down the mountainsides into big pipes, out of which it squirted onto the flanges of turbines that turned his paper machines. When the turbines were attached to dynamos hydro-electricity was produced, and the falling water was picturesquely christened "white coal" (*la houille blanche*).

Bergès' pioneer work started a movement. By 1911 French hydro-electric stations were yielding nearly 500,000 H.P. for the aluminum, calcium carbide, and other electro-chemical or electro-metallurgical industries, as well as for the general light and power needs of the region. Italy, devoid of black coal and apparently doomed to industrial insignificance, followed closely on France's heels. Her engineers improved transmission methods, sent current under high voltage over distances as great as 130 miles without serious leakage, built steam plants to supply power during dry seasons, and linked stations together in a network. Electricity invaded almost every town and village north of Rome, fed power to chemical works, turned the wheels of textile or automobile factories in Milan and Turin, and propelled Europe's first electric streetcar through the streets of Florence in 1890. From the south "hydro" spread to Switzerland, the hilly areas of central Europe, and Scandinavia. It compensated for lack of coal, but even where coal was available hydroelectricity was cheaper than thermo-electricity (made by steamdriven dynamos). Installation costs were higher but operating costs were lower, while the cleanliness and the decentralized production favored white coal at the expense of its black rival.

After 1900, and especially after 1918, the electrification of Europe proceeded rapidly. The harnessing of water was carried on with greater vigor. Italy in 1938 generated 3,500,000 H.P., against 500,000 H.P. in 1909. Russia rejoiced that a Communist government could get water into pipes, and its great plant at Dnieprostroi, where the Dnieper was dammed up, was one of the foundation stones of Soviet industrialization. The Irish Free State regarded the harnessing of the Shannon as an outward and visible sign of the constructive statesmanship of a self-governing people. At the same time the production of thermo-electricity was made far more efficient by building larger steam turbines and dynamos and by using lignite or other inferior coal. The amount of fuel required to produce a given quantity of power fell from 6 lb. in 1900 to 1.8 lb. in 1930, but some large stations used less than 1 lb. Thermo-electricity could now be made as cheaply as hydro. As the range of transmission was extended, "super-stations" served wider areas, supplanting the motley of small generators. Public and private interests joined hands to rationalize the industry: Germany divided its territory into four interconnected zones, and Great Britain in 1926 established a Central Electricity Board which by 1936 had built a "grid" that conveyed power from great stations to virtually every nook and cranny in the land. In each of these countries the output increased at least fourfold between 1924 and 1939. Emphasizing electrical generation in her Five-Year Plans, Russia raised her production sixfold during the thirties.

The Extraction of Metals. The development of machines and power generators was closely interrelated with the production of great quantities of metals, especially iron and steel. Iron ore deposits existed in places under an area stretching from Wales to south Russia and flanked by Sweden and Spain; but their increased exploitation in any region was doomed to be checked sooner or later by the exhaustion of the charcoal supply. England felt that check by 1700, and the charcoal bill in one furnace for which we have records rose from 62 per cent of total production costs in 1696 to 72 per cent in 1740. Réaumur warned France in 1721 that the spread of cultivation and the growth of the iron industry threatened the land with deforestation. Sweden took steps in 1633 to preserve her forests and during the next century forbade the erection of new furnaces or the unlimited expansion of output from the old ones. Swedish exports therefore stagnated, and British iron users supplemented the small, stationary (or even shrinking) yield of their own country's furnaces by importing a little from the American colonies but mostly by drawing on Russia, a land so well endowed with ore and wood that by 1750 it had become an important exporter of pig iron.

A way round the barrier was revealed by Abraham Darby's discovery (about 1709) that coke could be used for smelting and by his son's improvement on this pioneer work (about 1736). Adoption of the new fuel spread after 1750. Newcomen and then Watt engines were used to work bellows or air pumps which blew a draft into the furnace, and in 1828 Neilson, a Scot, discovered that by using waste heat from the furnace to warm the air before it was blown in he could reduce his coke bill by nearly half.

The metal that ran out of the furnace was cast iron. It contained as much as 5 per cent of carbon and other foreign matter; hence it would break rather than bend and was too brittle for use where strain or blows must be endured. For many purposes wrought iron or steel was needed, but to make either of these it was necessary to extract more carbon. In 1784 Onions and Cort independently patented methods of making the former. While a flame played down from the roof of a furnace on to liquid iron, a long puddling rod stirred the metal, thus bringing much of the carbon to the surface to be burned out and leaving the iron cleaner and tough. Cort also designed rollers through which white-hot iron bars were passed and turned into plates, rods, or other shapes.

Coke, puddling, and rollers lifted the British iron industry out of stagnation, put its technique ahead of that in other countries, and made its product the cheapest in Europe. Production had been less than 20,000 tons in 1740; by 1800 it had risen to 156,000 tons, and then almost trebled every twenty years to reach over 3,800,000 tons in 1860. With the dawning of the Iron Age a metal became plentiful for the first time in history, and the needs of the machine makers or the new railroad builders could be met. In 1825 bar iron cost about £10 a ton in Britain against £26 in France, and a country which so recently had been unable to meet its own requirements became the leading exporter of iron and ironware.

After 1860 the Iron Age gave place to the Steel Age. Steel can be described as iron with less than 1 per cent of carbon, and the task of production was therefore that of extracting more carbon than could be removed by puddling. It was being done by intense prolonged heating, the output was small, and in the early nineteenth century the best steel cost £50 a ton. Great Britain in 1850 was producing 3,000,000 tons of pig iron, but only about 40,000 tons of steel. Cheap mass production was made possible by Henry Bessemer. Son of a French refugee, Bessemer flitted from one invention to another, became interested in the making of cannon, searched for a better method of making wrought iron than the puddling process, and ended by finding a way to make steel. His method, announced in 1856, was as follows: Pour molten iron into a large container (a *converter*) which had a number of holes in the bottom; blow air through these holes into the liquid iron; as the oxygen combined with the carbon and silicon the impurities would be burned out, and to the cleansed iron the required amount of carbon could then be added. The process might take only twenty minutes, yet tons of steel could be made cheaply.

Between 1856 and 1870 the price of British steel fell about half, and production rose sixfold. Some kinds of iron refused, however, to respond to Bessemer's process, much to the angry dismay of ironmasters who had bought permission to use it. Chemical analysis soon revealed that the recalcitrant metal contained phosphorus, and 0.1 per cent of phosphorus sufficed to render iron useless to steelmakers. Bessemer strove in vain to remove the offender. Meanwhile William Siemens, a German living in England, developed a rival method of making steel. His "open hearth," perfected in 1867, was in essence a big shallow pan. Into it he poured liquid iron, on which he blew a hot stream of air and a torchlike flame of gas. The carbon was burned out slowly, the conversion could be controlled, samples could be taken out at any time for analysis, the steel was more uniform in quality, old scrap iron could be mixed with the new metal, and the hearth could hold a heavier load than one dared put in the largest converter.

Yet the German was as baffled by phosphorus as was the Frenchman and had to be helped out by a Cockney and a Welshman. In 1878 Thomas (a London police court clerk who studied chemistry in his spare time) and his cousin Gilchrist (a chemist in a Welsh ironworks) solved the riddle. They gave the converter or hearth a "basic" limestone lining. The phosphorus combined with the lining when the two came in contact, producing a slag which made a good phosphate fertilizer; the iron could now be turned into steel.

Few spare-time studies have exerted such far-reaching influence on history. The advance in steel production now became fast and furious. While British phosphoric ores could be used by the steelmen, the chief beneficiaries were Germany and the United States. The former awoke to a full realization of the value of Alsace-Lorraine, taken from France in 1871. In that year Lorraine had only twoscore little furnaces making cast iron; but underground, and spreading into Luxembourg, Belgium, and France, was one of the world's richest beds of phosphoric ore. The Thomas process therefore opened the door to a vast, rapid expansion based on this ore and on the Ruhr Valley's coking coal. By 1894, when the patent expired, Germany had already passed Britain in steel production and by 1913 was producing almost twice as much as her older rival. France also benefited a little, for she still had some of the ore; but she lacked good fuel, and as it was more economical to take the ore to the coke than the coke to the ore, much French ore went into German furnaces.

On the eve of World War I the iron and steel center of Europe rested on this ore bed and on Ruhr coke. An area smaller than Vermont contained two-thirds of the continent's furnaces, converters, and open hearths, producing 24,000,000 tons of steel against 8,000,-000 in Great Britain and 31,000,000 in the United States. Of the 29,000,000 tons of ore fed into German furnaces in 1913, three-fourths came from Lorraine. Steel as well as sentiment therefore demanded the retransfer of Alsace-Lorraine to France in 1919. Germany lost the sources of 72 per cent of her ore supply to France and Poland, and about a quarter of her iron and steel plants. Her output in 1920 was only about half that of 1913. France now had 95 per cent of the ore field but Germany had the coking coal. She developed her remaining ore beds, imported ore from Sweden and France, made far greater use of scrap, and built better plants to take the place of those she had lost. By 1929 her steel output had risen far above its former level, thus adding greatly to the productive capacity of the continent at a time when demand had ceased to grow at the rapid rate of the preceding five or six decades. When general depression came in 1929 output in all countries was cut down—in some lands by a half. Recovery and rearmament lifted it to a new high by 1939, while the Five-Year Plans had raised Russian production to a figure almost as high as that of Germany. Europe's

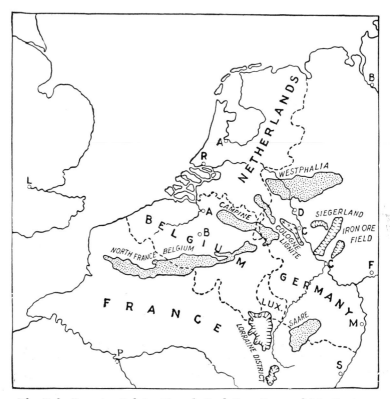

The Ruhr-Lorraine-Belgian-French Coal, Iron Ore, and Lignite Area

(From Blanshard and Visher, *Economic Geography of Europe*, McGraw-Hill Book Company, Inc., 1931.)

steel-producing capacity was being determined by preparations for war rather than peacetime needs.

Those needs had grown rapidly after the coming of the Steel Age. In 1860 steel began to be used for boilers, and far higher steam pressures could thus be developed. In 1863 the first steel locomotive was built, and Bessemer convinced the railroads that a steel rail would outlast twenty iron ones. As old railroads turned to steel and new ones were built in Europe or overseas, the railroad became a great customer of the converters and open hearths. Meanwhile the first steel ship was launched in 1863, cheap steel sheets made possible the growth of the canning industries, and cheaper galvanized iron, wire, and wire netting were useful to farmers and ranchers on all continents. Steel replaced iron in the world's navies, and armies needed it in ever increasing quantities. When Eiffel, the French engineer, completed his tower in 1889 he thought he had symbolized the Steel Age as Notre Dame Cathedral did the Middle Ages. But that tower was only a sight-seers' elevator shaft. The real temples were built on the other side of the Atlantic; the Flatiron Building in New York was the first steel-framed chapel of the new faith, the Woolworth Building its first cathedral.

Once steel could be made in abundance, the next task was to develop steel alloys, each possessing some special characteristic which fitted it for a particular duty. In 1850 Mushet produced tungsten steel, and from it tools were made that cut metal four times as quickly as did the ordinary steel tool. In 1888 Hadfield produced manganese steel, suitable for railroad crossings, curves, or other places where severe friction had to be borne. Armament makers sought steel that would give shells power to penetrate armor plate, then for armor plate that would resist these shells; and so on *ad bellum.* Chromium made steel rustless, vanadium gave it greater strength, and some alloys might be given a combination of virtues by being dosed with several stimulants. By 1914 the military and civilian use of alloys had become widespread. World War II created a demand for "super-alloys" suitable for jet planes, rockets, and projectiles.

Other Metals. Industry and transportation do not live by iron and steel alone. The nineteenth century needed the already well-known metals—copper, lead, tin, and zinc—and found at least one new one: aluminum. In the early nineteenth century the copper alloys (bronze and brass) ranked close to iron in general usefulness; cannon, bells, boilers, vats, piping, kitchen utensils, and metal parts of the early machines were made of them. Cheap iron displaced the non-ferrous metals from some uses, but new ones were found— copper for electric wires, zinc for galvanizing, and tin for coating steel sheets. The Cornish mines were the chief European producers of copper until about 1850. As they petered out, the Rio Tinto mines in Spain became famous, and Bulgaria, Norway, and Germany increased their output. But these supplies were insufficient; Europe had to rely increasingly on North America, Chile, and the Belgian Congo. By 1929 Europe consumed a third of the world's copper but produced only a fifteenth of it. She was also dependent on other continents for half her lead and zinc. The ancient glory had long since departed from the Cornish tin mines, leaving Malaya, Bolivia, and Nigeria to supply most of that metal. Only in the case of aluminum could Europe satisfy its own appetite for any important nonferrous metal.

COAL PRODUCTION
(in million metric tons)

	1800	1841	1871	1900	1913
United Kingdom	10	35	117	225	290
Germany and Luxembourg	1	3	29	{ 109 black[a] { 40 lignite	{ 190 { 87
France	1	3	13	33	41
Belgium	4	4	14	23	23
Other countries	..	..	...	...	50[a]
Total (black coal)	16	45	173	390	594

[a] Bituminous or anthracite.

Coal. British coal production in 1700 has been estimated at nearly 3,000,000 tons; that of the continent was negligible. In 1800 the British output was 10,000,000 tons, but this threefold increase was a mere prelude to the more than twentyfold expansion of the next century. Belgium, France, and Germany combined may have dug 6,000,000 tons in 1800, but by 1900 their output (excluding the inferior coal, lignite) was over 160,000,000 tons. The accompanying table tells the essentials of the story up to 1914.

Three factors caused this rapid growth in the production of a commodity that had been unknown to most Europeans in the eighteenth century. The first was the rising and widening demand for coal to supply "energy to the world's industries and warmth to those of its population who live in temperate climates" (Court). In the 1920's the world's customers for coal were, in order of importance, industrial steam engines, railroads, iron and steel producers, householders, electrical generating stations, gasworks, and steamships. Industry and the metal makers used nearly half the coal and the railroads nearly a quarter. For many years before 1914 the world demand grew about 4 per cent per annum.

The second factor was the growing ability to move coal cheaply from the pit head to the consumer. "Coales at a distance from Navigation are considered of no value," wrote the manager of a Welsh estate in 1747, and in the early nineteenth century the cost of transporting French coal to some markets was eight to ten times that of mining it. One reason for England's early development of mining was the proximity of the northeastern coal beds to the sea. As rivers were made navigable, as canals were cut, and as railroads linked mines to waterways or to a general railroad system, inland coal deposits could be profitably worked because markets were now within reach.

The third factor was the improvement in mining methods, the tapping of deeper seams, and the opening up of new coal fields. Improvement came by finding answers to three questions: How could mines be made dry and safe? How could more coal be hewed per pair of hands? How could coal be moved more easily to the pit mouth and on the surface? The steam engine helped to answer the first question by removing the water and by making possible an attack on deeper mineral deposits; but as this was done and men went farther underground the menace of chokedamp (which suffocated), firedamp (methane), and coal dust (which exploded) became more serious. To combat these unseen foes improved ventilation and illumination were necessary weapons. A second shaft was sunk, and a fire, or by 1840 a powerful fan, at the bottom of it made an upward draft which pulled fresh air down the first shaft. Davy's safety lamp (1815) reduced the risk of explosion by keeping flame and methane apart, and made possible the reopening of mines which had been abandoned as too "fiery." Disasters continued to occur occasionally, partly because of the growing use of explosives and also because coal dust might explode when mixed with methane. The discovery of this dust hazard (1845) led to still better ventilation and the use of explosives which gave less flame. Today explosions are the least important contributors to the death roll in European mine accidents.

The second problem, that of increasing the coal hewer's productivity, was not mechanically solved until nearly 1900. Eighteenth-century inventors had tried to put better equipment into the miner's hands. "Willie Brown's iron man" (1761) was a mechanical pick operated by levers, gear wheels, and a crank handle; but it was unsatisfactory, as were efforts to drive picks or circular saws by horsepower. No machine could be efficient until compressed air or electricity could be carried to the coal face to drive it. Hewing therefore remained a manual occupation in Europe until 1914, a task done with a pick and a few other simple tools and requiring a combination of human strength with considerable skill. By 1900 coal-cutting machines were rapidly coming into use in the United States, especially in the new fields of West Virginia and Illinois; but in Europe the thin or sloping character of some coal seams, the abundant supply and hostility of skilled labor to labor-saving devices, the lack of enthusiasm of the older mineowners, and the satisfactory financial returns from existing methods prevented their introduction. Only during and after World War I did the pressure of demand, the scarcity or high cost of labor, and the severity of competition lead to mechanization. In Britain the percentage of coal cut by machines rose from 8 in 1913 to 70 in 1939; in the Ruhr the increase was from 5 to about 90 per cent, and in Belgium and France the same trend was marked.

The third problem was that of improving the transportation of coal to the pit mouth. The crudest old method was to shovel the coal into baskets, which were then dragged by boys, women, or girls to the shaft and hauled, or even carried up ladders, to the surface. German metal miners had improved on this method in the sixteenth century by putting the baskets on wagons or sleds which were pulled on boards laid down parallel to form a track. This practice was copied in coal mines, and when English iron became cheap in the late eighteenth century iron plates with a flange on each edge took the place of wood. The plates were later replaced by rails; on these the wagons were pushed by boys, pulled by ponies, and later hauled by being attached to an endless rope or chain worked by a steam engine installed underground. Engines were by 1800 being used to lift the loaded wagons to the surface, and during the next twenty years mining engineers like Stephenson and Trevithick put engines on wheels, ran them on rails, and used them to supplement or supplant horses for hauling coal wagons from the pit head to a port or waterway.

A versifier who had known the bad old days burst into song:

> God bless the man wi' peace and plenty
> That first invented metal plates.

Draw out his days to five times twenty,
Then slide him through the heavenly gates.

To the more prosaic mineowner savings in underground transportation costs were important, for in the eighteenth century far more
labor was needed to move the coal than to hew it. Every improvement in haulage methods reduced the number of workers serving
the coal cutter and thereby increased the percentage of men actually
hewing. But it was only after 1900 that really far-reaching improvements became available—electric engines for hauling wagons, con-
veyor belts, and mechanical shovels to lift the coal onto the belts or
into the wagons. The adoption of these new devices in Europe was
impeded by such underground conditions as the narrow, winding,
or undulating nature of the roadways, by the thin seams, and by the
cost of installation. During the inter-war period the use of the con-
veyor belt became widespread, and in 1939 it moved about two-
thirds of the coal mined in Britain; but loading machines were introduced more slowly and the task of making the roads suitable for
efficient transportation had scarcely begun.

Slowly improving methods, an abundant labor supply, and the
opening up of new coal beds—some of them in remote regions
which went through a mining "frontier" stage—enabled the industry to meet the ever expanding needs and to become one of the most
important occupations. In Britain coal mining knit itself into the
fabric of economic life. In 1914 it employed 1,100,000 men, or one-
twelfth of the working population. It provided the only industrial
material in which the country was self-sufficing. In addition it contributed a tenth of the value and four-fifths of the volume of exports. In 1913 a third (over 90,000,000 tons) of the total output
went abroad to supplement the domestic production of Belgium,
France, and Germany; to supply lands devoid of coal, such as Italy
and Scandinavia; to fuel Argentina's railroads, replenish bins in
coaling stations the world over, and fill the bunkers of foreign ships
leaving British ports. Coal thus paid for part of the country's imports of food and raw materials, provided outward cargoes or ballast
for ships going out to deliver manufactured goods and fetch foodstuffs, and thereby made lower freight rates possible on both journeys. As in all countries, the industry employed workers under
conditions that were dirty, difficult, dark, and dangerous. It con-

demned them to live in regions that were usually dreary and often isolated. Relations between capital and labor might become harsh as trade unions grew in strength, and conflicts were bitter. But in general the owners' profits, landlords' royalties, and miners' wages were relatively high.

On the continent coal mining was insignificant until the second quarter of the century. By 1850 improved waterways and some railroads had reduced transportation costs and extended the range of sale. The expanding iron industry was turning from charcoal to coke fuel. Rich seams, discovered deep down in northern France, Belgium, and the Ruhr Valley began to be worked about 1840. From that time onward the German output increased rapidly both before and after the formation of the Empire, chiefly in the Ruhr-Westphalia region, Saxony, and Silesia. Deposits of brown coal (lignite) were being exploited by 1900 to supplement the supply of anthracite or bituminous coal. In 1913 the industry employed over 700,000 men and exported about a quarter of its output; but at the same time coal was imported, going all the way by water from Newcastle (England) to supply some of the needs of Berlin. Belgium exported and imported, but France had to supplement her own yield by buying from Germany and England.

Russia discovered very large coal deposits in the Donets basin about 1850, and large reserves of ore in the same region a little later. Both minerals began seriously to be exploited in the nineties, and by 1913 the output of coal of all kinds had risen to about 33,000,000 tons. Austria, Spain, and Holland were minor producers; but of the 730,000,000 tons of European black and brown coal dug in 1913, 40 per cent was mined in the British Isles and 38 per cent in the German Empire. The output of coal (excluding lignite) in these two countries had risen 45 per cent since 1900. The Hundred Years' Peace thus ended on a wave of record output and abounding prosperity for the coal fields. King Coal was healthy and merry.

War took many miners away, strained productive capacity in all countries, raised prices and wages, destroyed 200 mines in northern France, decimated Russian production, and forced Britain and Germany to abandon some of their export markets. The peace settlement gave Poland and France coal fields which had supplied Germany with a quarter of her fuel and ordered Germany to pay some reparations in coal. The revival of production in central and western Europe proved fairly easy, and by 1924 the yield was almost equal to the pre-war level. But there was no corresponding full restoration of demand and no sign of a return of that ever expanding market which had been normal before 1914. King Coal became sick, and instead of calling for pipe, bowl, and instrumentalists, he cried for subsidies, bounties, tax exemption, tariffs, lower wages, longer hours, and state purchase of coal at high prices.

The malaise of this basic industry was due to many factors:

1. Depression or stagnation in the heavy or export industries reduced coal consumption by iron and steel plants, factories, railroads, and steamships.

2. Former coal-importing countries which had coal beds were exploiting them more vigorously. Holland mined less than 2,000,000 tons in 1913, but in 1929 produced nearly 13,000,000 tons.

3. Substitute fuels grew in popularity, and hydro-electrical developments checked some demands for coal. Oil fuel, used by only 1,500,000 tons of merchant shipping in 1913, supplied heat for over 20,000,000 tons in 1925; the world's navies had installed oil burners, and the Diesel engine had won its spurs in ocean traffic. Lignite, "the Cinderella among the coals," found a fairy godmother, to the discomfiture of its bituminous and anthracite elder sisters. It was earthy and watery and gave only about a fifth of the heat provided by the same weight of black coal, but it was easily mined in open cuts, and German engineers had found improved ways to dry, pulverize, and mold it into briquets. It could be burned in the improved furnaces of electric power stations, and in 1922 a German chemist. Bergius, obtained liquid fuel from it. By 1929 Germany was mining 175,000,000 tons of lignite.

4. Marked economies were effected in the use of coal. Pre-war Europe had burned its cheap coal wastefully. Much heat and soot went up the chimney, the use of raw coal wasted valuable by-products, and the generation of steam power, electricity, and coal gas in thousands of plants involved losses from small-scale production. After World War I greater care was taken, for coal was now more costly. Boilers and furnaces were improved, central power stations were built, and the making of coal gas began to be centralized, with pipe lines carrying the product long distances to serve many industries which had formerly burned coal or coke.

The post-war coal industry was therefore confronted by sluggish demand. The 4 per cent annual increase in consumption of pre-war days gave place to one of only 0.3 per cent between 1913 and 1937.

Some home markets were no greater than they had been in 1913, and competition for the shrunken foreign markets was intense, with Poland, now in possession of the Upper Silesian mines, as a new rival to Britain and Germany. Lower wages, longer hours, price cutting, rationalization, and mechanization were weapons used in the struggle. Six years of discussion between owners, governments, and the League of Nations failed to produce any agreement to equalize wages—which comprised 70 per cent of mining costs—limit production, or share out markets. In 1929 depression descended on a world glutted with coal as it was with steel and wheat, oversupplied with mines that were being equipped with the new machines and capable of producing far more coal than was wanted, and flooded with coal's chief rival, oil.

During the depressed years (1929–1932) the output of coal fell to less than 72 per cent of the 1913 level in Britain and to 60 per cent in Germany. Only Russia, now in the first phase of her planned expansion, increased her production. Recovery did not lift the British output to more than 84 per cent of the 1913 figure, for half the old export market had been lost, and the domestic demand was down a little. Under the strain of World War II the yield dropped by 1945 to 175,000,000 tons, or 60 per cent of the 290,000,000 tons mined in 1913. In 1946 the mines were nationalized. Plans were set in motion for radical improvements in their layout, mechanization, and administration as a unit instead of as over 1,000 mines of varying size and efficiency operated by almost as many firms. The "target" was set at about 250,000,000 tons a year. This figure is well below the peak of 1913; but it is far above the 200,000,000 tons which was the objective for 1947. It is also an indication of the retreat of the coal industry from the predominant position it occupied during the nineteenth century. A country which had built up its great industrial fabric on coal and had once exported a third of its output emerged from World War II industrially starved and domestically shivering for lack of enough fuel.

In Germany the coal-mining industry revived rapidly after 1933, and by 1937 had regained the level of 1913. This was due to general recovery, to the rearmament drive, and also to the fact that Germany sought to obtain from coal some products which otherwise she would be obliged to import. Germany above all other countries exploited the knowledge that coal was not merely a fuel but also a chemical storehouse from which other things than heat could be drawn. As far back as 1792 Murdock, one of Boulton's mechanical geniuses, illuminated his house and office with coal gas, and a plant installed by him (1805) in a Manchester mill reduced the lighting bill from £2,000 spent on candles to £650. By 1820 gas companies were being formed to supply the leading cities with what seemed a miraculous maker of daylight. In the eighties Welsbach

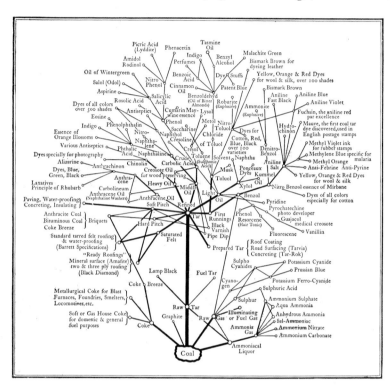

Coal's Family Tree

devised the asbestos "mantle," which was heated by a Bunsen burner and set a standard of illumination that the electric bulb only slowly equaled.

In addition to yielding a valuable gas, coal gave a liquid (coal tar) which soon roused the curiosity of chemists. Mansfield extracted aniline from it. In 1856 Perkin extracted from the aniline a mauve dye and then other colors ranging from purple to pink. Mankind had scoured the animal, vegetable, and mineral kingdoms in a search for colors for its cloths. It had used beetles, crocus blooms, shellfish, wood, plants, mosses, walnut peel, and bullock's blood. Perkin and his countless successors spared it from further search, as the picture of coal's family tree should make clear. On the twigs of that tree a thousand dyes are now to be found; but to reach them we must pass a motley of other tar by-products, including aspirin, wintergreen, saccharin, disinfectants, laxatives, perfumes, photographic chemicals, high explosives, and essence of orange blossom. Nearer the trunk or the roots are roofing or road materials, ammonia fertilizers, lubricating oils, and liquid fuel.

In the industrial exploitation of coal tar, as of fertilizers and electricity, Germany led the world. University research became intensive, technical schools poured out a stream of trained men, and chemical firms established large laboratories. Ruhr coking coal supplied plenty of tar, the production of fertilizers had created a strong chemical industry and a class of chemical engineers, and Germany therefore soon dominated the dye market. By 1913 six large companies were making about 88 per cent of the world's dyes and supplying textile manufacturers with a wider range of better dyes at a fraction of the old cost. During World War I other countries established dye works, government aid was given, and German patents or formulas were appropriated. By 1928 Germany was supplying only two-fifths of the market, or just a little more than did the United States and Great Britain combined.

The dye industry is naturally the most colorful example of the application of chemistry on a large scale. It found treasure in a waste product. Yet its achievement seems little more remarkable than do many others of the last fifty or sixty years, such as the production of rayon from wood pulp by a process patented by the Count de Chardonnet in 1884 and made practicable by 1900; the taking of nitrogen out of the air to make ammonia fertilizers, commercially practicable by 1913; the making of gasoline from coal by a process developed in Germany during the twenties and rapidly improved during that country's self-sufficiency drive in the thirties; the production of synthetic rubber from coal or oil, equally important to Germany's plans in the thirties and to other lands when Japan cut off the supply of natural rubber from the East Indies in 1941; and other less important efforts to obtain from materials abundantly at hand substitutes for commodities that are costly or scarce, or that come from abroad. If to them we add the achievements of the physicists in applying electricity to production, transportation, and communication, and their more recent work on the atom, the total result is a greatly increased understanding of nature, an enlarged ability to exploit its resources, and a power to use science for ends that may be more political than economic.

BIBLIOGRAPHY

General

Bogardus, J. F., *Europe: A Geographical Survey* (1934), chaps. 7 and 8, and sections describing chief industries of each country.

Bowden, W., Karpovich, M., and Usher, A. P., *Economic History of Europe since 1750* (1937), chaps. 6, 15, 19, 32, and the excellent Bibliography.

Bragg, W., *Creative Knowledge: Old Trades and New Science* (1927), chaps. 2–6.

Epstein, R. C., "Industrial Invention: Heroic or Systematic?" *Q.J.E.*, February, 1926.

Gilboy, E. M., "Demand as a Factor in the Industrial Revolution," in *Facts and Factors in Economic History* (1932).

Hatfield, H. S., *The Inventor and His World* (1933).

Marshall, A., *Industry and Trade* (1919), book i.

Nef, J. U., "The Industrial Revolution Reconsidered," *J. Ec. H.*, May, 1943.

Rossman, J., *The Psychology of the Inventor* (1931).

Rossman, J., "The Motives of Inventors," *Q.J.E.*, May, 1933.

Usher, A. P., *History of Mechanical Inventions* (1929), chaps. 7, 9, 11–13.

Wolf, A., *History of Science, Technology, and Philosophy in the 16th and 17th Centuries* (1936), chaps. 20–23.

Encyclopaedia of the Social Sciences: See the article on "The Industrial Revolution"; also the list of titles under Industry, vol. xv, pp. 551–552.

Special Industries or Countries

Ashton, T. S., *Iron and Steel in the Industrial Revolution* (1924).

Ashton, T. S., and Sykes, J., *The Coal Industry in the Eighteenth Century* (1929), chaps. 1–4.

Ballot, C., *L'introduction du machinisme dans l'industrie française* (1923).

Benaerts, P., *Les origines de la grande industrie allemande* (1933).

Bladen, V. W., "The Potteries in the Industrial Revolution," *Ec. Hist.*, January, 1926.

Blanchard, W. O., "White Coal in Italian Industry," *Geog. Rev.*, June, 1928.

Bowden, Witt, *Industrial Society in England toward the End of the Eighteenth Century* (1925), chaps. 1, 2.

Bowden, Witt, *The Industrial Revolution* (1928). An excellent collection of extracts from contemporary accounts of developments.

Burn, D. L., *Economic History of Steelmaking, 1867–1939* (1940).

Burn, D. L., "The Genesis of American Engineering Competition, 1850–1870," *Ec. Hist.,* January, 1931.

Clapham, J. H., *The Economic Development of France and Germany, 1815–1914* (1923), chaps. 3, 4, 10, 11.

Clapham, J. H., *Economic History of Modern Britain* (1926, 1932, 1938), vol. i, chaps. 5, 10; vol. ii, chaps. 2, 3; vol. iii, chap. 3.

Court, W. H. B., "Problems of the British Coal Industry between the Wars," *Ec. H. R.,* 1945.

Daniels, G. W., *The Early English Cotton Industry* (1920).

Dawson, W. H., *The Evolution of Modern Germany* (1908), chap. 3.

Day, C., *Economic Development in Modern Europe* (1942), chaps. 8–12, 15, 18, 25–28.

Dickinson, H. W., *Matthew Boulton* (1937).

Dickinson, H. W., *A Short History of the Steam Engine* (1939).

Fay, C. R., *Great Britain from Adam Smith to the Present Day* (1932), chaps. 13–16.

Fleming, A. P., and Brocklehurst, H. T., *History of Engineering* (1925).

Hamilton, H., *The Industrial Revolution in Scotland* (1932).

Hammond, J. L. and B., *The Rise of Modern Industry* (1926), chaps. 7–11.

Jeans, W. T., *The Creators of the Age of Steel* (1884).

Jenkins, Rhys, *Links in the History of Engineering and Technology from Tudor Times* (1936).

Knowles, L. C. A., *The Industrial and Commercial Revolutions in Great Britain during the Nineteenth Century* (1922), part ii.

Knowles, L. C. A., *Economic Development in the Nineteenth Century* (1932), part iii.

Lord, J., *Capital and Steam Power, 1750–1800* (1923).

Mantoux, P., *The Industrial Revolution in the Eighteenth Century* (Eng. trans., 1928), part ii, chaps. 1–4.

Miall, S., *History of the British Chemical Industry* (1931).

Redford, A., *Economic History of England, 1760–1860* (1931), chaps. 1–3, 9.

Roe, J. W., *English and American Tool Builders* (1916).

Sée, H., *La vie économique de la France, 1815–1848* (1927).

Veblen, T., *Imperial Germany and the Industrial Revolution* (1915), chap. 6.

Wadsworth, A. P., and Mann, J., *The Cotton Trade and Industrial Lancashire, 1600–1780* (1931).

XXII

THE DEVELOPMENT OF MODERN
TRANSPORTATION

The connection between changes in production and improvements in transportation was close. While some of the improvements were impossible till cheap iron and the steam engine were available, expanding production depended on greater ability to bring in raw materials and send more goods to a wider market. That ability came in two stages. In the first one the improved river, the canal, the good road, and the larger sailing ship enabled men to move greater quantities of cheap, bulky, heavy, or fragile commodities more quickly over long distances at lower cost. In the second, steam and (later) the internal-combustion engine increased further the size of the load, gave certainty of movement, defied climatic obstacles, added greatly to speed and flexibility, reduced costs still more, and gave the power to penetrate areas inaccessible by river or canal.

Improvements in inland transportation were so costly that they depended far more on state action and funds than did the developments in industry. Only in Great Britain were they undertaken by private enterprises which raised their own capital and made their own profit or absorbed their own losses. In most parts of the continent capital was scarce, the tradition of state enterprise was strong, the prospect of profit was too poor to tempt investors, and the military authorities needed facilities for quick movement of troops and supplies. Hence the state not merely undertook the work on rivers, canals, and roads, but either built and ran the railroads or subsidized private construction and operation.

ROADS AND WATERWAYS

The first thorough improvement in pre-railroad transportation was carried out in Great Britain. Having made many rivers more navigable by 1750 and discovered that freight rates fell by about

515

three-quarters when goods left poor roads for the water, the country became "canal conscious" when the Duke of Bridgewater's canal, completed in 1761, linked coal mines at Worsley with Manchester, seven miles away. The price of coal in Manchester fell by half and the duke extended his canal to the Mersey, offering rates one-sixth of those charged by land carriers. Between 1758 and 1807, 165 canal acts were passed, the rivers were further improved and joined together, and by 1830 England south of York was covered with a network of nearly 4,000 miles of navigable waterway.

The effects were far-reaching. Goods could be moved in tens of tons instead of hundredweights, freight costs fell, coal from inland mines became available, and farmers could serve distant markets. Prices were equalized between districts, passengers could travel cheaply, and Wedgwood ceased to worry about broken crockery. Canal construction employed armies of "navvies" (i.e., workers on "navigations") and offered a great field for investment. Porter estimates that at least £11,000,000 was spent on canals. Some canals failed, but those which served busy districts and had no costly engineering difficulties to surmount made large profits. In 1832 nearly thirty companies out of eighty paid 10 per cent or more; but forty distributed little or nothing.

The canal era was paralleled by a great period of road building. All road construction faced two questions: How could the necessary supply of labor, money, and material be obtained? What was the best method of constructing a durable surface? Statute labor or *corvée* was inadequate for the maintenance of much-traveled roads. On the continent central governments were assuming more direct responsibility for the main highways. They were still using *corvée* but supplementing it from the exchequer. England entrusted road improvement to local groups of citizens organized as turnpike trusts. The first trust was created in 1663 to take charge of a piece of road, and in the eighteenth century so many were set up that by 1830, 1,100 of them were dealing with 20,000 miles of highway. The trust consisted of local landlords, traders, clergy, and farmers. It had statutory power to borrow money, employ a surveyor, improve the road with hired and statute labor, and collect tolls which were expected to defray the cost of maintenance, pay the interest on the bonds, and ultimately redeem them. By 1830 over £7,000,000 had been borrowed, and over £1,300,000 was collected annually. This revenue was not enough; expenses often exceeded income, interest could not be paid, administration was in the hands of an unwieldy "promiscuous mob" of amateurs, and when railroad rivalry grew intense the trusts went bankrupt. Eventually statute labor was abolished (1835), local taxes were imposed, the trusts were disbanded, and road maintenance was recognized as a public obligation. That obligation was lightened as railroads relieved the highways of all but local traffic, and roads were adequate until the automobile came to tear up their surface after 1900.

By 1830 the second problem had been solved, for during the decades after 1750 Metcalfe, Telford, Macadam, and other road engineers had evolved methods of making hard-surfaced roads that would bear traffic all through the year. Competition and better surfaces had increased the speed of travel by coach from four miles an hour to six, eight, or even ten; but when the Liverpool-Manchester coach did one journey at fourteen miles an hour there were loud calls for a judicial inquiry into this attempted manslaughter. Travel by night and in winter became possible; the journey from Edinburgh to London, which had once taken fourteen days, was reduced to forty-four hours. Speed was productive of many accidents; it was costly in horseflesh; but it accelerated the movement of persons, packages, and mail. Horses could pull a far greater load on wheels than they had formerly carried on their backs. Freight wagons and livestock could get more easily and quickly to their destination. The country became more tightly knit together, and McCulloch declared in 1835 that "Manners as well as prices are reduced nearly to the same standard. . . . Everything is, as it were, brought to a level."

After 1830 the railroad challenged both waterway and road. It killed all long-distance road traffic by providing greater speed and safety, charging lower freight rates, and moving goods in greater loads than could be taken over the highways. It defeated the waterways by carrying even such cheap heavy commodities as coal at rates lower than those charged by canals. Some railroads assured their victory by buying or leasing canals and letting them stagnate or pass out of use. Thus the new private enterprise played havoc with the older ones by giving a better service. The canals were therefore only "an episode" (Fay)—an important one—in the transition from bad to good transportation. They attracted no fresh capital, few of them carried out any improvements, and their towpaths became little more than unhedged lovers' lanes.

In Germany inland water transportation needed three things: improvement of the six main rivers and their tributaries; the linking of these rivers, which flowed from south to north, by canals running generally east to west; and the provision of an outlet for the Rhine through German territory to the sea. The main rivers were

(From Bowman's *The New World*, copyright, 1928, by World Book Company, Yonkers-on-Hudson, New York.)

improved after peace came in 1815. The tolls and restrictions on Rhine traffic which Cologne and Mainz had claimed for centuries were abandoned, and the steam tug made upstream haulage easier after 1840. For a time railroad construction diverted capital and attention from the waterways, but after 1870 railroads, rivers, and canals were regarded as parts of a general transportation system which was to be developed by public enterprise. Money was spent lavishly on rivers and canals, and by 1903 the country had almost

9,000 miles of navigable waterway, of which over a quarter had been improved or made. The Rhine was rendered navigable as far up as Strasbourg almost the whole year round. Canals were planned on a wider, deeper scale than the narrow, shallow "cuts" of the earlier days. They were traversed by power-driven boats of 200 or more tons rather than by barges; but the ambitious *Mittelland* project for a canal along which vessels of 600 or more tons would steam through the heart of the country from the Rhine to the Vistula was not finally completed until 1938. In 1886 the Rhine-Ruhr area was joined by canal to the River Ems, thus providing a German outlet to the sea. But a canal made before 1850 to link the Main, a tributary of the Rhine, with the upper Danube remained narrow, shallow, and virtually unused. Its conversion into a "ship canal" had scarcely begun in 1939.

In 1929 German waterways transported 110,000,000 tons of freight, or one-fifth the amount moved by rail. Coal and coke were the chief cargoes. Sand, ore, bricks, grain, fertilizer, lumber, and other heavy cheap goods provided most of the rest of the loads. Half of these commodities went to or came from abroad. Berlin was a veritable inland port, as a third of the goods it bought came by water. Yet in Germany, as elsewhere, the waterway was a minor part of the transportation system. Its use was held up by frost in winter and low water at other times. The cost of construction and of later improvement was high. Its freight rates were lower than rail rates, partly because vessels used the rivers free of charge and paid canal dues which contributed little or nothing toward meeting the interest on the cost of making the waterway. These capital costs and some of the maintenance charges were met in Germany out of the profits made on the publicly owned railroads and out of the pocket of the taxpayer. A water freight rate large enough to defray capital charges in addition to those of operating the vessels would rarely have been lower than the rail rate.

After World War I, when the Rhine became part of the French frontier, French and Belgian railroads competed more keenly with the German lines and compelled them to lower their rates. This reduced the advantage which the Rhine had enjoyed, just at a time when the automobile and truck were stealing some of the river's passenger and parcel traffic. Meanwhile, the middle Danube, which once had provided 700 miles of waterway for the Austro-Hungarian Empire, lost much traffic when that Empire broke into pieces, and the use of the lower Danube shriveled with the collapse of the export trade in grain from Rumania. The river did, however, continue to serve as a channel by which the primary products of southeastern Europe—grain, ores, and Rumanian oil—were exchanged for the manufactured products of industrial central Europe. It was also a vital artery for such landlocked countries as Austria, Hungary, and Czechoslovakia. As Nazi Germany expanded her economic control in Danubia and then annexed Austria (1938), the Danube assumed great importance. Plans for making Vienna a port and for completing quickly the renovation of the Rhine-Main-Danube canal were announced, but had not been carried through when war came.

THE RAILROAD

The railroad came in two installments. The plate or rail track was in common use by the mid-eighteenth century for moving coal from the pit head to some waterway or to the place where it was to be burned. The laying of such a track from a mine to the Carron ironworks, two miles away, reduced the coal bill by three-fourths. Similar roads were used by stone quarries, and after 1800 at latest they were laid down on the outskirts of London, Sheffield, Munich, and other towns to serve as public toll highways. On the Munich wagonway it was claimed (1819) that a woman or child could pull a cart laden with three-quarters of a ton, and that one horse could do as much work as twenty-two horses did on a common road.

The engine came next. By 1801 Trevithick, a Cornish engineering genius, had an engine pulling trucks on rails around the mine at which he worked. In 1808 he built a steam railroad near London, but his lone engine ran off the track and he lacked money for its repair. He emigrated to install pumping engines for a mine in Peru, and thus let the pioneer's fame fall into the lap of another mining engineer, George Stephenson. Stephenson used an engine to pull coal trucks six miles from a mine to the River Tyne, and urged the promoters of a plate road between Stockton and Darlington to give steam and rails a trial. They agreed, and in 1825 his engine, weighing seven tons, hauled a train weighing ninety tons on the new line at four to eight miles an hour. At all speeds its chimney was red hot; but it did the work of forty teams of horses, the price of coal in Stockton fell by half, and only a financial panic late in 1825 checked a rapidly spreading epidemic of railway promotion.

Five years later even better results were obtained. The merchants and manufacturers of Lancashire completed a railroad which they hoped would liberate them from the "exorbitant and unjust charges of the water carriers." Their line from Liverpool to Manchester was opened in 1830. On it Stephenson's *Rocket* pulled a train thirty-one miles at an average speed of fourteen miles an hour; and as Huskisson, a prominent cabinet minister, was knocked down and killed, the opening ceremony received great publicity.

These two lines proved there was "something" in steam railroads. The Lancashire trains were soon running at twenty miles an hour, a result which went "far to strike space and time out of the calculations of the traveler." The number of passengers and the amount of freight rose rapidly, and the company earned 8.4 per cent on its capital. Soon other lines were planned. They had to wrestle with technical problems, as boilers burst, engines broke down, and construction costs exceeded estimates. Before they turned the first sod they had to fight the vested interest of the old order or rival projectors of the new. Canal stockholders, turnpike trusts, innkeepers, coach owners, horse breeders, and fodder merchants saw that they would be injured by "this smoky substitute for canals" and tried to stop its progress, while two or more companies might fight each other to obtain authority to build a potentially profitable line. The main battle, especially between rivals, was on the floor of parliament, and its costs during the boom years 1845–1847 were estimated at over £10,000,000, or enough to build a first-class line from London to the top of Scotland. If to this are added the sums spent in buying or leasing nearly a thousand miles of canal, the money used to build branches in order to forestall a rival, and the high prices paid for land, we get a glimpse at the cost of competitive private enterprise.

To the burden of initial costs was added that of speculation, extravagance, and mismanagement. The railroad was a new kind of bubble, to be blown up until it burst. In four frenzied years, 1844–1847, 628 railroad acts were passed, authorizing the raising of £250,000,000. These figures represent much solid achievement and a top layer of froth. The profits that were being made by some lines and the powerful "sales talk" of promoters like Hudson, the Railway King, were bait enough to catch eager, credulous investors. The cost of mismanagement or fraud also seems to have been heavy. Herbert Spencer in 1855 charged directors with multiform dishonesties, declared that the morality of railroad construction engineers was not far above that of railroad lawyers (he had been an engineer), and quoted an estimate that a quarter of the £280,000,000 already raised had been filched or squandered. While, therefore, many investors lost heavily, the railroads themselves were loaded with a burden of bonded debt far greater than it need have been.

The growth of the British railroad system is shown in the accompanying table. By 1850 the main routes had been built and the chief

UNITED KINGDOM RAILROADS

Year	Miles	Paid-Up Capital	Passengers
1838	500	. . . .	. . . .
1850	6,600	£ 240,000,000	73,000,000
1870	15,500	530,000,000	337,000,000
1890	20,000	897,000,000	818,000,000
1910	23,400	1,319,000,000	1,307,000,000

features fixed. Most companies had laid only short lines—ten to fifty miles—but competition, amalgamation, and leases gradually welded the fragments together. By 1850 the engineers had solved most of their early problems. Cheaper iron and better machine tools aided them, cheap steel was just over the horizon, and the electric telegraph, introduced in the forties, transmitted information about train movements. In the fifties hydraulic brakes were introduced, but Westinghouse's air brake (1868) gave much more satisfaction. Wood ties replaced stone blocks, rails became stouter and engines larger. By 1850 speeds of 30, 40, or 50 miles were well known, and 60 was "far from uncommon when in full motion." Edinburgh was 44 hours from London by stagecoach, but only 12 hours by train.

Effects of the Railroad. In 1850 two-thirds of the railroad revenue came from passengers. For their accommodation three classes of carriages and even of trains were offered. The first-class coach resembled three stagecoach bodies mounted on a chassis. The early second-class coach was cheerless, but had seats and a roof. Third-class passengers stood in open trucks on trains that started at inconvenient hours, dawdled along, and reached their destination at no fixed hour. In 1844, however, parliament insisted that they be given better service. This decree combined with competition to cause such improvement of the cheapest travel that second class was eventually abandoned, and by 1900 first class was used only by rich men or honeymoon couples. Cheap excursion fares permitted Demos to visit the coast, the inland scenic areas, and the capital. The cheap weekly or season ticket dispersed urban workers and opened a way of escape for "the sickly artisan, pent up in the densely populated city, or inhaling the pestilential atmosphere of the crowded manufactory."

After 1850 freight steadily grew more important than passengers, but even today British railroads draw a third of their revenue from the sale of tickets, as against a sixth in the United States. Coal and coke provided the greatest weight, and in 1913 supplied two-thirds of the tonnage; other minerals came next, and general merchandise ranked third in weight but first in yield of revenue. The carriage of mail began in the thirties, and when penny post came in 1840 the postal service became cheap as well as quick. The railroad ended long-distance driving of livestock along the highways; one of the earliest pictures we have of a freight train (1833) shows closed trucks of sheep, a wagon full of cattle, and open trucks in which green-coated Irishmen are trying to keep pigs in order. Milk and other farm produce could be sent quickly to market and fresh fish be distributed far inland.

For handling small consignments of produce and merchandise the railroads built up a rapid service. Regular freight-train schedules were in operation by 1850; rates were the same for small shipments and whole carloads; and the farmer, storekeeper, or manufacturer could send or receive his can of milk, sack of potatoes, bale of cloth, or packet of clothes cheaply and quickly. Even today the average consignment is only 500 pounds, the average load per car is about five tons, and the average car capacity is less than eleven tons—a fact which makes North Americans think they have strayed into a toy shop when they first see a British freight train.

The railroad reduced the time and cost of movement. By 1845 its fares from Liverpool to London were half (or less) those formerly charged by stagecoaches, and the journey had been shortened by nearly two-thirds. Road wagons had charged 12*d.* to 15*d.* per ton-mile and covered about twenty-four miles a day. Canal barges charged 6*d.* to 12*d.*, and their speed was lower than that on the road. In 1849 railways were carrying coal at 1*d.* and general merchandise for 2*d.* to 4*d.* They offered little time or opportunity for the thief to do his work, whereas on road and canal "a system of plunder of the most extensive nature" had prevailed.

The railroad provided new fields for employment of labor. In

1847 nearly 50,000 workers were operating British lines, 250,000 were building new ones, while many others were providing iron, rolling stock, building material, or the 700,000 tons of coal consumed by engines in that year. By 1907 over 600,000 persons were working on the railroads, doing all kinds of tasks—manual and mechanical, clerical and administrative, skilled and unskilled, regular and casual, sedentary and strenuous.

The railroad was a great new sponge for capital. By 1910 the paid-up capital invested in British railways exceeded £1,300,000,-000, of which bonds and guaranteed stock accounted for less than three-eighths, against three-fifths in the United States. "Home Rails," as these securities were called, were investments popular with all classes down to the better-paid wage earner. It soon became evident, however, that the railroads would not make fabulous profits. An early company might pay 6 to 10 per cent, but the heavy capitalization of most railroads forbade any such good return. Each mile of track bore a capital load of £34,600 in 1853 and of £64,000 in 1918, against about the same number of dollars in the United States. The dividend on common stock between 1850 and 1914 never reached 5 per cent and never fell below 3 per cent; but if anything were to happen to reduce receipts or to increase operating costs, the difference between these two figures—the "net receipts"— might become too small, when maintenance, interest, and tax charges had been met, to leave any money over for payment of even 3 per cent.

Finally, the railroad raised new problems of state policy. In the beginning parliament had readily given companies permission to build lines, in order to improve the country's transportation system, promote competition, and break monopolies held by canals, by roads, or by any one railroad in a district. In addition it imposed regulations, fixed some maximum fares and freights, protected the poor by demanding that a third-class train be run on each line each day at a penny a mile, and even coquetted with the idea of public ownership by decreeing (1844) that the state might buy the lines after twenty-one years.

After 1850 the state had to change its policy of fostering regulated competition to one of regulating the railroads' monopoly of inland transportation. The granting of preferential rates to some patrons was forbidden (1854), a Railroad and Canal Commission was set up (1873) to settle disputes between customer and carrier, and maximum rates were fixed (1888–1894). These rates gave none too generous a return on the capital sum, yet remained unaltered till 1913; but meanwhile employees became organized and demanded higher wages, coal and materials rose in price, and the gap between receipts and operating expenses steadily narrowed, as the following table shows:

OPERATING EXPENSES AS A PERCENTAGE OF RECEIPTS

1860	47	1920	97
1880	52	1929	78
1913	63	1937	80

The First World War therefore found the railroads nearing a crisis caused by overcapitalization, rising costs, and state control. "Home Rails" were falling in price on the Stock Exchange and the motor car was ceasing to be an unimportant curiosity. During the war the 26 main companies and 93 subsidiaries were run as a unit, at costs which rose till they swallowed virtually all the revenue. When peace came, the unscrambling of 119 eggs was neither desirable nor possible. Parliament, therefore, in 1921 merged them into four giant companies and divided the railroad map among them. A tribunal was set up to fix rates at levels that were expected to yield the same net revenue as was earned in 1913. Provision was made for cooperation between managers and employees in order to settle disputes and promote efficiency. Thus the railroads remained private property, but their public importance and their regional monopolies made their reorganization, regulation, and welfare matters of national concern.

That welfare proved to be elusive, for if King Coal was sick his iron horse was far from well. Receipts by 1929 were more than 50 per cent above those of 1913, but expenses had doubled and remained stubbornly at about 80 per cent of the income, against 63 per cent in 1913. Depression in the export industries reduced rail traffic, but far more serious was the loss of business to the bus, truck, and private car. In a land of short distances these newcomers could skim off the cream of the railroad's earning capacity. Railroad freight rates, regulated by the tribunal, were high on valuable goods but low on heavy cargoes and could not be reduced without considerable fuss. The road carriers were free to run what services they wished and charge what they pleased. They therefore offered lower rates to attract the valuable parcels, leaving the railroads to handle the coal, raw materials, and other less remunerative loads. Consequently the railroads were hard pressed even before depression came in 1929. In the lean years that followed they trimmed rates where they could, improved their services, secured tax relief, obtained permission to establish or acquire bus and truck services, and vigorously availed themselves of that permission. Like their American counterparts, they asked for a "square deal," persuaded parliament to regulate road vehicles plying for hire, and on the eve of World War II were conferring with the truck companies in a search for harmony over freight rates.

World War II cast a heavy burden on road and rail alike. In addition to meeting swollen military and civilian needs, they had to reverse the normal flow of much traffic. The eastern and southern ports, especially London, Southampton, and Hull, became bombers' targets. Cargoes which in peacetime would have gone there for distribution westward or northward now had to be received by western ports, such as Liverpool, and then be redistributed inland. Leased to the government and run under central control, the railroads showed great resourcefulness in meeting all demands, but virtually wore out their equipment in the process. In 1947 the Labor government sought power to nationalize all forms of inland transportation—water, rail, and road. The "dominant economic factor" was said to be "the need to plan road and rail services in a unified way, since otherwise the railways (which have heavy overheads and are obliged to take all types of traffic) cannot compete with the road services which are free to exploit only the most profitable lines." Another reason was the fact that the railroads, as private enterprises which were no longer profitable, could not hope to secure the funds needed for repair and renovation. The shades of the stagecoach drivers and the canal boatmen must be chuckling at the discomfiture of the enemy who drove them out of business.

Continental Railroads. The continent had its wagonways, and British success with steam traction led to the building of some railroads in most European countries by 1850. In this work British capital, equipment, and workers played a part. In 1841 Thomas Brassey took a small army of English and Irish "navvies" to build a line from Paris to Rouen. During the next two decades his men laid tracks in Belgium, Denmark, Australia, Canada, Argentina, and India. Railroads became a staple British export; but the system of private ownership did not export very readily. For this the lack of

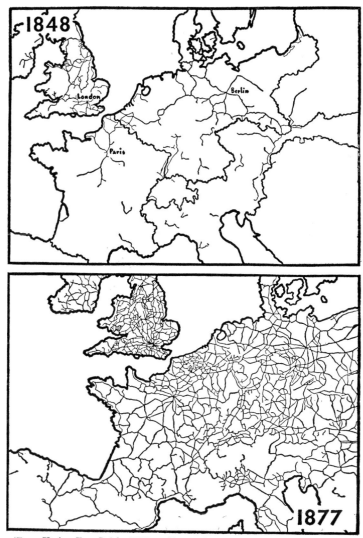

(From Varian Fry, *Bricks Without Mortar*, Foreign Policy Association, 1938.)

European Railroads

A comparison of these two maps helps to make clear several points: (1) the intense railroad building during the third quarter of the nineteenth century and the large outlay of capital and labor that was necessary; (2) the knitting together of the different parts of each country; (3) the creation of an international network of rails.

capital was partly responsible, but, in addition, "no continental state could treat railroads as individual commercial enterprises, because the problem of defending the country against invasion by land was always present" (Dunham).

Belgium. Belgium was the first state to plan a coordinated national system. She resolved in 1834 to turn the cockpit of western Europe into the railway hub by building two trunk lines, one from Ostend eastward toward Germany, the other at right angles to it from Antwerp to the French border. This railroad cross, completed by 1844, tapped trade with Prussia, Holland, France, and England. It was built with borrowed money and run by the state. Foreign railroad men praised the careful spending of the loans, the speed of construction, and the thorough study of engineering, fuel, and cost accountancy problems. Traffic was attracted by such low fares and freight rates that at first the lines did not earn enough to pay the interest bill. They did, however, help greatly in building up the foreign trade of Antwerp and contributed to the advance of factories, foundries, and mines in a country that was following more closely than any other in Britain's industrial footsteps.

In later years Belgium made two other innovations. (1) In 1872 she inaugurated a system of extremely cheap workmen's weekly tickets to induce urban wage earners to live in the rural areas. A journey of six miles to or from work cost only two cents, and any stalwart commuter who cared to travel sixty miles to his job could do so for five cents. In 1906 about a sixth of the working population used this opportunity to live where rent was low, fresh air less rare, and a plot of land available to provide a supplementary source of income. (2) In 1881 a system of light narrow-gauge railways was initiated to bring steam traction nearer to the farmer's gate. By 1910 about 3,000 miles had been laid; in 1927 they carried at least 4,000,000 tons of farm produce, fertilizers, coal, and other heavy materials, along with 50,000,000 passengers. Belgium had more railroad track per hundred square miles than any other country.

France. While British entrepreneurs and Belgian statesmen were busily building railroads to serve their small, crowded lands, France was debating. Her distances were great, most important places were a long way from Paris and from each other, and trains would pick up little local traffic on the way. Capital was scarce, costly, or shy, for investors preferred land or government bonds to company securities. The banks and the government could not find a satisfactory basis for cooperation in railroad building. As ministries changed frequently, policy changed abruptly, and meanwhile the bureaucrats who were in charge of inland transportation were skeptics, quick to see problems and difficulties but slow to find solutions. Not till 1842 did an official policy emerge, and meanwhile most of the few short lines built by private groups had come to grief.

The "Organic Law" of 1842 had two parts. (1) The railroad system was to consist of seven main lines radiating from Paris to the coasts or the frontier and two lines from Marseilles (one up the Rhone Valley and the other to the Bay of Biscay). (2) The system was to be a compromise between private and public enterprise. The central and local governments would provide the roadbed and lease it for a long period to some company which would then lay the rails, provide equipment, and operate the line. When the lease expired the whole property would pass to the state, but the company would receive compensation.

By 1850 most of the main lines were at work. During the next twenty years the length of track increased fivefold, and amalgamation reduced the number of companies from about thirty to six, which operated under leases granted for thirty or forty years. The system was still largely one of trunk roads with few branches. To encourage the laying of spur tracks the state agreed (1859) to guarantee the interest on funds spent on these lines, and extended the leases for a further ninety-nine years. This policy led to a doubling of the railroad mileage within ten years, but left some areas still unserved. During the seventies the state built lines to fill gaps, but the venture was a disastrous failure, partly because the roads were in regions of scanty traffic. In 1883, therefore, the railroad companies were offered a guarantee of enough money to pay interest *and* moderate dividends on the capital they had already spent as well as on any sunk in further construction. The money paid out to them by the state was not to be a gift, but a loan. They must pay interest on it, and repay it out of any excess profit they made.

Under such stimulation the railroad mileage doubled between 1880 and 1914. The Nord Company, which covered the northeastern industrial region, had sufficiently dense traffic to make ends meet without state aid. The P.-L.-M. (Paris-Lyons-Mediterranean) became an important international highway and soon paid its own way. But the other four companies drew heavily on the public purse until after 1900, and one of them, the Western, was so hope-lessly in debt that in 1908 the state took it over. The First World War, competition with motor vehicles, mounting costs of fuel and labor, and depression after 1929 plunged the lines back into financial difficulties. The state tried to help them to coordinate and modernize their services, divided some traffic between them and the road carriers, and shouldered some of their financial burdens, but all to little avail. By 1938 they owed the government far more (in depreciated francs) than the total of their capital issues. In that year they passed into the hands of one National Railway Company. As the state took 51 per cent of the stock of this company, the railroads thus became state owned and state controlled. It was recognized formally that an indispensable but unprofitable public utility must become a public burden.

Germany. Probably no area except Russia, Canada, and the American middle west benefited so much from railways as did Germany. The railroad bound her together economically and politically. It also knit her tightly into the fabric of continental Europe.

The early lines were short. The first one, built in 1835 from Nuremberg to Furth, was only 3½ miles long, and most of its immediate successors provided a suburban or interurban service or were portages from one waterway to another. In 1850, 15 lines were only 20 miles long or less. But by that date about 3,600 miles were at work, and the larger pattern was taking shape. Interstate junctions had been made, thus facilitating that internal free trade which had been inaugurated by the formation of the *Zollverein* (1834). Frederick List aptly described the railroads and the *Zollverein* as Siamese twins. Some lines linked Cologne with French and Belgian railroads; others ran toward Austria and Hungary. The first of many international agreements had been reached in 1846, providing for a standard width of track. Since Vienna was throwing out railroads in all directions, only fifty miles were lacking in 1850 to complete an iron road from Trieste on the Adriatic to the Baltic. Some lines had been built privately, others by state governments. Prussia in 1838 anounced its willingness to encourage private construction by buying bonds, guaranteeing payment of interest, and giving lines a monopoly for thirty years of the territory they were built to serve. In 1848, however, military considerations led the state to start laying a line from Berlin to the Russian border.

German engineers followed cheap American rather than costly British methods of construction and operation. They spent little

money on moving earth to make level roadbeds, took hills and valleys as they came, and laid only single tracks. Hence they built and
equipped the railroads for about a third of the British cost. They
used very plain passenger coaches, ran no expresses, put first to
fourth classes behind the same engine, added freight cars, and
stopped at all stations. Their trains were scheduled to go 11 to 25
miles an hour, but Von Moltke reported that "when the wind op-
poses the direction of motion, it delays it." Yet in Germany, as in
France, even this service had far-reaching effects in tying town and
country together, fostering interregional exchange of goods, stimulating industry, and encouraging commercial farming.

When the Empire was founded (1871) Bismarck tried to weld
the 12,000 miles of track, owned by about 70 state governments or
private companies, into one imperial system. He failed, and had to
be content with coordination through the Imperial Railway Office.
In Prussia he bought the private lines, built more, and laid light railways to help the Junkers. As Bavaria and other states pursued similar policies, the total mileage reached 40,000 by 1914. The opening
of the St. Gotthard tunnel in 1882 gave an outlet on the Mediterranean, and Genoa became almost a German port. As Russian lines
came westward, the eastward flow of German goods rose, supplying Russian factories and markets with German machines and
wares. When the railroad from Vienna through Belgrade to Constantinople was completed in 1888, the Balkans assumed a new
importance in the eyes of German businessmen and diplomats.
Meanwhile the railroads served the needs of the expanding trade
with Austria-Hungary, France, the Low Countries, and Britain.

Public ownership allowed Germany to fit her railroads into her
commercial as well as her military policy. Special encouragement
was given to industries and districts which sought foreign markets,
by lowering rates on exported commodities or on imported raw materials. Lorraine ore went to Ruhr coke at freight rates which
"largely cancelled the 150 miles of distance that lay between"
(Bowman). The railroads were not, however, allowed to be milch
kine, except for the waterways; they were run to yield a surplus,
and in 1911 had $90,000,000 left over after meeting working and
capital costs.

In 1919 the railroads were transferred from the states to the
Reich. They shared the general dislocation of the post-war years.
Currency inflation wiped out the debt incurred for their construc-

tion, and though their renovation was costly they secured modern equipment. By 1924 they were recovering their old efficiency and were regarded as a source from which reparations payments of about $200,000,000 a year could be collected under the Dawes Plan (1924). But the car, truck, and airplane could not be restrained, and the railroads estimated in 1929 that they were losing traffic worth $100,000,000 a year to their new rivals. When depression came in 1929 their freight earnings were cut in half, and recovery was slow. The Nazis, enthusiastic for motor transportation, poured vast sums of money into super-highways and aviation facilities but made no serious attempt to improve the railroads until 1939, when a four-year plan was inaugurated for renovating rolling stock. War taxed the railroads to the full, and at the end damaged them so severely that transportation was brought almost to a standstill. That damage impeded the restoration of coal production, the movement of ore, and the revival of the highly industrialized western regions.

Russia. To Russia railroads brought easier and quicker transport inside the country and an effective penetration of Siberia. The Crimean War (1854–1856) demonstrated the need for the former, and the length of track rose from 850 miles in 1855 to 15,000 miles in 1882. The early lines were built and operated by companies which were aided by state guarantees of interest or purchase of their bonds. This plan proved unsatisfactory, and in 1881 the state decided to embark on government ownership. Sergius Witte, who had advanced from the rank of stationmaster to be minister of communications (1888) and then minister of finance (1892–1903), reveled in buying up old lines and building new ones. Loans were floated at home and abroad, the mileage rose to 47,000 in 1914, and a third of the national debt was incurred for railroads.

Witte's efforts brought many more farmers into contact with domestic and foreign markets, but his most spectacular achievement was the building of the Trans-Siberian line (1891–1905). Siberia was virtually useless till the railroad reached it, and few people went there of their own will. Though built mainly for military reasons, the line had great economic value as a key to open the door on landlocked agricultural, forest, and mineral resources. Between 1893 and 1913 over 5,000,000 settlers crossed the Urals, and in the peak year (1908) the number of emigrants (760,000) equaled that entering the United States. Soon the westbound trains began to carry loads of grain and butter; branch lines went north to the forests, and south to Turkestan, where irrigation turned dry steppes into cotton fields.

War in 1914 quickly revealed the inadequacies of the Russian railroads. The network was unevenly spread, dense on the western front and the industrial areas of Poland and Moscow, but thin elsewhere. Rolling stock was insufficient in quality or quantity, tracks were flimsy, repair shops and engines were often equipped with German tools or parts. The semi-developed and lopsided system broke down, and its western lines were broken off by the loss of territory stretching from Finland to Poland. Many wagons and two-thirds of the engines were out of service in 1921.

An enormous task of reconstruction therefore confronted the Bolshevik rulers. By 1928 it had been almost accomplished, and from that point onward each Five-Year Plan earmarked about a sixth of the new capital investment for expansion or improvement of transportation. By 1938 the mileage inside Russia's inter-war boundaries had been increased from 36,000 to 55,000, largely by building lines in the north, Siberia, and central Asia. The conversion of the Trans-Siberian into a double track by 1932 facilitated the industrial expansion which took place east of the Urals during the thirties. Equipment was improved by using heavier rails, stronger locomotives, and larger freight cars. The emphasis was on freight services, especially heavy freight. In 1938 about 80 per cent of the goods hauled was minerals, lumber, and grain. Since Russia has no good highways and only mediocre waterways, the railroads had to bear the whole traffic burden. Hers were the only railways in the world to be expanding in mileage and in the volume of business in the two decades before 1939.

THE AUTOMOBILE AND THE AIRPLANE

Although Germans and Frenchmen contributed most to the development of the automobile engine before 1900, the motor vehicle influenced European civilian life less and more slowly than it did that of America. Production has never exceeded a tenth of America's highest annual output, and even in Great Britain, the most motorized country, there was only one gasoline vehicle to every seventeen persons in 1937, against one to every four in the United States. (In terms of cars per square mile of country or per mile of road the British density was much higher than the American.) Production was on a smaller scale than in Detroit, and prices were therefore higher, as were taxes and the price of gasoline. Middle-class and wage earners' incomes were lower; people traveled to work and went on holidays by cheap train, streetcar, bus, or bicycle; and old residential areas lacked room for garages. Nevertheless, the number of private car owners rose during the twenties and doubled during the thirties in France and England alike. Meanwhile, the bus and truck swarmed everywhere, subtracting traffic from the railroads but also adding greatly to the sum total of movement.

The automobile created large new fields of investment and employment; made new demands for steel, alloys, and other materials; produced new types of service occupations; revolutionized the old industry of roadmaking; and called for the expenditure of vast sums on highways. It made more of the population suburban or rural, changed the character of leisure and holidays, and gave more work to hospitals, insurance companies, and the police force. Finally, it forced governments to the conclusion that free competition between truck or bus operators, as well as between them and the regulated or state-owned railroads, was harmful, uneconomical, and dangerous. During the thirties most states therefore imposed licensing and other restrictions on commercial vehicles and tried to coordinate road and rail services.

Commercial aviation began when the First World War ended. Two companies started regular air services between London and Paris in 1919. Germany's central position and the ban imposed by the peace treaty on her possession of military planes led her to develop civilian lines. The country was soon covered with routes, and the pioneer companies were fused into the *Luft Hansa*. From the Tempelhof Airport near Berlin planes left for nearly every European capital. Paris was almost as active, with Le Bourget as its hub. England and Holland were too small for domestic services, and their developments had to be international or imperial. Like France they planned lines to remote points where their flag flew. France established quick contact with her North African empire, Syria, and Indo-China; Holland in 1930 began a service to her East Indies; Britain began flights to India (1929) and later to Singapore, Hong Kong, Australia, and the Cape.

The airplane brought speed impossible on land or sea, and traversed areas that could not be economically crossed by railroads. But it lifted only a relatively small paying load, its fuel and operating bills were large, and its depreciation costs were heavy. In

1927 the *Luft Hansa* found that of every 100 marks spent, 30 went to meet depreciation, 20 were absorbed in maintenance and repairs, and 14 were spent for fuel. These costs have not been materially reduced since the twenties, and meanwhile the growth in the number and size of planes has necessitated very large expenditures on airports, little of which is borne by those who use them. Hence commercial aviation has depended on its ability to attract the cream of the cream of traffic—small, valuable, or perishable goods that can afford to pay heavy freights, or passengers to whom time is more important than money. It must supplement its earnings by direct government subsidies or by indirect subventions in the form of ground facilities and substantial mail contracts.

COMMUNICATION

By 1700 state postal services were becoming common, but the modern system is largely the product of steam transportation and the practice of paying postage in advance. When Rowland Hill in 1837 analyzed postal costs, charges varied with the number of sheets of paper, the weight, and the distance to be covered. He found that distance made little difference in the cost of delivery; the heaviest expenses were incurred in weighing the letter, ascertaining the number of sheets, and collecting the money from the recipient. He therefore urged that all letters weighing a half-ounce or less be carried throughout the country for a penny (two cents), and that postage be paid in advance through the purchase of stamps or stamped envelopes. Penny post was inaugurated in 1840, the envelope appeared, and stamp collecting was born. Other postal facilities followed; other countries adopted similar methods. In 1875 the Universal Postal Union was established to smooth the passage of mail across frontiers.

Still quicker communication came with the electric telegraph, used first by the railroads but soon made available to newspapers and the general public and in most countries taken over or inaugurated by the state as part of its postal system. The first British telegraph company was formed in 1846. In 1851 its submarine cable to Calais forged a link with wires that soon stretched to Moscow and the Mediterranean. By 1865 the ocean cables went as far as Calcutta, in 1866 they crossed the Atlantic, and in 1871 they reached Australia. These wires over land and under water carried messages and news halfway round the world in a few minutes. They enabled men to buy or sell in what became, for stocks and the great staples capable of being graded, a world market.

Bell's transmission of the human voice over a wire (1876) brought the telephone into being, but twenty years elapsed before it won much favor in America or Europe. Technical improvements were needed to carry the voice more than a short distance. Governments which owned telegraph systems did not welcome a rival form of communication if it was privately owned. In Germany the telephone was adopted by the state and vigorously developed; but in Britain a long wrangle between the Post Office and the company which operated the service ended only with the government's purchase of the system in 1911.

Wireless telegraphy quickly found favor after the first dots and dashes went through the air across the English Channel in 1899 and across the Atlantic in 1901. Warships and the larger merchant vessels soon learned the value of the new ears and tongue, a lesson driven home in three letters—S O S—sent out by the "unsinkable" but sinking mammoth liner *Titanic* over the North Atlantic in 1912 and picked up by wireless-equipped vessels in the vicinity. Ability to communicate between shore and distant ship gave ocean communication something of the same flexibility that had come to transportation with the automobile. Wireless telephony—radio—made its public bow in 1920 but proved to be of far less economic significance to Europe than to North America. The broadcasting services grew up (or soon became) government systems, were maintained by the license fees of listeners, and did not "sell" time for advertising purposes. Each enjoyed a monopoly inside its national boundaries. Their function was to send forth entertainment, news, information, propaganda, appeals, and commands. They discharged that function with varied and sometimes terrifying competence.

SHIPS AND SHIPPING

The nineteenth century witnessed the triumph of the metal steamship over a greatly improved wooden sailing ship. It was more than a mere transfer of carrying business from one type of vessel to another; in addition it made possible such an increase in the mobility of people and goods as would never have been possible under sail.

Europe's merchant marine in 1800 consisted of a few big East Indiamen of 500 to more than 1,000 tons, which made the 10,000-mile journey to the Far East; a considerable number of full-rigged "ships" or barques, ranging from 400 tons down to about 150, which sailed the North Atlantic, went to Africa, and penetrated to the Levant or Baltic ports; and a swarm of smaller craft, running in size down to 30 tons or even less, which carried cargoes along the coasts or made short journeys across narrow seas. The average tonnage of the vessels entering British ports from overseas in 1816 was about 125 tons apiece with an average crew of 10 men; the figures for coastal craft were 80 tons and 5 men. In 1830 only 6 per cent of France's merchant ships were larger than 200 tons. Few ships were 200 feet long; the largest liner today is more than 1,000 feet in length.

The speed of ships depended partly on their design but more on wind and weather. So long as men had to rely on sails, the date of journey's end was uncertain. Given good weather, a vessel could cross from New York to Liverpool in thirty days and do the return trip in forty, in spite of the hostile winds and currents of the westward passage. But storms could delay her departure from port, drive her off her course, or wreck her. She might be becalmed in mid-ocean for days, a nerve-racking experience for passengers and a gloomy one for any captain who owned his ship, since every idle flap of the sails against the mast seemed like a dollar dropping out of his pocket. Winter journeys were avoided whenever possible, and the Baltic was closed by ice for about four months each year. If to climatic impediments we add such other items as the time required for overhauling and repairing the vessel and the primitive facilities for unloading or loading cargo, we can understand why the best "regular traders" plying the North Atlantic between New York and Liverpool did only two round trips a year and spent more time immobile than in motion.

The art of navigation, especially on ocean journeys, had improved considerably since 1600. The telescope was perfected by 1610, map making became more skillful, and coastal routes or approaches to port were marked by buoys and lighthouses. The sextant, invented in 1731, measured latitude more accurately than did the astrolabe. A chronometer (invented in 1772) and improved methods of lunar observation about the same time helped mariners to ascertain their longitude. By that time the way to healthier conditions aboard ship was being charted. During his long voyage to the Pacific (1769–1770), Captain Cook discovered that by keeping his ships clean and serving lime juice to his crew he reduced greatly the appalling toll of sickness and death and was virtually free from scurvy, a disease which killed more men on battleships than were lost in battle. By 1800 the British and French navies were giving some thought to the use of soap, brushes, hospitals, and doctors; lime juice—or rather vitamin C—defeated scurvy. But merchant ships were slow to follow the naval example.

Some maritime risks did not disappear until after 1800. Privateering played a large part in war at sea, especially in the Anglo-French conflicts which occupied 66 of the 127 years between 1689 and 1815. Each belligerent authorized private merchantmen to arm themselves and seize enemy ships, as, of course, did the regular warships. Between 1692 and 1697 the French took over 4,000 English and Dutch prizes. A fifth of the ships registered in Britain in 1811 had been acquired as prizes. During the War of 1812 American privateers captured about 1,300 British vessels, while the British were prevented from making an equal haul only by the fact that they had bottled up American merchantmen in harbor. Peace in 1815 brought an end to this long story of commerce-destroying, and the safety of some seas was further strengthened by extirpating nests of pirates in the Caribbean in 1816 and ending the menace of the Barbary pirates a little later.

When peace came the two largest merchant marines were those of Great Britain (with about 2,000,000 tons in 20,000 ships) and the United States (with 1,200,000 tons). France, Holland, and the other maritime states lagged far behind. The American merchant marine had continued after 1783 the expansion of colonial days. Abundant cheap timber gave it a great advantage—said to be as much as 40 per cent—over its rivals in building ships, and in 1793, when Britain joined the war against France, the United States became the only important neutral carrier in a world at war. Its merchant fleet worked overtime and almost trebled in size between 1793 and 1807; but after 1807 this advance was checked by the policies of embargo, non-importation, and non-intercourse with one or both of the main belligerents. The War of 1812 shut most of the ships up in port.

Peace released them in early 1815, but the big war ended a few months later and there were no more profits of neutrality for a hundred years. Instead a healthier traffic developed across the North Atlantic with cotton, breadstuffs, tobacco, and other staples flowing eastward and swarms of emigrants riding westward on vessels laden with manufactured goods. In 1818 a group of New York merchant-shipowners inaugurated a line of *packet* ships, which left New York and Liverpool on a fixed day each month all the year round. This innovation was quickly copied and larger vessels were built. By 1840, packets of 1,000 tons were crossing eastward in three weeks and westward in five, charging rates which were at least a third lower than those of 1820. But the advantage derived from cheap timber was rapidly diminishing as America's eastern forests disappeared, and ocean shipping became more competitive as reciprocal treaties removed some of the restrictions imposed by Navigation Laws. In that competition British and German vessels secured an increasing share of the traffic to or from American ports.

In the forties the American shipbuilder produced the *clipper*, the fastest and most beautiful sailing craft ever launched. It was five to six times as long as it was broad, its shape was streamlined, and it cut through the waves instead of bumping into them. The timing of this innovation was most fortunate, for it coincided with the emergence of demands for speed on long routes. Gold seekers were willing to pay high fares for a quick journey to the new El Dorado in California or Australia. Chinese ports had been opened to foreigners, and the first cargo of each season's tea crop delivered in London always fetched the best price. In the Crimean War France and Britain needed the speediest contact with that distant war zone. Hence the fifties wanted speed, and the clipper supplied it.

The Steamship. Into this world of sail the steam-driven vessel made its modest entry at the beginning of the nineteenth century. From about 1770 onward, men in France, Scotland, and America experimented with engines afloat. Fulton gathered up their ideas and some of their devices and bought a Watt engine. In 1807 inhabitants of the Hudson Valley saw "the Devil on the way to Albany in a saw-mill" as the *Clermont* traveled 150 miles upstream in 32 hours. In Scotland, Bell built the *Comet* (1811) and ran it for eight years between Glasgow and a port twenty-five miles away.

During the next ten years many vessels were put to work on the sheltered waters of lake, river, canal, or inlet; but in addition coastal journeys were undertaken, and steam ferries braved open seas between Wales and Ireland or between Dover and Calais. Experience quickly revealed the technical problems that must be solved, as boilers burst for lack of safety valves or the weight of the power plant broke the back of the wooden hull. It also showed the two basic economic problems: (1) A vessel which propelled itself was more costly to build and operate than was a sailing ship. (2) Its boiler, engine, water tanks, fuel, and the machinery for turning the paddle wheels occupied so much space that there was little left for passengers and cargo, especially on a long journey.

The technical problems were solved fairly quickly, the economic ones by a long series of improvements which enabled the steamship to challenge its rival in one field after another. Against its liabilities it could soon place some valuable assets, especially "celerity, certainty, and safety." Even when it was slow it was sure. Doldrums held no terrors for it. It was not helpless in a storm, need not go out of the way in search of favorable winds, and could enter or leave port under its own power. Hence it did more round trips in a year than a sailing ship, delivered its cargo on time, and was less liable to shipwreck. These advantages were realized during the twenties in coastal traffic and in short sea journeys between British and western or northern European ports. In the thirties the lines grew longer and thicker. The number of British steamships more than doubled, and continental shipowners began to acquire steam vessels. France and England established steam mail services to Egypt, from which point a "dromedary post" carried the mail across the desert to Suez at the top of the Red Sea, where it was picked up by steamers which carried it to India and then to China.

By 1840 the North Atlantic had also been opened up to the steamship. The problem there was to find enough room in the ship for the fuel that would be consumed on a journey of 3,000 miles. Lardner, the leading transportation expert of the period, declared that no ship would ever be able to carry enough coal. He therefore "had no hesitation in saying" that a non-stop run from Liverpool to New York was "perfectly chimerical, and they might as well talk of making a voyage from New York to the moon." The chimerical was, however, accomplished. In 1833 the *Royal William* made the shorter crossing from Nova Scotia to England, using steam all the way. In 1838 the *Sirius* and the *Great Western* steamed the westward passage from Liverpool to New York in 16½ and 13½ days respectively, or about half the time usually taken by the best packets.

On its return journey the *Sirius* overhauled a becalmed packet, took off the mail, and was soon out of sight. This episode convinced Samuel Cunard, a passenger on the packet, that Atlantic mail ought to be carried by steamers, and in 1839 he secured from the British government a contract to carry mails fortnightly between Liverpool, Halifax, and Boston, receiving a fixed annual sum that was virtually a subsidy. The first Cunarder left Liverpool on July 4, 1840, and reached Boston in seventeen days. If the ship had ended instead of begun its journey on July 4, Boston could scarcely have staged a greater celebration. Flags flew, toasts were drunk, Cunard received a silver vase, and Daniel Webster made a speech. Rapidly the service improved. Cunard began to announce dates of arrival as well as of departure and described himself as operator of an "ocean railway" which had replaced the "maddening irregularity insepara-ble from the days of sail" with almost clocklike regularity and speed. Unlike his American rival, Collins, his ships always reached their destination.

By 1850, therefore, the steamship had established itself firmly as the best vehicle for carrying passengers and mail. It was superseding "the use of sailing vessels for trading purposes also, where the distance to be accomplished is not very great [e.g., from Britain to Hamburg], and where the bulk of the goods to be conveyed is not considerable in proportion to their value" (Porter, 1850). But it still had far to go before it displaced sail. In 1849 it accounted for only about one-sixteenth of the tonnage on the British registry and for a ninth of the entries from foreign ports. For long journeys on routes devoid as yet of coaling stations and for the carriage of cheap, heavy cargoes steam was not yet ready. The world had probably 10,000,000 net tons of sailing ships, but only 750,000 of steamers, of which nearly 500,000 were on the rivers and lakes of North America.

The next sixty years saw European steam registration expand as follows:

Year	Europe, Net Tons	United Kingdom, Net Tons	Germany, Net Tons
1850	186,000	168,000	. . . . . .
1870	1,483,000	1,113,000	82,000
1890	7,816,000	5,043,000	724,000
1910	19,045,000	10,443,000	2,257,000

This growth was accompanied, and made possible, by important improvements in hulls, driving methods, engines, and fuel. The first two of these came when Brunel in 1839 planned a big iron steamer, driven by a propeller in place of the ungainly paddle wheel. An iron hull did not leak or become waterlogged, and its weight was little more than half that of a wooden vessel of equal capacity. Wooden ships could not safely exceed 300 feet in length, but the only limits to the size of an iron steamer were the strength of the engine, the amount of cargo available, and the ability of ports to accommodate the vessel. Steel proved an even better material than iron and began to be used for ocean-going ships in 1879. The average British steamship increased at least tenfold in size between 1850 and 1914.

The third improvement came when compound engines, with more than one cylinder, became efficient about 1860. Steamers equipped with them cut fuel bills in half, got more miles per ton of coal, had more spare space, and could compete with the sailing ship on long journeys to the Orient or to the lands of the east and southwest Pacific. On shorter runs the speed and size of vessels could be increased, and the race across the North Atlantic entered a new phase when the *Alaska* made the passage in less than a week in 1882. The turbine, introduced about 1900, required less steam, weighed less, occupied less room, but spun the propellers more quickly with less vibration. It therefore made possible the movement of destroyers at more than thirty knots and of giant liners at speeds which eventually crept up to thirty knots.

The fourth improvement came when oil began to be used as fuel by ocean vessels in 1904 and later was exploded in Diesel engines. A ton of burned oil produced nearly 50 per cent more steam than did a ton of coal yet took up 12 per cent less space. It was easily pumped aboard and could be stored anywhere. As it dispensed with an army of stokers, the labor cost of feeding the fires was greatly reduced. Much space was released for passengers or cargo, while the dirt, discomfort, and laundry bills of coaling days were eliminated. By 1914, 4 per cent of the world's merchant tonnage was burning oil; in 1939 the figure was 30. Meanwhile the Diesel engine, invented in 1903 by a German engineer, became highly satisfactory after 1920 for marine work. It was much smaller and lighter than a steam unit of equal power and needed no boiler, water tanks, or funnels. A ton of exploded oil gave as much power as did four tons of coal or nearly three tons of oil burned in a boiler furnace. It was therefore an efficient power unit and a great space saver. By 1938 22 per cent of the world's tonnage consisted of ships which put M.V. (motor vessel) instead of S.S. in front of their names.

All these improvements increased the superiority of steam over sail. The steamer's capacity for work eventually became four times that of a sailing vessel of the same tonnage. While the difficulties of construction and of handling sails limited the size of an iron or steel-hulled sailing ship to 5,000 tons, a steamship could go far beyond that size. Hence a 10,000-ton steamer "making eight round voyages a year in the North Atlantic trade will do in a year the work of at least a dozen sailing vessels of the largest type formerly employed in that trade" (Fayle). Certainty of movement and safety in all weathers increased; it became unusual for a ship to be late in reaching port and very unusual for it to be lost.

The sailing ship's capacity to resist attack was weakened by the exhaustion of those supplies of cheap ship timber which had been the basis of American shipping success, and by the opening of the Suez Canal in 1869. The Canal cut the distance from London to the Orient by at least 3,000 miles. Steamers went through it under their own power, but a windjammer would have to be towed through at great expense and would then find navigation of the Red Sea difficult for lack of wind. The struggle between steam and sail could therefore have only one result. It was fairly slow in coming, especially on long journeys to fetch Australian wool or wheat, Chile nitrates, or other cheap goods from remote places. But in 1893 the world's steam tonnage exceeded that under sail, a position reached in British shipping by 1883. In 1914 only 8 per cent of the world's shipping was driven by wind, and today one may travel all the oceans without seeing a vessel moving under a spread of canvas.

Types of Shipping. In 1914 the world had over 24,000 steamships engaged in coastal or overseas traffic. In size they were distributed as follows:

Over 10,000 gross tons	290
5,000–10,000 gross tons	1,770
2,000–5,000 gross tons	5,880
100–2,000 gross tons	16,500

The fast floating palaces of the North Atlantic route had already passed the 50,000-ton mark. They climbed up to more than 70,000 tons and a speed of about 30 knots in the 1930's. In spite of their wide renown they did only a very tiny fraction of the world's shipping work, for they carried little cargo, and very few harbors could give them berths. Their operation was made possible only by the large volume of passenger traffic on their route, the number of round trips that could be made in a year, the ability of rich Americans and Europeans to pay high fares, and government subsidies or well-paid mail contracts. The bulk of the passenger carriage on the North Atlantic and the whole of it on other oceans was done by vessels of much more modest bulk and speed. These medium-sized ships, usually 10,000 to 20,000 tons in size, steamed only 350 to 450 miles a day. They crossed the North Atlantic in seven or eight days or went from London to Australia in about five weeks, carrying at most 600 passengers and a large amount of miscellaneous cargo. Any attempt to shorten their journey would involve a much more than proportionate increase in the fuel bill.

Below these large and middle-sized vessels, numbering less than 300 in 1914, came a motley array of cargo and passenger ships or of freighters, moving at eight to fourteen knots and placing more emphasis on regularity, certainty, cheap operation, and low charges than on speed. Some of them, like their larger sisters, were liners; they belonged to a company which owned a long enough "line" of vessels to provide a regular service over a fixed route. Others were "tramps," free lances of the oceans, willing to go anywhere to fetch or carry almost any kind of cargo for the person who chartered them. Professor Kirkaldy has traced a chapter in the roving life of a tramp which left England in 1910, laden with rails and general cargo for western Australia. There she picked up lumber for Melbourne, where she loaded combine-harvesters for the Argentine. In Buenos Aires she took grain aboard for Mauritius and Calcutta, and in the latter port was filled with jute for Boston and New York. From New York she carried a cargo of American general merchandise to Australia, where the hold was filled with lead, wool, and wheat for England. When the ship reached London it had traveled 72,000 miles in 17 months, and put into port 31 times in 6 continents.

The typical tramp was about 2,500 gross tons. It had large cargo capacity, a speed rarely greater than eight knots, and hence a low fuel consumption—sometimes as low as one ton for every six miles. As such ships improved in efficiency they drove the sailing vessel out of one trade after another. Competition and economical operation reduced their freight rates by nearly half between 1885 and 1904, and in 1913 they comprised 60 per cent of the world's steam tonnage.

The oil tanker and the refrigerated vessel are the chief examples of ships built to carry a special cargo. The demand for gasoline and oil fuel grew so rapidly after 1900 that by 1938 a sixth of the world's tonnage consisted of tank steamers. The carriage of refrigerated cargo for long journeys across the equator became feasible when in 1880 a consignment of frozen Australian meat reached London. New Zealand followed with a shipload in 1882, and the Argentine in 1883. The first sale of New Zealand meat in London was fittingly described by the *Times* as "a prodigious fact," for refrigeration afloat opened a new world of possibilities to the southern producer, the European consumer, the ocean traveler, and the shipowner. As engineers solved the problems surrounding chilling and freezing, and as southerners became able to send out steady streams of good well-graded produce, Europe became a ready customer. By 1894 the cost of killing, freezing, and delivering New Zealand lamb in London was only four cents a pound. Liners turned part of their space into cool chambers, and special ships were built capable of carrying 150,000 carcasses. To the carriage of meat was gradually added that of dairy produce and fresh fruits. The southern hemisphere benefited most from this new contact with the great food markets of Europe; but the livestock, dairy, and fruit producers of North America and the Mediterranean lands also found those markets were now more accessible.

Interoceanic Canals. The Suez Canal, dug by De Lesseps and a French company, was opened in 1869. At first it was shallow, narrow, and unprofitable; a boat spent three days passing through it. But by 1880 the traffic and the profits were rising, and improvements since that date have made it possible for vessels of 20,000 tons or more to traverse it in about fifteen hours. The Canal reduced the distance between London and Bombay from 10,700 miles to 6,300; Hong Kong came 3,400 miles nearer to the Thames, and Yokohama 3,000 miles. The Mediterranean awoke to a new day, soon becoming the second most important ocean route. In 1913 about 5,500 ships passed through the canal, of which two-thirds were British. In 1938 the number was only a little greater, 6,200 in all, but the tonnage had grown nearly three-fourths. Half of it was British, and one-eighth consisted of Italian vessels bound to or from Mussolini's newly conquered Abyssinia.

When Suez began to pay dividends, De Lesseps and a group of French capitalists tried to repeat their success at Panama. In six years (1883–1889) the company spent $350,000,000 and then went bankrupt, victim of graft, a financial rake's progress, and the mosquito. Where it failed, the United States government, aided by Sir

Ronald Ross' discovery that mosquitoes spread malaria, succeeded and the Panama Canal was opened in 1914. Its chief effect was to shorten journeys between the two coasts of the Americas and to bring the west coast nearer to Europe. But it also brought that coast, along with New Zealand, Japan, and the eastern half of Australia, much nearer to New York than to London. The Canal therefore gave the American exporter an advantage over his British and German rivals in Pacific markets. The First World War presented him with an immediate chance to exploit that advantage. When peace came some ocean routes were changed. Ships which went from Europe via Suez to New Zealand and the Orient now returned home via Panama instead of through Suez or round Cape Horn. Rubber and tin from Malaya came that way to America, the world's greatest customer for these commodities. In return, cotton, fertilizers, and scrap iron went westward through the Canal to Japan. In 1939 two-thirds of the tonnage using the Canal was foreign —an indication of the extent to which trade routes had been affected.

Ports. Since the end of every sea voyage was a harbor, the growth in the size of vessels and volume of traffic called for drastic improvement in port facilities. Most of Europe's great ports had grown up as far upstream as could be reached by a seagoing vessel at high tide. Ships had to move carefully amid sand or mud banks and shallows, watching tides and currents and often requiring two or three tides to reach anchorage. London had an intricate navigation at the mouth of the Thames, the road to Amsterdam was treacherous and large vessels could not cross the bar into harbor, and at Liverpool the tide rose and fell thirty feet. Vessels drawing four feet of water needed a pilot for the seventy miles of estuary leading to Hamburg and large ones had to stop sixty miles downstream.

Since few ports had quays in the eighteenth century, ships dropped anchor or were tied to piles in midstream. Cargoes were unloaded into barges or small boats for transfer to shore. Harbors were therefore crowded, repeated handlings cost time and money, customs procedures were slow, and cargo landed on the bank or in open sheds was fair game for thieves who thronged the ports, ready to steal anything from a bag of coffee to an anchor. Meanwhile the ship lay idle, earning nothing. The most strenuous efforts were needed to get an ocean-going ship out of a terminal port in less than a month from the date of her arrival.

Port improvements called for three steps: the deepening of the channel, the provision of wharves, and the erection of warehouses. The steam dredge, first built in 1824, made the first possible and also led to the cutting of new "ship canals" from the sea to Amsterdam (1825), to Rotterdam (1872), and to Manchester (1894). In 1715 Liverpool made a wet dock, an artificial basin which boats could

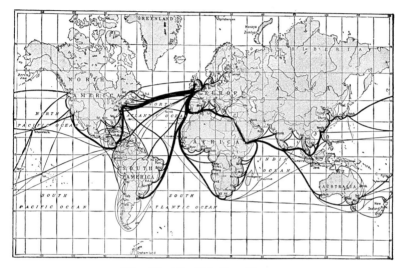

The World's Shipping Routes

The thickness of the lines is proportionate to the tonnage. (From Bowman's *The New World*, copyright, 1928, by World Book Company, Yonkers-on-Hudson, New York.)

enter at high tide; the entrance gates were then closed to keep the water in and the ship afloat. This device was widely adopted where the water level varied greatly with the tide, or where more wharf space was needed than was offered along the river bank, e.g., in London. Where conditions were favorable, open wharves or piers were constructed. In some places, especially Liverpool, these improvements were undertaken by an energetic municipal authority, but some political units lacked the power, capital, or enthusiasm, and the work was done by private dock and warehouse companies, as for instance in London, or, in the case of Southampton, by a railroad which served the district. Eventually the costly and complicated task had to be undertaken by legally created public bodies. The competition between rival dock companies and the lack of coordination on the Thames drove parliament in 1909 to establish a public trust—the Port of London Authority—which took charge of seventy miles of river, thirty-six miles of quays, and three thousand acres of land and water devoted to docks. By such provisions the "turnaround" time ships spent in port was greatly reduced, and their cargoes were more quickly deposited in storage or dispatched to their inland destination.

Shipping During and Between the Two Wars. In 1914 the world had about 43,000,000 gross tons of steamships engaged in coastal and overseas trade. Of these,

> 19,000,000, or 42 per cent, were British;
> 5,000,000, or 12 per cent, were German;
> 11,000,000, or 26 per cent, were owned by the rest of Europe.

Europe thus possessed 80 per cent of the total. Britain's preeminence in shipping was due to her priority in steamship building, her large imports of food and raw materials, great exports of coal and manufactured wares, widespread imperial and foreign banking and commercial connections, and also to the readiness with which capital had been obtained for the merchant marine. The victory over the American sailing ship had scarcely been completed when a new challenger appeared. In 1871 Germany had only 80,000 tons of steamers and 900,000 of sailing ships; but when she swung into her stride as manufacturer and exporter the expansion of her merchant marine became rapid. The government gave generous mail subsidies, foreign-built ships or shipbuilding materials were admitted duty free, and orders for battleships stimulated the growth of shipyards. Cheap iron and steel, low wages, and the rising transatlantic traffic in emigrants from central and eastern Europe also helped. By 1914 the German steam fleet of 5,000,000 tons seemed to be everywhere: the *Vaterland* (60,000 tons) was the largest floating hotel on the North Atlantic, liners ran to most continents, and German tramps were loading nitrates in Chile, phosphates in Oceania, and scrap tin or lumber in Tasmania.

During World War I over 12,000,000 tons of merchant shipping—nearly 8,000,000 of them British—were sunk, including many of the best and most modern. Such frantic efforts were made to repair this damage by building new ships that when the war ended the world's tonnage was larger than in 1914, many unfinished vessels were on the stocks, and the productive capacity of the shipbuilding industry had been vastly expanded. In the peace settlement Germany was deprived of virtually all her ocean-going ships, but she soon set to work to replace them with modern vessels. The United States, which in 1914 had only 1,000,000 tons of ships registered for foreign trade, emerged with 11,000,000 in 1920. Japan, Norway, Italy, Holland, France, and every other land—except Britain—expanded its merchant fleet at least twofold, sometimes with the aid of direct or hidden subsidies. By 1929, therefore, the world's fleet had risen from 43,000,000 tons (1914) to 68,000,000, an increase of 60 per cent. The new ships, somewhat larger and faster, were more efficient than their predecessors, and improved facilities had reduced their turnabout time. Hence the carrying capacity per ton increased alongside the growth in the number of tons.

If this growth had been accompanied by a comparable expansion in trade, all might have been well. In general, however, the volume of goods and persons seeking ocean transportation was no larger in 1929 than in 1913. Tariff obstacles and economic nationalism frowned on imports, and the stream of emigration was greatly reduced by the quota restrictions of the United States, the growing reluctance of other countries to take all comers, the exhaustion of free or cheap land in the New World, and the higher fares. Competition therefore became fierce for the sluggish volume of shipping business; subsidies permitted some lines to operate at a loss; and freight rates fell to pre-war levels or below. But as operating costs declined more slowly, shipping, like coal mining and the railroad, became a sick industry even before 1929.

When depression came, the sickness grew serious. The quantity of cargo fell by almost a third. The world's idle shipping quadrupled during 1930, and the remaining vessels ran with half-empty holds and short passenger lists. Unemployment stalked the water front, and five out of every six shipyards were in 1933 as silent as cemeteries. As the clouds lifted, some old ships were scrapped and new ones built, often with the aid of subsidies or of such cheap loans as those made by the British government to finance the construction of the *Queen Mary* and the *Queen Elizabeth*. But the world's total shipping supply was no longer growing. Rather it retreated somewhat—from nearly 70,000,000 tons in 1929 to 65,000,000 in 1939, thanks to a small decline in the British tonnage and the continued long fall of the American merchant marine from the peak reached after World War I. Only Japan and the smaller European countries had more ships than they possessed in 1913.

Within a few hours of the declaration of World War II the submarine claimed its first victim. By VE-Day in 1945 "enemy action" had sunk about 5,800 ships, with a total of 22,000,000 tons, flying the British flag and about half of them belonging to the British merchant marine. In December, 1941, American shipping became a target. Shipyard capacity was enlarged in Britain and still more in the United States to replace losses and meet the vast military or naval requirements. When peace came, ships could only slowly be released from service to resume their civilian tasks, but it was evident that when all had been demobilized the world would again have a superabundance of war-built vessels, many of them unfit for economical commercial operation. Britain, Norway, and Holland settled down to rebuild their depleted fleets, and the United States faced the task of deciding what to do with its swollen marine. Each was a difficult assignment.

BIBLIOGRAPHY

General

Bogart, E. L., *Economic History of Europe, 1760–1939* (1942), chaps. 4, 11, 19.

Clapham, J. H., *Economic History of Modern Britain* (1926, 1932, 1938), vol. i, chaps. 3, 9, 10, 12; vol. ii, chaps. 5, 6; vol. iii, chap. 6.

Clapham, J. H., *The Economic Development of France and Germany, 1815–1914* (1923), chaps. 5, 7, 10, 12.

Fay, C. R., *Great Britain from Adam Smith to the Present Day* (1932), chaps. 8–11.

Kirkaldy, A. W., and Evans, A. D., *History and Economics of Transport* (1924).

Knowles, L. C. A., *Industrial and Commercial Revolutions in Great Britain during the Nineteenth Century* (1922), parts iv, v.

Knowles, L. C. A., *Economic Development in the Nineteenth Century* (1932), part iv.

McPherson, L. G., *Transportation in Europe* (1910).

Porter, G. R. (ed. F. W. Hirst), *Progress of the Nation* (1912), chaps. 14, 28, 29.

Encyclopaedia of the Social Sciences: See list of articles on Transportation, vol. xv, p. 557.

INLAND TRANSPORTATION

Acworth, W. M., *The Elements of Railway Economics* (1924).

Hines, W. D., *Report on Danube Navigation* (League of Nations, 1927).

Jackman, W. T., *Development of Transportation in Modern England* (1916).

Jagtiani, H. M., *The Role of the State in the Provision of Railways* (1924).

Lewin, H. G., *Early British Railways, 1801–1844* (1925).

Sheldon, G., *From Trackway to Turnpike* (1928).

Sherrington, C. E. R., *A Hundred Years of Inland Transportation* (1934).

Walker, G., *Road and Rail: An Inquiry into the Economics of Competition and State Control* (1942).

Webb, S. and B., *The Story of the King's Highway* (1916).

OCEAN TRANSPORTATION

Berglund, A., *Ocean Transportation* (1933).

Chatterton, E. K., *The Mercantile Marine* (1923).

Fayle, C. E., *Short History of the World's Shipping Industry* (1933), chaps. 8–11.

Hardy, A. C., *Seaways and Sea Trade* (1934).

Jackson, G. G., *The Ship under Steam* (1928).

Johnson, E. R., and Huebner, G. G., *Principles of Ocean Transportation* (1920), part i.

Kirkaldy, A. W., *British Shipping: Its History, Organization, and Importance* (1914).

Salter, J. A., *Allied Shipping Control* (1921).

Siegfried, A., *Suez and Panama* (1940).

ARTICLES

Berglund, A., "The War and the World's Merchant Marine," *Am. Ec. R.*, June, 1920.

Dunham, A. L., "How the First French Railways were Planned," *J. Ec. H.*, May, 1941.

Lefranc, G., "The French Railroads, 1823–1842," *J.E.B.H.*, February, 1930.

Levainville, J., "The Economic Function of the Rhine," *Geog. Rev.*, June, 1930.

Magnes, J., "The Recovery of Germany's Merchant Marine after the War," *Harv. Bus. Rev.*, October, 1930.

XXIII

INDUSTRIAL AND COMMERCIAL ORGANIZATION

The two preceding chapters have been concerned chiefly with technological developments. It is now time to examine the organization of enterprises which used the new equipment, knowledge, and processes to make old or new products, to serve as private or public carriers, and to find markets. Three features stand out. The first was the spread of the factory system over industries which had formerly been domestic, its extension in occupations which had always gathered workers together, and its adoption from the start by new industries. The second was the growing importance of manufacturing industries and of mining in the economic life of what became Industrial Europe. The third was the accumulation of relatively large sums of capital for equipping and operating industry, commerce, and transportation.

The Growth of the Factory System and of Industrialization

The essence of a factory, or mill as it is called in some industries, is the congregation of wage earners in an employer's premises, working under his direction, with his equipment, on his materials. In labor laws and popular discussion a distinction has often been drawn between the factory and the workshop: the former has been defined as a place where mechanical power is used to drive machines; in the latter the work is done with tools or other equipment that can be operated by manual power. For our purpose, however, the important feature is the gathering of the workers together, whether in a machine-filled building, a mine, smelter, chemical works, or any place other than a home or tiny workshop. As we saw in Chapter XVI, this congregation of labor was essential in some industries because of the nature of the work, as in mining and shipbuilding, or of the equipment, as in sugar refining and cloth finishing. It was also becoming desirable in traditionally domestic occupa

552

tions if output was to be increased greatly or quality improved. An employer could save time by bringing in labor rather than putting out material, train men to do new kinds of skilled work, use greater division of labor, impose discipline, enforce regular hours, prevent embezzlement, and get his goods produced in a steadier stream. The putting-out system was neither a good technical school nor a satisfactory police system. There were obstacles, such as the cost of buildings, equipment, and supervision, and labor might be hostile; but these difficulties were being surmounted in some degree even before machinery and power added their economies to those already enjoyed by centralized production.

The factory system made its greatest advance when it annexed the most widespread domestic industry, clothmaking. Lombe's silk-throwing machines were at work in several factories by 1760. The early jennies and mules could be operated by hand at home, but enterprising persons erected a number of them in barns or converted adjacent cottages into spinning sheds. In 1771 Arkwright built a water mill at Cromford in Derbyshire, filled it with his frames, and by 1779 employed about 300 workers. Some manufacturers paid him heavy royalties for permission to use his machines, but others refused to pay, challenged his patent in court, and in 1785 succeeded in having it annulled. The adoption of spinning machines now became rapid. Grain or fulling millers installed and attached them to their water wheels. As the supply of suitable buildings was soon exhausted, new mills were erected—some of them tiny structures, others great boxes of brick, stone, and glass, with four, five, or six floors. By 1800 hundreds of them were strewn along the river banks of Lancashire, Yorkshire, and adjacent counties, as well as in the Glasgow region, and steam had begun to supplement water power. The yarn made in them was still woven on hand looms. Some employers were gathering those looms into mills, but most weavers remained at home, and the weaving shed filled with power looms was not common, even in the cotton industry, until at least 1830.

Cotton spinning was the only occupation to make a fairly rapid transfer from old to new conditions, and its story must not be taken as typical of what happened in industry generally. In other processes and industries the transition was more gradual and piecemeal, or the development was from small congregations of workers to larger ones. By 1850 the factory system was supreme in the production of cloth, paper, glass, pottery, metals, engines, and machines. This left large fields in the hands of the craftsman and outworker, such as the clothing, shoe, woodwork, food, and some small metalware industries. After 1850 most of these were mechanized, while the new industries born after that date often depended on patents and costly equipment and lived in factories almost from their birth. By 1900 there were only a few remnants of home or small workshop production, chiefly in occupations which served local retail needs.

As the new industrial organization advanced, Britain passed from a balanced agricultural-industrial economy to one that was overwhelmingly industrial and urban. In 1801 about 60 per cent of the people of England and Wales lived in rural districts or in towns with less than 2,000 inhabitants; but many of these—how many we cannot say—were part- or full-time industrial or mining workers. By 1841 the figure was just over 50 per cent and continued to drop until it reached 20 per cent in 1931. In 1841 agriculture employed 19 per cent of the working population, a fraction almost identical with that engaged in American farming in 1930; but the three big industries—textiles, metal, and mining—employed 20 per cent. By 1881 the population had nearly doubled, but agriculture engaged only 12 per cent of it. The "big three" still accounted for 20 per cent of the labor force, in spite of the removal of many children from mills and mines by labor laws; and the whole field of secondary industries employed about 45 per cent. Since that date the farming figure has sunk as low as 5 per cent (1936), but that of the secondary industries has remained about 45 per cent. In value of output the predominance of industry over agriculture was greater than it was in volume of employment.

The Spread of the New Industrialism on the Continent: *France.* In spite of laws banning the emigration of artisans and the export of equipment, a few spinning machines appeared in France soon after they were at work in England. British workers were procured to build and operate them, and in 1788 a cotton factory set up by a Manchester man was using Arkwright's frames and employing 600 workers. In 1782 a Watt engine was bought for the Creusot ironworks. Frenchmen were evidently watching the changes taking place in England, their government encouraged the introduction of machinery, their scientists were among the best, and fertile minds produced ideas about steam boats or vehicles, propellers, and other novelties. Further, the long war (1792–1815) created a great demand for munitions for the large armies. British goods were shut out of the French market and after 1806 Napoleon tried with some success to exclude them from the whole continent. Yet notwithstanding these favorable factors, French industry emerged from the war in 1815 only moderately expanded in metalwork and textiles and little changed in organization, equipment, or technique. Englishmen chuckled over the fact that some of Napoleon's soldiers had worn uniforms made of British cloth and regimental badges made in Birmingham.

Peacetime progress was slow until about 1830, when the iron, cotton, and coal industries began to move ahead. Old churches, confiscated during the Revolution, served as factories, and textile mills multiplied in Lille, Normandy, and Alsace-Lorraine. English workers were welcomed; it was said in 1824 that there were at least 15,000 of them in France. Coal mining expanded its output nearly sixfold between 1815 and 1848, thanks in part to better equipment for deeper mining and to improvements in canals, rivers, or roads, which reduced transportation costs. The production of iron grew fourfold, and by 1850 nearly half of it was being smelted with coke. But there were still impediments to the spread of the new industrialism. Much of the population was rural; it might not have enough land to yield a good income, but it did own too much to abandon, and preferred to divide its time between industry and agriculture rather than take a steady urban job. By contrast, many English villagers owned no land, inclosure had destroyed their little stake in the commons, and they were therefore foot-free to go to town. Capital may not have been scarce in France, but those who owned it were loath to take industrial risks. High tariffs made coal, iron, machines, and raw materials expensive. Finally, France was slow in finding such energetic captains of industry as those who were driving British enterprise along new paths. Consequently French industry in 1850 was still overwhelmingly a world of small-scale units; four people were engaged in domestic manufactures for every one in *"la grande industrie"* (textiles, iron, and mining); and technological advance had scarcely moved out of bottom gear.

Movement was more rapid after 1850, stimulated by the growth of railroad transportation, a keener interest in industrial investment, and a generally flourishing European economy. In 1860 an Anglo-French trade treaty removed the French ban on the importation of some goods, especially cottons, and lowered the tariff on others.

Keener competition from British wares shook weak firms or industries, but others met the challenge by overhauling their plants
and methods, and the lower tariff enabled them to import machines,
coal, and other necessaries more cheaply. The Franco-Prussian War
(1870–1871) jolted France badly, and deprived her of the flourishing Alsace-Lorraine textile industry as well as of the iron ore deposits, though at the time these were not highly valued. Within two
years Europe slid into a long period of depression, keen competition, and low prices for farm and factory products alike. French industrial advance was therefore slowed down, and did not regain
much pace until about 1890.

From that point onward progress was considerable until 1914.
The Gilchrist-Thomas process for converting phosphoric ore into
steel made possible the use of the considerable iron deposits which
France still held. In 1913 her steel output was three-fifths that of
Great Britain, in spite of the unsuitability of French coal for coking
and the need to import fuel. There were also promising developments in hydro-electricity and in the production of aluminum and of
the early automobile. By 1900 workers were leaving the country for
the town in greater numbers, investment and banking facilities had
improved, and a more energetic class of industrialists was in charge.

Yet in 1914 France stood third in the industrial list, as she now did
in population, since that of the United Kingdom had passed hers in
size. The expansion of her heavy industries was limited by her inability to supply all their coal needs. Her domestic market for
staple necessaries was limited by the fact that her population had
virtually ceased to grow. Her investors were pouring their money
into foreign loans—to Russia, Turkey, and other countries which
later proved to be bad risks—rather than into developing her own
industrial resources. Her silk industry was having trouble with
oriental and some occidental competitors. A great part of her industrial structure was still that of the small factory or workshop,
producing for local market or export those goods of artistic quality
and luxury which had been characteristic of her output for centuries. Her population was nicely balanced between rural and
urban, but the scales were just threatening to tip in favor of the
town, and there was scarcely enough labor to meet the full needs
of town or country.

Germany. German industry until 1850 was mostly in the hands of
urban craftsmen or of peasants who divided their time between

working their land and producing goods either for their own use or for some *Verleger* who took the wares away to market. The unit of production was small; Prussia in 1843 had fewer apprentices and journeymen than masters. The work was often part or spare time; only one linen loom out of every seven in Prussia provided its owner with the main part of his income. Some industries served substantial home or foreign markets, especially for linen cloth and hardware. These expanded somewhat when Napoleon's decrees shut British goods out of the continent but collapsed when peace reopened the door. Silesia's great linen industry was hurt by the competition of British mill-made fabrics, German shear steel and cutlery lost ground to products from Sheffield, while post-war tariffs excluded German goods from Russian and some other former markets.

The pioneers in introducing the new industrial technique to Germany were Prussian officials who were administering state mines, copper mills, cannon foundries, and saltworks. By 1780 some of them had become interested in the British novelties and visited England to see what they could learn, openly or by espionage. Stein, while director of mines, was sent across in 1786 "to inspect English mining and smelting procedures and the iron and metal foundries . . . and to study the application of machinery to these industries." The visitors secured drawings, bought cylinders, and persuaded workers to emigrate. By 1800 two Prussian state engine-building works were supplying the needs of the royal industries, and the smelting of iron by coke had begun.

After 1800, and especially after 1820, private enterprise gradually overshadowed this state initiative. Men in the Rhineland, Westphalia, Saxony, Silesia, Berlin, and the coastal cities built engines for mines, mills, railroads, and steamboats, introduced the puddling process and rollers for making wrought-iron plates or rails, launched steam vessels, and made textile machines. They secured British workmen and sometimes British capital, but gradually developed a native supply of both. Their work was carried on in more favorable surroundings when the *Zollverein* (1834) established free trade between seventeen states which held about two-thirds of the area and population of the later Empire, and thus offered a wider market to the German manufacturer. The coming of the railroads and river steamboats, the gradual mobilization of capital by bankers chiefly interested in financing industry, and the imitation of British or Belgian methods all helped to quicken development. Movement was most marked in the coal and iron industries, especially after the tapping of deep coal seams in the Ruhr. The introduction of textile machines became fairly common, while machine-making works, sugar factories, and chemical plants grew in number. Germany shared in the general European business expansion of the fifties and sixties, and by 1871 the coal-bearing regions had assumed a definitely industrialized appearance. The newborn Empire was still predominantly agricultural, with nearly half of its workers engaged in farming or forestry; but another third of them was making Germany the second or third most important industrial country in the world.

By 1914 the number of workers in industry had risen to two-fifths of the total labor force, and that in agriculture had fallen to one-third of a population which had grown from 40,000,000 to 68,000,000 since 1871. Industrialization had advanced so far that Germany was now the largest European producer of iron, steel, and chemicals, ranked high as maker of machines and textiles, and seemed destined to catch up with Great Britain in coal production. The acquisition of Alsace-Lorraine had given her a highly developed textile region and, more important for her future, had added beds of ore and potash to her own rich deposits of coal and potash. Technological advances, such as those made by Bessemer, Siemens, and Gilchrist-Thomas in steelmaking, those made in the use of coal by-products, the production of alloys, of electricity, and of improved machines, all were taken advantage of by a nation which believed in science and technical education. The support of the banks compensated for the lack of an adequate supply of private investors. The imperial government looked with favor on industrial expansion, gave tariffs to protect the iron and steel men, recognized the existence of cartels to limit cutthroat competition, and shaped railroad rates to assist export industries. Old industries mechanized themselves more vigorously and increased the size of their plants. Newer ones began on a large scale or quickly reached it. A vigorous campaign was launched to find foreign markets for goods which at first were often justly stigmatized as "cheap and nasty," but which gradually overcame that condemnation. The merchant marine and the shipyards helped to round out the picture of a comprehensive economy with "heavy" and "light" industries, with a powerful position in the center of a continent with which Germany did two-thirds of her foreign commerce, and with threads of trade or investment stretching to most parts of the outer world. In 1871 one-twentieth of the population lived in eight towns with more than 100,000 inhabitants each. In 1914 a quarter of her population resided in forty-eight towns of that size.

Russia. In the eighteenth century Russia had a number of industries which served domestic and foreign markets. Landlords operated workshops, mines, and smelters with serfs as laborers; merchants managed elaborate putting-out enterprises or collected workers into shops; the crown established a few industries to supply its luxury needs, and petty craftsmen met local demands. A writer in 1780 tells of a clothmaking firm which employed 900 looms and of a linen tablecloth maker who employed 4,000 workers. Russian leather (made by processes which were kept "top secret"), iron, copper, linen, sailcloth, and tobacco were exported in considerable quantities. As the iron industry of western Europe turned to coke fuel the demand for Russian metal declined, and the growth of the British linen industry combined with the growing use of cotton cloth to reduce the market for Russian fabrics. The domestic market remained, and behind high tariff walls the Russian cotton industry made some progress in adopting the new machines. But in comparison with any country to the west of her, Russia in 1861 was industrially very backward.

Emancipation in 1861 freed the serfs to go and work where they wished; but freedom meant little until railroads, better banking facilities, and more capital were available to stimulate industrial expansion. That expansion gathered a little speed during the eighties, and in the nineties the government embarked on a vigorous policy of industrialization in order to make the country as self-supplying as possible. Witte was as eager to build industries as he was to lay railroads. The tariff was raised high, foreign capitalists were invited to establish industries, and subsidies were offered to the makers of railroad equipment. The results were impressive but costly. The growth of textile mills, mines, metallurgical works, machine factories, and oil wells raised the industrial output about 8 per cent per annum during the nineties, against about 3 per cent during the sixties and seventies. The cost was borne by the peasants in the form of high prices and heavy taxes.

Depression and revolution checked the advance between 1900 and 1906, but as political conditions became both stable and less autocratic native and foreign capital flowed again into the industrial field. The number of large plants increased rapidly. The production of iron ore and steel had by 1913 risen to a third of the German figures, that of coal was about halfway between those of France and Belgium, and cotton from Turkestan was feeding a quickly expanding textile industry.

The First World War reduced the output of consumers' goods but stimulated that of heavy goods. Two revolutions, loss of territory, and civil war wrecked every kind of production. By 1920 the total output had fallen to a fifth of its pre-war level, but that of the larger industries was down to one-eighth or even less. The Communists had no precise idea of what they were going to do, except abolish private property and run industries as state enterprises. The government or the workers had appropriated most plants, but since everything—management, discipline, transportation, supplies of raw material or fuel or credit, and marketing machinery—had broken down or vanished, goods could not be produced to supply the peasants, and without those goods the Revolution would collapse.

The New Economic Policy (1921) therefore retained only the large industrial units as state enterprises. It left the swarm of smaller ones in the hands of cooperatives and individuals, or returned them to those hands. The state industries employed over four-fifths of the total labor force and possessed most of the worn-out capital equipment inherited from the "expropriated" owners. By dint of countless expedients, drawing on the public treasury for capital and operating expenses, restoring the currency, reestablishing foreign trade, improving organization, and tightening up factory discipline, the total output was brought back to its pre-war level by 1927. This achievement was, however, very uneven; the production of coal and oil more than recovered, but that of iron, steel, and consumers' goods lagged far behind. Not merely were the goods farmers wanted still scarce, but their quality was low and their price high, especially when compared with the prices peasants were paid for their produce. Rural discontent, recovery, alleged danger of attack from "capitalist states," and the need for deciding what to do next all combined to produce the first Five-Year Plan, formulated in 1928.

This plan laid out an ambitious program for the general reconstruction and rapid expansion of the whole economy—industry, agriculture, transportation, trade, electric power, housing, municipal services, and education. We have already seen how agriculture was collectivized and mechanized. For industry the plan envisaged a vast investment, especially in the capital goods industries; as much capital was to be invested yearly as the whole industrial plant was worth in 1913. This expansion and improvements in methods were to raise production about 20 per cent per annum; in five years the output of capital goods was to be trebled and that of consumers' goods doubled. The difficulties confronting such an effort were stupendous, but the result was a gain in output amounting to an average of about 15 per cent per annum. Some industries, such as those making machines, tractors, farm implements, and electrical equipment, went far beyond the figures assigned them; but the output of iron, steel, coal, chemicals, and such consumers' goods as cloth and shoes fell far short. Production costs were high, prices rose, and quality was often very poor.

The second Five-Year Plan, framed in 1932, called for a smaller percentage increase in production than did the first—about 14 per cent yearly instead of 20; it demanded improvement in the quality of goods; but its emphasis was still overwhelmingly on the capital goods industries. It was carried out more smoothly than was the first plan; unskilled laborers hurriedly pulled into factories were now acquiring some competence, incentives to work harder or more carefully were offered, punishment for the "economic crime" of poor work was made more severe, and administrators were learning how to handle the problems of planning. By 1937 the plan as a whole had been more than carried out; the production of "means of production" was a third higher than the figure set in 1932; the metalworking industries, which made machines and armaments, were 50 per cent above their allotted mark; steel, chemicals, and electricity did what was expected, but coal and oil failed to do so. Consumers' goods industries still had to be content with a very minor role. In 1938 less than three shoes were produced for each pair of feet; but that was better than the one-shoe output of 1930, and was part of the steady increase in supplies which made possible the abolition of rationing in 1935.

The third Five-Year Plan (1937) resembled its predecessors, but the shadow of rearmament lay more heavily over it. The annual increase in production was set at 12 per cent, but the fastest advance was to be in the production of chemicals, aluminum, and other metals. New plants were to avoid such already densely developed centers as Leningrad, Moscow, Kiev, or Rostov and be located farther east—on the Volga, in the Urals, and in Siberia. This eastward movement was in part a reaction against the "gigantomania" of the earlier plans; it was intended to reduce the long haul of raw materials from remote places to a few centers; and it was a strategic dispersion of production. Strategy also dictated that consumers' goods industries once more take a poor second place.

The result of this series of intense drives is seen in the following official figures of production in 1913, 1929, and 1938 (or 1940):

	1913	1929	1938
Engineering and metal goods industries (billion rubles at 1926–27 prices)	1,450	3,050	33,600
Electricity (billion K.W.H.)	1.9	6.2	39.6
Coal (million metric tons)	29	40	166 (1940)
Pig iron " " "	4.2	4	15 (1940)
Steel " " "	4.2	4.9	18.3 (1940)
Oil " " "	9.2	13.8	31 (1940)
Cotton cloth (billion meters)	2.2	3.1	3.5
Leather shoes (million pairs)	. . . .	48.8	213

The high lights of this table are (1) the great growth in size and diversity of the metal goods industries, as a result of which the large-scale production of machine tools and motor-driven vehicles—trucks, cars, tractors, planes, and tanks—became possible; (2) the quick advance in electrification; (3) the fourfold rise in the output of coal, iron, and steel, which by 1940 had lifted the U.S.S.R. to a position of equality with Germany as steel producer; (4) the slower increase in supplies of cotton cloth. The emphasis on the heavy industries justified itself in the war years by enabling Russia to meet most of the requirements of mechanized conflict. The development of eastern centers kept supplies forthcoming when the western and southern areas passed into German hands. The post-war objective announced by Stalin in 1946 called not merely for the restoration of devastated agricultural and industrial plants but for three or more five-year plans aiming at an output of coal, oil, iron, and steel three times that of 1939, in order that "our country be insured against any eventuality."

The Persistence of Handicrafts, Workshops, and Homework. With possibly two exceptions—cotton spinning and the Russian drive for industrialization—the "triumph of the factory system" was neither an overnight campaign nor a complete conquest of the industrial field. The speed at which the transfer from domestic or small workshop production to the factory took place was determined by the ability of the machine to produce satisfactory goods and also by the relative costs under the old and new orders. Factory spinning soon did more, better, and cheaper work; but as late as 1877 an English woolen-cloth manufacturer could contend that it was cheaper for him to pay a domestic hand-loom weaver seventeen cents for doing a certain piece of work than to pay a power-loom weaver seven cents, because the costs of wear and tear on the loom, of power, damage, waste, maintenance, supervision, "and other little *et ceteras*" more than ate up the difference between the two rates. The ready-made clothing trades lingered in the home long after factories had taken over a large part of the work; they did so because the sewing machine could be used and many women, though unable to leave home, were compelled to earn an income or supplement the inadequate earnings of the breadwinner by doing outwork at wages which made the product as cheap as that of a factory. In many minor occupations domestic or small workshop labor was cheap enough to delay the search for machines.

In some industries manual skill resisted displacement because the quality of the workmanship could not be mechanically reproduced, because the volume of demand did not justify machine production, or because the product had to possess some distinctive quality or pattern. Classic instances were (1) the Sheffield and Solingen cutlery industries, in which master cutlers worked in small shops producing high-grade knives, razors, and tools; (2) the Lyons cottage weavers of fine patterned silks; (3) makers of those expensive garments or personal and domestic accessories for which Paris and London were famous; and (4) the motley of peasant industries which made such things as Belgian lace, Harris tweeds, German toys, or Italian embroidery for tourists or for buyers who disliked factory products. There was also the army of local bakers, tailors, blacksmiths, job printers, carpenters, and so forth, an army reinforced in the twentieth century by the service or repair stations for radios, electrical appliances, cycles, and automobiles.

The extent of this petty production was therefore considerable even in the twentieth century. Germany's late industrialization kept many handicrafts strong until well after 1900; in 1925, 5 per cent of the population was employed in handwork, especially in cloth or clothes making or in peasant industries, and the money turnover of these occupations was said to be about 15 per cent of that of the whole country. In France there were about 2,300,000 small masters and homeworkers in 1921. In Great Britain a "sweated" industries exhibition in 1906 revealed that a great variety of goods were being made at home or in small shops by people who spent long hours at tedious, monotonous jobs for miserably low wages. The goods on display included most articles of clothing, cardboard and match boxes, chains, clay pipes, nails, tennis balls, brushes, bead decorations, jewel cases, military embroidery, and coffin tassels. The exhibition was not concerned with occupations in which the scale was small but the remuneration adequate; if it had been, the list would have been much longer. Thus European industry was not all crowded into giant factories. The American student may well remember that this is also true of his country. In 1939 there were 184,000 manufacturing plants in the United States. Of these, over 8,000 hired no labor, about 76,000 had from 1 to 5 employees, and a further 50,000 employed form 6 to 20 workers. In all, over 70 per cent of the plants could therefore be described as small. The European situation was not dissimilar.

The Commercial Unit. As a greater percentage of the population became urban and specialized in its work, as living standards rose, and as new kinds of goods or services were introduced, the number of persons engaged in commerce increased both absolutely and relatively. In Germany the percentage rose from 9 in 1907 to 12 in 1925. In Britain the "distributive trades" employed nearly 12 per cent of all insured workers in 1923 and 16 per cent in 1938. In France the distributors more than doubled in number between 1866 and 1906, but the population rose only 3 per cent, and Professor Gide jestingly predicted that at this rate all the French people would be tradesmen within two centuries.

In the wholesale field large warehouses and great sums of capital or credit were needed, though a surprisingly large number of men were able to find a little niche as brokers, jobbers, or agents. In retail trade the small store was almost as firmly rooted as was the peasant farm in the countryside. It was near the consumer, it needed little capital or credit, and the family supplied the labor. Retail distribution attracted those who had confidence in their ability to fight their own battles, to be free lances rather than privates. It was the hotbed of hope, and all too often the deathbed. Consequently, there was, in the 1920's, one retail store for every seventy-five to eighty persons in Italy, Germany, and Britain, but one for every forty Frenchmen. The overwhelming majority of them were small and "independent," the rest were cooperative societies, departmental or chain stores. The cooperatives had been spreading over Britain since 1844 and were covering the northwestern continental countries a little later. They sought to benefit their member-consumers by producing and distributing goods without profit. (See Chapter XXXI.) Department stores seem to have developed first in Paris about 1850 as a device for allowing the customer to find many kinds of goods under one roof instead of having to go from shop to shop to satisfy his needs. Chain stores came into being as outlets for the distribution by large manufacturers of such things as clothes or shoes, by large importers of such foodstuffs as tea, meat, and dairy produce, and by purchasers of large quantities of cheap goods such as could be sold in a "penny bazaar," the equivalent of an American "five and ten cent" store.

By 1914 the cooperatives were very strong, while the chain and department stores were spreading. During the First World War, when Britons had to register for their food supplies, half of them did so with 137,000 "independents," a quarter at the 5,500 cooperatives, and a quarter at 7,000 chain stores. The independent had only one-tenth as many customers to each shop as had his rivals. During later years he lost some ground to them, but new fields opened up before him. The growth of new suburbs, of new commodities, and of such new leisure activities as hiking, cycling, motoring, and eating away from home provided him with fresh opportunities to find a place in spite of, or away from, the giants. Some customers preferred his individual personality and service, others liked his willingness to sell on credit and to deliver goods. He rarely made a fortune, but he might scrape together a modest income, and if he failed, some optimist was usually ready to take his place.

THE INDUSTRIAL CAPITALIST

Of the men who developed or spread the new industrial order, some were landlords. In Scotland, Wales, England, Silesia, and Russia we find them exploiting the mineral resources of their estates, operating furnaces, forges, tin-plate mills, and (in Germany) owning large breweries. Some industrial entrepreneurs were merchants who became manufacturers as well. In 1792, Benjamin Gott, a Leeds merchant who bought woolen cloth from domestic clothiers, erected a mill which eventually employed a thousand workers engaged in every stage of production. When asked why he did this, he replied: "I was brought up as a merchant, and became a manufacturer rather from possessing capital than from understanding the manufacture. I paid for the talents of others in the different branches of manufacture." He was, however, influenced also by his frequent inability to procure sufficient goods in the public market and by his desire to make super-fine cloths which would break into the West of England's monopoly of those fabrics. In Scotland merchants who had shipped cloth to the American colonies and imported tobacco found their transatlantic trade suspended by the Revolution just at a time when the cotton machines were coming into use. They therefore transferred their capital from overseas trade to the production of yarn or to making glass and iron. David Dale, one of the most famous of them, erected a huge cotton mill at New Lanark in 1786. It was in this mill that his son-in-law, Robert Owen, was later to conduct his pioneer experiments as a model employer.

Similar instances of mercantile and landed enterprise can be found in most countries. Landlords and merchants were influential in getting the first German steam engines built, and merchants developed the deep mines in the Ruhr Valley. Italian traders and such landlords as Cavour put money into silk and cotton mills and hired Englishmen to serve as managers and teachers. Yet in general landlords were too busy with other interests and merchants had quite enough commercial calls on their time and capital to make them avoid the added worries of industrial production. Most of the initiative and enterprise therefore came from within industry.

They were supplied by men who had grown up in an industrial atmosphere—with its dust, dirt, noise, and smells. The ironmasters were descendants of many generations of smelters or makers of nails, chains, locks, clocks, and similar wares. Wedgwood had behind him four generations of potters; Boulton inherited a flourishing business and Krupp (1812–1887) a small ironworks in Essen. The early textile millowners, with few exceptions, had learned the industry from childhood in cottage or farmhouse, had developed putting-out businesses or were machine makers. Samuel Oldknow put out cotton to spinners and weavers, then turned a discarded silk-throwing mill into a spinning factory, and went on (about 1790) to build a larger one with sheds for weavers, dormitories for the pauper children he obtained from London, and homes for his other workers. Radcliffe saved money out of his wages as a weaver until he had enough to start his own firm. Eventually he fed yarn to a thousand looms, and could boast that his firm had all been raised "like a gathering snowball from a single spindle or single loom." Throughout the nineteenth (and even the twentieth) century the textile industry continued to offer scope for the rise of ambitious men from the ranks. An investigation made about 1910 revealed that 88 out of 139 cotton manufacturers in one Lancashire town were "self-made" men who had started their career as wage earners. In offering opportunity of this kind the textile industry was not alone.

The first problem to be faced by the industrial entrepreneur was that of raising the capital needed for equipping a new venture or for introducing improved methods and equipment into an old one. The sum might be quite small. Robert Owen, a draper's clerk in Manchester, borrowed £100 in 1789, went into partnership with a penniless skilled mechanic, rented a workshop, bought materials on credit, and soon had forty men at work making mules. Countless firms began with a few secondhand or rented machines in a rented room and with credit from the merchant who supplied the materials or bought the product. The larger ventures needed much more. A big textile mill, fully equipped, might absorb £20,000, Dale's mill at New Lanark changed hands in 1800 for £60,000, and the capital in the Carron ironworks rose from £12,000 in 1760 to £150,000 in 1771—yet was not enough to protect its owners from insolvency.

The financial records which have survived reveal the difficulties encountered when men faced the double task of sinking much capital in buildings and plant and of securing or retaining enough operating capital to carry on their business in its new or expanded form. Boulton plunged into trouble when he decided to build his Soho factory (1762), for that establishment eventually cost him £10,000 instead of the £2,000 which he had thought would be adequate. To keep its hundreds of employees busy he had to make great commitments in purchasing materials and in wages bills. He and his partner, Fothergill, sank all their own capital in the enterprise; he sold his own estate, poured the dowry of his first wife and then of his second wife into the firm, borrowed from friends, and mortgaged to London or Amsterdam bankers his Soho buildings and the premiums paid by users of Watt engines. The firm lost £11,000 in ten years on a capital of £20,000, was constantly on the verge of insolvency, and would have fallen over that edge if Boulton's good luck had not brought him into alliance with Watt. The income from

Watt's first patent saved the day, as Watt generously let his two-thirds of it be used to help meet Boulton's debts; and when the engine became capable of supplying rotary motion (1782) the demand for engines became so large that the royalties cleared away the debts, paved the way to profit, and made Boulton worth £150,-000 when he died.

Wedgwood's difficulties were almost as great when he began to build his Etruria factory and homes for his workmen (1769). "I must either collect in my debts, hire money, or take my place among the *Whereas's* [insolvents listed in the *London Gazette*]," he wrote to his Liverpool merchant partner. "Collect—Collect, my friend— set all your hands and heads to work—send me the *L'argent* and you shall see wonders— £3,000! £3,000?—aye, £3,000, not a farthing less will satisfy my Architect for the next year's business; so you must collect, or take a place for me in the *Gazette*." In Germany Krupp had to empty the purses of all his kinsfolk to raise the 50,000 thalers he needed for his first cast-steel plant, and that sum proved to be inadequate.

The second problem confronting the pioneer industrialist was that of getting his raw materials and of converting them into the kind of product he desired. The Liverpool cotton market was by 1800 sufficiently well developed to cope with the flood of fiber that was beginning to come in from the southern states, and Lancashire manufacturers had little trouble in getting supplies privately or at public auctions all the year round. But the markets for many other raw materials were less satisfactory; hence a woolen manufacturer might find it necessary to visit Germany to purchase his supplies, potters secured interests in clay deposits or in coal pits, as metal-working firms did in mines or refineries.

Building up a satisfactory labor force was a difficult task. Some textile domestic workers disliked the early mills and refused to work in them. The first millowners were therefore obliged to hire tramps (hoboes), Irish immigrants who swarmed into England or Scotland after bad famines, and adults or children from the poorhouses of the country. Wedgwood was "teased out of [his] life" by the lack of competent labor. He stumped on his wooden leg round the shops, broke badly made pieces of pottery, and chalked on the bench, "This won't do for Josiah Wedgwood." Boulton worked hard to create his skilled staff; trained "young plain Country Lads, all of which that betray any genius are taught to draw"; and was worried by the fact that the men he sent out to erect engines spent so much time getting drunk. Machines might be "labor-saving," but the labor they did need had to possess a considerable amount of skill.

Finally, there was the marketing problem. Some manufacturers were content to sell to existing merchants or sell through them on commission, and a large producer might be able to find a merchant willing to become his partner. But many industrialists set out to become their own salesmen. Boulton toured Britain trying to make the country "steam-mill mad"; his partner roamed over northern Europe seeking customers, and for a time Boulton entertained so many aristocratic visitors (and potential customers)—including even Catherine the Great—that his home "resembled an inn rather than a private house" (Dickinson). Wedgwood used showrooms and circulars, an energetic merchant-partner, and agents abroad. Humbler men were no less vigorous in their search for markets. One pioneer maker of men's suits, finding there were no retail stores willing to handle his product, pawned the clothes and threw away the tickets. Krupp went over the heads of ministers to persuade the crown to buy his guns. Many manufacturers went round, or sent traveling salesmen round, the commercial centers at home or abroad; they engaged foreign agents to receive and sell their wares on commission; or they dispatched a brother, son, or partner to live in such ports as Hamburg, New York, or Rio de Janeiro. In 1812 there were about 140 unnaturalized British merchants, most of them overseas partners, living in New York City, and probably at least as many more who had become naturalized citizens. If an industrialist's business was too small for him to use any of these selling methods, he might send a few bales of goods to be sold at public vendue by an auctioneer in a foreign city.

With much of his capital sunk in plant, the industrialist was more liable than the merchant to feel the pressure of those hard times which came with unpredictable frequency. Markets were upset when the American Revolution began; when France took up the American cause in 1778 and Holland did so a little later; when the European conflict began in 1792 and Britain joined it in 1793; when Napoleon tried to erect his "Continental System" (1806 onward) and shut British goods out of the lands he controlled; and when America's economic warfare of 1807–1812 led to armed conflict. Peace in 1763, 1783, and 1815 proved as dislocating as war had been. Buyers did not always promptly pay what they owed, even though long credit had been granted, and war gave them a good excuse for delaying payment to an enemy. Bread cast on the water in consigned goods returned slowly, the banking and credit structure was defective, and competition quickly became intense in any field which a pioneer had found to be profitable. When booms burst the whole business fabric crumpled, ushering in three or more lean years. The town of Bradford had four panics between 1836 and 1844; of 318 textile firms in existence in 1836, only 127 were alive in 1846. The bankruptcy list was no respecter of persons; the biggest merchants, manufacturers, and bankers were caught along with the minnows, and if an auctioneer was ever invited to dine at a rich man's house he must have spent much of his time wondering when the silver, glass, furniture, and wine cellar would come under his hammer.

When profits were made they had to be put back into the business until the firm seemed safely financed. The records of one well-rooted textile firm show that when it was bringing its buildings, power plant, and machinery up to date the partners plowed back over 60 per cent of the income they received from rent, interest, and profits during a period of six years; that in 1830 the figure was 85 per cent, and that it rose to 88 in 1831. If profit was, as some economists said, the reward of risk and interest the reward of abstinence, these men earned both.

Sometimes entrepreneurs received neither, or lost both. If they were more fortunate they eventually had money to spend according to their taste. Then some of them found satisfaction in vulgar ostentation, as for instance one *nouveau riche* who went to church in a bright yellow chariot driven by a coachman decked with gold braid and accompanied by three footmen in gaudy livery. Others became men of culture, if they had not been so already, philanthropists, patrons of art, science, letters and education, generous to their church and powerful in their party. They bought country estates and had their portraits done in oils by the fashionable painter of the day. When they died the second generation carried on, but often lacked the ability or the concentration on one objective possessed by the founder. It developed wider interests, in railroads, banking, or politics; it hunted, collected old furniture or books, obtained a title and sent its children to famous schools and ancient universities. Meanwhile the firm might lose its drive, become set in habits, assume that the methods which had brought success in the past would continue to do so, fail to keep its equipment and policies up to date, and ignore changes in market demands. If it continued solvent unto the third generation, its owners might sell out, break all connection with industry, and turn to the professions or a life of leisure. There is no law of nature decreeing that the third generation should be the last, and some firms had a longer life. Yet the story of many enterprises is summarized by the sad dictum, "Three generations from overalls to overalls," or in the happier schedule, "Three generations from overalls to bishop's gaiters, lawyer's wig, guardsman's uniform, or cabinet minister's knee-breeches."

THE SPREAD OF JOINT-STOCK ORGANIZATION

Until at least 1850 most of the burden of financing industrial expansion was borne by the one-man or family firm and the partnership. The same kind of unit also developed wholesale and retail trade, extended coal mining, built up merchant fleets, supplied some banking service, and prevailed not only in the older professions of law and medicine but also in such new ones as architecture, accounting, and journalism. If we count each firm as one, it is still by far the most common type of enterprise.

In England all partners, whether active or sleeping, shouldered unlimited liability for the firm's debts. In France, however, the *société en commandite* limited the liability of the passive partners to the loss of their investment and thus made it easier for entrepreneurs to induce outsiders to supply funds. During the eighteenth century the capital supplied by sleeping partners was cut up into shares known as *actions,* and these became transferable. Thus there developed the *société en commandite sur actions,* and it was given legal recognition in the *Code Napoléon* (1809). The active partners were liable without limit, but the shareholders had limited liability and an interest that could be sold. Germany followed the French practice with its *Kommanditgesellschaft* and its *Kommanditgesellschaft auf Aktien.* Such partnerships were easily formed, and might attract investors who felt that the unlimited liability of the managers would make these men careful with their own as well as with other people's money. That confidence was sometimes badly shaken.

The full joint-stock company (*société anonyme, Aktiengesellschaft*) emerged from its earlier limited field of distant trading in response to needs which could not be served by a partnership. Some enterprises, such as canals, waterworks, gas supplies, and railroads, were too large to be initiated and financed by private firms; others, such as mines in America or ranches in Australia, were too far away; and some were both too large and too far away. If, however, they were to be developed by joint-stock firms, four things were needed: (1) legislation which facilitated the formation of companies and defined their rights and obligations; (2) a supply of capital; (3) the development of the investing habit among the owners or controllers of that capital; and (4) a market in which new or old stocks and bonds could be sold.

Until 1844 no state allowed a joint-stock company to be created easily or cheaply. In France a charter was needed, and in England the Bubble Act (1720) required a charter or a private act of parliament. Lacking this expensive document, any firm which raised capital by selling shares was still only a partnership; it could not sue or be sued as a person, but all its members must plead or be cited individually; and if an English one became insolvent its members might have all their property seized to meet the firm's debts.

When a specific need arose, parliament was willing to take action; the canal promoters procured private acts, as did turnpike trusts, dock makers, insurance firms, and later the railroad builders; but there was no general law providing an open road to incorporation. Consequently a number of unincorporated companies came into being. Some of them had worthy reputable purposes, but boom times always produced a crop of disreputable promotions and issues of worthless stocks. In 1824–1825 that crop included companies which promised to exploit the mineral resources of newly liberated Spanish America, to find the treasure lost in the Red Sea when Pharaoh and his hosts were drowned, and to track other rainbows to their golden end. They used high-sounding titles, published enthusiastic accounts of meetings that never took place, and in various ways separated the public from some of its savings. The bubble of which they were a part burst in 1825, and four-fifths of the 600 new companies had vanished by 1827. The close connection between stocks, speculation, and original sin had once more been demonstrated.

Yet the need for the joint-stock company could not be gainsaid, and gradually that need was met. Since many provincial private banks collapsed in the crash of 1825, the establishment of joint-stock banks outside the London area was authorized in 1826. In 1844 parliament passed a general law for the easy formation of companies, and granted limited liability in 1856. One apparent reason for taking the second step was the well-known unhappy experience of a highly esteemed member of parliament who had invested £50 in a company formed under the act of 1844 but lost £50,000 because he and one other stockholder were the only ones possessed of enough property to meet the heavy debts of the firm when it went bankrupt. Company law took its full shape in 1862. A company could now be established by handing the state a "memorandum of association," signed by seven persons and giving the name, purpose, directors, and nominal capital of the firm. When it had raised enough money to start operations, it must file "articles of association." Thereafter it must supply the government with an annual statement of its capital, shareholders, and directors; publish each year a properly audited balance sheet; and use the word "Limited" at the end of its name. In return for this publicity, the liability of its stockholders was limited to the amount of nominal capital they held. Thus the privileges of easy formation and limited liability were to be paid for by such publicity as would let investors know how their money was being used, tell creditors the financial position of their debtor, and give competitors an idea of the strength (or weakness) of their rival. France moved in the same direction in 1867, and Germany in 1870.

Limited liability was a boon all entrepreneurs desired if they were to attract investors, but its price was one they did not like to pay. A company might therefore conceal its financial position by building up secret reserves, of which no one but the directors knew anything, by writing down too heavily (or too lightly) the value of its assets, or by other tactics which made its condition look weaker (or stronger) than it really was. Governments belatedly attacked these practices, placed heavier obligations on auditors, and made directors or managers personally—sometimes criminally—liable for the accuracy of financial statements. Yet it has proved to be impossible to enforce the demand for the truth, the whole truth, and nothing but the truth. In the words of one authority on accountancy, many published balance sheets have been "collectors' specimens rather than business guides" (Smails).

Private firms longed for limited liability, but were even less willing than the public companies to pay the price. They eventually got what they wanted when a German law (1892) and British laws (1892, 1907) allowed them to convert themselves into "private companies" enjoying limited liability. As such, they were not to have more than fifty stockholders; they could not sell their securities on the stock exchange; but since they were thus debarred from appealing to the public for funds, they need not file annual balance sheets. Many family firms and partnerships quickly took advantage of this combination of privacy and limited liability.

The spread of joint-stock companies depended not merely upon the state of the law but also on the supply of capital available, the willingness of owners to hand it over, and the development of machinery for bringing investors and investments together. In Britain by 1800 the supply of capital had grown large, the investing habit was well developed, and the Stock Exchange had its own premises. There were about four thousand holders of East India Company stock. Their stations and locations were widespread—"London merchants and bankers, shipowners and sea-captains, spinsters and widows of high and low degree, Scotsmen, clergymen, and 'Anglo-Indians' rubbing shoulders with Dutch burghers, Jewish diamond merchants, and the occasional noble Venetian or Chamberlain to the King of Poland" (Furber). The Bank of England's stock was in the hands of an equally motley army of about 2,000 investors; a sixth of them were Dutchmen, including professors of divinity at Utrecht; over a hundred lived in other European countries; half were Londoners; the rest included colleges, banks, and individuals in most parts of the British Isles, and the percentage of widows and spinsters was "extraordinarily high" (Clapham). Meanwhile the canal promoters had sold their stocks to people who lived in the districts that were to be served, and the growth of the national debt from about £230,000,000 to £800,000,000 during the long struggle with France was made possible by large-scale selling of war bonds.

With peace the investing habit soon became more deeply ingrained and widespread. The boom of 1824–1825 produced some company offerings that were sound. The new joint-stock banks were capitalized by local merchants and manufacturers to take the place of the private banks that had died in 1825. The early railroads appealed to local investors. Though there was no more need for war loans, the peacetime needs of governments in Europe, South America, and the United States soon grew great, and the interest rate they offered was high. Most of the loans they raised were eventually repudiated, but some remained good, as did some of the companies floated to exploit colonial or foreign land and mines.

It was the railroads that provided the greatest stimulus both to solid investment and to speculation. They offered wares to suit all kindes of buyers—bonds for the timid, preferred or guaranteed interest stock for the cautious, ordinary stock for the venturesome; and there was always the prospect that a company born in boom times might prove so profitable that its stock would rise to high prices. Newspaper advertisements, meetings, and other means were used to make the public stock-conscious. The Stock Exchange in London and markets in provincial towns dealt in railroad securities. Private bankers who had developed the art of "underwriting" government loans, i.e., taking the bonds of a new loan at a certain price and then trying to sell them to the public at a higher figure, helped to put company securities on the market. Thus the railroad booms, especially that of the mid-forties, broke "the crust of investment habits and opened up mass investment. . . . The Investment Revolution had started and a new phase of capitalism entered upon" (Shannon).

That phase was far from peaceful or uniformly profitable. The limited-liability company was capable of great use and abuse. Alongside companies which gathered capital together for production and transportation were those formed to benefit promoters and liquidators at the expense of investor and creditor. Every new wave of investment rose to a crest of overoptimism, speculation, and promotion for promotion's sake. After 1850 the lure of new issues of "Home Rails" subsided, only to give place to great expectations from railroad enterprise in the United States, Canada, and South America. Other seductive novelties were finance companies and hotels in the sixties; foreign mines, coal, iron, and skating rinks in the seventies; overseas land, gold, banks, and electricity in the eighties; bicycles in the nineties; rubber, gold, rayon, gramaphones, and holding companies in the present century. In each of them there appeared "bubble companies blown by men of strong lungs and brazen countenance" (Shannon), mines that were never dug outside a city office, speculators who did not all sell out in time, and investors who went empty away from the joint-stock racecourse.

The record of achievement was therefore checkered. Companies that were free from shallow or sinister intent might be sunk by uncharted rocks, unwise business policies, or general depression. Mr. Shannon has shown that one-third of the 20,000 British companies registered between 1856 and 1883 were very small or never got into action. Of the remainder, 28 per cent were wound up compulsorily as insolvent, 32 per cent were wound up voluntarily, and 11 per cent disappeared unnoticed. One out of every three died before its fifth birthday, one out of two before its tenth, and only 8 per cent were alive in 1929. The course of joint-stock history was liberally strewn with failure, fraud, and vain hopes, and the experience of the twentieth century differed little from that of the nineteenth. Out of 277 stock issues made in Britain during the boom year 1928, 101 were made by companies which had disappeared by 1933. Of 109 new firms 68 had vanished, and the stocks of 29 more had lost from four-fifths to all of their value.

Apart from the railroads the joint-stock company played its most important part as an organization suitable for the new and larger business units of the steel, chemical, and electrical age. On the continent it became popular later than in Britain. Capital there was less abundant and more shy, and its provision had therefore to be undertaken by banks which devoted most or all of their attention to the flotation and financing of companies. (See Chapter XXIV.) Thanks to their work and to the general expansion of German enterprise after 1870, the number of companies rose from 2,100 in 1886 to 5,400 in 1912 and doubled between 1913 and 1926. These figures, like the count of 10,000 public and 95,000 private companies in Great Britain in 1930, convey little idea of the extent of the economy that was under corporate control. The growth of some individual companies and the amalgamation of formerly independent units turned some companies into giants, in whose hands rested the management of the greater part of western Europe's banking and shipping, of British and French railroads, of the petroleum and tobacco trades, and of the steel, chemical, and electrical appliance industries.

The joint-stock company developed certain important characteristics. In the first place, its ownership was often widely dispersed. The list of stockholders in one British bank contained 65,000 names in the 1930's, the ownership of the railroads was at least as widely scattered, and a company might therefore have more owners than empolyees. This led to the second feature, the separation of ownership from management. The rank and file of the stockholders exerted little influence and did not attend the annual general meeting, except when roused by adverse reports and unprofitable results. Control lay in the hands of a few large or vocal stockholders, of the board of directors, and of the managing officers. As firms became interlocked with one another or with the banks, a comparatively small group of men might direct the affairs of many companies.

In the third place, the gulf between ownership and management was paralleled by gaps between labor and management and between owners and laborers. Personal contact—pleasant or otherwise—between wage earner and employer became increasingly difficult as firms grew in size. The wage earner knew only a foreman. Stockholders rarely knew much of the business or even of the country in which their money was invested. Their only concern was with the check that came out of the machine into which they had put their cash, or with market variations in the price of the stock they held. If one of them felt little responsibility for the Persian oil workers, Argentinian railroad men, Malay rubber cultivators, British seamen, Australian lead miners, and South African gold diggers who were producing profits for him, he could (or should) not be surprised if they in turn thought more of their own interests than of his. Large-scale enterprise and joint-stock organization were poor soils for the cultivation of any sense of mutual responsibility in investors, managers, or wage-earners.

The joint-stock company was only one of the devices for using the accumulating capital supply of the modern world. Private businesses saved and reinvested some of their income, and a company that had got well onto its feet might do the same. Savings banks, insurance companies, and friendly societies steered the savings of the middle and wage-earning classes into such safe investments as houses and public bonds. Finally, the state invested some of its tax revenue in public utilities or other pieces of necessary social equipment that were not likely to be provided by private enterprise. It did, however, usually need to borrow money to make such provision, and often that borrowing had to be done abroad, especially by the young countries of the New World or the undeveloped ones of the Old.

The accumulation and investment of capital in these various ways was one of the outstanding achievements of the nineteenth century. The world's railroads are said to have absorbed $100,000,000,000 in an age when a billion dollars seemed an enormous sum of money.

During the fifty years before World War I the British are estimated to have invested about a quarter of their annual income in one way or another, about 20 per cent of it at home and about 5 per cent overseas. By 1914 their external investments were worth $20,000,-000,000 and supplied the country with one-tenth of its national income. The "unearned" part of that income was now drawn largely from interest or dividends, for the day when real estate was the main form of property had passed. In 1913–1914, 45 per cent of the gross capital that came to the notice of British collectors of death duties consisted of stocks and bonds, while only about 20 per cent consisted of real estate. In Germany and France the trend was in the same direction; industrial and commercial capital was piling up, and a considerable quantity had already been invested abroad.

Capital Accumulation in the Soviet Union. By abolishing private enterprise the Communists closed the door on any further influx of those native and foreign investments which had built up the pre-revolutionary industrial and transportation equipment. The railroads had relied heavily on foreign loans, and a substantial part of the joint-stock capital invested in industries had been imported—a quarter of that in the textile industries, two-fifths in the iron, steel, and engineering enterprises, and nine-tenths in the mining industry. The Five-Year Plans had therefore to be financed within the country, by taking from the annual national income the funds needed for establishing new plants or industries and expanding old ones. Since there were no large income-receivers left, the subtraction must be made from the earnings of peasants and wage or salary earners.

The instrument used for this work was the State Budget. The Budget set forth the amount to be invested each year in building up the national economy as well as the sums to be spent on social and cultural services, defense, justice, and administration. During the first Five-Year Plan the financing of economic development accounted for two-thirds of the total expenditure, in the second Plan for about half.

The money needed to defray these capital and operating expenses was obtained chiefly by levying a turnover (or sales) tax. The government controlled virtually the whole trade of the country through the state or cooperative enterprises. It fixed the prices at which they obtained and sold goods, and it determined the rate of the turnover tax they were to pay. Its policy was to have the largest possible gap between the price the trading services paid for their goods and the price they got for them, and then to take the greater part of these monopoly profits by imposing a very heavy tax on them. It fixed low prices for the farmer's meat and grain, authorized the traders to sell them at high prices, and levied a turnover tax which swallowed up about 80 per cent of the receipts. For manufactured goods the gap between cost and sale price was likely to be smaller, but it was sufficient to allow the state to take a substantial share.

In 1936, "from every 100 roubles' worth of all goods sold on the internal market, 62.7 roubles were taken as indirect taxation [by the turnover tax] into the State budget" (Baykov), and the price level seems to have been about eight times that of 1928. Wage earners' incomes were thus largely swallowed up in purchasing costly food and the still scanty supply of consumers' manufactured goods. On the average, two-thirds of what they paid was tax, and on vodka the rate was 84 per cent.

Other sources of revenue were much less important. Those state enterprises which had reached the profit-making stage were allowed to keep part of the profits for capital additions or for rewarding outstanding employees; but the rest, ranging from 10 to 80 per cent, went into the Budget coffers. Actually the amount thus received was never large. Loans to the state from individuals were a more useful addition to the capital fund, and the quantity of bonds sold crept up steadily during the thirties; yet the total sales up to 1938 were only about one-third of the yield from the turnover tax of that year. Some minor taxes were even less productive. Russia's capital accumulation was therefore accomplished by depriving the present generation of the enjoyment of much of its income. The task of restoring the equipment destroyed by war and of achieving new objectives three times as high as those of 1939 may need "perhaps three new Five-Year Plans . . . if not more" (Stalin). This may mean that the deprivation will continue.

BIBLIOGRAPHY

Baykov, A., *The Development of the Soviet Economic System* (1947), chaps. 2, 7, 10, 11, 16, 19.

Berdrow, W., *Alfred Krupp* (Eng. trans., 1930).

Bogart, E. L., *Economic History of Europe, 1760–1939* (1942), chaps. 2, 9.

Bowden, W., Karpovich, M., and Usher, A. P., *Economic History of Europe since 1750* (1937), chaps. 7, 22, 24.

Clapham, J. H., *Economic Development of France and Germany, 1815–1914* (1923), sections 11–15, 18–22, 23, 33, 60–66, 70–76, 97.

Clapham, J. H., *Economic History of Modern Britain* (1926, 1932, 1938), vol. i, chaps. 5, 6; vol. ii, chaps. 4, 8; vol. iii, chaps. 3, 4.

Fong, H. D., *The Triumph of the Factory System in England* (1930), chap. 1.

Hunt, B. C., *The Development of the Business Corporation in England, 1800–1867* (1936).

Mantoux, P., *The Industrial Revolution in the Eighteenth Century* (Eng. trans., 1928), part iii, chap. 2.

Marshall, A., *Industry and Trade* (1919), book ii, especially chaps. 3, 4, 8.

Nussbaum, F. L., *History of the Economic Institutions of Modern Europe* (1933), part iv, chaps. 7, 9.

Redford, A., *Economic History of England, 1760–1860* (1931), chap. 6.

Roll, E., *An Early Experiment in Industrial Organization: A History of the Firm of Boulton and Watt (1775–1805)* (1930).

Sombart, W., *Der moderne Kapitalismus* (1922), vol. iii, pp. 712–948.

Stolper, G., *German Economy, 1870–1940* (1940), part ii.

Unwin, G., *Samuel Oldknow and the Arkwrights* (1923).

Articles

Allen, G. C., "Methods of Industrial Organization in the West Midlands," *Ec. Hist.*, January, 1929.

Chapman, S. J., and Ashton, T. S., "The Size of Businesses, Mainly in the Textile Industries," *J. Royal Stat. Soc.*, April, 1914.

Chapman, S. J., and Marquis, F. J., "The Recruiting of the Employing Classes from the Ranks of the Wage-Earners," *J. Royal Stat. Soc.*, January, 1912.

Cule, J. E., "Finance and Industry in the 18th Century; the Firm of Boulton and Watt," *Ec. Hist.*, February, 1940.

Furber, H., "The United Company of Merchants of England Trading to the East Indies, 1783–96," *Ec. H. R.*, November, 1940.

Gerschenkron, A., "The Rate of Industrial Growth in Russia Since 1885," *J. Ec. H.*, supplement, 1947.

Hartsough, M. L., "Business Leaders in Cologne in the 19th Century," *J.E.B.H.*, February, 1930.

Heaton, H., "Benjamin Gott and the Industrial Revolution in Yorkshire," *Ec. H. R.*, January, 1931.

Hower, R. M., "The Wedgwoods: Ten Generations of Potters, *J.E.B.H.*, February and August, 1932.

Hutt, W. H., "The Factory System of the Early 19th Century," *Economica*, March, 1926.

MacGregor, D. H., "Joint-Stock Companies and the Risk Factor," *Ec. J.*, December, 1929.

Postan, M. M., "Recent Trends in the Accumulation of Capital," *Ec. H. R.*, October, 1935.

Redlich, F., "The Leaders of the German Steam-Engine Industry during the First Hundred Years," *J. Ec. H.*, November, 1944.

Shannon, H. A., "The Coming of General Limited Liability," *Ec. Hist.*, January, 1931.

Shannon, H. A., "The First Five Thousand Joint-Stock Companies," *Ec. Hist.*, January, 1932.

Shannon, H. A., "The Limited Companies, 1866–1883," *Ec. H. R.*, October, 1933.

Encyclopaedia of the Social Sciences: See list of titles under Business and Industry, vol. xv, pp. 548 and 551. See especially articles on Captain of Industry, Industrialism, Homework (Industrial), Joint-stock Company, Partnership, Retail Trade.

XXIV

BANKING AND CURRENCY TO 1914

In Chapter XVI we saw how public banks and private bankers met the needs of early modern Europe by providing places in which money could be deposited, offering facilities for its withdrawal or transfer, making loans to the state and to businessmen, and issuing notes which supplemented the supply of metal currency. In 1789, on the eve of a turbulent quarter-century, these four services—deposit, transfer, loans, and notes—were being rendered by a few chartered public banks, some large private bankers or merchant-bankers, and a host of small banks. The number of public banks had grown recently, because most governments had felt the need for an agency to handle state finances and help industry or commerce. Frederick the Great in 1765 tried to repair the ravages of the Seven Years' War on his country's economy and his own credit rating by setting up one bank for deposit and transfer work, another one to discount bills, and a "big Lombard" or glorified pawnshop. In 1776 Turgot established the *Caisse d'escompte* (discount bank) to lend money to the government, discount bills, and issue notes. Russia, Denmark, and other countries took similar action, while in 1782 the Bank of Spain was created to wrestle with a depreciated currency and finance various economic projects.

Most of these new banks had checkered careers during the revolutionary period which began in 1789. Turgot's creation was submerged in the general financial wreckage when the revolutionary government's *Assignats* (treasury notes originally issued in small quantities and backed by the land which had been taken from the church, crown, and *émigrés*) were poured out in such vast amounts that by 1796 they were worthless paper. The Bank of Spain was besoviled by having large funds under the control of a director whose exuberant ideas earned him a reputation as "the John Law of Spain" and later by the wartime needs of the government and the deterioration of issues of treasury bills into an inflated paper currency. The war years also helped to complete the decline of Amsterdam. The

Dutch East India Company died in 1798, and the Bank of Amsterdam became insolvent. Many private banks and merchant-bankers continued their work; but the center of interest and strength had now moved across the North Sea to the new focal point of industry, foreign trade, shipping, investment, and banking—to Britain, and especially to London.

British Banking. The Bank of England was still chiefly servant and financier of the state, and as such it shouldered colossal war tasks between 1793 and 1815, raising loans, making short-term advances, and handling a greatly swollen revenue. Its private business was also growing rapidly. It made loans to the large trading companies, received deposits from some of London's leading bankers, and discounted bills of exchange for over a thousand clients drawn from every walk of the city's commerce and industry. Its discounting was most active in critical times when other bankers were loath to part with their cash for a bill which did not mature for some days or weeks; it had already become "the greatest and most accessible haven of storm-tossed traders and, at the last, of bankers also" (Clapham). As its notes were convertible into coin or bullion on demand, its reserves had always been greatly reduced in days of political or economic stress, but it had always succeeded in rebuilding them. In 1797, however, they were pushed to a dangerously low level as precious metal was needed to defray military or naval expenses abroad, to remit loans or subsidies to continental allies, to pay for grain imported in a year of bad harvest, and to meet the hoarding instincts of timid persons who feared that the country was going to the dogs and that the French were coming across. The government therefore gave the Bank permission to "forbear issuing any Cash in Payment until the Sense of Parliament can be taken on that Subject." This forbearance lasted until 1821. During all that time the Bank's notes were inconvertible; those who drew out their money or borrowed from the Bank must be content with pieces of paper.

In addition to the Bank, London had a goodly supply of private bankers who took deposits, honored checks, and made loans either directly or by discounting bills; also of merchant-bankers who accepted, discounted, and sold bills in addition to trading in commodities and handling shipping business. Some firms, such as the Barings, had become well known as loan underwriters, and many of them found in the war an opportunity to profit by raising public loans, transferring money to troops and allies, and financing the trade in war supplies. It was this kind of war work that did much to build up Europe's greatest private banking firm, the Rothschilds. One member of that family, Nathan, had gone from Frankfort-on-Main into the Manchester cotton trade and then moved on to London, where he gained both profit and prestige by devising methods for getting funds to Wellington in Spain. His brothers meanwhile were lending to Danish and other rulers, and by 1815 the five of them, stationed in five strategic centers—London, Paris, Vienna, Frankfort, and Naples—were on their way to eclipse the fame of the Fuggers. For seventy years the House of Rothschild had its finger in most financial pies. It made long- and short-term loans to governments, underwrote state and company securities, and raised the capital for railroad building in places as far apart as Austria and Brazil. It bought American cotton and tobacco, shipped them in its own vessels, and gathered in much of the gold that came to London. It played a large part in financing the Crimean War, the struggle for Italian independence, and the transfer to Berlin of the billion-dollar indemnity imposed on France in 1871. Disraeli did not exaggerate when he said that the seven great powers of Europe were England, France, Prussia, Russia, Austria, the Barings, and the Rothschilds.

Outside London, the provincial (or country) banks were gaining in numbers and strength before 1793. Then they were stimulated by industry's need for financial aid in producing armaments, woolen cloth, and other military supplies; by the expansion of the cotton trade and industry, which coincided with the war period; and by two trade booms during the years 1797–1802 and 1808–1810. The number of them in England and Wales rose from 230 in 1797 to about 800 in 1809. As they were private firms they could make their loans by issuing notes which, like those of the Bank, were incon-vertible after 1797. The size of the issue was therefore determined by the country banker's confidence in his local clients and in his ability to forecast trade prospects. His confidence was so high that by 1814 the total country bank note issue was equal to that of the Bank. When peace came, the stoppage of war orders was not counteracted by any great overnight emergence of civilian demand. The general price index fell from 194 in 1814 to 130 in 1816, bankruptcy stalked the industrial towns as it did the wheatlands, and the number of note-issuing country banks dropped from 733 in 1814 to 585 in 1817. The panic of 1825 dragged down another 70 of them, making their notes, which were an important part of the local currency, quite worthless.

Joint-Stock Banking. These bank failures emphasized two needs: for a stronger banking system with adequate capital and for some restraint on the issue of notes. The first was met by permitting joint-stock banks to be set up outside a range of sixty-five miles from the Bank of England (1826) and then inside that zone (1833). The provincial banks could issue notes, but those nearer London must not break the Bank's monopoly. Armed with these powers, groups of manufacturers and merchants founded banks in the industrial towns, put much capital into them, and imported managers from Scotland, a land of high repute for sound banking practices. By 1836 over a hundred had been set up, and some of them quickly established branches, a policy the Bank of England had been pursuing since 1826. The movement was overdone during the boom of 1834–1836, there was excessive or speculative creation of joint-stock banks, unhealthy extension of credit, overissue of notes, and disaster in 1836–1837. The formation of such banks was therefore made less easy and the issue of notes restricted (1844). During the rest of the century most of the remaining private banks became joint stock or were bought out (or beaten out) by their new rivals. The latter scattered branches widely and then began to amalgamate. Their number in Scotland fell from 36 in 1819 to 11 in 1873, and to 8 in 1928. England in 1844 had 400 banks, in 1891 only 143, and by the 1920's, 5 joint-stock banks (out of a total of 16) operated 8,000 branches and did five-sixths of the country's banking business. One of this "big five" absorbed 111 banks between its foundation in 1836 and its hundredth birthday.

The movement toward a few large units with a legion of branches was repeated on the continent. By 1914 the 36 largest German banks had 1,500 branches, and 5 of them controlled nine-tenths of the joint-stock banking of the country. The "big D's"—Deutsche, Disconto, Dresdner, and Darmstädter—fell in number from four to three when the first two amalgamated in 1929 and to two when the last two were merged in 1931. In France, Belgium, and most other western lands concentration came later and more slowly but produced the same pattern. Bigness was no virtue in itself, and might easily become a monopolistic menace; but it did tend to produce great aggregations of assets, to diversify interests, risks, and opportunities, to call for expert responsible direction, to limit cutthroat competition, and to make the state interested in saving a big bank from (possibly merited) disaster.

Note Issues. The crises of 1825 and 1836 provoked discussion about the principles that should govern the issue of notes. In the early forties about 280 British banks were handing out paper promises to pay legal tender—gold coin or Bank of England notes—on demand, and the plethora of such promises had been partly responsible for both crises. For two decades two questions were debated: Who should possess the right to issue notes? and What should control the size of the issue? One school of experts said banks should be free to expand or contract their issues as they pleased in accordance with the general growth or seasonal state of trade; their obligation to redeem notes on demand would be a sufficient check on the temptation to issue too many. The opposing school had a low opinion of the banker's ability to resist (or even recognize) temptation, and urged that the size of a bank's issue be related to the quantity of precious metal in the vaults.

The cynics won the day, and the Bank Charter Act of 1844 regulated the note issue in two ways. (1) It decreed that existing banks, except the Bank of England, could not increase the quantity of notes they had in use; that banks formed after 1844 could not issue any; and that when any old bank failed, changed its character, or amalgamated, its right of issue lapsed into the hands of the Bank. By 1900 only forty of the veteran banks were in existence; the last one disappeared in 1923, and the Bank of England's note monopoly became complete. (2) The act regulated that monopoly. The Bank was allowed to issue notes up to £14,000,000 on the security of its loans to the state; it could also put out notes equal to two-thirds the lapsed issues of the other banks, thus eventually bringing its "fiduciary" issue to nearly £20,000,000. Beyond that point every note must be backed in full with gold; every increase in the issue must be accompanied by an addition to the gold reserve; and if that reserve declined the note issue must be reduced accordingly. The notes were thus virtually gold certificates, as good as gold.

This plan had been proposed by the Bank. It made British bank notes safe, but it might also make the supply of them inadequate, since so much depended now on the supply of gold, and in 1844 no one could foresee that the gold famine would be broken within ten years by the discovery of rich deposits in California and Australia. The ending of uncontrolled note issue did not end the susceptibility of the business world to booms, and when those fevers reached their inevitable crisis the Bank might be compelled by a drain on its gold reserve to reduce its issue, recall some loans and refuse others to reputable but harassed firms, thus accentuating rather than allaying the trouble. In 1847, 1857, and 1866 this situation developed, but the Bank could legally do nothing to provide the additional loans that would relieve the tension. In response to panic-stricken clamor from businessmen—not from the Bank—the government on each occasion announced that if the Bank cared to issue notes for which it had no gold backing, thus breaking the law, parliament would be asked to take the necessary steps in granting forgiveness. This announcement was enough to allay the panics of 1847 and 1866, but in 1857 the Bank had to use the emergency powers granted to it.

An act that had to be suspended to save a situation seemed a poor statute, needing to be converted from cast iron to at least wrought iron or even to be given a bit of the quality of rubber. When Germany set up its Reichsbank in 1875 it copied the essentials of the British plan—a monopoly of note issue, some fiduciary notes, but a gold backing for the rest. In order, however, to cope with emergencies, the Reichsbank was allowed to put out uncovered notes, provided it paid a tax of 5 per cent on them and did not let its gold reserve sink below 30 per cent of the total issue. The tax would prevent the emergency power from being used too largely or too long.

France handled the problem in a quite different manner. In 1800 Napoleon established the Bank of France to restore public credit, issue notes, and discount bills. Like the Bank of England, it was privately owned, and given a monopoly of note issue in Paris (1803) and later throughout the land (1848). Unlike the Bank of England, part of its governing body was chosen by the state, part of its profits went to the treasury, and its notes, though convertible, were not tied to gold. Instead a maximum issue was fixed, and the figure was increased at various times as the need arose, to 6,800,000,000 francs ($1,300,000,000) in 1913. The Bank could therefore increase its issue with the growth of trade and vary it in accordance with business needs; but it prudently kept a very healthy metal reserve behind the paper, usually as high as 80 per cent.

Commercial Banking. The banks of issue did more than print notes and serve as bankers for the state. In France and Germany they went into what can be called retail banking. The Bank of France became nation-wide with hundreds of branches, allowed small customers to open deposit accounts, and discounted small bills for them. Its notes, supplemented by silver, gold, and these bills, were such an ample medium of exchange that there was little need to develop the use of checks in petty trading. The Reichsbank spread its services in similar manner through branches or sub-branches. Yet the greater part of the business of both banks was on a larger wholesale scale with the big firms, the other banks, and governments.

Until 1825 the Bank of England was sometimes correctly mis-called the Bank of London, since most of its private business was limited to that city. But when the crisis of 1825 destroyed many provincial banks it stepped out of London to set up branches in eleven provincial industrial and commercial centers. The branches were profitable: they attracted plenty of business in good times, and in days of crisis merchants and bankers flocked to them as they did to the head office, urgently seeking loans or trying to turn their bills into cash. The Bank's work therefore came to fit its name. In that work it competed to some extent with the private banks and with the new joint-stock ones as they were set up; but in the long run it became more their servant, in some respects their master. Eventually, though unintentionally and unwillingly, it emerged as a central bank for the whole banking system.

In its private dealings the Bank developed certain practices which seemed both safe and profitable—as it was a joint-stock company its stockholders expected profits. Until 1833 the usury laws forbade lenders to charge more than 5 per cent interest. The "Bank rate" at which the Bank lent money or discounted bills therefore remained at 4 or 5 per cent for many decades, in good and trying times alike. When the demand for help was heavy and urgent, the Bank rationed its available funds, limiting the amount a borrower could secure and also discriminating between first-class bills and those which were less sound. It also indulged in what a later age knows as "open-market operations": in slack times it put more of its notes into circulation by using them to buy exchequer bills or government bonds—"Consols" as they were called—from private owners, thereby getting for itself an interest-yielding security and giving the seller spending power which might help to stimulate the demand for goods. When it wanted the money back it sold them, and thereby reduced the note circulation. Sometimes it borrowed money from other banks in order to increase the supply needed for loans; sometimes it set out to buy gold to supplement the supply that came into its hands in the normal way of deposits.

After 1840 the Bank's most notable policy became that of adjusting the Bank rate according to the state of business and the size of its gold reserve. If conditions grew critical because the gold reserve had been drained low and the demand for help ran high, the Bank raised the rate on loans and discounts from the 2 or 3 per cent of easy-money times to as much as 6, 7, or 8 per cent and in the panic-swept days of 1857, 1866, and 1893 to 9 or 10 per cent. This action led the other banks to raise their rates; it made loans dearer, checked people's inclination to borrow more, and might induce them to reduce their debts. But it also raised the interest rate which banks paid on deposits. Some foreigners might therefore send funds to London to lend or deposit at the new attractive rate, or to pay off their debts, with the result that gold would flow back into the country and into the Bank's reserves.

The Bank rate was therefore intended to be a stimulant when borrowing and buying were slow, as a brake when they got too high, and as a guardian of the gold reserve. The practice was a rather clumsy, drastic device for regulating the volume and price of credit, and sometimes the situation had got so far out of hand that its application was painful or even disastrous to those who were innocent as well as to those who had been guilty of blowing the bubble too large. But so long as London was the center of international commerce and finance, a change in the Bank rate was immediately felt in every money market in the world.

The reverse was also true: every wind, whether zephyr or tornado, that swept through New York, Paris, Vienna, Melbourne, Buenos Aires, or any other center of any part of the world's economy was felt in the Bank and in the financial institutions that were crowded around it in the heart of "the City." Those institutions were of many kinds. Some were the private or the increasingly powerful joint-stock banks. They accepted deposits from all sizes of customers, and as their branches got within easy reach of more people the habit of depositing one's receipts in a bank and then drawing checks on them spread to small tradesmen and salaried or professional workers. Since the banks operated chiefly with money which belonged to depositors and must be paid back to them on demand, they could not let too much of it get too far away. They kept some of their assets in cash in their own vaults and tills or deposited it with the Bank, to be drawn out when it was needed and perhaps to be supplemented by a loan from the Bank if need arose. Some was lent for a few days or was repayable "at call"; some was used to buy Consols, which could be sold quickly in the stock market if the money was wanted. Experience suggested that about half the bank's assets should be kept in this "liquid" condition; the earnings on it were low, but liquidity was more important than income.

The rest of the assets could be put a little farther out of immediate reach, but not too far. They were used to discount bills which were a few weeks from maturing, especially foreign bills, for the domestic bill was being supplanted by the check. Some funds were lent for a period of six to twelve months to merchants or manufacturers. These loans were no longer made by handing over a sheaf of notes, but by placing the amount to the borrower's credit in his account and allowing him to draw checks on it; or they were made by allowing him to overdraw his account. There was, however, little long-term lending to supply plant for industry or transportation. Those who wanted fixed capital must obtain it out of their own pockets and profits or by selling stocks and bonds. The bank would help them in the commercial part of their enterprise by discounting the bills they drew on buyers or lending them money for a set short time, but it would not "invest" its funds. It engaged in "commercial banking" rather than "investment" or "industrial banking."

Other financial houses in the City were concerned chiefly with handling bills of exchange—accepting, discounting, buying, and selling. They used their own funds, accepted deposits, and borrowed from banks or the Bank. Some bill-dealing firms became so large that the collapse of one of them (Overend and Gurney) in 1866 converted a credit crisis into a panic. While their business in domestic bills diminished, that in foreign bills expanded with the growth of international trade, shipping, and investment. All roads led to London even more than they had to Amsterdam. When a Boston importer bought British goods it was natural that he should tell the exporter to draw the bill on Baring Brothers, who would accept it on the American's behalf; but his pride in his city's history may well have been hurt by the knowledge that he could not buy tea direct from Canton without getting someone in London to accept the bills drawn on him by the Chinese exporter; and if he therefore turned to importing coffee direct from Brazil he still had to make the same arrangement. All over the world sellers obtained payment from buyers through London for goods which never came near Europe. Bills accepted by London houses ranked as first-class paper in every continent. They were the paper money of world trade, and when war came in 1914 about £350,000,000 ($1,700,000,-000) of them were at large. Finally, the flotation and underwriting of colonial or foreign government and corporation securities became a big business, in which the Rothschilds and Barings played a prominent part but were by no means alone.

London in 1914 thus housed a financial system evolved to meet every kind of requirement. The Bank competed to some extent with the banks but was becoming more acceptable to them—and more conscious of itself—as a colleague, cooperator, and center. By keeping large deposits in the Bank, they made it a central reserve and obliged it to pay great attention to the protection of its gold supply. When a bank got into difficulties, as did the Barings in 1890 and two savings banks in 1911, the Bank led the others or cooperated with them in saving the situation from disaster. The concentration on London was emphasized further as banks were set up to specialize in handling public and private money affairs for China, Australia, and other remote regions, and when German, French, Japanese, and other foreign banks established branches in the City. One instance only need be given to illustrate this high centralization. China was defeated by Japan in 1894 and ordered to pay an indemnity from Peking to Tokyo. She did it by gradually building up the necessary sum as a deposit in the Bank of England, and when there was enough she drew a single big check ordering the Bank to pay the money to the account of the Japanese government in the London branch of the Yokohama Specie Bank. While the money was being accumulated, the Yokohama Bank asked the Bank of England to put it out on loan in the money market, and the sum was so large that it had some effect in keeping the Bank rate down at the low figure of 2 per cent.

Continental Investment Banking. Much continental banking was concerned with the needs of governments, the credit and transfer operations of trade, and the note issue. It resembled in essentials the work of the British banks and therefore need not be described. The chief difference lay in the addition of investment banking to commercial services, and in some instances to the formation of banks which were chiefly interested in supplying capital as well as short-term credit to industrial or transportation firms. An early instance was the *Société Générale pour Favoriser l'Industrie Nationale*, set up in Brussels in 1822 to serve as government banker, issue notes, lend money on mortgage, and provide funds for industries. It raised much of the money for this work by selling stocks and bonds and played an important part in the industrial development of Belgium. In France the Rothschilds dominated the field of underwriting and floating industrial and railroad companies until the *Crédit Mobilier* was set up in 1852 with the blessing of Napoleon III to challenge them. It sold its own bonds to raise capital, used the money to promote, finance, and buy the securities of new companies, and then sold some of its holdings to investors. Railroads, industries, mines, harbors, and ships were among the objects of its attention, but the task finally became too large and unprofitable, and collapse came in 1867.

Investment banking did its largest European job in financing Germany's industrial growth. Investors in stocks or bonds were neither plentiful nor willing, and people who wished to deposit money preferred savings banks, usually municipally owned ones, to ordinary banks. The German banks therefore had to play a substantial part in floating companies. One of them, formed in 1849 at Cologne, financed mining, steel, and machine-making joint-stock companies. The Darmstädter Bank (1853), the *Discontogesellschaft* (1856), and later creations supplied the needs of many manufacturers, metal producers, shipping firms, chemical works, and other ventures. They used their own money (received from the sale of shares) and customers' deposits to underwrite the stocks and bonds of new companies, sold some of these to the public, but (willingly or unwillingly) kept some. In addition they supplied their protégés with short-term credit. In return they had representatives on the companies' boards of directors, and brought pressure to bear whenever competition became destructive or fusion promised benefits. The Deutsche Bank in 1920 had representatives on the governing bodies of over 200 firms, while the Dresdner Bank had become closely bound up with Krupp. When German industry began to seek foreign markets the banks helped by establishing branches abroad or by setting up subsidiary banks to finance operations in the Levant, South America, and the Far East. They proved that whether trade follows the flag or not, it certainly follows the banks.

Foreign observers regarded this close alliance between industry and banking as one secret of Germany's rapid expansion. Englishmen scolded their own banks for not following the German example, and in Sweden the banking laws were amended (1911) to permit banks to purchase shares in industrial undertakings. But the record was far from spotless. Overexpansion was not avoided, overoptimism had no check from the bank office, short-term loans could not be recalled when depositors wanted their money, and disaster struck both bank and industry when it came. Investment banking raised as many problems as it solved, and intimate relations between industry and banking proved to be dangerous. Sweden recognized this by reversing its policy of 1911 in 1921 and 1933.

THE GOLD SUPPLY AND THE GOLD STANDARD

The growth of regulated note issues, the spread of bank deposits, the use of checks, and improvements in the machinery for making international payments permitted the nineteenth century to do most of its business with pieces of paper. Yet behind the printed or written paper slips lay a supply of precious metal. Every transaction was in terms of some "unit of account" (pound, dollar, mark, franc, etc.) representing a fixed weight of gold or silver, and every piece of paper gave its possessor the right to obtain metal disks if he wished. In domestic affairs the timid preferred the chink of coins to the crackle of paper, and in times of crisis most people were timid. In foreign transactions a debt could be paid or a transaction made by shipping coin or bullion if bills of exchange or drafts could not be bought at a reasonable price. Precious metal was thus the foundation of the commercial and credit structure, even if people rarely went into the basement to look at it.

A strengthening of that foundation was essential as the weight of the superstructure increased. During the second half of the eighteenth century there was a great revival of silver production in Spanish America and a considerable output of gold from Brazil. The silver spread over Europe or went to the Orient; the gold tended to reach London. During the war years coins gave place to paper money in the belligerent lands, and when currencies were restored to convertibility only Britain went onto a gold standard. The export drain on her far-from-ample gold supply helped to precipitate the crises of 1825, 1836, and 1847. In continental countries a bimetallic standard might prevail, as in France, where an ounce of gold was decreed to be worth 15.5 ounces of silver; but few gold coins circulated. In Belgium, Switzerland, and Italy silver was the officially favored metal, and when Holland in 1847 abandoned bimetallism

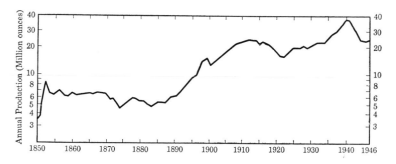

Estimated Gold Production of World (Excluding U.S.S.R.), 1850–1946
(In million fine ounces)

for silver monometallism she seemed to be voicing the continent's belief that gold was too scarce to be useful as a currency basis.

Within five years the situation had been relieved and reversed by the gold discoveries in California (1848) and Australia (1851). The world's output during the first half of the century averaged $16,000,-000 of gold a year (at about $20 an ounce), but that of 1853 was $150,000,000 and the annual average for 1851–1875 was $120,000,-000. The new fields showed signs of being worked out by the early eighties and the yield fell to two-thirds the peak output of 1853; but soon the cyanide process made possible the working of low-grade ores, and a number of new gold fields were discovered. The richest was on the Rand, near Johannesburg in South Africa. Gold was found there in 1884, production became large after the South African war ended in 1902, and by 1930 this field had yielded over $5,000,000,000 of gold. Close on the heels of the Rand discovery came smaller ones in west Australia, the Yukon, Ontario, and other places. The total output gave an annual average of nearly $400,000,-000 for the years 1901–1930.

Not all this treasure went to augment the monetary supply. The Orient continued to be a sink down which much of it disappeared into hoards or decorations, while jewelers, dentists, and others used it as raw material. Since 1900 about 45 per cent of the new gold has gone into those channels, but sufficient was left to increase the world's stock of monetary gold as follows:

1835............ 2	billion dollars (at $20 an ounce)	
1889............ 3.5	"	"
1909............ 6.8	"	"
1929............11.1	"	"

The rate of growth was irregular. From 1850 to 1873 it was 4 per cent per annum; during the quieter years 1873–1895, only 1.6 per cent. The boom period 1896–1914 lifted it to 3.7 per cent, but the rate between 1918 and 1930 was down to 1.8 per cent.

The Dethronement of Silver. The new gold made the spread of the gold standard possible, since there was now enough metal for currency and bank reserves. The golden flood also made the abandonment of bimetallism inevitable, for it was impossible to maintain a fixed legal ratio between the two metals. A government could decree that within its boundaries an ounce of gold was worth 15½ ounces of silver and that the gold in one twenty-franc piece was equal in value to the silver in twenty one-franc coins. But in the world's bullion market gold sank in price as it became more plentiful. In 1848 an ounce of gold cost 15.85 ounces of silver, but in 1859 one could buy it for 15.19 ounces; or, to put it another way, 19.17 silver francs would buy the gold that was in a twenty-franc gold piece. If bimetallism was to be maintained, the gold coins must be reminted and given a larger gold content to restore their value. This was impracticable, as it would have to be done frequently to keep up with every change in the relative value of the two metals. The alternative was to abandon the double standard. France, her franc-using allies (Belgium, Switzerland), and Italy tried to devise a modified bimetallism, but when the German Empire in 1872–1874 established its currency on a gold standard the silver cause was lost. Scandinavia, Holland, Austria-Hungary, Russia, the United States, and Japan soon joined the ranks of gold and in 1878 the franc-using countries suspended the free coinage of silver. Eventually only Ethiopia and China were left on the silver standard. Mussolini crossed the former off the list in 1936 and at almost the same moment American policy had raised the price of silver so high that China could not afford to retain it as the basis of its currency.

This dethronement of a metal which "for thousands of years had enjoyed equal privileges with gold" (Helferrich) greatly diminished the demand for silver. Its price fell from $1.25 an ounce in 1866 to 43 cents in 1903. It continued to be used in token coins, but the silver put into a shilling was not worth a shilling. At times it almost ceased to be worth mining for its own sake, and in the 1920's about 80 per cent of the yield was a by-product obtained in the extraction of lead, copper, or other metals which were needed in growing quantities by industry and which were mixed with silver in complex ores. When World War I and fourteen senators from seven American silver-producing states pushed its price up, mints reduced the silver content of coins and turned to the use of nickel or brass. The price plunged to 24 cents in 1932, was raised by Congress in 1933–1934, and went still higher during World War II. This only made silver less important than ever in the world's currency systems.

The Gold Standard. In 1914 the gold standard prevailed throughout Europe and most other parts of the world. The unit of account was expressed in terms of a fixed number of grains of gold. In Britain that unit, the pound, was equal to 113 grains, a quantity large enough to make a coin, known as the pound or sovereign, that was not too small for use; in fact, half-sovereigns were also made. In other countries where the number of grains was much smaller, gold coins contained five, ten, or more units (francs, marks, dollars, etc.). The coins were in general circulation, men carried them in special compartments of their purses or in small metal containers on the end of a watch chain, and supplies could be obtained on demand at any bank.

To most people that was all the gold standard meant, but to businessmen it might mean much more. Bullion was turned into coins freely and free of charge by the mints. Coins could be melted down if anyone wished to do so. Coin or bullion could be exported, and any debtor, buyer, or person who wished to deposit or invest money in a foreign land was free to ship metal if he found it cheaper to do this than to buy a bill of exchange or draft. If he did send gold, he knew that a sovereign was worth $4.87 in New York, 25.22 francs in Paris, or 20.43 marks in Berlin, since this was the "Mint Par of Exchange," the value of 113 grains in foreign units of account.

In practice it rarely was cheaper to send metal, for there was an international gold standard as well as a domestic one, with London as its financial center and clearinghouse. Through its operations each country could receive payment for its exports, pay for its imports, receive or send capital investments, borrow or lend for a short term, pay or receive interest, dividends, shipping charges, and insurance premiums, or carry out any other kind of monetary transaction without much movement of gold. There were always men in London who held claims on money in foreign cities, just as there were men in every foreign city who had claims on London. The former were willing to sell theirs (in bills or drafts) to those who needed money in a foreign currency to pay their debts to the latter. The sale price, the *rate of exchange,* was usually so near the Mint Par of Exchange that the cost plus postage was below that of packing, insuring, and shipping gold. If, however, the demand for claims exceeded the supply, the rate of exchange might rise so high that shipment would be as cheap or cheaper, and also would be necessary to cope with the excess of demand. When this happened, or when any other influence caused a serious drain on London's gold supply, the raising of the Bank rate and other steps brought enough gold back to restore the metal foundation for notes and credit to satisfactory strength. But no gold standard, domestic or international, could stand up under the burden of a world war. That breakdown will be examined in Chapter XXVIII.

Gold and the Price Level. The part played by gold in causing price fluctuations cannot be measured, since it was only one of at least three influences operating on prices. A large influx of gold increased the metallic and paper currency supply, expanded the basis on which credit could be granted, stimulated new demands for capital and consumers' goods in the countries which produced the metal, and thus tended to increase purchasing power and raise prices. The second factor was the relation between the supply of commodities and the demand for them. In times of boom and heavy capital investment the demand became intense and prices therefore rose. The third factor was the cost of production and transportation. The technological improvements in each of these fields, the great expansion in industrial and agricultural production, the cheapening of carriage on land and sea, and the raid on the fertile soils and subsoils of the New World were all cost-reducing factors.

The graph on page 598 shows the movement of English prices since the late eighteenth century. Two features of it are noteworthy.

The first is the jagged nature of the line, reflecting such immediate short-run influences as bad or good harvests, the outbreak or end of war, and the rise and fall of booms. The second is the alternation of long upward and downward trends. The war years 1792–1815, broken by peace in 1802–1803, comprised a period of rising prices. The Hundred Years' Peace revealed four phases.

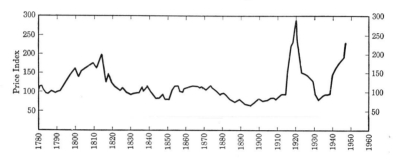

British Wholesale Prices, 1780–1947

(1780–1850, based on Silberling index; 1850–1947, based on Sauerbeck-Statist index)

1. *1815–1849.* The collapse of war prices occupied the first ten years; machinery, better roads, and then the railroad reduced the costs of making or transporting goods; but the supply of new gold was small and lack of an adequate supply caused trouble to the banking system on a number of occasions. Consequently prices fell about 55 per cent between their war peak and 1849, and nearly half of that decline took place between the early peace years and mid-century.

2. *1850–1873.* The inrush of gold gave the banks a larger reserve and increased the metallic currency of the leading countries by 30 per cent within a decade. The demand for goods of all kinds and for ships for the newly awakened lands as well as for buyers in old markets pushed prices up. In England they jumped 35 per cent between 1851 and 1854 and fluctuated about that level until the boom of 1873 took them up to nearly 50 per cent above the mid-century mark. Germany, Sweden, France, and the United States all witnessed price increases of about the same dimension.

3. *1873–1896.* In the third phase the price level fell almost without interruption in all countries, by about 40 per cent. The supply of new gold was much smaller than during the preceding period, and

there was a considerable demand for it by countries turning to the gold standard. Yet there are no indications that banks or business generally felt any shortage of gold, that their credit facilities were thereby restricted, or that they charged high interest rates because the demand for loans was higher than the supply. The causes of the great price decline must therefore be sought elsewhere—in the reduced costs of production and transportation, in expanded output, and for some capital goods such as railroad equipment or coal in a slackening of demand. (See Chapter XXVII.)

4. *1896–1914.* The outpouring of gold from South Africa, Australia, and other places came just about the time when the forces which had depressed prices before 1896 had exhausted themselves. The fertile lands in the United States had now been all shared out and settled, and American food products were being needed for home consumption; the supply of wool had been cut down by a long drought in Australia; low profit rates had slackened the rate of expansion in some industries, and low prices had made it difficult for many overseas areas to attract the capital needed for their development. The world's economy was ready for a new stimulus (or shot in the arm), and the new gold helped to provide it. Between 1896 and 1914 English prices rose 35 per cent, German 42, French 44, and Russian 52 per cent. The high cost of living was one of the acute problems of the years just before 1914.

BIBLIOGRAPHY

Bagehot, W., *Lombard Street* (1873).

Birnie, A., *Economic History of Europe, 1760–1930* (1930), chap. 6.

Bogart, E. L., *Economic History of Europe, 1760–1939* (1942), chaps. 5, 12, 20.

Brown, W. A., Jr., *The International Gold Standard Reinterpreted, 1914–1934* (1941).

Clapham, J. H., *Economic Development of France and Germany, 1815–1914* (1923), chaps. 6, 13.

Clapham, J. H., *Economic History of Modern Britain* (1926, 1932), vol. i, chaps. 7, 13; vol. ii, chap. 9.

Clapham, Sir John, *The Bank of England* (1945), vol. ii.

Conant, C., *History of Modern Banks of Issue* (6th ed., 1927).

Corti, E., *The Rise of the House of Rothschild* (1928); *The Reign of the House of Rothschild* (1928).

Fay, C. R., *Great Britain from Adam Smith to the Present Day* (1932), chap. 6.

Feavearyear, A. E., *The Pound Sterling* (1931).

Gregory, T. E., *Select Statutes, Documents, and Reports Relating to British Banking* (1929), Introduction.

Hawtrey, R. G., *Currency and Credit* (3rd ed., 1928).

Hawtrey, R. G., *A Century of Bank Rate* (1938).

Layton, W. T., and Crowther, G., *An Introduction to the Study of Prices* (1938).

Le Cheminant, K., *Colonial and Foreign Banking Systems* (1924).

Leavens, D. H., *Silver Money* (1939).

Marshall, A., *Industry and Trade* (1919), book ii, chap. 9.

Powell, E. T., *The Evolution of the Money Market* (1915).

Riesser, J., *The German Great Banks and Their Concentration* (1911).

Sayers, R. S., *Modern Banking* (1938).

Van Dillen, J. G. (ed.), *A History of the Principal Public Banks* (1934).

Whale, P. B., *Joint Stock Banking in Germany* (1930).

ARTICLES

Hamilton, E. J., "War and Inflation in Spain, 1780–1800," *Q.J.E.*, November, 1944.

Hidy, R. W., "Anglo-American Merchant Bankers, 1815–1860," *J. Ec. H.*, December, 1941.

Sayers, R. S., "The Question of the Standard, 1815–1844," *Ec. Hist.*, February, 1933.

Encyclopaedia of the Social Sciences: Articles on Banking (Commercial), Branch Banking, Central Banking, Credit Control, Investment Banking, Money Market, Bimetallism, Coinage, Gold, Monetary Unions, Money, Silver.

XXV

COMPETITION, COMBINATION, AND CONTROL

The economy of the nineteenth century was not merely more capitalistic and commercial than that of any preceding period but also more competitive. Those who ran it were given at times to glory in this last characteristic. "Competition" and "progress" were two of the most popular words in their vocabulary, and the first was deemed an important factor in causing the second. "Competition is the life of trade and the law of progress"—this was an unquestionable truism in 1850. The classical economists regarded competition as the road to maximum welfare, the spur to efficiency, the enemy of incompetence, the guardian of the consumer, and the best guarantee that no man got more of the national income than he deserved. The Western liberal political theorist, nurtured on British, American, and French ideas which had been the ammunition for revolutions in those countries, urged that the state should remove its restraints on thought and action, abolish any survivals of privilege and monoply, recognize equality of rights and opportunities for all, and thus provide a field in which the citizen was at liberty to pursue his own interests according to his talents. When the scientists began to talk about evolution their phrases seemed to support these views, for competition, the survival of the fittest, and the extermination of those who could not adapt themselves to the changing world were evidently the inexorable rules of nature as well as of society.

Competition was more than a concept or a slogan. It was also a fact, a condition which had always existed in some fields of enterprise but which now became more widespread with the disappearance of monopolies or regulations created by governments and the appearance of new fields in which men could strive with one another for the rewards. In overseas trade the gateway to Asia was thrown open with the passing of the East India companies and the forcible entry of Europeans and Americans into Chinese and Japanese trade.

The doors to the United States and Latin America were opened on equal terms to all comers with the ending of colonial status. The removal of prohibitions and scaling down of tariffs encouraged international competition. Meanwhile in domestic economies the abolition of guilds, the repeal of apprenticeship laws, the end of serfdom, and the removal of bans on migration or emigration made it legally possible for men to go where they wished or enter any occupation that attracted them. Dislike of monopolies might lead the state deliberately to foster competition and to frown on any action which was "in restraint of trade." Finally, the improvements in transportation and communication widened the area over which men could compete with one another.

Given this freedom and mobility, competition invaded almost every market in which goods, services, and labor were bought or sold. There was competition between old industries, methods, or commodities and new ones: Manual skill was challenged by machine work; merchants who obtained their goods by putting out material felt increasing and eventually irresistible pressure from those who employed factory methods; the sailing ship, canal, and stagecoach were pushed aside by the steamship and the railroad. There was competition between rival producers of the same goods or services; and if they were new goods or services the rush of manufacturers, traders, or wage earners into the field when once its attractiveness had been revealed usually created overcapacity, the rapid disappearance of the pioneers' high profits or wages, and cutthroat competition. There was competition between rival products or services—butter and margarine, rayon and other fabrics, gas and electricity, rail and bus. Finally, there was competition among buyers of nearly all kinds of goods.

Some of these rivalries were local in scope, some were waged between regions in the same country, but the larger ones had the international field as their battleground. Although the weapons were chiefly those of price and quality, other factors might influence the outcome, such as the terms of credit, ability to deliver goods regularly in the required quantity, and the skill of the advertiser in catching the purchaser's eye in cases where the buyer had no means of determining the relative merits of competing goods.

At its widest extent competition never covered the whole field. Business enterprises ranged over a semicircle from monopoly at one end, through what economists now call *duopoly* (where two firms control the supply), through *oligopcly* (where a small number hold the market), and past other stages of "imperfect competition" to the "pure" brand in which hosts of rivals are involved. Some enterprises had a natural monopoly almost from the start because their product —gas, electricity, water, streetcars, or telephone service—was unsuitable for competition. In Europe most of these public utilities began as public ventures or were acquired by the municipality or state at an early age. Some firms gained a virtual monopoly of a piece of market because their product possessed some distinctive quality, name, or trade mark, had been persuasively advertised, or had built up so much good will for itself and its makers that customers would never think of buying a rival article. Other businesses enjoyed a tariff monopoly or oligopoly if the customs rates were high, or a patent monopoly until the patent on their product expired, or a geographical monopoly if the nearest competitor was far away and freight costs were heavy. Some monopolies or oligopolies were the result of competition which had reduced the number of survivors to one or a few; and others were the outcome of a successful campaign to absorb or amalgamate independent firms in the interest of greater efficiency, higher rewards, or less competition.

Industries therefore varied greatly in the number of competitors and the severity of the competition. The older industries, such as textiles and coal mining, which took their modern form before 1850 grew up in hundreds, even thousands, of small or middle-sized private firms which competed vigorously with one another. But the later enterprises, such as steel or chemicals, tended to run to large size, joint stock, and heavy capital cost in all countries. The number of firms was small, and though the call to battle between these giants might at times be so alluring as to be irresistible, common sense bought by bitter experience and price wars suggested that it might be wise to avoid being too provocative, to limit competition to advertising the superior virtues of one's product, to reach some working agreement, or even to seek profit through union.

In periods of prosperity competition seemed to possess the virtues attributed to it. Demand more than kept up with the expanding supply of goods from old firms or from new ones that came into being; prices rose and profits were satisfactory. When, however, conditions changed for the worse, when the swollen capacity of the industry led to overproduction and cutthroat rivalry, so that no one knew who would be the next bankrupt, competitors might begin to wonder if they had not been worshiping a false god. Perhaps co-operation, rather than competition, was the life of trade and even the law of self-preservation. Competition was a means, not an end. The end was profit, and if competition jeopardized that end some better means must be sought. Or if competition was not at fault, perhaps the blame should be placed on that misleading adjective "free" which was always used as a prefix. Men ought to be free to compete, but should they be free to compete in any way they wished, or should the phrase be "regulated, orderly, controlled competition"? The state had already reached the conclusion that "free enterprise" did not mean freedom to employ children at too early an age or for excessive hours, to sell impure goods or use short weights and measures. Labor had also pointed the way. In its trade unions it was trying to develop a sense of community of interest among wage earners, to establish the principle that free competition for jobs should not be free to push wages below a recognized stand-ard, and from this defensive attitude it was passing on to fight for a higher standard. Capital took these three leaves out of labor's book and added many to them. It sought to foster a consciousness of community among rivals, to assure profit and then to increase it, by regulating, limiting, or eliminating competition.

Cartels. When rival sellers of the same goods or services took such steps the result has been called a *horizontal* association or combination; but those who took them used such names as *Kartell*, cartel, *comptoir*, syndicate, association, alliance, pool, conference, or institute. Whatever the name, there were three possible lines of action. (1) Rivals could agree on a minimum price; decide on a maximum total output and give each member a fixed quota; or divide the market, grant each member a monopoly over a part of it, and pledge themselves not to invade one another's preserves. (2) A central selling agency might be set up to enforce the agreement by taking out of the members' hands the marketing of their products. (3) Rivals might abandon this regulated competition in favor of partial or complete amalgamation into one firm.

If the compact was limited to the first method the title "cartel" was fitting, since a cartel is an agreement between sovereign powers, especially those at war with each other, which lays down certain rules to mitigate the rigor of the conflict.

Agreements on price or output or markets have a long history. The regulated companies, such as the Merchant Adventurers, tried to make their oligopoly profitable by limiting the quantity of goods each member could put on the market. From 1592 to 1844 the New-castle coaldealers had their Vend, which restricted output and regu-lated prices of the coal they sent by sea to London. In spite of denunciation by the Privy Council and a law "to dissolve the present and prevent the future combination of coal-owners, lightermen, masters of ships, and others to advance the price of coals" the Vend carried on until canals and railroads allowed other coal fields to get their coal cheaply to London and break the veteran monopoly. As early as 1717 the merchants who bought Welsh iron at the Bristol fairs always held a preliminary meeting "to determine ye rate of Iron." During the second half of that century ironmasters, potters, cutlers, glassmakers, and others met to fix prices, to agree on the maximum wages they were to offer, and to form associations in pro-tection of their interests against labor or the government. During the first two-thirds of the nineteenth century we hear less of such restrictive action, but since manufacturers and merchants often gathered together to discuss their common problems it seems safe to assume that discussion of prices was not unknown. After 1870 conditions became such that the regulation of competition was widespread in many countries. In the United States the "trust" be-came an ogre and "trust busting" a crusade. In Europe Germany led the way but she had followers in other lands.

The German movement began during the depressed years which followed the boom of 1871–1873. Victory over France and the for-mation of the Empire intoxicated the country and too many over-capitalized companies rushed into being, only to fall into difficulties or succumb when the bubble burst in 1873. The formation of *Kar-tells* was favored by many factors. In the first place, the tariff of 1879 sheltered the western heavy industries as well as the eastern rye growers from foreign competition. In the second place, con-cepts of free enterprise, competition, and *laissez faire* were never accepted in Germany as heartily as in Britain, France, or the United States. The common law of England was supplemented in America by state and federal laws to condemn acts in restraint of trade. Courts in those countries and in many other lands would not en-force a restrictive trade agreement on anyone who wished to violate it after having pledged himself to abide by it. They were more likely to praise the rebel and punish the plaintiffs for conspiracy. But when a Bavarian *Kartell,* formed in 1873 to check the decline of its members' income by regulating output and prices, sued a member for having exceeded his quota, the state court gave a verdict in favor of the *Kartell* on the ground that it was incumbent on businessmen suffering from depression to take joint action to restore prosperity. In 1890 the federal supreme court said that a *Kartell* contract was as valid as any other kind. Finally, in some German industries the number of competitors was small; agreement was more easily reached than where a multitude of firms existed, and the investment bankers could bring effective pressure to bear on their clients when the need arose.

Kartells therefore developed in a congenial legal and financial atmosphere. By 1906 nearly 400 of them were in existence, and by 1932 the sale of over 50,000 kinds of articles was controlled by 3,200 *Kartells*. They had been formed for a fixed period of time, such as five or ten years, but were renewed if their record seemed satisfactory. Most of them merely regulated prices, output, and markets, or one or two of these three aspects; but some of the more important ones marketed the goods of their members. Three of them merit description because they handled products which loomed large in Germany's economy—coal, steel, and potash.

Faced with overcapacity and low prices, the Westphalian coal producers formed *Kartells* in 1877 and 1878 to control exports and prices. These gentlemen's agreements failed because some of the members were not gentlemen, and because new mines were opened by men outside the *Kartell*. Prices therefore could not be kept up. In 1893 the Rhenish-Westphalian Coal Syndicate was set up to sell the coal of 170 mines which produced virtually the whole output of that region. It fixed the maximum output for each mine, its central bureau at Essen took delivery of all coal at a fixed price and then sold it at the best price it could obtain. Where rival coal (especially British and Belgian) could be brought in cheaply the bureau sold at low competitive prices; but on its own doorstep, where it had a geographical monopoly, it charged high prices. After defraying expenses it shared its surplus among the members in proportion to their quotas, whether they had produced up to them or not.

The Syndicate was periodically renewed and served as a useful body for handling fuel problems during World War I. When peace came the new republican government forced all mines into eleven similar syndicates and placed them under (1) an Imperial Coal

Union to fix quotas, allocate markets, and establish maximum prices; and (2) an Imperial Coal Council, consisting of representatives of producers, consumers, labor, and the state, to plan and control the industry in the general welfare. The Council did little, but the Union did much to restore and remodel the industry. Old mines or poor seams were abandoned, machinery was installed, new methods of wage payment were introduced, and "rationalization" became a combination of watchword and catchword. In the Ruhr field 77 firms closed their pits, leaving 70 companies with 175 mines to carry on more intensively and efficiently. These plans revealed a community of interest far surpassing the aims or methods of 1893. But the savings in wages and the increased productivity were countered by the heavy interest rate on the new equipment. The cost of production and the price were not appreciably reduced, and overcapacity still dogged the industry as the demand for coal failed to expand.

The second famous German *Kartell* grew up in the steel industry. In 1904 several *Kartells* which already controlled the sale of steel, rails, railroad ties, and girders formed the Steel Union (*Stahlwerksverband*) with headquarters at Düsseldorf. The Union handled the sale of steel in the raw, rails, girders, and other simple shapes; it only regulated the output of pipes, wire, rims, wheels, and other goods which required more manufacture or were not standardized. By 1914 it embraced thirty steelworks, sold its wares at home at a relatively high price, and let any surplus go abroad for sale at whatever price it could get. The export price was usually much below the home figure and the Union was accused of "dumping" goods overboard in order to maintain high prices in Germany. It knew, as every producer in every country was aware, that the cost of making a unit of goods was lower if production was large than if it was small. If only part of a huge output was sold in the protected market and the rest dumped abroad to be sold at bare cost or at a slight loss, the total profit would be larger than on an output limited to domestic demands.

The Steel Union also served as a valuable agency for industrial mobilization when war came. The industry's capacity was greatly increased and its profits were high. During the years of inflation up to 1923 these profits were put into the purchase of firms which used the industry's products or into horizontal amalgamations. Soon six giant firms, equipped with new works to take the place of those lost to France, were producing 90 per cent of the country's steel; but consumption at home and sales abroad did not absorb more than half the metal these plants could produce. German steel magnates therefore sought agreement with their foreign rivals, and in 1926 the Continental Steel Cartel came into being. It embraced all the European steel producers except those of Britain, Sweden, and Russia. For five years it was to limit the total output and allot quotas to each country, but no agreement could be reached on prices.

The third *Kartell* was important because it tried to bring order and profit out of the chaotic exploitation of potash, the one commodity in which Germany had a world monopoly. Potash mining was begun by the Prussian government in 1861 but passed over to private enterprise in 1865. Huge profits quickly attracted so much capital that overcapacity ensued, and competition combined with improved methods to reduce prices greatly, turning the profits into loss. In 1879 a *Kartell* was formed and in 1881 a sales syndicate was set up. The government insisted that domestic prices be kept low for the benefit of German farmers, but left the syndicate free to charge high prices on foreign sales. This policy was profitable for a time, but inevitably it induced firms outside the syndicate to expand their output and exports, especially to the American market. The syndicate's profits and much of its export trade therefore vanished. In 1910 the imperial government stepped in to restore "order." By forcing outsiders to sell only through the syndicate, it produced the first compulsory *Kartell*. It fixed maximum domestic prices and minimum export prices, limited total production, and allotted quotas to each firm. After the First World War the loss of Alsace-Lorraine broke Germany's potash monopoly and "the monster of unrestricted competition" loomed up. To fight it the sinking of new shafts was forbidden, inefficient mines were closed, and in 1926 the Alsatian producers were induced to agree that the world market be shared out in the ratio of 70 for Germany and 30 for France. By that time, however, the United States was beginning to produce potash, while Spain and Poland were developing a small export trade which could be a nuisance to the two big allies.

In Great Britain the praise of competition reached its loudest and ran as a sustained note through the long agitation which led to the adoption of free trade as the country's commercial policy by 1850. Yet " 'free and open competition' [was] never perfectly attained, or even universally and sincerely desired" (Clapham), and during the last quarter of the century the short step to association or the longer one to amalgamation was taken by so many industries that by 1914 "the trade without an association of some kind was rare" (Clapham). Most of these bodies were chiefly or solely concerned with presenting a united front in relations with labor or in handling legal, technical, and political matters; but some of them tried to benefit producers of commodities ranging from salt and steel to building materials and brass bedsteads by price or output agreements; and one or two of them had central sales bureaus. Since the railroads charged uniform freight or passenger rates, their rivalry had to express itself in the quality of the service offered. Shipping firms made agreements, called "rings" or "conferences," with one another and soon welcomed German, French, Japanese, Dutch, and other lines into what were the first really effective international cartels. They fixed freight rates and fares for most of the world's ocean lanes and tried to prevent outsiders from stealing the traffic by offering shippers a rebate of 10 per cent on condition that they did not patronize free-lance ships. This rebate was not paid until six months after the goods had been carried and was canceled if in the meantime the shipper was discovered to have been disloyal. Meanwhile British banks, decreasing in number as they grew in size through amalgamation, adopted uniform scales of charges; but they still competed vigorously with each other in every other way, and were a little startled at their own departure from the normal when in 1911 their representatives and those of the Bank of England decided to meet quarterly to discuss matters of common interest.

British conditions in general were much less favorable to joint action than were those in Germany. There was no legal sanction for restrictive compacts, and popular opinion was so hostile that those cartels which were formed tried to keep their existence a secret. As there was no tariff protection, foreign competition was always close at hand to check any attempt to push prices high. Further, in the two old staple industries the task of getting agreement between 3,000 cotton businesses or 1,700 coal-mining companies was an impossible one. British cartel development was therefore tardy and limited. In 1914 "more than three-quarters of the occupied people in the country were producing goods or selling services whose price or output had been affected in no appreciable manner by association among those for whom they worked; and the influence of association over the trades of the remaining quarter was patchy" (Clapham). Associations of firms were less important than were the efforts to secure economies and benefits through the amalgamation of firms into larger operating units; and the combination of general pre-war prosperity and rising prices made cartels seem unnecessary.

After World War I conditions were very different. In the difficult twenties and depressed thirties, with the old industries on the sick list, free competition seemed to be costly and *laissez faire* might mean "let things alone to die." During the war the government had worked with trade associations and thus strengthened them. Now it had to be interested in the state of the ailing industries, partly because of the heavy unemployment among their workers and partly because foreign trade must be built up if the nation was to pay for its imports. As we saw in Chapter XXII, the railroads were amalgamated into four large units. One government after another wrestled with the problems of the coal industry, encouraging and in 1930 ordering the formation of regional cartels to restrict output, allot quotas, and fix minimum prices. Plans were made for compelling firms to amalgamate as a first step toward weeding out inefficient mines and raising productivity. The cartelization was carried out successfully, but the mineowners resisted the reorganization scheme so forcefully that it was shelved. Some voluntary amalgamations and improvements did take place during the inter-war years, but much of the task of overhauling the industry remained to be done when the mines were nationalized in 1946. Meanwhile the iron and steel industry was told to reorganize itself when it was given tariff protection in 1932. It did much amalgamating and set up a central agency to handle imports and exports. The cotton industry, burdened with excess capacity when it lost the Asiatic market to India and Japan, tried everything that could be suggested from within and without. Most of its efforts, whether cartels or amalgamations, failed to produce satisfactory results, but in 1936 parliament gave the industry power to eliminate surplus mills and machines and to compensate their owners by making a levy on the mills which still remained in operation. The shipbuilders had already worked out a similar scheme for eliminating surplus shipyards. Thus industrial associations, under government persuasion or compulsion, strove to achieve order, or at least an orderly retreat, by plans that left little room for individual free enterprise.

International Cartels. We have already noted the existence of international cartels in steel, potash, and shipping. Such cartels were born soon after national ones appeared. European rail makers in 1883 formed one to stabilize the market at a time when the demand for rails had fallen far below the industry's swollen capacity. It was strengthened in 1904 and welcomed American producers into the fold soon afterwards. In the armament industry a few giant producers supplied a limited number of customers and could therefore easily share out the market. At least forty international cartels had been made by 1896, chiefly as a result of German initiative after bouts of price cutting. By 1914 more than a hundred cartels had crossed national boundaries, controlling the sale of aluminum, electric bulbs, plate glass, bottles, enamelware, tobacco, and many other commodities which were produced by a few large firms or were in the hands of national cartels.

War broke many of these compacts, but when peace came they were soon mended and many new ones were added affecting steel, coal, potash, synthetic rubber, rayon, nitrates, dyes, non-ferrous metals, linoleum, paper, wood pulp, and other manufactured goods or minerals. All these commodities were produced by a few large national monopolies or oligopolies, American, British, German, French, Canadian, or Japanese. If these giants fought each other the battle would be bloody and costly to all of them, no matter who won. The Germans were anxious and aggressive. Their shrunken steel and potash industries could either fight or sign a treaty of peace with the expanded French industries. Their powerful chemical industry and dye ex-monopoly now confronted greatly expanded British and American firms. Since neither side wished a fight, amicable agreements were reached. Some of them perished in the great depression after 1929, but some survived and others were made, so that by 1939 about 180 international cartels were known to exist, with American firms participating in nearly two-thirds of them.

These treaties between high contracting industrial powers shared out markets by regions, so that British chemicals did not come to the United States and American products stopped out of the British Empire; by quotas, such as that which allotted Germany 40 per cent of the steel export market and admitted France's right to 32 per cent; or by commodities, when each member of the cartel was freed from the competition of his associates in the production of a particular line of goods. Sometimes sales organizations were set up, and the harmony of interests might be strengthened by interlocking ownership through the reciprocal exchange of stock, by combining to set up a subsidiary company for some special task, by exchanging information concerning processes, or by sharing the use of patents.

Government Cartels and Controls. While big firms thus developed policies of reciprocal restriction during the inter-war period, sometimes with government approval, primary producers were unable to save themselves without considerable state aid and even initiative. They were so numerous and scattered that a spirit of solidarity was hard to create and harder to convert into practicable plans. Some ambitious political cartels were therefore hatched on their behalf. In 1922 the rubber planters of Ceylon and Malaya, faced with a severe fall of prices from the post-war level, induced the British government to put into effect the Stevenson Plan for balancing supply and demand at a reasonable price by regulating exports. Under this Plan the quantity of rubber a planter was permitted to export went down as the price fell but expanded as it improved. The price promptly rose a little from the low figure of 13 cents a pound (1922) and then shot upward unexpectedly when America, recovering from the depression of 1920–1922, began to buy great numbers of cars and to equip them with balloon tires. By 1925 rubber was selling at $1.25. This exorbitant price provoked tiremakers to reclaim more old rubber, tempted planters to smuggle out surplus rubber which they could not export legally, and stimulated Dutch planters and natives (who had refused to cooperate with the British plan) to increase their output greatly. Prices therefore fell rapidly after 1926 to 40 cents in 1927 and to 20 cents by 1929. The Plan was abandoned in 1928; it had brought temporary advantage to the participants but benefited outsiders at least as much and led the industry to a vast expansion of capacity. By 1932 overcapacity and depression had pushed the price down to 4 cents and the Dutch now eagerly suggested that a new plan be devised. In 1934 all the Asiatic rubber-producing regions came to terms, an International Rubber Restriction Committee was set up to restrict new planting and fix quotas for each territory, and the governments of the eight rubber territories agreed to cooperate with the Committee. The second effort was therefore more successful than the first and was in operation until the area was seized by the Japanese in early 1942. The price rose to about 20 cents and fluctuated somewhat, especially when the Committee failed to anticipate moderate increases in demand, but never went so high as to stimulate a new distention of planting.

Sugar rivaled rubber in its inter-war sufferings and called for international control. In 1931 agreement was reached between the cane growers of Java and Cuba and the beet growers of five European countries. This scheme, known as the Chadbourne Plan, provided for restricting output, reducing acreage, rationing exports, and eliminating surplus stocks. The governments of the sugar-producing countries blessed the Plan and offered to pass whatever legislation was needed to make it effective. Yet it was a dismal failure, for while the participating producers reduced their crops other countries increased their output of sugar. In 1937 a new international agreement was reached; this time the governments shouldered a great part of the responsibility and most of those who had sugar-producing areas participated. Other commodities, such as tea, wheat, beef, and coffee, were the subject of "orderly marketing" schemes during the thirties, most of them with government sanction and aid; and meanwhile the domestic production and marketing of some foodstuffs came under state or state-supported control in virtually all European countries, as well as in other continents, including all parts of North America.

Critique of Cartels and Controls. Cartels and controls were aimed at raising prices to a satisfactory level and at keeping them there either by fixing a minimum figure or by limiting the supply of goods put on the market. They rested on compacts that ran for ten, five, or fewer years, that expired unless renewed and could be modified in the light of experience. Since they did not interfere with the actual methods of production, each firm could be as efficient as it wished. They were most effective where the number of producers was small, the product capable of standardization and mass production, the supply of raw materials scarce or localized, and where patents, tariffs, large capital requirements, and transport costs impeded external competition.

Where these conditions prevailed, prices were maintained at fairly stable levels, and although they might not rise much in prosperous times they were very slow to fall during depressions. In the lean years after 1929 some German *Kartells* were disciplined by the government for holding prices up while the world level was falling fast. In fixing prices a cartel tried to assure a profit to its least efficient members. This policy gave a higher reward to the more efficient plants and prevented the weeding out of the incompetents unless the cartel deliberately closed them down, which happened in few cases. Price policies therefore might tend to accentuate overcapacity by stimulating members and outsiders to expand their operations. To maintain the price level it might be necessary for members or their sales bureau to withhold some of the product from the market and let it accumulate in stock piles; but these piles became so large just before 1929 that they could no longer be financed, and their dispersion under duress helped to make the crash of that year more severe. In the international field even the most imposing cartels rarely included all producing areas, and often the outsiders were regions of low-cost production. Prices, quotas, and market allocations were therefore exposed to unwelcome interference in good times and to damaging blows in bad ones.

No cartel or control was sufficiently flexible to respond promptly to changes in the economic weather, much less to forecast those changes accurately. There was a tendency to maintain prices in depressed days, regardless of the fact that the community had smaller spending power and must either buy less or seek substitutes. The supply of goods was either cut down too much or too little to meet changes in demand. When most of the cartels and controls of the twenties had been wrecked by the depression, the new ones that were set up tried to escape some of the mistakes of their predecessors. Their price and other policies were more moderate and cautious, often too cautious. Attempts were made to keep production in closer step with demand, large stocks were not to be piled up, and the consumer was to be given more consideration. Yet the outsider was often as sharp a thorn in the flesh as before, and the calculations of probable market demand were often far off the mark. When America, under the pressure of low prices and New Deal policies, cut down its production of cotton by 2,000,000 bales the growers in other continents raised theirs by 7,000,000 bales. The Chadbourne sugar scheme overestimated the importing capacity of the United States, underestimated the probability that outside countries would increase their output, and was caught unawares by the simultaneous decline of imports and the increase of production in India and the Japanese Empire. The second rubber scheme had just got its restrictions working satisfactorily when a large outburst of consumption caught the market short of supplies and stimulated a wave of unhealthy speculation. Hence experience showed that "the technique of artificial control is apt to require superhuman foresight" (Rowe) and that controlled markets were almost (or quite) as devoid of that foresight as were those which were entirely free.

But all market calculators were soon to lose their yardsticks as a new element of demand crept in. By 1936 or soon afterwards rearmament needs began to be powerful influences on the market for many commodities. Purchases for making munitions or for building up government stock piles grew large. The task became one not of restraining production but of spurring it to greater yield.

Amalgamations and Holding Companies. The cartel movement for the regulation of competition was accompanied, supplemented, and in some industries supplanted by one which abolished competition by knitting firms tightly together under unified control or merging them fully into one large corporation. The elimination of competition was not the only motive behind this movement, but it was rarely absent. A producer might try to protect himself from rival buyers by acquiring the source of supply of his raw materials and fuel, and then go on to protect his market by getting hold of the users or sellers of his product. This kind of policy, spreading downward and upward, has been called a *vertical* combination or an integration. It has a long history. Wedgwood bought a three-fourths interest in one Cornish clay company and joined with thirteen other potters to form another, thus securing his material at cost price instead of having to buy it in a competitive market. He also entered into partnership with a merchant and set up his own sales organization. As the British iron industry grew after 1760 on coke fuel, ironmasters bought coal mines and limestone quarries. After being charged high prices by coal and ore producers, Albert Krupp acquired coal mines in Germany, iron mines in Spain, and a fleet of ore boats. He also provided himself with a sure market for some of his raw steel by developing the manufacture of guns. His successor took over a large machine-making plant, built railroad rolling stock, and in 1896 bought a shipyard which became famous as the birthplace of many submarines at Kiel. By amalgamation or absorption one Sheffield steelmaking firm built up a similarly self-sufficing enterprise with ore mines in Spain; coal mines and limestone deposits in England; coke ovens, blast furnaces, convertors, and rolling mills; factories to make cannon, projectiles, small arms and ammunition; engineering works and shipyards. A soap magnate (Lever) secured control of the sources of his ingredients in places as far away as Africa and Australia. A chain-store grocer (Lipton) began to process some of the goods he sold and then acquired tea plantations. Breweries bought an interest in "public houses" in order to gain sure and exclusive retail outlets for their product. The British cooperative movement began with retail stores and then went on to erect a wholesale organization and to manufacture goods. Eventually it included farming, ownership of tea and palm-oil plantations, banking, insurance, and operation of a few ships.

Integration led to diversity of enterprise in place of the specialization in one process or product that had characterized most early industrial enterprises. It also led to great size and sometimes to great strength. Meanwhile horizontal amalgamation of firms doing the same kind of work offered greater freedom from the prospect of damaging competition than a cartel could assure, and also gave a chance to secure the economies of large-scale buying, production, selling, and research. If, in addition, integrated rivals united horizontally, the result might be a further strengthening of organization.

Closer union, whether vertical or horizontal or both, was obtained in at least three ways. (1) Community of interest was achieved in the "concern" (*Konzern*). A group of independent businesses retained their separate legal entities but adhered to a common policy under the direction of some central authority which directed both production and sale. Their directorates might be interlocked; a bank or individual might own sufficient stock in each of them to force a common purpose on them; or they might exchange stock in one another. They divided the field of production, shared patents or processes, and did not get in one another's way. (2) One company purchased the others or a new company was formed to take them all over. (3) A "holding company" was set up for the express purpose of securing a majority of shares in several operating companies. It got them by giving their owners its own stocks or bonds, and possibly some cash as well. The owners might be induced to make the exchange by being offered two or three times as much face value of stock as they surrendered; thus the new firm had the task of producing profits and interest on a larger volume of securities.

These developments were visible in Europe in the eighties—the decade of the first phase of the American trust movement—and in the case of British banks and railroads even earlier. Amalgamation brought American meat exporters and British importers together (1889), and ended competition between German and British makers of dynamite by setting up what was probably the world's first holding company, the Nobel Dynamite Trust Company (1886). The Scots sewing cotton firm of J. and P. Coats amalgamated with

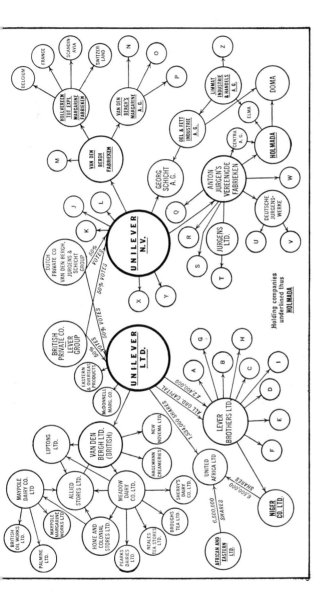

The Soap and Margarine Combine

The dairy, tea, and other stores represented by the circles in the top left corner are large groups of chain stores selling dairy produce and groceries. The circles containing letters A-Z include a hundred and forty subsidiaries which are concerned with fishing, whaling, sealing; producing, transporting, or selling soap, oilseeds, candles, jam, cocoa, margarine, vegetable oils, perfumes, cattle foods, and candies; or operating grocery stores, fish shops, and restaurants. They are located in Great Britain, Holland, Belgium, France, Germany, Scandinavia, Switzerland, Ireland, Nigeria, the Congo, the Dutch East Indies, North America, and Australia. (From the *Economist*, reprinted by permission of the Editor.)

four British rivals in 1895–1896, obtained a controlling interest in smaller firms, gradually spread to the continent and America, and eventually held a virtual monopoly of the world's thread industry. In similar fashion, by buying, integrating, and building, Lever started out in the nineties on the road that made him the colossus of the soap world, with factories in many lands and plantations or trading posts in Asia and Africa. In 1929 Lever Brothers joined hands with the Margarine Union, which had been formed by the amalgamation (1927) of two Dutch companies and controlled most of the continental margarine and soap trades. The diagram on page 617 gives some idea of the ramifications of this Anglo-Dutch combination. Few European or American faces or clothes could now be washed without using the product of Unilever; but cleanliness was not the only service that was offered. British shipping had its amalgamations as well as its conferences, and one of them—that of Cunard with White Star—was made in 1934 at the government's request. By that time most of the country's banking was in the hands of the big five, and in 1926 the Imperial Chemicals Industries, Ltd., was born as a holding company to obtain stock in three large firms and about fifty small ones which produced chemicals, dyes, and dynamite.

In Germany combination was strongest in the steel, electrical, and chemical industries. In 1926 the United Steel Company fused four large firms into a giant integration. In 1925 thirteen chemical and dye companies united in the *Interessen Gemeinschaft Farbenindustrie Aktiengesellschaft* (Associated Dyestuffs Industries Company), popularly known as I. G. Farben. This step brought to a head a process of concentration which had been going on since 1904, and brought together the makers of dyes, pharmaceutical chemicals, heavy industrial chemicals such as acids and alkalis, synthetic nitrogen, liquid fuel, rayon, explosives, and camera films. With the whole chemical field as its parish, I. G. Farben set out to seek cartel agreements with its counterparts in other countries. On the continent it got them easily and quickly, using the big stick of threatened cutthroat competition if a treaty was not signed. With the giant units of Britain and America pacts providing for harmonious cooperation, division of markets, and exchange of information or patents were also negotiated.

In the international field one of the chief combinations was that to control the supply of petroleum products. Of these products

Europe had a pitifully inadequate supply and must draw on outer continents. In 1907 the "Royal Dutch Company for the working of petroleum wells in the Netherlands Indies" united with a British company, the Shell Transport and Trading Company. Each of them was already an international holding company, and Royal Dutch-Shell therefore controlled hundreds of subsidiaries in all parts of the world. It also made friends with two smaller rivals operating in Persia and in Burma, and was therefore in a strong position to meet, peacefully or otherwise, the United States giants.

Combination came sometimes as a natural growth by the expansion of a leading firm or through a recognition within the industry that the step was desirable. But in several cases before 1914 and still more after 1920 the initiative came from some outsider, either a promoter with a persuasive tongue or an investment bank which believed that the troubles of an industry could be cured and its profits restored by union. Severe dizziness is the only reward for any attempt to follow the colossal promotion projects of British, Belgian, French, American and other financiers during the 1920's. The advantages of super-large-scale production and the benefits of rationalization or oligopoly or integration were sought by some of them; but others were gigantic financial manipulations by megalomaniacs. The chief industries affected were electrical generation, appliances and power, wood pulp, rayon, chemicals, and non-ferrous metals; but no industry or continent was immune from attack. Great rivals fought each other for control; American financiers, investment bankers, industrial firms, and funds were mobilized to seek foreign conquests; and Europeans welcomed them or warred with them. The canton of Glarus in Switzerland, the principality of Lichtenstein, and the duchy of Luxembourg offered the promoters of holding and super-holding companies "liberal" laws and low taxes in order to induce them to make their headquarters in those states, much as New Jersey and Delaware did in the United States.

Of the many grandiose plans one of the most notorious began when Ivar Kreuger, a Swedish engineer, fused the matchmaking firms of his country and set out to build a hierarchy of holding companies which secured control of match factories in forty-three countries and hence of 80 per cent of the world's output of matches. By lending $350,000,000 to penniless governments he secured the match monopoly in thirteen countries. From playing with matches he went on to gain interests in banking, iron ore, telephone equip-

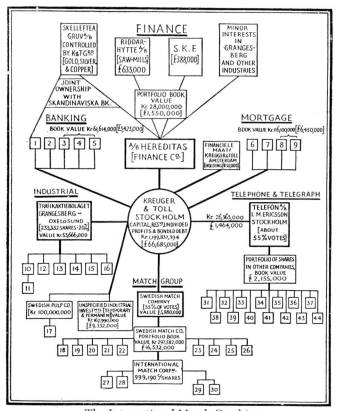

The International Match Combine

Squares 10–13 and 15 handled iron ore; 14 was a railroad; 16 was a power and engineering firm; 17 controlled thirteen large producers of sulphur pulp; 18–30 were match companies in Scandinavia, Great Britain, Poland, Peru, San Domingo, and other places; 31–44 manufactured or operated telephones. (From the *Economist,* reprinted by permission of the Editor.)

ment, paper, railroads, ball bearings, and anything else that caught his eye. He floated vast issues of stock in London, Amsterdam, and New York. In every place the glamour of his reputation, combined with the prospect of profits from the monopolies, caused money to flow freely into his hands. The price of matches rose, but Russia remained outside Kreuger's empire, ready to undersell him with better wares. Believing that ends justified means, the mastermind used heterodox accountancy methods, borrowed on false securities, and forged bonds. But the whirlwinds of 1929 blew over his skyscraper of matchboxes, a lot of short-term loans could not be met, and in 1932 a tawdry suicide in a Paris hotel bedroom ended the career of the northern Napoleon.

Many such figures strutted as supermen on the world stage during the twenties. Some made their exit by death, some went to prison, but some found legal loopholes and skillful lawyers. To them the production of commodities for sale seemed less important than the production of stocks and bonds for sale. They gave the public what it wanted and supplied a demand that seemed just as real as was that for rayon or radios. Their contribution to the productive efficiency of the industries with which they toyed was negligible or was countered by the heavier burden of capital charges imposed on production. Europe, like America, had little cause to be thankful to the wizards who waved their wands over its pocket. During the thirties there was no scope for the financial superman; but the havoc he had already wrought among investors, creditors, producers, and wage earners did much to set the stage for the political superman who followed him.

Conclusion. From the developments described in this chapter it is evident that competition in the twentieth century is a shriveled, puny descendant of the vigorous fellow and popular myth of the mid-nineteenth century; that from many fields he has been virtually shut out by entrepreneurs who prefer not to have him about; that he is admitted to others only on condition that he behave himself at the end of a chain; but that he is far from dead and displays a capacity for breaking out of bounds in unexpected places at unwelcome times. "We are much more conscious nowadays of the wastes of competition than of its stimulus to efficiency. In industry after industry unrestricted competition has been superseded by planned control" as a result of "the general discrediting of laissez faire in modern times." In these words two English scholars (Jones and Pool) described the situation in their country in 1939. It has yet to be seen whether planned control is free from wastes or provides a stimulus to efficiency. Meanwhile in later chapters we shall see how competition was welcomed and then rejected in the fields of international trade and in the labor market.

BIBLIOGRAPHY

Brady, R. A., *Business as a System of Power* (1943).

Carter, G. R., *The Tendency toward Industrial Combination* (1913).

Clapham, J. H., *Economic History of Modern Britain* (1926, 1932, 1938), vol. iii, chaps. 4, 5.

Domeratzky, L., *The International Cartel Movement* (U.S. Dept. of Comm., Trade Information Bulletin, No. 556 [1928]).

Hexner, E., *International Cartels* (1945).

Intergovernmental Commodity Control Agreements (International Labor Office, 1943).

Jones, G. P., and Pool, A. G., *A Hundred Years of Economic Development in Great Britain* (1940), chaps. 8, 12, 15.

Levy, H., *Monopolies, Cartels and Trusts in British Industry* (1927).

Levy, H., *Industrial Germany* (Eng. trans., 1935).

Liefmann, R., *Cartels, Concerns, and Trusts* (Eng. trans., 1932).

MacFadyean, A., *History of Rubber Regulation, 1934–43* (1944).

Macgregor, D. H., *Industrial Combination* (1906) parts i, ii.

Marshall, A., *Industry and Trade* (1919), book iii.

Plummer, A., *International Combines in Modern Industry* (1938).

Rowe, J. W. F., *Studies in the Artificial Control of Raw Material Supplies* (Royal Economic Society, Special Memoranda, Nos. 23, 29, 34 [1930–32]).

Rowe, J. W. F., and others, *Stocks of Staple Commodities* (Royal Economic Society, Special Memoranda, Nos. 3, 17, 24, 69 [1927–37]).

Stockder, A. N., *German Trade Associations* (1924).

Stocking, G. W., *The Potash Industry: a Study in State Control* (1931).

Warriner, D., *Combination and Rationalization in Germany, 1924–28* (1931).

Whittlesey, C. R., *Government Control of Crude Rubber* (1931).

ARTICLES

Domeratzky, L., "Cartels and the Business Crisis," *Foreign Affairs*, October, 1931.

Hartsough, M. L., "The Rise and Fall of the Stinnes Combine," *J.E.B.H.*, February, 1931.

Hurstfield, J., "The Control of British Raw Materials Supplies, 1919–1939," *J. Ec. H.*, 1944.

Encyclopaedia of the Social Sciences: Articles on Cartel, Combinations (Industrial), Competition, Cutthroat Competition, Employers' Associations, Export Associations, Holding Companies, Interlocking Directorates, Monopoly, Price Stabilization, Restraint of Trade, Stabilization (Economic), Trusts, Unfair Competition, Valorization; Hudson, G.; Leverhulme, Lord; Melchett, Lord; Ballin, A.; Stinnes, H.; Kreuger, I.; Nobel, A. B.; Loewenstein, A.

XXVI

INTERNATIONL TRADE TO 1914

During the Hundred Years' Peace (1815–1914) the total value of the world's international trade grew from less than $2,000,000,000 to $40,000,000,000. This twentyfold expansion, during a period in which the world's population only doubled, is one of the outstanding facts and factors in the economic history of the nineteenth century. After World War I the figure rose, largely because of higher prices, to $69,000,000,000 in 1929; but the years of depression witnessed a great decline in the volume of trade and a greater fall in prices, which drove the total value down to $23,000,000,000 in 1934. From that low point it had risen only to $28,000,000,000 in old dollar values (but to $47,000,000,000 in devalued dollars) on the eve of World War II.[1] Its volume had, however, regained more than half its loss and was about nine-tenths that of 1929.

Europe was chiefly responsible for the expansion and for some of the later decline. The exchange of goods between Europeans of different nationalities or between them and the inhabitants of other

VALUE OF WORLD TRADE AND PERCENTAGE DONE BY:

Year	Value	United Kingdom	France	Germany	U.S.A.	Rest of World
1840	$ 3 billion	32%	10%	. .	8%	. .
1880	7 "	25	11	9%	10	45%
1900	20 "	21	8	12	11	48
1913	40 "	17	7	12	11	53
1929	69 "	14	6	10	14	56
1938	47 "	16	5	8	11	60

[1] These figures count every commodity twice, once as an export from one country and then as an import into another. To get the actual value of goods involved the figure should be divided almost in half, with the imports a little larger than the exports to allow for the cost of insurance and freight. In 1934 the dollar was devalued by about 40 per cent; hence the difference between the two totals given for 1938.

623

continents accounted for two-thirds of the world's trade in 1913 and for 56 per cent in 1930. The accompanying table shows the part played by the leading countries. The United Kingdom was throughout the largest trader, because of her growing need for imported foods and raw materials, her export of coal and manufactures, and her considerable *entrepôt* trade. Her share of the expanding traffic declined as the commerce of other countries grew; yet in 1913 her overseas trade comprised a sixth of the world's total, in the inter-war period it accounted for a seventh, and in 1938 it enabled her to claim she was "the best customer of thirty-one of the world's countries." France came second—a rather poor second—in the early nineteenth century, but Germany rapidly climbed into that position after industrialization and federation came, and by 1913 one-eighth of the world's trade crossed her borders or touched her ports. The export of farm produce and the import of manufactured goods made the United States the largest non-European foreign trader at an early stage of the nineteenth century, but the country's relative position remained little changed, at about one-tenth of the total business, until World War I expanded her exports and post-war needs or opportunities kept them large. With the coming of the depression (1929) America's share of world trade slipped back to its old fraction and remained there until war enlarged it once more.

The growth of foreign trade increased greatly the dependence of many European economies on external buyers and sellers. In 1800 Britain could just about feed herself. By 1914 she was importing more than half of her foodstuffs, and for every dollar spent on imported food, drink, and tobacco another dollar was spent on overseas raw material and sixty-six cents on manufactured goods. In return Britain exported about a third of her coal output, 4,000,000 miles of cotton piece goods (or nearly 80 per cent of her output), chiefly to the Far East, 100,000 miles of woolens, large quantities of iron and steel, engines, machines, chemicals, steamships built for foreign buyers, along with a great variety of other articles, such as books, clothes, crockery, shoes, and liquor. In all, these exports accounted for a third of the country's total output from farm, mine, and factory.

Germany's industrial growth soon began to give her economy a similar pattern, though with a smaller dependence on food imports. By 1913 probably a fifth of German production was exported. France remained relatively self-sufficing, but some of the smaller countries which concentrated on the production of farm or factory staples bought and sold so heavily abroad that their foreign trade per capita exceeded that of the big industrial nations.

FOREIGN TRADE PER HEAD OF POPULATION, 1929

Denmark	$252	France	$102
Holland	243	Germany	97
Belgium	227	U.S.A.	77
Switzerland	213	Italy	46
United Kingdom	196	Poland	21
Sweden	158	U.S.S.R.	6

European foreign trade was chiefly intracontinental. Great Britain was the only country to do more trade outside Europe than within. In 1913 her exports were divided almost equally among Europe (34 per cent), the British Empire (37 per cent), and foreign countries outside Europe (29 per cent). Her five best customers were India, Germany, Australia, the United States, and France; the five chief markets in which she bought were the United States, Germany, India, France, and the Argentine. Each list contains two European countries and three distant ones; but if we grouped together the seven small countries on the continent's western fringe, from Norway to Portugal, their total trade with Britain would put them second on each list. Germany's dependence on other continents, though growing, was still small. In 1913 three-fourths of her exports went to near-by countries, and over half her imports came from them. Her eastern and southern neighbors did at least a quarter of their foreign trade with her, and her national economy "formed the very center of the economic system of the European continent" (Rosenberg). The rest of Europe had only slight contact with remote lands. Denmark sent nine-tenths of its exports to Britain, Germany, Norway, and Sweden; Belgium in 1926 sold almost 60 per cent of its exports to its four neighbors; and Holland sold 65 per cent to four. Czechoslovakia, an inland industrial country, bought or sold only 15 per cent of its goods outside Europe, while Sweden, with some highly developed industries and a good merchant marine, did three-fourths of its foreign business with its own continent on the eve of World War II.

Europe's international trade can be divided into three classes: (1) exchange of tropical and semi-tropical products for those of tem-

perate or cold zones; (2) exchange between agricultural and industrial areas; (3) exchange between industrial regions. The first
class was chiefly intercontinental. Europe could draw on its Mediterranean lands for some semi-tropical products; but when areas with
the same kind of soil and climate were settled in America and the
antipodes, and when refrigeration became possible, Greece, Italy,
and Spain were supplemented by California, Florida, South Africa,
and Australia. As there was no suitable European area large enough
for growing much cotton and the Ottoman Empire was slow to seize
its opportunity, favorable conditions in the United States tied Europe to the cotton states of the south. As early as 1828 some Lancashire men saw the danger of relying mainly on one source of supply
and urged manufacturers and the British government to encourage
the growth of cotton elsewhere. The American Civil War reinforced
these pleas and led to expanded cultivation in India, the West Indies,
Guiana, Natal, Australia, the Ottoman Empire (especially Egypt),
Brazil, and other regions. The yield was inferior, costly, and unsuitable for some purposes; manufacturers were glad to get back to
the American supply as soon as possible; and when peace reduced
the price of cotton some of the mushroom growth ended. After 1900
American preeminence became less secure. The yield per acre de-
creased and the boll weevil forced cultivators to grow plants which
matured early enough to escape that pest but produced a poorer
fiber. Meanwhile cotton growing spread in other continents, and
cotton manufacturing developed in the Orient. In 1930 Lancashire
and the southern states could bewail in unison the loss of their old
supremacy, for although Asiatic mills had captured Lancashire's
low-grade trade the world's spindles were using more cotton grown
outside the United States than inside. Ten years later they were
using very much more.

Though no other commodity from warm latitudes approached
cotton in importance, the combined demand for rice, cocoa, coffee,
tea, silk, copra, cane sugar, spices, bananas, jute, palm oil, and rubber created a large volume of trade. The demand for many of these
commodities was elastic, and the quantity sold depended largely on
the price. Hence cheaper production and reduced ocean freights
brought them within the reach of the middle classes and then of
wage earners. Further, the nineteenth century needed more and
more oils and fats for dressing leather and making soap, paint,
linoleum, margarine, lubricants, salad or cooking oil, and candles.

Since the supply of animal fats was inadequate, the oilseeds of the tropics were raided. Coconuts, cotton seeds, palm kernels, and various nuts were crushed to yield oil, the refuse was made into cakes for fattening cattle, and the husks could be made into paper. Finally, the tropics produced rubber. Until 1900 the supply came solely from Brazil and the Congo, but after that date the "wild" rubber from those areas was rapidly supplanted by the "tame" product of plantations in Ceylon and the East Indies. Most of these new or expanding demands for tropical produce became acute after about 1860 and led European entrepreneurs and governments to develop a keen interest in "darkest Africa," India, the East Indies, and Oceania.

The second kind of international trade was that between agricultural, forest, or mineral areas and industrial regions. Industrial Europe bought food and raw materials from Agricultural Europe and supplemented them by drawing increasingly on those New World temperate zones in which transplanted European animals, grains, and fruits could flourish. American foodstuffs were not unknown in eighteenth-century Europe, but their influence was seriously felt only after 1850. South American hides were being shipped to Europe by 1800, and by 1900 the Argentine was becoming Europe's chief beef provider. By 1820 Australian wool had appeared in London auction rooms, and in 1850 Australia, South Africa, and South America supplied two-thirds (50,000,000 lbs.) of Britain's wool imports. In 1913 over half the world's wool was produced in the antipodes, and the position has not changed since. Little of the fiber was retained for domestic manufacture; Australia, the chief producer, sent at least four-fifths of her clip across the equator, chiefly to Europe. The southern hemisphere also supplied a large part of the artificial fertilizers used in Europe.

Europe's forest products grew in importance as the growth of factories and towns increased the need for building lumber, as coal mines required pit props, and then as wood became the raw material for paper. Sweden's exports of dressed lumber rose tenfold between 1850 and 1900, only to be overshadowed by those of pulp and paper after 1900. Sweden and Spain were the two chief sources from which the iron industries of Germany and Britain drew part of their ore. For her non-ferrous metals Europe had to rely increasingly on other continents. Of oil she had enough so long as it was used chiefly for lamps and lubrication. The Nobel brothers began systematically to

exploit the Baku oil fields in 1873, and by 1900 that region was producing half the world's oil. After 1900 the Baku yield declined just
as the automobile was changing the nature and size of the demand.
War and revolution threw the Russian industry into chaos. The Bolsheviks restored order and their Plans increased production threefold, but little of the oil went abroad. The rest of Europe had to draw
what it could from Rumania but rely chiefly on the Americas, the
Dutch East Indies, Persia, and Iraq.

The third kind of international exchange was that in manufactured
products between industrial countries. Industrialization did not
breed a group of continental facsimiles of Britain. As it spread it
might reduce the need for importing some kinds of industrial goods,
but no country could hope to make everything, much less to do
everything better than did everybody else. Differences in natural resources, in labor costs, in technical knowledge, tradition, and equipment, and priority in developing a new industry gave some manufacturers in each country a temporary or permanent advantage over
foreign rivals in both domestic and foreign markets, and therefore
made each industrial nation a good customer of the others.

The French, for instance, were best in silkwork, in making certain
woolen fabrics, and in luxury goods, but not in making steel, machinery, electrical appliances, and cheap mass-produced wares.
England excelled in making fine yarns or fabrics, leather, and certain
machines; for a time she was far ahead of others in weaving cheap
cottons; her woolen industry was good at producing the whole range
from super-fine to shoddy; and she could place coal in some continental markets at a lower price than was asked for domestic fuel.
But Englishmen who wanted chemicals, dyes, and many kinds of
machines were best served by German or American manufacturers.
German potash, dyes, lenses, electrical equipment, and tools had
high repute abroad, while German toys, crockery, trinkets, knitwear,
and watches ranked alongside Yorkshire shoddy, some Birmingham
hardware, some American tools, and (later) Japanese cottons, cups,
and matches as wares of low quality and price bought by the poorer
sections of Europe's population. In countless cases the finished
product, such as yarn or a special steel, of a manufacturer in one
country was the cheapest available raw material for an industry in
another. Hence the exchange of industrial products among the manufacturing countries of Europe was larger than that with the agricultural nations. Germany sent three-quarters of her industrial ex-

ports to her "rivals," Britain was in 1913 her best customer, and in turn she bought more from Britain than did any other country except India. Discussion of international trade in terms of rivalry, conflict, and war usually ignored these fairly important facts.

Influences on the Development of International Trade. The volume and character of international exchange were influenced by the quantity of goods seeking a purchaser, the growth in the number of potential buyers, and the removal of economic or political barriers across the path between buyer and seller. The changes in industrial and agricultural methods made possible the pouring out of some commodities in a volume far beyond local or national needs. Long before the law of "diminishing cost of production" or of "increasing return" had ceased to operate, the pile of Lancashire cottons or German steel was greater than could be sold to domestic consumers, and the manufacturer must seek foreign buyers.

In his search he was helped by the growing accessibility of areas that had been politically barred. The American Revolution opened the door on equal terms to all countries, though a long time elapsed before continental industries had many goods to send through it, and British exporters continued to supply most of America's manufactured imports. When Napoleon drove the Portuguese royal family from Lisbon to Rio de Janeiro in 1807, direct trade with Brazil became legal, and within a year over sixty British firms had established themselves in the new capital. As the Spanish-American colonies became independent during the next few years, traders could openly cultivate them and forget about the fierce struggles with the *guarda costas.* By 1830 Latin America was buying about a ninth of all British exports, and continued to be a good customer from that time onward. Frenchmen went out there to sell their special lines after 1815 and have maintained a strong hold on the luxury market ever since. Germany in due course embarked on a vigorous commercial campaign in South America. Hides, wool, beef, coffee, metals, wheat, and fertilizers paid for the goods Latin America bought.

Asia was opened wider to foreign traders by installments. American merchants were no longer restricted by the British East India Company's monopoly after 1775, and that monopoly was revoked for India in 1813, for China in 1834. India was a pleasant market, for the Company had prepared the way, and the cheap cottons provided Europe at last with a commodity that it could barter for oriental products. China had given the white man scant respect and few trading privileges; but her defeat in the first Opium War (1840–1842) led to the opening of five ports, the cession of a pirate's rock, Hong Kong, to Britain, and the fixing of the Chinese tariff at a mere 5 per cent. France and the United States quickly followed Britain's lead in claiming concessions, and the second Opium War (1856) opened more ports. Two years earlier the United States had pushed open the door which Japan had kept closed since 1638, and Europeans quickly slipped in. The Asiatic market gradually grew in importance. By 1850 it was taking a sixth of British exports, in 1913 more than a fifth; four cotton pieces out of every ten made in Lancashire were sold in the Orient. No other country made much impression, for India, China, and Japan took only 4 per cent of Germany's exports; but Holland found an increasingly valuable market and source of supplies in her East Indian empire.

The emigration of Europeans and the export of capital promoted the outflow of goods and the production of return cargoes. Between Waterloo and the end of mass emigration in the 1920's, about 55,-000,000 people left Europe to make their homes in other continents. Some 19,000,000 of them went from the British Isles (especially Ireland), 9,000,000 from Italy, 6,000,000 from Germany, 5,000,000 from Austria-Hungary, 4,000,000 from Spain, and about 2,000,000 from Scandinavia. The United States took 36,000,000 of them and South America about 10,000,000, though we do not know how many of these returned home. Canada got over 4,000,000, especially when the opening up of her prairies was begun in earnest after 1896. Australia and New Zealand received a smaller number, and their periods of greatest attraction were immediately after the gold discoveries (1851) and during the years just before World War I. The emigrants played their part in pushing back the various frontiers—farming, ranching, lumbering, and mining—and in supplying enterprise or labor for the industrialization of their new home. That industrialization reduced the demand for some goods formerly imported, but it only changed the nature rather than the volume of external trade.

Capital Investments. With the flow of labor went a stream of capital; but the capital also went where the white man could not settle, i.e., to the tropics, and some of it took a much shorter journey from one European country to another. After 1815 London became a reservoir from which loans and investments poured forth to the continent and farther afield. Lenders' fingers were burned by the defaults of governments or companies in Greece, Spain, Portugal, Spanish America, and the United States; but they got better, and after 1868 an international Association of Bondholders helped to bring a greater measure of security to creditors and a heavier sense of responsibility to borrowers. British investors were chiefly interested in the political and economic development of the New World. Only a twelfth of their pounds had been put into the continent by 1914. Their money flowed more and more toward British colonies and dependencies as these grew in importance, yet more than half the $20,000,000,000 worth of bonds or stocks which they owned in 1914 was outside the Empire. Latin America had $4,000,000,000 of it and the United States almost as much, far more than had been invested in India, Australia, or Canada.

No other country had such a large stake abroad. France began to export capital about 1850, and by 1914 her investments amounted to nearly $9,000,000,000. Little of this sum (perhaps 10 per cent) had gone into her colonies, either the few old ones, such as Martinique, or the new ones in Africa and Asia which Ferry and his fellow enthusiasts for colonies began to accumulate after 1880. The old sugar islands had been ruined by the competition of beet sugar and the abolition of slavery. The new colonies had little economic value and neither the French people nor the investors were interested in them. French capital went rather to Latin America and the United States—the Sante Fé Railroad was virtually French property in 1914—but mostly into government loans in eastern Europe. Paris was the largest market in the world for government securities, largely because Frenchmen were traditionally more interested in what seemed safe gilt-edged government bonds than in industrial securities, which the *Crédit Mobilier* and the Panama fiasco had shown were dangerous. When, therefore, France found an ally in Russia (1894), French investors subscribed over $2,000,000,000 to Russian loans and supplied a third of all the foreign joint-stock capital put into Russian industry up to 1914.

Germans invested a little money in American western railroads during the 1860's and 1870's, and by that time merchants of Hamburg or Bremen were developing trade on the coast of Africa or the islands of the western Pacific. When Germany got her share of Africa and the islands in the great partition of the eighties, some funds were invested there; but the resources of these colonies were too meager to yield profits, and the greater part of the $6,000,000,000 which Germans had invested abroad by 1914 was in the Americas, the Turkish Empire on the road from Berlin to Bagdad, or the Shantung concession which Germany had won in the scramble for Chinese ports and spheres of influence. Holland meanwhile was a steady investor in her East Indies, and Belgium put money into her Congo rubber colony.

The Balance of Trade and of Payments. These capital movements influenced international trade in two ways. In the first place the capital was exported to its destination largely in the form of goods or services. In times of heavy investments by Europeans (see Chapter XXVII) outbound ships bulged with cargoes of consumers' or capital goods, sent not merely to pay for goods received but also to transfer the capital. When the annual trade statistics were published they might therefore show that the lending or investing nation had a "favorable commodity (or visible) balance of trade," exporting more than it imported, while the borrowing country had an "unfavorable" commodity balance, receiving more goods than it sent out. In the second place the payment of interest or dividends might for a time be made out of new loans but ultimately had to be met by shipment of goods from the debtor country, which gave her a favorable balance and made the creditor country's balance unfavorable. In 1914 Britain was earning about 5 per cent ($1,000,000,000) on her overseas investments. If she had collected it in full she would have received a billion dollars' worth of imports for which she did not have to make return payments, and her commodity balance would have been "unfavorable" to that extent on that account alone. This sum was not, however, all collected; much of it was left overseas to be invested. Germany was similarly entitled to $400,000,000 from her external investments but did not gather it all in.

Imports of goods represented more than payment for commodity exports, investment of capital, or receipt of interest and profit. They could be payment received for "invisible exports"—shipping or banking services, insurance premiums, or tourist expenditures. In 1913 British shipowners earned nearly £100,000,000 by carrying foreign persons or goods for foreigners, and in effect were paid by being given goods to take back home. When American tourists were transported, entertained, and fed in Europe, the host received payment in imports of goods. When a London accepting house, insurance broker at Lloyd's, or banker rendered a service to clients in other countries, his remuneration came in the form of additional imports.

When we gather together this medley of visible and invisible items in the relations between people living in different countries, the balance sheet of *payments* is very different from the balance sheet of *commodity* exchanges. The latter in 1913 ran as follows for a number of important countries:

	Commodity Imports (million $)	Commodity Exports (million $)	Surplus of Exports (+) or Deficit (−) (million $)
Canada	634	432	−202
Russia	708	783	+75
U.S.A.	1,894	2,330	+436
France	1,642	1,327	−315
Germany	2,563	2,403	−160
Netherlands	1,575	1,239	−336
Italy	702	483	−219
United Kingdom[a]	3,568	2,862	−706

[a] Including gold and silver.

Canada in that year was still importing capital in great quantities for prairie settlement and for industrialization farther east, and therefore had a considerable surplus of imports. Russia was borrowing less heavily than in the days of Witte's railroad and industrial program, and her exports of goods to pay interest therefore exceeded her imports of new capital. The United States was no longer a great importer of capital and was now investing some abroad in her new empire, in Canada, and elsewhere; but in addition her obligations as debtor, as patron of foreign ships, and as incorrigible tourist obliged her to export a large surplus of goods yearly. France, Germany, and the Netherlands were creditors and ship operators, and the first two also drew much from tourists. Italy had little capital invested abroad, but her emigrants remitted large sums to relatives at home or brought capital back when they returned from exile, while her tourist traffic gave her much spending power in francs, pounds, and dollars.

The outstanding figure in the last column of the above table is that for the United Kingdom. Since 1854 the British commodity balance had been weighted constantly on the import side in spite of heavy capital exports at times and of the reinvestment overseas of income earned there. In 1913 the excess of imported goods was about $700,000,000; in 1929 and 1931 it was almost three times that figure. Against these sums the country could place the following estimated invisible exports (in millions of dollars):

	1913–14	1928–29	1930–31
Shipping, net income	460	630	390
Investments, net income	1,020	1,220	830
Financial and other fees, commissions, etc.	170	510	260
Total invisible exports	1,650	2,360	1,480
Less excess of imports	700	1,850	1,990
Balance of payments	+950	+510	−510

When all the excess imports had been paid for out of the invisible exports, there was still nearly a billion dollars left over in 1913 for reinvestment overseas. In 1929 the surplus was half that sum; but depression then reduced the invisible exports so drastically that they fell short of doing their normal duty by half a billion dollars, with consequences which will be described later. (See Chapter XXIX.)

Multilateral Trade. When examining early modern trade we saw that some of it was triangular or even more multilateral. As the whole world became more closely knit in a trade network, round-about trade played an increasingly important role in helping people to sell goods to one country and obtain payment in goods from another. In Chapter XXII we followed a tramp steamer which moved seven cargoes between thirty-one ports in six continents. It would not be fanciful to say that the western Australians who bought the first cargo of British goods paid for it by selling goods to eastern Australians; that they in turn paid by selling to South Americans, who did likewise by selling to Indians, who sold to Americans, who sold to Australians, who rounded out the transaction by sending goods to England and thus secured the money to pay the original exporter as well as to remit some interest and dividends due to British investors.

Dr. Hilgerdt has shown how this multilateral trade developed during the half-century before World War I. That period was marked by the establishment of the gold standard in most parts of the world after 1870, a step which gave exchange stability to the world's currencies; by the growing importance of tropical areas and their products; by the expansion of the temperate regions of the New World (the American west, Argentina, Canada, South Africa, and Australasia); by the industrial emergence of the United States and Germany; by some industrial growth and great agricultural expansion in continental Europe outside Germany; and by the con-

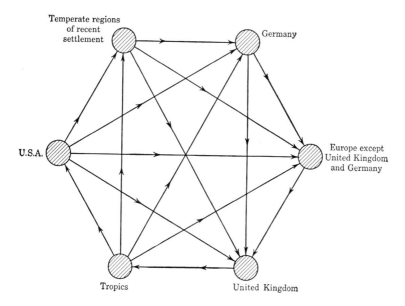

The System of Multilateral Trade, as Reflected by the Direction of Balances of Merchandise, 1928.

The region at which a line starts shipped more goods to the region to which the arrows point than it received therefrom; e.g., the tropics sent more goods to the United States, the temperate regions, Germany, and the balance of Europe than it received from them, but it received a surplus of goods from the United Kingdom.

tinued development of Britain as manufacturer, shipper, exporter, and investor. Hilgerdt therefore finds the world economy taking the shape of a hexagon, as shown on the accompanying diagram.

Three of the angles were large industrial countries, each flanked on both sides by predominantly agricultural regions; but each of the six points had direct connection with the other five as well as a route round part of the hexagon. The goods which flowed along any one line did not cancel each other out by a bilateral balance of exports with imports. The United States, for instance, was the greatest buyer of tropical coffee and rubber and a large purchaser of jute; but the countries supplying these products did not buy much from the United States, since they needed to use their export balance for purchasing European goods and also for paying their obligations to European investors whose capital had made possible the development of the region. The United States therefore paid for some of its invisible imports and for some of its tropical products by sending produce to Europe; but it paid a large part of both by selling industrial goods (machines, cars, oil) to the developing temperate zones, without buying much from them in return, since it produced the same things as these countries did—wheat, meat, and dairy produce. They in turn shipped wheat, wool, meat, and other farm produce or raw materials to Europe, including Britain and Germany. Germany paid for part of these imports by selling her manufactured goods to the rest of Europe, and the rest of Europe paid for some of them by shipping Scandinavian butter, lumber, or iron ore, Mediterranean fruits, and French textiles to Britain. Inside the hexagon there were simpler triangular transactions, such as Malayan rubber to America, American cotton to Britain, and British manufactures to Malaya; and there was a great amount of bilateral trade. By a combination of these trade movements each nation was able to pay for what it bought and creditors could collect their dues. The ultimate creditor was often a British investor, whose market stood wide open to receive whatever debtors cared to send.

Commercial Policy. International trade was (and still largely is) a matter of personal or corporate buying and selling. With the exception of Russia since 1917, nations did not trade with one another as political units. Germany did not sell to England; individuals in Germany sold to Englishmen. The latter bought from Germans rather than from fellow countrymen or Americans if they found that Germans offered a better or cheaper article. The Englishman got more value for his money, and the German got more money for his value than he would have done by putting all his wares on the German market or by not producing them at all.

To this exchange across frontiers eighteenth-century governments applied restrictive policies which were inspired by their own concepts of what they needed in order to be economically and financially strong or were prompted by the pressure of groups which sought to secure and retain privileges over their fellow countrymen or foreign rivals. War, traditional animosities, the need for revenue, balance-of-trade considerations, the desire to bring a new industry to birth and protect it in infancy, or the power of a vested interest had surrounded all nations except Holland with high tariffs or prohibitions and guarded their ships with Navigation Laws. Smugglers knew a dozen ways of "free-trading" in sugar, tobacco, wool, silk, or other heavily taxed and prohibited goods, and one of the strongest arguments in favor of lower tariffs was the admission that high duties provoked smuggling.

On the eve of the French Revolution fact and theory were combining to challenge the old policies. The American Revolution had blown a gaping hole in Britain's imperial trade and navigation system, and attempts to repair it by shutting American ships or goods entirely out of the remaining British transatlantic colonies were of little avail. Meanwhile the new industrial technology was making the manufacturers of cottons, metalware, and pottery eager to exploit their advantage in foreign markets, especially the French. In the realm of theory Smith's *Wealth of Nations* (1776) expounded the doctrine that the wealth of all nations would be increased if each area specialized in that line of production for which its physical and human resources fitted it and the specialists were free to exchange their cheap goods regardless of national boundaries.

A chance was offered to bow a little to these new winds when in 1786 the inveterate enemies, France and Britain, signed a trade treaty by which the latter admitted French wines and spirits to Britain at much lower tariff rates (but still excluded silks) in return for lower French tariffs on British cottons, pottery, and iron. As Britain produced no wine, no native interest was hurt. Portugal, for whose benefit French wines had long been heavily taxed, was shrinking as a market for British goods, while France promised to be a very good one. French wine producers, harassed by low prices since the seventies, were glad to have easier access to the British market; but most French manufacturers cried, "Ruin!" though some of them sent delegates to England to learn the secrets of British production.

Revolution and war prevented the treaty from having a fair test, and for two decades after 1793 trade was regarded as a weapon to be used by each side against the other. France promptly began to evolve a policy which would ruin the "isle of shop-keepers." British goods and ships were to be excluded from France and from every other country that she came to control. Thus Britain would find "her vessels laden with useless wealth wandering around the wide seas, where they claim to rule as sole masters, seeking in vain from the Sound to the Hellespont for a port to open and receive them" (Napoleon, 1807). This loss of markets would ruin her industries and prevent her from supplying her allies with goods; she would have to pay her debts and her subsidies in gold, and thereby wreck her credit. The accumulation of these disasters would bring her economy to the ground and drive her rulers as suppliants to a peace table.

By 1806 Napoleon was in a position to impose this policy on a great part of the continent and later to gather in most of the remainder. But he was never able to enforce it fully outside France. The subject countries were apathetic or hostile; the Dutch were such incorrigible smugglers that Napoleon was frankly told, "You might as well prevent the skin from sweating" as try to stop them; and France could not supply goods to take the place of those she tried to shut out. The British had no intention of being ruined, and whenever one port was closed they always found another through which their wares could enter the forbidden land.

By lasting so long, the war of 1792–1815 made the distorted economy become almost a new normal condition, habituated to high costs and prices, higher customs and excise taxes, new taxes on everything that could be thought of (including an income tax in Britain), swollen agricultural production, expanded industries to meet war needs or to benefit from wartime protection, and an inflated paper currency. When peace shattered war demands and price levels, producers in every land cried out for help. English landlords and farmers had for a decade lived in a world where the price of wheat averaged 11/6 (almost $3.00) a bushel, against about 6/– ($1.50) in the decade before 1793. They now clamored successfully for protection; by a new Corn Law (1815) wheat imports were forbidden so long as the domestic price of grain did not exceed 10/– a bushel; and a tax of 6d. a pound was imposed on foreign wool. Meanwhile the old order continued, with its prohibition of some imports (especially silk) and of some exports (especially wool and machines), its tariffs on all manufactured goods and on such raw materials as cotton or hemp, its navigation laws, preference to colonial products (including one on lumber granted in 1807), its bounties on exported linens, and its taxes on exported coal as well as on many manufactured goods. It was a cumbrous combination of protection and of a desperate search for revenue to meet the crushing burden of national debt.

The continent emerged from the war even more protection-minded than ever. Russia in 1810 had decreed a prohibition of all manufactured imports and in 1822 changed this ban to high tariffs on only the less important articles. Austria used prohibitions and prohibitory duties; French tariffs of 1816, 1822, and 1826 shut out textiles and many other goods; Prussia in 1818 strove to protect both her old industries and her wartime offspring. In the United States, industries born before or during the War of 1812 were afforded protection by the tariffs of 1816, 1818, 1824, and 1828.

After 1820 the tide slowly began to turn in Britain. As Europe settled down to peace, with no great dispute to disturb the international horizon, the demobilization and demilitarization of commercial policy became possible. Some cabinet ministers, parliamentarians, manufacturers, and merchants came more and more under the influence of the economists' contention that free trade was a policy which would, in the words of a London merchants' petition (1820), "render the commerce of the world an interchange of mutual advantages and diffuse an increase of wealth and enjoyments among the inhabitants of each state." For that interchange British manufacturers equipped with the new technique were more than ready. They had little to fear from foreign competitors in the home market or anywhere else, provided they could get rid of the duties on imported raw materials and their workpeople could draw freely on any cheap food that was available outside the country. Some of them wanted free trade in farm products because they feared that protection for agriculture would provoke primary producing lands to retaliate by encouraging the development of their own manufactures. Any exporter who received news reports from his American partner or agent knew well that one of the most popular protectionist arguments was the assertion that Britain kept its doors closed to the staple farm products of the region north of the Potomac.

While the manufacturers, especially the cotton men of Lancashire, were eager for free trade, the shipowners clung tightly to their Navigation Laws, the agrarians to their Corn and other laws, the colonial interests to their preferences on sugar, lumber, and grain, and the finance ministers to any levy that helped to keep the national purse replenished. The progress from protection to free trade was therefore gradual, fitful, but eventually complete. During the twenties Huskisson took some important preliminary steps; in the thirties little was done, but Peel resumed the journey during the forties, and Gladstone completed it in the fifties. The Navigation Laws were modified a little by making reciprocity treaties after 1823 but were not repealed till 1849 and 1854. With repeal the ports were thrown wide open on equal terms to the vessels of all nations. Other countries went nearly as far, but some, including the United States, retained the coastal trade for their own vessels. The tariff was reduced and rid of its prohibitions by Huskisson, duties on raw materials were abolished, and restrictions on exports disappeared. In 1840 there were still 1,150 items on the customs list, but few of these were needed to protect British industries. Seventeen of them yielded 95 per cent of the customs revenue, and the receipts from at least 600 of them were not worth collecting. By 1860 the list had been cut down to forty-eight items, and in 1882 only twelve imported articles were taxed, all of them for revenue purposes only. The income tax was reintroduced by Peel in 1842 to fill the gap made in the revenue by the tariff reductions; it was to be a "temporary fiscal engine," but it became far from fleeting. Colonial products lost their preferences as duties were reduced or disappeared. When colonies received self-government during the forties and fifties they gained control of their own commercial policies. Canada used this power to negotiate a reciprocal trade agreement with the United States in 1854 and to impose a moderately protective tariff on imports (including British) in 1857.

Few of these steps created much fuss. England's economy was strong enough to dispense with protection. Even the lamentations of the shipowners, a group notorious for making "loud and continued complaints of distress" as well as for being "numerous, wealthy, and influential" (Porter), had a hollow, untrue ring. But the repeal of the Corn Laws was a long, noisy, bitter battle which might have gone on indefinitely if a calamity had not ended it. The Laws were amended in 1828 and 1842 to replace the door which did not open until the price rose to 10/– a bushel with an open door through which grain could always come on paying a duty that rose as the price fell. In 1839 the Anti-Corn Law League was formed to agitate for the repeal of any duty on grain imports. For seven years it bombarded the country with well-organized propaganda—pamphlets, newspapers, lectures, mass meetings, and speeches in parliament. Peel resisted its attacks, for he wished to introduce free trade in food gradually as part of his general program. In 1845, however, he was faced with the tragic facts of a second consecutive bad harvest in England and a potato blight in Ireland. To relieve the latter he threw Irish ports open to wheat and bought American corn. Then in 1846, accepting the inevitable, he carried through parliament a law which provided that in 1849 grain was to be admitted on payment of a nominal duty of three cents a bushel. In 1869 that little levy disappeared.

Peel's repeal of the Corn Laws was bitterly opposed by many of his own Tory party. They prophesied that he would ruin the country's agriculture. The only thing he did ruin was his own career. There was no great supply of foreign grain available for pouring into British ports until the seventies, and British farmers enjoyed more than a quarter of a century of unprecedented prosperity. (See Chapter XVIII.)

Trade Policies on the Continent. Free trade also had its prophets. Cobden and others frequently asserted that if Britain adopted "free trade in all its simplicity" there would not be a tariff in Europe that would not be changed "in less than five years" to follow her example. The forecast was correct in some measure, apart from the time limit, for up to 1870 there was a widespread trend toward freer trade. In France, English theory and policy found some admirers. One of these, Chevalier, resigned his chair in political economy to become a member of Napoleon III's government, and persuaded the emperor to let him negotiate a commercial treaty with England (1860). By that agreement France abolished prohibitions on British goods and reduced many duties; in return French silks and wines were given easier access to British markets, and most other goods already enjoyed free entry. More important still, each country promised the other "most-favored-nation treatment." If France subsequently signed a treaty which gave some other country lower rates than England enjoyed, these rates were automatically to apply to British goods as well.

This treaty helped French wine and silk producers and jolted French industrialists out of their highly protected indolence. Manufacturers who had clamored most loudly against the treaty "prospered exceedingly. The stimulus of foreign competition forced them to enlarge their factories and improve both their machinery and their methods of production" (Dunham), and the state helped them through the transition by lending money. Meanwhile France made similar treaties with other powers between 1860 and 1866. In each case she received and granted lower duties, and some of these were passed on to British goods. Other countries made treaties with one another, and thus spread a network of low-tariff agreements over European trade.

Germany in 1815 was a geographical expression. Each of the thirty-eight states had a tariff round its borders, many had provincial tariffs inside as well, transit dues had to be paid when goods passed through one state to get to another, while differences in currencies and commercial law impeded exchange. The fusion of the states into a Customs Union (*Zollverein*) and later into an empire was largely the work of Prussia. In 1818 that state, by far the largest in the region, began to put its tariff house in order as part of the general reconstruction begun by Stein a decade earlier. It abolished internal customs, allowed raw materials to enter free, discarded most prohibitions, and imposed moderate duties on manufactured imports. Gradually a number of small states came inside the Prussian customs system, and the free-trade area was widened. The central and southern states, disliking Prussia's economic advance, formed customs unions of their own; but they generally came out second best in struggles with Prussia, and by 1834 seventeen states had agreed to form the *Zollverein*. By 1854 most of the others had entered; the ancient free ports of Hamburg and Bremen stayed out, and Prussia kept Austria out because she wished to prevent that powerful southern rival from exerting any influence in Germany.

The *Zollverein*, by sweeping away all interstate customs barriers, established a large free-trade area. Around it was a customs frontier against the outside world. The duties collected there were shared out among the states in proportion to their population. At first those duties were based on the Prussian tariff of 1818. There were no prohibitions, and the rates were moderate, even though they were raised somewhat in the forties under pressure from textile and metal manufacturers. After 1850 the trend was downward; the wool and grain exporters of Prussia, like the cotton exporters in America, were free traders, and their rulers saw that low tariffs would prevent protectionist Austria from wishing to enter the Union. In 1862 Prussia signed a trade treaty with France and forced the other states to accept it. Germany in 1870 was therefore a free-trade market of 40,-

000,000 people, knit together by roads, rivers, and railroads, and linked to neighboring countries by rails and low-tariff agreements.

In other lands the trend toward liberal international intercourse was also evident. Holland pared her tariffs almost completely away between 1845 and 1877, the Scandinavian countries did the same, and Belgium repealed her Corn Laws in 1850. Russia moved away from prohibition and high tariffs and discovered that she thereby reduced smuggling but increased her revenue. In Italy Charles Albert of Piedmont (1831–1848) allowed grain and raw silk to be exported, and cut down tariffs which had been so high that half the country's imports were smuggled. After 1848 Cavour went far on the road to commercial liberation.

The Return to Protection. Looking over the commercial scene about 1860 Disraeli concluded that protection was not merely dead but damned. Within twenty years the danger of writing political obituary notices was evident, for protection became very much alive in the seventies and put free trade on the defensive or forced it to retreat in most parts of the world. Three chief factors were responsible for this change in attitude and policy. In the first place the economic climate became much less congenial. The free-trade era, covering roughly the third quarter of the century, had been marked by high prices, high rates of interest or rent or profit, heavy capital investments, and generally by rich rewards for enterprise. The collapse of an almost world-wide boom in 1873 and the agricultural invasion a year or two later ushered in a quarter of a century during which all these rewards were much lower or were even lacking. (See Chapter XXVII.) In this period, known as "the Great Depression" until a deeper one deprived it of its right to that title, entrepreneurs turned to their governments with pleas for protection, relief, and aid.

In the second place, recent political events had strengthened nationalist sentiment and added two large new national states to the European family. These victorious newcomers, the German Empire and the kingdom of Italy, were exuberant, aggressive, but a little nervous about their place in the family, and therefore eager to pursue policies that would make them strong. France, defeated, weakened, and bitter, must find some way to regain her strength. Austria-Hungary, barred from exerting influence to the north, looked southward to the Balkans. Russia, faced now with a big power on the west, must see to its defenses on that frontier and to its prospects in the Balkan region. The national state had supplanted the early modern dynastic state, but its aims, standards of value, and methods remained almost the same. Three weapons were essential: diplomatic efforts to strengthen one's position and weaken that of others; a strong army built of conscripts and equipped with the newest kinds of armaments; and a national economy so well developed at all points that it could produce the goods needed by the nation in peacetime or war. "Blood and iron" might have put the German Empire together, as Bismarck said; but coal and iron, vigorously exploited and serving as the foundation for heavy and light industries, were equally indispensable twin resources.

In the third place, national treasuries were confronted with the task of raising much more revenue to defray the rising costs of military and naval services, to meet interest bills on money borrowed for state-owned public utilities, to encourage desirable enterprises, and to provide such growing social services as education or public health.

The low-tariff era ended in Germany, Austria, France, Italy, and Russia almost simultaneously between 1878 and 1882. In Germany the abolition of duties on iron imports just before 1873 exposed the market to a glut of foreign iron; the textile industries were hit by the absorption of the efficient Alsace mills; and the eastern rye growers were shaken by the impact of Russian grain. For a time Bismarck passively regarded the depression as "one of those stagnations as they periodically recur in course of time" and disappear in due course. But as it deepened, leaving the federal and state treasuries with growing deficits, a tariff began to look like a stone that would kill at least three birds: It would protect and please the western heavy industrialists and the eastern landlords who had swung almost overnight from their free-trade faith as exporters to one of protection; it would give these two groups a common bond and remove one of the worst sectional conflicts in the Empire; it would give the federal government a large revenue, provide Bismarck with plenty of money for building up the army, and liberate him from dependence on the Reichstag for annual grants of funds for the military machine. The tariff imposed in 1879 embodied a combination of protection and revenue motives, but in later years the former became stronger, especially for farm produce.

France lost its chief free-trade advocate when Napoleon III disappeared. Thiers, head of the protectionist group that hated the emperor's policy, wished to cope with the crushing deficit and burden of war debt by raising the tariff, but the trade treaties stood in the way and the last of them did not expire till 1877. Industrial depression, agricultural competition, and financial need grew great, and in 1881 tariff rates were raised somewhat. As in Germany the agriculturalists demanded and got more and more protection as prices sank. In 1892 the whole tariff was put on a higher level and also on a new basis. Two schedules of rates were prepared—a maximum and a minimum, similar to the new German "general" and "conventional" lists. By making concessions to France a country could get the benefit of the minimum. If the maximum rates were high enough foreigners could be frightened into granting substantial concessions to French products; if the minimum rates were high enough a generous protection was provided even against favored rivals. Thus the tariff became a bargaining weapon. A weapon it certainly proved to be; its use led to endless bickering and to tariff wars when one side retaliated against the other for some real or imaginary act of discrimination. France had such wars with Italy and Spain, and Germany had a fierce one with Russia. Schedules were frequently altered; France made thirty changes between 1892 and 1913.

The tariff history of Austria, Russia, and Italy ran on similar lines, leading five of the six great powers to what at the time seemed high protectionist policies. Britain and the small western countries moved slowly or stood still. The latter took advantage of the cheap food from overseas and became dairy specialists. In Britain the rural interests were politically too weak, the industrialists and wage earners too strong to permit the taxing of imported food and raw materials. Every depression evoked demands from some manufacturers for "retaliation," "fair trade," or some other plan for hitting countries that taxed British goods; but when better times returned the agitation went into recess. In 1903 Joseph Chamberlain began a campaign for "tariff reform" and imperial preference. On the one hand he felt that the industrial maturing of Germany and the United States was producing conditions far different from those of the palmy days when Britain was the workshop of the world. On the other he had developed a belief in the potential economic value of the Empire, a belief which had been unpopular for at least half a century. He therefore proposed "tariff reform" to protect British industry against the products of ill-paid foreign workers, the surplus of the dumpers, or the onslaught of American trusts. Imperial preference was to be granted by levying duty on imported food, but with a lower rate on that from the dominions and the colonies than on produce from foreign countries. In return the dominions and the colonies would admit British goods at preferred rates, though some enthusiasts talked of Empire free trade, of an imperial *Zollverein*, with goods passing duty free between one member of the family and the others.

These proposals were in such flat contradiction to the policy of the preceding sixty years that they threw the country into intellectual and emotional turmoil. Certain criticisms were hard or impossible to answer. (1) A tariff would not help British export industries. (2) Duties on food would raise the cost of living, while those on manufactured imports would enhance the price of some goods which were the raw material of many industries. (3) The overseas empire supplied only about a third of Britain's imports and bought only about a third of her exports. Preference would therefore benefit the less at the expense of the greater. (4) The dominions, wedded to protection and the development of their own infant industries, would give only such preferential rates as were innocuous to their own manufactures. These arguments were repeated and refuted *ad nauseam* during the years 1903–1914; the Conservative party eventually adopted protection and preference, but the free traders (Liberals) were in power from 1906 onward, Labor was strongly opposed to tariffs, and the country's policy therefore remained unchanged.

On the continent protection was supplemented by encouragement. Bounties were given on some products, such as sugar. The building of a merchant marine was fostered by admitting shipbuilding materials duty free, granting lower railroad rates on goods that were to be exported in native ships, lending funds at low rates or free of interest for ship construction, paying Suez Canal dues, and giving subsidies. One French subsidy was so generous that a ship could steam round the world carrying only ballast most of the way and make a profit. Obstacles were placed in the path of food imports by veterinary or pest-control rules. Foreigners could be forced to build factories and make goods inside a country instead of at home by restricting the validity of patents.

The period of new protectionism was one of revived interest in colonies, especially in Africa and the Pacific islands. Africa had just about ceased to be regarded as a slave reservoir when the need for its palm oil and rubber began to be felt. German merchants from Hamburg and Bremen, British and other traders operated along the coasts, but no European government pegged out any claims. In the sixties and seventies explorers who penetrated to the interior brought back glowing reports of the potential wealth of such regions as the Congo basin. Portugal, France, and the king of Belgium now began to assert claims to sovereignty. Since these claims would have shut foreign traders out of their preserves, British and German merchants persuaded their governments to intervene, and the result was a peaceful division of the African map in or after 1884.

Neither the British nor the German government had any desire to undertake the administration of its new colonies, and the work was left to chartered trading companies similar to the old East India companies. These failed, for they lacked the funds, will, and experience needed to control the natives and protect themselves. By 1900 the task of government therefore had to be assumed by the possessing state, and the traders were left free to do their best with the concessions of land, mineral deposits, or other assets that were available. Actually none of them did very well. The new colonies in Africa, like those in the Pacific islands, were poor markets, scanty suppliers of raw materials, and climatically unfit for housing a large white population. Since their trade was "open door," accessible to all comers, few manufacturers suffered if their country was outside the imperial circle or benefited much because it was inside. The imports of Britain's tropical African possessions were worth only about $2.00 per head in 1911, and less than half of them came from Britain. Germany in 1910 drew only half of one per cent of her total imports from her colonies, and sent only three-quarters of one per cent of her exports to them.

The Position in 1914. On the eve of World War I an incorrigible free trader could find evidence that the protectionist tide had spent its force. The flood of farm produce from the virgin soils was rising less rapidly, and the areas capable of being opened up by mechanical transportation were almost all gone. The price curve had turned upward in 1896, and it seemed probable that the statesman's task would soon change from that of keeping imported food out to that of finding countries which had any to spare. In Germany the growth of industry and towns had outstripped the native yield of food and raw material; prices were rising rapidly, and a bad harvest in 1912 caused a widespread outcry for lower tariffs on food. The alliance between the manufacturer and the farmer was breaking down. The former now wanted cheaper primary products as well as easier access to foreign markets; the latter retaliated by attacking the tariff which made manufactured goods unnecessarily dear, and meanwhile wage earners were feeling the pinch of the rising cost of living. In America Woodrow Wilson's election in 1912 was followed by a marked downward revision of the tariff in 1913, and British elections fought on the tariff issue in 1910 revealed a solid mass of free-trade orthodoxy.

In comparison with the policies of later decades, those of 1914 now look like free trade or at most like very moderate protection. As Professor Heckscher remarks, trade followed largely the same channels as it would have done under free trade; the tariffs prevented those channels from being worn quite so deep and choked them a little at some points. The constructive factors were more powerful than the restrictive, and were probably stronger in the decade before 1914 than at any earlier period. During those years overseas investment, which had been relatively small and fitful since the seventies, revived and reached the record volume of possibly $15,000,000,000 for the ten years. The value of international trade doubled, the exchange between the big industrial rivals grew steadily larger, while the contributions made by such newcomers as the Canadian prairies, the southern hemisphere producers of cargoes for the refrigerated ships, the rubber plantations in the East Indies, the oil wells of Central America and Persia, the South African gold fields, and the manufacturing industries of the United States and Japan were all poured into the stream of bilateral or multilateral trade.

How World War I diminished and dislocated this trade we shall see in Chapter XXVIII.

BIBLIOGRAPHY

Ashley, P., *Modern Tariff History* (1910).
Ashley, W. J., *The Tariff Problem* (1911).
Barnes, D. G., *History of the English Corn Laws, 1660–1846* (1930).
Benaerts, P., *Les origines de la grande industrie allemande* (1933), chaps. 1, 2.

Bland, A. E., Tawney, R. H., and Brown, P. A., *English Economic History: Select Documents* (1914), section iii, pp. 689–711.

Bogardus, J. F., *Europe: A Geographical Survey* (1934), chap. 9.

Bogart, E. L., *Economic History of Europe, 1760–1939* (1942), chaps. 3, 10.

Bowden, W., Karpovich, M., and Usher, A. P., *Economic History of Europe since 1750* (1937), chaps. 4, 12, 16, 17, 18, 20, 30, 31.

Bowley, A. L., *England's Foreign Trade in the Nineteenth Century* (1905).

Clapham, J. H., *Economic Development of France and Germany, 1815–1914* (1923), sections 16, 23, 28, 29, 47, 55, 67, 78, 88.

Clapham, J. H., *Economic History of Modern Britain* (1926, 1932), vol. i, chap. 12; vol. ii, chap. 6.

Clough, S. B., *France: A History of National Economics, 1789–1939* (1939).

Dawson, W. H., *Evolution of Modern Germany* (1908), chap. 4.

Day, C., *History of Commerce* (1907), chaps. 34–42.

Dunham, A. L., *The Anglo-French Treaty of Commerce of 1860* (1930).

Fay, C. R., *Great Britain from Adam Smith to the Present Day* (1932), Introduction and chaps. 2–5, 7.

Fay, C. R., *Imperial Economy . . . 1600–1932* (1934).

Feis, H., *Europe the World's Banker, 1870–1914* (1930).

Hoffman, R. J. S., *Great Britain and the German Trade Rivalry, 1875–1914* (1933).

Horn, E. E., *Organization of the English Customs System, 1696–1786* (1938).

Jenks, L. H., *Migration of British Capital to 1875* (1927).

Knowles, L. C. A., *Industrial and Commercial Revolutions in the 19th Century in Great Britain* (1922), part vi.

Knowles, L. C. A., *Economic Development in the Nineteenth Century* (1932), part v.

Levasseur, E., *Histoire du commerce de la France de 1789 à nos jours* (1912).

Levi, Leone, *History of British Commerce* (1872).

List, F., *The National System of Political Economy* (Eng. trans., 1904).

Ogg, F. A., and Sharp, W. R., *Economic Development of Modern Europe* (1926), chaps. 12–14, 16, 28.

Ohlin, B., *Interregional and International Trade* (1933).

Porter, G. R. (ed., F. W. Hirst), *Progress of the Nation* (1912).

Viner, J., *Dumping* (1923).

Wagner, A., *Agrar- und Industriestaat* (1902).

White, H. D., *French International Accounts, 1880–1913* (1933).

The Network of World Trade (League of Nations, 1942).

Henderson, W. O., "The Rise of German Industry," *Ec. H. R.*, April, 1935.

Articles

Henderson, W. O., "Germany's Trade with her Colonies," *Ec. H. R.*, November, 1938.

Hilgerdt, F., "Multilateral Trade," Am. Ec. Ass., *Proceedings*, 1943.

Jenks, H. L., "British Experience with Foreign Investments," *J. Ec. H.*, supplement, December, 1944.

Sée, H., "The Normandy Chamber of Commerce and the Commercial Treaty of 1786," *Ec. H. R.*, 1930.

Snow, E. C., "The Relative Importance of Export Trade," *J. Royal Stat. Soc.*, June, 1931.

Encyclopaedia of the Social Sciences: See list of titles under Commerce, Economic Policy, and Tariff, in vol. xv, pp. 549, 550, and 556.

XXVII

BUSINESS FLUCTUATIONS TO 1914

The economic course of the last two centuries, like that of earlier periods, did not flow smoothly or in a straight line, but was marked by alternations of prosperity and depression. The years of prosperity were characterized by growing demands for goods and services, plentiful employment, increased investment on old lines and on at least one new one, more requests for bank loans, rising prices and wages, higher interest rates and profits, a general confidence that all was right with the world, and consequently a widespread readiness to speculate in commodities and securities. Then suddenly or gradually these conditions were reversed: all curves except those of unemployment and bankruptcy turned downward, profits became meager, investment dried up, and the optimists of yesteryear decided that the world was going to the dogs. Two, three, or more gloomy years ensued before the clouds lifted and signs—sometimes false signs—of recovery revealed themselves; but eventually the road seemed clear and movement was resumed along it at a quickening pace through familiar scenery to the usual destination. The experience of the nineteenth century suggested that the normal pattern of economic life was one in which conditions got better, got ready to get worse, got worse, remained bad for a time, and then got ready to get better. In the twentieth century new factors disturbed the old normal, making prosperity harder to attain, relapse more severe, and recuperation more tardy.

These ebbs and flows affected social and political life as well as economic welfare. As the business curve rose, so did the marriage rate, the consumption of alcohol, tobacco, or other non-essentials, and the number of convictions for drunken or disorderly conduct; but larceny, petty theft, and the calls on charity declined. There was usually "a not negligible amount of overwork and strain, an intensification of industrial strife, a burgeoning of cupidity and fraud" (Robertson). There was a lack of radical proposals in domestic

651

politics, but a bumptiousness in international relations, so that friction might lead to war, since each side felt sufficiently strong and wealthy to take the risk. Depression turned most of these conditions and attitudes around. If it lasted long enough a wave of mutual recrimination might sweep the country, with everybody blaming everybody else—the little man attacking big business, the debtor denouncing the creditor, most people condemning the foreigner, and, as was the case in Germany after 1873 and 1929, with "anti-Semitism [rising] as the stock market fell" (Sontag). Radical schemes for social, political, and economic reform found favor; governments had to give relief or provide relief work, and some of their emergency measures involved changes in policy which persisted after the depression was over. Discontent found an outlet in anti-machine riots between 1750 and 1850, when starving men saw in the new equipment the thief that had stolen the bread out of their mouths. It sometimes overthrew governments at the ballot box or at the barricades. In the twentieth century hard times played a large part in making distressed people willing to accept or unable to resist the rise of dictators. Statesmen obsessed and harassed by depression after 1929 had no will, energy, or money to spare for restraining the aggressive policies of Japan, Germany, or Italy. A curve tracing business fluctuations would therefore be an illuminating frontispiece to any book on modern political history.

Early students of business fluctuations were impressed by the fact that the intervals separating the tips of booms were roughly of equal length. In the seventeenth century the complaints of bad trade came every eight to ten years. After 1760 crises descended on the British economy in 1763, 1773, 1784, 1793, 1803, 1810, 1815, 1825, 1836, 1847, 1857, 1866, 1873, 1883, and 1893. Some of these were caused by the beginning or end of a war, but in peacetime there was a cyclical movement occupying about ten years. From 1893 to 1914 trouble came more frequently—in 1901 in Germany, in 1907 in America and Britain—but was less severe. After World War I the dates of descent were 1920, 1929, and 1937. Meanwhile detailed research has shown that inside the decennial cycle there were smaller fluctuations which occupied about three years; and that the decennial cycles were in turn parts of longer swings, called secular trends or cycles, in which an upward movement of prices, profits, and stimulus to investment lasted about a quarter of a century and then gave place to a downward trend for about the same length of time. The years from 1815 to about 1845 comprised a downward secular trend; those from the mid-forties to 1873 an upward swing; the trend from 1873 to 1896 was downward, that from 1896 to the end of World War I was upward, but from 1920 onward the road ran downhill again. Thus the evidence suggests three kinds of fluctuations: the secular cycle covering about fifty years, the decennial business cycle, and the short-run fluctuation which we may call a cyclette.

Booms and depressions varied in range and intensity. The severity of the bad times was often proportionate to the intensity of the boom which had produced them, but it was also determined by the nature of the secular trend. If that trend was upward the pains were not very severe and recovery came fairly quickly; but if it was downward the opportunities for getting back to profitable enterprise were slow in appearing. The capital goods industries were especially active in boom days but prostrate in depression. Farmers and manufacturers of consumers' goods continued to pour out fairly large streams of wares in dark days. They made little profit, and when prosperity returned their increase in net earnings came through higher prices rather than from a large increase in the volume of business. Whole countries might stand apart, flourishing while most of the others were ailing, or vice versa. Nevertheless, the growing commercial and financial interdependence of the world in the last hundred years has tended to make nations companions in disaster or good fortune.

The booms of the first half of the nineteenth century usually ended with a loud bang as the bubble burst. With little warning a credit crisis emerged and degenerated into a panic. The financial heart seemed to stop beating, bankruptcy stared men in the face, and in a few days or weeks business was headed for the abyss. After the panic of 1866 the British banking system learned how to avert or deal with these crises, and henceforth business slid down a hill instead of falling over the edge of a precipice. France also succeeded in avoiding sudden disasters, but Germany was severely shaken in 1901, as was the United States by panics in 1901, 1903, and 1907. These led to the establishment of the Federal Reserve System in 1913 to serve as a brake on financial exuberance, and it was therefore possible in 1914 to believe that crises were now things of the past. The events of 1920 and 1929 showed that this belief was ill founded.

Causes of Fluctuations. Every serious depression produced its crop of analysts who searched for an explanation of that particular misfortune or for the causes of fluctuations in general. Some of the theories were fantastic; others canceled each other out; but the serious ones differed rather in the emphasis which contemporary conditions made them place on different factors. The differences reflected the great variety of points at which something could go wrong with the economic machine, with the judgment of those who operated it, with the power supply that drove it, and with the external political or social environment. In a simple agricultural economy the weather alone was a sufficient guarantee that the reward for man's labor would fluctuate. In the early modern economy, dominated by commerce and agriculture rather than by industry, the combination of weather, war, and mercantile mishaps or misjudgments of market opportunities could turn sunshine into gloom. If the modern economy had been able—which it was not—to eliminate all these ancient hazards, its own innovations in the technique and organization of industry or transportation, its need for large sums of fixed capital, and the ease with which rivals could compete would still have created sufficient new elements of instability to insure that even the most expansive periods of its growth were filled with fluctuations.

Though no two business cycles were quite alike in their character or in the extent to which they were influenced by some special or extraneous event, certain general factors played a part in taking business up into a boom, dragging it down, and pulling it out of the slough of despond. Of these the first and most important was personal—the optimism, self-confidence, and forgetfulness of the farmer, manufacturer, banker, trader, and investor. The desire of these men was to obtain as much income as possible. In dark days they might become very pessimistic, condemn themselves for their recent follies, make vows of caution, and resolve never again to let themselves be caught in the trap of a trade boom. But after a while, when demand began to expand and prices crept up from their low point, the unpleasant memories faded, pessimism gave way to optimism, and the vows were forgotten; or if the older men remembered them a new generation had entered the field eager to buy its own experience. Improving trade eventually begat overoptimism, which begat the conditions that led to depression, which begat pessimism, whose child was overpessimism, which is where we began to trace the cycle. This psychology of the entrepreneur was "the dominant cause of the rhythmic fluctuations . . . the backbone of the explanation . . . but other bones must be added from elsewhere" (Pigou).

As optimism spread and strengthened its hold, enterprise expanded in every direction. Industrialists independently decided that conditions justified an increase in output, and this decision proved to be safe for a time but not indefinitely. If the commodity was comparatively novel, such as a new kind of cloth or a bicycle, the pioneer producer was soon followed by so many competitors that the supply eventually saturated the market. When the news spread that a market, especially a foreign one, for some article was good, a flood of wares would soon descend upon it, partly to fill orders actually received but partly because merchants or manufacturers consigned goods there on their own account. Meanwhile the expansion of production sharpened the demand for materials, credit, and labor and eventually raised their cost so much that the margin left for profit was pared down at just about the time when the market was so well stocked that further increases in the price of the product were impossible. By that time the demand for labor might also have compelled employers to engage inferior workers and to bring old machines back into use, thus lowering the average productivity of their operations. In the urge to expand, new buildings and machines might be ordered, but these sometimes did not become available until the crest of the boom was passed. In these and a host of other ways merchants and manufacturers overextended themselves until they were caught with an oversupply of goods or by a dangerous relation between costs and prices. They had not intended to be caught; they were going to know when to stop this time; but they had been unable to call a halt even if they remembered to want to do so.

In agriculture man was less the maker of his weal or woe and more the plaything of climatic variations which affected not merely him but the whole economy. So long as western Europe depended on its own farm supplies a bad season raised food prices to such an extent that consumers had far less income left for buying manufactured goods, and farmers lost some of their purchasing power if higher prices did not counteract the effect of short crops. Years of bad harvest were usually periods of depression; a turn to better yields frequently helped greatly in stimulating recovery; and the return of poor harvests might help to wreck prosperity because emergency food imports might have to be paid for by exporting gold, thus draining reserves and forcing the banks to reduce their loans.

Every modern period of prosperity was swept by a great wave of investment for the production of capital goods—machines, buildings, roads, canals, railroads, ships, power generators, metals, etc. In this respect the modern economy differed from its predecessors. While the capital was being spent large quantities of material and labor were needed, but when it was gone and the new equipment had been erected the demand shrank almost to vanishing point. In the case of railroads three or four waves of investment were needed to supply England, Europe, and then America with the new transportation service, and each of them produced the same outburst of energy followed by years of lassitude until the next stimulus was applied. The same experience was undergone by industries that made durable consumers' goods. Bicycles, cars, sewing machines, and furniture lasted for years; people bought them in prosperous times but were then out of the market for a long time. Hence the capital goods industries and those producing durable consumption goods proceeded by "bumps and jerks," and "most of the great upward and downward swings of trade in the nineteenth century, from the great English railway boom of the 'forties to the great German electrical boom of the late 'nineties, can be explained in terms of . . . the essential bumpiness and jerkiness of the process of investment in capital equipment" (D. H. Robertson). The troubles of the 1930's sprang partly from the fact that the production of capital goods, consumers' durable articles, and primary products had developed both rapidly and simultaneously during the twenties to the point of "glut and indigestion," and that relatively few new capital requirements emerged to attract investors or revive the capital goods industries until rearmament began.

The growth of investment added new causes of instability. In the first place, it made speculation in securities a much more widespread habit, practiced in part with borrowed money. Every boom had at least one new field to which buyers were lured by the prospect of being able to sell nicely printed pieces of paper at a higher price than they had paid for them. In the second place, new stocks were usually issued and sold for only a fraction of their nominal value, with the understanding that the holder was liable for "calls" for other fractions later on until he had subscribed the full amount. The buyer drew on his bank deposits or borrowed to make his first payment; when calls came he might have to withdraw or borrow still more; and the result was a reduction of the funds available for productive or commercial use, often at a time when they were badly needed to cope with crisis. In the third place, investment bankers froze their funds when they underwrote an issue of securities, expecting to thaw them out by selling the stocks or bonds; but a quick or complete sale was not always possible and the banker was therefore unable to discharge his commercial function or even, in crisis, to meet his obligations to his depositors. Such a situation, as we shall see, almost shipwrecked the Barings.

Finally, the credit machinery played its part in causing fluctuations. During depressed times people left their savings in banks for want of something better to do with them. The banker therefore welcomed any sign of a resumption of requests for loans in order to get his deposits back to work. Recovery made such requests more numerous and the prospect that they would be granted grew more favorable. The banker could go a long way before the ratio between his liabilities and his reserves sank dangerously low; the growing practice of granting overdrafts or of allowing the borrower to draw checks seemed to keep lending under control, while money lent "on call" or put into bill discounting looked almost as good as cash in hand. On the basis of the credit thus granted, a whole superstructure of credit and debt was erected. Every merchant or manufacturer was both debtor and creditor; at any given moment he owed money to the bank and to the people from whom he bought goods, and in turn he was owed money by those to whom he had sold his wares.

When, however, bank ratios became endangered either by over-liberal lending or by a drain on reserves, the bankers changed their tune from major to minor key, raised their rates, refused to grant new loans or extend old ones, and asked for the return of money out on call. The collapse of some large firm, a sudden break in commodity or stock prices, an increase in the Bank rate, a diplomatic crisis, news of harvest failure, or some other untoward event might frighten them. Whatever the cause, this application of the brake to lending shook the credit fabric. Borrowers were driven to sell goods, stocks, or any other property they possessed in order to lay their hands on cash; their own debtors could not be relied on to pay their debts on time, for they in turn were also creditors of debts that had become unsure. If this scramble for liquidity came when industry and investment were in a fairly healthy condition the damage might be limited and the trouble brief; but if they also had developed boom characteristics, then the credit crisis toppled over the whole house of cards (or paper).

The Chief Fluctuations, 1760–1914. The crises of the sixteenth to eighteenth centuries were caused by commercial excesses or mishaps, the closing of markets by war or tariff, the collapse of prices on the coming of peace, speculation in commodities or stocks or bonds, political upheavals, famine, the repudiation of royal debts, or the failure of some large venture. The end of the Seven Years' War in 1763 broke prices and punctured the credit balloon which had been blown up to finance the combatants. Its most spectacular event was the ruin of creditors in Amsterdam and Hamburg when the king of Prussia was unable to honor some of his short-term promissory notes. Recovery soon came in Europe and across the Atlantic, only to lead to excessive lending by some Scots banks, to speculation in East India Company stocks, to an attempt at cornering the alum supply, and other similar antics. These provoked a serious crisis in 1772–1773, which wrecked many Scots bankers, ruined two of the three leading Amsterdam merchant-banking houses, and plunged the staple industries into a depression which in England was prolonged by the American colonists' boycott of British goods on the eve of the Revolution.

That Revolution and the Anglo-French war to which it led caused an inflation of credit, of prices, and of industries supplying the needs of armies and navies. When it ended there was the usual deflation, and the flood of goods which British exporters consigned to the United States or which American importers ordered soon stopped (1784–1785) as it became evident that buyers in the new nation lacked the means to pay for them. As American exports revived, this lack was remedied, and by 1790 prosperity had returned to most countries except France, now advancing on its revolutionary road. In Britain it was a prosperity marked by some new features, for the period was one of cotton-mill building, of the widening use of steam, of the early puddling furnaces and coke-fed blast furnaces, and of other technical advances. It was also a time of widespread turnpike improvement and of a veritable boom in canal projects. Hence capital was being sunk in industrial and transportation equipment as well as used to finance production and commerce.

The outbreak of war in 1792–1793 ended the boom with a severe crisis, and for the next twenty-two years the conflict influenced economic conditions for belligerents and neutrals alike. France did not emerge from its early revolutionary dislocation until about 1795; its attempt to ruin England did not prevent its own economy from being seriously depressed in 1797–1799, a fact that helped to carry Bonaparte into power; and control of most of the continent after 1806 was of little avail in saving France or its subject nations from depression in 1810–1811. Loss of sea power and some aspects of French commercial policy impeded the influx or raised the price of cotton, sugar, and other materials from the outer world, thus injuring such industries as sugar refining and cotton clothmaking.

In Britain business conditions swung back and forth between good and bad. Prosperity came from the production of military supplies and the shipment of goods as subsidies to allies; from the ability to treat the mounting influx of American cotton and the investment of more capital in the new equipment; from the possession of such control of the seas and oceans that markets in Europe, Asia, and the Americas could all be reached; and from the fact that when neutral Americans carried goods from the West Indies or the American mainland to the continent they spent much of their freight earnings as well as the money received for their own exports in the purchase of British manufactured goods. Adversity came with bad harvests, with the collapse of prices when peace was made in 1802, with the shock given to trade by the resumption of the war in 1803, and when the obstacles erected from 1806 onward by Napoleon and the United States became really insuperable. These two attempts to wreck British trade were frustrated for a time by finding new doors into Europe and by the opening up of the Latin American market in 1808. But too many goods were poured out there, the returns were disappointing or even ruinous, and in 1810 the trade collapsed just as Napoleon was managing to close the northern European ports to British goods and ships and as the United States was embarking on its most successful effort to shut them out of her harbors. Since the continent and the United States had bought about two-thirds of British exports, the years 1810–1812 were therefore dark, with unemployment accentuated by famine; but 1812 saw Napoleon's grip on Europe begin to break, and by 1814 the ports were open.

Into them British manufactures and reexported colonial produce were poured in expectation of a ready market; but the continent was too exhausted and too poor to buy much. The American market, opened by the signing of peace at the end of 1814, was more promising but not sufficiently hungry to absorb all the flood of goods which British exporters sent or American importers ordered during 1815. The end of the wars therefore brought, not "peace and plenty," but "peace and beggary." Agriculture lost its high prices without shedding its high costs. Industry lost its high-priced army orders and found that its expanded productive capacity was too great or its output too costly for the civilian demand. Bad harvests, a potato famine in Ireland, bank failures, and the demobilization of large armies all added to the stress of transition to peace. Every western European town and many an American one had its bread lines and soup kitchens.

Out of this gloom Europe crept after 1820, was walking by 1823, and then accelerated its pace so much that it tripped and fell in 1825. Production and trade rose quietly at first, then began to feel the effect of a rising tide of new investment. Since the British government was no longer borrowing for war and was converting some of its debt to lower interest rates, those who had money to invest had to find other places in which it could be put to work. They did not need to search long. The Rothschilds, Barings, and others were floating loans for European governments at prices which yielded at least 5 per cent—but sometimes 7 or 8 per cent—against the 4 per cent or less on British bonds; and by 1824 the new South American republics, from Mexico to Argentina, had been joyfully welcomed into the loan market. By 1825 British capitalists had lent these republics or invested in their mineral resources at least £20,000,000, and merchants had sent vast consignments of goods—including a famous shipment of ice skates to a region near the equator. Meanwhile private firms were plowing their own profits and borrowing money to expand their mills, metalworks, and mines, while in 1824–1825 over 600 joint-stock companies were projected, of which about 250 actually came into being with plans for docks, British or foreign mines, insurance, gaslight, water supplies, canals, and the first railroads.

This flood of domestic and overseas investment produced its inevitable froth of fraudulent promotion; one loan was floated for a non-existent republic, and the only silver that interested some Mexican mining companies was that which they took out of investors' pockets. The raising of the £50,000,000 actually subscribed for loans and stocks imposed a heavy strain on the banking system. The spending of this money stimulated the demand for raw materials and finished goods, pushing prices up and provoking speculation in such things as cotton. The export of some of the capital was, in effect, done in gold. The general optimism led the country banks greatly to increase their note issues, while the circulation of bills of exchange was expanded.

All went merrily until the fall of 1825, when disquieting signs appeared on the horizon. The harvest of 1824 had been poor, and that of 1825 was worse. The price of the new stocks and bonds began to drop seriously, the returns on consignments were disappointing, well-founded doubts arose concerning the ability or intention of some governments to pay the interest on their debts, and the banks were so laden with bills that they dared lend no more. Then some banks closed their doors, the list of bankrupt firms in the *Gazette* jumped to abnormal length, November brought crisis, and December was "a month of bankruptcies" which reached a panicky week of terror when six London banks and countless country banks stopped payment. The toll of loss continued high throughout 1826; investment dried up overnight and production declined. Of the 250 companies formed during the boom only 127 were alive in 1827, which is both a measure of the wreckage and a reminder that a considerable part of the investment remained as a durable addition to the country's capital equipment.

Seven years went by, years of underemployment, low profit, false recovery, poor seasons, and occasional violent popular discontent before the curves began to rise again to the next boom, that which reached its crest in 1836. For that recovery domestic and foreign influences were again responsible. The harvests once more became bountiful, technical improvements appeared in the textile, coal, and iron industries, and capital flowed into the newly legalized joint-stock banks as well as into railroads after the Liverpool to Manchester line had shown in 1830 what the new form of transportation could do. The external stimulus came this time, not from Latin America, but from the United States, where settlement was being rapidly pushed west. Many of the canals, roads, and other "internal improvements" were financed by the sale of state or local bonds in London; much of the credit needed for trade across the North Atlantic was provided by British merchant-bankers; and many American banks borrowed money in England in order to lend it at higher rates at home. Since America was a ready borrower and buyer and Britain equally ready to lend or sell, British exports to the United States rose 125 per cent between 1832 and 1836, and the flow of capital or credit carried some gold as well as goods.

In the fall of 1836 the Bank of England, worried by this drain of gold, began critically to scrutinize its loans to firms engaged in transatlantic underwriting or commerce. At almost the same moment the boom was collapsing in America and by the spring of 1837 most of the banks in that country were closed. British creditors and exporters could not collect their debts, many of them were thereby ruined, and the losses continued to mount as one state after another defaulted on its bonds. Since most of western Europe had shared in the boom the interdependence of countries and continents made the depression widespread, severe, and long. A promise of revival was wrecked by the closing of the Bank of Belgium in 1838, then by the American suspension of specie payments in 1839, and then by bad harvests in 1839 and 1840.

After six disastrous, dark, dreary years, conditions in 1842 became favorable for a fresh advance. Good harvests and cheap food laid a sound foundation for general recovery. Savings had accumulated and banks were therefore eager to lend money or discount bills at very low rates. In the Far East China was expected to provide a larger market for cottons and other manufactured goods after she had been obliged in 1842 to open her doors wider. The greatest stimulus came, however, from the railroad, now recognized as such an invaluable servant that all countries wanted as many lines as they could afford. France in 1842 had decided on its railroad plan; Belgium was hard at work constructing its two trunk lines; but the center of what became a veritable railroad mania was in Britain. During the years 1843–1848 there was proposals for the formation of over 1,400 companies with a total capital of £700,000,000. Only a fraction of these actually came into being, chiefly during the years 1843–1845 which comprised the period of the boom, and some of them "had no other purpose than to furnish profits for their promoters" (Morgan). By the end of 1848 about £200,000,000 had been collected from investors and 3,000 miles of new track were open. The construction work stimulated the demand for labor and materials, but the calls made on stockholders were not easily met even in good times. Those sent out in 1847 were heavy, equal to 70 per cent of the total declared value of the country's exports, and by that time conditions had become bad throughout western Europe. The harvests of 1845 and 1846 were very poor from Ireland across to Germany; the failure of the American cotton crop of 1846 raised the price of raw material to the cotton manufacturers; the Bank of France was struck by a crisis in 1846 and had to borrow gold from London; and better crops in 1847 reduced grain prices, ruining dealers whose stocks had been bought at a higher figure as well the banks which served them. The total effect in 1847 was a drain on the Bank of England's reserves, a rush of distressed borrowers seeking help, and a panic which was allayed only when the government authorized the Bank to increase its fiduciary note issue in violation of the Bank Charter Act. (See Chapter XXIV.)

The troubles of 1847 led to depression, deepened by revolutions on the continent in 1848 and the fear of a Chartist uprising in Britain. But the gloom was not prolonged for, without being aware of the fact, the world's economy was just rounding a very important corner. New stimuli to investment and enterprise were added almost overnight to the old ones. The gold discoveries in 1848 and 1851 produced the first of "a series of erratic outbreaks of economic activity along the Pacific coast of North America and in Australia which suddenly transformed vast scantily populated areas into regions producing enormous quantities of raw material for a highly industrialized Europe" (Innis). Capital, labor, goods, and ships rushed to those regions during the next few years, and the gold which came back was a powerful aid to lending in good times as well as an eagerly awaited import in days of crisis.

To the demand for goods for the new Pacific communities was added that which came from the moving frontier of North America. The United States' railroad system grew from 9,000 to 31,000 miles during the fifties, and that of Canada from 66 to 2,000 miles. Nearer home railroad gangs went to work in most parts of Europe. In Germany industrial expansion was rapid and investment banks were springing up to finance it. In France the *Crédit Mobilier* was active, setting a pattern that was copied in most other countries of central and western Europe. Britain felt the demand from all these regions for capital and consumers' goods; she supplied rails, engines, machines, experts, and laborers; and her exports jumped 60 per cent between 1848 and 1853. Nearly a quarter of them went to the United States in 1856, for the memory of the defaulted state bonds had faded sufficiently to let British investors buy American railroad bonds and to make English bankers grant almost unlimited credit to American buyers.

This "feverish and gold-dazzled activity of the mid-fifties" (Clapham) was too fast to last. It ended with the quick collapse of the American boom in the fall of 1857. In October alone about 1,400 American banks closed their doors, many railroads defaulted on their bonds, and remittances to European creditors could not be made. This news staggered London, Liverpool, Hamburg, and other centers. Panic swept the money market so rapidly that the Bank of England was obliged to use the emergency power granted it to issue fiduciary notes. On the continent boom conditions had developed so far on their own account that a crash would have come even without American aid. Consequently 1857 was a year of crisis and disaster in most parts of the world.

So also was 1873. Business had recovered fairly quickly after 1857, in contrast to the tardy recuperation after 1825 or 1836. The American Civil War disturbed Europe's cotton industry by shutting off the supply of raw material; the Austro-Prussian War of 1866 and the Franco-Prussian War of 1870–1871 caused some nervousness; but the whole economy was still buoyant, especially in the years 1871–1873. Prices, interest rates, and profit yields were high, and investors found plenty of opportunities at home or abroad. Capital still flowed in great quantities into railroads in Europe and outside, as for instance into the 25,000 miles of track laid in the United States during the four years 1869–1872. The iron industry expanded still farther to supply the rails and metal for rolling stock, the new Bessemer plants multiplied, the rising demand for coal was met by opening new mines, while machine makers and consumers' goods industries flourished. Industrialization and the promotion of companies— honest, reputable, and otherwise—reached a new peak in Germany with the receipt and expenditure of the billion-dollar indemnity paid by France. During the years 1868–1875 "government-loan contractors deluged the London market with the bonds of nearly every country of Europe, the Near East, Latin America, and the United States, at high rates of interest and attractive discounts" (Jenks). Every country drew sustenance from the rich man's table, farmers were prosperous, and wages rose so high that London *Punch* published drawings of British coal miners drinking champagne.

In June, 1873, Vienna began to have financial trouble, which spread rapidly up to Berlin and down to Rome, leaving a trail of bankruptcy. In September New York had its "Black Friday" as banks closed. The American debacle helped to intensify the continental break; the prices of commodities, stocks, and bonds fell in all countries, and the world settled down to the inevitable aftermath of liquidation, hopeful that the discomfort would be brief. The hope proved to be a vain one. The economy had rounded another corner: the long upward secular trend which had run since the late forties was now replaced by a downward trend which lasted till 1896. It was marked by the serious, almost unbroken decline in prices and by a heavy fall in the earnings of capital. British wholesale prices dropped during each of seventeen years out of the twenty-three; their total decline was from an index number of 152 to 88. The interest return on gilt-edged securities and bank loans fell, as did private profits, company dividends, rents, and the market price of stocks.

This "Great Depression" of prices and profits was obviously more than a mere reaction to the boom of 1871–1873; it was also a double result of the vast pouring of capital into railroads, steamships, capital goods industries, mines, and overseas developments during the preceding quarter-century. In the first place, while the construction was going on there was a heavy demand for materials and labor, higher prices for both, and a great expansion of productive capacity for supplying such things as rails, coal, engines, and ships. Now that the construction was finished, at least for the time being, industrial capacity was excessive. The iron and steel masters, for example, could produce 2,500,000 tons of rails in 1873, but consumption declined to about 500,000 tons. Hence the price of rails fell 60 per cent between 1872 and 1881. In the second place, the investments of the third quarter-century opened up new areas of cheap or free land and gave those who settled there cheaper transportation to market. By the fourth quarter the consequences became evident in the arrival of the flood of cheap grain in western European markets.

Although the downward secular trend was partly the result of past investment, it was accentuated by the decline in new investment. After 1873 the failure of some overseas governments and corporations to pay their interest bills emphasized once more the danger of thinking that a high interest rate outweighed high risk. Foreign bonds and stocks became unpopular, and capital tried to find work at home, even though the reward there was smaller. Sometimes it helped to develop a new industry, sometimes to reequip and make an old industry more efficient and thereby enable costs to be reduced to counteract low prices. In most cases the return was small, those who received it grumbled, and when a new temptation came from overseas they might succumb to it. By 1879 they were ready for such a lure as came from the American west with its revived appetite for railroads; but by 1883 that boom had spent itself, and the years till 1886 were dark once more. From 1886 to 1891 hopes were raised again by the discovery of gold in South Africa, French plans for a Panama canal, more American railroads, the promise of great developments in Argentina, Australia, and New Zealand, and the organization of cartels or trusts to restrict competition. The good old days seemed to have returned; over £2,000,000,000 of new capital was collected in London alone in three years, 1888–1890, prices rose a little, shipowners bought new modern vessels, and the heavy industries worked night and day. But the canal project failed, the South American bonds proved unreliable, and Baring Brothers, who had underwritten them but were unable to sell all of them, faced bankruptcy in 1890. The brief investment boom therefore vanished. Prices resumed their fall, banks broke in Australasia in 1892–1893, and in America the railroads, the banks, and the Stock Exchange collapsed in 1893.

These two decades were heavy with gloom but devoid of any panic in London, Paris, Berlin, or Vienna. When the Barings tottered, the Bank of England swiftly mobilized British private and joint-stock banks in a plan to guarantee that the veteran firm's liabilities would be met in full, and thus averted a panic which would have been frightfully severe. Joint action coped with minor crises, and there was some collaboration between the Bank of France and its British counterpart. Western Europe was therefore better able to absorb the shocks of disaster and panic from the outer world. In other fields of enterprise the lean years led entrepreneurs to joint action in the formation of cartels and in the application of pressure on governments. As the vote was now possessed by most or all men and political parties had taken shape, calls for succor could not be ignored, and every government took steps which were intended to give a measure of security against the impact of depression.

The period of low reward for capital was one of good returns to labor. Labor organization grew weaker in the bad years but regained numerical strength whenever conditions improved. In Britain, as in

a less degree on the continent, it was strongest in the skilled occupations, and may have played some part in preventing the pre-1873
gains in wage rates from being lost during the depressed seventies
and in raising them during the eighties. Since, however, the percentage of workers enrolled in unions was still small, other factors,
such as the demand for labor and the increased productivity which
came when more capital equipment was provided for each worker,
may have been chiefly responsible for the fact that money wages
stood still or increased while the price of food and of manufactured
articles fell. Hence *real* wages and consequently the general standard of living rose during most of the "Great Depression." Mr.
Rostow estimates that they went up between 1874 and 1900 by an
average of 2 per cent per annum if no account is taken of unemployment, and by 1.85 per cent if unemployment is taken into consideration. For some men that consideration was important. Boilermakers,
shipbuilders, and other capital goods producers enjoyed full employment when capital was flowing abroad to equip new regions
or was being put into reequipment at home; but when the job was
done, 10 to 20 per cent of the workers became unemployed. For the
rest of the wage-earning population, however, the period was one
in which between 90 and 98 per cent were employed at wages which
bought a little bit more each year than they had done the year
before.

To farmers, industrialists, bankers, and the whole "capitalist class"
as British socialists were now calling them, or "bourgeoisie" as the
continental Marxian socialists labeled them, the best thing about the
last quarter of the century was its end. After more than twenty lean
years the downward secular trend stopped in 1896. Between 1896
and 1914 the British wholesale price index rose in twelve years out of
the eighteen, stood still in three, and dropped a little in only three;
its total climb was from 88 to 117. The comparable figures for France
were 82 to 118; for Germany, 81 to 120. On such a rising curve enterprise and investment could safely ride at home in the new electrical,
automobile, chemical, turbine, and rubber industries or in the older
textile, metal, coal, and shipbuilding fields. The riding was once
more good abroad. South of the equator Africa was proving to be
the richest gold mine ever discovered; Australia got over its long
drought after 1902; New Zealand was producing butter that rivaled
the Danish product and lamb that could be carried frozen halfway
round the world; Argentina was becoming a vast cattle ranch for

Europe; and all these lands wanted more railroads, capital equipment, and consumers' goods. In the Far East Japan could use some foreign capital and China must have some if the spheres of influence were to be profitable. In Europe Russia was the new industrial frontier, Siberia a new rural frontier, and both needed rails. The Turkish Empire, the "sick man of Europe," had assets that almost everybody except the Turk seemed eager to develop, and the Nile Valley might regain its ancient fertility if capital gave it proper water control. To the west the United States was now largely self-supplying in capital and industrial goods, but still open to receive any quantity of labor, while Canada, now getting into her stride, was still mostly wilderness northwest of Toronto and a few miles north of the St. Lawrence.

Here were all the conditions for an upward secular trend, marked first by domestic investment and then by capital exports. That it could not avoid excesses and relapses was made evident in the collapse of the overexpanded German electrical industry in 1901, and again when the "rich man's panic" which swept Wall Street in 1907 "brought the most complete interruption in its banking facilities that the country has experienced since the Civil War" (Sprague). But the damage done by such storms was slight, quickly repaired, and caused no serious check to the general trend. By 1905 capital exports began to loom large in all countries that had money to invest. In Britain they rose above a billion dollars in 1912 to make a total of $5,000,000,000 in eight years. The volume of European emigration rose, still flowing chiefly to the United States but in a growing measure to Canada, Latin America, and Australasia. The value of international trade doubled in thirteen years. Perhaps the capital export was excessive; it seems to have caused some branches of the domestic economies, such as housing, to be starved, and may have caused others to lag behind in productivity by depriving them of capital for better equipment or obliging them to pay a high price for it. But the overseas fields offered a higher rate of interest or chance of profit than was available at home, the tax reductions from gross income were smaller, the new ventures such as growing tame rubber tempted the venturesome, and some of the relatively new big borrowers were superb salesmen of their "unbounded potentialities."

The Hundred Years' Peace thus ended on an optimistic note for those who provided capital and ran enterprises. There was little sign in 1914 that saving was outrunning the demand for funds, though

Canada and some other areas had passed beyond the peak of their immediate needs and had built some railroads which could not hope to pay their way except under very favorable circumstances. For labor, as for people who lived on fixed incomes, the note was not so cheerful. All estimates show that the real wages, even of well-organized workers, were a little lower in 1914 than they had been in 1900. Unions were struggling to raise them by striking when collective bargaining failed, and unorganized occupations were going through the stormy stages of organizing, fighting for recognition, and in some cases or countries making up for their weakness by voicing revolutionary aims or resorting to violent methods. (See Chapter XXXI.) In Industrial Europe the standard of living of wage earners (as expressed in real wages) had risen, with only brief interruptions, since about 1850. The check to this improvement after 1900 was therefore an event of disquieting importance to a large part of Europe's population.

BIBLIOGRAPHY

Beveridge, W. H., *Unemployment* (1909, 1930), chaps. 3, 4.

Clapham, J. H., *Economic Development of France and Germany, 1815–1914* (1923), section 35.

Clapham, J. H., *Economic History of Modern Britain* (1926, 1932, 1938), vol. ii, chap. 9; vol. iii, chap. 1.

Hansen, A. H., *Cycles of Prosperity and Depression in the United States, Great Britain, and Germany* (1921).

Hawtrey, R. G., *Good and Bad Trade* (1913).

Hyndman, H. M., *Commercial Crises of the Nineteenth Century* (1908).

Levi, L., *History of British Commerce* (1872).

Mitchell, W., *Business Cycles: the Problem and Its Setting* (1927).

Rosenberg, H., *Die Weltwirtschaftskrisis von 1857–1859* (1934).

Rostow, W. W., *British Economy of the Nineteenth Century* (1948).

Schumpeter, J. A., *Business Cycles*, (1938).

Sombart, W., *Der moderne Kapitalismus* (1922), vol. iii, chap. 35.

Thorp, W. L., *Business Annals* (1926).

Wells, D. A., *Recent Economic Changes* (1890).

ARTICLES

Beales, H. L., " 'The Great Depression' in Industry and Trade," *Ec. H. R.*, October, 1934.

Heaton, H., "An Early Victorian Business Forecaster," *Ec. Hist.*, January, 1933.

Henderson, W. O., "Trade Cycles in the 19th Century," *History*, July, 1933.

Newbould, J. T. W., "The Beginnings of the World Crisis, 1873–1896," *Ec. Hist.*, January, 1932.

Rosenberg, H., "Political and Social Consequences of the Depression of 1873–96 in Central Europe," *Ec. H. R.*, 1943.

Rostow, W. W., "Investment and the Great Depression," *Ec. H. R.*, May, 1938.

Rostow, W. W., "Investment and Real Wages, 1877–86," *Ec. H. R.*, May, 1939.

Rostow, W. W., "Explanations of the Great Depression, 1873–96," *Ec. Hist.*, February, 1940.

Silberling, N. J., "British Prices and Business Cycles, 1779–1850," *Rev. of Econ. Statistics*, 1923.

Encyclopaedia of the Social Sciences: articles on Boom, Business Cycles, Conjuncture, Crises, Inflation and Deflation, Promotion, Stabilization (Economic), Unemployment.

XXVIII

ECONOMIC CONSEQUENCES OF THE
FIRST WORLD WAR

Economic issues had little to do with provoking the First World War. To lay the responsibility, as has often been done, on the shoulders of "imperialism" or "capitalism" is not illuminating, if only because there is no acceptable definition of either word. General references to a struggle, race, or rivalry for colonies, markets, natural resources, raw materials, and fields for investment are irrelevant or misleading. The instances given to support them ignore the fact that the distribution of colonies in Africa and of spheres of influence in China was done fairly amicably; they are capable of quite different interpretations—in terms of prestige, strategy, or diplomatic triumph; and in many cases "the capitalist, instead of pushing his government into an imperialistic enterprise in pursuit of his own financial gain, was pushed or dragged or cajoled or lured into it by his government" (Viner). It is true that competition between the nationals of different countries could, especially in depressed times, "foster warlike emotions among those sections of the population . . . which think instinctively in fighting terms" (Clapham); but during the early twentieth century competition was no bar to prosperity. No powerful economic group or class in any large country either desired war or was advocating economic policies likely to cause war. The conflict was rather the outcome of the changes wrought in European interstate relationships by Germany's rapid rise to a commanding political, military, and economic position in the heart of Europe, of her outspoken determination to be a first-class power outside Europe and on the oceans, and of the antagonisms which were thereby generated between her and her allies on the one hand and the nations which refused to make way for her on the other.

The war was full of surprises. The first of these was the fact that it broke out. Several critical incidents had occurred during the preceding decade but had all been settled by diplomacy or by con-

671

ferences at which one or more of the big powers had given way a little. There was widespread confidence outside Germany, and even inside, that the Social Democratic party in the Reichstag would be strong enough to prevent war by refusing to grant money for the conflict. There was also a belief, based on a recent book written by Norman Angell and called *The Great Illusion,* that since war "did not pay" the victor, it was a thing of the past in societies dominated by economic considerations. Finally, the less optimistic were convinced that while a war might be unavoidable it would end quickly because no belligerent could finance it for more than a few months.

The second surprise was the inability of the generals to end the war quickly. German strategy was based on a lightning dash through Belgium to knock out France in a few weeks; then sufficient troops were to be rushed from the western to the eastern front to deliver a similar final blow to the slowly mobilizing Russians, while the Austrians dealt with the Serbians. All would therefore be over by Christmas. Instead of lasting four months the war lasted over four years; instead of being fought on one front at a time it developed many fronts; instead of being decided by maneuver leading to encirclement or great battles it settled down to trench warfare between more and more heavily defended front lines stretching from the North Sea to the Swiss frontier. At sea there was no immediate great encounter of massed fleets. The mighty battleships stayed in port to avoid mines and submarines, and the only trial of strength, the Battle of Jutland, came when the war was twenty-two months old. There was no early breakdown of the financial machinery.

From these two surprises others followed as the unexpected pattern of a long war emerged. (*a*) The quantity of munitions consumed passed all expectations. Within two months both sides were running short of supplies, and the demand rose relentlessly to the very end, even though the airplane, tank, and motor truck were used in a far smaller measure than in the later conflict. (*b*) The food problem assumed gigantic dimensions; the blockade gradually cut off supplies from the Central Powers, the submarine brought Britain near to starvation, the withdrawal of men and horses from the countryside reduced the supply of labor and power, fertilizers were not fully procurable, and bad weather spoiled the harvest in crucial years. Rationing was therefore inevitable in all lands. (*c*) The demand for industrial raw materials mounted far more rapidly than production could be increased. Again the blockade and submarine reduced the quantity that could be imported, and thus emphasized the need for increasing domestic production or finding substitutes. The rationing of civilian supplies of manufactured goods was therefore necessary. (*d*) The labor problem was intensified by the competition between the army's need for men and production's need for workers. In countries which began the war with conscript armies, millions of men—15,000,000 in Russia alone—were called to the colors, largely regardless of their occupations. In Britain, which entered the conflict with only 250,000 professional soldiers and a system of voluntary enlistment, men were accepted without any thought of the effect on production; the need for a larger army compelled the country to adopt conscription (1916), and the total number of men in uniform at some stage of the war reached 5,500,000. The result in every land was a scarcity of labor at vital spots. (*e*) The financial problem was acute for two reasons: firstly because no government made many of the things it needed and must therefore pay for its purchases from private producers, and secondly because no country was completely self-supplying, and must find ways to pay for the goods it needed to import in great quantities at a time when it was less able to export goods and services.

No belligerent country was ready with plans for the economic mobilization that was necessary to cope with the production and financial problems of the home front. Germany was the first to remedy that defect. The blockade soon pinched or cut her channels of supply; the occupation of Belgium and northeastern France added to her industrial resources; relations between the government and the cartels or big firms were intimate, and Rathenau, who took charge of mobilization, was a businessman of great ability. By April, 1915, the machinery for controlling the German economy had been built but needed to be amplified as the problems of food and raw materials grew more acute. In Russia the central government was so incompetent that little could be done until voluntary committees took up the task, and their efforts were too late to prevent the economy from cracking. France's economic mobilization was rendered difficult by the loss of her eastern mining and industrial regions. The brunt of Allied economic mobilization therefore fell on Great Britain. In that country the early popular belief that "Business as usual" was a possible war slogan was soon shattered. In May, 1915, the Ministry of Munitions was set up, and as other problems emerged ministries or boards were established to handle such things as shipping, food, and raw materials.

This marshaling of industrial, human, and financial resources was marked by improvisation, blunders, and high cost; but it achieved its purpose to such an extent that at the end of 1916 neither side had been able to gain any marked superiority. In the spring of 1917 Russia dropped out of the Allied line, but the United States came in. The American fleet helped to deal with the now serious submarine menace; dollar loans relieved the strain on the Allies' virtually vanished supply of external purchasing power; but more than a year went by before American troops were available in force, and meanwhile Germany, released from the worries of an eastern front, was able to concentrate men and material for a massive assault in the west in the spring of 1918. The attack, or rather a series of five attacks, pushed back the Allied line and nearly broke it—but not quite. Despite the pounding they had received, the Allies still had enough strength to stage a counteroffensive, with a unified command at last and with the assurance that American troops were reaching the front in significant numbers.

By early August the German high command realized that it could not win the war. By the end of September it knew that stark defeat lay ahead and insisted that the Berlin government seek peace. The Armistice was signed on November 11, 1918. The Treaty of Versailles was signed on June 28, 1919, exactly five years after a young nationalist fanatic had fired his revolver point-blank at an Austrian archduke and his wife in an obscure Balkan capital city. The world then settled down to face the economic and other problems created by those years of war as well as by the terms that were written into the peace settlement.

The economic problems were due to distortion and dislocation rather than to destruction. True, the destruction had been great. Of 65,000,000 men mobilized by the belligerents, at least 10,000,000 were killed or permanently disabled. The effect of this loss of relatively young men was felt in the economic, political, and intellectual life of the inter-war decades; and meanwhile the fall in the birth rate during the war years helped to hasten the day of stationary populations in the countries of western Europe. The direct destruction of capital equipment was limited to ships at sea, to the deterioration of farm lands for lack of labor and fertilizers, and to the damage done in the fairly narrow belt which became the war zone on the western front. Finally, the savings of four years were devoted to destruction rather than to productive investment, and those of earlier years were rendered worthless by inflation.

Yet many of these material losses were made up fairly quickly. By 1924 the British national income equaled that of 1914; by 1925 the French devastated areas were producing more than they had done in 1913; by 1928 the German real income per capita was perhaps 15 per cent above the pre-war figure, in spite of the fact that recovery did not begin until 1924; and Russia had regained its former level of production by 1926–1927. Continental Europe's agricultural output, especially of grains and livestock, fell about a third during the war but was almost back to its old volume by 1929.

Dislocation and Distortion of Currencies and Values. The pre-war economy had rested on a domestic and world-wide exchange of goods and services at prices that were expressed in terms of a monetary system, based on gold, which provided a medium of exchange and a measure of value. The war dislocated the economy at every point. In the first place, it disturbed domestic exchange by creating a great demand for some goods and services—iron, steel, coal, munitions, ships, woolen cloth, and transportation—and reducing or repressing that for others, such as luxuries and cotton cloth. Consequently some industries increased their capacity, their prices, and their wages beyond points that were likely to be tenable when peace came.

In the second place, the war disturbed international exchange by preventing customers from drawing on their old sources of supply and obliging them to do without the goods or services, go elsewhere for them, or take steps to supply their own needs. When eastern Europe's grains could not flow through the Dardanelles, western Europe looked to North America and the antipodes for supplies, thus stimulating the vast expansion of cultivation in the New World. When Germany was prevented by the blockade from importing oil and nitrates, she set up plants to make the former from coal and the latter from the air. When the outer continents could not get their goods carried by British or German ships or obtain their usual supply of manufactured goods from western Europe, some of them, especially the United States, built their own merchant fleets, they went to Japan or the United States to buy goods, or they began to manufacture the wares for themselves. Consequently when peace set the belligerents free to resume their former business activities, they found that others had taken their place as producers, sellers, and shipowners, and that the newcomers, unwilling to relinquish their new equipment, were disposed to supply their infant industries with whatever protection seemed necessary to insure survival.

In the third place, the whole currency, credit, and financial system was deranged by the ever growing needs of war finance. That system had been kept under control by two ropes—the gold standard and the governmental practice of trying to keep the budget balanced. Neither of these ropes could stand the strain of war; each broke or was frankly cut. The total monetary cost of the war to the European belligerents has been estimated at about $170,000,000,000. There were three possible ways of meeting it—taxation, borrowing, and printing paper money. Britain met about a quarter of its bills by increasing and widening its tax levies, most of the rest by borrowing so heavily that the national debt jumped twelvefold between 1914 and 1919; and a little by the issue of inconvertible governmental "currency notes." These circulated alongside the Bank of England notes and took the place of the gold coins which had promptly vanished from circulation into bank reserves or private hoards. Other countries were unable or unwilling to pay much of their war costs out of taxes and relied almost entirely on borrowing. The funded French national debt incurred by selling bonds rose sevenfold, the German nearly twentyfold. In addition there was much unfunded short-term debt.

Balanced budgets therefore disappeared. So also did the gold standard. Much of the borrowing was done chiefly through the expansion of bank credits in Britain and by the expansion of the note issue in France and Germany. In France the ceiling on note issue was raised and by 1918 the circulation had grown fivefold; in Germany the paper currency multiplied sixfold. This would have been impossible if the gold standard had been maintained, since the claims of the noteholders for gold would have exhausted the reserves in a very short time. In every belligerent country the right to convert notes into gold, to withdraw coins from banks, to melt them down, or to export them had sooner or later to be revoked. There was now no brake on the amount of credit the banks could grant or of notes that the printer could produce. The ever mounting government demands for goods could be paid for, but no restraint had been applied to the general public's spending power, such as might have come from heavier taxation or widespread rationing.

Prices therefore rose throughout the war years in belligerent and neutral countries alike. At the time of the Armistice British prices were about 130 per cent above their pre-war level, and in other countries the figure was still higher. When the fighting stopped, a replenishment boom developed in the victorious countries, especially Britain and the United States. Devastated areas began to be rebuilt, soldiers needed civilian clothes, houses were wanted, warehouse shelves were empty, and manufacturers scrambled for supplies of raw materials or equipment. Purchasing power was great, with war-time savings, soldiers' bonuses, and war profits itching to be spent. Government spending diminished slowly, as peace loans replaced war loans or as the printing press supplied continental treasurers with much of their revenue. Government controls were removed quickly, particularly in the United States, for statesmen forgot that when a big game or fight ends there is still a difficult traffic problem to be handled if people are to get smoothly and safely to their homes. Financiers bought up businesses, recapitalized them at in-flated figures, and sold the shares to a public of pigeons. Farmers bought more land. Banks were swept along by the jubilant stream and their loans were generous. Prices therefore rose during 1919 and early 1920 even more quickly than they had in the war years. If 1913–1914 is taken as 100, the British wholesale index stood at 230 when the fighting ended but went above 310 in early 1920. For other countries the index numbers for 1920 read as follows:

France 509	U.S.A. 228
Germany 1,965	Holland (a neutral)...292
Italy 624	Sweden (a neutral)...359

In the spring of 1920 this "victory ball" ended. A speculative bubble in silk burst in Japan, famine and rebellion descended on China, the monsoon rains which decided the fate of India's crops were scanty, and the price of silver broke. Some consumers had spent their savings, others went on strike against exorbitant prices, and the most urgent demands had been satisfied. Finally, some governments, especially those in London and Washington, dras-tically reduced their spending, while the Bank of England and the Federal Reserve Board, feeling that the credit supply had become excessive, raised their bank rates. All these factors combined to shatter the boom. Between the spring of 1920 and that of 1921

British wholesale prices dropped from 313 to 195 and continued their headlong descent till they found relative stability at a level about 50 per cent above the pre-war figure. American prices fell within the same year from 228 to 151 and then also settled down at about 50 per cent above the level of 1913. Thus even in the best-regulated economies of the years 1913–1921 witnessed a very marked inflation and then a deflation of the supply of currency, bank credit, spending power, and prices.

On the continent the inflation road was longer, rougher, and steeper. In Germany all efforts of the new republican government to balance the budget by devising new or heavier taxes failed in face of the interest burden on war loans, the cost of caring for war victims, and the obligation to make reparations payments. Expenditure exceeded revenue by two or three to one during the years 1921–1922; but it rose to ten to one in 1923 when the French occupied the Ruhr district (January) and the government had to feed the workers who were waging passive resistance against the French as well as to compensate industrialists for their losses.

This gap between receipts and expenditure was filled by getting notes from the Reichsbank. At first the additions to the note issue were moderate; but as prices rose, as the purchasing power of the mark sank both at home and abroad, and as revenue became increasingly inadequate, the outpouring of paper swelled into a flood. "In the last months before the collapse more than 300 paper mills worked at top speed to deliver notepaper to the Reichsbank, and 150 printing companies had 2,000 note presses running day and night to print the Reichsbank notes" (Stolper). In addition to lending lavishly to the state the Bank lent money at low interest rates to industrialists. They used these funds to extend their plants or to buy any others that could be procured. Then when the debt had to be repaid, the value of the mark had fallen so low that the paper handed by the debtor to the Bank was almost worthless, and the borrower had got his extension or his purchase virtually for nothing. As the mark notes sank in value, people who received them hastened to turn them into goods before their purchasing power shrank still more. Consequently there was a "flight from the mark" which in turn helped to reduce the value of the paper still further.

As a result of all these factors the index of German wholesale prices rose as follows:

```
January, 1913........................1.
January, 1920........................12.6
January, 1921........................14.4
January, 1922........................36.7
January, 1923 .....................2,785.
July, 1923........................74,787.
November 15, 1923........750,000,000,000.
```

In Russia taxes met a third to an eighth of the government's expenditures between 1918 and 1924. A decree of 1919 authorized the printing of as much paper money as was needed to carry on the government, but by 1921 this paper had become so worthless that the collection of taxes in money was temporarily discontinued in favor of taxes in kind. Under NEP, conditions improved, a balanced budget drew nearer, and new banks were developed to supply credit. Yet the printing press only slowly ceased to be "the main source for covering the deficit of the State Budget, and the note issue took on astronomical dimensions" (Baykov). Prices on the eve of the Bolshevik Revolution had been 13 times their pre-war level. By January, 1921, they were 16,800 times higher, and in January, 1923, the figure had risen to 21,242,000. To remove some of the zeroes, the new ruble of 1922 was declared to be worth 10,000 of the old ones, and the ruble of 1923 was valued at 100 of the 1922 vintage or 1,000,000 of the earlier printings. In Austria and Poland inflation was only a little less extravagant. In France, Italy, and Belgium the note issues rose almost tenfold. Only Britain and the neutral countries (Scandinavia, Holland, Switzerland, and Spain) managed to keep their currencies relatively "strong."

The currency dislocations had their international repercussions. The fall in the domestic purchasing power of a country's money was usually preceded by a decline in its external purchasing power in terms of currencies which did not depreciate. Its rate of exchange went down; a German therefore had to pay more marks to obtain a dollar's worth of cotton, while on the other hand an American paid fewer dollars to purchase a German camera. The extent to which currencies depreciated varied greatly. British money had suffered the least at home and abroad during the war. The printer had not worked so hard. By shipping gold, by maintaining a considerable export trade, by selling securities abroad, by borrowing from American bankers, and after April, 1917, by obtaining loans from the

American government, London was able to "peg" the exchange value of the pound at $4.76. When the peg was pulled out (1919) the rate dropped as low as $3.20 in early 1920, but then began to recover. British goods therefore did not become more than a third cheaper through exchange depreciation. German wares sank to ridiculously low prices to holders of strong currencies, and some time usually elapsed before an increase in domestic prices made articles dearer to the foreigner. French goods or charges to tourists went low as deficit financing by loans and paper pushed the franc lower and lower until 1926; and the same was true in Italy and Belgium. While, however, buyers liked to pick up these bargains, producers in countries with undepreciated currencies cried out against the unfairness of competition from "cheap currency" countries.

This plea added one more to the many reasons that were being advanced for higher protective tariffs. War-born or war-expanded industries demanded that they be "safeguarded," insisted that they were "key industries," pleaded that doors which had shut out enemy goods be not opened, and pointed out that if imports were kept down (while exports mounted) a country's rate of exchange would be improved as its balance of trade became more favorable. Meanwhile the new states which had appeared on the map needed revenue from customs and felt that in building up industries they would give substance to their national pride as well as strike a blow at their former ruler. Competition through currency depreciation therefore coincided with other factors to provoke a wave of protectionism. It helped to make some minor breaches in the British free-trade wall by the Safeguarding of Industries Act of 1921; and it was a useful plea on the lips of Americans who secured an emergency tariff in 1921 and the Fordney-McCumber tariff of 1922.

The final dislocation was in the crisscross of payments that had to be made across national frontiers. As we saw in Chapter XXIV, these payments were made through the international gold standard machinery. The payments which the people of any one country had to make abroad for goods, services, or debt charges could be met out of the proceeds of the goods and services they sold abroad, the return on their overseas investments, or, in the case of the new, growing countries, out of the influx of new capital. The war had blocked or narrowed many trade channels, so that debtors or importers could not always sell enough abroad to pay for what they owed or for what they needed to buy. Britain and Germany especially found that foreign markets lost during the war were not easily regained. In neither country had the staple export industries regained their old position in 1929. In Germany's case the loss of Alsace-Lorraine obliged her now to import iron ore from that region, and hence she had to increase her exports in order to pay for it.

Reparations. On top of this difficulty in meeting commercial obligations there had been imposed two political obligations—the reparations which Germany had to pay to the victors and the inter-Allied debts. Reparations could not be expected to cover the whole gigantic cost of the war and were limited by the Armistice to payment for "all damage done to the civilian population of the Allies and their property by the aggression of Germany by land, by sea, and from the air." In the Versailles Treaty (1919) this limitation was expanded to include the money paid by Allied governments in pensions and separation allowances. The total obligation was thereby considerably increased and was not definitely assessed until 1921, when it was fixed at $33,000,000,000. Pending the determination of that figure, Germany was called on to begin making reparations in kind. To repair the damage done by her submarines, she handed over all merchant ships above 1,600 tons and part of her fleet of smaller craft and fishing boats. To restore the devastated areas, she was called on to deliver farm animals, machines, tools, building materials, etc. to France and Belgium. To compensate for the destruction of coal mines, she must cede the Saar mines and deliver considerable quantities of coal to France, and in addition she must supply up to 25,000,000 tons of coal annually for ten years to France, Belgium, and Italy. Property and securities owned by German individuals or corporations and lying outside the country's borders were to be thrown into the pool, as was any gold or silver that was available. All these deliveries were to be credited to the German government; against them would be set the cost of armies of occupation and other Allied expenses, and the net balance would be counted as reparations payment. Since it could not be expected to cover more than a small part of the total bill, the balance would be paid in cash or in kind during a period of thirty to forty years.

The reparations problem went through several sorry stages as its various facets became clear. The question, How much *ought* Germany to pay? was settled in 1921. The answer to the second question, How much *could* she pay? only time could answer, especially as it was closely connected with the third question, How could she make payment? and with the fourth, What would the creditors be willing to accept? Once the physical properties and goods listed above had been transferred, further payment depended on two conditions: (a) the ability of German manufacturers, merchants, and shipowners to build up a large surplus export of goods and services, and thus accumulate a great quantity of claims to dollars, pounds, francs, or other foreign currencies; (b) the ability of the German government to accumulate a large balance of receipts over expenditures, and to use this surplus for buying these claims from its people in order to hand them over to the Reparations Commission.

Neither of these was possible. The German economy was scarcely in a condition to export enough to pay for what it must import, much less accumulate a large surplus. Its exports of goods and services were reduced by the loss of important mineral and manufacturing resources to France and Poland: by the loss of shipping earnings with the surrender of its merchant marine; and by the tariff policies which its creditors had adopted to keep out its dyes, chemicals, and other staple products. The foreign exchange was therefore not available in adequate quantities, and if it had been there the government lacked the funds needed for purchasing it, except those supplied by the printer.

By early 1922 the Reparations Commission was being obliged by the pressure of facts to reduce the installment Germany was expected to pay and to permit more of it to be paid in kind. In mid-1922 Germany asked for a two-year moratorium on cash payments, and although this was not granted the payments were eased and Germany was left to pay chiefly in goods. A small failure in the delivery of telegraph poles, lumber, and coal led the Reparations Commission in late 1922 to declare, Britain dissenting, that Germany was in "voluntary default," and the Franco-Belgian occupation of the Ruhr followed, in January, 1923. This action, perfectly legal under the Versailles Treaty, brought life to a standstill in a region which housed 10 per cent of Germany's population and 80 per cent of her coal and steel production. German passive resistance failed and was abandoned in September; but France failed to get much reparations. Consequently the occupation served "both to bring France to a realization that only a reasonable reparation [could] be collected and to bring Germany to the knowledge that it [could not] avoid its payment" (Dawes). Inflation and reparations had got so bad that the only thing left for them both to do was to get better.

Inter-Allied Debts. The second political obligation created by the war was that of repaying loans made between the Allies. Almost from the outbreak of hostilities Great Britain made loans to her colleagues. By April, 1917, when the United States entered the war, she had lent nearly $4,000,000,000; by October, 1919, the figure had risen to $8,700,000,000, partly by loans of British funds and partly by relending money borrowed from the United States. Of this sum, pre-Bolshevik Russia had received a third, which was now repudiated; France and Italy had been lent a little less; and the balance had gone to the British dominions, Belgium, or other smaller allies. France had lent less than $2,000,000,000, nearly half of it to czarist Russia. Meanwhile Britain and France borrowed a little from American private lenders before the United States entered the war; but their borrowing capacity and their ability to pay for American products by selling securities or shipping gold had been well-nigh exhausted when the United States declared war. That declaration eased the financial position greatly, for by the time the Armistice was signed Washington had lent over $7,000,000,000—half of it to Britain and most of the rest to France and Italy. By October, 1919, additional loans to old or new borrowers and the accumulation of interest (at 5 per cent) had raised the figure above $10,000,000,000.

Put another way, the network of intergovernmental debts was as follows: The financially poor countries owed France, the United Kingdom, and the United States $10,000,000,000; France was creditor for $2,000,000,000 but owed the United States and the United Kingdom $5,000,000,000; the United Kingdom was creditor for $9,-000,000,000, but owed the United States $4,000,000,000. The United States was creditor to the tune of $10,000,000,000. Germany was debtor for $33,000,000,000.

In the peace negotiations the United States insisted that the loans she had made must be regarded not as subsidies but as ordinary commercial debts; that they must be paid in full with interest; and that they had no connection whatever with reparations, which the American delegates endeavored to keep at a low figure. To Europeans the connection between what they received from Germany and what they had to pay as debtors seemed very real and intimate. Their fight for large reparations was therefore stiffened in part by the knowledge that their own heavy burden of external debt was not to be eased. When, by 1922, the realities of the reparations problem were becoming manifest, Britain announced that it was prepared to abandon further claim to reparations and all claims on its own debtors if this renunciation formed part of a general plan. If this was impossible, Britain would try to collect only enough from Germany and the debtors to pay its own debt to the United States. It would prefer the first alternative, since "a general settlement would be of more value to mankind than any gains that could accrue even from the most successful enforcement of legal obligations" (Lord Balfour).

Such a policy would have meant a net loss of $5,000,000,000 to Britain, and of $10,000,000,000 to the United States; but the British per capita loss would have been $110, the American $83. It would have been cheap at that price; but it seemed too dear to France, and so the Ruhr occupation was tried. It was unacceptable to the United States, and so in 1923 America's debtors were invited individually to fund their debts. Country after country did so during the next three years. The principal sum was not reduced, but the interest rate was dropped from 5 per cent to 3.5 for Britain, to 1.6 for France, and to a mere 0.4 per cent for Italy. Payments were to be spread over 62 years and would total about $22,000,000,000. To make them, the debtors would need an excess of exports of about $300,000,000 a year—two-thirds of it British—and the United States would need to help them by being willing to receive an excess of imports of the same value.

Readjustment and Recovery. The Ruhr fiasco and the collapse of German paper currency marked a divide between the days of dislocation and the return to political and economic conditions which seemed to grow more and more healthy until 1929. The Germans set out to rebuild their own currency and were given a powerful helping hand from outside. In November, 1923, scarcely two months after both sides had called a truce in the Ruhr, the government issued a new paper note, the Rentenmark, worth 1,000,000,000,000 old marks. With it went the assurance that the issue would not be inflated, but that the budget would be balanced; and meanwhile everybody knew that the Dawes Committee had been appointed (November, 1923) to study the reparations question. In such circumstances the new paper was accepted by the German people and stability was restored. Inflation had destroyed the value of government bonds, mortgages, savings bank and cooperative society accounts. The savings of the middle class and the income of people who lived on interest or fixed salaries had been rendered worthless. Government steps to compensate such sufferers did not restore the interest-yield-ing documents to more than a quarter of their former value. Debtors emerged scot free and most of the government's own debt had been wiped out.

The Dawes Committee was one of two appointed by the Repara-tions Commission to examine the reparations problem and Ger-many's financial condition. Although the United States had officially turned its back on the whole peace settlement, two Americans (Charles G. Dawes and Owen D. Young) shared with delegates from France, Belgium, Britain, and Italy in the deliberations, and Dawes was chairman of the more important committee. The report was ready by the spring of 1924, and by that time changes in the governments of France, Germany, and Britain had placed in power men who were not bound by the unhappy policies of the preceding four years. The Dawes Plan was therefore accepted by all concerned as at least a temporary arrangement. It provided for lower annual payments by Germany, starting at about $250,000,000 a year and rising gradually to $625,000,000. It required that this sum be pro-vided from certain taxes levied and earmarked for reparations and from the earnings of the large industries and the railroads. It put an Agent-General in Berlin to supervise the collection and transfer of the money. Finally, to help start the Plan, a loan of $200,000,000 was to be floated.

The Dawes Plan worked amazingly well. The payments were made in full on time. In fact all seemed to be running so smoothly that by 1928 the time seemed ripe for replacing the temporary Plan with a permanent one which would look after the admittedly long remaining period during which Germany must pay reparations. The Young Plan, accepted by all concerned in January, 1930, was to do this. It set forth a series of payments which stretched till 1988—the date on which most Allied debt installments to the United States would terminate. The total capital payments were to amount to about $9,000,000,000, instead of the $33,000,000,000 which had been fixed in 1921. Germany was freed of the foreign supervision which the Dawes Plan had imposed on payments, on the Reichsbank, and on the railroads. She was to be trusted to pay her annual installment into a new bank, the Bank of International Settlements, which was to be set up at Basel in Switzerland. The whole matter looked as if it was settled once and for all on a sound businesslike basis.

The Dawes years witnessed a remarkable recovery in Germany.

Men set to work to make up for the years of frustration. The rage for "rationalization" swept industry, mining, transportation, and agriculture alike, with a consequently large investment of new capital. New plants, machines, and methods were introduced, chemistry and electricity worked wonders, productivity rose, German competition became formidable in many markets, a newly built merchant marine appeared on the oceans, and by 1929 exports almost equaled in volume (but exceeded by a third in value) those of 1913. Wages and profits were higher. Builders were active everywhere erecting new houses, apartment blocks, suburbs, stadiums, swimming pools, schools, hospitals, and automobile highways. A visitor to Germany in 1928 found it almost impossible to believe that this was the land of whose tribulations he had read in 1918–1923.

The secret of this transformation was the release of Germany's pent-up energy and the tapping of foreign purses. With the Dawes Plan Germany had become a new frontier to be developed by foreign investors. There were three reasons for this: a desire to build Germany up as a counterbalance to a France that seemed desirous of dominating Europe; a troubled Anglo-American conscience which had been persuaded that Germany was overharshly treated at Versailles; and the fact that lenders or investors could get at least 2 per cent more in Germany than elsewhere. American, British, Dutch, and Swiss bankers, industrialists, and investors were therefore willing to send their money to Germany—first for the Dawes loan, then to purchase government, municipal, or other kinds of bonds, to deposit in banks, to make short-term loans, to buy stock, or to plant branch firms. Americans were the largest suppliers of this capital. The agents of investment bankers scoured Germany looking for places that could be persuaded to borrow money, so that the bankers could earn fat commissions by floating the bonds on the American market.

In all, foreigners seem to have invested and lent about $6,000,-000,000 between 1924 and 1931. Out of this sum Germany paid about $2,500,000,000 in reparations, financed her economic reconstruction, and built the new public and private edifices; some of her wiser citizens invested about $2,500,000,000 abroad. The countries which received the reparations used part of them to pay their debts to Britain and the United States, and Britain used her receipts of reparations or debts to help meet the annual installment of $200,000,-000 to the United States. So long, therefore, as the stream of money flowed into Germany all was well for that country and its creditors; but since "hardly one penny of [Germany's] payments came from Germany's own resources" (Stolper), the position was as precarious as it was pleasant.

The Restoration of the Gold Standard. Between 1923 and 1928 about thirty currencies struggled back to the gold standard or to a modified version of it. This was an indication of the extent to which most countries had surmounted their immediate post-war difficulties and were getting their budgets balanced and their economies onto a fairly stable basis. In each case the restoration of the gold standard involved the answering of two questions: (1) How many grains of gold were to be put into the unit of account? (2) How should gold be used?

Where the currency had been smashed beyond repair, a new unit was adopted, such as the Rentenmark (equal in value to the old gold mark and worth about twenty-four cents) or the chervonets (equal to ten prerevolutionary gold rubles) which Russia adopted. Where the currency had been only damaged it was devalued. The French franc had fallen by mid-1926 to about one-seventh of its pre-war value, thanks to the inability or refusal of the government to defray current expenditure and reconstruction costs out of taxes, loans, or reparations receipt and the consequent reliance on new notes to fill the gap. When in 1926 more resolute financial policies were adopted, the franc regained some of the lost ground and in 1928 was officially revalued at one-fifth its pre-war gold value, or 25.5 francs to the dollar. Belgium devalued its currency by the same amount, Italy by three-fourths. In each case owners of money paid the price, but those who owed money (including the state) had their burdens lightened, while French, Belgian, or Italian goods were made cheap to foreigners who imported them or went touring to buy them.

Britain in 1925 returned to the gold standard with the pound *at its old value,* i.e., $4.87. Many experts insisted that this rate was too high and suggested a lower figure, such as $4.20. Full restoration benefited some people but hurt others. The owner of pounds invested overseas got more pesos or dollars in interest; the English buyer of American cotton once more got $4.87 worth of it for his pound, but the foreign buyer of British manufactured goods or coal had to give more francs or dollars for them, and might find he could get them more cheaply elsewhere. The British export industries were therefore handicapped by the return of the old unit of account, though this was not the only cause of their difficulties in regaining lost markets. Attempts to reduce miners' wages in order to lower the price of coal led to a long, disastrous strike in 1926. Further, the Bank of England had to maintain its gold reserve and yet be ready to meet demands for gold for export. To do this it was obliged to keep its Bank rate higher than might otherwise have been necessary, and this tended to keep interest rates high, thus discouraging enterprise. But again, this was only one of many discouraging factors in the general situation.

Gold did not regain its old accessibility under the new currency plans. During the war it had been gathered into central bank reserves, gold coins had disappeared, and people had become accustomed to paper money. The gold remained mobilized under the new versions of the gold standard. Beyond a certain but greatly increased fiduciary issue, the paper of the central banks must be supported by a minimum percentage of gold in France and Germany and be fully backed in Britain, except when emergency made an increased issue necessary. Thus the link between paper and gold was rewelded, and the volume of the paper currency was related once more to the size of the reserve. But the public's right to convert notes into gold was not fully restored. People could not get gold coins for notes; they could get bullion bars, weighing 400 ounces under the British plan and worth about $8,000. Since free minting was not restored, these bars were useless except to persons who wished to export metal. Gold was therefore limited to two functions: it served as a reserve within the country, and it supplemented the available supply of foreign exchange in making payments abroad. It was in large measure the base of a "gold-exchange standard."

There were some doubts whether the newly established gold standard would be able to stand up. If it was to do so, each country must be able to keep enough gold both to serve as an adequate reserve and to meet any calls that were made for export. There were three reasons for fearing that this would not be the case. In the first place, the output of new gold was scarcely adequate to meet the world's monetary and other requirements. In the second place, the dislocations in the balance of commercial payments and the burden of the intergovernmental payments would normally call for far larger settlements of debts in gold than had been the case in pre-war days. True, the loans and investments in Germany and other countries were taking care of the situation for the time being. But how would indebted governments and individuals pay their foreign creditors if and when the influx of dollars, pounds, or guilders dried up?

The third disturbing condition was the way gold became distributed and redistributed. The gold standard could not operate unless the gold stood fairly still and did the job expected of it. Instead, it flowed about in alarming quantities and if it did settle down it was in Paris or New York. France had always held much gold—twice as much as Britain did in 1913. During the years when the value of the franc was falling, shrewd or nervous Frenchmen exported their capital, in gold if they could lay hands on it, to safer places, there to lodge till stability returned. The banks in which it rested could use it to expand their credit facilities. When French confidence returned in 1926 the émigré capital, or "hot money" as it came to be called, was brought back home, and in 1928 the government decreed that it be brought back in the form of gold. This deprived its temporary custodians of a great quantity of their store of treasure. Still more gold came into France as interest or reparations payments, tourists' spendings, and the purchase price of goods that were cheap in terms of a four-cent franc. By 1929 the French gold reserve was nearly double its value in 1925 and comprised 16 per cent of the world's supply.

The United States received much gold in payment for war supplies before 1917, and even larger quantities arrived between 1920 and 1924 as "hot money," as investments, and as payment of debts or of purchase price. The influx stopped when America began to export capital (1924–1928), but started again when that export subsided and was replaced by an inrush of foreign funds for use in the soaring stock market. By 1929 American gold holdings were 60 per cent above their level of 1920 and accounted for 36 per cent of the world's monetary gold. The United States and France therefore held over half the total world reserve in 1929. In that year Britain had no more than she held in 1913. Her share of the world stock had sunk from 10 to 7 per cent, yet with this small reserve she had to protect her gold standard and try to play her role as international banker. Germany's reserve had climbed since stabilization but was no larger than in pre-war days and began to fall again in 1929. Apart from France, the United States, and Japan, every important country had less gold than before the war.

The financing of the post-war world economy was therefore no longer centered in one city but divided among three—London, Paris, and New York. Their central banks cooperated occasionally, as, for example, to stabilize the currencies of Belgium, Poland, and Rumania; but for the larger job of serving the world's needs they had no unity or even uniformity of policy. New York and Paris lacked the equipment, the experience, and, more important, any vital abiding interest in the task. While London was so wrapped up in overseas trade and investment that its domestic and external outlooks were almost indistinguishable, the interests of the other two were predominantly domestic. Basically self-sufficing, they were not free-trade markets in which debtors could pay their dues by sending whatever goods they wished. French external trade was of secondary importance, and her investments were traditionally regarded as means to desirable diplomatic ends.

America was a sub-continent, vast in resources, productive power, and income; there was enough opportunity at home for investment, trade, and the production of most of the things that were needed. New York, New England, and Chicago were tied up with the rest of the country as London was tied up with the rest of the world. The economy was as violent in its fluctuations as was the climate; the booms were colossal, the depressions cataclysmic. Apart from the cotton and tobacco producers, interest in exports was secondary. Except for raw materials, interest in imports seemed almost unpatriotic. Apart from the outflow of capital for extending American corporations, foreign investment was artificially and violently stimulated in the mid-twenties by the prospect of high interest rates for bondholders, high commissions for the underwriters, and full employment for the graduates of business schools; and the movement subsided almost as quickly as it had risen when better bargains seemed to be offering in the nation's stock exchanges.

American high policy was not interested in the role which the United States had come to occupy in the world's economy, or rather in what is now better called the political economy. Public opinion was too isolationist to allow bankers or the government to recognize openly "the existence of other central banks and other governments with whom we share mutual interests." The "central banking organization [was] too overcomplex, too decentralized, and too much subject to regional pressures to act quickly and decisively in the international sphere" (Viner). The Federal Reserve authorities were willing during the mid-twenties to help Europe get onto its feet; to keep interest rates low in order to prevent money from coming to America, especially since this "easy money" policy also aided depressed American farmers; and to encourage investors to buy foreign bonds. But many of the bonds proved worthless, and meanwhile easy money encouraged the rising tide of stock speculation at home. In the hope of checking the latter, the interest rate was raised. This step failed to halt the tide; it helped to stop foreign investment and in addition induced Europeans to send their funds across the Atlantic for speculation or for supplying loans to the speculator. Thus neither France nor the United States used its accumulating gold to serve world investment or trade needs. The gold was either sterilized or domesticated, and meanwhile Britain, with scant reserves and a precarious trade balance, could not play its former role in full, while Germany was living on borrowed money.

The Years of Prosperity. The weaknesses inherent in the reestablished gold standard did not fully reveal themselves until 1931. The outstanding feature of the years following the return of gold was the considerable measure of recovery that Europe was making. Even by 1925 the output of primary and manufactured goods was near or above pre-war levels, and the production of the newer goods—electricity, electrical apparatus, automobiles, and rayon—was mounting. The old stalwarts—coal, shipbuilding, steel, cottons, and woolens—were still sick from excess capacity, fierce competition, and fallen prices, and two-fifths of Britain's unemployed army of a million workers belonged to these industries. Meanwhile farmers everywhere complained that the price of their produce had fallen too near the cost of production, but that the price of the industrial goods they needed to buy and of the money they had to borrow remained too high. In France, Germany, and Italy tariffs were raised to protect grain from competition which came from the New World, for Russia and Rumania were still out of the market.

While, however, some industries lacked customers, others found plenty. Building enjoyed a boom and flourished as it tried to catch up with the arrears in the supply of houses, offices, shops, movie theaters, and public buildings. The war had made private building, especially of rented houses, unattractive and unprofitable by imposing restrictions on rents, increasing taxes on real estate, and raising the interest rate on loans. As private enterprise was therefore unwilling to put a roof over people's heads, governments had been obliged to step in and either build the houses or subsidize the private builder. By 1929 a million houses had been erected in one or other of these ways in England; Germany had by 1930 put up 1,500,-000 houses, largely with public funds or aid; municipal authorities in Vienna and many other cities had built great apartment blocks for workers, cleared slums, and constructed new suburbs. Meanwhile middle-class people had paid for the construction of their own homes. Further, governments spent vast sums making or remaking roads to bear the growing load of motor traction. Consequently the construction industry was very busy during the twenties, and according to one estimate it employed a seventh of the industrial population of western Europe in 1925.

The second stimulus came from the demand for consumers' comforts and luxury goods or services such as bicycles, cars, radios, furniture, more clothes, shop-made bread and cakes, entertainments, and holidays. Higher wages and the smaller families that resulted from the declining birth rate—the "retreat from parenthood"—gave many people more money to spend on these things after the necessaries of life had been bought. This spare cash was less plentiful in Europe than in North America, but there was enough of it to provide business for a great number of new enterprises producing the goods, of stores selling them, and of service stations ranging from those which repaired cars and "wireless sets" to those which preserved feminine beauty. Hence the decline in the number of miners, weavers, and shipbuilders was counterbalanced by an increase, sometimes very substantial, in the number of workers in these other occupations. The production of building material and of the new commodities or services called for considerable capital outlay in new plants, as also did the rationalization of industries. The combined result was an increase of 30 per cent in the industrial output of France between 1925 and 1929, of 22 per cent in Germany, and of 13 per cent in the United Kingdom.

The growth of international trade was even more marked. In 1914 the value of world imports had been about $20,000,000,000; by 1929 it was nearly $36,000,000,000. Perhaps two-thirds of this increase was accounted for by higher prices, but there still remained a substantial measure of growth in volume. Some of it was explained by the revival of foreign investment on a large scale. In this the United States played the largest part, so large that American private foreign investments increased from less than $4,000,000,000 in 1914 to $17,-

000,000,000 in 1929, and the country switched over from being a debtor for less than $4,000,000,000 to being a creditor to the extent of $8,000,000,000, apart from the intergovernmental debts.

While much of the capital had gone to Germany, no country in the world was omitted from the list of dollar-receivers; even Russia granted a concession. Some of it was used to repay debts; some of it went out in the form of consumers' goods to be eaten or worn and some of it in the form of capital goods to equip production. Meanwhile the British resumed their overseas investing habit, and by 1929 had restored their holdings to the pre-war figure of $20,000,-000,000. Like the dollar, the pound often was used to develop resources; Australia, which stood second to Germany as a borrower in the twenties, obtained a billion dollars from London and New York for internal improvement; Canada received much capital for the development of her forest, mineral, and water resources; the East Indies expanded its rubber plantations; Latin American oil, mineral, and sugar production was further developed with the new influx of capital.

These expansions in production, trade, and investment dissipated much of the earlier gloom and gave ground for economic and political optimism. The world had, by an accident for which all seemed responsible, blundered into a tragic war. Having paid the price, it was now recovering and would never let such an accident happen again. Germany was admitted to the League of Nations by the front door in 1926, the United States was growing accustomed to using the side door, and Russia, having abandoned its dream of raising revolution abroad in favor of raising crops and factories at home, seemed destined to become a tolerated member of the family of nations. A World Economic Conference in Geneva (1927) said the time had come to begin reducing or removing the trade barriers piled up during the war and the years since its end. Export and import prohibitions, it was agreed, had produced "deplorable results," especially as there were now 7,000 miles of new customs walls in consequence of the appearance of new states on the European map. The delegates of fifty nations therefore agreed to do something. Some trade treaties were negotiated, some prohibitions disappeared, and proposals for a "United States of Europe," for a European Economic Union, or at least for a tariff truce were discussed. Discussions on naval disarmament were stalled in 1927 but made headway in 1929. In 1928 the Briand-Kellogg Pact, pledging nations to forswear war as an instrument of national policy, was signed by most countries; and in the same year the Young Committee was called into being to put reparations on a permanent businesslike basis. The European optimist thus had abundant congenial food to nourish his temperament. His American counterpart believed that his land had entered a "new era" of permanent prosperity, that its economy, now "come of age," had established its residence on a higher "plateau," and that the abolition of poverty was just beyond the next range of hills on a still higher plateau.

The End of Prosperity. The years just beyond were to prove that mankind was really experiencing a business cycle cursed with postwar complications. Till 1928 production and purchase advanced at about the same pace, and the efforts of cartels, farmers' pools, and other schemes for price maintenance had not yet piled up large unsold stocks or provoked a great increase of production. But in 1928–1929 hints of saturation began to be evident; prices of foodstuffs and raw materials began to fall a little more quickly from the level—40 to 60 per cent above 1913 figures—which they had maintained since the early twenties; and surplus stocks grew large enough to overshadow the market. By mid-1929 mineral prices were breaking, wool brought much lower returns in the auction rooms, while bumper wheat crops in 1928 and the revival of Russian exports wrecked grain prices. This fall came just at a time when the flow of capital to primary producing countries and to Germany had been checked. Hence the debtor primary producing countries could no longer pay their interest or pay for their imports out of new loans, but must do both by exporting produce that was shrinking rapidly in value and supplement it with gold from their bank reserves. Soon they had to reduce their imports, and some of them had to default on their interest payments. The silver countries were also hit by a rapid fall in the price of silver.

The depression which began in 1929 thus started largely as a result of increasing stringency in the agricultural borrowing lands. As prices of primary products continued to sink during the next three years, the loss of purchasing power by their producers was a serious blow to manufacturing industries. Some of these industries had probably reached the crest of expansion by 1929, especially those engaged in building and construction, in supplying reequipment capital goods, or in providing consumers' durable goods. There were beginning to be houses and apartments to let, hotels were not full, and more cars and radios were being made than could be sold. But this slackening off in industry was not marked until the third factor exerted its devastating effect in the collapse of the almost world-wide stock market boom.

That boom began to gather a little impetus in the United States in 1927. One index number for American common stocks rose from 100 in 1926 to 117 in 1927, to 148 in 1928, and then shot up to 291 in September, 1929. This American boom was accompanied by a more modest one in Europe. In London the price of industrial shares rose from 120 in early 1927 to 150 in 1929. The German share index rose about 40 per cent during the same period, and similar movements took place in all financial centers, with much larger increases in the price of new or speculative issues.

Signs of trouble appeared in Europe before they were apparent in America. In January, 1929, an Italian bank came to grief after "bulling the Bourse." A Belgian bank nearly foundered after financing an unprofitable cork trust. A big Viennese bank nearly sank under the load of embarrassed firms it was supporting, and a Rothschild had to withdraw funds from New York to save it. Just at that moment (September) the arrest of a flashy British promoter for forging stock certificates upset London, sent prices diving down, forced the Bank to raise its rate, compelled investors to sell their American stocks to get funds, drove British lenders to pull their loans out of the New York call market, and thus added one more cloud to the already threatening Manhattan sky. Within a month that sky was jet black as a selling panic swept Wall Street. By Christmas stocks had lost a third of their value; but that was not the end, for eventually the loss amounted to three-fourths. Thus the major boom in America and the minor boom in Europe had ended. To the fall in the price of primary products was added that in the price of all other things that men offered for sale.

For three years the gloom grew relentlessly deeper in every part of the world. Stock market prices dropped nearly half in London, two-thirds in Berlin, and three-fourths in Amsterdam. Wholesale price index numbers fell between 30 per cent in Great Britain and nearly 50 per cent in Holland. Primary products suffered much more severely: a League of Nations composite index for eight of them fell nearly 70 per cent by 1932. This decline in two or three years was greater than that in any preceding two or three decades, and the shrinking pains were consequently more acute. At the worst a fifth to a quarter of the wage earners were out of work—over 3,000,000 in Britain, over 6,000,000 in Germany, and 13,000,000 in the United States. But in the capital goods industries every second worker was a victim of the collapse in the great construction and equipment boom. The League of Nations index number for industrial activity in Europe (excluding Russia) fell 30 per cent between 1929 and 1932, as did the output of raw materials; but that of foodstuffs scarcely declined at all. The volume of world trade declined about a third and its value two-thirds. No aspect of the economy, no part of the world, escaped the devastation. Even Russia, wrapped up in its first Five-Year Plan but still far from completely insulated from the capitalistic outer world, felt the effect when the prices of the primary produce it exported to exchange for capital goods imports shared in the general price slaughter and thus bought far fewer of the goods Russia needed. And Russia had its own peculiar troubles—those which came from the attempt to convert the peasants to collectivist farming, to liquidate the kulaks, and to fight a devastating famine.

BIBLIOGRAPHY

See end of Chapter XXIX.

XXIX

THE ECONOMIC HISTORY OF
A DECADE, 1929–1939

In September, 1929, the depression which few had been expecting broke out for all to see. In September, 1939, the war which most people had come to regard as inevitable became a reality. The intervening decade, probably one of the most tense and exhausting in modern history, can be divided into two halves. The first five years saw the world descend deeper and deeper into the slough of economic despond and then creep painfully a little or a long way back toward unspectacular prosperity. During the second five years economics, politics, minds, and emotions became increasingly obsessed by the strident voice that came out of loud-speakers from a German microphone, by the use of force and the threat of force, by the apparent futility of all efforts at peaceful settlement of international differences, and by the thankless task of rearming for a second trial of strength within a generation.

For the first two years (1929–1931) the depression was an almost uninterrupted downward movement of prices, production, trade, and employment. Governments tried to cope with the situation by raising tariffs, propping up some prices, giving relief, subsidizing unemployment insurance funds, and assuring the public that the worst was over. They were wrong, for in the summer of 1931 the combined cumulative burden broke the financial, credit, and banking system and caused a third crisis which was quite as serious in its effects as the stock market and price crises had been. Governments therefore had to search for more fundamental remedies, and put the economy still further under the influence of state control and management. Rarely have governments worked so hard as they did in the thirties. But whether their policies dealt with commerce, credit, or currency, whether they sought to bring relief, recovery, reform, or reconstruction, they were nearly all conceived on a national basis rather than on any concept of international action to deal with a problem that obviously was world-wide in scope. Hence the depression accentuated economic nationalism and consequently political nationalism. The world economy built up by the nineteenth century had been shaken by World War I; it was now shattered by the scramble for self-preservation in the years after 1929. Each nation took unilateral action regardless of the effect on others or of the readjustment which foreigners would need to make in the production and sale of their products. They in turn appealed to their governments for action which in turn necessitated more readjustments; and so the vicious circle was traversed, with a maximum of derangement and little apparent benefit to many.

Commercial Policies. Some government policies affecting agriculture, competition, and industrial reorganization have been described in earlier chapters. Two general groups of policies remain to be examined here: those dealing with commerce and with currency. There had been some increase in tariffs during the twenties, but that tendency seemed to have spent itself, and in September, 1929, the League of Nations Assembly was actually discussing the proposed tariff truce when the ground began to shake under its very feet. The first important step in the new movement toward higher tariffs was taken when Congress in 1930 passed the Hawley-Smoot Act. This tariff revision was to have been limited to farm produce but ended by raising the rates on virtually everything to an average of about 40 per cent. This step looked to America's debtors like a piece of "brutal egoism"; combined with the shrinkage of American demand for imported raw materials and the ending of capital exports, it presented those debtors with an insoluble problem, which will be examined later.

Other countries raised tariffs on farm or industrial products, so that by 1931 the rates in most continental countries were 60 to 100 per cent higher than in 1929. Wheat was protected in France by a duty of about 200 per cent, rye in Germany by one of 300 per cent. But the most important European tariff step was the abandonment of free trade by Great Britain after the financial crisis of 1931. In spite of some imposition of duties during and after World War I, four-fifths of British imports were still duty free in 1930. In 1931, however, the country found that its balance of payments was about $500,000,000 on the wrong side. Its imports had declined only a little, for distressed foreign producers poured through its open ports the goods they could not sell anywhere else—at home or abroad. But its visible exports were down because of the shrinkage of capital exports and overseas demand; and its "invisible exports" (interest on investments, shipping earnings, and commercial fees) had dropped almost a billion dollars as a result of depressed conditions abroad. (See Chapter XXVI.) The country therefore could not pay its way without shipping gold or selling securities, thus living on its capital. Hence the tariffs of 1931–1932 were imposed partly to correct this situation but also because the government placed in power in 1931 was protectionist in principle.

The new British tariff imposed a moderate basic duty of 10 per cent on all imports except a few foods and raw materials; but this basic rate could be increased and grew to 20 per cent (or more) on most manufactured articles. Imports from the dominions and colonies were admitted either duty free or at lower rates than were charged on goods from foreign sources, and in 1932 the mother country and the dominions met at Ottawa to negotiate a number of trade agreements which provided further mutual preferential concessions.

In most countries the tariff was supplemented by three other protective weapons. In the first place, the actual quantity of goods to be admitted was limited by fixing a quota. Goods that had to be sold somehow, somewhere, might jump a tariff, and trade treaties might prevent rates from being raised. France discovered this fact when in 1930–1931 her exports fell away while imports poured in. She therefore began to limit the admission of lumber and wine (August, 1931), and within a year had over 1,100 commodities on the quota list. She might fix a total limit, or set the amount to be sent by each country, and the quota could be arbitrarily altered at a moment's notice. Many other countries followed her example.

In the second place, imports were checked by controlling the sale of foreign exchange. If an importer could not get dollars he could not buy American goods. If he could get no foreign bills or drafts he could import nothing. In some countries the government established a prior claim to foreign exchange in order to pay its interest bills abroad; in other cases priority went to those who wished to import certain goods or buy from certain countries, but other buyers could get no foreign exchange. Hence it might be impossible for a German agent to send a British or American author the royalties collected on the sale of his works. British firms which had sent cloth or clothes to Vienna or the Balkans could not get payment except by taking produce (e.g., a quantity of hams) and selling it in England. Some governments took this bilateral barter to great lengths; Poland agreed to exchange coal for Bulgarian tobacco and for liners built in Italian shipyards; Brazilian coffee was exchanged for Rumanian oil or Ruhr coal. In many trade treaties each country pledged itself to buy a certain quantity or proportion of its imports from the other. In an Anglo-Russian agreement (1934) Russia promised to buy more goods from Britain until her purchases nearly equaled her sales to that country. Denmark, almost completely dependent on the British butter market, consented to buy 80 per cent of her coal from Britain in return for being guaranteed a fixed share of the British butter and bacon market.

This bilateral trading reached its highest point in the relations between Nazi Germany and the countries of Danubia and the Balkans. Tariffs impeded Germany's sale of manufactured goods in some important foreign markets; tariffs, quotas, and low prices made it difficult for southeastern Europe to sell her primary products abroad at prices that were satisfactory. Germany had formerly protected her agriculture against these regions. Now she turned around, bought what they had to sell at prices that were above the world market level, but paid for them in "blocked marks" which could be spent only in purchasing German goods. France and Britain were uninterested economically in the area, and Germany was therefore able to bind it to herself, even before she annexed Austria. But here, as in all the bilateral bargainings, obstacles were placed in the way of that multilateral trade which formerly had carried goods and payments round to the spot where they were needed or due. The total value of international trade was not increased; little bits of it were diverted and fenced off.

In the third place, the abandonment of the gold standard in 1931 allowed countries to use their depreciated currency as a device for keeping out imports but expanding exports. This policy will be examined in a moment. In general, therefore, the impact of depression drove commercial policies to new aims and methods. "From a mere tariff subsidy to aid and protect certain domestic industries, the goals aimed at have shifted to the protection of the balance of payments, the stability of the currency, and even to the more ambitious program of autarchy or self-sufficiency" (Hansen). Trade had become regimented and controlled as much as in a wartime "economics of siege" (Hancock), and self-sufficiency had been embraced as a desirable ideal by those who could not sell abroad the things they had to offer. When recovery came the controls imposed, often in a panicky mood in the dark days, were not easily removed or were not removed at all. They had created vested interests and cut deep channels out of which it was not easy to escape, even if a country wished to escape.

Currency and Credit Policies. The depression quickly made the problem of international commercial and intergovernmental payments more serious. When dollars and pounds were no longer being exported, the supply of them available to debtors shriveled up. The shrinkage in the supply of dollars was the more serious; how serious it eventually became is seen from the following table:

	1929	1932
Dollars made available to foreigners by American purchases of goods or services and new investments	$7.4 billion	$2.4 billion
Dollars required by foreigners to meet fixed debt service to U.S.	.9 "	.9 "
Balance of dollars available to foreigners for purchase of American goods and all other purposes	6.5 "	1.5 "

The fall by two-thirds in the first line was due partly to the abandonment of overseas investment, but most of it was the result of a great decline (70 per cent) in the value of American purchases of goods and services overseas. The second line shows that debt obligations to the United States stood unchanged. Consequently, as the third line reveals, if foreigners had met those debt obligations in full they would have had only 23 cents available in 1932 for buying American exports against $1.00 in 1929. This was not enough, even allowing for the fall in the price of goods. Deprived of American loan dollars, Germany found it difficult to pay reparations to the Allies or interest to the American creditor, and some of the Allies found it hard to pay their installments to Washington without digging into their gold reserves. German, British, and Austrian gold reserves were reduced, while those of France and the United States rose even more rapidly than in the twenties. Countries which owed pounds were in a less serious situation, since they could ship whatever goods they had to London; but the decline in prices made it necessary to send far more goods to pay the same amount of debt.

Central Europe soon began to show the effect of this dollar shortage, especially since so much of its recovery had been financed with American loans. London tried to bolster Vienna and Berlin with loans as the gold reserves of their central banks sank lower. By the spring of 1931, however, the breaking point was being reached. In May the largest Viennese bank, the *Kredit Anstalt,* fell and the government forbade gold exports. If that bank was broken, what others could be solvent? Certainly not the German investment banks, tied to their sick heavy industries. Germans and foreigners therefore rushed to withdraw their deposits and short-term loans. In the first half of 1931 foreigners pulled out $500,000,000 of these, and natives got as much as they could. In July the Darmstädter Bank closed its doors and the German government not merely shut the rest of the banks to prevent them from crashing but stopped the payment of all short-term loans to foreigners.

With a first-class financial crisis thus coming to the boiling point, President Hoover in June suggested a moratorium on all inter-governmental debts—reparations and inter-Allied—for a year. This was agreed to, reluctantly by France and very slowly by Congress. In August an international conference of bankers, held at Basel, made a "standstill agreement" to suspend all payment of foreign loans for six months.

The events in Vienna, Berlin, and Basel hit Britain hard, for the Bank of England could not get its continental loans back just at a time when short-term foreign depositors were rushing to withdraw their funds, largely in gold, from British banks. This drain rapidly became so serious that the government suspended the right to demand bullion for notes (September 21, 1931). In other words, Britain went off the gold standard. Her action started a stampede. The pound soon sank to about $3.50. Countries which did most of their trade with Britain let their exchanges fall to keep them at par with the pound. By the end of 1931 ten European countries were off gold and a dozen had severe restrictions on the traffic in currency. Only France, Holland, Belgium, and Switzerland—the gold *bloc* as distinct from the "sterling group" or the dollar *bloc* of North America—remained faithful to gold, but badly shaken. In the bank crisis of March, 1933, the United States not merely stopped the export of gold but ordered those who had any to hand it over to the Federal Reserve banks.

So ended the post-war "experiment of operating a worldwide international gold standard with a decentralized credit system in an unbalanced world economy" (Brown). The British let the pound find its own level without gold support, and at one time it dipped to

$3.20. For a brief period this made British goods cheap to owners of undepreciated francs or dollars, but this advantage to British exporters was short lived, for other currencies soon fell. When the United States stopped gold exports the dollar sank as much as the pound had done. The Japanese let their currency sink by 60 per cent, and the price of their goods fell nearly twice as much as had those of British wares.

It soon became clear that few people were going to benefit by this competitive exchange depreciation, and that the gold *bloc* was suffering acutely by keeping its currency at the values fixed in the twenties. In 1933 a World Economic Conference was therefore held in London to see if international cooperation could stabilize currency and exchanges. Preliminary discussions between London, Paris, and Washington (including both Presidents Hoover and Roosevelt) had reached agreement on the need for stabilization and other concerted steps; but the Conference had scarcely met when a message from President Roosevelt blasted any hope of success by repudiating all idea of collaboration and announcing that the United States intended to pursue an isolationist policy in search of a "sound internal economic system" with a currency which would be so manipulated as to raise prices to a satisfactory level and then keep them there generation after generation.

Each nation now went its own way, and the United States took two fateful steps. In 1934 it raised the price of gold from $20 to $35 an ounce, and started buying silver at prices far above the market rate. The hope that these acts would raise farm prices was doomed to disappointment. The silver policy was, as we have seen, a fiasco in the United States and a disaster to China. The gold policy made gold dearer to public and private buyers everywhere and benefited only the gold-mining regions of the world. To them an increase of 75 per cent in the price of their product was equivalent to a first-class gold discovery. By 1939 they were mining two-thirds more ounces of gold than they had in 1933.

This vast outpouring of metal flowed chiefly to America and the United Kingdom. France was no longer an attractive home, in spite of the devaluation of the franc by one-third in 1936 and a tripartite agreement with London and Washington which tried to keep the franc, pound, and dollar relatively stable. France's domestic politics were disturbed, her position in Europe was uncertain, her trade balance and budget were far out of balance on the wrong side.

Hence gold did not go there; instead there was a flight of capital from the country, the gold reserve sank lower, and further devaluation was necessary (1938). Meanwhile the British bought and built up a larger reserve than they had ever had before, but their receipts were small when compared with the stream that flowed deep and wide to the United States. Some of it came seeking the $35 or paying for goods and securities. Some sought safety as the shadows grew darker over Europe and remained the property of those who sent it. The result was a net influx of $8,000,000,000 between the end of 1934 and the beginning of World War II. The monetary stock in September, 1939, stood at $16,600,000,000, and of this sum $10,-000,000,000 belonged to foreigners.

What to do with their heaps of gold the Americans and British scarcely seemed to know. A little of it was used as an "exchange stabilization fund" which could be drawn on to prevent wild variations in the foreign exchange rate. If the remainder had been allowed to operate freely as basis for bank credit, the volume of loans would have been so vast and the purchasing power so expanded as to precipitate a boom and consequent disaster. When this danger seemed faintly imminent in the United States (1936–1937), the government took steps to restrict bank credits, bought all gold entering the country, put it into an "inactive fund," and thereby caused what was called a "recession" (rather than a depression), which was felt all over the world. The symbol of this fear of gold was a huge massive vault, built at Fort Knox, Kentucky, in which the gold was buried. In Britain the banks already had plenty of funds available to supply all borrowers' needs at low rates of interest, the Bank rate stood at 2 per cent from 1932 onward, and the government was pledged to "cheap money" in the interest of recovery. But the risk of a runaway was ever present, and steps were therefore taken in 1936–1937 to "manage" the supply of credit to prevent it.

Recovery. During the summer of 1932 signs appeared that the worst was over and that recovery might be on its way. Its arrival was delayed by the American financial crisis in the winter of 1932–1933, but when that was over the business curves began to turn upward. Their progress was no longer disturbed by the problem of intergovernmental debt payments. At the Lausanne Conference in mid-1932 Germany's creditors agreed to settle the whole reparations account for $750,000,000, provided that they in turn got their debt to the United States lightened. America did not grant this re-

lief, so the agreement never came into effect; but that was imma-
terial, for Germany did not pay any more—even of the $750,000,000
—and no one was disposed to try to make her do so.

In December, 1932, the Hoover moratorium expired and the next
installment on the American debt was due. Raising the money would
have been well-nigh impossible in the prevailing condition of national finances, and remitting it to America was possible only in
metal in view of the collapsed state of world trade. Britain dug into
her gold reserve to pay her installment of nearly $100,000,000; Italy,
Czechoslovakia, Latvia, Lithuania, and Finland paid in full, a mere
$3,000,000; but France, Poland, and the other states sent none of
their total dues of $25,000,000. When the next installment was due
in June, 1933, the British sent $10,000,000 in silver, some other
states sent their mites, but France and the rest again defaulted. Since
Washington took no steps to reconsider the whole changed situation,
no further payments were made, except by Finland. Thus the outstanding debts due to the United States, the loans made by the
British, and reparations—about $50,000,000,000 in all—were all
wiped out by default. Payment was impossible, but recognition of
that hard truth was not easy.

With the debts and the banking crisis out of the way, recovery
made considerable progress. How much of it was a normal revival of
the economy and how much the result of governmental policies we
have no way of measuring. In all countries recovery was in the domestic field rather than because of any great revival of international
trade. In Britain a low interest rate encouraged capital investment in
railroad improvement and the development of the electrical supply;
but its chief effect was to stimulate an outburst of building and slum
clearance. About a quarter of the new investment of capital went
into housing. The tariff guarded the home market for some industries
and gave birth to some new ones, including a large crop of American
branch factories. The government kept its budget balanced, but its
financial policies affected the economy in many ways since about a
fifth of the country's national income passed through the public
purse. Some of this sum represented a transfer from high to low incomes, through taxation, unemployment assistance, and social services; hence it maintained mass consumption and the industries which
supplied the general body of consumers. Much of the rest was invested by the various units of government in houses, highways,
public utilities, and the like. The index of production rose from 84

in 1931 to 118 in 1936; unemployment declined as industrial expansion took care not merely of many who had been out of work but
also of young people coming into the labor market. The physical output per worker was in 1935 about a quarter larger than it had been a
decade before, an improvement equal to the record in the United
States. The workers' real earnings were up a fifth, while in America
they had declined. In short, the bulk of the population was now
better off than it had been before the depression.

In overseas trade British recovery was not so marked. In 1937
exports were nearly 50 per cent higher than their low depression
point but were only three-fourths of their value in 1929. In 1913
Britain had exported 33 per cent of its total output; in 1924 the
figure was 27, in 1930 it was down to 22, and in 1937 to 15 per cent.
This decline was the result of the shrinkage of world trade rather
than of a fall in Britain's share of that trade, for the share was retained during the inter-war period. It was part of the shift in the
center of interest from external to domestic markets. Yet while the
country was earning more of its growing income at home it was still
vitally dependent on imports for much of its food and raw materials.
Britain's visible imports during 1936–1938 exceeded her visible exports by an annual average of $1,900,000,000. Of this excess about
$1,700,000,000 was paid for by invisible exports. The net adverse
balance of payments therefore had to be met by exporting gold,
borrowing, or selling securities. Any of these methods meant living
on capital, which was not a healthy situation.

Imperial enthusiasts were disillusioned by the operations of the
imperial preference schemes hatched at Ottawa in 1932. The notion
of a self-sufficing empire was never seriously entertained, but recovery showed how impossible such a concept was. There was an
increase in intra-imperial trade, but in 1938, 60 per cent of Britain's
imports were still drawn from foreign sources, and 55 per cent of
her exports were bought by foreign customers. "Imperial self-insuf-
ficiency" was manifest in still more ways: in Canada's close interdependence with the United States, in Australia's need for wool
markets in Japan and the United States, in the unwillingness of
Australia and Canada to expose their dairy farmers to the competition of New Zealand butter, and finally in the dominions' discovery
that the British market was not a bottomless pit into which they
could pour their primary products without any thought of the welfare of the British farmer. By 1938, therefore, there was little en-

thusiasm left for the Ottawa compacts, since they tied everybody's hands in negotiations with foreign countries. At that time Mr. Cordell Hull, the American Secretary of State, was pushing his trade-treaty program. Consequently Canada and the United Kingdom made treaties with America. By these pacts each of the first two surrendered some of its claims to preference in return for easier access to the American market, the United States bought its way into the British and Canadian markets, and the corners of the "North Atlantic triangle" were welded more firmly.

Recovery was disappointing in two other respects. At the best there was still a distressingly large mass of labor that could find no one to hire it and an equally large mass of savings or potential bank credit that could find no attractive use. In the depth of the depression 20 per cent of Britain's insured workers had been wholly or partly unemployed. The figure sank to 11 per cent in 1937 but rose again to 13 per cent (or 1,800,000 persons) in 1938. Meanwhile people were saving in all sorts of ways and places—banks, insurance companies, building societies, and undistributed profits. Yet even when all the current capital demands had been satisfied, there was still idle capital and credit and no sign of any such vast new need for it as had come with the building of the railroads in the nineteenth century. World War I had absorbed the savings of the early twentieth century, and the developments of the twenties had swallowed up their large share. But in the thirties the supply was outstripping the demand; there were no new regions overseas left to be opened up, except Siberia, which was not a field for foreign capital; and there was no revolutionary innovation to create a demand for funds for the reequipment of Europe or America. Hence the spectacle of unemployed labor, which had to be supported since no one could be allowed to die of starvation, and the mountain of unemployed capital. Capitalism seemed to stand condemned because it could not put all the available resources to work.

This situation worried economists and led them down new paths of thought. They began to think about the national income and the way it was spent. Was too much of it being saved? Would it be better to impede savings and stimulate spending by transferring through taxation more of the income of the saving class to those who lacked enough to maintain a decent standard of living? If the savers were guaranteed social security from the cradle to the grave, they might be less concerned with preparing against a rainy day. Or, to approach the matter from another angle, history showed that when investment was large, employment was always good. Since private and public investment was now unable to use all the available capital and labor, should the state try to fill the gap by using more tax revenue and even borrowing money for a program of capital investment? The debate was getting well under way when Germany showed, as Russia had done before it, how to create full employment of all resources.

Recovery in Germany. Germany also had shown signs of recovery in 1932, especially after the Lausanne Conference agreed that reparations were to be reduced to a mere trifle. Deflationary policies had been followed in 1930–1931, based on the desire to cut costs—interest, rent, wages, and government pay rolls—so that producers would be compensated for falling prices, and to keep the budget near balance by heavy taxation. One effect of those policies was a reduction in the purchasing power of the mass of the population and widespread discontent which reflected itself in the swing to extreme left or right in five general elections held during 1932. When the deflating government was displaced in mid-1932 its policies were reversed. Taxes were reduced, the wage and salary cuts were restored, and public-works programs or subsidies to private builders were begun, regardless of the effect on the budget. A good harvest reduced the need for imported food. The tide of bankruptcy began to ebb. The banks, thanks to a transfusion of government capital in their hour of crisis in mid-1931 and then to the shedding of the reparations burden, were regaining health and reduced their discount rates from 7 per cent at the beginning of 1932 to 4 per cent at the end. But the American relapse and a very wintry winter in 1932–1933 pushed unemployment up to the record figure of 7,000,000. In January Hitler became chancellor. In March the Nazis came a little short of gaining a majority in the Reichstag, but they possessed enough power to smash their opponents, and pushed through the Reichstag an Enabling Act which established the dictatorship of the National Socialist German Workers' party and government.

The program on which the Nazis had risen to power was more "national" than "socialist." It appealed to the hates and hopes of the "German race," of the "German people," whose veins were filled with "German blood," whose superiority over non-Aryans and Slavs was unquestionable, and whose destiny it was to be united regardless of historical boundaries under a mighty leader. The socialist part of the original program was a queer motley of appeals to all—especially wage earners, peasants, and little businessmen—who had a grievance against some part of the economic order. It included demands for a ban on immigration of foreign workers; for abolition of "incomes acquired without work" and the consequent obligation of every citizen to work with his hands or brain; for confiscation of war profits; for nationalization of businesses which had become trusts and the sharing out of the profits of large enterprises; for more assistance to the aged; for the "creation and maintenance of a healthy middle class," by extirpating department stores and granting all government contracts to small producers or dealers; for land reforms, abolition of interest on farm loans, and a ban on land speculation; and finally, for a "ruthless struggle" against those whose activities were injuring the common weal and the death sentence for common criminals, usurers, profiteers, and others "whatever their creed or race."

This program, hatched in 1920 by a handful of unhappy workmen who disliked foreigners, communists, and capitalists, caught the eye of Hitler and the band of frustrated army officers for whom he was working. To them it seemed a good lure which might be used to attract German laborers to a cause aimed at the military revival of Germany. Hitler preached the two sides of the program and won converts. The party grew. At first the quickest way to success seemed to be by use of force, but one such attempt in cooperation with an army officers' attempt to overthrow the republican government ended in disaster, and Hitler went to prison to write *Mein Kampf.*

With force ruled out, the democratic method was tried and the party developed its powerful propaganda technique, its organization, and its private army. It made little impression on the working class in general, for most of them were bound to their unions and the Social Democratic party or to the Communist party. But it attracted the younger men who found jobs hard to get, the small shopkeepers who were being hurt by department and chain stores, the small manufacturers who found the competition of big industry severe, the farmers who had to pay high interest on their loans, the salaried and middle class who had seen their savings wiped out by inflation, the anti-Semites, and finally some big businessmen who saw in this new party a shield against the left-center socialists and the left-wing communists.

The strength of this appeal varied inversely with the business curve. In 1924, when conditions had not yet improved much, the party won thirty-two seats at an election. In prosperous 1928 it won only a dozen and seemed doomed to extinction. But depression proved that the seed had been well planted in the right places. In election after election the upper and lower middle class, the younger unemployed, and the big industrialists raised the strength of the party, by the use of democratic machinery, to a point from which the new rulers could snatch power and smash that machinery.

The political economy of which the new rulers took control was one in which the ties between economics and politics were already close. They always had been, since at least Bismarck's time or even that of Frederick the Great. The connection between the banks and industry, between them and the state, and between the large land-lords and the state had been strengthened by the First World War. Protection and that war had exphasized the concept of self-sufficiency. The state was an entrepreneur, running the railroads, operating potash and coal mines; the king of Prussia was in 1914 probably the largest coal merchant in the world, with 12,000,000 tons for sale. Public utilities were publicly owned, while after 1900 the generation of electricity, city transit, housing schemes, docks, and many other undertakings were "mixed" enterprises owned jointly by private and state or municipal proprietors. The Weimar Republic extended state participation or control. It regulated some cartel prices and took ultimate responsibility for fixing wages. It imposed controls on coal and potash. It founded new banks, and in 1931 supplied the tottering banks with so much new capital that it became virtually their owner. Finally, by taxes, insurance schemes, and the public utilities, the state handled a large part of the national income; it has been estimated that the taxes and insurance contributions accounted for a fifth of the income. Thus the state already had control over a large part of the economy and a policy which aimed at self-sufficiency. The Nazis extended their grasp to take control of the rest. Their only innovation was in the "technique of domination," the use of coercion, and the suppression of dissent.

The first task was to help the farmer and reduce unemployment. The end of winter and the revival of business outside Germany did that to some extent, but the Nazis attacked the problem from many sides. Agriculture was put under various controllers who were to make the country as self-sufficing as possible. The prices of wheat and rye, already fixed, were raised far above the world price, but this gave more help to the Junker than to the peasant, since the latter did not grow much cereals. Interest rates on farm loans were lowered still further. An inheritance law declared that land holdings above a certain size were inalienable, but must pass from one generation to the next and could not be seized by creditors if the owner defaulted on his debts; but this sheltered only medium and large estates and left the peasant unprotected. Self-sufficiency was not achieved, for although the country could produce barely enough cereals in good years to meet requirements it could not get from its own soil enough cattle feed to nourish enough livestock to meet the domestic need for animal products. Actually production in general did not increase; food for man and beast had to be imported, but the farmer was relieved of high interest costs, given high prices, and therefore began to feel better.

Unemployment was reduced by starting more ambitious public-works programs, especially roads and buildings, by evicting married women and young men from their jobs, and by removing Jews and supporters of the old opposition parties from government posts, law, and medicine. The public-works program was financed by short-term loans from the Reichsbank, in the hope that this priming of the pump would stimulate the economy, induce private investors to put their money to work, and thus yield taxes from which the loans could be repaid. This hope was only in part justified by the results, and the loans had to be paid by selling bonds; but the unemployment figures certainly did fall and the government claimed the credit for having cut the number of men out of work in half by early 1935. The banking situation was somewhat eased by mobilizing all foreign exchange which was in private hands under a threat that non-surrender would be counted as treason, by paying off some foreign debts, and by forcing foreign creditors to accept part payment in scrip which could be spent only in buying German goods.

In 1935 Germany set out on the real course that the Nazis intended to pursue, and henceforth rearmament overshadowed all other economic considerations. In that year conscription was introduced, then extended from one year to two, the rebuilding of the navy was begun, and the covers were removed from plans for building a large air force. In 1936 the demilitarized Rhineland was reoccupied in defiance of all concerned, and the building of fortifications began at full speed. Military roads were constructed all over the countryside. Munitions plants worked overtime. Unemployment vanished and gave place to a shortage of labor.

These steps required the conversion of Germany to a "preparedness economy." Some thought had been given to such conversion in the United States, where plans had been prepared for the mobilization of industrial plants on "M Day" if that day should ever be ushered in by war. Germany took over the plan, but recognized that success required plans for all the preceding letters from L back to A. Also that the preparedness must be "total": it must cover all aspects of production, capital supply, taxes, borrowing, and prices; control cultural, emotional, and communication media for influencing the civilian population; and provide gas masks, emergency fire fighters, hospitals, and evacuation schemes. Such comprehensive plans could not be left to be superimposed on the peacetime economy; that economy must be geared in advance to the task, by telling capital where it could be invested and controlling its export, by directing production to supply what would be needed, by anticipating and breaking bottlenecks, by persuading or compelling labor to cooperate, and by planning foreign trade in order to gain self-sufficiency where possible, determining the quantity and nature of goods to be moved, and seeking economic allies or vassals.

Russia's Plans had contained a great element of preparedness from the start, with their emphasis on the heavy industries, motor vehicles, and planes. It had been possible for a dictatorial government to shape them as it wished, with little fear of resistance or dissent, especially after the peasant had been brought under control by collectivization. Germany's plans took shape when her first Four-Year Plan of 1933 was followed by the second one announced in 1936. Mass production and self-sufficiency were its two objectives. The first was already almost achieved, but the second called for a tremendous effort to produce substitutes for imported materials, especially textile fibers, oils, iron ore, rubber, non-ferrous metals, and essential foodstuffs. The public was promised a higher standard of living through the increased supply of consumption goods that would be made available with the production of raw materials within the Reich; but that promise was not kept.

The Plan was relentlessly carried out. New plants appeared to produce synthetic rubber and gasoline, to make wool substitutes from straw and fish albumen, to work low-grade domestic ores, and even to squeeze oil from grape pips. Though self-sufficiency proved to be unattainable, every possible step was taken to get as near to it as possible. To avoid grain imports, farmers were forbidden to feed their cattle with the grain which they had been obliged to use because they could not import fodder. This cut down the number of livestock and the supply of fats; hence fats must be imported or rationed, and rationed they were in 1937. No cloth was to be made of pure wool, and flax must take the place of cotton.

Since imports were unavoidable, the character of foreign trade must be fitted into the general plan. No commodities could enter or leave the country unless some controller gave permission. In addition, the destination of exports and the source of imports must be regulated. If the United States would not buy many German goods, Germany would get her cotton from South America, and by 1938 four-fifths of her supply came from that source. With other countries barter or clearinghouse agreements controlled the exchange of goods. With the weaker ones the terms virtually guaranteed that Germany would get much of what she required in return for small quantities of such goods as she cared to hand over.

Preparedness was very costly, even though costs were kept down by fixing prices, profits, and wages. In 1935 Germany was already spending $400,000,000 on rearmament, but by 1939 the plans called for $2,500,000,000, or about two-thirds of the national revenue. The bills were paid by a combination of heavier taxation, a higher yield as recovery made enterprise more profitable, and large-scale borrowing. The revenue doubled between 1932 and 1937; the expenditure on unemployment disappeared, but the 6 per cent tax on wages for the unemployment insurance fund continued to be collected, and all profits over 6 per cent were taken by the state. Taxes therefore took about 30 per cent of the national income. The acknowledged national debt also doubled between 1932 and 1937, but there was an unacknowledged debt as well, which was supposed to be too large to be disclosed. The amount of paper money also doubled, though this was no longer of great importance since the inflation of credit was now being carried out by bank credit rather than through the printing press.

In this way Germany achieved full employment of all her resources. By 1938 her unemployment figure was down to 450,000, which was accounted for by the sick, temporarily disabled, or persons moving from one job to another. That moving was now forbidden without state permission, for the labor shortage was acute.

Capital was also fully employed, but only in those directions to which the state steered it; the capital market was reserved for meeting state needs, and industry had to finance its own expansion out of its own funds. Yet full employment did not reveal itself as the happy condition which economists expected. With prices, wages, interests, and profits fixed, with the mobility of capital and labor alike restricted, and with the state taking a larger share of the national income, full employment was not the same thing as full enjoyment, for the standard of living sank lower.

Britain turned seriously to a preparedness program in 1937 and France in 1938. In those two countries there could be no dictation, and the transformation was therefore difficult and patchy. There were still 1,800,000 unemployed persons in Britain in 1938 and 1,200-000 in August, 1939, the month before the war broke out. By 1941 the figure was down to 350,000 and by 1942, to 160,000. The United States passed through a similar experience. In early 1940, when preparedness had scarcely begun, the census revealed that while 45,000,000 persons had jobs, about 5,000,000 were "seeking work" and a further 2,500,000 had found it only in public relief projects. Within two years the number of workers had risen high and the scarcity of labor was becoming acute. Thus preparedness and war succeeded in shelving the problem of unemployed capital and unemployed labor which had baffled the thirties. The task of repairing the physical damage or wear and tear of war and of maintaining the armed services of the victorious powers at more than their pre-war strength kept the problem on the shelf long after the fighting had stopped.

BIBLIOGRAPHY

Benham, F., *Great Britain under Protection* (1941).

Bogart, E. L., *Economic History of Europe, 1760–1939* (1942), chaps. 15, 17, 18, 20, 23.

Bowden, W., Karpovich, M., and Usher, A. P., *Economic History of Europe since 1750* (1937), chaps. 33, 35, 36, 37, 40, 41.

Bresciani-Turroni, C., *The Economics of Inflation* (Eng. trans., 1937).

Brown, W. A., Jr., *The International Gold Standard Reinterpreted, 1914–1934* (1941).

Bruck, W. F., *Social and Economic History of Germany from William Iı to Hitler* (1938).

Day, J. P., *Introduction to World Economic History since the Great Waı* (1937).

Guillebaud, C. W., *The Economic Recovery of Germany, 1933–1938* (1939).

Haight, F. A., *French Import Quotas* (1935).

Hancock, W. K., *Survey of British Commonwealth Affairs: II. Problems of Economic Policy, 1918–1939* (1940).

Hansen, A. H., *Fiscal Policy and Business Cycles* (1941).

Heaton, H., *The British Way to Recovery* (1934).

Keynes, J. M., *The Economic Consequences of the Peace* (1919).

Liepmann, H., *Tariff Levels and the Economic Unity of Europe* (1938).

Morton, W. A., *British Finance, 1930–1940* (1943).

Ogburn, W. F., and Jaffé, W., *The Economic Development of Post-War France* (1929).

Ohlin, B., *The Course and Phases of the World Economic Depression* (1931).

Pigou, A. C., *Some Economic Consequences of the Great War* (1930).

Robbins, L., *The Great Depression* (1934).

Stolper, G., *German Economy, 1870–1940* (1940).

ARTICLES AND REPORTS

Clay, H., "The Export-Import Economy of the United Kingdom," *Ec. J.,* July, 1942.

Gardner, W. R., "Central Gold Reserves, 1926–1931," *Am. Ec. R.,* March, 1931.

Kindersley, R., "British Overseas Investments," an annual article in *Ec. J.,* e.g., June, 1930, 1932, 1933.

Preston, H. H., "Europe's Return to Gold," *Harv. Bus. Rev.,* April, 1931.

Smith, L., "England's Return to the Gold Standard," *J.E.B.H.,* February, 1932.

Britain and World Trade: A Report by PEP (1947).

Employment Policy (British White Paper, 1944).

League of Nations: *World Economic Survey* (annual 1930 onward); *Memorandum on Commercial Banks, 1913–29* (1931); *Report of Gold Delegation of Financial Committee* (1932); *The Network of World Trade* (1942); *International Currency Experience* (1944).

Macmillan Committee: Report on Finance and Industry (British Parliamentary Paper, Cmd. 3897: 1931).

The United States in the World Economy: The International Transactions of the United States during the Inter-War Period (U.S. Dept. of Comm., 1943).

XXX

LABOR CONDITIONS AND REGULATIONS

The outstanding features in the history of European labor during the last two centuries are (1) the increase in the proportion of the population engaged in industry, mining, transportation, and commerce; (2) the increase in the percentage working under factory conditions and dependent entirely for its income on the sale of its labor; (3) the growing importance of labor problems in politics; (4) the development of labor organizations; and (5) a long-run lifting of the standard of living.

The Distribution of Occupations. The following table gives the percentage of the total "gainfully occupied" persons in each main

	Agri- culture	Manu- factur- ing	Mining	Trade	Communi- cation and Trans- port	Profes- sions	Personal Service
England and Wales	7	43	5	14	10	6	13
Germany	30	39	3	12	5	4	..
France	25	38	2	11	6	3	5
Belgium	19	40	7	11	8	3	6
Holland	24	36	2	12	10	6	..
Switzerland	26	44	..	12	5	5	6
Rumania	80	8	..	3	2	1	..
Russia	80	6	..	1	2	2	..

occupational group in the 1920's or 1930's The figures are only roughly comparable between countries.

The first six countries in the table were well developed industrially. The last two joined with Poland, Bulgaria, and Lithuania in having over three-fourths of their workers engaged on the land, but the Five-Year Plans reduced the predominance of the farming class in Russia, and by 1937 agriculture seems to have employed

716

only about 60 per cent of the population. All the industrial countries except Britain had a large farming class. In all of them manufacturing (including building) provided about two-fifths of the jobs. This fraction, reached in Britain by 1870 and in Germany by 1900, apparently was a limit beyond which little or no further growth took place; in fact the tendency was for it to shrink a little.

The fourth column shows that trade, including finance, absorbed between 10 and 14 per cent of the labor force in industrial countries but was an insignificant occupation in rural lands. Transportation and communication employed between 5 and 10 per cent of the workers in the economically advanced countries, but only 1, 2, or 3 per cent in Agricultural Europe. If we add the fourth and fifth columns together, we see that in the west one worker out of every five or six was engaged in moving or marketing.

The last two columns indicate the large part played by professional and personal service. No one has written the history of domestic service, yet in slave economies and ever since it has been an important kind of work. The number of female domestic servants in England in 1830 was probably more than 50 per cent greater than that of the workers in the cotton industry, and only six English cities in 1851 had populations greater than the army of "general domestic servants" employed in London homes. Conditions on the continent were probably similar. In 1931, 2,400,000 persons in England and Wales were engaged in "personal service." About 1,300,000 of them were female domestic servants, but their occupation was becoming less attractive because of the shorter hours and higher wages in industry and commerce or in the hotels, restaurants, and other places which were growing in numbers to serve the needs of a population that was spending less of its time at home.

The number of professional workers reflected the degree of economic maturity and diversity of each country. In 1931 there were 750,000 of them in England and Wales, rendering those skilled services which modern society requires. The doctors and lawyers played a larger part in guarding life and property; but to these ancient highly organized and disciplined occupations had been added those of the accountant, engineer, teacher, architect, and scientist, each resting on a body of skill and knowledge acquired by long training and tested by some examining board. In western Europe one worker out of every twenty was rendering professional service of some kind. Finally, a small but growing number was engaged in some branch of government service as the need grew for central or local officials to care for such things as public health, labor laws, highways, and the collection of taxes.

If we divide occupations into primary, secondary, and "tertiary," and include transportation, commerce, and the services in the last class, the modern trend of employment has shown a relative decline in the primary group, an increase to some point of stability in the secondary, and a great increase in the tertiary fields. In Britain tertiary employments engaged about 40 per cent of the workers in 1871, but 53 per cent in 1936; in France the figure rose from about 20 per cent in 1861 to 36 per cent in 1930; and similar developments in other continents were exemplified by the rise in the number of tertiary workers in the United States from 25 per cent in 1880 to 46 per cent in 1937.

Migration and the Labor Supply. The expansion of industry, transportation, and commerce, accompanied by the rise of industrial and commercial towns, called for migration or even immigration to supplement the local labor supply. Much industry had been carried on in country districts because that was where the food supply was most accessible; but improved transportation allowed industry to move to places where coal and raw materials were most easily available, and the labor and food could be brought to them. In England between 1800 and 1850 there was comparatively little long-distance migration from the south and east to the north or west, but rather a series of short journeys. The growing manufactures and the higher wages they offered drew people in from the hinterland, the void thus created was filled by people from the ring farther out, and so forth. There was a little long-distance transfer of pauper children and their elders, but the strange brogue most commonly heard in the industrial hives of England and Scotland was Irish. At one time the boat fare from Belfast to Glasgow was only 6d. (12 cents). By 1850 one-tenth of the population of England and Wales was Irish-born—a fact that influenced wages, housing conditions, and public health.

In England, as in most other countries, the capital city was a powerful magnet, drawing ambitious young people from far afield. Those cities combined politics and pleasure with commerce, finance, and industry. Their very size attracted light industries which used relatively little fuel or material and which needed to be near the consumer rather than near coal or iron; and their position at the heart of the financial and transportation systems made them economic as well as political capitals. The influx of population and industry into them or into communities within easy reach of them was continuous throughout the nineteenth century but reached the dimensions of a flood in the inter-war years. By 1937 Greater London housed 8,700,000 residents, or nearly a quarter of the population of England and Wales; it produced nearly a quarter of the country's industrial output, and was therefore doomed to be a bomber's target. Greater Paris held an eighth (5,000,000) of the French people, while the Berlin area contained 4,500,000 persons, of whom only a quarter had been born there.

Women's Work. Of the "gainfully employed" in the 1920's, about three-eighths in Germany and Great Britain were female. The transfer of some industries to the factory and the rise of new occupations affected the economic position of women in many ways. The factory took spinning out of the home, and for a time the machines made that process one done by men with the aid of children or young persons. Then the power loom took weaving out of the home and made it a woman's job. Married women had to decide whether they would go to the mill and neglect their homes or stay at home and become economically dependent on other members of the family. For a time some refused to go or let their children go; but this hostility gradually broke down and the mill eventually provided work of various kinds for persons of both sexes and all ages. To it women went to work while they were single and also as long as they could after marriage. About 65 per cent of the labor in the British textile industry was female in the 1930's; in some Lancashire towns 40 per cent of the married women and 50 to 60 per cent of all the women worked if they could find employment.

The rise of the ready-to-wear clothing industry offered another field to women workers, and they comprised two-thirds of the English labor force in that occupation in 1931. In the preparation of tobacco they held three-fourths of the jobs and in the pottery industry half of them. In other occupations where great physical strength was not needed, where a task could be quickly learned, where semi-automatic machines had to be fed, where standardized parts were assembled, or where nimble fingers were essential, women did the work as well as men and were willing to accept lower wages. As these light industries increased greatly in number and size during the twentieth century, the scope for female factory labor was widened. In non-factory occupations—commerce, hotels, retailing, clerical work, and the like—women supplied nearly half the labor force in the inter-war decades. In "personal service" they held four-fifths of the jobs. As better secondary, technical, and university education facilities became available for girls after 1900 and as mechanical office equipment came into wider use, still other avenues to employment were opened up. In 1931 there were three times as many stenographers as there were soldiers and sailors; the teaching profession was a large field for educated women, though not so predominantly feminine in its elementary and secondary branches as in North America; and nursing, law, and medicine had a steadily increasing number of women practitioners. In the professions as a whole there were more women than men.

The heavy industries remained in men's hands. Women were excluded directly by law from working in coal mines, indirectly from some continuous processes by the ban on nightwork, and by trade-union restrictions from other occupations. During the First World War women entered many of these industries, but when peace came the old conditions were restored, only to be discarded again when war returned in 1939. The social structure of English agriculture limited the large farmer's wife to domestic duties, and in 1931 only 5 per cent of the land workers were female, against over 40 per cent in France and over 50 per cent in Germany. In many other walks of life, among better-paid wage earners and the middle class, convention decreed that a woman should quit her job when she married. She worked only if it was necessary to supplement her husband's income, and in 1931 less than 10 per cent of British wives worked for wages. On the Continent the peasant's wife worked hard, the practice of industrial homework lasted longer, women entered the usual factory occupations and retained many of those which they had annexed during the First World War. For a time during the depressed thirties Nazi and Fascist rulers told women their role was that of wife and mother, and they were removed from jobs that men wanted; but with the coming of rearmament many of them were recalled. In Russia, on the other hand, women were enrolled in such vast numbers to help carry out the Plans that the total number engaged in work of all kinds rose from 3,300,000 in 1929 to 9,300,000 in 1937. In the latter year they provided about 35 per cent of the labor force, which was about the same as in England and Wales. They accounted for a quarter of the workers in agriculture, two-fifths of those in "large-scale industry," a fifth of those in construction and transportation, and over half of the teachers and public-health workers.

Labor Conditions. Of the 19,000,000 gainfully occupied persons in England and Wales in 1931, at least 16,000,000 were wage or salary earners. In other industrial countries the fraction was similar: at least four-fifths of the working population depended for its income on the sale of its labor to some employer. The wage earner's material welfare was therefore determined by his ability to make a sale, by the price he obtained, by the regularity and duration of his employment, by the conditions under which he worked, and by the price he had to pay for the goods he needed as a consumer.

Most of the conditions of employment which we associate with the modern factory had been common features of the domestic or small workshop industrial order (see above, Chapter XVI). Wage-earning had a long history. Long hours—twelve a day, or from sunrise to sunset, and even more in busy seasons—had always been general, and the only new feature was the extension of the field over which the discipline of regular working hours prevailed. The employment of children had always been regarded as normal, necessary, and even beneficial, and the frequent instances of maltreatment of apprentices suggest that cruelty had not been absent from the craftsman's workshop. The new aspects of child labor were the gathering of children together in large numbers, the discipline and strain of hours at the machine, and the higher earnings. Modern industry introduced new dangers to health, life, and limb, but put some ancient ones to flight. It destroyed the value of some old kinds of skill but created many more new ones. Boredom, monotonous repetition, physical strain, wet feet, poisonous fumes, and low wages paid in truck were not new factory products. The really important innovation was the dawning consciousness that some labor conditions were inhuman and then that they were bad economics as well as bad humanics.

Improvement in labor conditions and earnings was made *possible* by the increased productivity of industry. It was brought about, bit by bit, through the building up of a body of labor laws and the growing ability of labor organizations to influence the terms on which their members sold their labor. Let us therefore first examine the development of labor legislation, leaving the story of labor organization till the next chapter.

The State Regulation of Working Conditions

The first factory act was passed in 1802. Little more was done till the thirties, but by 1850 important steps in legislation and enforcement had been taken. After that date the area of control was expanded more easily, new principles were introduced, and by 1914 the leading industrial countries had comprehensive codes regulating most aspects of the labor contract.

The movement did not originate in any broad economic or political philosophy. It spent its childhood in an atmosphere generally hostile to state intervention. Its early triumphs were tolerated only on the ground that they dealt with children who were unable to bargain with an employer and whose economic well-being therefore could not be left to *laissez faire* and the play of free enterprise. The motive force was humanitarian.

The awakening of western Europe to a consciousness that certain things were cruel, intolerant, and inhuman was one of the most remarkable events of the late eighteenth and early nineteenth centuries, just as the revival of intolerance and cruelty is one of the most tragic features of the twentieth. Liberal political theory may have been partly responsible, by its stress on the rights of the individual or by Bentham's plea for the maximization of pleasure, the minimization of pain, and the greatest good for the greatest number. The work of Howard and Beccaria led to prison reform, a gradual softening of the penal code, and a more sparing use of the death sentence. In the religious field Wesleyans, Quakers, evangelical Episcopalians, and, later, High Churchmen worked among the poor and gave new meaning to the brotherhood of man. In literature Mrs. Gaskell, Kingsley, Disraeli, and Dickens made people uncomfortable about economic and social conditions merely by describing them. The agitations of Wilberforce for slave emancipation, of Owen, Oastler, and Shaftesbury for factory reform, and of others for education or public health were all indications of a new kind of social conscience, of a critical attitude toward time-honored practices, and of a belief in the possibility of human betterment.

The task of awakening this conscience was hard, and some results came slowly. The reformer sometimes overdid his denunciations, saw evils only when they were far enough away from his own personal interests, was motivated by political partisanship and personal spleen, or was consumed by an intolerance that defeated or delayed his purpose. Further, "there is a limit—very soon reached—to the amount of workman-like creative legislation or administration of which any government is capable in a given time" (Clapham), and within that limit other issues enjoyed a higher priority of urgency and importance than did factory legislation. Yet in the long run, bit by bit, the community and the legislators came to look on industrial conditions through new spectacles and decided that some of them ought to be changed.

Labor legislation developed by answering a series of questions: 1. Which workers were to be protected? The early answer was, Only those unable to fight their own battles. This at first meant children, then young persons, then women. Men were supposed to be strong enough to look after their own interests. Indirectly, however, the regulation of hours of labor for women and young persons influenced the hours of men who worked in the same industries. Eventually the myth of masculine might was abandoned. Laws dealing with the safety of ships, wages, the eight-hour day, workmen's compensation, social insurance, and health or safety requirements affected male labor directly. The scope of protection also gradually spread from factories to mines, workshops, stores, homeworkers, and even to agriculture.

2. At what age should persons be allowed to begin work? Once an age limit was fixed, the tendency was to raise it by stages from nine years to thirteen, fourteen, and then still higher.

3. For what hours should work be permitted? Should nightwork or overtime be allowed? What statutory holidays should be provided? The answer to these questions was a gradual reduction in the length of the working day from twelve toward eight, the prohibition of nightwork for women, and the provision of legal holidays or weekly days of rest.

4. What should be done to protect the health, strength, and safety of workers? Gradually rules were framed dealing with sanitation, ventilation, the fencing of machinery, the control of dangerous or poisonous trades, and all other aspects of the working environment. As occupational diseases became better understood, protective measures became more effective.

5. Could or should the state regulate wages? Employers and economists thundered a unanimous "No"; but after 1900 the dis-

covery of sweating, the power of some labor groups, and the problems created by war led to the erection of machinery for the regulation of some wages.

6. All the above questions referred to the person at work. But what happened to the worker who could not earn an income, the victim of sickness, accident, old age, or unemployment? Could he be left to depend on his savings, family, friends, or union, or to fall back on the hated poor relief? The number of such persons was too great and the resources at their disposal were too scanty to make this method adequate. Workmen's compensation might take care of the victim of accident, but the needs of the others must be met by insurance schemes in which employer, employee, and the state participated.

In answering these questions different countries pioneered. Great Britain led in dealing with minimum age, maximum hours, and working conditions. Germany was the first to deal with insurance, and Australia led in wages regulation. International imitation was widespread. England dealt with sweating by copying wages boards from Australia and with health insurance by adopting the German method. But she pioneered in unemployment insurance, and Germany copied that scheme from her. Many laws made national and compulsory the conditions voluntarily established by the best employers. Most of the things which reformers advocated were already to be found in the better factories or were urged by employers who wished to adopt them but were prevented by the competition of their rivals. This policy of bringing backward employers up to the standards prevailing elsewhere was applied to the international field when the International Labor Organization was set up in 1919 to work for uniformity of labor regulation throughout the world.

The First Stages. The first factory act (1802) was passed to protect British pauper children who had been handed over by local poor-relief authorities as apprentices to some cotton factory owners. The treatment of these paupers had often been bad when they were forced onto tradesmen or craftsmen; it was no better if they remained in the relief authority's hands, and in the early factories apprentices were at the mercy of their master or of his manager or foreman. That children of six should work twelve hours or more, that a rush of orders should be met by working two shifts of twelve hours, that discipline should be enforced with fist or lash, that food and bedding should be frugal, and that fevers should sweep over mills and towns crowded with paupers and Irish—all these things were natural, but protest against them was inevitable. Hence the "Health and Morals of Apprentices Act" passed with little opposition. It dealt with: (1) *Sanitation.* Mill walls and ceilings must be whitewashed twice a year; ventilation and lighting must be adequate. (2) *Hours.* The working day was not to exceed twelve hours, and nightwork must be abolished. (3) *Education.* Instruction in the three R's must be provided. (4) *Inspection.* Two visitors—one a local justice and the other a clergyman—were to inspect mills, and offending employers were to be fined.

The act achieved virtually nothing. It applied only to apprentices in cotton factories, but "free" children were now available in increasing numbers. The visitors did not do their job, and the country was too busy wrestling with Napoleon to bother about little labor problems. Here and there, however, employers were improving working conditions of their own accord, and when peace came one of them—Robert Owen—went out to preach the cause of factory reform. Owen (1771–1858) was a Welshman who made a fortune in Scotland and lost most of it trying to plant an ideal community in America. He was the father or sponsor of nearly every modern labor movement. Cooperation, trade unionism, friendly societies, the eight-hour day, factory laws, and socialism owed much to this man who "started out to help the masses and ended by wanting to change the whole system" (Cole).

Owen's first chance came when, as son-in-law and junior partner of David Dale, he became manager of the New Lanark cotton mills in 1800. Of the 2,000 workers, 500 were pauper apprentices, and many of the remainder were "addicted to theft, drunkenness, and falsehood" (Owen). For twenty-three years he experimented in making a model mill and a model village. He gave up using pauper apprentices, forbade children under ten to work and sent them to school instead. He limited hours to twelve a day, less 1¾ hours for meals. He established a store to sell food at cost, improved houses, provided medical care, set up a sick fund, and founded a savings bank. Though his plans frightened his partners, he made profits, and New Lanark became one of the seven wonders of Britain. Visitors went to see it and sometimes to study it. Owen's influence was great even in high quarters, and his views on factory reform and other matters were given respectful attention. Then in 1817 he shattered that influence by making an attack on religion. The prestige of a reforming businessman was changed into the menace of an atheistic radical visionary. His political power faded, and the factory act for which he had fought was a pale reflection of his proposals.

That act (1819) forbade children under nine to work in cotton factories; thus an age limit was introduced. "Young persons," i.e., those from nine to sixteen years, must not work more than twelve hours, i.e., a seventy-two-hour week. In 1825 Saturday work was limited to nine hours, and in 1831 the upper age was raised to eighteen years. There was still no inspection worth the name, no provision dealing with women, and no regulation of any industry except cotton. But by 1831 a storm had blown up which led to the first really effective piece of labor legislation.

The storm king was Richard Oastler. Factories had been multiplying in the Yorkshire woolen industry, and during the twenties many of the larger employers had not merely provided good conditions and limited hours but decided that legislation was as necessary for woolen factories as for cotton. One of them interested Oastler in the question. Oastler had failed in business and become agent for a large landlord, but he spent much of his time in anti-slavery or other agitations. In 1830 his interest, hot temper, and lurid vocabulary were switched from owners of Negro slaves to "factory slave-owners." His blistering letters to the press and his speeches demanding a ten-hour working day aroused great enthusiasm and equal resentment. As a propagandist he has had few peers. Committees were formed, supported by employers, clergymen, doctors, and wage earners. Countless mass meetings were organized, and lobbying was persistent. Michael Sadler persuaded parliament to appoint a committee to investigate factory conditions. This inquiry was far from being judicial; much of the evidence given by carefully coached youngsters was either suspect or at least partisan, and there was no cross-examination of the witnesses. Yet the committee's general conclusion that the labor of children and young persons needed to be regulated could not be gainsaid and was supported by a royal commission which studied the matter more critically in 1833.

The result was the Factory Act of 1833. It did not provide for a simple ten-hour day, but it did take many important steps. (1) It applied to cotton, wool, and linen mills. (2) No child under nine could be employed. (3) Children between nine and thirteen years were not to work more than nine hours a day or forty-eight hours a week, and must spend three hours a day in school. Compulsory education thus began in a factory act. (4) Young persons (thirteen to eighteen years) must not work more than twelve hours a day or sixty-nine a week, and no one under eighteen years could work on the night shift. (5) Effective inspection was provided. Four full-time inspectors were appointed to enforce the act and bring offenders to court.

To pass an act was one thing, to enforce it was another. The inspectors faced a herculean task, confronted with the apathy of some parents and the hostility of some employers. Children seldom had birth certificates, and forged certificates were often presented. Factory clocks were not always reliable, schools were not everywhere available, teachers were often illiterate, and fines were sometimes so light that employers escaped any real punishment. Yet the inspectors stuck to their task. The best employers supported them, fines became heavier, school facilities improved, the inspectors stressed the importance of safety and sanitary precautions, and the long depression from 1836 to 1842 and some improvements in machinery reduced the need for young workers and long hours. The agitation for a ten-hour day continued, led by Lord Shaftesbury, who had become champion of factory reform in 1832. In 1844 children (under thirteen) were ordered to spend not more than 6½ hours in the factory and the other half-day in school. Women were put under the same time limit as young persons, i.e., a maximum sixty-nine-hour week. In 1847, 1850, 1853, and 1874 the ten-hour day became the rule for young persons and women in textile mills, and since many men could not work without female or juvenile aid their hours were automatically restricted.

Every step in this story had been bitterly fought by some employers. The plea of complete *laissez faire* was rarely urged, for it obviously could not be applied to children. Opponents rather contended that factory labor was not bad in itself, that the work was light and healthier than at other places in which children worked, that the labor was productive of thrift and preferable to loafing or getting into mischief in the streets, and that factory conditions were not in general as black as in those particular extreme cases to which the reformers gave such noisy publicity. Further, they argued, industry could not bear the cost of reduced hours; overhead costs had to be met, reserves must be built up, competition was fierce, and when the employer had plowed into his business all that it needed he had little margin left over. To reduce working hours by a twelfth or to impose a ten-hour day would more than wipe out that margin. The danger of competition from lands which had no labor laws was stressed, and textile manufacturers asked why their industry should be singled out for interference while workers in other occupations remained untouched.

The employers' case could not be dismissed as the lies of a lobby. Their enterprises were often skating on very thin ice; their need for fixed and operating capital was intense and incessant; the protest of the reformers was an attack on old labor conditions which many self-made employers had endured themselves; and the motives of the reformers were not always disinterested or free from party politics. If the landlords who denounced the grimy north would look at the wages or the houses of laborers on their estates, or at the London slums and tenements from which much of their own income was drawn, they might remember a proverb about glass houses. As for Oastler and some of his colleagues, their vehement language, their refusal to accept anything less than their full demand, and their occasional exhortations to violence or sabotage alienated some supporters and stiffened the resistance of some opponents.

The textile industry managed to survive its tribulations. Regulation equalized competitive conditions at one important point, mechanical improvement reduced the dependence on young fingers, and after 1850 brighter days came for both capital and labor. Meanwhile other industries were subjected to regulation. In 1842 the foul conditions under which pauper apprentices, free children, and women were working in some mines were exposed. Boys under ten, women, and girls were therefore forbidden to work underground and mine inspectors were appointed. In the sixties and seventies regulation was extended to all kinds of factories and workshops, the employment of women and children in agricultural gangs was restricted, and the long fight to prevent the sweeping of chimneys by sending children up them ended successfully (1875). The safety of ships, passengers, and crew was guarded by providing (1876) for inspection of vessels, preventing unseaworthy ones from sailing, investigating wrecks, issuing certificates to officers, and marking a line (the Plimsoll line) on the side of ships and forbidding vessels to take on any more cargo when the line had reached water level.

The minimum age for beginning work was supplemented by a minimum age for leaving school, and the joint result was that work could not begin till the twelfth to fourteenth birthday. Health and safety precautions were imposed by legislation or by local sanitary rules. Industries which were exposed to special danger from fumes or the handling of poisons (e.g., potteries, leadworks, paint factories, and match factories) were subjected to laws or to orders prepared by government experts after 1900. By that year retail trading had become subject to regulation by limiting the hours of labor and by demanding a weekly half-holiday. Outworkers, the survivors of the putting-out system, received attention in 1891. Their homes were to be inspected by the local health officer, and they were to be given detailed "particulars" of the work to be done and the rate of pay.

In most of this legislative advance the interests of women, young persons, and children were paramount, but after 1900 the state began to respond to pleas for aid to male adults. In 1908 the eight-hour day was imposed on coal mining. In 1912 the miners gained another point by securing the imposition of a legal minimum wage on the industry. While the state thus granted the wishes of one of the strongest groups of wage earners in the kingdom, it protected the weakest by establishing "trade boards" to fix minimum wages for sweated industries (1909). It also took up the task of providing insurance against sickness and unemployment (1911) and in that work there was no distinction between the sexes.

Continental Factory Legislation. France and Germany lagged behind Britain in framing factory acts. France passed its first child-labor law in 1841 but provided no inspectors till 1874, and its labor code was largely a product of the early twentieth century. Prussia started to protect children and young persons in 1839 and provided inspectors in 1853; but there, as in other German states, the laws were slow in becoming effective. Bismarck was indifferent or hostile to labor legislation, hated the Social Democrats who were advocating it, and believed that other things, especially insurance against loss of income, were more important than were restrictions on working conditions. Little was done, therefore, until 1891, when an industrial code was drawn up. It ran along familiar lines and was frequently amended or supplemented by law or administrative decree. After the revolution of 1918 an eight-hour law was passed. In other countries the rise of factories eventually led to similar action.

Industrial Fatigue. The motive behind early factory reform was humanitarian or political. Labor laws placed human welfare above profits. By 1900, however, there was some recognition that output was not strictly proportionate to the length of the working day, and some study of industrial fatigue had been made. In America efficiency experts, such as F. W. Taylor, were experimenting, and in Germany Ernst Abbe noticed that output increased when he reduced working hours at the Zeiss optical works at Jena from nine to eight. During the early stages of World War I the factory laws of every country were suspended in order to expand production. Men and women alike worked seventy to eighty hours a week, and some men even longer. The results on the work and the worker were disastrous, and in Britain especially the factors that influenced output began to be seriously studied.

The conclusions reached from these studies showed that shorter hours, safe and sanitary conditions, and most other items of factory legislation were good not merely for the employee but also for the employer, since they staved off industrial fatigue. That fatigue reduced the quantity and lowered the quality of the product, caused spoiled work and damage to tools or machines, was responsible for many accidents and much sickness, roused a feeling of staleness and resentfulness and thus provoked industrial unrest. Once this many-sided relationship was recognized, many questions cropped up. What, for instance, was the optimum working day? The evidence showed that a sixty-hour week was more productive than a longer one; that for women and for men's heavy work a fifty-four-hour week was the most productive, and that in some circumstances one of forty-eight hours was the optimum. Long working periods, say of four or five hours, needed to be broken by a rest pause. Good lighting, adequate ventilation, the removal of dust and fumes, the provision of seats and of facilities for obtaining good meals—all these measures improved the productivity of the plant.

Such discoveries provided a basis for further legislation and gave employers guiding principles on which they could formulate labor policies far in advance of the minimum conditions required by law. There was consequently a fairly general improvement in working conditions and a shortening of hours during the inter-war period. The production needs of World War II placed a great strain on peacetime practices. The danger of air raids led to the "black-out," which prevented light from going out and fresh air from coming in, necessitated more use of artificial light, and generally made the working environment unsatisfactory in a continent which had not gone far in air-conditioning. When Germany broke loose in western

Europe in the spring of 1940, and the British had to leave most of their equipment behind at Dunkirk, the urgent need for quickly expanded production led to the suspension of British factory acts and the call to a twelve-hour day seven days a week. The output jumped for a few crucial weeks but quickly fell back to its old level as workers reached the point of exhaustion. The limits on women's working hours were therefore restored, and a new study was begun of the methods needed to promote the health, safety, and welfare of factory workers. But the war years remained a period of abnormal strain on all kinds of workers. The prevention or cure of industrial fatigue was impossible.

International Aspects of Labor Legislation. Almost every proposal for industrial legislation encountered the objection that it would harass native industries in competition with lands that had backward labor laws or none at all. As early as 1850 Le Grand, a Swiss factory reformer, was urging that this obstacle be removed by persuading governments to take common action, but without avail. In 1890 an international convention at Berlin approved a few simple proposals, such as the non-employment of children in mines. A convention at Berne in 1905–1906 recommended that the use of phosphorus for making matches be restricted, since it produced a bone disease known as "phossy jaw." Beyond this, little was accomplished until World War I gave an opportunity for more ambitious effort. It is hard now to recapture the enthusiastic belief of those days that from the conflict there would emerge not merely a better international order but also a better social order. The "war to end war" was also to end social injustice. While peasants were stirred by being promised land, wage earners were urged to intensify their efforts by promises of better working conditions and rewards. World War II was less rich in promises.

Labor's demand for the fulfillment of these promises (and the fear of the specter in Russia) led to the inclusion in the Covenant of the League of Nations of a pledge that all members would "endeavour to secure and maintain fair and humane conditions of labour for men, women and children . . . and for that purpose will establish and maintain the necessary international organizations." Part XIII of the Treaty of Versailles created the organization and stated the two principles that were to guide its work. (1) "Universal peace . . . can be established only if it is based upon social justice." (2) "The failure of any nation to adopt humane conditions of labour is an obstacle in the way of other countries which desire to improve the conditions in their own countries." The essentials of social justice included the living wage, the eight-hour day, the abolition of child labor, the restriction of work by young persons and women, the payment to men and women of "equal remuneration for work of equal value," and the right of workers to form associations.

To promote the attainment of these objectives was the task of the International Labor Organization. All members of the League were automatically members, and other countries could join if they wished. The Organization consisted of an International Labor Office and an annual conference. To the latter each country sent delegates representing the government, employers, and wage earners. Any "draft convention" or "recommendation" that was approved by two-thirds of the conference was forwarded to the member governments, who were pledged to submit it to the "competent legislative authority." The "authority" could accept or reject the proposal as it thought best; it was under no compulsion except that of considering the recommendations made by the conference.

The first conference was held in Washington in 1919, the second in Genoa in 1920, and the later ones met in Geneva, where the Office became an efficient bureau of research and information on every aspect of labor problems. The Washington meeting achieved more in a month than had been accomplished in thirty years, for the delegates agreed on proposals bearing on hours of labor, nightwork, child labor, and many other topics. Genoa examined questions of employment on ships; and the Geneva conferences dealt with a wide range of subjects. By 1935 about 70 draft conventions or recommendations had been approved by the conferences, and about 650 ratifications had been made by different governments.

The net effect had not been great on the countries with advanced labor laws, but backward lands had been brought far forward. The new states created by the war were provided with laws ready made and the leveling up of industrial legislation was substantial. Hours of labor tended to move toward the eight-hour day in Europe and were subjected to control and reduction in Asia. Provisions for health, accident prevention, unemployment aid, and factory inspection became more thorough, and freedom to associate in trade unions spread in some regions, though it was later lost in lands that succumbed to dictatorship. The living wage, "equal pay for equal work," and many other objectives which seemed to be just round the corner in 1919 remained there; but the efforts of the Organization gave large sections of Europe's working population a protection undreamed of before 1914.

Most of this advance was made before depression hit the world. From 1930 onward the chief concern was to find jobs rather than to regulate them. National considerations overrode all others, and the International Labor Organization shared in the general breakdown of attempts at international cooperation. In 1939, when war came, its headquarters moved to Montreal. In 1944 it resumed the practice of holding annual conferences and then became incorporated in the United Nations organization. But the economic problems and the atmosphere after World War II were very different from those of 1919.

Industrial Insurance. The development of compulsory insurance of wage earners was Germany's pioneer contribution to the worker's welfare. Imperial Germany had its Marxian Socialists, whose growing strength and talk of an impending social revolution worried Bismarck, especially when the gloomy days of the seventies and eighties gave support to their contention that capitalism was doomed to an early collapse. Germany also had its "state socialists," many of them university professors, who urged the extension of state activity for the amelioration of the wage earner's lot. This policy was far closer to the German concept of statesmanship than was *laissez faire,* and Bismarck accepted it, refusing to be scared by the charge that it was socialistic. He was also wise enough to see that tangible tokens of state solicitude might wean the laboring class from the Social Democrats. That solicitude should deal less with the conditions under which men worked and more with the dread insecurity of work and income that hung like Damocles' sword over the wage earner. The wise and valuable policy was to provide insurance against insecurity.

Insurance against loss of income was part of the policy of some friendly societies and trade unions. Bismarck extended these voluntary efforts into a nation-wide scheme, based on two principles: (1) All workmen in certain occupations were compelled to insure themselves. (2) All parties contributed to the premiums; the funds were built up by payments from the employer, the employee, and in some cases the state. These principles—compulsion and tripartite contribution—were first translated into a sickness insurance plan, which began in 1883 with 10 per cent of the total population but was extended till in 1926 it covered a third (21,000,000 workers). In 1925 it was expanded to cover the worker's dependents and the middle class as well, thus embracing 60 per cent of the population. Contributions amounted to about 2 per cent of wages, of which the employer paid two-thirds. When a worker fell sick, he received free medical attention and medicine, and half to three-fourths of his wages for six months. Gradually other benefits were added, such as X-ray or dental work, hospital care, maternity benefits for workers' wives, and treatment for rickets, tuberculosis, etc. The extension to the whole family was accompanied by increasing attention to preventive work and to raising the general level of working-class health. In 1929 the total cost of the scheme was about $415,000,000, or about $10 per head of the insured population.

Accident insurance was established in 1884. Premiums were paid entirely by the employer; but for the first thirteen weeks a victim of accident was technically a "sick person," drawing on the sickness fund. After that period he drew on the accident fund as long as he was disabled; if he was permanently totally helpless he obtained full wages, and if he was killed his dependents received a pension up to three-fifths of his wages. These liabilities induced employers to take great care to prevent accidents. Old-age and invalidity insurance came in 1888. Employer and employee contributed equally to pay the premiums, and the state added something. If a person became unable, through illness, to earn more than a third of the usual wage he was classified as an invalid; otherwise he began to draw old-age benefits at seventy. Actually most people became eligible before they reached threescore and ten.

Germany never regretted these schemes, and frequently extended or improved them. They put a bottom to poverty—except that which came from unemployment. The sickness plan was widely copied abroad, and by 1930 twenty-five countries had compulsory systems while fifteen had voluntary ones. Great Britain in 1911 established its twin health and unemployment insurance scheme. Workmen's compensation laws of 1897 and 1906 had made employers financially responsible for all accidents to their workers. A non-contributory old-age pension plan had been established in 1908. Two of the fields covered by insurance in Germany had therefore been cared for, the first by making the employer liable, the second by drawing the pension money out of the public purse. The health insurance plan followed the German trail into territory that had already been well explored. It was financed by payments from wage earners, employers, and the state. The scope of the scheme was so wide that by 1928 about 15,000,000 workers (nearly nine-tenths of the employed class and a third of the total population) were assured of medical attention and of some income while absent from work because of sickness.

Unemployment Insurance. Unemployment was still a little-known problem, with no adequate statistics concerning its extent, variations, or character. Its solution called for two preliminary steps: helping the workless man to find a job and giving him support until he did. A private employment exchange was set up in Berlin (1883) and proved useful in bringing together employers who wanted men and men who wanted work. The depression of 1893 led to the establishment of public exchanges, and a nation-wide system was gradually evolved. Britain established a similar system of "labor exchanges" in 1909. Meanwhile the provision of a small sum of money for unemployed members became part of the policy of some labor unions. Since this was a far better method than leaving men to beg or appeal for poor relief, some continental city governments supplemented the payments made by the unions.

The first really important step, however, was taken in the British scheme of 1911. The plan was a modest, cautious, compulsory insurance contract for seven occupations, chiefly capital goods industries, whose employment cycle was fairly well known. The employee paid five cents a week, the employer the same, and the state added three cents. When a man had paid dues for a certain time he became eligible to draw 7/– ($1.75) a week for fifteen weeks in one year. He obtained the money at the local labor exchange, and the exchange could test the genuineness of his unemployment by offering him any suitable job it had on its books.

At its inception the scheme covered only 2,250,000 employees; but in 1916 over a million women munitions workers were brought under its wing, and in early 1920, while the post-war boom was still rampant, the range was widened to include all workers except those in agriculture, domestic service, the government, and the higher clerical ranks. By 1930 nearly 12,000,000 persons were insured. Even with this extension the plan might have remained actuarially sound if unemployment had retained its pre-war size and character. But it did not do so; instead it became so heavy and so many men were out of work for so long that the funds were often exhausted and workers were often still jobless when their last benefit payment had been received and spent.

The choice confronting the government was either to let these men seek assistance from the poor-law authorities or to continue the insurance benefits beyond the prescribed term. The poor-law system had neither the organization nor the money for such work, and in addition reputable workers resented the badge of "pauper" that became attached to all who sought poor relief. The benefits therefore continued to be paid out of the insurance fund; the scheme thus ceased to be purely an insurance plan based on a contract and became in part a relief fund for men of unemployed status. The benefits were now far above the original weekly sum; most of the burden was borne by the contributions of employers and of those men who were actually at work; but the income from these sources was insufficient to meet even pre-depression needs, and in 1928 the fund was $125,000,000 in debt. When depression came the debt jumped to nearly $600,000,000 in 1931.

Well-informed and sympathetic critics pointed out the danger of this drift from insurance benefits to relief. They felt that it was preventing the state, employers, and unions from attacking the causes of unemployment, and feared that the system was partly responsible for maintaining wages at too high a level, since unions no longer had to support their unemployed members and therefore resisted any reduction of wages to rates at which employment could be given. When the financial crisis came in 1931 the brake had to be applied to what had become popularly known as "the dole." In 1934 the plan was reorganized on an insurance basis, but men who still lacked work when their benefits expired were told to seek "assistance" from a new "Unemployment Assistance Board" which dispensed public funds according to the "needs" of the applicant. Recovery from the depression eased the cost of both insurance and assistance. The insurance scheme became solvent again and the new Board in 1940 found other work to do. It shed the word "Unemployment" from its name, for there were now no unemployed, and took over the task of assisting victims of German bombing raids.

A few continental countries adopted unemployment insurance based on the British pattern. The German scheme of 1927 tried to avoid some of England's mistakes but did not have enough time to build up much reserve before the hard times came. In 1931 the government, faced with a deficit of $365,000,000 in the fund, virtually abandoned the insurance aspects of the scheme. British and German experience made it clear that in a deep depression no insurance plan could cope with the whole unemployment problem without substantial aid from the public purse; but it also showed that such plans were more efficacious for coping with distress than was any scheme improvised during an emergency or based on charity.

This lesson was learned by the United States, and led to the Social Security Act of 1935. The title was exaggerated, since only about half the working population was covered by the unemployment and old-age insurance provisions, and sickness insurance was not touched. Yet it was one more recognition of the fact, hammered home by the intense, widespread unemployment of the early thirties, that there must be public planning to minimize unemployment and public forethought if those who were unable to find work were not to be left to beg, starve, or steal.

The various insurance schemes aimed at providing against interruption and loss of earning power of wage earners and lower-paid salary earners. But social security against want in modern industrial communities was not fully covered by them. On the one hand they did not include high-salaried workers or people who worked for themselves. On the other they did not take cognizance of the fact that some wage earners, even when fully employed, did not earn enough money to meet basic needs if their families were large; and often the old-age pensions were inadequate. Governments in various countries had tried to meet unsatisfied family needs by providing maternity bonuses, widows' pensions, children's allowances, meals for children at school, free medical services, and various other subsidies to income out of the public treasury; and in addition the same funds were tapped for unemployment assistance and general poor relief.

In thinking about its post-war reconstruction problems the British government in 1941 asked a committee headed by Sir William Beveridge to survey "the existing national schemes of social insurance and allied services." The "Beveridge Report" showed that while British social security policies provided for "most of the many varieties of need through interruption of earnings and other causes," there were "serious deficiencies which call for remedy" and need for coordinated administration. In place of the many separate pieces and policies, the plea was made for a single all-embracing scheme which would insure the *whole* population from the cradle to the grave against the major economic risks of life, providing uniform benefits which were adequate for living costs and financed by uniform contributions from the beneficiary, his employer if he had one, and the state.

The Report was indorsed by the wartime coalition government in 1943, and in 1946 the Labor cabinet embodied it in legislation. The plan, which was to come into operation in July, 1948, provided for a single weekly contribution. In return for this the benefits available to the contributor and his dependents would include unemployment pay, sickness pay and free medical service, maternity and widows' benefits, guardians' allowances for orphans, old-age pensions, and burial allowances. In addition, under a separate law, allowances for all children beyond the first in each family were provided in 1945. The operation of this comprehensive plan will, like that of the unemployment part of the United States social security scheme, make an interesting chapter in the history of the next depression if full employment is not maintained.

BIBLIOGRAPHY

Beveridge, W. H., *The Past and Present of Unemployment Insurance* (1930).

Beveridge, Sir William, *Social Insurance and Allied Services* (the Beveridge Report) (1942).

Birnie, A., *Economic History of Europe, 1760–1930* (1930), chaps. 12, 14.

Bland, Tawney, and Brown, *English Economic History: Select Documents* (1914), pp. 502–524, 571–618.

Burns, E. M., *British Unemployment Programs, 1920–1938* (1943).

Carr-Saunders, A. M., and Wilson, P. A., *The Professions* (1933).

Clapham, J. H., *Economic Development of France and Germany, 1815–1914* (1923), sections 17, 49, 68, 69, 70, 80, 81.

Clapham, J. H., *Economic History of Modern Britain* (1926, 1932, 1938), vol. i, chaps. 8, 14; vol. ii, chaps. 10, 11; vol. iii, chap. 7.

Cole, G. D. H., *Robert Owen* (1925).

Day, C., *The Distribution of Industrial Occupations in England, 1841–1861* (1927).

Driver, C., *Tory Radical: The Life of Richard Oastler* (1946).

Fay, C. R., *Great Britain from Adam Smith to the Present Day* (1932), chaps. 16, 17.

Florence, P. S., *Economics of Fatigue and Unrest* (1924).

Goldmann, F., and Grotjohn, A., *Benefits of the German Sickness Insurance System* (1928).

Hutchins, B. L., and Harrison, A., *History of Factory Legislation* (1911).

Johnston, G. A., *International Social Progress* (1924).

Pinchbeck, I., *Women Workers and the Industrial Revolution* (1930).

Polany, K., *The Great Transformation* (1944).

Redford, A., *Labour Migration in England, 1800–1850* (1926).

Schwenitz, C., *The Road to Social Security* (1943).

Vernon, H. M., *Industrial Fatigue and Efficiency* (1921).

Williams, H. (ed.), *Man and the Machine* (1934).

The Treaty of Versailles, part xiii.

ARTICLES

Derry, T. K., "Repeal of the Apprenticeship Clauses of the Statute of Apprentices," *Ec. H. R.,* January, 1931.

Florence, P. S., "The Theory of Women's Wages," *Ec. J.,* March, 1931.

Gregory, T. E., "Rationalization and Technological Unemployment," *Ec. J.,* December, 1930.

Oualid, W., "Foreign Workers in France," *Int. Lab. Rev.,* August, 1929.

Renold, C. G., "The Present Position of Skill in Industry," *Ec. J.,* December, 1928.

Shannon, H. A., "Migration and the Growth of London, 1841–1891," *Ec. H. R.,* April, 1935.

Ward, G., "The Education of Factory Child Workers," *Ec. Hist.,* February, 1935.

Encyclopaedia of the Social Sciences: See list of articles on Labor and Industry in vol. xv, pp. 551 and 552.

Students who have access to the publications of the International Labor Office will find there a mine of information. See especially the *International Labor Review* (monthly), *Industrial and Labor Information* (weekly), and the numerous special reports and studies. The *Labour Gazette* (British), *Monthly Labor Review* (U.S. Bureau of Labor Statistics), and Canadian *Labor Gazette* contain much European news on labor affairs.

XXXI

THE LABOR MOVEMENT

While the state erected some defenses around labor, wage earners built some for themselves. The trade union sought to protect the worker as earner; the consumers' cooperative society served him as spender; and when unions joined forces with socialist parties or built up a party of their own the labor movement ran on three wheels—unionism, cooperation, and politics.

The story of trade unionism has three facets. The first is the actual building of the organization, the search for the best type of structure, and the effort to win and keep members. This task was easiest among skilled workers—printers, cloth dressers, cutlers, shipwrights, mechanics, and others who possessed qualities of hand or head gained by long training and who felt a sense of group solidarity as well as a desire to protect their talents. The organization of semi-skilled, unskilled, casual, or women workers was difficult, came late, and was least successful.

The second aspect of the story is the union's relationship with employers. The central aim was to "take wages out of competition," to replace individual contracts between workman and employer by collective bargains, and to obtain standard rates, standard hours, and standard conditions which would prevent anyone from undercutting his fellows by offering to work more cheaply. The first step toward this objective was "recognition"; employers had to be persuaded or compelled to recognize the union and to deal with its official as a representative of their own employees. This was often regarded by employers as unjustifiable interference and dictation by outsiders, as a pill too bitter to be swallowed. The fight over recognition was therefore frequently long and fierce; but sooner or later recognition was conceded, thus paving the way to peaceful negotiation, to conciliation, or even to willingness to accept the arbitration of some third party. In the last resort each side retained the right to fight—

740

labor by striking, the employer by locking the men out of his plant; but that last resort became more remote and was reached only after all efforts had failed to find a mutually acceptable settlement.

The third aspect of the story is the changing relationship between unions and the state. At first governments in all countries were hostile: unions were illegal in England until 1824 and until forty or more years later on the continent. When they ceased to be illegal they did not immediately become legal persons, and even when legal personality had been granted them some of their actions might still be unlawful. Their bargains with employers were not contracts enforceable in court. The state was not interested in the way capital and labor were dealing with each other, and there was no reason why it should be if those dealings ran smoothly. When, however, occasional outbursts of industrial warfare demanded public attention by causing considerable economic injury and dislocation to the whole community, the state was obliged to abandon its indifference toward capital-labor relationships. It might take steps to mediate in disputes, foster conciliation, offer to arbitrate, or pass some law which settled a first-class conflict. On the continent during and after World War I, governments went much farther. Sweden in 1915 declared that collective bargains were legally binding and ordered each side peaceably to observe them. Australia had been building up a whole system of compulsory arbitration since before 1900. Post-war Germany, France, and Italy took steps to encourage or command collective bargaining, to settle disputes if the parties failed to do so, and to make settlements generally binding. In the United States governments swung almost overnight during the 1930's from hostility or indifference to policies which made collective bargaining virtually compulsory.

While these changes took place in the attitude of the state toward unions, there were changes in the attitude of unions toward the state. A hostile state naturally made unions hostile; but when wage earners secured the vote and became political-minded, especially after about 1870, the platforms of old political parties began to be influenced by the demands which unions made or by the need for their support. In Britain the new Labor party's program combined various economic, social, and political reforms, such as workingmen desired, with hopes of a gradual approach to a socialist state in which the "means of production, distribution, and exchange" would be publicly owned. On the continent the language of labor leaders was more revolutionary, but the accomplishment was only mildly reformist until Russia put talk to the test.

Trade Unionism in Great Britain. Throughout the eighteenth century industrial wage earners became more and more accustomed to joint action. A town or village inn provided a natural meeting place in which to discuss their problems. Sometimes they came together to resist an attack on their wages or hours or to demand an improvement, and dispersed when the dispute was over; but in some occupations there were associations which may have started as clubs to help the sick and unemployed but had gone on to protect the employed as well. Some of them were strong enough—and on occasion violent enough—to enforce their demand for a minimum wage, to forbid the employment of "snakes" (non-members), to fix a maximum age for the indenturing of apprentices, and to ban the introduction of new machines or processes. The member of a union in one part of the country was welcomed and looked after by kindred groups in other areas if he went seeking work. The last decade of the century witnessed a great increase in this organized activity. Men employed in the cotton mills formed societies, miners were grouping together, cloth finishers were protesting against new equipment, and various workers were demanding that the old apprenticeship law of 1563 be enforced to check the entry of untrained men into factory jobs. High prices, war strain, and revolutionary ideas ruffled the water at times.

Combinations by workers to bring pressure on employers to secure higher wages or shorter hours were regarded by British common law as conspiracies. Employers sometimes took cases to the quarter sessions or assize courts, but these courts met so infrequently that offenders had time to run away. At various times from 1720 onward employers therefore petitioned parliament to pass laws making combination in their particular industry an offense that could be summarily dealt with by a local justice. About forty such laws were passed, and in 1799 the London millwrights, harassed by a strike which brought their work to a standstill, asked for one. Wilberforce suggested that it might be better to pass a *general* act than to continue doling out more private laws. This was done; then the first "combination law" as it came to be called was repealed in 1800 in favor of another one which required action by two local judges (instead of one) and included a provision for arbitration of disputes between masters and men.

The combination laws were almost dead letters and little more was heard of them until an agitation began later on for their repeal. There were very few prosecutions under them, more under the common law, and still more under a provision of the act of 1563 which forbade men to leave work unfinished. This last weapon was most useful against men who went on strike. Yet in spite of the triple legal threat, unions continued to grow, even if they had sometimes to grow underground. Masters either did not dare or did not wish to attack them, and in the well-organized occupations collective bargaining continued more or less openly. In 1824 a parliamentary inquiry found that all attempts to ban combinations had been ineffective except in producing mutual irritation and distrust and giving a violent character to some unions, thus rendering them dangerous to the peace of the community. This verdict, given at a time when war emotions were well on the road to complete demobilization, led to the repeal of the combination laws (1824) and the removal of the taint of conspiracy from labor associations. The result was an open outburst of organizing activity and a series of strikes, for trade was booming and workers wished to lift their wages above the levels of the preceding depressed years. Frightened by this new birth of freedom, parliament in 1825 said that while combinations were not illegal any act of violence, threat, intimidation, or force was a penal offense. Unions could live but must walk circumspectly.

During the next quarter-century labor spent much of its time chasing mirages. The period was one of expansion and of change. The former was marred by severe depressions after 1825, after 1836, and in 1847–1848. The latter injured those manual workers, such as handloom weavers, whose labor faced growing competition from machines, and at the same time created new working conditions which often were unpleasant. Men who did not like what was growing up around them listened to those who painted pictures of a new and easily attainable heaven on earth. The air was full of agitation and proposals of all kinds, not merely for such things as parliamentary reform, factory acts, or the repeal of the Corn Laws but for more fundamental changes such as the abolition of alcohol, meat, private property, and competition. In France the drawing of blueprints for Utopia went on apace. The ideas of Saint-Simon, Proudhon, Fourier, and Louis Blanc found much favor, since they envisaged a happier social system that could be created almost overnight by the adoption of some such rational principle or policy as the abolition of private property and the planning of production for the benefit of all.

In England and for some years in America Robert Owen prophesied the dawning of a cooperative commonwealth if only enough little cooperative communities were set up to serve as examples. Then he became fascinated by the potential power of labor organization and in 1833 founded the Grand National Consolidated Trades Union. Into this "one big union" he sought to gather existing local craft unions and also to cover the country with lodges which would enroll all kinds of workers, male and female, skilled and unskilled, rural and urban. This mighty army would use its invincible force to demand an eight-hour day and stage a general strike if its request was rejected. It would then proceed to "transform existing society into a Socialist community by taking over industry and running it cooperatively" (Cole).

The "Consolidated" was aggressive in temper, tongue, and tactics. Its leaders seemed to expect that the walls of Jericho would crumble before their manifestoes. Employers replied by producing what became known as "the Document," and demanded that their employees sign this declaration that they were not members of a union, under pain of losing their jobs. Strikes and lockouts, often marked by great violence, ended disastrously for labor. In 1834 six farm laborers of Tolpuddle (Dorsetshire) who were organizing a lodge were arrested and "transported" to Australia for having taken secret oaths (in violation of an old forgotten law passed at the time of a naval mutiny in 1797). Finally, the union was torn with internal dissension and was dead before the panic of 1836 ushered in dark days for labor and capital alike.

During the next ten years Chartism was the new gospel. Salvation was to be won by securing a parliament consisting of representatives chosen under secret ballot by universal male suffrage at annual elections and paid a salary for their services. The agitation for such parliamentary reform was mixed up with a motley of economic panaceas and was conducted, especially in depressed times, by torchlight processions, plots for revolution, machine-breaking, and strikes. It was both an irritant and a stimulant; it failed to realize any of its political program, but it did stir its opponents to advocate the repeal of the Corn Laws and the passage of the ten-hour factory act and other measures which improved labor conditions.

Amid the noise and the grandiose schemes some local craft unions of skilled workers had managed to grow, and in 1851 they created what became known as the New Model for labor organization. That model was the Amalgamated Society of Engineers (A.S.E.), created by a fusion of several local or sectional unions of engineers, machinists, blacksmiths, and kindred metalworkers. It limited membership to certain properly trained skilled artisans. Its constitution concentrated control in the central office in London and imposed strict discipline on the branches, especially in such matters as starting a strike. Its officials were competent administrators rather than Owenite visionaries or Chartist firebrands, and their business was to develop collective bargaining and settle disputes peacefully whenever possible. It welcomed publicity, avoided the fantastic secret society ritual of some of its predecessors, and set out to destroy the bourgeois distrust of unionism by letting all see that it had no revolutionary or subversive intentions. Finally, it was a friendly society as well as a trade union. Its members paid large weekly dues and in return received aid when they were sick, unemployed, or old, as well as when they were on strike. This aid kept members loyal and solid.

The New Model worked well, not merely because it tried to be "calm, prudent, temperate, and enlightened" (Cole), but also because it was born at a good time, at the beginning of the upward secular trend. Other skilled trades copied its policy. Between 1851 and 1890 the fourteen largest unions disbursed nearly £8,000,000 in benefits. About half this money went to help unemployed members and nearly a quarter to the sick; 8 per cent was spent on giving members a decent funeral, and only 6 per cent was strike pay. Unionism had evidently found the right track. In the sixties its legal position became obscured by the courts but seemed to be cleared up by acts of 1867 to 1876. Under these laws unions could register, and thus buy, hold, and protect property. The right to strike was assured, strikers could peacefully persuade others to leave their work, and no action taken by a union was to be illegal unless it would be illegal if committed by an individual. Further, the union was a registered body but not a corporation. Its funds could not be called on to pay for any damage or loss of trade caused by a strike. This immunity was shattered in 1901 when the Taff Vale Railway Company sued the union to which its striking employees belonged and was granted £23,000 for damage done when two hundred men left their jobs without giving notice. In 1906, however, the Trade Disputes Act repaired the rent in union immunity and said that unions could not be sued for breaches of contract or "tortious acts" committed in the course of a labor dispute.

Collective Bargaining. Recognition came slowly; in the thirties, the fifties, and later some employers resorted to the use of "the Document." When it had been granted, the way was open for peaceful discussion of disputes, and in 1860 the Nottingham hosiery trade established a conciliation board. On it sat an equal number of representatives of each side, and if it failed to reach agreement an arbitrator was called in. Below it were district and factory subcommittees which settled most matters without bothering the central board. During the discussions work continued undisturbed; but if in the last resort the arbitrator's award was unsatisfactory to either side, a strike or lockout was permissible.

The Nottingham plan or something akin to it was widely copied. Most large industries established permanent machinery and methods of procedure for dealing with disputes or with matters that might lead to disputes. Acts of 1896 and 1908 gave the Board of Trade power to arbitrate or appoint a conciliation board if asked to do so by conflicting parties, or to mediate between disputants if it saw a chance of bringing a quarrel to an end. Between 1900 and 1909, 7,500 disputes—750 a year—came before the 300 boards or standing joint committees. Only 104—10 a year—went away unsettled to cause a stoppage of work. These figures suggested that the day of industrial warfare was passing; but the years 1911–1913 belied the hope, for war in the mining, transport, and other industries shook the country, and a scheme was hatched for a "Triple Alliance" of miners, railroadmen, and water transport workers, binding 1,350,000 workers together (1914). Yet in 1911 about 4,500 disputes went to conciliation or arbitration, and only 13 of them led to a stoppage of work.

The Spread of Unionism. After 1890 unionism spread from the skilled crafts both upward and downward. In 1888 the ill-paid girls in a London match factory struck successfully. In 1889 ten thousand dock workers paralyzed the port of London for five weeks, attracted world-wide support in their claim for six pence an hour, and won a great victory. These successes contradicted the belief that unskilled or casual workers could not be organized. At the same time the "blackcoat brigade"—teachers, clerks, shopworkers, civil servants, musicians, and actors—began to realize that in days of rising prices the preservation of their standard of living could be guaranteed only by united action. Between 1892 and 1913 the membership of British unions rose from 1,600,000 to 4,100,000.

This broadening of membership was accompanied by changes in policy and methods. The unskilled unions could not collect high dues from low-wage workers, could not undertake friendly society work, but must concentrate on improving labor conditions. Some of their leaders were soaked in the ideas of Henry George, William Morris, John Ruskin, or even Karl Marx, for a wave of economic self-criticism was sweeping the country as it had done in the 1830's. The Great Depression was making farmers and other entrepreneurs dissatisfied with their lot. The better-paid wage earners were well off, but there was much concern over that fraction of the population —a third, if London was a fair sample—which was living below a meager poverty line. Young intellectuals had formed the Fabian Society (1884) and were seeking ways to reach socialism by install-ments through national and local political action. Some workmen were buying red ties and reading Robert Blatchford's peppery socialist newspaper, the *Clarion*. A few were trying to understand the translated first volume of Marx's *Capital*.

Even the old unions felt the need for adding the political weapon to their armory. In 1874 the miners of Northumberland won a seat in the House of Commons for their leader, Thomas Burt, and in 1885 ten unionists were elected, but they had no distinct Labor creed and ranked as good loyal Liberals. In 1900, however, various socialist bodies and the Trades Union Congress (which was the heart of the trade-union movement) came together in what became known as the Labor party in 1906. The unions supplied the funds, many of the candidates, and most of the votes, while the socialists supplied many of the planks for the platform. In 1909 a court ruling (the Osborne judgment) forbade the unions to make political levies on their members, but an act of 1913 permitted them to do so, provided that members who did not wish to contribute to a party which was not theirs could claim exemption.

Organized labor now had a chance to pursue its aims along two roads. On the political road it was soon able to accomplish much. It won 29 seats (out of 50 contested) in an election of 1906, and 42 (out of the 670 in the House of Commons) in 1910. It supported social legislation introduced by the Liberal government, and as that government was dependent on the Labor vote for a majority after 1910 the new party's influence was greater than its size. The reversal of the Taff Vale and Osborne judgments, the payment of members of parliament, and the introduction of insurance schemes and old-age pensions helped the unionist and his union. Laws improving workmen's compensation, giving the miner an eight-hour day and a minimum wage, establishing trade boards to eliminate sweating, stamping out the last traces of nightwork for women in industry, and improving conditions in retail stores—all these owed much to the presence of the small but strategically strong Labor group in parliament.

Valuable as these reforms were, they brought the socialist part of the party's program no nearer to fulfillment. Further, they did nothing to check the wave of rising prices or to lift wages. Some wage earners therefore grew dissatisfied with political action and listened to ideas that were slipping across from France. In that country labor leaders were declaring that French experience had proved the state was useless to wage earners, that political action was futile, and that economic ends must be sought by industrial means, which meant by strikes. This combination of high prices, disillusion, and imported ideas was partly responsible for the outburst of strikes between 1910 and 1913. The strikes did some good, forced some wages up, and drove parliament to provide a minimum wage for miners. But they were costly, drained union funds, and brought to light the strength of the employers' organizations. Hence war in 1914 found both sides strengthening the weak spots in their armor, making alliances, and filling war chests.

Labor and World War I. By early 1915 it was evident that the conflict was going to be a mechanic's war. The Munitions Act of 1915 organized capital and labor for such a fight. Labor accepted compulsory arbitration, virtually abandoned the right to strike, and agreed to the suspension of all trade-union rules which "might restrict production or employment." Unionism had kept the boundary lines between crafts almost as clear as did the medieval guildsman. One job was a bricklayer's task, another a mason's; the shipwright and the boilermaker, the plumber and the coppersmith all had their preserves marked out by rule or tradition, and the line between the skilled man and the laborer was equally sharply drawn. Now all such restrictions were to be cast aside for the duration of the war, and skilled labor could be "diluted." In return for these sacrifices by labor, employers' profits were to be limited and all excess profits were to be handed over to the state. Eventually the whole field of mining, manufacture, and transportation was controlled by the state. The wage-regulating activities of the trade boards were extended, and farm laborers' wages were fixed in the same way. There was much inevitable friction, delay in adjusting wages, suspicion of victimization, and hatred of profiteering. In addition, nerves were wracked by overtime, deficient food or housing, long casualty lists, and growing doubt concerning the real aims of the war.

Peace brought a great release of discontent, a brief boom in employment and prices, a welter of ideas, and a vast expansion in union membership. The enrollment in 1920 (8,350,000) was double that of 1913. The high prices led to strikes in quest of higher wages, and when the boom burst strikes sought to prevent wage cuts. In three years (1919–1921) 3,700 disputes affecting 6,000,000 workers involved a loss of 150,000,000 working days.

With prices falling, the post-war boom collapsing, and the staple industries headed for difficult days, attempts to prevent wage reductions were futile. The engineers were locked out for three months in 1922; the miners were locked out when they refused reductions in wages in 1921 and 1926; and on each of these three occasions labor was defeated. In the 1926 coal struggle the miners had for a few days the support of the General Council of the Trades Union Congress, which since 1921 had been a headquarters staff of the union world. The Council called a general strike in May, and for nine days virtually no trains, buses, or streetcars moved, no newspapers were printed, no building work was done, and no power was generated. But the strike leadership was weak and confused, the government took a strong line, the country refused to be paralyzed, and the strike collapsed. The miners resisted till November before admitting defeat. The stoppage damaged the coal industry and many others as well. It led parliament to pass a law banning general strikes and forbidding unions to collect political levies except from members who definitely said they wished to pay them. From the tragedy of 1926 onward there were very few disturbances of industrial peace

The gains of the war years were by no means all lost during the twenties and thirties. The range of collective bargaining remained widespread and even included the civil service. In 1931 the earnings of about 8,000,000 workers were determined by collective bargaining or by the state. The trend to a shorter week was not reversed. The high money wages of the war years did not fall as much as did prices, and Professor Bowley estimates that *real* wages in general were almost a third higher in 1937 than in 1914. This improvement was most marked in the newer, expanding industries, the unskilled, and other low-paid occupations. In Britain as in most other countries the gap between the worst-paid and best-paid workers was greatly narrowed, not so much by lowering the wages of the latter as by raising those of the former. For this development, repeated in World War II, trade unionism could claim only a part of the credit.

The Labor Party. During the inter-war period the political wing of the labor movement displaced the Liberal party as one of the two chief parties in British politics. In 1918 it widened its appeal to attract "workers by hand and brain," with a platform of social reform and of socialism to be reached by a gradual process of parliamentary action. Though snowed under in the election held just after the Armistice (1918), Labor won nearly 200 seats in 1923 and ran the government with Liberal support until it was defeated by the Conservatives in 1924. Five years later Labor came back to power again with Liberal support; but the steps that were deemed essential to cope with the financial panic of 1931 offended many of the Labor rank and file, split the party, and led to an election in which a few Labor leaders, a few Liberals, and an army of Conservatives were returned as a "national government" with a huge majority, smothering the official Labor party in the landslide. In effect the Conservative party ran Britain for the next nine years. Then in the dark days of the German blitz over western Europe, Neville Chamberlain gave place to Winston Churchill and a national government containing several Labor leaders (May, 1940).

This coalition carried the country through the rest of the war but was dissolved when victory came in Europe. The election of July, 1945, astounded everybody, including Labor. That party won about 400 seats, against about 50 in 1931 and 150 in 1935, thus gaining an overwhelming majority in the House of Commons and receiving the sort of untrammeled power that democratic peoples have so often conferred on governments in time of crisis. Such power carried with it the triple responsibility for handling the problems of domestic reconversion, dealing with the international settlement, and turning the party's socialization program into policy.

Of the three, only the last concerns us here. The question of private versus public ownership had long since ceased to be argued on grounds of abstract principles. In the early days of the socialist agitation the plea for a change had often been inspired by the belief that "production for use rather than for profit" would end "exploitation" and divert large sums of profit from private pockets to higher wages for the worker as well as lower prices for the consumer. Though this desire to eliminate the "bloated capitalist" might still appeal to some, the emphasis had shifted by the inter-war years. There were few profits to be distributed from land, railroads, steel, or coal nowadays. Public enterprise came to be regarded as the only way to reorganize and refinance these sick veterans and make their efficient operation once more possible. It was advocated as a more rational and economical way of rendering such services as electrical generation, radio broadcasting, port facilities, or city transportation; and Conservative governments were responsible for the creation of the "public corporations" which generated and transmitted the electricity (1926), operated British radio (1927), and managed London's traffic service (1933). Finally, some services, such as overseas aviation and the Bank of England, were so intimately connected with the government that public ownership seemed a logical step.

Labor's list of enterprises slated for nationalization reflected these considerations. The Bank of England was nationalized in 1946 by buying with government bonds the shares of the stockholders. Coal mining became a public enterprise at the beginning of 1947, inland transportation at the beginning of 1948, and civil aviation in 1946. The rest of the list of achieved or proposed transfers included overseas cable and radio communication, electrical supply, and possibly parts of the iron and steel industry. The omissions from the list were notable—manufacturing industries, agriculture, commerce, shipping, and most banking. It was officially claimed that the completed program would cover only 20 per cent of the economy, leaving the remainder "under private ownership and 'free enterprise.'" These percentages mean little in view of the vital importance of the central bank, coal, and the railroads to the rest of the economy. The quality and cost of the goods and services they render, the wages level and the political power their employees enjoy, and the methods that are used to provide incentives to full effort and innovation all will influence conditions and results throughout the country's enterprise.

Unionism on the Continent. Labor associations came later to the continent than to Britain. Only after 1890 was much progress made. By 1912, however, there were about 7,000,000 unionists, half of them in Germany. War and its aftermath brought a great expansion in membership and influence, but depression and dictatorship caused a heavy decline in strength or economic power.

The late start was in part due to the late industrialization. It was also partly due to the fact that many skilled workers were employees in small shops. Only in mining, railroad work, the heavy metal industries, and the textile mills were large numbers of workers gathered together. The predominance of women in the mills and complicated piece rates weakened unionism in the textile industry. In the other occupations the opposition of employers and of the state was protracted and bitter. There were many benevolent despots among German industrialists, paternal and philanthropic, ready to pay good wages and provide for their people's welfare; but some despots were not benevolent, and all alike regarded the union official as an impertinent intruder. They refused to recognize or negotiate, formed employers' unions, talked labor matters over in their cartels, and resorted frequently to the lockout with the frank intention of smashing a union or exhausting its funds.

The hostility of the state died slowly, and some outburst of revolutionary sentiment or socialist propaganda often put new life into it just when it seemed to be expiring. The restrictions imposed on labor associations in France in 1791 were not fully withdrawn till 1884. Belgium in 1866 allowed unions to be formed, but its penal code contained a clause against strikes till 1921. In Germany unionism really got going in 1868, under the auspices of two socialist bodies which in 1875 fused into the Social Democratic party. Bismarck therefore made little distinction between the political and industrial wings when in 1878 he set out to kill the socialist movement, and he declared both of them illegal. In ten years over a hundred unions were compulsorily dissolved. Not till 1890 was the ban removed; the unions' legal position was unclear for much longer. In Russia a limited permission to organize was granted in 1906. These hostile attitudes fell far short of achieving their full purpose —men found ways around them and still more under them—but they did prevent normal development.

The close association between socialism and unionism led to the establishment of non-socialist associations. The "Radical" unions which Max Hirsch began to form in Germany in 1868 repudiated political action, sought amicable relations with employers, and did friendly society work. After 1890 the Catholic Church began to form unions, for it feared that its laity might be drawn into the socialist fold and imbibe the anti-religious doctrines often preached there. German unionism therefore marched under three banners—"free" (Social Democratic), Radical, and Christian. The armies were very unequal in size, for while the free unions in 1913 had over 2,500,000 members, the Christian unions had only 350,000 and the Radical only 100,000. This division of forces was found in other countries where Catholicism was strong, e.g., in Austria, Holland, and Belgium. In some countries differences of nationality divided workers: Czechs and Germans had separate camps in Bohemia; Belgium had its socialist unions, its Catholic unions, and also its Flemish and Walloon groups. In all cases the non-socialist or anti-socialist bodies were relatively small.

Continental unionism was seen at its best in the German free unions. They were few in number but large in size; in 1914 there were only 47 of them and in 1931 only 30, against over 1,100 in Great Britain. The German Metal Workers' Federation was for a time the largest union in the world, with 900,000 members in 1928. The giants were allied in the General Commission of Trade Unions which was founded in 1890 to direct developments when the ban on unionism was lifted. Though the free unions worked in close contact with the Social Democratic party, their business was economic, not political. They concentrated on securing better wages, hours, and working conditions and provided friendly society benefits. The large-scale and heavy industries were the most difficult to influence, but even there some concessions had been won before 1914. In 1910 alone nearly 10,000 "movements" (collective bargains) reduced hours for 1,300,000 workers and increased wages for 800,000. Of these movements, two-thirds were settled peacefully. Some unions ran labor exchanges, much money was spent on libraries, lectures, classes, and daily or weekly papers, and the General Commission ran a school for training union officials.

The First World War greatly strengthened the Social Democratic party and the unions. The former voted for the war credits when the conflict began and occupied a more responsible position in the country's affairs as the years went by. The unions gained in prestige and experience because of the part they played in helping to deal with wartime labor problems. When revolution came, the strength of the party and of the unions helped to avert the threat of a Communist seizure of the country. One Socialist became president of the new republic and another its first chancellor. A flood of workers and ex-soldiers raised union membership from about 3,000,000 in 1913 to over 9,000,000 in 1920.

All things therefore combined to insure that the new Weimar constitution and the laws of the Republic would guarantee labor's position, rights, and wishes in the most generous terms. The state regarded collective bargaining as the best assurance of the public welfare, and the free unions as the official voice of labor in such bargaining. It offered to mediate if discussions were not going smoothly. If a bargain was not reached, the mediator was to make his own proposal for a settlement; if either side accepted this proposal it became binding on the other; and all settlements, however reached, were to be made legally binding not merely on the contracting parties but on the industry generally. There were also to be works councils in each factory; in them elected representatives of the employees would discuss with the employer such matters as accident prevention, health, pension funds, and working conditions, and examine complaints of unfair dismissal. There were to be district councils, and at the head a Central Economic Council which would advise the government on industrial matters and initiate or examine bills dealing with social or economic questions. Finally, the eight-hour day was established by law, and the constitution provided for the socialization or public control of industry. Industrially and politically the German labor movement thus attained a position of power and responsibility.

That position was in large measure retained during the twenties. During the chaos and inflation of 1919–1923 labor tried to keep prices down and, failing in that, to push wages up; and in one crucial period in 1920 a general strike seemed to help in breaking a monarchist *Putsch*. When conditions became more stable in 1924, collective bargaining advanced, and in 1929 three-fourths of all wages and salaries were determined either by voluntary agreements or by the decisions of mediators who had become in effect judges in labor courts. The unions welcomed these courts, since the verdicts they gave were usually higher than could have been obtained by negotiation between employers and the union. In the opinion of employers and some outside observers, however, the rates fixed were too high to allow profitable employment of all available workers, and they stimulated industries to "rationalizing" efforts at labor-saving which increased the volume of unemployment. Meanwhile the party remained fairly strong. In 1928 it provided the leading members of the Reich cabinet and controlled the government of the leading state, Prussia. Though no longer the left wing, it was confronted by the traditional attacks from the military, conservative, and capitalistic right; but in addition it was under constant heavy fire from the Communists and from the Nazis. It had thus become almost "middle of the road," shot at from both sides, and its own strategy lacked imagination or resolution in dealing with its enemies.

By mid-1933 the organized labor movement had been wiped out. In January of that year the unemployment figure stood officially at 6,000,000, and there may have been another million unrecorded; over two-fifths of the unionists were entirely out of work; and Hitler became chancellor. Then followed the rapid destruction of the party and of the unions, the arrest of their leaders, and the seizure of their property. Freedom of association, the right to strike or lockout, and the whole machinery of collective bargaining all vanished. The property and funds of the unions were annexed by the Labor Front, that part of the Nazi scheme of government to which was allotted the task of handling labor affairs. The new policy was to be guided by the principles of unity in place of class struggle, and of leadership by the employer under strict control from the state.

The Labor Front regulated wages and hours. It promptly forbade changes in the former but raised the latter, especially when rearmament created a labor shortage. It allowed the old shop councils to continue but filled them with party nominees. It set up "Social Honor Courts" to punish "leaders" (employers) who exploited their "followers" or "retinue" (employees) and to deal severely with followers who started agitation among their fellows. It preached the need for better factory conditions and surroundings. It organized and directed the facilities for leisure, recreation, and vacations as a vast "Strength through Joy" tourist and holiday accommodation service. It managed the social insurance schemes and collected the workers' contributions for them, as well as a 6 per cent wage tax for the unemployment reserve fund and another levy which was to be spent on the Front's general activities. It assumed authority over employers' associations.

These policies, decked out in sentimental labels and amounting to a complete regimentation of labor, would have been empty mockeries if they had not been accompanied by a marked revival of employment to which they contributed little. The eviction of Jews, non-Nazis, and women from their jobs found work for some who had been idle. Relief work found much more, and the general world recovery which became noticeable in the spring of 1933 helped to cut the number of unemployed in half between 1932 and 1934. Conscription and rearmament reduced the figure still more and by 1938 there was a scarcity of labor.

This recovery brought an intensification, rather than a relaxation, of control. In 1938 universal labor conscription was definitely established. Men were bound to their jobs and could be moved wherever they were needed. The limit on the working day was extended from eight hours to ten and removed from the munitions industry. The seizure of Austria and of part of Czechoslovakia added to the potential labor force available for conscription. When war came, prisoners or inhabitants of occupied territories passed under control, to be used as laborers and to be transported to other regions if need ' be. The International Labor Office estimated in 1945 that at least 30,000,000 foreigners, including men and their dependents, passed under such control and that a considerable number of them were transferred willingly or otherwise to German soil, thus helping to create the "displaced persons" problem of post-war days. There had never before been such a vast mobilization or migration of foreign labor; there had never before in modern times, save in Soviet Russia, been such a peacetime economic conscription of subjects by their own state as that which Germany carried out before 1939; and there had never been such a vacuum created in the voluntary organization of labor as that of 1933.

French Syndicalism. In most other continental countries unions and the parliamentary socialist movement grew side by side. If the unionist had a vote he cast it for socialist candidates and for their program, which talked in Marxian phrases of class struggle and social revolution. That revolution, according to Marx, would come inexorably some day when capitalism, operating under "the laws of motion" which governed its actions, broke down, fell apart, or exploded; but its coming might be hastened if socialists gave it a helping hand and prepared themselves for the great day. The assistance could be of two kinds: the one peaceful and parliamentary, the other violent; the one a triumph of words, the other the victory of action. The first seemed the most acceptable, easy, and safe. "The proletariat cannot effect the passing of the means of production into the ownership of the community without acquiring political power," said the Erfurt Social Democratic program of 1891. Hence the cause of political democracy had to be advanced by fighting for fully representative responsible legislatures, with freedom of speech, association, and press. Then elections had to be fought in the faith that some day one of them would return such a large majority of socialists to the legislature that socialism could be ushered in by passing the necessary laws. Pending that time, socialist parties could fight for better labor laws or social services and fight against militarism, aristocratic or plutocratic privilege, or imperialism.

By the early twentieth century there was enough experience to show that this path was doomed to be long and tedious, strewn with obstacles and marked with false guideposts. Elections were hard to win, wage earners were slow in becoming class-conscious, and when a socialist party gained some influence its leaders, especially those who were admitted to such coalition cabinets as were common in France, quickly mellowed from a bright red to a pale pink or even a yellowish hue. On the soapbox men waved the class-struggle sword; when they got into office they swallowed it. They discovered that legislative power availed little if the civil service, army, and courts were in hostile hands. In their obsession as a pressure group with the interests of their supporters they had failed to see the wider problems of politics. They had taken capitalism for granted as a system that would continue to provide jobs and wages while they attacked it. Then when they got into office they were confronted by the realities, complexities, and limitations of political action and either failed to cope with them in time or had to do so by taking steps which alienated their supporters. In short, political effort did not move any country much nearer to socialism or even do much to improve the wage earner's lot under capitalism.

The search for a shorter cut than through the ballot box therefore began to attract those who were disillusioned as well as those who were temperamentally malcontents. To Frenchmen the general strike seemed to offer a better way. The class struggle should be fought with industrial, not political, weapons. If every worker in every industry put down his tools at an agreed signal, capitalists would soon admit defeat and in sheer despair would surrender their property. Instead, however, of handing the industries over to the state to be run by a civil service and a minister who would be as bad an employer as his predecessor, the victorious strikers would keep the industries in their own hands. The miners would run the pits, the railroad men would operate the railroads, and so forth. The fighting unions of today would become the producing and controlling groups of tomorrow.

This doctrine—known as syndicalism because a French union is called a *syndicat*—became the program of the *Confédération Générale du Travail* (the C.G.T.), formed in 1895 to unite countless small unions which had been divided in allegiance between several socialist factions. The C.G.T. sponsored some strikes, but they were neither general nor successful. It staged anti-military or anti-patriotic demonstrations; but when the test came in 1914 it turned patriot, cooperated with the government, and made friends with the socialists. In 1920 it did call a general strike to enforce its demand for the nationalization of the railroads, but was badly beaten and terribly weakened.

By that time a new approach to social revolution had become visible. The Bolsheviks had regarded their Russian venture as the first stage of a general European-wide revolt. "Final victory is possible only on a world scale," said Lenin, and could be won only by strategical and tactical methods of a new brand. Parliamentary action was useful only in providing a sounding board for communist propaganda, for discrediting capitalists and socialists alike, and for pouring sand into political bearings. The revolution must come through an eventual *coup d'état*, skillfully and patiently prefaced by building new unions, infiltrating into key positions in old ones, capitalizing on every legitimate labor grievance, inventing causes for strikes if none existed, weakening the loyalty of armed forces and the police, and seeking employment in public or private places where influence could be wielded or valuable information picked up. This general destruction of solidarity and morale would open the door, when the time was ripe, for the seizure of key economic and political points by a militant revolutionary minority, the establishment of a dictatorship by this group (but called a "dictatorship of the proletariat"), the liquidation of the bourgeoisie and the bourgeois state, and so on to whatever was necessary in consolidating the victory and defying the counter-revolution.

The failure of the German Communists to capture control of the revolution in their country in 1918 was a bitter disappointment, for a communist Germany was regarded as a vital bulwark against an attack on Russia and as an easy route to western Europe. The Communist International, formed in Moscow in early 1919, did not, however, lose heart. It worked hard on Germany and in close cooperation with the Communists in that country, and its skill in sowing dissension inside the labor movement, as well as hatred outside, eased the way for the Nazi dictatorship.

France ranked second only to Germany as a field for Communist energy. The political socialist movement split in 1918 when most of its members went off to form a Communist party. The C.G.T. was similarly divided and the Communist wing was ejected in 1922, going off to form unions and a federation of its own which was ever ready to rush into disputes for propaganda purposes, even when the hope of victory was slight. Rid of its reds, the C.G.T. turned to the policies it had spurned in its turbulent youth—to collective bargaining, shorter hours, better wage contracts, friendly society benefits, and a social insurance law. There was plenty of work for it to do, as French labor conditions lagged behind those of Britain or Germany. But depression checked the improvement, recovery was delayed by the unwillingness to devalue the franc, while the political scene was darkened by fascist developments at home, the resurgence of Germany on France's eastern border, and the developments in Italy and Spain.

Faced with this multiple menace, the C.G.T. and its Communist enemy amalgamated; the unions joined with the Socialist and Communist parties; one or two other parties came in, and the Popular Front thus created swept the polls at a general election in 1936. Victory was followed by steps to fulfill part of the Front's pledges: a forty-hour week with no reduction in pay, several extra holidays with pay, wages increases, enforcement of collective bargains, the nationalization of the Bank of France, and plans for nationalizing the armaments industry. Most of these reforms may have been long overdue, but they were unrealistic and irrelevant in face of France's domestic crisis and of the European situation. Their tragic effect was to reduce French production at the moment when Germany was adding to working hours and industrial man power. Violent attacks on "the two hundred families" who were said to control the Bank of France were destructive and disturbing to the economy rather than helpful. The policies of 1936 did little to help France get ready for 1939.

Fascism. Syndicalism found fertile soil in Italy. Disputes between sharecroppers and landlords, between rural laborers and owners of great estates, or between factory workers and employers produced a dreary round of "social war, short truces, social war again, martial law" (Finer) in the days before 1914. The parliamentary system worked badly, with too many weak parties full of factions. Labor was divided between Catholic and socialist unions, and by 1914 about 100,000 members had adopted the syndicalist creed. During the war this number was increased, and communism won converts after 1917. When peace came the social war broke out again with added fury. High prices, unemployed ex-soldiers, land hunger, broken promises made by political leaders, and dissatisfaction over Italy's share of the spoils of victory all combined to foment unrest. Some workers evicted owners from their factories and carried on production till they ran out of raw materials. In the country districts estates were seized. Socialists, many of them now Communists, won wider control of local administration, nearly doubled their number in the national legislature, but did nothing to restore order.

Contributing to this wild welter and as raucously radical as any communist, or syndicalist, or anarchist, was Mussolini and his *fascio* (bundle of sticks bound together) of about twoscore followers. Mussolini in his time had explored and expounded most leftist doctrines, including anarchism; he had left the editorship of the Socialist party's paper and the party in 1914 only because of his sudden conversion to the belief that Italy should enter the war on the side of the western powers. His fascist band began with all sorts of demands for economic and political change: a republic with universal adult suffrage, international disarmament, suppression of the stock exchange, dissolution of the banks, the transfer of land to peasants and of factories to the workers. Food riots were encouraged; the stay-in strikes were welcomed as steps to social upheaval.

By 1921 fascism had taken a swing from left to right. Landlords, industrialists, and middle-class shopkeepers felt the need for some refuge and had apparently decided that fascism was the least unsafe harbor—partly on the assumption that a skilled poacher would sometime make a good game warden. The influx of bourgeois and upper-class youths changed Mussolini's outlook. He now sprang forth as champion of order, property, and country against socialists and internationalism. Various cities were invaded and "cleaned up." Then in late 1922 the Fascists decided to march on Rome, where order and stability seemed to be returning to economics and politics. The government did not proclaim martial law, the march was successful, and Mussolini was invited to become premier.

Only part of the sequel concerns us. Mussolini's policy was the suppression of both political and economic opposition. He had no good precedents to guide him in the destruction of liberal democratic institutions and therefore must work out his own methods. By manipulating the electoral laws he gained a majority in the legislature, used his power to pass repressive laws against the press, freedom of association, and voluntary organizations, and in 1928 reduced elections to a plebiscite in which voters were asked whether they approved of a long list of candidates containing about four hundred names. The first plebiscite, in 1929, revealed that the list was approved by 92 per cent of the voters; later dictators were able to do better than that. Parliamentary opposition was thus blotted out.

Meanwhile labor organizations were brought to heel. The doctrine by which this action was justified was enunciated in the Charter of Labor (1927). All individual and class interests must be subordinated to the national welfare, solidarity, and unity—as seen by the Fascist party. The state claimed the right to control all forces of production in the interest of "the moral, political, and economic unity" of the nation. Private enterprise was accepted as the most efficacious way to get work done, but the labor of the entrepreneur, technician, and manual laborer was a "social duty." Employers and employees were free to organize, "but only the syndicate legally recognized and under the control of the State" had any power. Translated into law and stripped of much that was verbiage, these declarations provided for one union in each industry or profession. Each would bargain collectively with the employers' association for that occupation and make agreements binding on the whole industry. Strikes and lockouts were made penal offenses, and any dispute not settled by discussion must go to a labor court. The union officials were appointed by the state, not by the members.

By such provisions the state hoped to keep a tight grip on industry, preserve industrial peace, and prevent labor associations from becoming centers of opposition either to employers or to the party in power. But peace was no guarantee of prosperity, and during the depressed thirties the state extended its control over both capital and labor much further. When Mussolini looked abroad for triumphs, trying to make a country with at best only second-class resources into a first-class power, wage earners and employers alike enjoyed little peace, plenty, or freedom.

Unionism in Russia. Italy and Germany defeated the advocate of the class struggle and put him under authoritarian control in the interests of a controlled capitalism and of an all-powerful one-party state. Russia put him under similar control in the interest of communism and of what was sometimes described as "the conscious vanguard of the working class—the Communist Party." In 1917, trade unionism was weak in Russia. Between the two revolutions of that year, and still more after the second, workers took charge of factories, managers were evicted, new ones were elected, committees or councils were everywhere, and workshops became talkshops. Workers' control of the syndicalist type and labor laws superior to those of the capitalist world were promised. Soon, however, the destruction of capitalism and that of production began to appear synonymous. To keep the wheels turning labor was conscripted, militarized, and tied to its job. Membership in unions was made compulsory, the unions in turn were subjected to complete government control, and strikes were forbidden. The workers' committees were shorn of most of their power, but union and party officials had a voice in factory management.

The New Economic Policy (1921) put the large industries in the hands of state trusts. The directors of these trusts were frequently under fire from the workers' committees or from party and union officials, and unionism developed some of the characteristics of a watchdog for labor. With the inauguration of the Five-Year Plans, the unions were told they had a double duty. While they must continue to protect the cultural, living, and economic interests of their members, they must also stimulate the workers' interest in increased production. The latter was a tremendous task because of the great demand for additional labor, the raw character of the peasants who were pulled into industry, and the heavy "labor turnover" such as took place in 1930, when for every 100 jobs 176 persons were hired and 152 dismissed. To "put the Plan over" was far more important than bothering much with the other side of the union's work—education, recreation, or the protection of members from "exploitation." Management now managed, the day of "workers' control" had gone, and the business of the unions was to be "the most permanent collaborators of the State" in the drive for fulfillment of the production objectives of each successive Plan.

For that drive two stimuli were used—deterrents to poor performance by the worker and incentives to good performance. The former comprised a code of strict discipline. Late arrival at work, absenteeism, and bad workmanship were punished by very heavy fines, deductions from wages, public denunciation, or even loss of job with the consequent loss of living space, ration card, and social security benefits. Incentives took many forms. In the beginning communist doctrine had favored the equal reward of all workers or held out the promise of "to each according to his needs." It had frowned on all thought of different rates for different qualities of work. That equalitarian practice had to be shed quickly, and by 1920 piecework rates, with bonuses for those who did more than a prescribed amount of work, were being paid. During the years of NEP the advocates of equal pay had regained some ground, but the results were so unsatisfactory that in 1931 Stalin denounced the practice and demanded that wage rates be made proportionate to the skill, character, and quantity of the work done. By 1935, 70 per cent of the hours worked were paid for on piece-rate scales, and these scales rose on all work done above a certain amount (or production norm) per day or week. This "premium-bonus system," violently denounced as a trick for speeding up by the wage earners of all capitalist countries, was the keystone of Soviet wage policy. In addition to material incentives there was public praise; honors and decorations were awarded to outstanding individual producers or groups; factories competed with each other as if they were football teams; "shock troops" went round showing laggard workers how to do more and better work; and training schools turned out an endless stream of young people who had been given some of the technical competence that was essential if the quality and quantity of production were to be raised.

In this crusade for production the unions played a large part, and their traditional task of protecting the workers' interests against employers faded more and more into the background. There was virtually no collective bargaining to be done; in the first place, there were no longer—in theory at least—two sides to make a bargain, and in the second place, wages and hours were details to be determined as part of a general plan for the whole economy. In each plan a general wages fund was allocated and distributed among the various industries. To earn that money workers had to increase the total volume of production, reduce production costs, and raise their individual productivity. There was no fear of unemployment to stimulate them to work hard lest they lose their jobs. Instead there were the deterrents to laziness, the monetary incentives of high earnings, the honors and praise of their fellows and superiors, and, for those who were capable of feeling it, a sense of "labor patriotism." Further, while the state accepted the principle of the citizen's right to work it also emphasized the corollary principle of the obligation to work. As ruler, policy maker, and employer it determined the conditions under which that obligation was discharged; the function of the unions was to see that the conditions were carried out rather than to determine, criticize, or oppose them.

Consumers' Cooperation

Consumers' cooperation was intended originally to be producers' cooperation as well. Owen and other utopian socialists of the early nineteenth century believed that society could be regenerated by setting up communities based on the principles of mutual coopera- tion, common property, and equal means of enjoyment. These com- munities would produce all that their members needed; employment and enjoyment would go hand in hand. Though all such plans failed, the belief in them died hard. When a group of Rochdale (Lanca- shire) weavers considered what could be done to improve their miserable condition and established the Rochdale Pioneers' Society (1844), their program embraced not merely the opening of a retail store; in addition they hoped to secure houses, manufacture goods, buy or lease land, and "as soon as practicable . . . proceed to ar- range the powers of production, distribution, education, and gov- ernment, or, in other words, to establish a self-supporting home colony of united interests."

This was almost pure Owenism; but the starting point was not a model village. It was a small store in a mean street, selling flour, butter, sugar, oatmeal, and candles. A flour mill, a cotton mill, a Turkish bath, a sick and burial club, and a building society were in later years added to the list of the Rochdale Pioneers' activities, and the cooperative movement which sprang from their success grew to great dimensions as producer. But it never reached a point where it could employ more than a small fraction of its members, and its policy centered on serving them as consumers rather than on finding them jobs.

Even a little retail society required capital, rules, and working principles. The Pioneers combined the desirable features of experiments that had gone before in societies that had failed; they made them work and then made them known over a wide field. These features were as follows:

1. Capital was provided by the members in units of £1, payable in small installments and withdrawable on demand. Members could also use the society as a savings bank, but on capital and deposits alike only a fixed rate of interest was paid.

2. The best obtainable goods were to be supplied and full weight or measure was to be given. This rule was almost a revolution in retailing in an age when flour was often adulterated, tea colored with Prussian blue, sand mixed with sugar, and the price of milk rose as the quantity of water fell. "Traders treated the workingman's stomach as a sort of wastepaper basket" (Fay), and there was little effectual state action to get pure food until about 1875 in England, 1876 in Germany, and much later elsewhere. The Pioneers were thus far ahead of commercial practice and public policy.

3. Sales were for cash, and market prices were charged. The first part of this rule avoided bad debts, but it tended to shut out the very poor or improvident who were accustomed to being in debt to the grocer, as well as middle-class families habituated to the charge account. The second part of the rule meant that no attempt was made to sell "at cost," for costs were not known at the time of sale. By selling at market price the society had a net surplus left over when all expenses, including interest on capital, had been met. In a private store this surplus would be the tradesman's profit. In a joint-stock company it would be distributed among the stockholders in proportion to their capital. In a cooperative society it was returned quarterly or semi-annually to the consumer from whom it had been taken, in the form of a "dividend on purchases" and in proportion to the amount of his purchases. In some societies this "divvy" was often 15 per cent during the early twentieth century, and the family which spent most of its income at the "co-op" received a substantial sum on "divvy day."

4. The Pioneers were democrats, imbued with Chartist ideas of manhood suffrage, vote by ballot, and annual elections. They decreed that "the principle of one member one vote should obtain in government, with equality of the sexes in membership." Management was in the hands of elected officers and committees, and frequent financial statements were issued. The principle of "one mem-

ber one vote," as distinct from "one share one vote," was natural in an association of consumers rather than of capitalists. The grant of votes to women came seventy-three years before it came in national politics.

5. The Pioneers knew the shortcomings in their own education and saw the need for cooperative propaganda. They resolved that "a definite percentage of profits should be allotted to education." In 1852 the rule was made that 2½ per cent of the surplus should be spent in educational work. At that time an effective system of state elementary education was still two decades away, while secondary schools, libraries, and adult education were still more remote.

The Pioneers succeeded where hundreds of earlier societies had failed. The dividend bound wage earners to the store just as friendly society benefits bound them to the new model unions. The Rochdale society grew from 28 members in 1844 to over 20,000 in 1913, the funds from £28 to £400,000, and the employees from one part-time salesman to over 400 workers. Other towns and villages set up societies, especially in the industrial midlands and north, and later in the south.

By 1900, 1,440 retail societies had 1,700,000 members.
In 1914, 1,385 " " " 3,050,000 "
In 1932, 1,200 " " " 6,760,000 "
In 1945, 1,060 " " " 9,200,000 "

The last membership figure is about one-fifth of the total population of Great Britain, and since a member is usually the head of a family it can safely be interpreted as indicating that at least half the population was obtaining some of its supplies from retail cooperative societies. In 1945 the share capital of these societies was over £160,-000,000, and the sales amounted to £300,000,000.

From retail distribution the next step was to production or to large-scale purchase. Some societies began to produce part of the goods they sold; but importation and production needed some central organization which would serve all the retail societies. In 1863 the English Cooperative Wholesale Society (C.W.S.) was established with headquarters in Manchester. Five years later a Scottish C.W.S. was formed. The capital was supplied by the retail societies, and on it a fixed rate of interest was paid. The C.W.S. procured, made, and sold goods to the member societies and at the end of the year distributed any net surplus among them in proportion to their purchases. The dividend-on-purchases principle was thus applied to wholesale as well as to retail trade.

The C.W.S. took cooperation into world trade. Soon its name plate appeared on doors in Ireland, New York, Rouen, Copenhagen, Hamburg, Montreal, Sydney, Colombo, and elsewhere. From overseas purchase to production overseas was sometimes a desirable step. Tea plantations were bought in Ceylon, a concession was obtained in Sierra Leone, and for a time 10,000 acres of wheat land were held on the Canadian prairie. Some goods from Europe were carried to England in C.W.S. ships, but the economies did not justify the building up of a large fleet. The really great successes came in the processing or making of consumers' goods in factories scattered over the country. Foodstuffs, cloth, clothes, shoes, tobacco, soap, furniture, coal, and other commodities could be obtained from C.W.S. plants. In 1872 the C.W.S. began banking, and eventually kept current accounts for 1,000 societies and 12,500 unions, friendly societies, and kindred bodies. The net surplus was distributed in proportion to the amount of custom. Insurance work began in 1872 and was gradually extended to cover most risks. In 1904 a collective life insurance plan was formulated under which all the members of a retail society were automatically insured without exception or medical examination. The capital for these wholesale, banking, and insurance activities amounted to £200,000,000, all of it supplied by the retail societies.

The administration of this huge, varied business was conducted on democratic lines. Control rested in the hands of meetings of delegates from the member societies and management was directed by elected committees consisting of men who belonged by birth, training, and sympathy to the wage-earning class. The failures were few, the successes substantial. Critics could point out that management had been conservative, reluctant to step into new fields, honest but humdrum. This was not entirely the leaders' fault, for often the brake was applied fiercely by the members, and progressive officers might be dethroned if the plans they presented for capital outlays seemed to threaten the size of the "divvy." One result of this conservatism was that members had to look to other sources for many of the semi-luxury goods which a rising standard of living allowed them to purchase. Critics could also point out that this great organization of consumers gave scant thought to the welfare of its employees. Workingmen, themselves stalwart unionists, might, when clothed with authority as committeemen or directors, resent the claims put forward by officials of the unions to which their members belonged. This criticism faded rapidly during the twentieth century. The growth of unionism among cooperative employees and the frank facing of the labor problem by management resulted in a complete unionization of the 350,000 employees and placed the cooperatives far ahead of their competitors as employers in the distributive trades.

On the continent consumers' cooperation spread among townspeople almost as easily as agricultural cooperation spread among farmers, and in rural regions the same society served the peasants both as producers and as consumers. In 1929 it was estimated that there were 40,000,000 members in 60,000 consumers' societies in about 30 countries. The strongholds were Germany and Russia, but all northern Europe had its stores and wholesale societies, and during the thirties the building of houses became an important cooperative enterprise. Germany had 4,000,000 members; France had 3,500,000 members and 7,500 stores; in Hungary, Switzerland, Czechoslovakia, Denmark, and Finland one-tenth or more of the population was enrolled.

Russia began late, but after 1905 the growth of consumers' cooperatives was rapid. By 1914, 10,000 societies were at work, and by 1917 the number had risen to 35,000. In the first troubled period of revolutionary years (1918–1921) the Bolsheviks nationalized all trade, set up some state trading machinery, but let the cooperatives continue to operate under the control of the Food Commissariat. The New Economic Policy (1921) freed them from that control, returned what was left of their property and goods, gave them liberty to buy and sell and (in 1924) to resume payment of dividends on purchases. The movement went ahead rapidly. Membership rose from 11,000,-000 in 1918 to 43,000,000 in 1930. The central wholesale organization, *Centrosoyus,* operated elevators, mills, cold-storage plants, canning factories, soapworks, etc., and in 1926 the cooperatives handled half the trade in agricultural produce as well as a considerable part of that in manufactured goods. The state trading organizations conducted about a quarter of the trade, and private dealers did the rest.

Under the Plans the private trader was eliminated, and the field was left to be served by the state and cooperative services. In 1935, when rationing was abolished, the state took over all urban distribution and limited the cooperatives to rural trade. The societies which handled it were either consumers' organizations or producers' groups of farmers or industrial handicraftsmen. In 1939 they did about 85 per cent of the countryside's business and about 40 per cent of the trade of the whole nation. Capital was drawn from the members in the form of entrance fees and annual membership dues. The societies paid dividends on the purchases of their members. But they were not free to determine prices and in general were a controlled part of the Soviet economic system. The "co-op" and the union, labor's two outstanding expressions of the urge to voluntary association, had become instruments of the state.

Conclusion. The dream of Owen and the Rochdale Pioneers that cooperation could create a new social order has faded. In the production and distribution of necessaries of life cooperation found a large field for service, one that has not yet been fully occupied; but the provision of comforts and luxuries, as well as public utilities, transportation, and the heavy industries, was beyond its reach or vision. In its own field it faced not merely the irrepressible little "neighborhood store" but also the chain or department stores with their great capital resources, aggressive policies, elaborate displays of advertisements, and low prices. In its struggle with them it had a tradition of working-class loyalty and middle-class good will. Its basis—the interest of the consumer—is one that is universal; yet consumers are the least capable of being stirred to joint action. Producers of all kinds spring together to protect and push their sectional desires, and governments respond to appeals or commands which are often the expression of the crudest group selfishness. In such company consumers have little hope of making their voices heard, and their joint actions in defense have achieved only the modest successes described above.

BIBLIOGRAPHY

Baykov, A., *The Development of the Soviet Economic System* (1947), chaps. 2, 7, 13, 18.

Bergson, A., *Soviet Wages* (1944).

Bogart, E. L., *Economic History of Europe, 1700–1939* (1942), chaps. 6, 13, 21, 23.

Bowden, W., Karpovich, M., and Usher, A. P., *Economic History of Europe since 1750* (1937), chaps. 21, 26, 39.

Bowley, A. L., *Wages and Income in the United Kingdom since 1860* (1938).

Carr-Saunders, A. M., and others, *Consumers' Cooperation in Great Britain* (1938).

Clapham, J. H., *Economic History of Modern Britain* (1926, 1932, 1938), vol. ii, chaps. 4, 11; vol. iii, chaps. 5, 8.

Cole, G. D. H., and Postgate, R., *The British Common People, 1746–1946* (1947).

Fay, C. R., *Cooperation at Home and Abroad* (1920).

Fay, C. R., *Great Britain from Adam Smith to the Present Day* (1932), chaps. 19, 20.

Finer, H., *Mussolini's Italy* (1935).

Ford, G. S. (ed.), *Dictatorship in the Modern World* (1935).

Gide, C., *Consumers' Cooperative Societies* (1921).

Haider, C., *Capital and Labor under Fascism* (1930).

Laidler, H. W., *Social Economic Movements* (1944).

Levine, L., *Syndicalism in France* (1914).

Montgomery, B. G., *British and Continental Labor Policy* (1922).

Müller, H., *Geschichte der deutschen Gewerkschaften* (1918).

Pitigliana, F., *The Italian Corporative State* (1933).

Richardson, J. H., *Industrial Relations in Great Britain* (1933).

Rühle, D., *Karl Marx* (1929).

Sanders, W. S., *Trade Unionism in Germany* (1916).

Saposs, D., *The Labor Movement in Post-War France* (1931).

Sombart, W., *Socialism and the Social Movement* (Eng. trans., 1909).

Sturmthal, A., *The Tragedy of European Labor, 1918–1939* (1943).

Webb, S. and B., *History of Trade Unionism, 1666–1920* (1920).

ARTICLES

Anselmi, A., "Trade Associations and Corporations in Italy," *Int. Lab. Rev.*, January, 1935.

Childs, S. L., and Crottet, A. A., "Trade Unions in the Soviet State," *Ec. Hist.*, January, 1933.

George, M. D., "The Combination Laws," *Ec. H. R.*, April, 1936.

Hammond, J. L., "The Industrial Revolution and Discontent," *Ec. H. R.*, January, 1930.

Hewes, A., "The Transformation of Soviet Trade Unions," *Am. Ec. R.*, December, 1933.

Logan, H. A., "The State and Collective Bargaining," *Canadian J. of Ec. and Pol. Sc.*, November, 1944.

Plummer, A., "The General Strike During One Hundred Years," *Ec. Hist.*, May, 1927.

Encyclopaedia of the Social Sciences: See list of titles on Labor, Socialism, and Cooperation in vol. xv, pp. 552, 556, 550. See especially the articles on Trade Unions, Socialism, Syndicalism, the Labor Movement, Bolshevism, Russian Revolution, Gosplan, Fascism, National Socialism, Consumers' Cooperation, Producers' Cooperation, Collectivism.

INDEX